Contributions to Finance and Accounting

The book series 'Contributions to Finance and Accounting' features the latest research from research areas like financial management, investment, capital markets, financial institutions, FinTech and financial innovation, accounting methods and standards, reporting, and corporate governance, among others. Books published in this series are primarily monographs and edited volumes that present new research results, both theoretical and empirical, on a clearly defined topic. All books are published in print and digital formats and disseminated globally.

More information about this series at http://www.springer.com/series/16616

Sinem Derindere Köseoğlu
Editor

Financial Data Analytics

Theory and Application

Springer

Editor
Sinem Derindere Köseoğlu
formerly Istanbul University
Avcılar/Istanbul, Turkey

ISSN 2730-6038 ISSN 2730-6046 (electronic)
Contributions to Finance and Accounting
ISBN 978-3-030-83798-3 ISBN 978-3-030-83799-0 (eBook)
https://doi.org/10.1007/978-3-030-83799-0

This Springer imprint is published by the registered company Springer Nature Switzerland AG.
The registered company address is: Gewerbestrasse 11, 6330 Cham, Switzerland

Preface

Around 3300 BC, Mesopotamian merchants used clay tokens to track debts and payments. Around 2500 BC, Mesopotamians started to use money, which soon found its way into Egypt. Fast forward 5000 years, the volume of worldwide equity trade reaches about 35 trillion US dollars a quarter, with finances fueling the dreams of every business and entrepreneurial activity. For every world-changing dreamer throughout history, there are countless numbers of data analysts who never make it to the cover pages of top business magazines, but whose work is what enables dreams to morph into viable businesses that support millions of employees and their families. It is the innovators and entrepreneurs' role to lay out a vision, but when asked on what basis they think they would be successful, they point to market analysis and financial analysis reports and forecasts. Mathematics, statistics, and computer programming are the tools that amplify the contributions of those who work diligently behind the scenes. They are the ones who help us distinguish between an outlier which is an error in data reporting and one that is a prelude to the next economic boom. They are the ones who educate us about investments that do not make sense, and about the ones that will enable us to provide for our families. This book is a humble contribution to the data analyst's toolset, wrapped in our warmest expressions of gratitude.

Istanbul, Turkey

Sinem Derindere Köseoğlu

About the Book

Financial Data Analytics: Theory and Application

It is evident that big data analysis has touched all walks of our lives. There is enormous structured and unstructured data generated every moment in the financial industry in the digitalized era. The data can be used to create strategies for related parts of the industry. This huge data should be analyzed in a logical manner, and then policy and pathways should be suggested at the end of the data analysis. Data analytics is the science of examining raw data to conclude this information. It is used to enable companies, investors, and organizations to make better decisions as well as to verify and disprove existing theories or models. Researchers are now able to reach all these with less effort through existing programming dialects like R and Python®. The R and Python programming approaches take researchers to another degree of logical and business thinking.

This book is aimed to be an efficient resource addressing many applications of data analytics in the financial industry. Digitization in finance has enabled technology forms such as advanced analytics, artificial intelligence (AI), machine learning (ML), deep learning (DL), natural language processing (NLP), and network analysis to penetrate and transform how financial institutions compete in the market. Large companies, organizations, banks, and financial institutions adopt these technologies to execute digital transformation, meet consumer demand, and bolster profit and loss. As the finance sector rapidly moves toward data-driven optimization, companies, organizations, and investors must keep up with these changes in a deliberate and comprehensive manner. Therefore, it is determined that the most important aim of this book is that the audience learn and get insight on why, when, and how to apply many financial data analytics techniques in real financial world situations within a single book. As the primary purpose of this book, all the main aspects of analyzing financial data—statistics, data visualization, big data analysis, machine learning, and time series analysis—are attempted to be covered in depth both in a theoretical and a practical manner.

The most important subjects in finance today and in the future, including data processing, knowledge management, machine learning models, data modeling, visualization, optimization for financial problems, financial econometrics, and decision-making, are planned to be emphasized in this book. The importance and strength of the book are to explain the subjects along with real practical examples. Along with both applications and theory, it is set out to give examples and applications under real financial data. The audience will get familiar with the sense of programming improvement to actualize financial investigations through coding.

The book contains 13 theoretical and practical chapters, divided into 3 parts. Computer programming in R or Python is used in some of these chapters. Part I, *Introduction and Analytics Models*, includes chapters between 1 and 5. Chapter 1 introduces the latest changes in the financial industry, particularly with a focus on the development of financial technology and financial data analytics. Chapters 2 through 4 introduce the audience to four main types of data analytics types: descriptive and diagnostic, predictive, and prescriptive analytics since the main purpose of data analytics is to define data, model, predict, and suggest policies. Chapter 5 in Part I includes the financial empirical study of data analytics and modeling. Chapters 6 through 8 belong to the Part II that is named as *Machine Learning*. Chapters 6 through 8 belong to Part II that is named *Machine Learning*. Chapters 6 through 8 provide different machine learning techniques. As the data which will be analyzed is huge (big data), the curse of dimensionality should be reduced so that traditional methods in machine learning could be more effectively utilized. Therefore, Chapter 6 gives dimension reduction techniques in machine learning. Then, Chapter 7 gives one of the algorithms for classification and regression in ML: Random Forests. Chapter 8 provides some empirical studies of machine learning and deep learning algorithms in finance. Chapter 9 discusses the natural language processing (NLP) algorithms and shows the usefulness of them by an empirical analysis.

Chapters 10 through 13 are in Part III titled *Technology-Driven Finance*. Chapter 10 deals with the optimization of regulatory economic-capital structured portfolios with application to emerging markets with theoretical foundations, modeling techniques, and machine learning algorithms. Chapter 11 gives data science for the insurance business as the insurance companies are one of the important institutions of the financial industry. Chapter 12 explains the key areas in network modeling, and the theoretical discussion is complemented by two easily digestible empirical applications. Since financial technologies grow rapidly, cyber hygiene has also been important than ever before, and therefore, Chapter 13 explores the concepts of cyber hygiene and the risks of end users' behaviors from cloud services to security measurements.

Contents of the chapters are explained as below:

The first chapter, titled ***"Retraining and Reskilling financial participators in the digital age"***, introduces the latest developments in the financial industry, particularly with a focus on financial technology (FinTech) and financial data analytics. The chapter also explores what skills do finance workforce are needed in the digital age.

Moreover, discussions are given on various types of technology that learners may encounter and potential challenges they may experience during learning. Furthermore, related learning theories and approach are systemically reviewed. Overall, this chapter provides a practical reference for financial professional on reflecting how they can learn effectively through microlearning in the fast-changing digital age.

Data science process contains basic steps such as business understanding, data understanding, data preparation, modeling, evaluation, and deployment. In the second chapter titled "***Financial Data Analytics Basics***" first steps of data analytics for financial data are handled. In this chapter, data science, data types, financial time series data properties, data analysis techniques, and data analysis processes are explained. In addition, R program has been handled as an introduction here. This chapter covers working with data structure and data frames, importing data from different data sources, data preparation (cleaning data, handling missing data, and manipulating data) using some statistical functions, analyzing financial basic time series characteristics, and data visualization with R codes.

The third chapter, titled "***Predictive Analytics Techniques: Theory and Applications in Finance***"**,** is about predictive analytics. It presents several models related to predictive analysis. The chapter covers five models: logistic regression, time series analysis, decision trees, multiple linear regression, and RFM (recency, frequency, monetary) segmentation with k-means. The models are presented with moderate mathematical depth and with an emphasis of building a working software implementation in R.

The fourth chapter, titled "***Prescriptive Analytics Techniques: Theory and Applications in Finance***," is *about* predictive analytics. It examines several key models and techniques associated with prescriptive analytics. The chapter includes 5 models: sentiment analysis, association rules, network analysis, recommender systems, and principal component analysis. The scenarios and models are presented with moderate mathematical rigor, emphasizing the practical aspect, supported by a complete and detailed R code.

The fifth chapter, titled "***Forecasting Returns of Crypto currency - Analyzing Robustness of Auto Regressive and Integrated Moving Average (ARIMA) and Artificial Neural Networks (ANNs)***," focuses on predictive modeling by applying auto regressive models and machine learning models. This chapter contributes to the book by the application of univariate models with a step-by-step approach. For application of autoregressive and machine learning models, the study has considered the technology-based asset class that is cyptocurrency, and Bitcoin has been considered as an underlying asset to predict its prices. Autoregressive conditional moving average (ARIMA) and artificial neural networks (ANNs) have been used to forecast the prices of Bitcoin. The theoretical cum practical explanation of the paper will be useful for researchers, regulators, and investors. Finally, the chapter analyzed the robustness of the model among the two. In true sense, the chapter is the valuable contribution in the field of financial analytics.

In the sixth chapter, titled "***Machine Learning in Financial Markets: Dimension Reduction and Support Vector Machine,***" dimension reduction techniques are explained in detail. Recent progress in active portfolio management strategies such as multi-factor investing is encouraging researchers to use advanced dimension reduction techniques borrowed from machine learning and statistics. An example could be factor investment for equities in which a practitioner selects a reduced set of factors such as value, size, quality, and low volatility among more than 150 factors. It is interesting that each year more than 5 factors are being introduced by academics and quantitative researchers in investment companies such as HedgeFunds. Factor investing is not limited to equities and is used for many asset classes. Alternative investment is such an attitude to invest in a global multi-asset world that the number of features that a data-scientist needs is more than 100 features if a rigorous quantitative analysis for portfolio management is essential. Although these active managers charge investors with a big amount of fees, but as Robert Arnott the father of factor investment says: "Many investors prefer comfort chasing, what is popular and loved, rather than pursuing what is out of favor. The markets do not reward comfort." Investors cannot get a good alpha unless they forget index tracking which is so popular and try to use multi-factor investing in order to discover the underlying causal variables that generates alpha. The chapter starts by reviewing major dimension reduction methods and shows the connection with different ideas in finance such as CAPM (capital asset pricing model), APT (arbitrage pricing theory), risk parity, and statistical arbitrage. One of the most important methods of classification is support vector machine (SVM), and its connection with dimension reduction is explained and a practical example in algorithmic trading in Forex is explained. After reading the chapter, the reader may realize how dimension reduction and classification can play a big role in different contexts in finance.

In the seventh chapter, titled ***"Pruned Random Forests for Effective and Efficient Financial Data Analytics,"*** random forests are explained as classification and regression methods in machine learning. Random Forest is a highly performing classifier and regressor. It has been applied successfully in several financial applications. However, and owing to the need for rapid decision-making in many financial applications, reducing the inference time of Random Forests is highly desirable. CLUB-DRF and eGAP are experimentally proven Random Forest pruning methods, which reduce the size of the classifier significantly, leading to acceleration of the inference process. Thus, the chapter shows experimentally both the efficiency and effectiveness of pruning Random Forests using CLUB-DRF and eGAP on four financial data sets. As demonstrated experimentally, CLUB-DRF is more efficient, while eGAP is more effective. As per the financial application requirements, either of these two methods can be applied. If accuracy is more important, eGAP is likely to be the first method of choice. On the other hand, CLUB-DRF is applied when inference time is the more important criterion.

The eighth chapter, titled "***Foreign Currency Exchange Rate Prediction Using Long Short Term Memory,"*** analyzes the performance of machine learning (ML) and deep learning (DL) algorithms by focusing on the exchange rate of 22 countries based on US dollar. The overall performance of all ML and DL algorithms is good, but the performance of deep learning algorithms (LSTM) is better than others. Currency exchange rate forecasts help brokers and businesses make better decisions. It is necessary to evaluate the flows involved in international transactions.

In the ninth chapter titled ***"Natural Language Processing for Exploring Culture in Finance: Theory and Applications,"*** authors discuss the natural language processing (NLP) algorithms and shows usefulness of it by an empirical analysis. It is pointing out that culture has been given little attention in the study of finance; this chapter integrates literature on culture in finance and research on NLP. The chapter surveys a variety of NLP algorithms, including bag-of-words, TF-IDF, sentiment analysis, cosine similarity, word embeddings, and topic models, and demonstrates their implementation in R. The chapter also presents the usefulness of NLP to exploring culture in corporate decision-making by analyzing Warrant Buffet's letters to Berkshire Hathaway's shareholders from 1977 to 2019. As a result, this chapter makes both theoretical and methodological contributions. First, by introducing text mining algorithms, the chapter connects theories of culture to literature on finance decision-making. The findings have important implications for corporate governance, corporate culture, and managerial communication. Second, the chapter shows how to apply NLP methods, which are relatively new in finance, to discover and map cultural or semantic patterns in finance texts. This indicates that applications of NLP are ripe for the advancement of financial data analytics.

In the tenth chapter, titled ***"Financial Networks: A Review of Models and the Use of Network Similarities,"*** network models are explained by supporting examples. The increasing availability of big data and the growing belief in the explanatory power of interconnected agents and systems have made network science more popular than ever before. This chapter on the use of network science provides a historical overview of the increasing importance of network modeling in economics and finance by offering a detailed review on the methods and subjects of network applications. This review is complemented by a detailed discussion on three sub-fields (agent-based modeling, stock correlation networks, and calculating network similarities). The goal of the chapter is to demonstrate the vast number of possibilities available to researchers and practitioners interested in entering the field, as well as providing two easily digestible network applications that can be used to analyze micro-level, meso-level, and macro-level economic and financial phenomena.

In the eleventh chapter, titled "***Optimization of Regulatory Economic-Capital Structured Portfolios: Modeling Algorithms, Financial Data Analytics and Reinforcement Machine Learning in Emerging Markets***," the author Mazin A. M. Al Janabi examines the optimization of regulatory economic-capital structured portfolios with application to emerging markets. The theoretical foundations, modeling techniques, and machine learning algorithms are based on Al Janabi model. This chapter discusses from a regulatory portfolio management standpoint the application of liquidity-adjusted risk modeling techniques in obtaining optimal and investable economic-capital structures. In particular, in this comprehensive research methods case study the author implements a robust approach to optimal regulatory economic-capital allocation, in a liquidity-adjusted value at risk (LVaR) context. In effect, the observed market-microstructures patterns and the obtained empirical results are quite interesting and promising for practical optimization techniques, portfolio management purposes, and operations research models in financial institutions management, particularly in the wake of the aftermaths of the 2007–2009 financial crisis. In addition, the proposed quantitative portfolio management techniques and optimization algorithms can have important uses and applications in expert systems, machine learning, financial data analytics, smart financial functions, and financial technology (FinTech) in big data ecosystems. Likewise, it can aid in the development of regulatory technology (RegTech) for the global financial services industry, and can be of interest to professionals, regulators, and researchers working in the field of financial engineering and FinTech, and for those who want to improve their understanding of the impact of innovative quantitative risk management techniques and optimization algorithms on regulatory challenges for financial services industry and its effects on global financial stability.

In the twelfth chapter, titled ***"Transforming Insurance Business with Data Science,"*** data analytics is explained for insurance business. Insurance industry is a critical component of the modern financial infrastructure. The adoption of data science in the insurance industry in the USA was slow and gradual in the early 2010s. After seeing successful use cases of credit card companies and banks, the pace has been picking up in recent years. However, there is a lack of a formal methodology that offers a general approach to solve insurance business challenges using data science. In this chapter, Wayne Huang draws from his experience in process innovation and data analytics to describe how data science can play a transformative role in the insurance industry. He first gives an overview of data science's role in an insurance company. Then, the data science challenges in each stage of an analytics project life cycle are discussed. Frameworks and examples for managing each of the challenges are also provided. In the end, an example is demonstrated to showcase a complex business challenge in managing the customer journey and calculating customer lifetime value in a life insurance company. Throughout the chapter, the author highlights that data science is not just about developing advanced analytics models. It is equally important to help business partners see the opportunity of a business challenge and ensure the analytics solution can deliver value to the business. This topic is pragmatically significant and important to data science practitioners and students who are interested in the insurance business.

The thirteenth chapter, titled "***A General Cyber Hygiene Approach for Financial Analytical Environment,***" examines the cyber hygiene for financial environment. Cyber hygiene relates to the practices and precautions users take with the aim of keeping sensitive data organized, safe, and secure from theft and outside attacks. Moreover, cyber hygiene is a reference to the practices and steps that users of computers and other devices take to maintain system healthy and to improve online security services especially for the financial analytical platforms. These practices are often part of a routine to ensure the safety of identity and other details that could be stolen or corrupted. The real value of a cyber hygiene program for organizations is the advantages it will offer. This book chapter will investigate the cyber hygiene knowledge of concepts, the knowledge of threats, and the behaviors of end users. In addition, this chapter provides a survey to explore the cyber hygiene habits of end users. Furthermore, it would explore the concepts of cyber hygiene, the understanding of risks and the behavior of end users in a thorough and modified manner, and spanning from cloud services to security measurements. They are designed to educate the consumer and his or her organizations' actions based on processes and behavior.

Contents

Editor and Contributors

About the Editor

Sinem Derindere Köseoğlu got **Associate Professor of Finance** degree in January 2014 from Inter-University Council in Turkey. While doing her master's, Dr. D. Köseoğlu commenced her academic career as a research and teaching assistant for the School of Transport and Logistics at Istanbul University in 2004. Following her master's graduation, Dr. D. Köseoğlu began her PhD studies in Finance at the same university in 2006. She has held a PhD with a dissertation of "Analysis of Risks in International Maritime Transportation Industry and Factors that Affect Cargo Ship Investment Decisions" since 2010. Her article entitled "Market Risk of Index Futures and Stock Indices: Turkey as a Developing Country vs. Developed Countries" was selected as the best paper by the World Business Institute. She was also the international editor and three-chapter author of the book *Valuation Challenges and Solutions in Contemporary Businesses*. Her last article title "Is Palladium Price in Bubble?" has been published by *Resource Policy* which is a 3.185 impact factor journal. Dr. Derindere Köseoğlu is now a consultant and trainer. She gives classes in introduction to finance, corporate finance, financial management, financial planning, financial analysis, financial mathematics, risk management, and firm valuation. She has valued many companies for many different purposes such as acquisition, merging, liquidation, and ownership structure changes. She provides consultancy in financial issues to the companies.

Contributors

Mohamed M. Abbassy has a PhD and MSc in computers and artificial intelligence. He is currently **assistant professor** at the faculty of computers and artificial intelligence, Beni-Suef University. Mohamed has +17 years' experience in digital transformation and artificial intelligence. Mohamed is Infrastructure and Network Consultant in the Ministry of Higher Education. He is IT Consultant in Arabia Artificial Intelligence Company and in many other places. He is IT unit director in Beni-Suef University. Mohamed has many publications published in many ranked peer-reviewed international journals and international conferences. His research interests are in artificial intelligence, machine learning, data privacy and anonymization, gene analysis, and bioinformatics.

Menatalla Abdalla PhD Program Director of Business Information Systems, Lecturer of Accounting.

Menatalla Abdalla is the Director of the Business Information Systems Program at Galala University, Egypt. She is also a Lecturer of Accounting at Alexandria University, Egypt. Before joining the academics, Menatalla worked as a Financial Coordinator at Unilever Mashreq for a few years. After that, she has joined Alexandria University for teaching and research. She received her PhD degree in Accounting Information Systems from Alexandria University in 2018. Menatalla's research interests include topics in financial accounting, auditing, and information systems. In addition, as part of a program funded by Ford Foundation at the American University in Cairo, she participated in a research study investigating equity in higher education in Egypt.

M. Z. Abedin is an **Associate Professor of** Finance at the Hajee Mohammad Danesh Sci. & Tec. Univ., Bangladesh. Dr. Abedin continuously publishes academic paper in refereed journals. Moreover, Dr. Abedin served as an area editor of Sage Open, an SSCI journal, and an ad hoc reviewer for many academic journals. His research interest includes data analytics and business intelligence.

Mazin A. M. Al Janabi is a full research professor of finance and banking and financial engineering at EGADE Business School, Tecnologico de Monterrey, Santa Fe campus, Mexico City, Mexico. He holds a PhD degree (1991) from the

University of London, UK, and has more than 30 years of real-world experience in science and technology think tanks, engineering enterprises, financial markets, and academic institutions and in many different roles. He has worked for top international financial groups (e.g., ING-Barings and BBVA) where he held several senior management positions, such as Director of Global Market Risk Management, Head of Trading Risk Management, and Head of Derivative Products. Prof. Al Janabi has a strong interest in research and developments within emerging economies and has several publications in international refereed journals, books, and chapters in books. Furthermore, his research and developments in quantitative finance have been formally classified in the academic literatures as "Al Janabi Model" for Liquidity Risk Management (Liquidity Adjusted Value-at-Risk, LVaR Model). Prof. Al Janabi has published in top-tiered journals such as *European Journal of Operational Research*, *Journal of Forecasting*, *International Review of Financial Analysis*, *Physica A: Statistical Mechanics and its Applications*, *European Actuarial Journal*, *Annals of Operations Research*, *Applied Economics*, *Economic Modelling*, *Review of Financial Economics*, *Journal of Asset Management*, *Service Industries Journal*, *Journal of Modelling in Management*, *Studies in Economics and Finance*, *Emerging Markets Finance and Trade*, *Journal of Risk Finance*, *Journal of Banking Regulation*, and *Annals of Nuclear Energy*, among others. He received several awards for excellence in teaching and research and his biography is featured in Who's Who in the World (2013–present) and in Who's Who in Science and Engineering (2016–present).

Isac Artzi is **Associate Professor and the Program Lead of the MS in Computer Science and MS in Data Science** at Grand Canyon University. Dr. Artzi teaches and conducts research in the areas of machine learning, virtual reality, and theory of computation. Prior to GCU, Dr. Artzi had a rich and diverse career highlighted by developing interactive multimedia educational systems at Michigan State University, developing satellite-based distance education technologies at Gilat Satellite Networks Ltd., and patenting application streaming technology at AppStream in Silicon Valley (acquired by Symantec). Recently, Dr. Artzi launched the *Journal of Transdisciplinary Computational Sciences*, where he serves as the Executive Editor. Dr. Artzi has a BS in Computer Science from Ben Gurion University and an MS in Computer Science from Michigan State University. He completed doctoral studies in Educational Systems Development at Michigan State University, earned a PhD in Instructional Design at Capella University, and the Data Science Specialization program at Johns Hopkins University.

Indira Bhardwaj is an academician with more than 20 years of teaching experience across institutions in India. She has done her FDP from IIM Indore. Her PhD is from AMU in Understanding Corporate Value Using Intellectual Capital Assets. Her research interests include corporate valuation and corporate finance. Her other areas of interest include sustainable management and sustainability reporting. Her corporate work experience includes being Knowledge Manager with a Forbes KPO

EduMetry engaged in Assessment of Learning using Learning outcomes. She has worked as an Assessment Faculty with a few universities of the USA and SE Asia including Butler University, U21Global, UniSIM Singapore, George Washington University, University of Northern Iowa, Sonoma State University, and Capella University. She has also worked as Assessment Content Developer for Cengage Publications. Her work experience also includes Academic and Research Associate at IIM Indore. She takes workshops on Critical Thinking and Career Counseling for students. She is a Member of ASSOCHAM National Council for Skill Development and a Member of CII Regional Committee on Higher Education

Cantay Caliskan has been trained as a computational social scientist and received his PhD in 2018. He is a faculty member in the Data Analytics Department at Denison University in Granville, Ohio. His research interests include computational social science, emotions in politics, social media, US Congress, networks of lobbying, and the politics of renewable energy. Cantay presented his research in various conferences and events including APSA, MPSA, Political Networks, and Microsoft Research New England Machine Learning Day. Currently, he is working on several research projects on the diffusion of information in social media and the quantification of emotions in politics.

Fahmida Tasnim Dhonno is a final year student of Bachelor in Business Administration (BBA) of Hajee Mohammad Danesh Science and Technology University, Bangladesh. Currently, he works as a research assistant in the Department of Finance and Banking of this university. He has good expertise in manuscript writing.

Waleed M. Ead has a PhD and MSc in computers and artificial intelligence. He is currently **assistant professor** at the faculty of computers and artificial intelligence, Beni-Suef University. Waleed has +15 years' experience in digital transformation and data analytics. He is the general supervisor of the artificial intelligence and intelligent system unit and the director of the SAS® Artificial intelligence lab. Waleed is Management Information System Consultant in the Ministry of Higher Education. He is IT Consultant in Arabia Artificial Intelligence Company and in many other places. He is e-learning unit director in Beni-Suef University. Waleed has many publications published in many ranked peer-reviewed international journals and international conferences. He has many MSc research students in data privacy and medicine gene personalization. His research interests in artificial intelligence, machine learning, data privacy and anonymization, gene analysis, and bioinformatics.

Khaled Fawagreh is a Lecturer in the department of Information Technology at Prince Mohammad Bin Fahd University, Khobar, Saudi Arabia. He holds a PhD from the school of Computing Science & Digital Media at Robert Gordon University in the UK, an MSc in Computer Science from Dalhousie University in Canada, and a BSc in Computer Science from York University in Canada. His main research areas are data mining and machine learning.

Mohamed Medhat Gaber is a **Professor in Data Analytics** at the School of Computing and Digital Technology, Birmingham City University. Mohamed received his PhD from Monash University, Australia. He then held appointments with the University of Sydney, CSIRO, and Monash University, all in Australia. Prior to joining Birmingham City University, Mohamed worked for Robert Gordon University as a Reader in Computer Science and at the University of Portsmouth as Senior Lecturer in Computer Science, both in the UK. He has published over 200 papers, coauthored 3 monograph-style books, and edited/coedited 6 books on data mining and knowledge discovery. His work has attracted well **over five thousand citations**, with an **h-index of 38**. Mohamed has served in the program committees of major conferences related to data mining, including ICDM, PAKDD, ECML/PKDD, and ICML. He has also co-chaired numerous scientific events on various data mining topics. Professor Gaber is recognized as a Fellow of the British Higher Education Academy (HEA). He is also a member of the International Panel of Expert Advisers for the Australasian Data Mining Conferences. In 2007, he was awarded the CSIRO teamwork award.

Mahmudul Hasan is a running bachelor student in the Department of Computer Science and Engineering at Hajee Mohammad Danesh Science and Technology University, Dinajpur - 5200. He works on machine learning and data science.

Jing-Mao Ho is visiting **Assistant Professor** of Data Science at Utica College. He received his PhD in Sociology from Cornell University and MS in Computer Science from National Taiwan University. He does theoretical and empirical research at the intersection of social science, statistics, and computer science.

Wayne Huang is Head of Data Science at Pacific Life Insurance Company. He has extensive experience in leading large analytics and technology projects, solving complex business problems. He is also Adjunct Professor at Columbia University and Stevens Institute of Technology. He holds a PhD from Stevens Institute of Technology, an MBA from the State University of New York at Albany, and a BS from National Central University in Taiwan. His research interest is in data analytics and process innovation.

Kelvin Leong is the **Professor in Financial Technology and Data Analytics** at the University of Chester. He started his academic career at the Hong Kong Polytechnic University as a lecturer in accounting and finance in 2007. In 2013, he joined Glyndwr University, Wales, UK, as a senior lecturer, and then had been promoted as Principal Lecturer and Professional Lead in Finance in 2016. He has a weekly column on *Hong Kong Commercial Daily* (HKCD).

Farshad Noravesh got his BS degree in Electrical Engineering from Tehran University in 2005. He dropped out his PhD in Manchester University in Electrical Engineering in 2008. He then got a master's degree from Amirkabir University (Tehran Poly-technique) in Aerospace Engineering in 2010. He is now a software developer in TriAset and works as a quant to implement portfolio optimization and risk management to provide solutions for banks around the world. His personal research in pure and applied math as well as machine learning led him to discover algorithms and paradigms that are currently missing in classical finance and algorithmic trading.

Md. Fazle Rabbi is an **Associate Professor** in the Department of Computer Science and Engineering at Hajee Mohammad Danesh Science and Technology University, Dinajpur - 5200. He completed his bachelor's degree from HSTU and MSc degree from Jahangirnagar University. *His research interest includes data science, machine learning, and computer security.*

Abdullah Shahid is a PhD Candidate in Sociology at Cornell University. He received his MSc in Management and MBA in Finance. He studies organizations and networks in financial markets using statistical and computational methods.

Sudhi Sharma has more than 13 years of experience in teaching finance and econometrics. She has done PhD from MLSU, Udaipur, and a Certified Equity Research Analyst. She possesses proficiency in R, Advance Excel, EViews, SPSS, and STATA. As a resource person she has delivered sessions on financial modeling, econometrics, and IO modeling. She has published her research papers in ABDC and Scopus indexed journals. She has completed projects titled "Evaluation of Handloom Mega Cluster Development Scheme-Virudhnagar (Tamil Nadu)" and "Evaluation of Impact of Technology Up gradation on Handloom Mega Cluster Development Scheme—Varanasi (U.P.)" submitted to Handloom Commissioner, Ministry of Textiles, Government of India.

Ayrin Sultana is from Bangladesh. Currently, she studies at Huazhong University of Science and Technology, China, under the Chinese Government Scholarship from September 2019 session. Her present major is in Finance at the School of Economics. Her master's study will be finished in June 2021. She has completed her Bachelor of Business Administration (BBA) degree and an MBA (Major in Finance) degree from the University of Rajshahi, Bangladesh. She has been serving as an Assistant Professor at Hajee Mohammad Danesh Science and Technology University, Bangladesh, from 2014 to date. Her research interest fields are in corporate finance, real estate finance, corporate governance, corporate social responsibility, and stock market behavior.

Anna Sung is a **senior lecturer in accounting and finance** at the University of Chester. She has cross-disciplinary background in finance, technology, business, biotechnology, and higher education. Anna is a pioneer in FinTech education. Before joining the University of Chester, she was the program leader of the UK's first undergraduate degree dedicated to FinTech and was the Founding Centre Lead of the FinTech Innovation Centre at Glyndwr University. She has worked for universities in both Hong Kong and the UK.

Part I
Introduction and Analytics Models

Retraining and Reskilling Financial Participators in the Digital Age

Kelvin Leong and Anna Sung

Abstract In recent years, coding is an emerging topic in the financial industry. The concepts behind these topics are reskilling and retraining, that is, financial professionals need to be equipped with new knowledge and skills. This chapter will introduce the latest changes in the financial industry, particularly with a focus on the development of FinTech (Financial Technology) and Data Analytics and then will explore what skills do finance workforce are needed in the digital age. Furthermore, discussions will be given on various types of technology that learners may encounter and potential challenges of their learning in the digital age. What follows is a review of how do people learn. Finally, a discussion about microlearning will be given as a solution and recommendation.

Keywords Reskilling · Retraining · Digital transformation · Finance education · FinTech · Data analytics · Financial technology · Education technology

1 Introduction

This chapter aims to provide a comprehensive review of reskilling and retraining for financial professionals in the digital age, covering the topics from the background to the suggested solution. Instead of focusing on any specific financial data analytics techniques, this chapter help learner to reflect how to learn the new skills and knowledge according to their personal context. More specifically, the learning objectives of this chapter include:

- To understand the latest trend in the financial industry and the emerging needs of reskilling and retraining for financial professionals
- To understand what skills do financial professionals are needed in the digital age
- To appreciate the new opportunities of learning with technologies

K. Leong (✉) · A. Sung
University of Chester, Chester, UK
e-mail: k.leong@chester.ac.uk; a.sung@chester.ac.uk

S. Derindere Köseoğlu (ed.), *Financial Data Analytics*, Contributions to Finance and Accounting, https://doi.org/10.1007/978-3-030-83799-0_1

- To review the challenges that learners might encounter when they are learning with technologies
- To reflect how humans learn and reflect how humans can learn better
- To understand the importance of microlearning in the digital age

2 Background

Financial industry plays an important role in the functioning of the global economy. The financial industry is a section of the economy made up of many individuals and organisations that provides financial services. This section will introduce the latest changes in financial industry, particularly with a focus on the latest development of FinTech (Financial Technology) and Data Analytics. In addition, this section will also explain why reskilling and retraining are urgently needed in the field. More specifically, a discussion will be given on how the latest development of FinTech (Financial Technology) and Data Analytics affect the job market in finance world with reference to related figures.

2.1 The Development of FinTech (Financial Technology) and Data Analytics

Like many other industries, technology is becoming ever more central in the finance industry. As a result, Financial Technology (FinTech) has become an emerging topic in the business world.

There are many definitions of FinTech. In brief, FinTech can be considered as any kind of innovative idea with the purpose to improve financial service processes while the ideas could also lead to new business models or even new businesses (Leong & Sung, 2018). The development of FinTech has changed the finance ecosystem in many different ways, omnichannel payments, cryptocurrency, alternative finance, etc. are only a few examples with huge impacts on finance systems.

It is worth mentioning that the development of data analytics and FinTech goes hand in hand. In fact, there is increasing use of data analytics in various industries and organisations, including the finance industry. The driving force behind the growth of data analytics and FinTech is the rising popularity of the Internet of Things (IoT). The enormous collection of connected sensors, devices, and other 'things' represent over billions of IoT worldwide and they are making a significant contribution to the volume of data collected. Furthermore, the changing market needs and customer expectations lead businesses to need timely information and data from various sources in order to help them to improve business performance. As a result, skilled talents become more and more demanding in the market.

2.2 Reskilling and Retraining for Financial Professionals

Although the development of FinTech and data analytics is emerging, a lack of digital skills is the most significant barrier preventing businesses from achieving their goals in today's fast-changing world, particularly in the post-COVID-19 age. In fact, billions of people in the world need to be retrained and reskilled to become 'digital workers'.

On the other hand, global job market has been significantly impacted by the development of technologies and data analytics. According to the report presented by the World Economic Forum in October 2020, more than 54% of working adults worry about their current jobs in the next year. However, these workers are exceeded by those who think their employers will help them retrain on the current job for the jobs of the future (67%). In addition, the report also estimated that by 2025, 85 million jobs may be displaced by a shift in the division of labour between humans and machines. Moreover, 50% of all employees will need reskilling by 2025, as the adoption of technology increases. Furthermore, in the financial industry, a previous study estimated European and US banks would cut another 1.8 million jobs in the next decade with the growth of FinTech.

In recent years, the global job market is changing dramatically in financial industry. For example, hiring in financial sector is facing new challenges, particularly the process of hiring has changed dramatically, video interviewing has become more common for those looking to hire, and employers should also expect that today's recruitment process is longer in the past due to the skill shortage. Moreover, as more technologies deliver instant gratification, responding quickly to changing customer needs becomes a practical challenge for many businesses and therefore relevant talents become emerging. In order to meet the fast-changing customer needs, the features of microservices architecture, such as simple to develop, simple to deploy and simple to test, are considered important in the market. It also creates the demand for related workforce.

In brief, workforce is always an important asset for any organisation. For a business to successfully achieve digital transformation, employees must always be learning and be encouraged and supported by the business to always be learning. Actually, the financial industry has a pervasive problem with its workforce. On one hand, many employers suggested that skills shortages hindered their businesses' ability to innovate effectively, on the other hand, many employees feel struggling with new changes. In this regard, the first challenge among financial professionals is that there are many new knowledge and skills to learn.

3 What Knowledge and Skills Do Financial Professionals Are Needed in the Digital Age?

This section will explore what knowledge and skills do financial professionals are needed. In fact, the role of a financial professional is evolving rapidly in the digital age. Many new technical skills have been identified consistently as the most in-demand skill in the industry. Other than technical skills, non-technical skills are also very important. Both of these technical and non-technical skills will be discussed in this section. Moreover, other than the skills, an individual's personality often makes them more adaptable to certain jobs; therefore, this section will also discuss the relationships between personality type and career development.

In brief, skills can be generally classified into two categories: hard skills and soft skills. Hard skills concern a worker's ability to do a specific task while soft skills are more about the way they do them, for example, how workers adapt, collaborate, solve problems, and make decisions. The following sections will review the emerging hard and soft skills in the financial industry.

3.1 Emerging Hard Skills for Financial Professionals

In general, hard skills include specialised knowledge and technical abilities, such as auditing, financial reporting, bookkeeping, or using specific software, etc. Very often, hard skills are easier to be defined and measured than soft skills.

In recent years, coding and programming are the two emerging topics in the financial industry. In fact, as the industry becomes more automated and technology-driven, financial professionals with relevant skills are going to be more in demand. In practice, coding and programming can be used to support a variety of situations. These situations include developing payment apps, designing automated investment advisory chatbots, setting up accounting systems or programming money transmitting platforms, etc.

There are many different types of programming language in the world and some of them are summarised as below:

- Python

  As an emerging skill, Python has seen maximum adoption in the finance industry because it is easy to use and has fast process speed. Very often Python has been used to develop scalable web applications. The syntax in Python helps the programmers to do coding in fewer steps as compared to other programming languages, such as Java, C or C++, etc. Moreover, it has a huge library as a development resource and has a wide developer community. Python is also very suitable for data analytics which is at the heart of a finance job. A lot of finance start-ups are using Python as their core programming language.

- Java

  Java has widely been used to build enterprise-scale web applications for many years. It is an Object-Oriented and general-purpose programming language that helps to create programmes and applications on any platform. Moreover, Java is also the preferred language for Android-related apps development. Furthermore, Java has an English-like syntax, which makes it the perfect language for beginners, therefore, like Python, Java is also a great programming idea for financial professionals to begin with.
- JavaScript

  Unlike Java, JavaScript is a client-side language. The JavaScript code is executed on the user's processor instead of the web server thus it saves bandwidth and load on the webserver. Therefore, JavaScript has also been considered as the 'front-end programming language'. It is widely used to construct interactive interface applications. However, the client-side JavaScript does not allow the reading or writing of files. It has been kept for security reason. Moreover, another limitation is that the browser interprets JavaScript differently in different browsers. It means that the developers of JavaScript must run the codes on various platforms before publishing.
- C and C++

  Both C and C++ are also very popular programming language and have a long history. C is a general-purpose, procedural computer programming language supporting structured programming while C++ is created as an extension of the C programming language, or 'C with Classes'. C and C++ are two of the oldest and most efficient programming languages that still continue to dominate the realm of programming. C and C++ have been considered as the backbones of almost all low-level systems. In practice, many operating systems and filing systems are all written in C/C++. Therefore, these programming languages are suitable for financial professionals who want to become system-level programmer.
- SQL

  A lot of data be generated in the financial industry every day, and many of them are stored in databases. SQL stands for 'Structured Query Language', it can be defined as a databased related programming language designed for managing relational databases and performing different kinds of operations on the stored data. SQL was initially developed at IBM in the early 1970s. Currently, SQL has been considered as a standard database language by many relational database management systems such as Oracle, Informix, Posgres, SQL server, MySQL, MS Access and Sybase.
- R

  Machine learning is a key topic of AI, while R provides an effective framework with built-in libraries to support developers to build powerful Machine Learning based solutions. Created in the 1990s, R was designed as a statistical platform for effective data handling, data cleaning, analysis, and representation. According to a survey conducted by an executive recruiting firm in 2017, out of all surveyed data scientists, 40% prefer R and 26% Python (https://www.burtchworks.com/2017/06/19/2017-sas-r-python-flash-survey-results/).

Therefore, R programming language is a suitable skill for people who want to develop their career in the data analytics field. In fact, many organisations use R because its function covers powerful statistical analysis as well as graphics generation for data visualisation.

- The importance of Microsoft Excel as a non-programming technical skill

  Other than the programming language, financial professionals should also be good at some other non-programming technical skills, one of the most important skills is Microsoft (MS) Excel. MS Excel is easy-to-use software that is widely used to store and organise data in many industries. MS Excel is a spreadsheet software and application developed by Microsoft for various operation systems such as Windows, MacOS, Android and iOS. It has various functions which are widely used, like calculation, graph production, pivot tables, and a macro programming language called Visual Basic for Applications (VBA) in which users can create tailor-made automation. MS Excel is widely used in the finance industry because it is easy to use and includes powerful financial functions.

In summary, the syntax in Python helps the developers to do coding in fewer steps as compared to other traditional programme languages. It means that Python can be used to develop new applications in a faster way, this feature is even more important in today's fast-changing. Moreover, Python has huge machine learning libraries and machine learning is a key topic in AI. Therefore, Python has also been considered the most demanding coding skill in the finance sector.

3.2 *Soft Skills for Financial Professionals*

Hard skills refer to measurable abilities that are developed over time through practice or study; Soft skills, on the other hand, are abilities that enable people to fit into a working environment or work effectively with others. In brief, soft skills are the combination of people skills, cognitive skills, social skills, communication skills, emotional intelligence and personality traits, etc.

According to '*The Future of Jobs report*' published by the World Economic Forum (2020), the sector of Financial Services and Investment will go through a significant change, the change includes major job growth for new technical roles, some of these examples are information security analysts, data analysts and database and network professionals. Moreover, the report also indicated that the significant sources of future job growth in the sector come from emerging markets' rising middle class and young populations. In fact, by comparing different sectors, the report also suggested that a significant skills disruption is expected to occur, specifically in the sector of Financial Services and Investment. Furthermore, nine skills were suggested in the report as becoming more important in the sector, including: *Social skills, Cognitive abilities, Process skills, Resource management*

Table 1 The nine emerging soft skills in future

Social Skills • Coordinating with Others • Emotional Intelligence • Negotiation • Persuasion • Service Orientation • Training and Teaching Others	***Cognitive Abilities*** • Cognitive Flexibility • Creativity • Logical Reasoning • Problem Sensitivity • Mathematical Reasoning • Visualisation
Process Skills • Active Listening • Critical Thinking • Monitoring Self and Others	***Resource Management Skills*** • Management of Financial Resources • Management of Material Resources • People Management • Time Management
Systems Skills • Judgement and Decision-making • Systems Analysis	***Content Skills*** • Active Learning • Oral Expression • Reading Comprehension • Written Expression • ICT Literacy
Technical Skills • Equipment Maintenance and Repair • Equipment Operation and Control • Programming • Quality Control • Technology and User Experience Design • Troubleshooting	***Complex Problem-Solving Skills*** • Complex Problem Solving
Physical Abilities • Physical Strength • Manual Dexterity and Precision	

Source: World Economic Forum (2020)

skills, Systems skills, Content skills, Technical skills, Complex problem-solving skills, and Physical abilities. More detailed descriptions of these nine skills were provided in Table 1.

3.3 *Personality Type and Career Choices in Financial Industry*

As said, other than the skills, an individual's personality type and their preferences can make them easier to work in some tasks but harder to work in other tasks. As a result, in order to achieve career success, it is vital to match an individual's career to the individual's personality type. A good match can boost professional fulfilment when an individual's job matches his/her own attitude, values, and preferences. Furthermore, job-related stress is lower when an individual's responsibilities at the workplace correspond to own personality-related preferences. Otherwise, if job requirements conflict with a personal personality type that may result in significant dissatisfaction.

In fact, the Fintech and data analytic sector in financial industry is growing, and there is a variety of new roles in the sector, such as business analyst, app developer, AI consultant, compliance expert, cybersecurity analyst, data scientist, etc. Obviously, expecting a financial professional to do well in all types of roles is impossible.

There are many theories around which personality types suit specific job roles. More advanced personality measures also provide insights into an individual's work preferences. Certain jobs in the Finance sector often require particular personality types to fulfil the job nature and employers often search for talents who can adapt to the job and fit in well with the organisation's culture. In this regard, Myers–Briggs Personality Type Indicator, also known as the MBTI (The Myers & Briggs Foundation, n.d.-a) is a popular personality measure widely used in many organisations.

The MBTI, in brief, is a self-report inventory that is designed to help people to identify their type of personality, their strengths and preferences. Individuals are classified into one of the 16 different personality types under 4 pairs based on the individual's answers to the questions on the MBTI inventory.

Financial professionals who are interested in the MBTI can find the 16 types of personality from the Myers & Briggs Foundation's official website.

Given the key purpose of reskilling and retraining is time-consuming and requires time and effort, therefore, financial professionals should have a better understanding of their own personality type before investing time, money and effort.

4 Learning with Technology in Digital Age

Once financial professionals understood their own personality types and identified their career routes, the next step is to consider how to prepare themselves for the new roles or to take new responsibilities in the digital age, that is, being ready for reskilling and retraining as a learner.

However, learners should manage their expectations in future that more and more learnings with technology are the trend. As a result, this section briefs various types of technology that learners may encounter. Understanding what types of technology will be used in learning can help learners to learn better.

4.1 Multimedia

Multimedia is a good way for communication because the content of multimedia can be easily understood (Sung et al., 2020). In practice, the most common type of multimedia is video. By definition, video is an electronic medium or platform which can record, copy, playback, broadcast, and display of moving visual media. As a sequence of many pictures, video can be a great tool to assist learners in gaining a better understanding of learning content. Moreover, video is one of the foundational tools of e-learning.

In brief, a key benefit of using video in learning is that allows learners to interact, explore and digest the content at their own pace by providing visual examples. This is an important point because human brain processes visual information much better and faster than processing text, therefore, picture has always been used to support learning. The beauty of video is that it consists of many pictures and is supported by audio content. Therefore, abstract knowledge and skills can be easier to understand by video illustration and demonstrations.

There are many reasons to use video for reskilling and retraining in finance. For example, learners can use video as an anytime, anywhere learning platform and revisit complex procedures as many times as they need to. Moreover, given video can be stopped and replayed as many times as needed, video can increase knowledge retention. Furthermore, the interactive features of video players can be used to promote learner's own learning results. Many studies have reported that the use of short video allows for more efficient information processing and memory recall. According to previous studies, the advantages of using digital video in supporting learning include: enhancing communication skills and team working, facilitating thinking and problem solving, inspiring and engaging learners, encouraging learner autonomy, providing evidence source relating to skills and knowledge, increasing learner motivation and enhanced learning experience, etc.

In order to take most of the benefits from video, learners should have carefully chosen video and use video in a way that is best fit for their own style. Following key points should be taken into consideration when using video in learning. Firstly, the title of a video can help learners to find the right content, irrelevant content just wastes learners' time. For example, if a learner wants to learn about the basic concept of Python instead of practical examples, the learner may find the videos with 'introduction', 'what is', 'basic concept', etc. in the titles are more relevant than with 'Step and step', 'how to use Python to extract something', etc. in the titles. Secondly, learners should understand that narration is an important element in video. This is very common to use instructional videos for training purpose. Learners could gain a better understanding of a topic which is combining screen capture animation with narrative description. However, it is important to remember that most of the content can be visually presented and learners can learn better through visual elements. Therefore, before deciding to watch a video for learning purpose, quickly scan the videos and choose the one which has rich visual elements that can improve learning results. Thirdly, people nowadays have an incredibly short attention span, as a result, choosing a short video is always important. The rule of thumb is to choose a video with a duration of 5–10 min. Fourthly, image quality is important as well. Brightness, contrast, saturation, and sharpness often affect learners' mood on the video, and then learners' motivation of learning.

Other than the video, immersive technology, as a new emerging topic of multimedia, is a new trend in reskilling and retraining in recent years. Therefore, learners should also expect that more and more immersive technology-related learning opportunities will be found. According to a previous report, in 2018, the market size of the global virtual reality in education had reached US$656.6 million, more importantly, virtual reality is only a type of immersive technology.

Immersive technology refers to any technology that attempts to mirror a physical world by using digital means to create a sense of immersion.

In learning, and daily communication, sensation plays an important role. As per Sung et al. (2020), sensation plays an important role in influencing human behaviour. In general, human has five types of sense, these are sight, smell, hearing, taste and touch. These five types of sense are five different ways on how humans connect their real-world surroundings. Moreover, these senses can also stimulate cognitive and emotional responses. Immersive technologies can stimulate the senses by creating new user experiences digitally, and the created experience could be used to help to develop changes in users' behaviour to meet the goals of reskilling and retraining.

Virtual reality (VR) is a very popular type of immersive technology. VR refers to using technology to create immersive environments. VR can be used to enhance learning and student engagement. One of the key features is that VR allows us to create any real or imagined environment, for improving interactions. There are many applications of VR in finance. For example, given some finance topics are related to situations that are not easy or impossible to experience in person, such as the impacts of global warming on the economy in some distant countries. Using VR can help a learner to experience the impacts effectively and impressively without the need of doing field trips. Besides, VR can help the learner to better learn the conceptual idea. Given many finance topics are very conceptual, VR learning materials could be used to enable learners to interact with different scenarios; therefore, learners can better understand different outcomes.

Given finance is a complex topic and involves different types of stakeholders, using VR can facilitate learners to share their own insights and experience to create new understanding.

Other than VR, there are other immersive technologies have been proposed and developed to support learning. These technologies include: Augmented reality (AR), Mixed Reality (MR) and Extended Reality (XR). Augmented reality (AR) refers to the technology that expands human physical world view by adding layers of digital information layer onto it. Unlike Virtual Reality (VR), AR does not create the whole artificial environments, in other words, AR does not replace the real world; instead, AR appears in direct view of an existing environment and adds layers to it, these layers could be sounds, videos or graphics, etc. Furthermore, Mixed Reality (MR) takes Augmented Reality a step further. MR merges real and virtual worlds to produce new visualisations and environments, where physical and digital objects co-exist and allow real-time interactions. Extended reality (XR) is the new term that covers virtual, augmented and mixed realities. It involves all real-and-virtual combined environments and human–machine interactions through the use of computer and wearable technology.

There are many opportunities and benefit to use immersive technologies. However, learners should ensure they are safe during these environments, in particular using these technologies in self-learning. In fact, there are potential risks of using immersive technology, such as motion sickness, panic attacks and eye strain, etc. Therefore, learners should read all setup and operating instructions provided with the immersive equipment carefully. This is also important to review the hardware and software recommendations for use of the immersive equipment. Moreover, a comfortable virtual reality experience requires an unimpaired sense of motion and balance. Learners should not use any immersive equipment when they feel tired, sleepy, under emotional stress or anxiety. On the other hand, learners should stop use the immersive equipment when suffering from cold, flu, headaches, migraines, or any related illness. Learners may also consult with their medical doctor in advance before they use any immersive equipment if they are elderly, pregnant, have pre-existing binocular vision abnormalities or other serious medical conditions.

In brief, the development of immersive technologies benefits from enabling wearable technology. As per Sung et al. (2020), wearable technology refers to any kind of electronic device that can be implanted in the user's body, incorporated in clothing, worn as accessories, or even tattooed on the human's skin. In brief, wearable technology is a kind of physical platform that can deliver digital experiences to learners. The application of wearable technology in supporting learning has been proved effective according to previous cases. It is worth mentioning that the development of related technologies is not complex and is affordable. Therefore, it can be expected that wearable technology will become more and more common due to its low cost.

4.2 Collaborative Technologies

Other the multimedia, collaborative learning with technologies is a promising way in finance reskilling and retraining. Collaborative technologies offer a range of new ways of supporting reskilling and retraining by enabling learners to share and exchange ideas during learning. Collaborative technology refers to tools and systems designed to better facilitate group work, both in workplace and remote, and can be called Computer-Supported Cooperative Work (CSCW). A key benefit of CSCW is enabling collaboration in different modes, such as, co-located or geographically distributed, and synchronously (same time) or asynchronously. This benefit, of course, relates to work-based learning. The core functions for collaborative technology in learning include sharing information (such as messages, files, data or locations), or other documents between learners.

Many collaborative technologies are software tools, one typical example is email. They are also known as group software. Group software can be classified by its function and the major types of group software include communication tools, conferencing tools and coordination tools. These tools can be used to support learning in different ways. For communication tools, they can support learners to share data, information, files or other attached documents between users or groups of users. Some examples include, but are not limited to, email system, voice mail, website, and wikis, etc. Compared with communication tools, conferencing tools do not only support information sharing functions, but they often are used to facilitate interactions. Some relevant examples include internet forums, online chat systems, instant messaging, videoconferencing, etc. In practice, MS team and Zoom are some of the popular conferencing tools in the market. Coordination tools generally refer to the more complex collaborative technologies and they often be used for managing group activities as well. Some examples of coordination tools include electronic calendars, online proofing platform and workflow system, etc. Overall, collaboration technologies provide platforms for learners to share knowledge with people beyond their teams or even organisations, with who they would not usually interact with in a physical setting. In a small collaborative group supported by technology, when a question is raised, different learners across the world can have different answers and learner can learn not only new things from one another, but also understand different perspectives. Furthermore, using collaboration technologies can help create a more engaging learning experience for learners.

4.3 Artificial Intelligence

Artificial intelligence (AI) is a hot topic in our daily life today. Some people fear that many jobs will be displaced by artificial intelligence (AI). However, AI can serve as an ideal platform to support reskilling and retraining.

As early as the 1950s, Minsky and McCarthy have been considered the fathers of the AI field. They suggested AI as any task performed by a programme, software or a machine in human way (Haenlein & Kaplan, 2019). In brief, AI is the sub-branch of computer sciences, and it has a focus on developing machines that can think and work like humans. Very often, robots are used as an interface between users and AI. Robots can be designed for many learning purposes without increasing costs significantly. Moreover, robots can be presented in many different forms, with or without a physical shape, such as a chatbot. A chatbot is a computer programme powered by artificial intelligence (AI) which simulates conversations with human users. Chatbots are often used as a cost-effective solution to improving experience and satisfaction. A key advantage of using Chatbot is that it can be leveraged to increase learner's engagement with timely tips and offers, so learners might consider setting up a Chatbot through a social media platform, such as on social media or on a webpage, and then the Chatbot can continuously stay active on the internet and help answering questions instantly according to the programmed interactive responses, and set reminders to remind staff to do revision or training. Depending on the design, the data collected from the conversation between the learner and the Chatbot could also be analysed to gain a deeper understanding of the learner's learning progress, behavioural patterns or other key findings that could be feed-forward to help learners to learn better and to improve the Chabot.

In order to get the most from learning with AI and robots, there are some points that should be taken into consideration. Firstly, learners should not be scared by the technologies; they are only a tool designed by humans in order to help humans do tasks. Second, learners should remember that robots are powerful, but they are designed for a specific purpose, in other words, they can perform certain tasks only. Therefore, do not expect robots to be able to do anything and everything; some people are disappointed when they find that robots cannot answer the questions that the robot was not designed for. For example, do not be expecting a Chatbot can do tax calculations if the Chatbot is not designed for this purpose. Thirdly, bear in mind that robot can make mistakes, just like humans, because it is made by humans. Blindly believing in the content, suggestions and advice provided by robots is dangerous. There is a real case example where a person asked a smart device to tell her about the cardiac cycle as part of her revision to become a paramedic. The device suggested that violently stabbing herself could relax the human strain on the planet; of course, this does not make sense and is both inhumane and unethical. Therefore, learners should always reflect on what they have been taught by a robot, using their sense, experience and logic. Fourthly, robots do not have emotions, therefore, learners do not need to feel bad about asking the robot the same questions over and over again to support their learning.

5 The Challenge of Learning in the Big Data World

Although there are many platforms, opportunities and enabling technologies for people to learn, there is no lack of challenges.

In the following, this section will discuss the challenges of learning with technologies. The discussion can help financial professionals to anticipate what potential challenges they might encounter, and then to have better preparation before they face the challenges.

5.1 Challenges of Learning with Technologies

Reskilling and retraining, particularly through self-learning way, is a very different experience from studying in a classroom setting. There are benefits to be sure, for example, learners can study at a time that suits them, learners can vary their study schedules each week to match changing work or family commitments, they can learn anyway that suits them, etc. However, there are also challenges associated with it. These challenges can be broadly classified into two categories: learner related and technological related (Rasheed et al., 2020).

5.2 Learner-Related Challenges

Reskilling and retraining with technologies may make the learning process more efficient and flexible. The common key personal characteristics of a successful reskilled and retrained learner include, but are not limited to, autonomy, responsibility, being proactive, persistence, self-efficacy, and self-regulation. However, holding the above personal characteristics does not enough to guarantee the success of learning. There are also many factors that would affect the learning effectiveness.

Among others, a key challenge of reskilling and retraining is self-regulation. Self-regulation can be considered as the ability to independently self-organise and complete tasks without external support. There are different reasons associated with self-regulation challenges, such as procrastination, lack of self-regulation skills, difficulty of getting online help-seeking, limited preparation before class, poor time management, etc. Firstly, procrastination has widely been considered a psychological dysfunction behaviour. In practice, procrastination can be caused by various reasons, such as difficulty, poor time management, time consumption, pleasure, etc. Previous studies had indicated that this is human nature to value immediate gratification over long-term needs. Besides, there are two kinds of self-regulation: behavioural self-regulation and emotional self-regulation. Self-regulation is an important factor in online learning because it is the ability to act in an individual's long-term learning interest and consistent with the person's deepest values. In other words, self-regulation allows learners to manage their behaviours and emotions while still focusing on the learning task at hand. Poor time management is a common issue for learners. Some learners are unable to achieve their learning goals within the scheduled time. Their reasons are not because they have been distracted or procrastinated. Instead, the reason is that they understate the required time to learn or they overstate the time they can have to learn. Very often, isolation and lack of interaction are the reasons for loneliness in reskilling and retraining. Moreover, the difficulty of getting help-seeking is also a typical challenge. Many reskilled and retrained learners get confused and sometimes get intimidated by seeking help. Some instructors use online discussion forums as a tool to offer online help, however, previous findings suggested that some learners feel less comfortable in sharing or inquiring about every help, and are reluctant in detailing such inquiry because they perceive online discussion forums as less private than other channels, such as email.

5.3 Technological-Related Challenges

There are two major types of technological-related challenges, including technological literacy/ competency challenges and technological Sufficiency Challenges.

Technological literacy can be understood as the level of familiarity, knowledge and proficiency in terms of how learners demonstrate the use of technology in their daily activities. Some learners find difficulty in learning with technologies because they lack technological competency. With the growing popularity of mobile and social media technologies, many people, particularly younger generations, also be described as digital natives, have become more digitally literate in their daily lives. However, previous research surprisingly suggested that although digital natives frequently use information and communication technologies during their non-learning activities, they are reluctant to engage with features such as instant messaging and social networking as part of their learning environment. In fact, many studies indicate that technologies are more likely to increase distraction rather than improve learning. There are various reasons for the distraction, including challenges in handling different user interfaces, overly complex technology, poor understanding of learning arrangement, etc.

Another type of technological related challenge is the technological sufficiency challenge, some related problems such as insufficient access to technology, inequality of technological accessibility, outdated technology. In fact, the rapid development of technology even increases inequality. One example is Internet, on one hand, new experiences be introduced in learning based on various technologies such as VR, AR, etc., on the other hand, learners with low bandwidth and slow processing speeds lead them to experience technical difficulties in learning.

5.4 The Age of Big Data

Other than the challenges listed above, an even bigger challenge for learners is that they are surrounded by a huge volume of data. In fact, a situation of today's world is that a huge volume of data and information have been and are being generated, processed, transmitted and recorded due to the fast development of various IoT devices. In the big data environment, it is very easy to get bombarded with information. Information overload has created many potential issues, such as it can reduce human attention span. One of the examples is in the music industry; according to a previous study, the average time that passed before the audience would hear the vocals on any radio song was 23 s in the past, but it takes just 5 s in average in 2017 as per (Gauvin, 2017). Another effect is that the huge volume of data and information would encourage people to selectively receive new information from daily life. In foreseeable future, professionals need to realise that the data volumes will continue to grow, that means financial professional will even deal with more information and very likely the information is real-time and in different formats. This situation is negatively affecting financial professionals when they learn new skills.

6 How Do People Learn?

In order to overcome the learning challenge in the big data age, people need to know how learning takes place. Therefore, we are back to the very fundamental in this section to review related learning theories and concepts. This review is important because understanding how people learn can help them learn more effectively.

6.1 Related Theories of Learning

Understanding how humans learn can help learners to achieve better reskilling and retraining results. In very brief, learning is an information process in our brain. Our brain receives information coming in, then manipulates it and stores it ready for future use—this forms a learning process.

Cognitive load plays an important role in human learning. Information Processing Theory (Atkinson & Shiffrin, 1968) is a cognitive theory that focuses on how information is encoded into our memory. As per the theory, when humans receive information, that piece of information is first briefly stored in sensory memory; it then being moved to working memory (i.e. short term memory), and then the information is encoded and stored in the long-term memory, as either: semantic memories (i.e. concepts and general information), procedural memories (i.e. processes) or images. During the information process, some information would be forgotten, that is not being transferred further to the next step.

When the sensory information is passed into working memory, it will be either processed or forgotten. Sensory Information are things that the brain collects from human senses that give human information about the world around us.

However, a key issue of learning is that working memory can generally hold only between five to seven items of information at any time. Therefore, human cognitive processes filter information, deciding what is important enough to save from human sensory memory to short-term memory, and ultimately to encode into our long-term memory. Human cognitive processes include thinking, perception, remembering, recognition, logical reasoning, imagining, problem-solving, our sense of judgement, and planning. More specifically, the processed information in long-term memory is stored in knowledge structures called 'schemas' as a piece of organised information, such as different categories of documents, colleagues, policies, etc. There are also behavioural schemas for actions like operating a machine, using an equipment, updating a record, etc. The more practice on those schemas, the more effortless and effective those behaviours would become.

As explained above, working memory has limited capacity. Therefore, a potential issue of reskilling and retraining is cognitive overload, which refers to the processing demands associated with the learning tasks exceed our working memory capacity (i.e. cognitive processing capacity). Therefore, the limitation on working memory capacity should be taken into consideration during reskilling and retraining.

In financial industry, particularly under the highly competitive, fast-changing environment and in the age of big data, humans receive a huge amount of incoming sensory information. Sensory memory filters out most of this information, but impressions of the most important items are kept long enough for them to pass into working memory.

Although working memory capacity is limited, the use of working memory can be used more efficiently in two ways. Firstly, humans process visual and auditory information separately, and the two types of information will not compete with each other in working memory. Making use of both visual and auditory information at the same time is one way to optimise the use of working memory. Secondly, working memory treats an established schema as a single item, and a highly practiced schema requires only minimum cognitive load. In other words, if pre-training or briefing is done before introducing a more complex task will help learners to build up established schemas that can optimise the use of their working memory. This practice also means that learners can understand and learn more complex and difficult information.

7 Solutions and Recommendations

As mentioned in previous sections, human is living in the big data world and human have only limited capacity to process information. In this last section, as a summary, microlearning is introduced as an effective learning approach for retraining and reskilling financial professionals in the digital age.

In recent years, microlearning has been considered a promising topic in work-based learning. Microlearning refers to an educational approach that offers bite-sized, small learning units with just the necessary amount of information to help learners achieve a goal. In brief, the key benefits of using microlearning include (1) better retention of concepts, (2) better engagement for learners, (3) improving learners' motivation, (4) engaging in collaborative learning, and (5) improving learning ability and performance (Hug, 2005).

Although there are many versions or definitions of microlearning, in practice microlearning often refers to well-segmented, bite-sized chunks of data on any single topic, and normally calibrated to a few minutes duration for users to access at any time or location, of their preference.

Big data plays an important role in the development of microlearning. In the age of Big Data, human attention span is decreasing. In comparison to the traditional approach that face-to-face study times are scheduled, it is now people expect to learn instantly anytime, anywhere. In the workplace, people used to have information at their fingertips, finding the answers they need within minutes. This has dramatically changed people's expectations of workplace learning. Also, more and more employees are preferred to taking control of their own learning. A previous survey (Mazareanu, 2019) suggests that 80% of employees are learning when they need it. Accordingly, the need for on-demand training, or just-in-time learning, is growing. This trend also facilitates the development of microlearning.

From the retraining and reskilling perspective, microlearning should be a key topic in talent development topics. In practice, microlearning can facilitate knowledge acquisition in the workplace by engaging and motivating employees to communicate and apply what they have learned. On the other hand, many learners prefer on-demand learning and access to up-to-date information in a timely manner under the current competitive business environment; therefore, microlearning is ideal for this purpose. Furthermore, microlearning is effective at increasing the feelings of confidence and accuracy in the work of dairy personnel.

It is worth mentioning that in the big data age, people have become habituated to having on-demand access to knowledge. They want to be able to learn just when they require. In fact, contemporary learners have enjoyed a technology-rich environment that has socialised them towards expectations of rapid information exchange and a tendency towards reduced or non-textbook reading. Moreover, on-demand learning and microlearning often go hand in hand. However, we consider on-demand learning is a double-edged sword, particularly in this fast-changing big data age. Nowadays people are facing more and more new issues and challenges. How people respond to an issue depending on what they know. But human knowledge is not born naturally; it is obtained through learning, and knowledge obtained from their learnings gradually construct their frame of reference. In recent years, the boom of technologies enables many new opportunities for people to acquire knowledge in different ways through the Internet. On this, self-directed learning without guidance and supervision could lead to several risks, such as obtaining inaccurate information, learning from false knowledge, making a judgment based on unreliable sources, etc. More importantly, once a view is formed, it will not easily be changed, instead, the view will be strengthened because people prefer to perceive what they want to receive in knowledge while ignoring opposing viewpoints, that is, selective perception. As a result, that knowledge with a clear specific opinion would be less likely to spread out to the people with the opposite opinion. Instead, like-minded people within the same group would be easier to obtain similar information and the information would reinforce their existing views as an 'echo chamber' effect. Given microlearning plays an important role in on-demand learning, learners should carefully learn in the right direction.

8 Conclusion

Instead of focusing on any specific financial data analytics techniques, this chapter review how to learn new skills and knowledge according to personal context. In fact, technology is becoming even more important in the finance industry in recent years and billions of financial professionals in the world need to be retrained and reskilled to become 'digital workers'. In addition to the emerging hard and soft skills, this chapter also reviews the importance of personality type and career choices in the financial industry. Financial professionals should better understand their own personality type before investing time, money and effort in retraining and reskilling.

Once financial professionals understood their own personality types and identified their career routes, they should prepare themselves for the new roles or take new responsibilities in the digital age. In this regard, financial professionals should realise that learning with technologies is the trend. Although there are many platforms, opportunities and enabling technologies for people to learn, there is no lack of challenges. Therefore, understanding how humans learn can help learners to achieve better reskilling and retraining results. Moreover, a key recommendation in this chapter is about why and how microlearning can help learners to learn effectively in the big data world. Hopefully, this chapter can facilitate financial professionals to reflect on how to reskill and retain themselves to meet the future ever-changing financial industry. It is worth mentioning that machine learning revolution and how to handle big data are two key challenges and hot topics in future, financial professionals are recommended to develop their own coding skills in these directions.

Acknowledgment No specific grant or funding was received from any funding organisations for this research.

References

Atkinson, R. C., & Shiffrin, R. M. (1968). Human memory: A proposed system and its control processes. In K. W. Spence & J. T. Spence (Eds.), *The psychology of learning and motivation* (Vol. 2, pp. 89–195). Academic.

Gauvin, H. L. (2017). Drawing listener attention in popular music: Testing five musical features arising from the theory of attention economy. *Musicae Scientiae, 22*(2), 291–304.

Haenlein, M., & Kaplan, A. (2019). A brief history of artificial intelligence: On the past, present, and future of artificial intelligence. *California Management Review, 61*(4), 5–14.

Hug, T. (2005). "Microlearning: A new pedagogical challenge", Microlearning: Emerging concepts, practices and technologies after e-learning. In *Proceedings of microlearning 2005* (pp. 13–18). Innsbruck University Press.

Leong, K., & Sung, A. (2018). FinTech (Financial Technology): What is it and how to use technologies to create business value in fintech way? *International Journal of Innovation, Management and Technology, 9*(2), 74–78.

Mazareanu, E. (2019). Time employees take to learn worldwide. Retrieved from https://www.statista.com/statistics/885973/time-employees-take-to-learn-worldwide/.

Rasheed, R. A., Kamsin, A., & Abdullah, N. A. (2020). Challenges in the online component of blended learning: A systematic review. *Computers & Education, 144*, 103701.

Sung, A., Leong, K., & Cunningham, S. (2020). Emerging technologies in education for sustainable development. In F. W. Leal, A. Azul, L. Brandli, P. Özuyar, & T. Wall (Eds.), *Partnerships for the goals. Encyclopedia of the UN sustainable development goals*. Springer.

The Myers & Briggs Foundation. (n.d.-a). MBTI basics. Retrieved from https://www.myersbriggs.org/my-mbti-personality-type/mbti-basics/

The Myers & Briggs Foundation. (n.d.-b). The 16 MBTI types. Retrieved from https://www.myersbriggs.org/my-mbti-personality-type/mbti-basics/the-16-mbti-types.htm

World Economic Forum. (2020). *The future of jobs report 2020*. World Economic Forum. Retrieved from https://www.weforum.org/reports/the-future-of-jobs-report-2020

Basics of Financial Data Analytics

Sinem Derindere Köseoğlu, Waleed M. Ead, and Mohamed M. Abbassy

Abstract There is enormous structured and unstructured data generated every moment in the financial sector in the digitalized era. The data can be used to create strategies for related parts of the financial sector. Even though some statistical properties of financial data have been studied using data from various sources for over half a century, the availability of big data in the financial sector and the developed applications of computer-intensive techniques for investigating their properties have opened new horizons to analysts in the sector in the last two decades. Digitization in the financial sector has enabled technology forms of advanced data analytics. In this book, most of these financial data analysis issues are tried to be addressed. This chapter is handled as an introduction to the subject. Therefore, in this chapter, data science, data types, financial time series data properties, data analysis techniques, and data analysis processes are explained. In addition, RStudio has been handled as an introduction here. This chapter covers working with data structure, working with data-frames, importing data from different data sources, data preparation (cleaning data, handling missing data, and manipulation data) using some statistical functions, analyzing financial basic time series characteristics, and data visualization with RStudio.

Keywords Data science · Data types · Data analytics · Descriptive statistics · Financial time series characteristics · Data preparation · Basic R codes

S. Derindere Köseoğlu (✉)
Formerly Istanbul University, Istanbul, Turkey

W. M. Ead · M. M. Abbassy
Faculty of Computers and Artificial Intelligence, Beni-Suef University, Beni-Suef, Egypt
e-mail: waleedead@bsu.edu.eg

S. Derindere Köseoğlu (ed.), *Financial Data Analytics*, Contributions to Finance and Accounting, https://doi.org/10.1007/978-3-030-83799-0_2

1 Basic Terminology of Data Science

Data science is the process of examining raw data to conclude that useful information and knowledge. Big data has lots of power. It has information and knowledge that exist in the real world, but these are unknown to the researcher and are needed to be revealed. It should be just known how to use this data and how to use this information from data. Therefore, using scientific methods to analyze the big data and extracting information it contains is called ***Data Science***.

Data science contains all steps of the collection, processing, presentation, and interpretation of measurements or observations. Data, on the other hand, is the main material that data science deals with.

Big Data is defined as large and complex data and sets of information from a variety of sources that increase rapidly. That is too large and too complex to be handled by traditional methods and software. Therefore, it needs to be used more developed computer-intensive techniques. Even if there are many definitions of big data, big data includes **"4 Vs"** concepts known as **Volume, Variety, Velocity, and Veracity** (Das, 2016). In addition, Cackett (2016) adds **Value** concepts to these.

- **Volume:** It is related to how much data it contains. Big data can range from terabytes to petabytes.
- **Variety:** It is about how many kinds of data are in the data set. It refers to the different variations of the big data. It contains a wide variety of formats and sources such as e-commerce and online transactions, financial transactions, social media interactions, etc.
- **Velocity (Speed):** It is related to how fast data is produced. Since the data generating speed is very high, data needs to be gathered, stored, processed, handled, and analyzed in relatively short windows.
- **Veracity:** It is related to data uncertainty. The data may be inconsistent, incomplete, ambiguous, and delayed, so it is thought that the data is uncertain.
- **Value:** This represents the utility that can be extracted from the data.

Financial Data *also* covers a huge amount of variety. In financial data science, one can come across many different kinds of data and each of them requires different approaches and techniques. For instance, macroeconomic variables, price quotes, common stock prices, commodity prices, spot prices, futures prices, stock indices' values, other financial market indexes, financial tables information such as balance sheets, income statements, and cash flow statements, financial news, financial analyst opinions, financial transactions, research reports, signals, or any other data or information whatsoever available through the trading platforms can be financial data.

1.1 Classifications of Data

In big data analysis, analysts come across many different types of data. They can be categorized depending on many aspects. According to the different aspects data can be classified as ***Qualitative Data vs. Quantitative Data; Structured vs. Unstructured data***; ***Cross-sectional vs. Time series vs. Panel Data; Deterministic vs. Stochastic Time Series data*** (Fig. 1).

Qualitative (Categorical) data is obtained by dividing data into nonnumerical groups. For example, data regarding whether a person is a woman, or a man can be transformed into categorical data by coding 1 for male and 2 for female. The result of the mathematical operation like 1 + 2 is not meaningful. Qualitative Data types are expressed in more detail as nominal (classified), ordinal (sorted/ordered), and binary data.

- ***Nominal data:*** It is a data type that has two or more answer categories and does not contain a sequential order, and marital status (married, single), gender (female and male), and eye color (blue, green, brown) can be given as examples.
- ***Ordinal data (Ordered Data):*** A data type that has two or more categories but specifies order. Examples of this data type are education levels (primary school, secondary school, high school, university, and postgraduation), competition degrees (1., 2., and 3.), and the development levels of provinces (1. Region, 2. Region, 3. Region, 4), and income status (low, medium, and high). In summary, nominal data can only be categorized but ordinal data both can be categorized and ranked.

Quantitative (numeric) data includes numbers, and it can be performed arithmetic operations, such as addition, subtraction, multiplication, and division. Examples of quantitative data are stock prices, GDP rates, money supply, interest rates, exchange rates, sales volumes, and salaries. Quantitative data are also divided into two classes: ***Continuous and discrete data.*** It is obtained by continuously variable measurement. If an infinite number is significant between two measurements, it is called **continuous data**. Salary and income can be examples of continuous data. The ***discrete data*** type is expressed as an integer, there are no intermediate values. Qualitative variables are often discrete. For example, it can be said 1, 2, 3 women, but not 2.5 women.

The *discrete data can be* binary, nominal, and ordinal. When numbers are given to the categories the data will be quantitative binary, nominal, and ordinal. For instance, if 1 and 0 are given to the yes and no variables, then the data will be quantitative discrete binary data.

The continuous data can be classified as **interval and ratio**. Interval Data is the data with equal distance between values with no natural zero. If it is mentioned a variable such as annual income measured in dollars, there are four people who earn \$5000, \$10,000, \$15,000, and \$20,000. The intervals are equal. Ratio Data is also data with equal distance between values but with natural zero. That is interval data can be categorized, ranked, and equally spaced. Ratio data can be categorized,

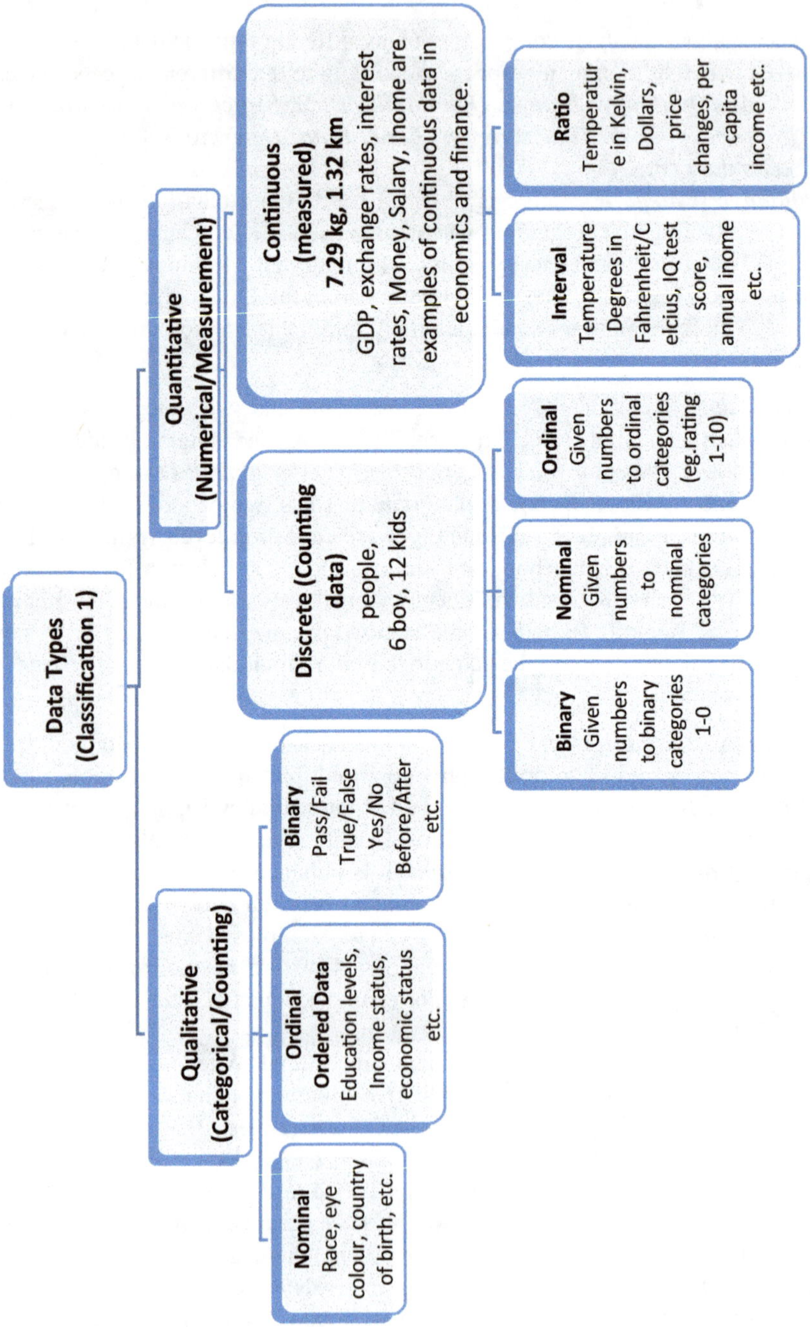

Fig. 1 Qualitative vs. quantitative (numeric) data. Source: Authors' own creation

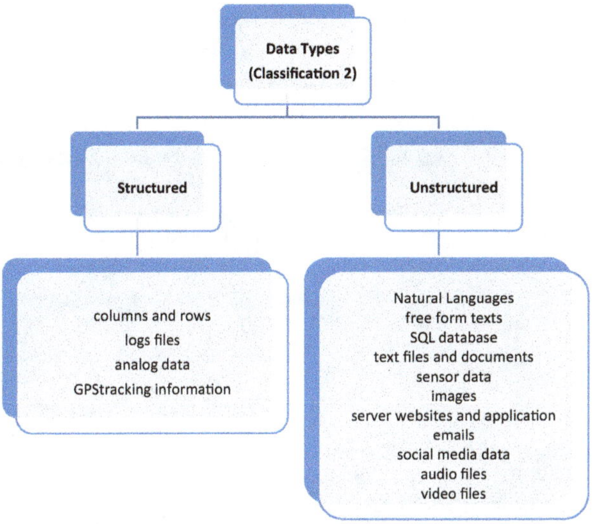

Fig. 2 Structured vs. unstructured data

ranked, equally spaced, and has a natural zero value. Since ratio data has a real/absolute zero value, the ratio between variables can be calculated.

The second classification for data is done depending on if it is structured and unstructured as in Fig. 2.

If the data is organized, it can easily be searchable in related databases. This is called **structured data.** Structured data is generally stored in tables in databases. Unstructured data has no defined format, it is stored in more irregular chunks in databases. A typical example of unstructured data is that of simple text files, images, videos, etc. It is a heterogeneous data source that contains a combination. The Google Search result page is an example of unstructured data. Unstructured data turns into structured data after going through the processes.

Today, the size of unstructured data is beyond multiple zettabytes as its size increases drastically. 10^{21} bytes equal to 1 zettabyte, or a billion terabytes combined into one zettabyte. Looking at these numbers, it can be understood why the Big Data name might be given and it can be imagined the difficulties that arise in its storage and processing.

Natural Language Natural language is a kind of unstructured data. Tweets, social media posts, blog posts, forum posts, and text data are examples of natural data. it is more difficult to process since it needs knowledge of specific data science techniques. Natural Language Processing (NLP) technique is used to extract meaningful and desired information from this kind of data (Cielen et al., 2016).

Machine-Generated Data Machine-generated data is all data that is created by computers, operating systems, processes, infrastructures of software, or other machines without any human intervention (Cielen et al., 2016). Web page requests,

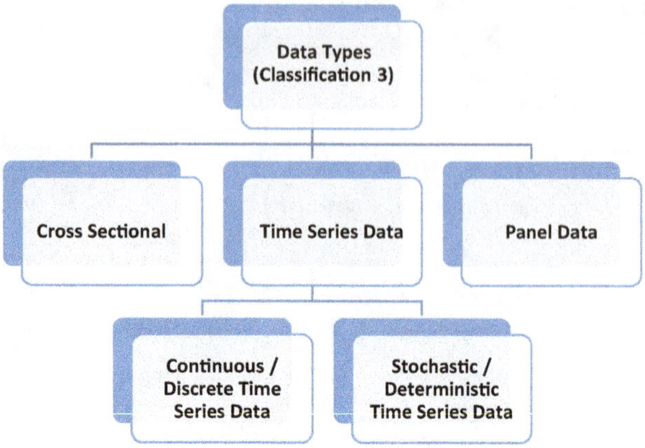

Fig. 3 Cross-sectional vs. time series vs. panel data

clickstreams, telecom calls, and network management logs can all be given as examples of machine-generated data.

Another classification for data is done depending on if the data time series, cross-sectional, and panel as in Fig. 3.

Cross-Sectional vs. Time Series vs. Panel Data

Time Series Data: The series that indicate the distribution of the values of the variables/units according to any time intervals such as day, week, month, and year are called time series. In other words, data indicating the change of values of one or more variables over time are called time series data. Stock market indices, exchange rates, and interest rates are some examples of financial time series examples. Most of the data is financial time series in Finance and Economics.

Continuous time series vs. discrete time series: Time series with data recorded continuously over time are called continuous time series, and data that can only be observed at certain intervals, usually equal intervals, are called discrete time series. While the series belonging to engineering fields such as electrical signals, voltage, and sound vibrations are examples of continuous time series; the interest rate, exchange rate, sales, and production volume data are examples of discrete time series. Asset and derivative prices in finance are examples of continuous time series. Stock prices, option prices are mostly modelled by continuous time financial models.

Another classification for time series data is used as deterministic and stochastic time series data. ***Deterministic vs. Stochastic Time Series:*** The time series which can be predicted exactly are deterministic time series. When the time series can be partly determined by past values; however, the exact prediction cannot be possible, it is mentioned in stochastic time series.

Cross-Sectional Data: Data collected from different units at a certain point of time is called cross-sectional data. In such data, time is fixed, but there are different units monitored in fixed time. In general, surveys provide cross-sectional data. This is one-dimensional data set. Trading volume data of 100 common stocks at the end of a year is an example of financial cross-sectional data. In addition, if one want to examine the financial position of many companies at a certain point of time, e.g., in

2020, they examine financial statement tables in 2020 for those companies, which are cross-sectional data. In general, analyzing cross-sectional data aims to examine similarities and differences between different units at a certain point of time.

Panel Data: Panel data shows the change in both time and cross section units. For instance, the ten states of the USA as a 5-year wheat production. Panel data are different from cross-sectional over time data because it deals with the observations on the same subjects at different times whereas the latter observes different subjects in different time periods.

Other important issues about data are ***Frequency (Time Scale) of the data, Time period (Duration) of the data,*** which affect the results of the empirical study. ***Frequency (Time Scale) of the data:*** Financial time series can be examined for different time scales such as daily, weekly, monthly, and annual (Taylor, 2007). Depending on the frequency of the data, daily, weekly, monthly, or annual returns are calculated. ***Time period (Duration) of the data:*** The duration of calendar time covered by a time series should be as long as possible (Taylor, 2007). The minimum number of years of data required is a controversial issue.

Closing prices, opening prices, high and low prices, and trading volume can also be useful to obtain additional information.

As can be seen, there are many different types of financial data and all of them have their own characteristics. According to the data type, financial data analysis should take shape. While time series analysis and techniques are a major area, cross-sectional data analysis and modelling are another major area. Different approaches are also used in modelling depending on whether the time series is discrete or continuous. In addition, each analysis and modelling have different usage areas in finance. For example, cross-sectional modelling plays an important role in empirical investigations of the Capital Asset Pricing Model (CAPM) or modelling financial time series analysis in continuous time series are popular for derivative asset pricing (Mills & Markellos, 2008). In addition, time series should be modelled differently depending on the characteristics. For example, if the kurtosis coefficient is greater than 3 in the financial time series, it shows that many observations in the series are accumulated in the tails, which indicates that it is appropriate to analyze the series with GARCH models (Tsay, 2002).

When all these variations are considered, it is understood that the field of "financial data analytics" is quite a wide field. Special types of data need special types of processing.

1.2 Data Analytics Types and Data Modelling

Data Analytics Methods and Techniques In the literature, it is seen that there are many different approaches to grouping methods and techniques. The main purpose of any data analysis is to suggest policy and pathways. Therefore, no matter which group it belongs to, the main purpose of data analytics is to define data, model, predict, and suggest policies. These operations already constitute the data analysis process. There are four main types of data analytics in general: Descriptive, Diagnostic, Predictive, and Prescriptive Analytics.

(a) **Descriptive Analytics:** This analytics type is expected to give answer for the question: *"What is happening?"* It is the first step of data analyzing by using historical data. The analysis shows the general patterns of the data. Descriptive analytics provides future probabilities and trends and gives an idea about what might happen in the future.
(b) **Diagnostic Analytics:** This analytics type is expected to give answer for the question: *"Why did it happen?"* This type of analysis tries to answer the root cause of a defined problem/business question. It is used to determine why something happened.
(c) **Predictive Analytics:** It is used to answer the question: *"What is likely to happen in the future?"* It generally uses past data and patterns in order to forecast the future. Forecasting and prediction are the main aim of analytics. Data mining, artificial intelligence, and time series analysis are some of the techniques used under Predictive analytics.
(d) **Prescriptive Analytics:** This analytics type is expected to give answer for the question: *"What should be done?"* This analytics step is related to give pathways and suggest policies. It is aimed to indicate and develop the right action to be taken for policy makers. Prescriptive analytics uses these parameters to find the best solution.

In summary, Descriptive analytics uses historical data and shows the patterns of the data, and predictive analytics helps to predict what might happen in the future. Lastly, Prescriptive analytics uses these parameters to determine the best policies.

Descriptive Analytics

- Descriptive Statistics: Mod, Mean, Median, Frequency, Range, Volatility
- Distribution Analysis, Skewness, Kurtosis
- Exploratory Analysis

Diagnostic Analytics

- Tells how this happen what the descriptive analytics show.
- Tells How do you Drill down the data happened.
- Why did it happen?

Predictive Analytics

- Time series analysis
  - Decomposition of time series:

    Trend analysis
    Seasonality

    Cyclical variations
    Random factors

  - ARIMA
  - GARCH
  - Vector autoregressive (VAR)
  - Regression based time series analysis
  - Deep learning for financial time series
  - Machine learning for financial time series

- Regression

  - Linear regression

    Multivariate regression analysis
    Generalized regression analysis

  - Logistic regression

    Logit/probit regression analysis
    Discrete choice analysis

- Classification
- Clustering/segmentation analysis

  - K-means

- Structural equation modelling
- Factor analysis / principal component analysis
- Decision trees
- Anomaly detection
- Artificial intelligence

  - Neural networks
  - Machine learning
  - Deep learning
  - Natural language processing (NLP)
  - Bayesian networks

Prescriptive Analytics

- Optimization

  - Heuristics (particle swarm optimization—PSO, genetic algorithm—GA)

- Simulation

  - Monte Carlo simulation
  - Markov chain
  - Simulation over random forest

- Sentiment analysis
- Network analysis

- Association rules
- Recommender systems
- Results/outcomes
- Reporting
- Decision-making

2 Data Science Process and Descriptive Analytics

Data science process contains basic steps. Brown (2014) handled data science processes as six main steps: *"Business Understanding, Data Understanding, Data Preparation, Modelling, Evaluation, and Deployment."* In literature, these are defined and titled some different steps. Therefore, it is given in Table 1 that what they mean or what different terms are used for these steps. In this chapter, it is given **data understanding and data preparation steps** with R. Other steps are given in other chapters of the book (for example, chapters "Predictive Analytics Techniques: Theory and Applications in Finance" and "Prescriptive Analytics Techniques: Theory and Applications in Finance").

Most of the data scientists spent much time in preparing their data for the required analysis to be performed. The data preparation step can be summarized into three steps. First, extraction; import/extract the data from the different sources. Second, transform; that involves the data manipulation steps such as handling the missing values and the outliers. Third, visualize your data to check regularity. Figure 4 depicts the required libraries for the data analysis steps.

Table 1 Data science steps

Steps	Definition
Business understanding	Defining project objectives and setting goals. Identifying the problem
Data understanding	Data collection and initial insights about data, descriptive statistics, and visualization
Data preparation	Importing data, data exploration and manipulation, data cleaning, structuring data
Modeling	Developing predictive, descriptive, and prescriptive models: e.g., clustering It should be tried using multiple algorithms related to project objectives
Evaluation	Understanding the models' quality Diagnostic measures Testing set Statistical significance tests
Deployment and visualization	The model is deployed into a limited/test environment Getting feedbacks, strategic decisions Data visualization (Graphs, plots, heatmaps)

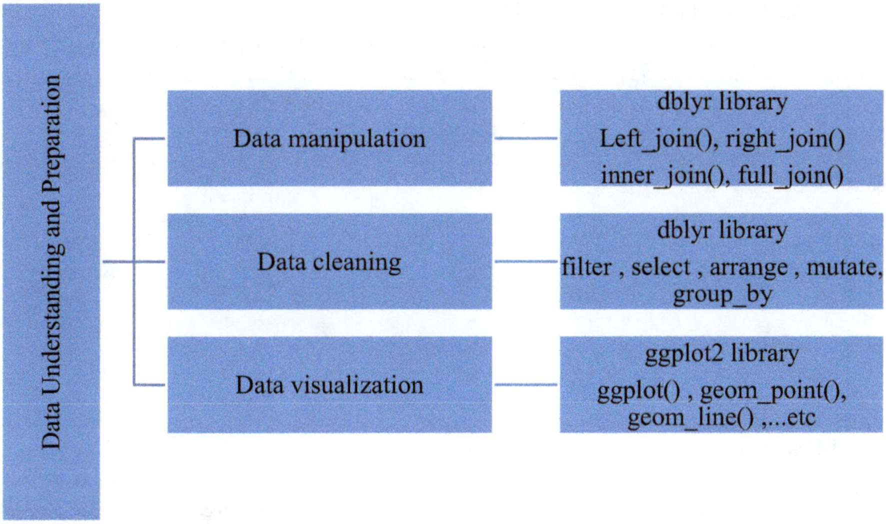

Fig. 4 Data understanding and preparation with RStudio

Data are everywhere. Discovering insights from such data are also more required to build the correct business decision. Furthermore, building a predictive generalized model can reshape any business strategy and its market share. Therefore, data analysts need to program their model, transform the data, and discover the hidden insights and finally need to present the discovered insights with the business owners/ strategy respective. Such predefined programming analytical life cycle needs a productive and flexible tool that can be integrated with others. R language is one of the solutions. R, it is a free programming language developed by the Robert Gentleman Ross Ihaka and in 1993 as an open-source project, that possesses a comprehensive catalogue of graphical, statistical, and analytical methods. Many industries use R in their analytical journey such as healthcare, government, finance, consulting, and academic research purposes. First, you should install the R IDE from the official website https://www.r-project.org. In addition, for ease of use the anaconda platform (https://www.anaconda.com/) to run the R codes.

Studio Cloud is also a hosted version of the integrated development environment (IDE) for R, RStudio in the cloud. This version is provided for making it easy for users to practice data science. There are many advantages of using RStudio.

- Financial data analytics without the hardware hassles.
- Analyze your data using the RStudio IDE, directly from your browser.
- Share projects with your team, class, and workshop.

One of the main advantages of R use analytical journey and working with different data sources such as CSV file, excel sheet, and any platform as showing below.

Collecting Data from Different Data Sources

Data collected from different data sources with different formats such as excel files, csv files, HTML files, STAT files, SAS files, SPSS files. R can connect with different functions to the different data sources formats. After the data was imported, it can be dealt with it as a data frame as explained before.

Read CSV File

Read CSV file

```
PATH <- 'https://raw.githubusercontent.com/guru99-edu/R-Programming/master/mtcars.
csv'
df <- read.csv(PATH, header =  TRUE, sep = ',')
length(df)
```

Read Excel File

The library library(readxl) is required to import excel files. so, you must load it first. After the readxl library installed, many EXCEL examples are also imported. You can explore it by executing the command readxl_example().

```
# Store the path of `datasets.xlsx`
example <- readxl_example("datasets.xlsx")
# Import the spreadsheet
df <- read_excel(example)
# Count the number of columns
length(df)
```

If your excel file has multiple sheets, it can be selected any sheet like the following. In addition, it can be specified the number of rows imported and the column names. The following two examples will show that.

Example 1

```
example <- readxl_example("datasets.xlsx")

excel_sheets(example)
```

Output 1

```
[1] "iris"     "mtcars"   "chickwts" "quakes"
```

Example 2

If you have many sheets in your workbook you can specify the sheet name or the sheet index to be manipulated.

```
example <- readxl_example("datasets.xlsx")
quake <- read_excel(example, sheet = "quakes")
quake_1 <-read_excel(example, sheet = 4)
identical(quake, quake_1)
```

Output 2

```
## [1] TRUE
```

Example 3
This example shows how to read a specific row of data from the sheet excel file.

```
# Read the first five row: with header
iris <-read_excel(example, n_max =5, col_names =TRUE)
# Read rows A1 to B5
example_1 <-read_excel(example, range = "A1:B5", col_names =TRUE)
dim(example_1)
```

2.1 Financial Time Series Characteristics and R

Most of the financial data consist of time series data. Therefore, financial time series data needs to be mentioned in detail. In no doubt each asset, each market, and each time period have their own characteristics and properties. However, empirical results show that there are some common characteristics of financial time series data. The forecasting of the financial time series analytical life cycle consists of main starting phases; data preparation, create and explore the time series, feature engineering, data visualization, smoothing, and stationarity in the time series. We added an example for each of these processes for the financial time series. The whole complete code will be available for the reader.

Unlike the traditional regression predictive model, data frames are organized in specified order based on their time series of occurrence. Therefore, it is good to use the time series to make accurate predictions of the future. The following set of demonstrated examples of financial time series with R, we use the Istanbul stock Exchange Index (ISE100) from 2019 to 2020 to demonstrate the basic characteristics of ISE100. Data are available for the reader. First, the analyst must import the required set of libraries to work will.

Example 4. Load and Explore the Data (Check the Date Format for the Time Series Column)

```
# adjust display settings
%matplotlib inline
plt.rc('figure', figsize=(18, 3))
pd.set_option('display.float_format', lambda x: '%.6f' % x)
pd.options.display.max_rows = 20
```

```
# load dataset
dataframe = pd.read_csv('datasetReturnISE100.csv',
                        index_col='DATE',
                        dtype={'ISE100': np.float32},
                        parse_dates=True,
                        date_parser=lambda date: pd.datetime.strptime(d
ate, '%Y-%m-%d'),
                       )
```

Example 5. Display a Few Lines of the Time Series

```
# display first few lines of a time series
dataframe.head()
```

	datasetReturnISE100
DATE	
2019-03-14	0.008477
2019-03-15	0.012410
2019-03-18	0.002549
2019-03-19	-0.014901
2019-03-20	0.000938

Financial Returns

Many financial time series consists of prices, such as spot prices (stocks, precious metals, commodity, exchange rates, macroeconomic variables), future prices (commodity futures, financial futures). Most researchers examine returns rather than asset prices (Tsay, 2002). Historical returns are calculated as follows:

One period historical return:

$$r_{t+1} = \frac{P_{t+1} - P_t}{P_t}$$

One period logarithmic return:

$$\log\left(r_{t+1}\right) = \ln\left(\frac{P_{t+1}}{P_t}\right)$$

2.1.1 Volatility and Extreme Values of Asset Returns

The characteristics and dynamic nature of financial time series are quite different and challenging (Al-hnaity & Abbod, 2016). For instance, their variances and standard deviations of returns are mostly relatively large. In finance, the volatility of returns is extremely important. It shows the risk of the asset. Risk and return relation is the core logic in finance. Since the volatility of the asset returns is remarkably large, the returns mostly contain extreme returns and large volatility means that the returns diverge from a specific mean in a noticeably short time. We can see this volatility from the graphs.

Example 6. Data Visualization (Line Plot)

```
# create a time series
s = pd.Series(dataframe.unstack().values, index=dataframe.index)
# basic plot
s.plot()
```

Figure 5 indicates the time plots of daily log returns of Istanbul Stock Exchange 100 (ISE100) from March 14, 2019, to April 08, 2020. This figure shows the high volatility of this stock index.

There are many different risk measures. Although there are many criticisms about standard deviation, it is still the most famous risk measure. Risk can be measured mathematically by standard deviation. Range, semi-variance, a lower partial moment can be also used for risk measurements.

Mean of asset returns:

$$\overline{r}_i = \frac{\sum_{t=1}^{n} r_i}{n}$$

Variance of asset returns:

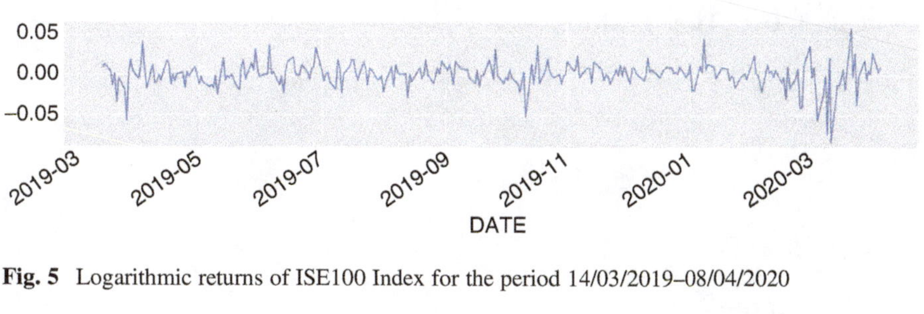

Fig. 5 Logarithmic returns of ISE100 Index for the period 14/03/2019–08/04/2020

$$\text{Var}(r_i) = \sigma_i^2 = \frac{\sum_{t=1}^{n} [r_i - \overline{r}_i]^2}{n-1}$$

Standard deviation of asset returns:

$$\text{Std}(r_i) = \sigma_i = \sqrt{\text{Var}(r_i)}$$

Some Other Descriptive Statistics

$$\text{Range} = \text{Max value} - \text{Min value}$$

$$\text{Mid range} = \frac{\text{Max Value} + \text{Mid Value}}{2}$$

Quartiles
1st quartiles = 25% th value

2nd quartiles = 50% th value

3rd quartiles = 75% th value

Descriptive statistics give a general tendency of the time series.

Example 7. Descriptive Statistics of a Financial Return Series
In this code, we can get the main descriptive statistics of a financial time series.

```
# calculate descriptive statistics
s.describe()
```

```
count    279.000000
mean      -0.000338
std        0.016189
min       -0.084162
25%       -0.006801
50%        0.000000
75%        0.008223
max        0.058104
dtype: float64
```

Example 8. Date Time Feature

```
df = pd.DataFrame()
df['year'] = [s.index[i].year for i in range(len(s))]
df['month'] = [s.index[i].month for i in range(len(s))]
df['value'] = s.values.tolist()
df.head()
```

	year	month	value
0	2019	3	0.008477
1	2019	3	0.012410
2	2019	3	0.002549
3	2019	3	-0.014901
4	2019	3	0.000938

Example 9. Lag Features of ISE100 Return Series
Sometimes we want to see the different lags of the financial time series.

```
values = pd.DataFrame(s.values)
df = pd.concat([values.shift(1), values], axis=1)
df.columns = ['t', 't+1']
df.head()
```

	t	t+1
0	nan	0.008477
1	0.008477	0.012410
2	0.012410	0.002549
3	0.002549	-0.014901
4	-0.014901	0.000938

Example 10. Sliding Window Features
We can see different lags together with sliding windows:

```
values = pd.DataFrame(s.values)
df = pd.concat([values.shift(3), values.shift(2), values.shift(1), valu
es], axis=1)
df.columns = ['t-2', 't-1', 't', 't+1']
df.head()
```

	t-2	t-1	t	t+1
0	nan	nan	nan	0.008477
1	nan	nan	0.008477	0.012410
2	nan	0.008477	0.012410	0.002549
3	0.008477	0.012410	0.002549	-0.014901
4	0.012410	0.002549	-0.014901	0.000938

Example 11. Summary Statistics Across the Sliding Window Features (Rolling Mean)
We can also calculate summary statistics for sliding windows:

```
values = pd.DataFrame(s.values)
shifted = values.shift(1)
window = shifted.rolling(window=2)
means = window.mean()

df = pd.concat([means, values], axis=1)
df.columns = ['mean(t-1,t)', 't+1']
df.head()
```

	mean(t-1,t)	t+1
0	nan	0.008477
1	nan	0.012410
2	0.010444	0.002549
3	0.007480	-0.014901
4	-0.006176	0.000938

Example 12. Related to the Above Example

```
values = pd.DataFrame(s.values)
width = 3
shifted = values.shift(width - 1)
window = shifted.rolling(window=width)

df = pd.concat([window.min(), window.mean(), window.max(), values], axi
s=1)
df.columns = ['min', 'mean', 'max', 't+1']
df.head()
```

	min	mean	max	t+1
0	nan	nan	nan	0.008477
1	nan	nan	nan	0.012410
2	nan	nan	nan	0.002549
3	nan	nan	nan	-0.014901
4	0.002549	0.007812	0.012410	0.000938

2.1.2 Distribution Characteristics of Asset Returns

Since the large volatility and having extreme values, the distribution of asset returns is mostly not normal and generally high kurtosis (heavy tailed/fat tailed) and skewed. Normal distribution refers that simple returns are independently and identically distributed (iid) as normal fixed mean and variance. Lognormal Distribution refers that the log returns of a financial asset are iid as normal with mean and variance. In a normal distribution, the mean, mode, and median values of the returns are equal, and the distribution is symmetrical with respect to the arithmetic mean. However, many empirical results show that the asset returns have wider spreads. This contradicts the normal distribution assumption. Modeling such series with normal distribution does not give reliable results (Tuna & İsabetli, 2014).

The function of normal distribution of returns:

$$f(r_i) = \frac{1}{\sigma_{r_i}\sqrt{2\pi}} \mathrm{e}^{-(r_i - \overline{r_i})^2/2\sigma_{r_i}}$$

where $\overline{r_i}$ *average of returns, and* σ_{r_i} standard deviation of returns, and $\pi \cong 3.14159$ and $\mathrm{e} \cong 2.71828$.

Skewness in Asset Return Distribution The skewness coefficients, which are accepted as the third moment, are in general different from "0" for asset returns. Skewness statistics are used to estimate the symmetry of the distributions (Taylor, 2007). A skewness coefficient greater than 0 indicates a positive return, while the opposite indicates a negative return. The fact that the skewness coefficient is different from 0 is also a situation that disrupts the normal distribution (Tsay,

2002). The empirical distributions of asset returns are in general skewed to the left, as negative returns are generally greater than positive returns (Hatipoğlu, 2015).

The skewness of the returns:

$$S(r_i) = \frac{\sum_{t=1}^{n} [r_i - \bar{r}_i]^3}{(n-1)\sigma_{r_i}^3}$$

Kurtosis in Asset Return Distribution The kurtosis coefficients, which are considered as the fourth moment, are different from "3" for asset returns. If the kurtosis coefficient is different from 3, it also disrupts the normal distribution (Tsay, 2005: 9). Asset returns have in general high kurtosis (which means heavy tails/fat tails and peaked center relative to the normal distribution). The distribution of asset returns is increasingly positive kurtosis while the frequency of data increases (Cont, 2001; Sewel, 2011).

The kurtosis of the returns:

$$K(r_i) = \frac{\sum_{t=1}^{n} [r_i - \bar{r}_i]^4}{(n-1)\sigma_{r_i}^4}$$

Example 13. Skewness, Kurtosis, and Jarque Bera Statistics

```
print(s.skew())
print(s.kurtosis())
print(stats.jarque_bera(s))
```

```
-1.000162
5.366248
Jarque_beraResult(statistic=366.3234408460616, pvalue=0.0)
```

According to the Jarque–Bera test statistics, index returns are not normally distributed. Negative skewness shows that the distribution of index returns is skewed to the left. It shows a decreasing trend in index returns. Since the kurtosis coefficient is greater than 3, it indicates that many observations in the series have accumulated in the tail. Since the Kurtosis coefficient is greater than 3, the distribution is peaker than normal, which approves leptokurtic distribution and means higher return volatility.

It can be drawn histogram, density, box plot, and **multiple scatter** of time series.

Example 14. Data Visualization (Histogram, Density, and Box Plot)

```
s.plot()
```

```
s.plot(style='k.')
```

```
s.plot(style='k.')
```

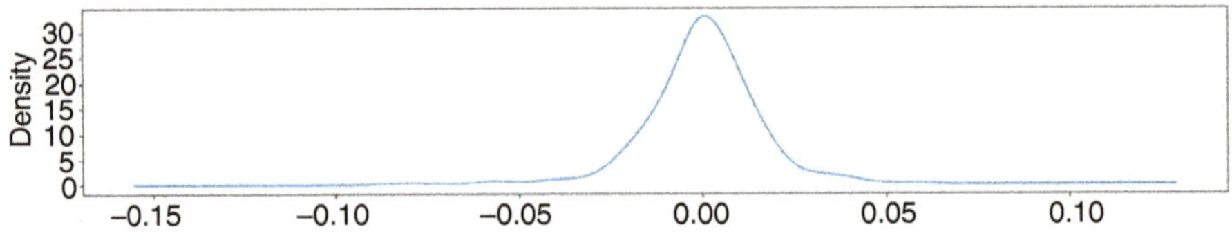


```
df.head(10).T.boxplot()
```

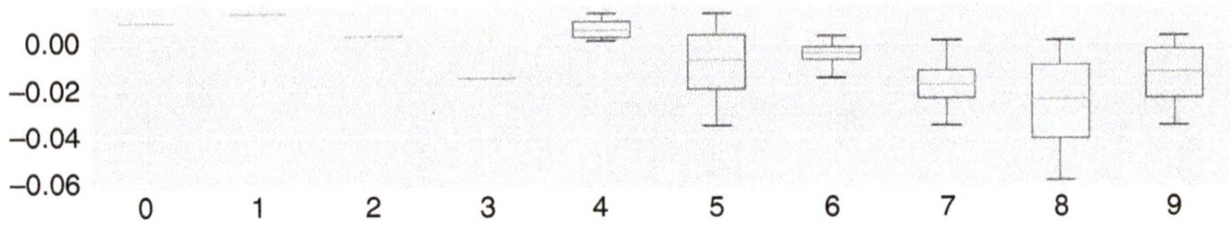

Example 15. Multiple Scatter

```
# create multiple scatter plots
values = pd.DataFrame(s.values)
lags = 8
columns = [values]

for i in range(1,(lags + 1)):
    columns.append(values.shift(i))

df = pd.concat(columns, axis=1)
columns = ['t+1']

for i in range(1,(lags + 1)):
    columns.append('t-' + str(i))
df.columns = columns

plt.figure(1, figsize=(15,9))
for i in range(1,(lags + 1)):
    ax = plt.subplot(240 + i)
    ax.set_title('t+1 vs t-' + str(i))
    plt.scatter(x=df['t+1'].values, y=df['t-'+str(i)].values)
```

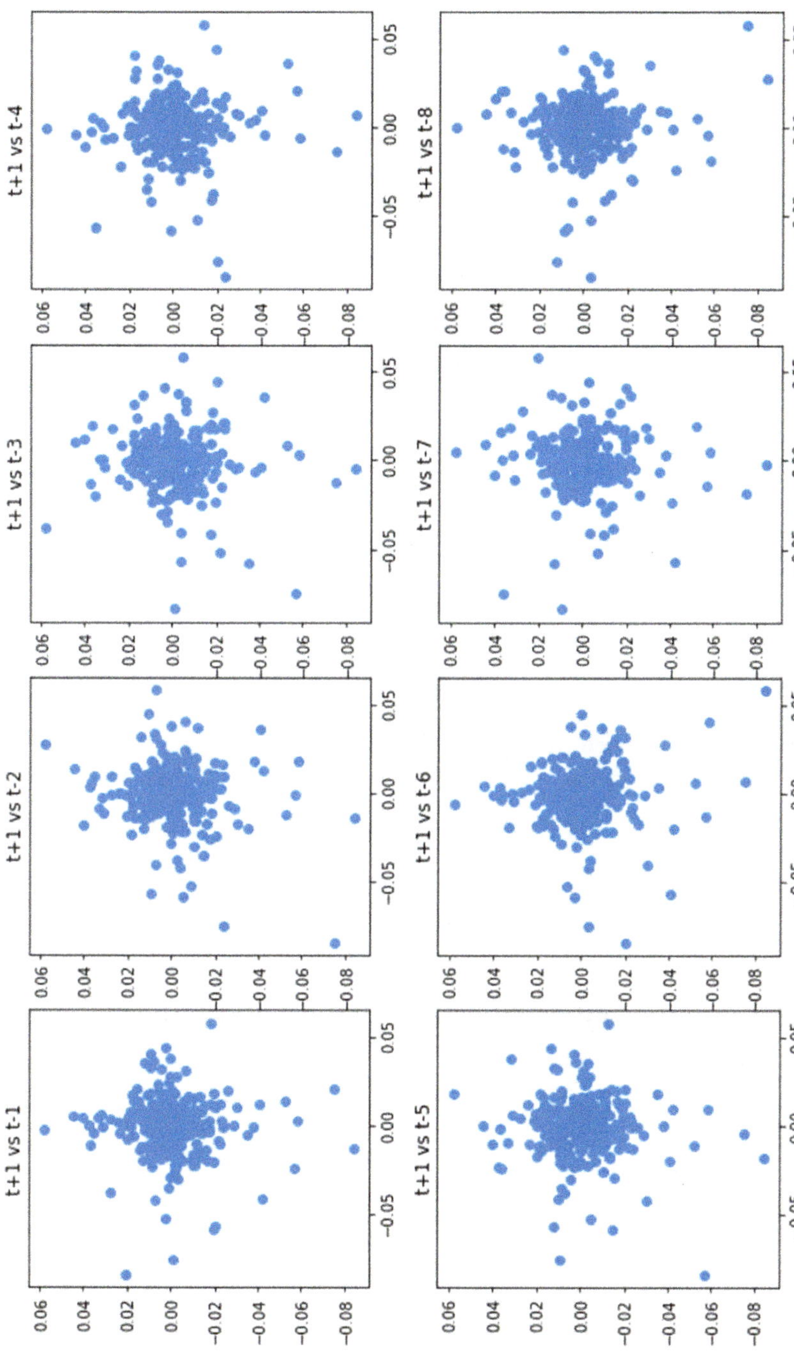
t+1 vs t-1
t+1 vs t-2
t+1 vs t-3
t+1 vs t-4
t+1 vs t-5
t+1 vs t-6
t+1 vs t-7
t+1 vs t-8

2.1.3 Stationarity Characteristics of Financial Time Series

If the time series is stationary, it means that the *mean* and *variance*, and the *correlation structure* of the series and lastly *lags of the series* do not change over time. Stationarity can be tested with ADF test statistics.

In unit root test, it can be expressed the dependent variable Y_t according to the random walk model (stochastic) as follows:

$$Y_t = \mu + \phi_1 Y_{t-1} + u_t$$

In DF (Dickey & Fuller, 1979), it is tested that $\phi = 1$ against $\phi < 1$ in the above equation.

$H_0 = \phi = 1$ unit root, not stationary

$H_1 = \phi < 1$ no unit root, stationary

Depending on $\Psi = 0(? - 1 = \Psi)$ equations are created as:

$$\Delta Y_t = \Psi Y_{t-1} + u_t$$

The test statistics of the model is as below:

$$\Psi / \mathrm{SE}(\Psi)$$

If estimated test statistics is less than the critical value, H_0 is rejected and concluded that the series are stationary.

In the ADF (Augmented Dickey Fuller Test) unit root test, the following pattern is applied to show the delay number p. And the test statistics is the same as DF unit root test.

$$\Delta Y_t = \Psi Y_{t-1} + \sum_{i=1}^{p} \alpha_i \Delta y_{t-i} + \beta_t + u_t$$

Asset return series are in general stationary since they are calculated as the first differences of prices. However, it can be seen calendar effects like the January effect, and weekend effect.

Example 16. Performing ADF Stationarity Test

```
# calculate stationarity test of time series data
X = s.values
result = adfuller(X)
print('ADF Statistic: %f' % result[0])
print('p-value: %f' % result[1])
print('Critical Values:')
for key, value in result[4].items():
    print('\t%s: %.3f' % (key, value))
```

```
ADF Statistic: -10.000092
p-value: 0.000000
Critical Values:
        1%: -3.454
        5%: -2.872
        10%: -2.572
```

According to test results, test statistics is less than all critical values so ISE100 index return series is stationary.

2.1.4 Dependence (Autocorrelation/Serial Correlation/Serial Dependence/Mean Reversion)

Correlation coefficient between two asset returns is calculated as below:

$$\rho_{i,j} = \frac{\mathrm{Cov}_{i,j}}{\sqrt{\sigma_i^2 \sigma_j^2}} = \frac{\sum_{t=1}^{n} (r_{it} - \overline{r}_i)(r_{jt} - \overline{r}_j)}{\sqrt{\sum_{t=1}^{n} (r_{it} - \overline{r}_i)^2 \sum_{t=1}^{n} (r_{jt} - \overline{r}_j)^2}}$$

$\rho_{i,\,j}$ measures the strength of linear dependence between i and j.

Correlation can be in returns (r_t), in absolute value $|r_t|$ and squared returns $(r_t)^2$, and in volatility $\left(\sigma_{r_t}^2\right)$.

Dependence in Returns When the linear dependence between r_t and its past values r_{t-1} is for interest, the concept of correlation is generalized to **autocorrelation** (Tsay, 2002). Then the correlation coefficient between r_t and r_{t-1} is calculated as below:

$$\rho_{r_t, r_{t-l}} = \frac{\mathrm{Cov}_{r_t, r_{t-l}}}{\sqrt{\sigma_{r_t}^2 \sigma_{r_{t-l}}^2}}$$

$\theta_{r_t, r_{t-l}}$ called the lag-l autocorrelation of r_t. For example, the lag-1 sample autocorrelation of r_t is:

$$\rho_1 = \frac{\sum_{t=2}^{n} (r_t - \bar{r})(r_{t-1} - \bar{r})}{\sqrt{\sum_{t=1}^{n} (r_t - \bar{r})^2}}$$

The autocorrelation of financial returns is mostly insignificant. There sometimes exit only small anomalies. Analysts in general require to test many autocorrelations of r_t together for financial analysis. According to the meaningful results for financial applications, there needs to be zero joint autocorrelation. Box and Pierce (1970) propose the Portmanteau statistics to test whether jointly several autocorrelations of r_t are zero or not.

$$\theta'(n) = T \sum_{l=1}^{n} \widehat{\rho}_l^2$$

$$H_0 = \rho_1 = \rho_2 = \ldots \rho_n = 0$$

$$H_1 = \rho_i \neq 0$$

Ljung and Box (1978) develop $\theta'(n)$ statistics. It is formulized as below:

$$\theta(n) = T(T+2) \sum_{l=1}^{n} \frac{\widehat{\rho}_l^2}{T-l}$$

The sample autocorrelation function (ACF) of r_t refers to the function $\widehat{\rho}_1, \widehat{\rho}_2, \widehat{\rho}_3 \ldots$. If all the ACFs are zero, it is called the white noise series. The absence of autocorrelations in returns gives some empirical evidence for "randomwalk" models of prices in which the returns are considered to be independent random variables.

Dependence in Volatility (Heterogeneity vs. Homoscedasticity of Asset Returns) One another feature of financial asset returns is that the autocorrelation of volatility is not zero. Volatility of financial asset returns in general shows positive autocorrelation. In financial asset return series, volatility movements follow each other, high volatility is followed by high volatility and low volatility is followed by small volatility. This is called "volatility clustering" due to the fact that these volatility movements tend to cluster in time. The different instinctive attitudes and future expectations of investors who invest in the financial market affect the frequency and volume of transactions and cause volatility clustering (Engle et al., 1990). Therefore, it can be difficult for financial asset returns to assume homoscedastic.

Example 17. ARCH Tests

```
X = s.values
model = arch_model(X)
model.fit()
```

```
Iteration:      1,   Func. Count:      6,   Neg. LLF: 1.8170361447461885e+18
Iteration:      2,   Func. Count:     17,   Neg. LLF: -777.9379394669091
Optimization terminated successfully    (Exit mode 0)
            Current function value: -777.9379400775828
            Iterations: 6
            Function evaluations: 17
            Gradient evaluations: 2
```

```
                     Constant Mean - GARCH Model Results
==============================================================================
Dep. Variable:                      y   R-squared:                       0.000
Mean Model:             Constant Mean   Adj. R-squared:                  0.000
Vol Model:                      GARCH   Log-Likelihood:                777.938
Distribution:                  Normal   AIC:                          -1547.88
Method:            Maximum Likelihood   BIC:                          -1533.35
                                        No. Observations:                  279
Date:                Thu, Feb 11 2021   Df Residuals:                      278
Time:                        14:52:25   Df Model:                            1
                                 Mean Model
=============================================================================
                 coef    std err          t      P>|t|       95.0% Conf. Int.
-----------------------------------------------------------------------------
mu         8.0221e-04  7.863e-04      1.020      0.308 [-7.390e-04,2.343e-03]
                              Volatility Model
============================================================================
                 coef    std err          t      P>|t|      95.0% Conf. Int.
----------------------------------------------------------------------------
omega      2.6114e-05  1.541e-06     16.949  1.955e-64 [2.309e-05,2.913e-05]
alpha[1]       0.1000  4.204e-02      2.379  1.738e-02   [1.760e-02,  0.182]
beta[1]        0.8000  2.371e-02     33.738 1.625e-249     [  0.754,  0.846]
============================================================================

Covariance estimator: robust
ARCHModelResult, id: 0x28b43a75370
```

Example 18. Portmanteau Statistics for Autocorrelation Testing

```
sm.stats.acorr_ljungbox(s, lags=[10], return_df=True)
```

	lb_stat	lb_pvalue
10	17.503799	0.063933

Note that the sm is the statistical model library that has been imported before. In addition, the Ib_stat is the test statistics and the Ib_pvalue is the pvalue based on the Chi-square distribution.

Example 19. Creating Correlation Plots

```
# create an autocorrelation plot
autocorrelation_plot(s)
```

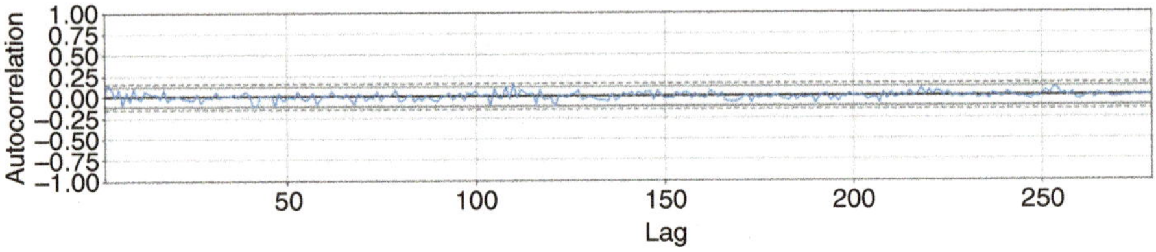


```
# autocorrelation plot of time series as a line plot
plot_acf(s, lags=50)
plt.show()
```

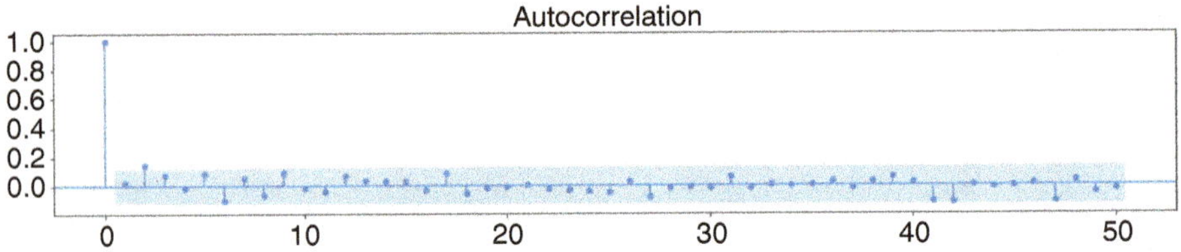

Example 20. Creating an Autocorrelation Plot

```
# create an autocorrelation plot, using only the last 100 entries
autocorrelation_plot(s[-100:])
```

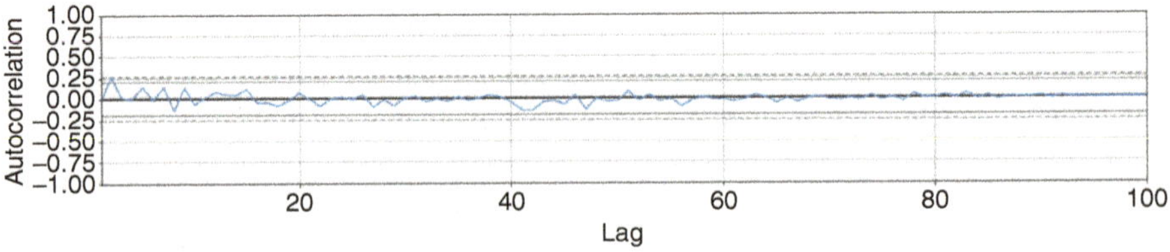

```
# autocorrelation plot of time series as a line plot
plot_acf(s[-100:], lags=50)
plt.show()
```

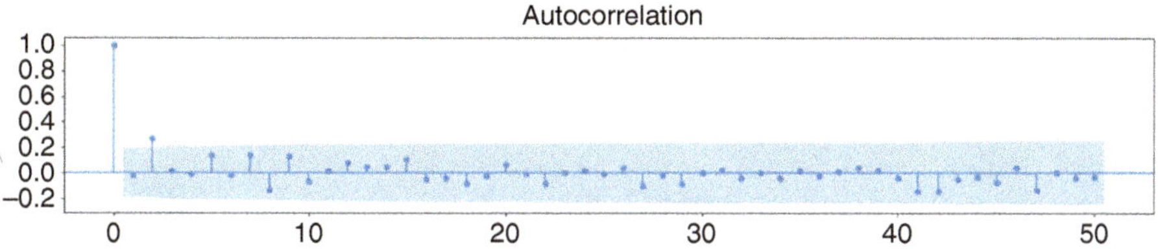

2.2 *Smoothing*

Smoothing is a useful technique in the data preparation. It is a technique applied to time series to remove the fine-grained variation between time steps. It is pretty important in time series pre-processing, especially as the data may be variant or has a noisy value. One of the most used smoothing techniques is the moving average techniques which filter the time series data from the noisy random data and transform it for prediction. In Moving Average Smoothing, each observation is assigned an equal weight, and each observation is forecasted by using the average of the previous observation(s). Using the time series X_1, X_2, X_3, ..., X_t, this smoothing technique predicts X_{t+k} as follows:

$$\text{St} = \text{Average}\ (x_{t-k+1}, x_{t-k+2}, \ldots, x_t), \qquad t = k, k+1, k+2, \ldots N$$

where k is the smoothing parameter.

Example 21. Applying Smoothing to the Data

```
# tail-rolling average transform
rolling = s.rolling(window=3)
rolling_mean = rolling.mean()
# plot original and transformed dataset
s[-100:].plot()
rolling_mean[-100:].plot(color='red')
```

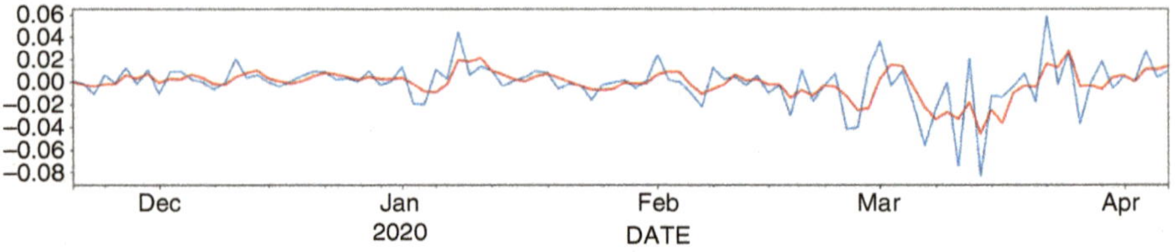

Example 22. Use Average as a Prediction After Smoothing
Note in this example, we use the average value as a prediction value. Moreover, the moving average model for predictions can easily be used in a walk-forward manner. As new observations are made available (e.g., daily), the model can be updated and a prediction made for the next day.

```
# prepare problem
X = s.values
window = 3
history = [X[i] for i in range(window)]
test = [X[i] for i in range(window, len(X))]
predictions = []

# walk forward over time steps in test
for t in range(len(test)):
    length = len(history)
    yhat = np.mean([history[i] for i in range(length-window,length)])
    obs = test[t]
    predictions.append(yhat)
    history.append(obs)
    #print('predicted=%f, expected=%f' % (yhat, obs))
rmse = np.sqrt(mean_squared_error(test, predictions))
# print('RMSE: %.3f' % rmse)
# plot
plt.plot(test)
plt.plot(predictions, color='red')
plt.show()
```

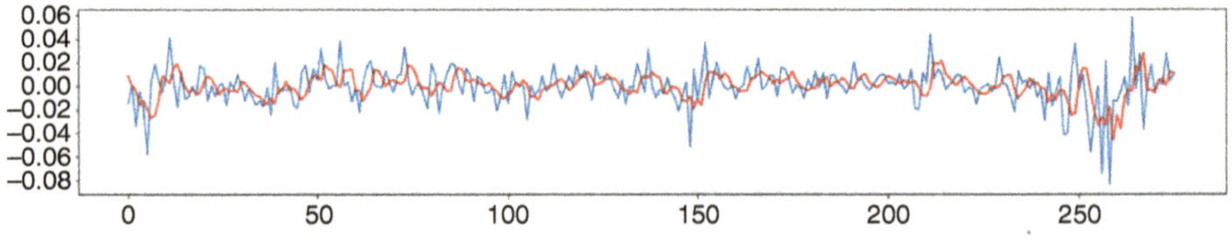


```
# zoom plot
plt.plot(test[:100])
plt.plot(predictions[:100], color='red')
plt.show()
```

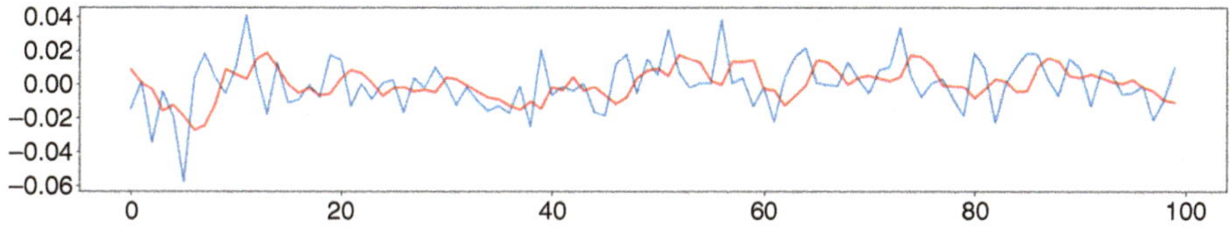

Example 23. Model Validation (Split, Train, Test)

This an important example for the prediction modelling problem. Moreover, when we build a model on a dataset, we should divide the dataset into two or three parts; train data part, validate data part, and optional test data part. This is done due to ensure the validity of the prediction model to be generalized to the new comping datasets.

```
# calculate a train-test split of a time series dataset
X = s.values
train_size = int(len(X) * 0.66)
train, test = X[0:train_size], X[train_size:len(X)]
print('Observations: %d' % (len(X)))
print('Training Observations: %d' % (len(train)))
print('Testing Observations: %d' % (len(test)))
```

```
Observations: 279
Training Observations: 184
Testing Observations: 95
```

```
# plot train-test split of time series data
plt.plot(train)
plt.plot([None for i in train] + [x for x in test], color='r')
```

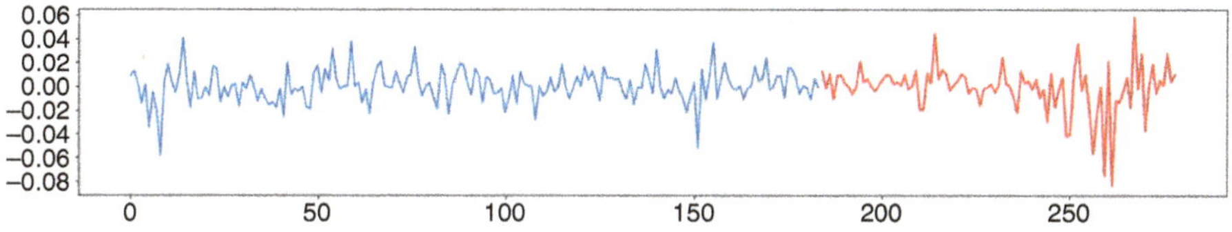

Example 24. Model Validation (Multiple Split, Train, Test)

Example 24. Model Validation (multiple split, train, test)

```
# calculate repeated train-test splits of time series data
X = s.values
splits = TimeSeriesSplit(n_splits=3)
index = 1
plt.figure(1, figsize=(15,9))

for train_index, test_index in splits.split(X):
    train = X[train_index]
    test = X[test_index]

    print('Observations: %d' % (len(train) + len(test)))
    print('Training Observations: %d' % (len(train)))
    print('Testing Observations: %d\n-----' % (len(test)))

    plt.subplot(310 + index)
    plt.plot(train)
    plt.plot([None for i in train] + [x for x in test], color='r')
    index += 1
plt.show()
```

```
Observations: 141
Training Observations: 72
Testing Observations: 69
-----
Observations: 210
Training Observations: 141
Testing Observations: 69
-----
Observations: 279
Training Observations: 210
Testing Observations: 69
```

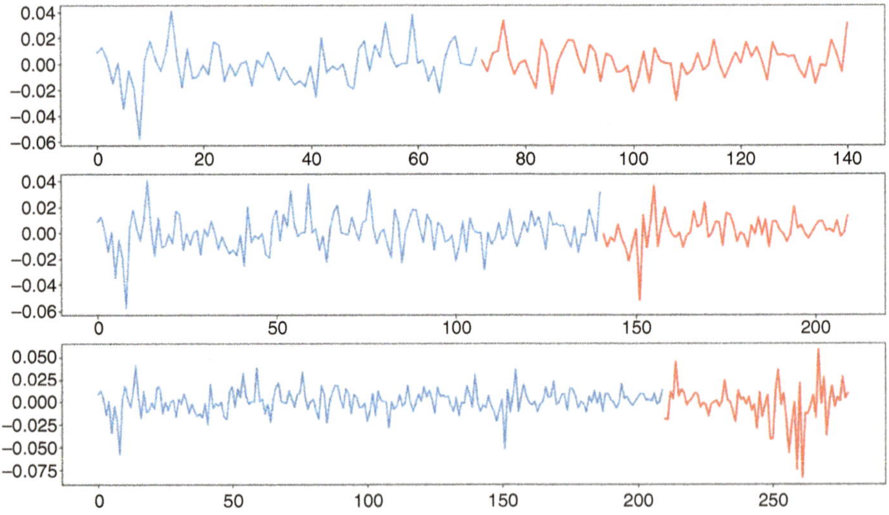

Model Persistence for Forecasting

Many steps are followed for such purpose. Such steps will be conducted in each of the following example. Recall, when the train set expanding each time step and the test set is fixed at one-time step ahead is called walk-forward validation.

Example 25. Model Persistence for Forecasting

```
# Create lagged dataset
values = pd.DataFrame(s.values)
df = pd.concat([values.shift(1), values], axis=1)
df.columns = ['t', 't+1']
# split into train and test sets
X = df.values
train_size = int(len(X) * 0.66)
train, test = X[1:train_size], X[train_size:]

train_X, train_y = train[:,0], train[:,1]
test_X, test_y = test[:,0], test[:,1]

# persistence model
def model_persistence(x):
 return x
# walk-forward validation
predictions = []
for x in test_X:
    yhat = model_persistence(x)
    predictions.append(yhat)
rmse = np.sqrt(mean_squared_error(test_y, predictions))
print('Test RMSE: %.3f' % rmse)
```

```
Test RMSE: 0.029
```

Example 26

```
# plot predictions and expected results on the test data
plt.plot(train_y[-50:])
plt.plot([None for i in train_y[-50:]] + [x for x in test_y])
plt.plot([None for i in train_y[-50:]] + [x for x in predictions])
```

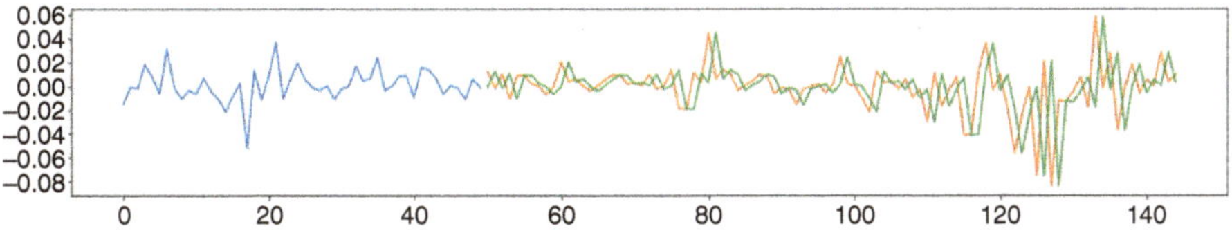

Example 27. Residual Error of Forecasting

```
# calculate residuals from the above persistence model
residuals = [test_y[i]-predictions[i] for i in range(len(predictions))]
residuals = pd.DataFrame(residuals)
# plot residuals
residuals.plot()
```

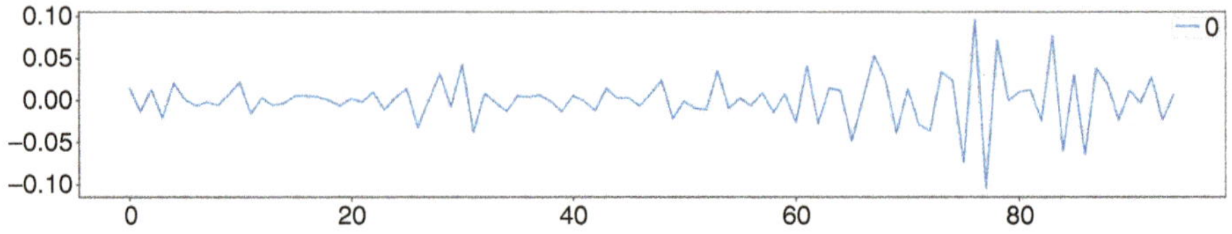

```
residuals.describe()
```

	0
count	95.00
mean	0.00
std	0.03
min	-0.10
25%	-0.01
50%	0.00
75%	0.01
max	0.10

Example 28. Density Plot of Residuals

```
# density plot
residuals.plot(kind='kde')
```

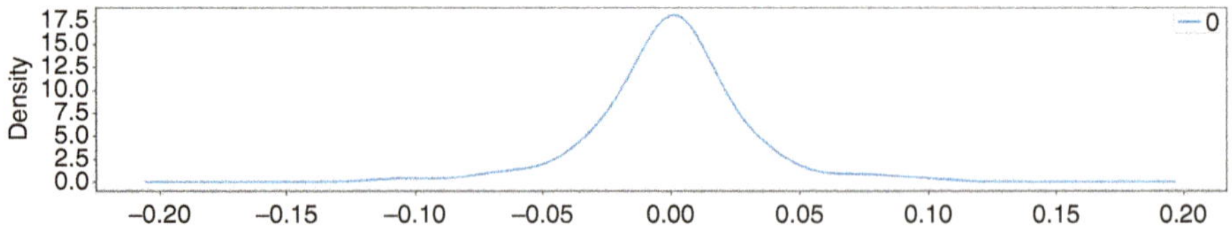

```
qqplot(residuals, line='r')
plt.show()
```

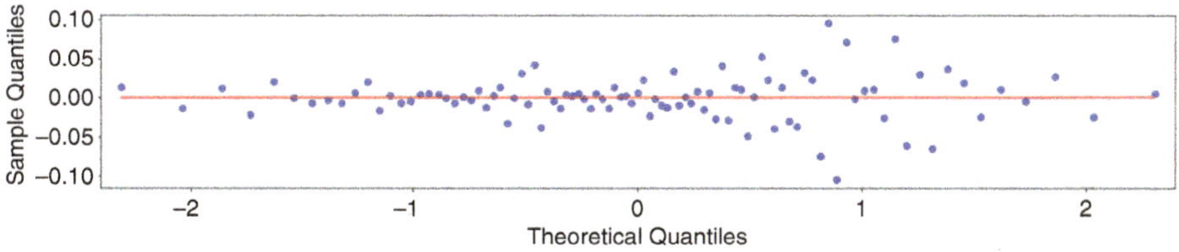

Example 29. Autocorrelation Plots of Residuals

```
autocorrelation_plot(residuals)
```

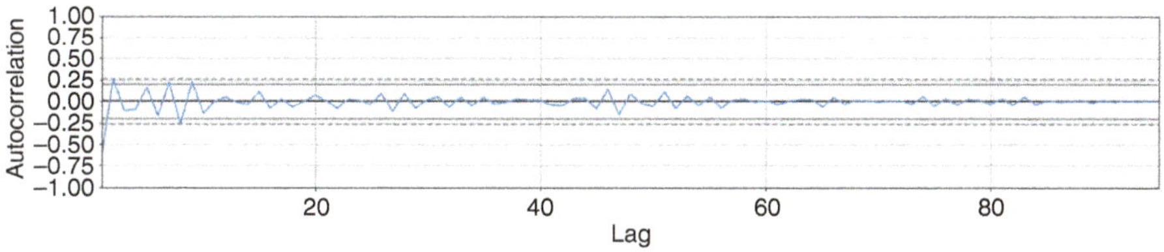


```
# autocorrelation plot of residuals as a line plot
plot_acf(residuals, lags=20)
plt.show()
```

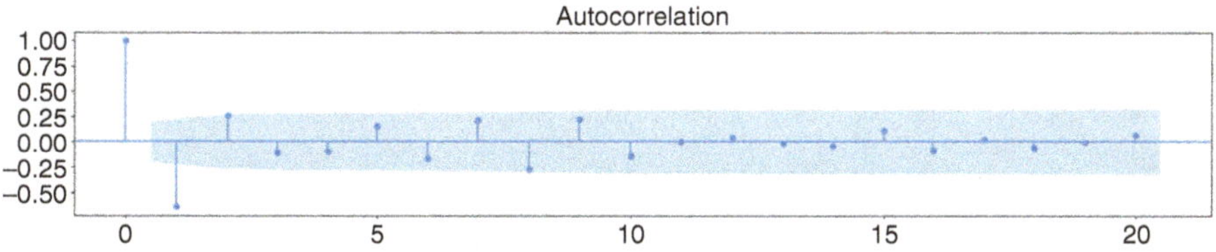

Example 30. Labeled Data Target as Low, Medium, and High

One of an important issue in the financial forecasting is to reframe the data into a classification problem and a labeled data target as low, medium, and high. Then predict such new targets labels.

```
# Create lagged dataset
values = pd.DataFrame(s.values)
df = pd.concat([values.shift(1), values], axis=1)
df.columns = ['t', 't+1']
def make_discrete(row):
    if row['t+1'] < 0:
        return 'low'
    elif row['t+1'] > 3:
        return 'high'
    else:
        return 'medium'
# apply the above function to reassign t+1 values
df['t+1'] = df.apply(lambda row: make_discrete(row), axis=1)
# Randomly sample 10 elements from the dataframe
df.sample(n=10)
```

	t	t+1
116	0.018230	low
213	0.010598	medium
89	0.017975	medium
27	-0.009429	medium
223	0.007613	low
82	-0.009469	low
142	-0.001132	low
85	0.008293	low
73	0.002508	low
42	-0.025754	medium

3 Summary

This chapter is an introduction to data analytics. After the basic concepts of data analytics are given, data types, data analytics techniques, and data modelling are classified. In this way, the conceptual framework of the following chapters contained has been tried to be given. The first step of data analysis is to prepare the data and so to reveal the basic pattern of this data. For this reason, this introductory chapter, it is shown how data is extracted from different file sources with R and how these data are prepared for the next steps of analysis. Since the first step of the data analytics is to calculate descriptive statistics, the codes of the calculations such as mean, standard deviation, correlation, and autocorrelation were given in the R. Financial time series have a special importance among the data in the financial industry. Therefore, the basic initial calculations for time series are explained together with the R codes.

References

Al-hnaity, B., & Abbod, M. (2016) Predicting financial time series data using hybrid model. In *Intelligent systems and applications*. Springer.

Box, G. E. P., & Pierce, D. (1970). Distribution of residual autocorrelations in autoregressive integrated moving average time series models. *Journal of the American Statistical Association, 65*, 1509–1526.

Brown, M. S. (2014). *Data mining for dummies*. Wiley.
Cackett, D. (2016). Information management and big data, a reference architecture. *White paper*. Oracle, 2013. Web. 20 Nisan 2016.
Cielen, D., Meysman, A. D. B., & Ali, M. (2016). *Introducing data science, big data, machine learning and more, using Python tools*. Manning.
Cont, R. (2001). Empirical properties of asset returns: stylized facts and statistical issues, research paper. *Quantitative Finance, 1*, 223–236.
Das, S. R. (2016). *Data science: Theories, models, algorithms, and analytics*.
Dickey, D. A., & Fuller, W. A. (1979). Distribution of the estimators for autoregressive time series with a unit root. *Journal of American Statistical Association, 74*(366a), 427–431.
Engle, R. F., Ng, V. K., & Rothschild, M. (1990). Asset pricing with a factor arch covariance structure. *Journal of Econometrics, 45*(1), 213–237.
Hatipoğlu, M. (2015). Doğrusal OLmayana Zaman serisi modelleri ve Gelişmekte Olan Ülke Borsaları Üzerine bir uygulama, doktora tezi, Eskişehir.
Ljung, G. M., & Box, G. E. P. (1978). On a measure of a lack of fit in time series models. *Biometrika, 65*(2), 297–303. https://doi.org/10.1093/biomet/65.2.297
Mills, T. C., & Markellos, R. N. (2008). *The econometric modelling of financial time series* (3rd ed.). Cambridge University Press.
Sewel, M. (2011, January 20). Characterization of financial time series. *Research note*.
Taylor, S. J. (2007). *Modelling financial time series* (2nd ed., p. 27). World Scientific Publishing.
Tsay, R. S. (2005). *Linear time series analysis and its applications* (Series in probability and statistics). Wiley.
Tsay, R. S. (2002). *Analysis of financial time series, financial econometrics*. Wiley.
Tuna, K., & İsabetli, İ. (2014). *Kocaeli Üniversitesi Sosyal Bilimler Dergisi, 27*, 21–31. https://dergipark.org.tr/tr/download/article-file/251847

Predictive Analytics Techniques: Theory and Applications in Finance

Isac Artzi

Abstract This chapter presents several models associated with predictive analysis across disciplines. While the models are presented to appeal to finance professionals and learners, they were chosen because of their wide use across disciplines. The chapter covers five models: logistic regression, time series analysis, decision trees, multiple linear regression, and RFM (Recency, Frequency, Monetary) Segmentation with *k*-means. The models are presented with moderate mathematical depth and with an emphasis on building a working software implementation in the R programming language. The theoretical justifications are weaved with the software creation, under the premise that seeing the model work provides the necessary encouragement to learn the theory (in a different book perhaps). Some datasets are accessed from public repositories, while other are synthetic and have been created specifically for this project. Each model is built to be used in finance as well as in any discipline in which similar questions are asked of the data.

Keywords Modeling · Logistic regression · Time series · ARIMA · Decision tree · *k*-means · Multiple regression · Machine learning · Segmentation

1 Introduction

This chapter is *about* predictive analytics. It does not and cannot cover a field on which dozens of books and thousands of research papers have been written. It does address key areas, tools, methods, and concepts and presents them through the lens of the Finance discipline. Key elements of Calculus, Linear Algebra, Statistics, and Computer Programming (in R) combine to create an abstract discipline, *predictive*

Supplementary Information The online version of this chapter (https://doi.org/10.1007/978-3-030-83799-0_3) contains supplementary material, which is available to authorized users.

I. Artzi (✉)
Grand Canyon University, Phoenix, AZ, USA
e-mail: isac.artzi@gcu.edu

S. Derindere Köseoğlu (ed.), *Financial Data Analytics*, Contributions to Finance and Accounting, https://doi.org/10.1007/978-3-030-83799-0_3

analysis, which transcends the worlds of science, business, engineering, social studies, sports, healthcare, cyber security, climatology, and other. Calculating the mean of two variables x and y, is the same whether they represent the weighs of a bag of potatoes, or the amount of time spent writing chapters in this book. On one hand an effort was made to present topics on predictive analytics in a manner that connects with the finance practitioner. On the other hand, it is equally important for finance practitioners to be exposed to methods, tools, and approaches in other fields and disciplines. There is a lot to be learned from observing a familiar tool, used in a very different context. If one learns about customer segmentation as an exercise in marketing, they might be misled into thinking that this method has been devised specifically for marketing. However, the same technique used to segment customers, can be used by an autonomous vehicle attempting to prioritize actions in response to multiple events occurring on the road and nearby. The more awareness one develops of the separation between the abstract theory and practical implementation, the more likely is he or she to realize that they possess a much broader set of abilities that can be applied in areas not yet contemplated. The ability to transcend disciplines is a catalyst for creative thinking, for cross-disciplinary collaboration, which is how new ideas and innovative approaches are born. In some respects, predictive analysis is a branch of applied mathematics, as is computer programming. Mathematics stands out as the unique discipline, whose abstract tools and concepts are indispensable, unchanged, in all other disciplines. Therefore, it is highly recommended that professionals in all walks of life, but finance professionals, because they are the main audience for this book, follow the mathematical undercurrents that are alluded to in this chapter and plan a journey into fields they have never explored before. This chapter is not a mathematical chapter. Mathematical concepts are mentioned with minimal depth, only to provide the necessary context for the critical thinking and implementation in computer code. The chapter takes a practical approach by conveying the message that once one understands the big picture, one can implement a computer model that works. The project of constructing a multiple linear regression model (for example) should serve as the justification for learning why does linear regression works the way it does. The ability to see the method of multiple linear regression in action and actually make a prediction, should serve as the motivator to pick another book on statistics and perhaps another book on R programming, and really examine these concepts in depth. Doing it in reverse, starting with the theory and gradually moving on to examples and then implementation, delays the point at which learners or professionals finally understand what the end goal is. Fortunately for some, computers can perform k-means clustering in seconds, using two lines of code. Unfortunately for others, the number of those capable of writing the software that empower analysts to do their job in a few simple steps, is in danger of shrinking. This chapter focuses on the big picture of the theory and detailed software implementation, with the hope that more professionals and learners will be encouraged to learn how the implementations work behind the scenes and perhaps stimulate some to develop their own R packages to perform other tasks.

2 Background

An old Danish proverb popularized by the famous physicist Niels Bohr, states that *"Prediction is hazardous, especially about the future..."* (Shapiro, 2006). A presentation of predictive modeling techniques is of outmost importance in a book covering analytics in Finance. Predictive modeling is heavily anchored in Statistics, a subjective discipline. In turn, Statistics is anchored in Linear Algebra and Calculus, both very objective branches of Mathematics. Professionals and researchers who intend to use statistical methods must recognize the necessity of developing the skills of telling stories with and about data. While these stories are often subjective and analysis results may vary from one practitioner to another, they rest on a solid foundation of precise mathematical tools and concepts. Novice and advanced professionals alike, are prone to overlook the apparent paradoxical relationship between the precision and deterministic character of Mathematics, the nuanced presentations in Statistics, and the art of data-driven storytelling.

3 Main Focus of the Chapter

3.1 On Predictive Analytics

Throughout the chapter, the reader is invited to contemplate a variety of scenarios, in which the same data may be used to tell a different story, sometimes by two professionals employing the same methodology. Predictive models attempt to offer an array of possible outcomes, paired with plausible explanations on why a certain phenomenon is more likely to occur than another. No one can predict the future with certifiable certainty, but one can empower decision makers with the ability to assess the likelihood of a scenario and prepare contingency plans for a variety of outcomes. Market stability and predictability is a coveted state by all business and finance professionals. However, business success depends on the ability of decision makers to detect trends, undercurrents, emerging patterns, and the likelihood of change.

Throughout the chapter, the reader is invited to contemplate a variety of scenarios, in which the same data may be analyzed from a different perspective, using a different model. In some cases, the source of data is a widely used Internet-based repository. In other cases, the data is synthetic and was created specifically to illustrate certain points in this chapter.

There are some similarities across models in the approaches to treating data, visualizing, and interpreting the analysis results. Therefore, an attempt has been made to reduce duplicity in the interest of exposing the reader to a broader range of tools. However, the reader should view individual steps presented in each model as potential methods that can be applied in other models. Thus, the chapter provides a richer set of tools and potential mixtures of approaches, which enable one to tackle different, more complex tasks than the ones described here. The chapter presents five models widely used in predictive analytics, across multiple disciplines. The context has been adapted to better illustrate an application in finance, but the underlying mathematical, statistical, and computational aspects are the same as in any discipline.

The first model is *Logistic Regression*. Often, there is a need to categorize an item or a phenomenon in a binary manner: "yes/no," "accept/deny," "buy/sell," "true/fake news," etc. This example analyzes a dataset of loan applications, with the objective of predicting whether a particular loan would be approved or declined. Logistic regression is widely used in such predictions and the model provides a peek behind the scenes to how banks can make decisions within seconds—if an appropriate machine learning software is in place. The model can be adapted to address any data and context seeking binary predictions.

The second model is *Time Series Analysis*. Information can be static, like car engine specifications, or dynamic, like changes in the value of an asset over time. This model is analyzing historical data documenting the performance of the Microsoft stock (NASDAQ:MSFT). It employs techniques like moving averages, exponential smoothing, and ARIMA to predict the future value of the stock. While the context of the application is finance, the same model can be applied to any scenario (often in conjunction with other models) in which time-based data is available. This could be predicting traffic volume, climate change, or demands of computer storage.

The third model is *Decision Tree*. The prediction of an outcome in a scenario can be accomplished by multiple methods. This example tackles the same problem and synthetic dataset as the logistic regression model, to demonstrate that analysts have choices in methodology and implementation. Unlike logistic regression, decision trees can lead to one of multiple outcomes. In this case, the model predicts whether a bank loan will be approved. The model can be easily adapted to be used in any context for which data is available like predicting which employee will become a manager, whether a company will choose to merge with another, or whether a newly introduced product will be successful.

The fourth model is *Multiple Linear Regression*. As the name implies, this model shows how multiple factors can be analyzed simultaneously to predict an outcome. In this example, the context is predicting the quality of wine, using information about its chemistry. The nature of the prediction is a continuous variable, ranking the wine on a quality scale. Linear regression is used in practically every discipline, ranging from assessing efficacy of vaccines, car engine failures, university admissions, or the fate of a recently planted tree. The model is sufficiently detailed that it can be repurposed to any scenario.

The fifth and last model is *Recency, Frequency, Monetary (RFM) Segmentation with k-means*. This is a more complex, which consists of two models, often used separately. RFM is a model for ranking the outcomes of analysis of observations. The *k*-means model is used to categorize observed events. The combination of the two creates a two-step prediction: (1) outcomes ranking; and (2) grouping outcomes into categories. The model analyzes a large dataset of historical shopping patterns in a store. It then ranks all customers based on their store visit patterns and amount of money spent. The customers are then grouped into categories, which can be later harnessed by store managers. For example, one category could be targeted for credit card offers, while another with a coupon, whose value can be tailored to the customer category.

3.1.1 Programming in R

While prior knowledge of R is not required, an aptitude for reading, writing, and executing computer programs is desired. The programming examples consist mostly of adaptations of mathematical and statistical concepts to the syntax of R, a language created specifically for statistical computing. It is highly recommended to inspect the code and identify the libraries used, and install the relevant R packages.

4 Solutions and Recommendations

The challenges outlined above, have generated myriads of research projects over the course of the last few hundred years, dating back to 1662 with John Graunt's and William Petty's work on census methods (Seager, 1900). The sections below provide a modest introduction to several predictive models and analytical techniques. These models are representative examples of several hundred currently in use if we account for variations and tweaks for specific scenarios. The emphasis is placed on defining concrete scenarios and objectives and presenting a plausible approach to tackling it, including the mathematical and statistical foundation and a computer-based solution in the R programming language.

Each model presented in this chapter is representative of a category of models used in a representative area of finance or business analytics. Consequently, this chapter is far from being comprehensive, but provides a solid foundation, which the reader is encouraged to regard as a steppingstone rather than a definitive guide.

It is worth remembering that predictive analysis is simply an application of abstract statistical and mathematical tools and concepts. As such, there is nothing different in analyzing datasets in finance from datasets in biology or history. The models are abstract, and they treat numbers as abstract symbols. It is the human analyst who adds a specific context-based interpretation and meaning. Otherwise, predicting the future value of a stock is no different than predicting the future number of cars on a road. The reader is encouraged to seek applications of the models presented in this chapter, in other disciplines, and learn how other professionals are using the same tools to tell their story about data. Then, return to the context of finance with fresh perspectives.

4.1 Predictive Model 1: Logistic Regression

4.1.1 Foundation

Logistic regression is used to make predictions with a binary outcome. For example, should a bank approve a loan, should a student be admitted to college, should a candidate be hired for a job, or which are better long-term investments: stocks or real estate. Useful case studies are discussed in Saha et al. (2016) and in Turvey et al. (2010). The treatment of logistic regression in this chapter is succinct, with a focus on practical applications, a more in-depth coverage can be found in Chen and Chen (2021). An even more comprehensive coverage is available in Hilbe (2018). While many questions and scenarios are possible, the mathematical and statistical foundation is the same.

4.1.2 Advanced Organizer

Figure 1 summarizes the steps involved in implementing logistic regression.

Given the binary outcome of an event $y = \{0, 1\}$, with probabilities P and $1 - P$, the Logit function is defined as:

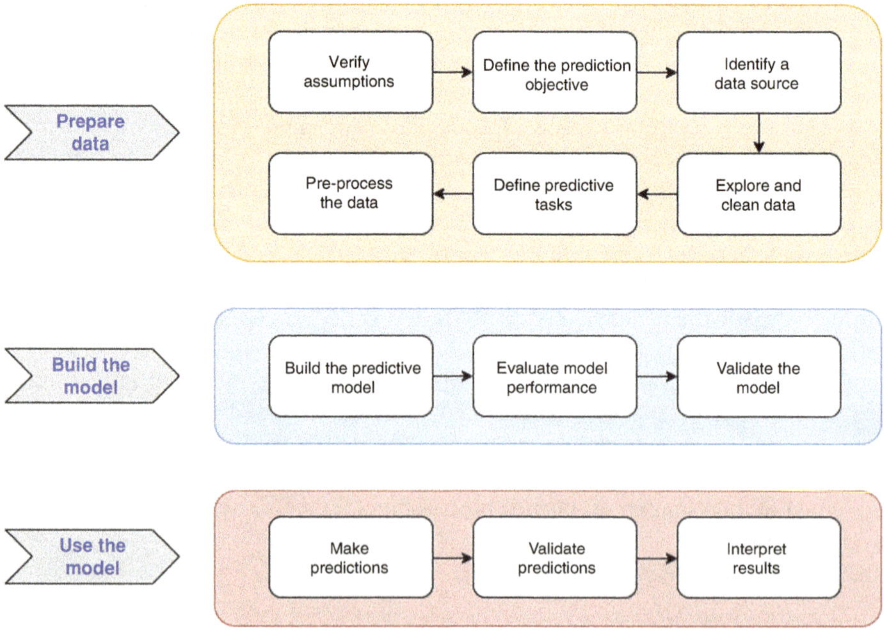

Fig. 1 Logistic regression advanced organizer

Fig. 2 Sigmoid function

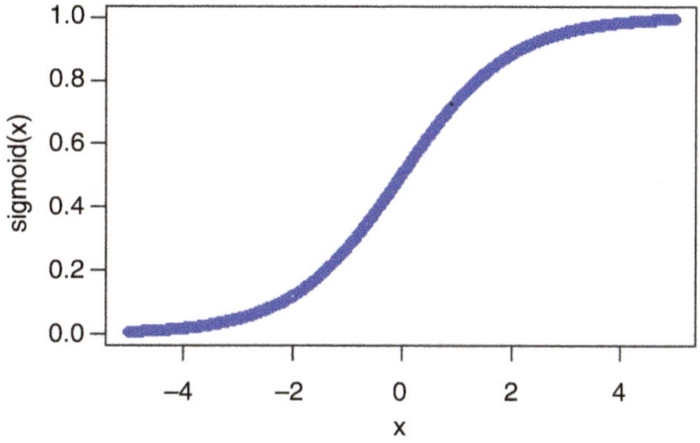

$$\ln\left(\frac{P}{1-P}\right) = \beta_0 + \beta_1 x_1 + \beta_2 x_2 + \cdots + \beta_n x_n$$

where:

- $x_1, x_2, \cdots, x_n$ are independent variables
- β_0 is the logistic regression model intercept
- $\beta_1, \beta_2, \cdots, \beta_n$ are the logistic regression coefficients

The *odd ratio* is defined as $\frac{P(y=1)}{P(y=0)}$, thus the visualization of the logistic regression curve has a sigmoidal shape, like the one in Fig. 2:

```
sigmoid = function(x) {
   1 / (1 + exp(-x))
}

x <- seq(-5, 5, 0.01)
plot(x, sigmoid(x), col='blue')
```

4.1.3 Assumptions

Before deciding whether logistic regression is an appropriate model, the following must be verified:

1. The outcome is a discrete, binary variable.
2. Low sensitivity to overfitting and underfitting, since errors significantly impact predictions.
3. No multicollinearity between the independent variables.
4. A linear relationship must exist between the independent variables and the log odds.

These assumptions will be verified as part of the evaluation of the validity of the model. This model is often used in machine learning applications, used to automate financial tasks.

4.1.4 Objective

Given a dataset with data about loan applicants, predict which loans will be approved and which ones will be declined.

4.1.5 Data Source

The data is synthetic and available in the file *LoanApproval.csv*, included with this book. It mimics the type of information typically collected by banks, in the process of applying for a loan. It consists of 20,000 loan applications with the following variables: *Amount, Term, Income, Interest, PMT, FICO Score,* and *Approval.* The *Approval* is a binary number, 0 or 1.

4.1.6 Data Exploration

We will now load and inspect the dataset.

```
loan.df <- read.csv("LoanApproval.csv")
head(loan.df)

##   Amount Term Income Interest      PMT FICO Approval
## 1 267941  180  52113     5.67 2213.548  667        0
## 2 383713  120 119598     9.13 4887.752  698        1
## 3 481244  360 105437     5.29 2669.383  592        0
## 4 382845  120  56441     4.84 4030.790  657        0
## 5 315850  120  76856     5.11 3367.087  850        0
## 6 479333  360  52634     3.78 2228.033  737        0
```

Since the data has been synthetically produced, it is clean. However, it is always a good idea to check for missing data:

```
# Check for missing values
sum(is.na(loan.df))

## [1] 0
```

Since there are no missing values, we can proceed with reviewing the descriptive statistics of the data:

```
summary(loan.df)
```

```
##        Amount               Term             Income            Interest
##  Min.   :100003   Min.   : 120.0   Min.   : 40002   Min.   :3.000
##  1st Qu.:201018   1st Qu.: 591.8   1st Qu.: 60403   1st Qu.:4.640
##  Median :301578   Median : 841.5   Median : 80701   Median :6.250
##  Mean   :300552   Mean   : 839.2   Mean   : 80275   Mean   :6.253
##  3rd Qu.:399165   3rd Qu.:1091.2   3rd Qu.:100142   3rd Qu.:7.870
##  Max.   :499997   Max.   :1341.0   Max.   :119985   Max.   :9.500
##       PMT               FICO           Approval
##  Min.   : 265.8   Min.   :580.0   Min.   :0.0000
##  1st Qu.:1010.0   1st Qu.:647.0   1st Qu.:0.0000
##  Median :1518.1   Median :716.0   Median :1.0000
##  Mean   :1645.8   Mean   :715.6   Mean   :0.5717
##  3rd Qu.:2157.4   3rd Qu.:784.0   3rd Qu.:1.0000
##  Max.   :6284.6   Max.   :850.0   Max.   :1.0000
```

4.1.7 Predictive Tasks

The task will be to build a logistic regression model and then use the model to predict whether a loan will be approved. The prediction will be based on what the system has "learned" after analyzing prior loan applications and decisions.

4.1.8 Data Pre-processing

In preparation for building the model, the data will be split into two sets, one used for training and another for testing. While there are no particular rules for the split ratio, 70:30 and 80:20 are common. The split will be performed by selecting a random sample of 80% of the dataset, while the remainder 20% will be used to test the model. Once trained, the model could be used to test new data. The seed is used to ensure reproducibility.

```
set.seed(2)
# Split the data 80:20
train.sample <- sample(c(1:dim(loan.df)[1]), dim(loan.df)[1]*0.8)

train.df <- loan.df[train.sample,]
valid.df <- loan.df[-train.sample,]
```

4.1.9 Build the Predictive Model

The model is built around the premise that *Approval* is a function of *all* other independent variables:

Approval ~ Amount, Term, Income, Interest, PMT, FICO Score

We will use the built-in *glm()* function, which is used to fit generalized linear models, specified by giving a symbolic description of the linear predictor and a description of the error distribution. Below is the output generated by the *glm()*

function, most notable being the coefficients table, showing the β_i values (*Estimate* column in the code output) in the logistic regression model.

```
logit.reg <- glm(Approval ~ ., train.df, family="binomial")
options(scipen = 999)
summary(logit.reg)
```

```
##
## Call:
## glm(formula = Approval ~ ., family = "binomial", data = train.df)
##
## Deviance Residuals:
##     Min       1Q   Median       3Q      Max
## -3.3219  -0.3068   0.0588   0.3159   4.0306
##
## Coefficients:
##                  Estimate     Std. Error z value            Pr(>|z|)
## (Intercept) -33.4730324755   0.5907816384 -56.659 < 0.0000000000000002 ***
## Amount        0.0000069204   0.0000007372   9.388 < 0.0000000000000002 ***
## Term         -0.0004581318   0.0001043286  -4.391           0.0000113 ***
## Income        0.0000350569   0.0000013316  26.327 < 0.0000000000000002 ***
## Interest      0.2742599441   0.0326412195   8.402 < 0.0000000000000002 ***
## PMT          -0.0024536796   0.0001315489 -18.652 < 0.0000000000000002 ***
## FICO          0.0449704850   0.0007318188  61.450 < 0.0000000000000002 ***
## ---
## Signif. codes:  0 '***' 0.001 '**' 0.01 '*' 0.05 '.' 0.1 ' ' 1
##
## (Dispersion parameter for binomial family taken to be 1)
##
##     Null deviance: 21824.8  on 15999  degrees of freedom
## Residual deviance:  8382.6  on 15993  degrees of freedom
## AIC: 8396.6
##
## Number of Fisher Scoring iterations: 6
```

Notice that the *p-values* of each variables are nearly zero, which means they are all significant (as indicated by the *** next to them.

The model predicts that (for example) given an increase by one unit of *Term*, the log odds of approval will decrease by 0.00046. Similarly, the higher the interest, the higher the approval odds. It is important to remember that this is synthetic and not actual data, and its purpose is to demonstrate how the model is implemented in R. The reader is invited to experiment with other datasets and different variables.

4.1.10 Model Performance Evaluation

To evaluate how well does the model work, it is essential to compare the predicted probabilities vs the actual ones:

```
logit.reg.pred <- predict(logit.reg, valid.df[,-7], type="response")

# Compare first 20 sampled actual vs predicted values

data.frame(actual = valid.df$Approval[1:20], predicted = logit.reg.pred[1:20])

##      actual    predicted
## 4         0 0.0003643066
## 6         0 0.5590936006
## 8         0 0.0486341970
## 9         1 0.1410227119
## 12        1 0.8032381411
## 15        0 0.0004744004
## 19        0 0.0027561282
## 25        0 0.2514103102
## 54        0 0.8223301924
## 57        0 0.0041490117
## 58        1 0.9857249097
## 60        1 0.9802270016
## 63        1 0.9966634325
## 86        1 0.9940780098
## 88        0 0.0450417430
## 91        1 0.6502499105
## 105       0 0.0391793696
## 116       1 0.9903811015
## 118       1 0.7289381145
## 125       0 0.3711320422
```

A nonscientific spot-check reveals that borrowers #4, #8, and #88 were not approved, and the model predicted their approval being closed to zero. In contrast, borrowers #12, #58, #60 were approved, as predicted by the model. There is no expectation that the results would be perfect (see borrowers #6, #54), but this is the nature of probabilistic models. However, there is some cause of concern regarding the accuracy of the model, which will be addressed in the following sections.

4.1.11 Model Validation

A better indication of the validity of the model is to produce a *Gain and Lift* chart (Fig. 2), which is commonly used to measure the performance of predictive classification models:

```
library(gains)

gain <- gains(valid.df$Approval, logit.reg.pred, groups=length(logit.reg.pred))

# plot Lift chart

plot(c(0, gain$cume.pct.of.total*sum(valid.df$Approval))~c(0,gain$cume.obs),
xlab="# records", ylab = "Cumulative", main="Lift Chart", type="l")

lines(c(0, sum(valid.df$Approval))~c(0, dim(valid.df)[1]))
```

The gap between the blue line and the red line (Fig. 3) indicates the gains made from using the predictive model to predict who will be approved for the loan.

It is now time to address the concerns indicated earlier, which noted that a predicted probability of 0.85 was listed as not approved. We will measure the *Variance Inflation Factor* to test multicollinearity to verify that indeed all variables are independent:

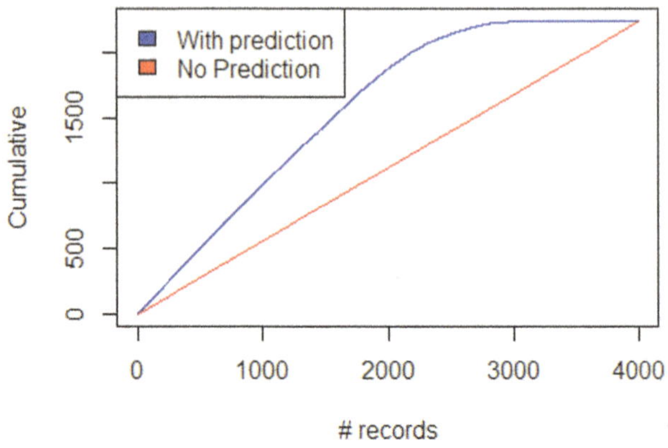

Fig. 3 Gain and Lift chart

```
library(car)

vif(logit.reg)

##     Amount       Term     Income   Interest        PMT       FICO
##   9.130721   1.203997   1.202346   4.829287  13.970800   1.537851
```

It turns out that the variables *Amount* and *PMT* have VIF values larger than 5–10, which indicate multicollinearity. Regardless of whether this agrees with our intuition (especially since this is a synthetic model created to illustrate a point), these variables need to be removed and the model simplified:

```
theFormula = Approval ~ Term + Income + FICO
logit.reg <- glm(formula = theFormula, train.df, family="binomial")
options(scipen = 999)
summary(logit.reg)

##
## Call:
## glm(formula = theFormula, family = "binomial", data = train.df)
##
## Deviance Residuals:
##     Min       1Q   Median       3Q      Max
## -3.5141  -0.3762   0.1040   0.4218   3.1300
##
## Coefficients:
##                  Estimate   Std. Error z value             Pr(>|z|)
## (Intercept) -29.429859055  0.468332847 -62.840 < 0.0000000000000002 ***
## Term          0.000289757  0.000088131   3.288              0.00101 **
## Income        0.000030041  0.000001203  24.972 < 0.0000000000000002 ***
## FICO          0.038495507  0.000592843  64.934 < 0.0000000000000002 ***
## ---
## Signif. codes:  0 '***' 0.001 '**' 0.01 '*' 0.05 '.' 0.1 ' ' 1
##
## (Dispersion parameter for binomial family taken to be 1)
##
##     Null deviance: 21824.8  on 15999  degrees of freedom
## Residual deviance:  9764.9  on 15996  degrees of freedom
## AIC: 9772.9
##
## Number of Fisher Scoring iterations: 6
```

The revalidation of the simplified model presents a more acceptable table of coefficients (actual vs predicted):

Fig. 4 Gain and Lift chart

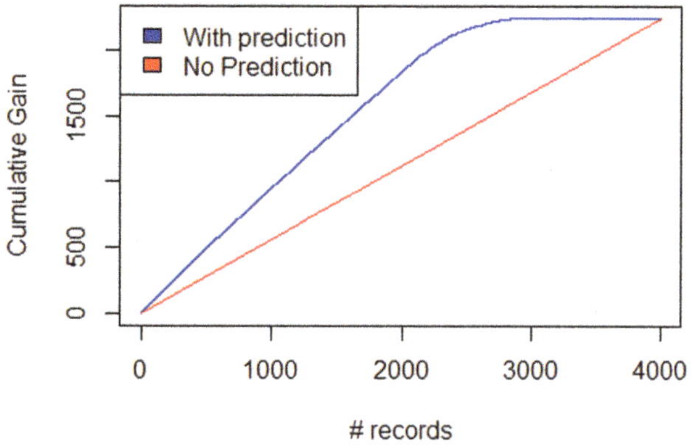


```
logit.reg.pred <- predict(logit.reg, valid.df[,-7], type="response")

# Compare first 20 actual vs predicted values

data.frame(actual = valid.df$Approval[1:20], predicted = logit.reg.pred[1:20])
##     actual  predicted
## 4        0 0.08256333
## 6        0 0.65176345
## 8        0 0.13720866
## 9        1 0.53292887
## 12       1 0.75980466
## 15       0 0.02221238
## 19       0 0.01110265
## 25       0 0.77215229
## 54       0 0.85714011
## 57       0 0.01013471
## 58       1 0.97301111
## 60       1 0.91994956
## 63       1 0.99200132
## 86       1 0.97988038
## 88       0 0.05111092
## 91       1 0.66416830
## 105      0 0.09768163
## 116      1 0.98216346
## 118      1 0.67934399
## 125      0 0.43476915
```

Indeed, in the new table, although only 20 records are shown, there are no “red” flags. As with the original model, we need to examine the Gain and Lift chart (Fig. 4):

```
library(gains)

gain <- gains(valid.df$Approval, logit.reg.pred, groups=length(logit.reg.pred))

# plot Lift chart


plot(c(0, gain$cume.pct.of.total*sum(valid.df$Approval))~c(0,gain$cume.obs), xlab="# r
ecords", ylab = "Cumulative Gain", main="Gain and Lift Chart", type="l", col="blue")

lines(c(0, sum(valid.df$Approval))~c(0, dim(valid.df)[1]), col="red",
      legend("topleft",c("With prediction","No Prediction"),fill=c("blue","red")))
```

Finally, we need to retest for multicollinearity as well:

```
library(car)
vif(logit.reg)

##      Term    Income      FICO
## 1.004261 1.151184 1.155397
```

As expected, all the values are smaller than 5–10, hence no multicollinearity exists. To reiterate, with this data, *this* is the improved model. Another dataset, perhaps with say, 15 variables, will pose different challenges to the analyst. However, the process of improving the model would be the same.

4.1.12 Make Predictions

We are now ready to make predictions using the model and the 20% entries in the test data prepared earlier. The results below indicate which borrowers should be approved and which ones should be declined, but only **if the probability of the decision exceeds 80%**. This probability can be changed and the reader is encouraged to explore with different values.

```
logit.reg.prob <- predict(logit.reg, test.df, type="response" )
logit.reg.prob.df <- data.frame(logit.reg.prob)

# Extract only decisions made with a probability higher than 80%
approvals <- ifelse(logit.reg.prob.df > 0.8, 1, 0)
head(approvals, 20)

##     logit.reg.prob
## 4                0
## 6                0
## 8                0
## 9                0
## 12               0
## 15               0
## 19               0
## 25               0
## 54               1

## 57               0
## 58               1
## 60               1
## 63               1
## 86               1
## 88               0
## 91               0
## 105              0
## 116              1
## 118              0
## 125              0
```

4.1.13 Validate Prediction

In the previous section, we validated the model. One final step to conclude this model, is to validate the predictions, by measuring their accuracy. One such measure is the use of a *confusion matrix*, that will test for misclassification errors.

```
table(test.df$Approval, approvals)
##    approvals
##        0    1
##    0 1623  134
##    1  632 1611

classification.error <- mean(approvals != test.df$Approval)
classification.error

## [1] 0.1915

accuracy <- 1 - classification.error
accuracy

## [1] 0.8085
```

4.1.14 Results Interpretation

While the above results are subject to interpretation, a misclassification error of 0.19 and an accuracy of 0.80 are considered acceptable by some and needing improvement by other. In addition, we will request a final "stamp of approval" in the form of *Receiver Operating Characteristic (ROC)* curve and *Area Under the Curve (AUC)*, as shown in Fig. 5. The curve illustrates the relationship between *sensitivity* (i.e., the true positive rate or *tpr*) and *1-specificity* (i.e., the false positive rate or *fpr*):

```
library(ROCR)

approvals <- predict(logit.reg, newdata = test.df, type="response")
predictions <- prediction(approvals, test.df$Approval)

# Plot True Positive Rate (tpr) vs False Positive Rate (fpr)
logit.reg.performance <- performance(predictions, measure="tpr", xmeasure="fpr")
plot(logit.reg.performance, col="red")
```

Fig. 5 Receiver operating characteristic (ROC) curve

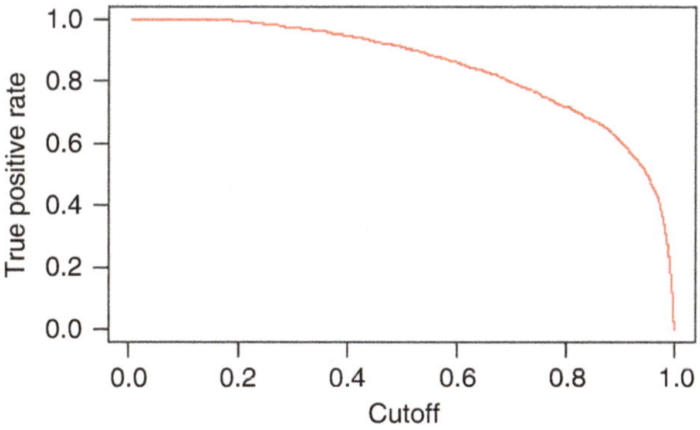

```
AUC <- performance(pred, measure="auc")
AUC <- AUC@y.values[[1]]
AUC
## [1] 0.9442274
```

The closer the curve approaches 1.0, the better the performance of the model. An AUC value >70% is considered acceptable. Therefore, the calculated AUC of 94.4% means that the model is highly accurate. Recall that we only looked at approvals with a cutoff probability of 80%.

4.1.15 Conclusion

We presented a predictive model, logistic regression, particularly suited for situations in which only a binary answer is expected, such as Yes/No. While the scenario referred to loan approvals it may just as well be used to decide whether to hire an individual, to invest in a company, or whether to retire at a given age. The model is simple and straightforward to use and validate. The reader is encouraged to examine the references provided and dig deeper into the variety of nuances and uses, as well as recommendations for improving the accuracy of logistic regression, especially when tested on data collected from real sources.

4.2 *Predictive Model 2: Time Series Analysis*

4.2.1 Foundation

Within the broad variety of data types, structures, and sources, time-based data is of particular importance in the world of finance. Time is the essential factor in calculating appreciation and depreciation of assets, and directly affects all aspects of business, banking, monetary policy, fiscal policy, and trade. Simply put, a *time series* is a dataset with information collected over time. Time series *analysis* consists of investigating changes over time, detecting patterns in those changes, and predicting what changes might occur in the future. Time series analysis has been the subject of many books and research publications. Very useful and relevant case studies are presented in Ahmar and del Val (2020), Abreu et al. (2019), and David et al. (2017). For a detailed study of time series analysis in general, the reader is invited to consult Kitagawa (2020), while for a more Finance oriented text, Chan (2010). There are numerous methods and steps one could use for detecting patterns and making predictions, but at the heart of this section, are the widely used *Holt-Winters* model and the *Auto**R**egressive* ***I**ntegrated* ***M**oving* ***A**verage (ARIMA)* model, which is a family of models.

Given a series of observations at times $T_1, T_2, \ldots, T_n$, we distinguish between two models:

$$\text{Multiplicative combination}: T_{i+1} = (L_i + B_i) \times S_{(i+1-m)} \times N_{(i+1)}$$

$$\text{Fully additive combination}: T_{i+1} = (L_i + B_i) + S_{(i+1-m)} + N_{(i+1)}$$

where:

- T_{i+1} is the time series *Value* observed at step $(i + 1)$
- $(L_i + B_i)$ is the estimated *Level* (i.e. local mean) at step $(i + 1)$
- $S_{(i+1-m)}$ is the estimated *Seasonal variation* at step $(i + 1 - m)$
- $N_{(i+1)}$ is the observed noise at step $(i + 1)$

The *Holt-Winters* model is used to forecast time series data that has a trend, and can be used whether seasonality is present or not

$$F_{i+k} = (L_i + k \times B_i) \times S_{(i+1-m)}$$

where:

- F_{i+k} is the *Forecast* at step $(i + k)$
- $(L_i + B_i)$ is the estimated *Level* (i.e., local mean) at step $(i + k)$
- $S_{(i+1-m)}$ is the estimated *Seasonal variation* of period of length m at step $(i +1 - m)$

The *ARIMA* model is a general class of models for forecasting time series. As the term *ARIMA* indicates, the model is an aggregate of three analytical steps:

1. The *AR* component measures the relationship between the series and past lags.
2. The *I* component transforms a series with lags into a stationary one.
3. The *MA* component measures the error at time t and its correlation with past errors.

A nonseasonal is an *ARIMA(p, d, q)* model, where:

- p is the number of auto-regressive terms
- d is the number of nonseasonal differences needed for stationarity
- q is the number of lagged forecast errors

The predicted value Y is a constant and/or a weighted sum of one or more recent values of Y and/or a weighted sum of one or more recent values of the errors.

We distinguish three values for d:

If $d = 0$ then $y_t = Y_t$

If $d = 1$ then $y_t = Y_t - Y_{t-1}$

If $d = 2$ then $y_t = (Y_t - Y_{t-1}) - (Y_{t-1} - Y_{t-2})$

Therefore, the general ARIMA forecasting model is given by:

$$\widehat{y}_t = \mu + \phi_1 y_{t-1} + \cdots + \phi_p y_{t-p} - \theta_1 e_{t-1} - \cdots - \theta_q e_{t-q}$$

where θ_i are the moving average parameters

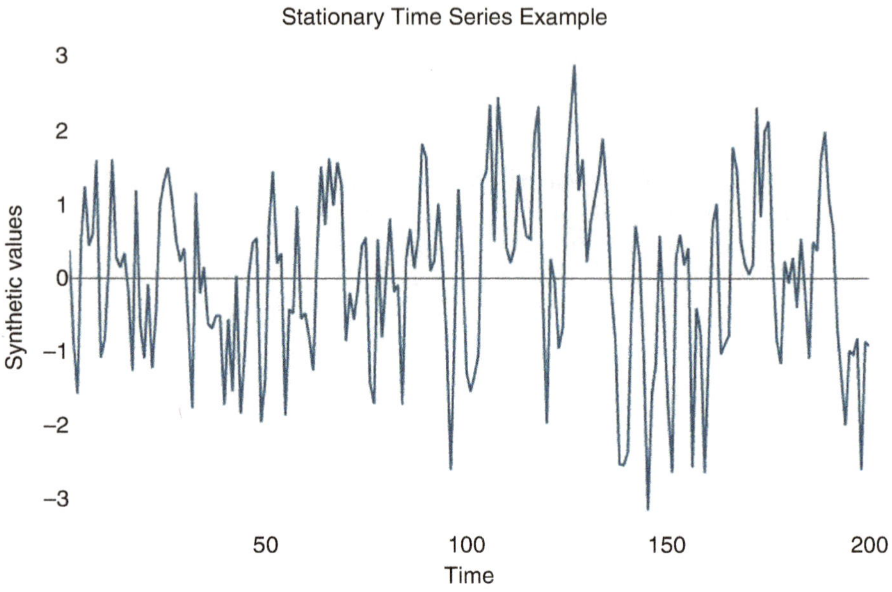

Fig. 6 Simulated stationary time series

In the model presented below, we will use an ARIMA(1,0,0) equation, which is a *first-order auto-regressive model.* The time series we will be working with is stationary and auto-correlated, therefore, we can predict using multiples of its own, with the addition of a constant: $\hat{Y}_t = \mu + \phi_1 Y_{t-1}$.

Entire books can be written not only about ARIMA but about each variation of the models. Within the constraints of this chapter, it is best to discuss the particulars of the model while engaged in implementing it. For a more detailed treatment of this topic, the reader is invited to consult (Dixon et al., 2020). Here is an example (Fig. 6) of a synthetic, stationary time series, the kind typically using an ARIMA forecasting model:

```
library(TSstudio)
stationary_ts <- arima.sim(model=list(order=c(1,0,0), ar=0.5), n=200)
ts_plot(stationary_ts, title="Stationary Time Series Example",
        Ytitle="Synthetic values", Xtitle="Time")
```

It is beyond the scope of this chapter to examine nonstationary time series and their conversion into stationary. The reader is encouraged to explore the resources cited, and apply the concepts presented here to other types of time series.

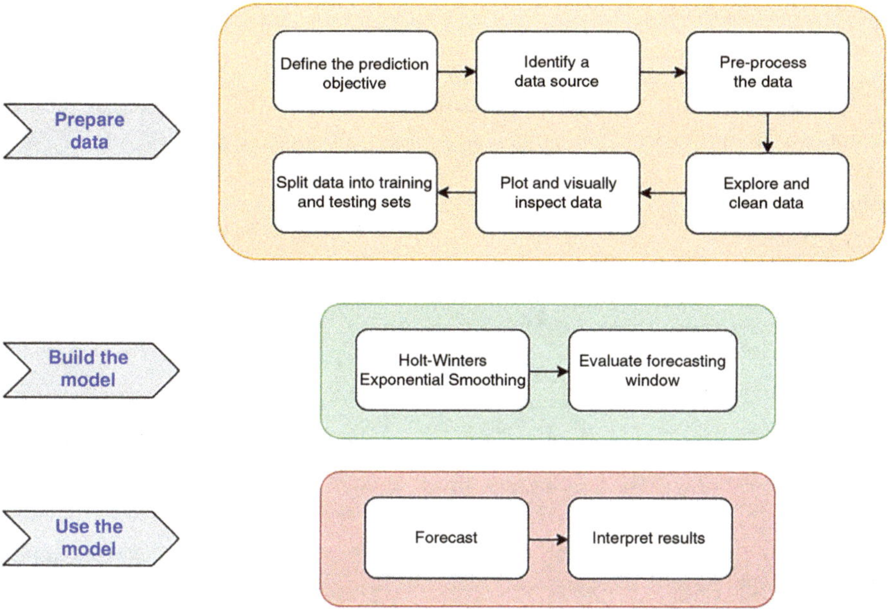

Fig. 7 Overview of the ARIMA process

4.2.2 Advance Organizer

Figure 7 provides an overview of the ARIMA process:

4.2.3 Assumptions

For data to be considered stationary, the following are assumed:

1. The *mean* and *variance* of the series do not change over time.
2. The *correlation structure* of the series does not change over time.
3. *Lags* do not change over time.

4.2.4 Objective

Given a stationary time series representing the values of Microsoft stock (NASDAQ: MSFT), predict the future value of the stock.

4.2.5 Data Source

Kaggle website: https://www.kaggle.com/szrlee/stock-time-series-20050101-to-20171231?select=MSFT_2006-01-01_to_2018-01-01.csv . The data includes the following variables: *Date, Open, High, Low, Close, Volume, Name*, for a total of 3019 days of trading.

```
library(forecast)

stock_value <- read.csv("MSFT_2006-01-01_to_2018-01-01.csv")
head(stock_value)

##          Date  Open  High   Low Close    Volume Name
## 1 2006-01-03 26.25 27.00 26.10 26.84  79974418 MSFT
## 2 2006-01-04 26.77 27.08 26.77 26.97  57975661 MSFT
## 3 2006-01-05 26.96 27.13 26.91 26.99  48247610 MSFT
## 4 2006-01-06 26.89 27.00 26.49 26.91 100969092 MSFT
## 5 2006-01-09 26.93 27.07 26.76 26.86  55627836 MSFT
## 6 2006-01-10 26.65 27.02 26.59 27.00  64924946 MSFT

tail(stock_value)

##             Date  Open  High   Low Close   Volume Name
## 3014 2017-12-21 86.05 86.10 85.40 85.50 17990745 MSFT
## 3015 2017-12-22 85.40 85.63 84.92 85.51 14145841 MSFT
## 3016 2017-12-26 85.31 85.53 85.03 85.40  9891237 MSFT
## 3017 2017-12-27 85.65 85.98 85.22 85.71 14678025 MSFT
## 3018 2017-12-28 85.90 85.93 85.55 85.72 10594344 MSFT
## 3019 2017-12-29 85.63 86.05 85.50 85.54 18717406 MSFT
```

Note that weekends are obviously not included, which means that the data is not exactly a set of 3019 days, but trading days.

4.2.6 Predictive Tasks

The key tasks will be to prepare the data, then apply the Holt-Winters exponential smoothing algorithm, This will be followed by an implementation of the ARIMA model to predict the value of the MSFT stock.

4.2.7 Data Exploration and Pre-processing

Let us first transform the raw data into a time series (Fig. 8). Note that the ts() function requires that the frequency of data collection is specified. The number of days in a year is approximately 365.25. Accounting for leap years are beyond the scope of this chapter.

```
value.ts <- ts(stock_value$Close, start = c(2006,1,3),frequency = 365.25)

# Visualize the time series
plot(value.ts, xlab="Time", ylab="Stock value in $", ylim=c(0,100))
```

The data is not particularly easy to explore visually, beyond noticing a clear upwards trend. Therefore, it is always helpful to zoom into a smaller time frame and examine changes in data (Fig. 9).

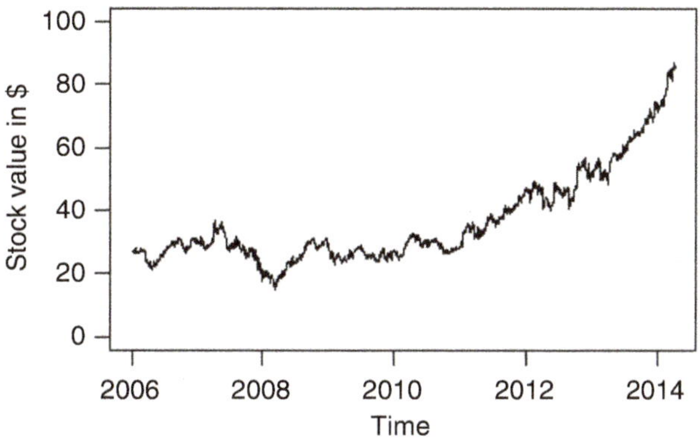

Fig. 8 Time series of MSFT values 2006–2017

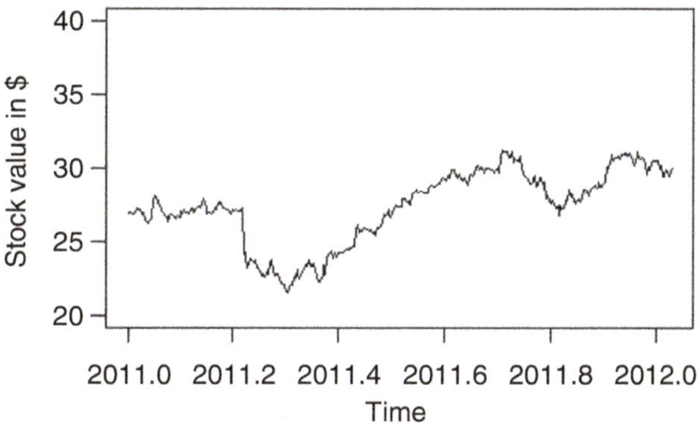

Fig. 9 Zoom into the MSFT time series for a period of 2 years

```
value.ts.zoomin <- ts(stock_value$Close, start = c(2011,1,1),
                       end = c(2012,12,31),frequency = 365)

# Visualize the time series
plot(value.ts.zoomin, xlab="Time", ylab="Stock value in $", ylim=c(20,40))
```

An important aspect of time series is the presence of *seasonality*. In the quest for identifying patterns, a key characteristic is the existence of seasonal trends. For example, is there a spike in data at a particular interval (e.g., once a month)? The *tbats()* function in can test for seasonality:

```
fit <- tbats(value.ts)
seasonal <- !is.null(fit$seasonal)
seasonal

## [1] FALSE
```

The test result is FALSE, which means there is no seasonality.

A second essential exploratory step is to determine the presence of a *trend* (Fig. 10). To assess this, we will examine the *central moving average (CMA)*. For that purpose, we need to create a new time series object, consisting of the moving averages:

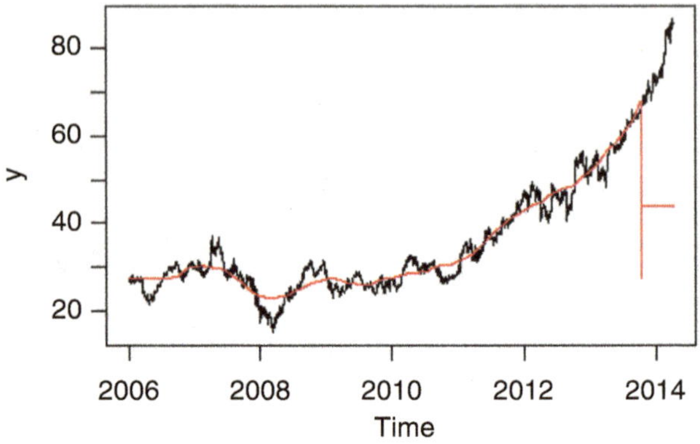

Fig. 10 Trend detected (red line)

```
# Plot Central Moving Average (CMA)
library(tsutils)

cma <- cmav(value.ts, outplot=1)
```

The structure of the new time series (CMA) and its first six values, are shown below:

```
head(cma)

## Time Series:
## Start = 2006
## End = 2006.01368925394
## Frequency = 365.25
## [1] 27.26921 27.26921 27.26921 27.26921 27.26921 27.26921
```

It is often useful to examine data using multiple tools. While the model presented in this chapter is limited in scope, the tools presented may prove useful in other instances. For example, the decomposition of the time series into *data, seasonal, trend,* and *error (remainder).* We will show this using two different functions: *decompose()* (Fig. 11) and *ggplot2* (Fig. 12):

```
decomposed <- decompose(value.ts, type="mult")
plot(decomposed)
stlRes <- stl(value.ts, s.window = "periodic")
lines(trendcycle(stlRes),col="red")
```

Alternative time series decomposition:

```
library(ggplot2)
autoplot(cbind(
        Data=value.ts,
        Seasonal=seasonal(stlRes),
        Trend=trendcycle(stlRes),
        Remainder=remainder(stlRes)),
        facets=TRUE) +
  ylab("") + xlab("Day")
```

A final confirmation (Fig. 13) of the existence of a trend and the absence of seasonality is computed with the *seasplot()* function:

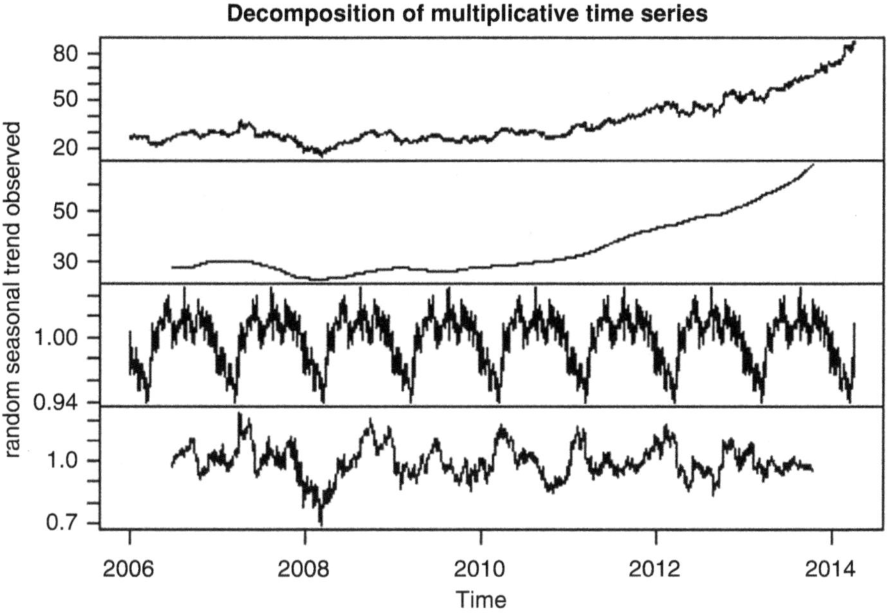

Fig. 11 Decomposition using the decompose() function

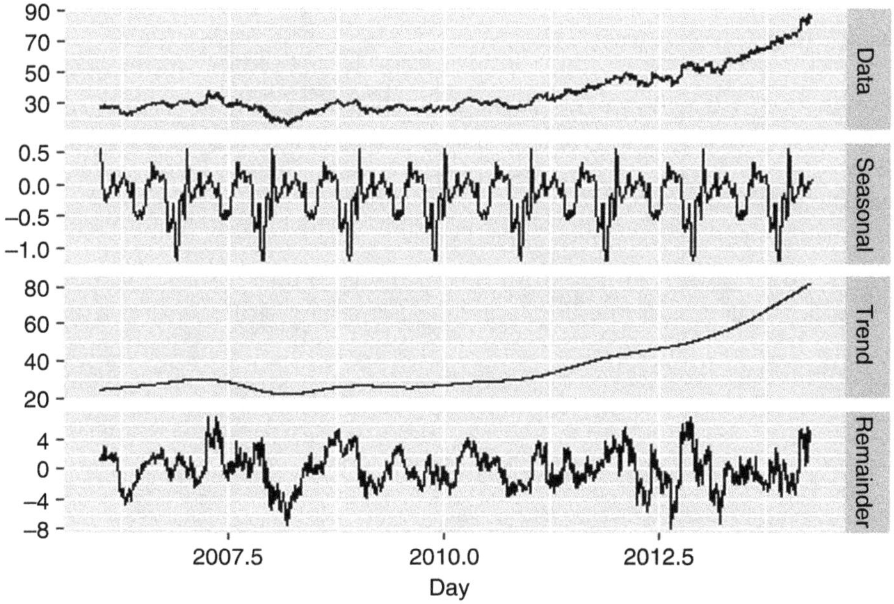

Fig. 12 Decomposition using the autoplot() function

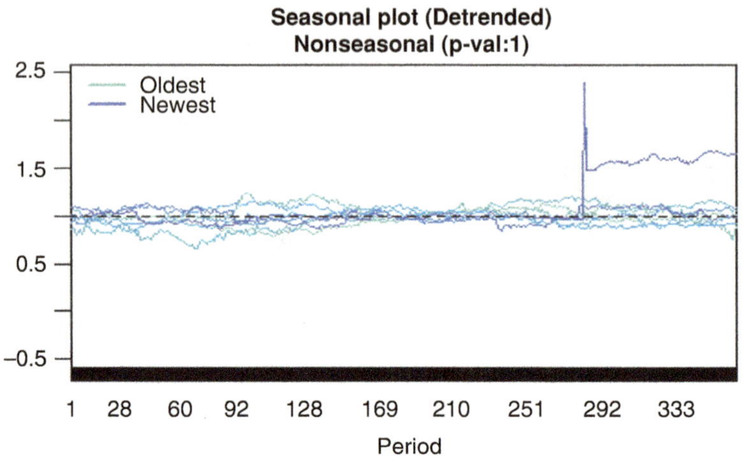

Fig. 13 Time series seasonality test

```
seasplot(value.ts)
## Results of statistical testing
## Evidence of trend: TRUE  (pval: 0)
## Evidence of seasonality: FALSE  (pval: 1)
```

4.2.8 Build the Predictive Model

Now that we have developed a better understanding of the data, we can start building a predictive model. We will start with an *exponential smoothing* fit, using the *Holt-Winters* model. The code below forecasts a few values into the future and provides an estimated interval:

```
# Calculate the sum of square errors (SSE)
value.ts.forecast$SSE

## [1] 959.275


value.ts.forecast <- HoltWinters(value.ts, beta=FALSE, gamma=FALSE)
head(value.ts.forecast) # Show the first few values

## $fitted
## Time Series:
## Start = 2006.00273785079
## End = 2014.26283367556
## Frequency = 365.25
##                 xhat    level
## 2006.003 26.84000 26.84000
## 2006.005 26.96594 26.96594
## 2006.008 26.98925 26.98925
## 2006.011 26.91247 26.91247
## 2006.014 26.86164 26.86164
## 2006.016 26.99568 26.99568

##
## $x
## Time Series:
## Start = 2006
## End = 2014.26283367556
## Frequency = 365.25
```

```
##    [1] 26.84 26.97 26.99 26.91 26.86 27.00 27.29 27.14 27.19 26.99 26.83 27.02## [3
001] 81.08 81.59 82.78 82.49 84.16 85.23 85.58 85.35 84.69 86.85 86.38 85.83
## [3013] 85.52 85.50 85.51 85.40 85.71 85.72 85.54
##
## $alpha
## [1] 0.9687703
##
## $beta
## [1] FALSE
##
## $gamma
## [1] FALSE
##
## $coefficients
##       a
## 85.5456
```

```
Value.ts.forecast2 <- forecast:::forecast.HoltWinters(value.ts.forecast, h=6)
head(value.ts.forecast2)
```

```
## $method
## [1] "HoltWinters"
##
## $model
## Holt-Winters exponential smoothing without trend and without seasonal component.
##
## Call:
## HoltWinters(x = value.ts, beta = FALSE, gamma = FALSE)
##
## Smoothing parameters:
##  alpha: 0.9687703
##  beta : FALSE
##  gamma: FALSE
##
## Coefficients:
##      [,1]
## a 85.5456
##
## $level
## [1] 80 95
##
## $mean
## Time Series:
## Start = 2014.26557152635
## End = 2014.81040383299
## Frequency = 365.25
##   [1] 85.5456 85.5456 85.5456 85.5456 85.5456 85.5456
##
## $lower
##             80%      95%
##   [1,] 84.82342 84.44113
##   [2,] 84.54011 84.00783
##   [3,] 84.32066 83.67221
##   [4,] 84.13494 83.38818
##   [5,] 83.97098 83.13742
##   [6,] 83.82255 82.91042
##
## $upper
##             80%       95%
##   [1,] 86.26778  86.65008
##   [2,] 86.55110  87.08337
##   [3,] 86.77055  87.41899
##   [4,] 86.95626  87.70302
##   [5,] 87.12023  87.95378
##   [6,] 87.26866  88.18079
```

```
# The accuracy decreases as the time progresses into the future
plot(forecast(value.ts.forecast2))
```

4.2.9 Results Interpretation (of the Holt-Winters Output)

The estimated value of the **alpha parameter** is approximately 0.97. Since it is nearly 1, it follows that the most recent observations are weighted more heavily in the forecast. Understandably, the accuracy decreases as time progresses into the future. This is evident numerical by the growing intervals, as well as visually in Fig. 14 (the fanning out).

A forecast using the ARIMA model exhibits the same behavior (Fig. 15):

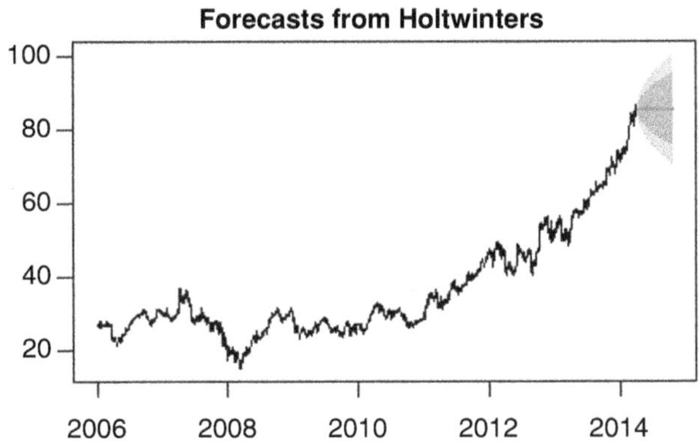

Fig. 14 Forecast by Holt-Winters method

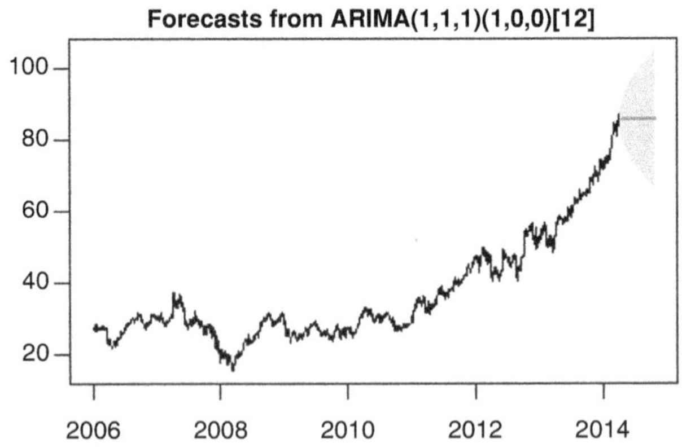

Fig. 15 Forecast by the ARIMA model

```
# Forecast with auto.arima()

value.ts.arima <- arima(value.ts, order=c(1,1,1),seasonal = list(order = c(1,0,0), per
iod = 12),method="ML")
value.ts.arima

##
## Call:
## arima(x = value.ts, order = c(1, 1, 1), seasonal = list(order = c(1, 0, 0),
##     period = 12), method = "ML")
##
## Coefficients:
##          ar1      ma1    sar1
##       0.7899  -0.8235  0.0173
## s.e.  0.0801   0.0738  0.0184
##
## sigma^2 estimated as 0.3171:  log likelihood = -2549.43,  aic = 5106.86

library(lmtest)
coeftest(value.ts.arima)

##
## z test of coefficients:
##
##       Estimate Std. Error  z value Pr(>|z|)
## ar1   0.789855   0.080091   9.8619   <2e-16 ***
## ma1  -0.823469   0.073803 -11.1576   <2e-16 ***
## sar1  0.017323   0.018447   0.9391   0.3477
## ---
## Signif. codes:  0 '***' 0.001 '**' 0.01 '*' 0.05 '.' 0.1 ' ' 1

predictions <- forecast:::forecast.Arima(value.ts.arima,h=200, level=c(99.5))
plot(forecast(predictions))
```

4.2.10 Conclusion

Since the data source is deemed reliable and it has been examined using multiple methods, it is fair to conclude that several outcomes have been established. Most notably, that there is no seasonality in data, and there is a definite trend. Consequently, an exponential smoothing approach can be used to extend the trend and make a prediction about future values. These values exhibit a decrease in accuracy as time progresses. With 80% confidence, we can say that the next value is within the interval `[84.82342, 86.26778]`. When the confidence increases to 95%, the predicted boundaries for the first predicted value is `[84.44113, 86.65008]`. These intervals increase over time, making predictions less accurate. The model presented here provides a solid foundation for analyzing any time series. However, due to space constraints many analytical concepts have been left out, such as the detection of *cyclical patterns*, tweaking the parameters of the model, and comparing several prediction methods.

4.3 *Predictive Model 3: Decision Tree*

4.3.1 Foundation

Decision tree is a supervised learning algorithm that makes a sequence of decisions based on predefined rules. Widely used in machine learning, one can learn more about decision trees in Lantz (2019). Educational examples of implementations of decision tree models in finance are presented in Ünkaya and Sayin (2019), Zhao (2020), and Teng and Lee (2019). The tree consists of a set of nodes N, differentiated by three categories (Fig. 16):

- N_{root} is the top (or initial) node, in which the data is stored, ready to be processed.
- $N_{decision}$ is a node at which a rule is consulted and a decision is made regarding the next course of action.
- $N_{terminal}$ is a node at which a decision is made, also known as *leaf node*.
- N_{child} or N_{parent} are descriptors (rather than functions) of the relationship between a node and its successor or predecessor.

In addition to nodes, two important concepts must be defined:

- *Branch* is a subtree, a subset of the original tree.
- *Pruning* is the process of removing a branch or even an entire subtree in the process of improving the efficiency of the computational tasks.

Since a decision tree makes a final prediction because of traversing a path from N_{root} to a $N_{terminal}$, often it is worthwhile to eliminate portions of the tree that are found to be redundant, resulting in a smaller tree, with a shorter path to a final decision.

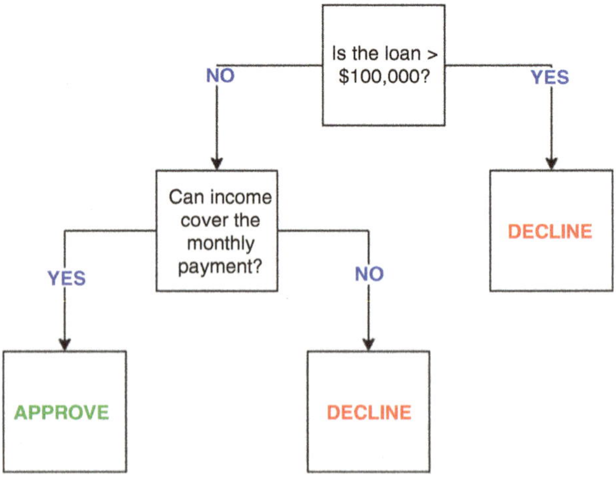

Fig. 16 An example of a decision tree

At its core, a decision tree is a simple construct that helps one reach a conclusion after a succession of decisions, as illustrated in Fig. 16. Additional concepts will be explained and demonstrated in the sections below.

The above description and implementations have been in part adapted from Kroese et al. (2019).

4.3.2 Advance Organizer

Figure 17 provides a high-level review of the key steps in building and using a decision tree predictive model.

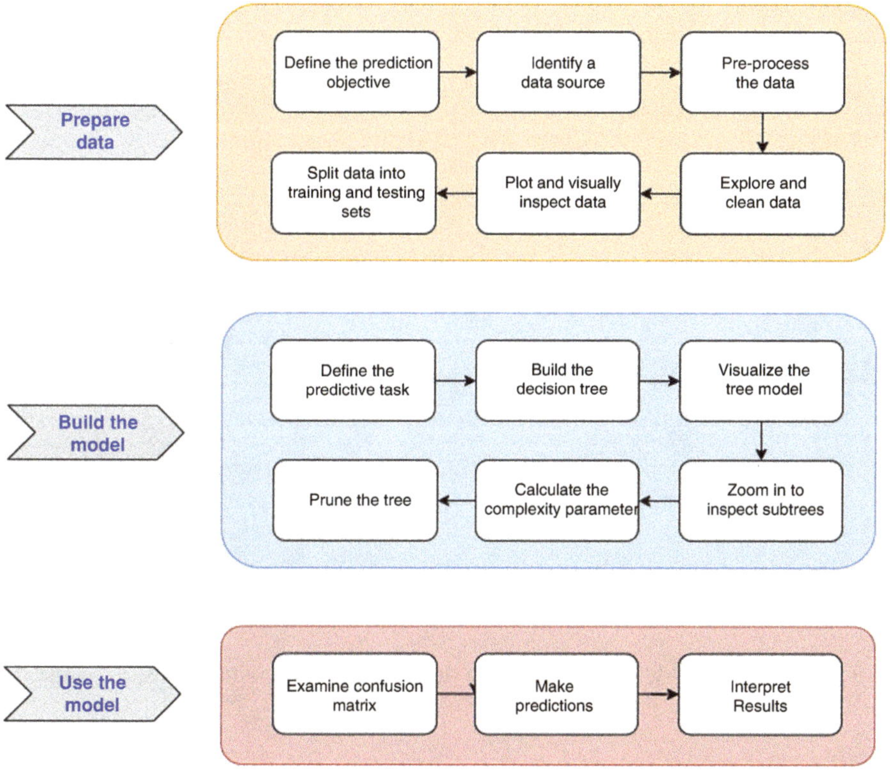

Fig. 17 Overview of key steps in implementing a decision tree model

4.3.3 Objective

Given a dataset with data about loan applicants, decide whether to approve the loan or not.

4.3.4 Data Source

The data is synthetic and available in the file *LoanApproval.csv*, included with this book. It mimics the type of information typically collected by banks, while processing loan applications. It consists of 20,000 loan applications with the following variables: *Amount, Term, Income, Interest, PMT, FICO Score,* and *Approval.* The *Approval* is a binary number, 0 or 1.

Note that this is the same dataset used in Model 1. This exercise provides a different approach to solving the same problem and is intended to instill the principle that *the best tool is the one that works for you.*

```
loans <- read.csv("LoanApproval.csv", header = TRUE, sep = ",")
loans.df <- data.frame(loans)
head(loans.df)

##   Amount Term Income Interest      PMT FICO Approval
## 1 267941  180  52113     5.67 2213.548  667        0
## 2 383713  120 119598     9.13 4887.752  698        1
## 3 481244  360 105437     5.29 2669.383  592        0
## 4 382845  120  56441     4.84 4030.790  657        0
## 5 315850  120  76856     5.11 3367.087  850        0
## 6 479333  360  52634     3.78 2228.033  737        0

tail(loans.df)

##       Amount Term Income Interest       PMT FICO Approval
## 19995 466206 1336  67080     5.59 2176.1193  671        0
## 19996 193532 1337  71840     8.26 1332.2838  600        0
## 19997 259017 1338 116486     4.20  915.0947  693        1
## 19998 367886 1339  45735     9.04 2771.5276  743        0
## 19999 498659 1340  91754     7.15 2972.2138  739        1
## 20000 197674 1341 117606     3.63  608.5622  703        1
```

4.3.5 Data Exploration

It is always a good idea to examine the data, its structure, and values, to gauge the best approach to analyzing it:

```
# The data structure
str(loans.df)

## 'data.frame':    20000 obs. of  7 variables:
##  $ Amount  : int  267941 383713 481244 382845 315850 479333 254761 236815 293288 23
0175 ...
##  $ Term    : int  180 120 360 120 120 360 360 180 180 120 ...
##  $ Income  : int  52113 119598 105437 56441 76856 52634 109797 46623 89154 113933 .
..
##  $ Interest: num  5.67 9.13 5.29 4.84 5.11 3.78 7.65 5.09 8.47 6.88 ...
##  $ PMT     : num  2214 4888 2669 4031 3367 ...
##  $ FICO    : int  667 698 592 657 850 737 696 679 697 583 ...
##  $ Approval: int  0 1 0 0 0 0 1 0 1 0 ...

names(loans.df)

## [1] "Amount"   "Term"     "Income"   "Interest" "PMT"      "FICO"     "Approval"

class(loans.df)

## [1] "data.frame"

summary(loans.df)

##      Amount             Term            Income          Interest    
##  Min.   :100003   Min.   : 120.0   Min.   : 40002   Min.   :3.000  
##  1st Qu.:201018   1st Qu.: 591.8   1st Qu.: 60403   1st Qu.:4.640  
##  Median :301578   Median : 841.5   Median : 80701   Median :6.250  
##  Mean   :300552   Mean   : 839.2   Mean   : 80275   Mean   :6.253  
##  3rd Qu.:399165   3rd Qu.:1091.2   3rd Qu.:100142   3rd Qu.:7.870  
##  Max.   :499997   Max.   :1341.0   Max.   :119985   Max.   :9.500  
##       PMT              FICO          Approval     
##  Min.   : 265.8   Min.   :580.0   Min.   :0.0000  
##  1st Qu.:1010.0   1st Qu.:647.0   1st Qu.:0.0000  
##  Median :1518.1   Median :716.0   Median :1.0000  
##  Mean   :1645.8   Mean   :715.6   Mean   :0.5717  
##  3rd Qu.:2157.4   3rd Qu.:784.0   3rd Qu.:1.0000  
##  Max.   :6284.6   Max.   :850.0   Max.   :1.0000
```

Since the data has been synthetically produced, it is clean. However, it is always a good idea to check for missing data:

```
# Check for missing values
sum(is.na(loan.df))

## [1] 0
```

Since there are no missing values, we can proceed.

4.3.6 Predictive Tasks

The task will be to build a *decision tree* model and then use the model to predict whether a loan will be approved. The prediction will be based on a succession of decisions until an answer is produced.

4.3.7 Data Pre-processing

As it is common in many predictive models (and often used in supervised machine learning applications), we will now split the data into *training* and *testing* sets. The recommended split ratio is left to the analyst to decide, after considering the size of data, its reliability, common practices in the field, and other. The reader is advised to explore with different ratios and compare the outcomes. In this case, we will split the data 70:30, with 70% of the observations assigned to the training set.

```
set.seed(22)  # set seed for sample reproducibility

library(caTools)
sample <- sample.split(loans.df$Approval, SplitRatio=0.7)

loans.df.train <- subset(loans.df, sample==TRUE)
loans.df.test <- subset(loans.df, sample==FALSE)

head(loans.df.train)

##       Amount Term Income Interest      PMT FICO Approval
## 1   267941  180  52113     5.67 2213.548  667        0
## 3   481244  360 105437     5.29 2669.383  592        0
## 5   315850  120  76856     5.11 3367.087  850        0
## 7   254761  360 109797     7.65 1807.566  696        1
## 9   293288  180  89154     8.47 2882.968  697        1
## 10  230175  120 113933     6.88 2658.313  583        0

head(loans.df.test)

##       Amount Term Income Interest      PMT FICO Approval
## 2   383713  120 119598     9.13 4887.752  698        1
## 4   382845  120  56441     4.84 4030.790  657        0
## 6   479333  360  52634     3.78 2228.033  737        0
## 8   236815  180  46623     5.09 1883.839  679        0
## 12  166778  180  51337     5.17 1333.686  753        1
## 14  266744  360  69390     7.32 1832.346  667        0
```

There is not much else to do at this point, other than proceeding with building the decision tree model.

4.3.8 Build the Predictive Model

The *rpart()* function in R pretty much performs all the heavy lifting of building the decision tree, as illustrated in the code below. The nodes of the tree are indented to show the decision path. For example, node 24 tests whether the PMT $\geq$ 2509.668 and then proceeds with assessing the income (nodes 58 and 49). Node 48 leads to a denial of the loan with 100% probability (due to income being less then 61,538.5), while node 49 launches a new path of decisions. This tree is easier to view in Fig. 18.

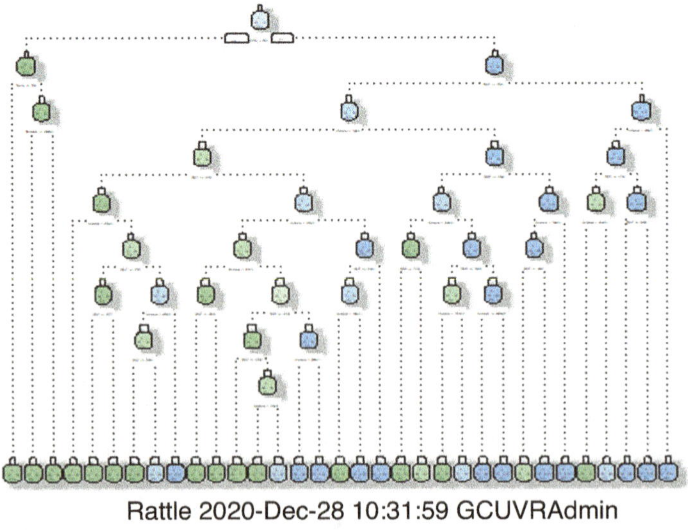

Fig. 18 The high-level visualization of the entire decision tree created by rpart()

```
library(rpart)
approvalModel <- rpart(Approval ~ ., data=loans.df.train, method="class", parms=list(
plit="information"), cp=-1)

approvalModel

## n= 14000
##
## node), split, n, loss, yval, (yprob)
##       * denotes terminal node
##
##   1) root 14000 5996 1 (0.428285714 0.571714286)
##     2) FICO< 680.5 5159    1 0 (0.999806164 0.000193836)
##       4) Term>=150 5137    0 0 (1.000000000 0.000000000) *
##       5) Term< 150 22    1 0 (0.954545455 0.045454545)
##        10) Amount>=245136 15    0 0 (1.000000000 0.000000000) *
##        11) Amount< 245136 7    1 0 (0.857142857 0.142857143) *
##     3) FICO>=680.5 8841  838 1 (0.094785658 0.905214342)
##       6) PMT>=1882.593 3072  812 1 (0.264322917 0.735677083)
##        12) Income< 70279.5 1146  409 0 (0.643106457 0.356893543)
##          24) PMT>=2509.668 535   35 0 (0.934579439 0.065420561)
##            48) Income< 61538.5 384    0 0 (1.000000000 0.000000000) *
##            49) Income>=61538.5 151   35 0 (0.768211921 0.231788079)
##              98) PMT>=2797.498 100    2 0 (0.980000000 0.020000000)
##               196) PMT>=2876.504 88    0 0 (1.000000000 0.000000000) *
##               197) PMT< 2876.504 12    2 0 (0.833333333 0.166666667) *
##              99) PMT< 2797.498 51   18 1 (0.352941176 0.647058824)
##               198) Income< 65171.5 29   11 0 (0.620689655 0.379310345)
##                 396) PMT>=2645.584 15    0 0 (1.000000000 0.000000000) *
##                 397) PMT< 2645.584 14    3 1 (0.214285714 0.785714286) *
##               199) Income>=65171.5 22    0 1 (0.000000000 1.000000000) *
##          25) PMT< 2509.668 611  237 1 (0.387888707 0.612111293)
##            50) Income< 54936 294   68 0 (0.768707483 0.231292517)
##             100) Income< 47257 163    3 0 (0.981595092 0.018404908)
##               200) PMT>=1930.011 144    0 0 (1.000000000 0.000000000) *
##               201) PMT< 1930.011 19    3 0 (0.842105263 0.157894737) *
##             101) Income>=47257 131   65 0 (0.503816794 0.496183206)
##               202) PMT>=2124.008 73   10 0 (0.863013699 0.136986301)
##                 404) PMT>=2254.283 44    0 0 (1.000000000 0.000000000) *
##                 405) PMT< 2254.283 29   10 0 (0.655172414 0.344827586)
##                   810) Income< 51515.5 14    0 0 (1.000000000 0.000000000) *
##                   811) Income>=51515.5 15    5 1 (0.333333333 0.666666667) *
##               203) PMT< 2124.008 58    3 1 (0.051724138 0.948275862)
##                 406) Income< 49235.5 16    3 1 (0.187500000 0.812500000) *
##                 407) Income>=49235.5 42    0 1 (0.000000000 1.000000000) *
##            51) Income>=54936 317   11 1 (0.034700315 0.965299685)
##             102) PMT>=2385.436 51   11 1 (0.215686275 0.784313725)
##               204) Income< 58886.5 11    0 0 (1.000000000 0.000000000) *
##               205) Income>=58886.5 40    0 1 (0.000000000 1.000000000) *
##             103) PMT< 2385.436 266    0 1 (0.000000000 1.000000000) *
##        13) Income>=70279.5 1926   75 1 (0.038940810 0.961059190)
##          26) PMT>=3199.259 226   70 1 (0.309734513 0.690265487)
##            52) Income< 82633 59    4 0 (0.932203390 0.067796610)
##             104) PMT>=3330.482 46    0 0 (1.000000000 0.000000000) *
##             105) PMT< 3330.482 13    4 0 (0.692307692 0.307692308) *
##            53) Income>=82633 167   15 1 (0.089820359 0.910179641)
##             106) PMT>=3885.611 21    7 0 (0.666666667 0.333333333)
##               212) Income< 107074.5 13    2 0 (0.846153846 0.153846154) *
##               213) Income>=107074.5 8    3 1 (0.375000000 0.625000000) *
##             107) PMT< 3885.611 146    1 1 (0.006849315 0.993150685)
##               214) Amount>=496377.5 7    1 1 (0.142857143 0.857142857) *
##               215) Amount< 496377.5 139    0 1 (0.000000000 1.000000000) *
##          27) PMT< 3199.259 1700    5 1 (0.002941176 0.997058824)
##            54) Income< 73775 112    5 1 (0.044642857 0.955357143)
##             108) PMT>=2946.612 7    2 0 (0.714285714 0.285714286) *
##             109) PMT< 2946.612 105    0 1 (0.000000000 1.000000000) *
##            55) Income>=73775 1588    0 1 (0.000000000 1.000000000) *
##       7) PMT< 1882.593 5769   26 1 (0.004506847 0.995493153)
##        14) Income< 44363.5 315   26 1 (0.082539683 0.917460317)
##          28) PMT>=1725.821 32    7 0 (0.781250000 0.218750000)
##            56) Income< 42824 21    0 0 (1.000000000 0.000000000) *
##            57) Income>=42824 11    4 1 (0.363636364 0.636363636) *
##          29) PMT< 1725.821 283    1 1 (0.003533569 0.996466431)
##            58) PMT>=1684.405 7    1 1 (0.142857143 0.857142857) *
##            59) PMT< 1684.405 276    0 1 (0.000000000 1.000000000) *
##        15) Income>=44363.5 5454    0 1 (0.000000000 1.000000000) *
```

4.3.9 Model Visualization

The above tree shows the actual decisions being made by the model and help creating an auditing trail to assess its validity. The *rattle* package in R creates a visual of the same tree that assists in following the logic of decision-making.

```
library(rattle)

## Loading required package: tibble
## Loading required package: bitops
## Rattle: A free graphical interface for data science with R.
## Version 5.4.0 Copyright (c) 2006-2020 Togaware Pty Ltd.
## Type 'rattle()' to shake, rattle, and roll your data.

library(rpart.plot)
library(RColorBrewer)
#Create the decision tree
fancyRpartPlot(approvalModel)
```

Obviously, the tree depicted in Fig. 18 is only useful to convey the high-level complexity of the model. To get a better insight into the model created, we will zoom in and focus on a small portion of the tree up to the fourth depth level (Fig. 19).

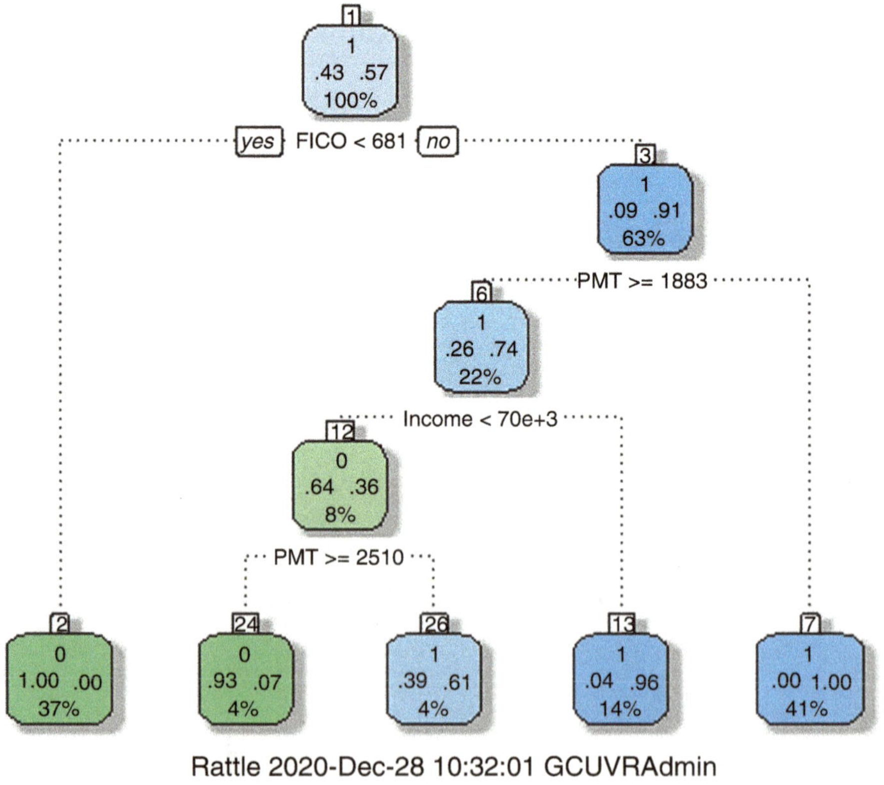

Fig. 19 Detailed visualization of the first four levels of the decision tree created by *rpart()*

```
# Show the tree at depth=4 for better visualization

approvalTreeModel <- rpart(Approval ~., data=loans.df.train, method="class", parms=lis
t(split="information"), maxdepth=4, minsplit=2, minbucket=2)

approvalTreeModel

## n= 14000
##
## node), split, n, loss, yval, (yprob)
##       * denotes terminal node
##
##  1) root 14000 5996 1 (0.428285714 0.571714286)
##    2) FICO< 680.5 5159    1 0 (0.999806164 0.000193836) *
##    3) FICO>=680.5 8841  838 1 (0.094785658 0.905214342)
##      6) PMT>=1882.593 3072  812 1 (0.26q 4322917 0.735677083)
##       12) Income< 70279.5 1146  409 0 (0.643106457 0.356893543)
##         24) PMT>=2509.668 535   35 0 (0.934579439 0.065420561) *
##         25) PMT< 2509.668 611  237 1 (0.387888707 0.612111293) *
##       13) Income>=70279.5 1926   75 1 (0.038940810 0.961059190) *
##      7) PMT< 1882.593 5769   26 1 (0.004506847 0.995493153) *

fancyRpartPlot(approvalTreeModel)
```

One should always attempt to improve every analytical model. In the case of decision tree, the improvement is achieved by pruning branches that add unnecessary complexity and redundancy in the decision-making process. The pruning is conceptually like excluding insignificant variables in the logistic regression model. The *complexity parameter (cp)* is a measure of the size (i.e., complexity) of the tree. If the addition of a variable results in an increased *cp* value, then that potential branch is pruned. Thus, the *cp* value helps avoiding over-fitting a model. Here is a calculation and visualization of the *cp* values for the model created so far.

The optimal value of *cp* is calculated by the *printcp()* function and visualized in Fig. 20. Notice that the smallest *cp* value is 0.1:

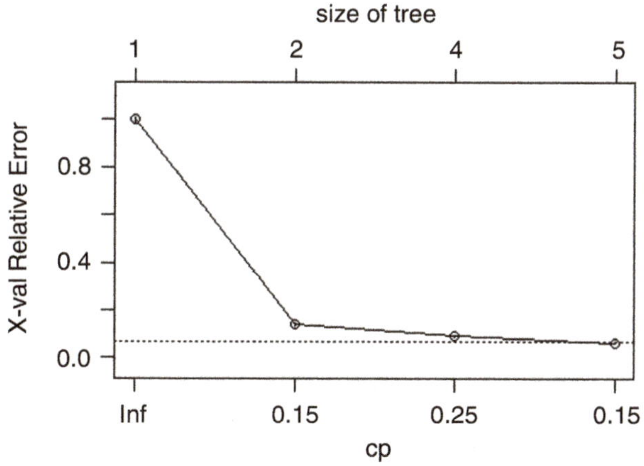

Fig. 20 The cp value and tree size

```
printcp(approvalTreeModel)

##
## Classification tree:
## rpart(formula = Approval ~ ., data = loans.df.train, method = "class",
##     parms = list(split = "information"), maxdepth = 4, minsplit = 2,
##     minbucket = 2)
##
## Variables actually used in tree construction:
## [1] FICO   Income PMT
##
## Root node error: 5996/14000 = 0.42829
##
## n= 14000
##
##          CP nsplit rel error   xerror      xstd
## 1 0.860073      0  1.000000 1.000000 0.0097647
## 2 0.027352      1  0.139927 0.139927 0.0046838
## 3 0.022849      3  0.085223 0.089893 0.0037967
## 4 0.010000      4  0.062375 0.064710 0.0032393

plotcp(approvalTreeModel)
```

From the output above and Fig. 19, we notice that the optimal $cp = 0.01$. Therefore, a good threshold for pruning is a value slightly higher, 0.02. We can now feed this threshold into the *prune()* function and generate a much simpler (thus more efficient) decision tree (Fig. 21).

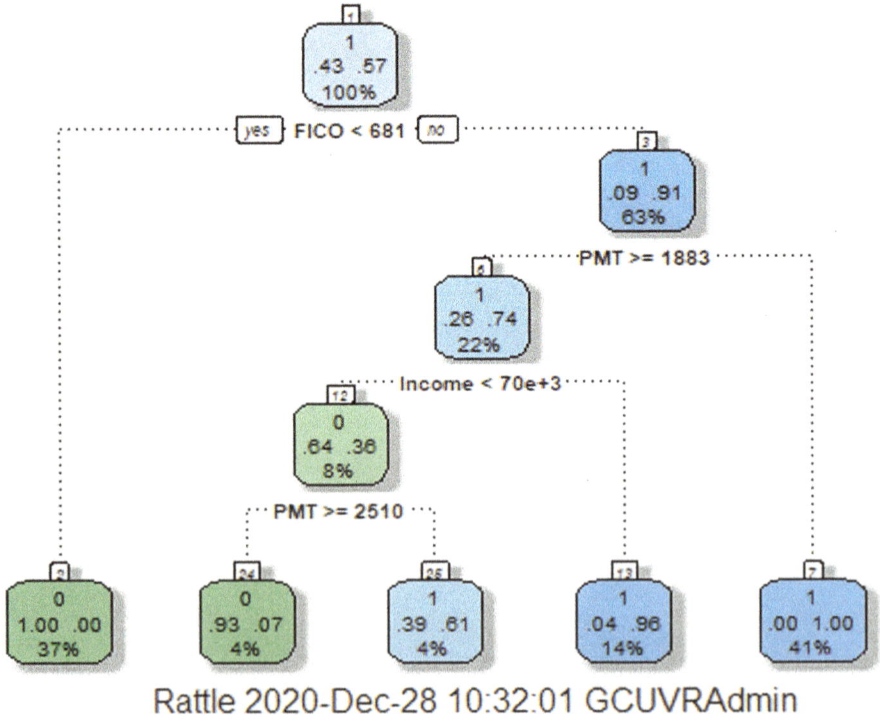

Fig. 21 The much smaller pruned tree model

```
# The pruned tree model
# Since the cp value is greater than 0.01, set to 0.02
approvalTreeModel.pruned <- prune(approvalTreeModel, cp=0.02)
approvalTreeModel.pruned

## n= 14000
##
## node), split, n, loss, yval, (yprob)
##       * denotes terminal node
##
##  1) root 14000 5996 1 (0.428285714 0.571714286)
##    2) FICO< 680.5 5159    1 0 (0.999806164 0.000193836) *
##    3) FICO>=680.5 8841  838 1 (0.094785658 0.905214342)
##      6) PMT>=1882.593 3072  812 1 (0.264322917 0.735677083)
##       12) Income< 70279.5 1146  409 0 (0.643106457 0.356893543)
##         24) PMT>=2509.668 535   35 0 (0.934579439 0.065420561) *
##         25) PMT< 2509.668 611  237 1 (0.387888707 0.612111293) *
##       13) Income>=70279.5 1926   75 1 (0.038940810 0.961059190) *
##      7) PMT< 1882.593 5769   26 1 (0.004506847 0.995493153) *

# Show the pruned tree

fancyRpartPlot(approvalTreeModel.pruned)
```

4.3.10 Making Predictions

Now that we created an efficient decision tree model, we can proceed with making predictions about loan approvals. First, we will examine the *confusion matrix*:

```
table(loans.df.test$Approval, loans.df.test$Approval_Class )

##
##        0    1
##   0 2419  151
##   1   19 3411
```

The confusion matrix enables the calculation of the probability of misclassification:

```
classification.error <- mean(loans.df.test$Approval_Class != loans.df.test$Approval)
classification.error

## [1] 0.02833333

accuracy <- 1 - classification.error
accuracy

## [1] 0.9716667
```

The probability misclassification is very small, 0.028, which means the accuracy of the model is 97%, giving us confidence in its prediction ability.

We can now finally make predictions using the decision tree, by applying it to the test data we created in the beginning. The *predict()* function is using the pruned tree to predict the whether loans would be approved. The first and last six loans are shown:

```
probMatrix <- predict(approvalTreeModel.pruned, newdata=loans.df.test, type="prob")
probMatrix.df <- data.frame(probMatrix)

#Show the matrix, where X0 denotes prob(No) and X1 denotes prob(Yes)
options(scipen = 999 )
head(probMatrix.df)

##             X0          X1
## 2  0.038940810 0.961059190
## 4  0.999806164 0.000193836
## 6  0.387888707 0.612111293
## 8  0.999806164 0.000193836
## 12 0.004506847 0.995493153
## 14 0.999806164 0.000193836

tail(probMatrix.df)

##                X0          X1
## 19988 0.004506847 0.995493153
## 19991 0.004506847 0.995493153
## 19995 0.999806164 0.000193836
## 19997 0.004506847 0.995493153
## 19999 0.038940810 0.961059190
## 20000 0.004506847 0.995493153
```

4.3.11 Results Interpretation

The results are straight forward, a loan is either approved or not and the decision can be easily audited by traversing the pruned tree. Borrowers #2 and #12 are predicted to be approved with high probabilities, approaching 100%, while borrower #6 has only a 61% chance of being approved. Keep in mind that the data used in this model is synthetic and some decisions may be contrary to common sense. Its purpose was to provide a context in which to construct a predictive model, with the risk of generating some questionable decisions when examined by human logic. Therefore, the reader is encouraged to test this model on actual bank data, update the variables (there will probably be many more than presented here), then tweak the parameters of the model accordingly.

4.3.12 Conclusion

We used the same dataset for loan approval in two different models. While a decision tree is an alternative to logistic regression in many cases, the tree is not limited to binary answers. In other scenarios, we may want issue decisions like: *Approved, Declined, Approved with conditions,* and *Declined until a certain date.* The analyst must wage factors like computational efficiency, ease of implementation, and accuracy of prediction, when comparing decision trees and logistic regression for binary answers problems. A decision tree model can be easily expanded to include additional rules, which will add more branches for new decision paths. The seasoned analyst is encouraged to explore additional ways to improve and expand the model, after experimenting with different scenarios.

4.4 Predictive Model 4: Multiple Linear Regression

4.4.1 Theoretical Foundation

Multiple Linear Regression is often viewed as the workhorse of predictive analysis across multiple disciplines (McCarthy et al., 2019). Discussed in a multitude of texts, Searle and Gruber (2016) and Hay-Jahans (2017) provide the necessary depth warranted by this topic, together with an abundance of R programming examples. The variety of uses of MLR in finance is represented in studies such as Gul and Khan (2019), Liang et al. (2020), and Vieira et al. (2019).

The model uses a set of independent variables $(x_1, x_2, \ldots, x_n)$ to predict the value of a dependent variable Y. The relationship between the two is defined by:

$$y = \beta_0 + \beta_1 x_1 + \beta_2 x_2 + \cdots + \beta_n x_n + \varepsilon$$

where:

- y is the dependent variable
- β_0 is the model intercept
- $x_1, x_2, \ldots, x_n$ are the independent variables
- $\beta_0, \beta_1, \ldots, \beta_n$ are the linear regression coefficients
- ε is the error term

Before performing multiple linear regression or to validate the model, several assumptions must be verified:

1. *Linearity*—There is a linear relationship between the independent and dependent variables.
2. The residuals (difference between predicted and actual values) are normally distributed.
3. *Homoscedasticity*—The variance of ε does not change for all independent variables.
4. *No multicollinearity*—Independent variables are not multicollinear.
5. ε_i—The error terms should not be correlated with each other.

Since the model attempts to fit a relationship between independent and dependent variables, we need to measure how good is the fit. This is accomplished by calculating R^2:

$$R^2 = 1 - \frac{\text{SSE}}{\text{SST}}$$

where:

- SSE is the Sum of Squares due to Error (i.e., the variance explained by the model)
- SST is the Total Sum of Squares (i.e., the total variance)

A deeper coverage of the linear regression than the one synthesized here, is presented in Kleinbaum et al. (2013).

4.4.2 Advance Organizer

Figure 22 depicts the key steps involved in building and using a multiple linear regression model.

4.4.3 Objective

Given a dataset of characteristics of wine types, predict their quality and thus their suitability for the market.

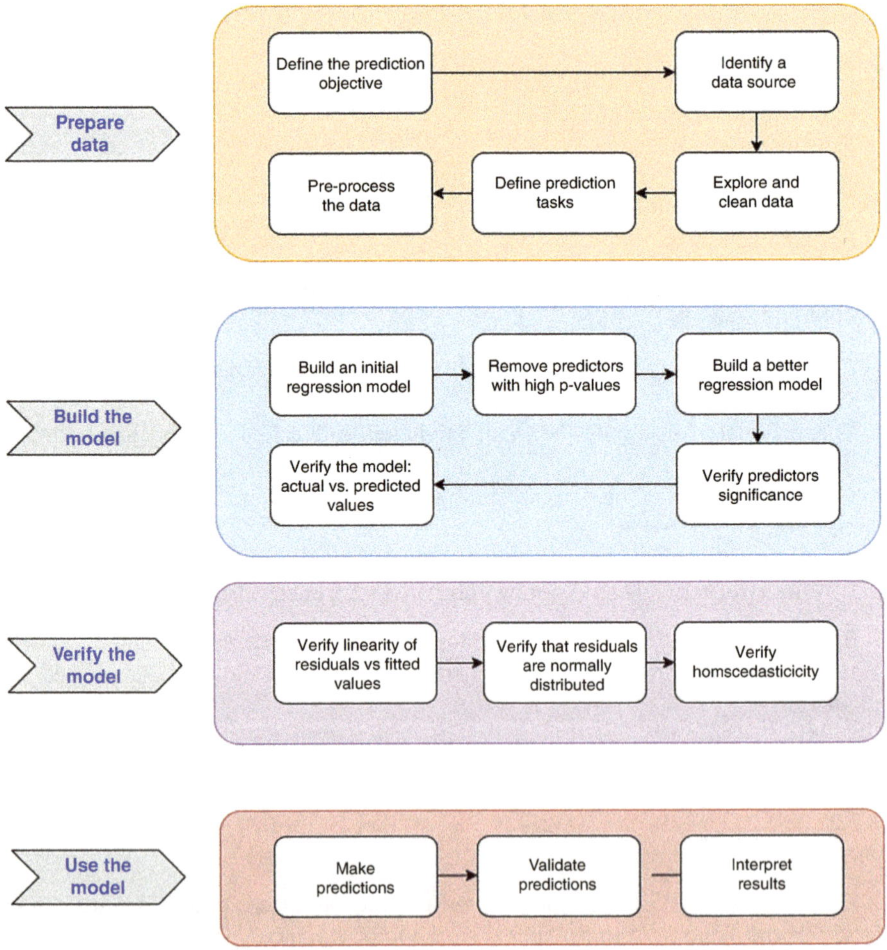

Fig. 22 An overview of the multiple linear regression process

4.4.4 Data Source

The data was downloaded from the free repository at UC Irvine, https://archive.ics.uci.edu/ml/datasets/Wine+Quality.

Let us first read the data into a data frame and inspect it. Note that the data includes 11 predictors of wine quality,

```
wine <- read.csv("winequality-white.csv")
wine.df <- data.frame(wine)
head(wine.df)

##   fixed.acidity volatile.acidity citric.acid residual.sugar chlorides
## 1           7.0             0.27        0.36           20.7     0.045
## 2           6.3             0.30        0.34            1.6     0.049
## 3           8.1             0.28        0.40            6.9     0.050
## 4           7.2             0.23        0.32            8.5     0.058
## 5           7.2             0.23        0.32            8.5     0.058
## 6           8.1             0.28        0.40            6.9     0.050
##   free.sulfur.dioxide total.sulfur.dioxide density   pH sulphates alcohol
## 1                  45                  170  1.0010 3.00      0.45     8.8
## 2                  14                  132  0.9940 3.30      0.49     9.5
## 3                  30                   97  0.9951 3.26      0.44    10.1
## 4                  47                  186  0.9956 3.19      0.40     9.9
## 5                  47                  186  0.9956 3.19      0.40     9.9
## 6                  30                   97  0.9951 3.26      0.44    10.1
##   quality
## 1       6
## 2       6
## 3       6
## 4       6
## 5       6
## 6       6

tail(wine.df)

##      fixed.acidity volatile.acidity citric.acid residual.sugar chlorides
## 4893           6.5             0.23        0.38            1.3     0.032
## 4894           6.2             0.21        0.29            1.6     0.039
## 4895           6.6             0.32        0.36            8.0     0.047
## 4896           6.5             0.24        0.19            1.2     0.041
## 4897           5.5             0.29        0.30            1.1     0.022
## 4898           6.0             0.21        0.38            0.8     0.020
##      free.sulfur.dioxide total.sulfur.dioxide density   pH sulphates alcohol
## 4893                  29                  112 0.99298 3.29      0.54     9.7
## 4894                  24                   92 0.99114 3.27      0.50    11.2
## 4895                  57                  168 0.99490 3.15      0.46     9.6
## 4896                  30                  111 0.99254 2.99      0.46     9.4
## 4897                  20                  110 0.98869 3.34      0.38    12.8
## 4898                  22                   98 0.98941 3.26      0.32    11.8
##      quality
## 4893       5
## 4894       6
## 4895       5
## 4896       6
## 4897       7
## 4898       6
```

4.4.5 Data Exploration and Cleaning

Some initial eyeballing of the basic descriptive statistics of the data can help inform the course of action later, when we will build the linear regression model. Examining the structure of the data provides another perspective of the predictors, their types, and names:

```
# The data structure
str(wine.df)

## 'data.frame':    4898 obs. of  12 variables:
##  $ fixed.acidity       : num  7 6.3 8.1 7.2 7.2 8.1 6.2 7 6.3 8.1 ...
##  $ volatile.acidity    : num  0.27 0.3 0.28 0.23 0.23 0.28 0.32 0.27 0.3 0.22 ...
##  $ citric.acid         : num  0.36 0.34 0.4 0.32 0.32 0.4 0.16 0.36 0.34 0.43 ...
##  $ residual.sugar      : num  20.7 1.6 6.9 8.5 8.5 6.9 7 20.7 1.6 1.5 ...
##  $ chlorides           : num  0.045 0.049 0.05 0.058 0.058 0.05 0.045 0.045 0.049 0
.044 ...
##  $ free.sulfur.dioxide : num  45 14 30 47 47 30 30 45 14 28 ...
##  $ total.sulfur.dioxide: num  170 132 97 186 186 97 136 170 132 129 ...
##  $ density             : num  1.001 0.994 0.995 0.996 0.996 ...
##  $ pH                  : num  3 3.3 3.26 3.19 3.19 3.26 3.18 3 3.3 3.22 ...
##  $ sulphates           : num  0.45 0.49 0.44 0.4 0.4 0.44 0.47 0.45 0.49 0.45 ...
##  $ alcohol             : num  8.8 9.5 10.1 9.9 9.9 10.1 9.6 8.8 9.5 11 ...
##  $ quality             : int  6 6 6 6 6 6 6 6 6 6 ...

names(wine.df)

##  [1] "fixed.acidity"        "volatile.acidity"     "citric.acid"
##  [4] "residual.sugar"       "chlorides"            "free.sulfur.dioxide"
##  [7] "total.sulfur.dioxide" "density"              "pH"
## [10] "sulphates"            "alcohol"              "quality"

class(wine.df)

## [1] "data.frame"
```

An examination of the basic descriptive statistics and a check for missing values helps gaining a better understanding of the possible impact of certain variables in the regression model:

```
summary(wine.df)

##  fixed.acidity    volatile.acidity  citric.acid      residual.sugar
##  Min.   : 3.800   Min.   :0.0800   Min.   :0.0000   Min.   : 0.600
##  1st Qu.: 6.300   1st Qu.:0.2100   1st Qu.:0.2700   1st Qu.: 1.700
##  Median : 6.800   Median :0.2600   Median :0.3200   Median : 5.200
##  Mean   : 6.855   Mean   :0.2782   Mean   :0.3342   Mean   : 6.391
##  3rd Qu.: 7.300   3rd Qu.:0.3200   3rd Qu.:0.3900   3rd Qu.: 9.900
##  Max.   :14.200   Max.   :1.1000   Max.   :1.6600   Max.   :65.800
##    chlorides        free.sulfur.dioxide total.sulfur.dioxide    density
##  Min.   :0.00900   Min.   :  2.00      Min.   :  9.0        Min.   :0.9871
##  1st Qu.:0.03600   1st Qu.: 23.00      1st Qu.:108.0        1st Qu.:0.9917
##  Median :0.04300   Median : 34.00      Median :134.0        Median :0.9937
##  Mean   :0.04577   Mean   : 35.31      Mean   :138.4        Mean   :0.9940
##  3rd Qu.:0.05000   3rd Qu.: 46.00      3rd Qu.:167.0        3rd Qu.:0.9961
##  Max.   :0.34600   Max.   :289.00      Max.   :440.0        Max.   :1.0390
##        pH           sulphates          alcohol          quality
##  Min.   :2.720   Min.   :0.2200   Min.   : 8.00   Min.   :3.000
##  1st Qu.:3.090   1st Qu.:0.4100   1st Qu.: 9.50   1st Qu.:5.000
##  Median :3.180   Median :0.4700   Median :10.40   Median :6.000
##  Mean   :3.188   Mean   :0.4898   Mean   :10.51   Mean   :5.878
##  3rd Qu.:3.280   3rd Qu.:0.5500   3rd Qu.:11.40   3rd Qu.:6.000
##  Max.   :3.820   Max.   :1.0800   Max.   :14.20   Max.   :9.000

# Check for missing values
sum(is.na(wine.df))

## [1] 0
```

We confirm that there are no missing data and can proceed with further preliminary steps. The next step is to assess whether certain variables are correlated. If, yes, we will remove them from consideration as predictors, as only one of a pair of correlated variables adds new information to the model.

```
# Calculate the correlation between all variables

cor(wine.df)

##                      fixed.acidity volatile.acidity  citric.acid residual.sugar
## fixed.acidity           1.00000000      -0.02269729  0.289180698     0.08902070
## volatile.acidity       -0.02269729       1.00000000 -0.149471811     0.06428606
## citric.acid             0.28918070      -0.14947181  1.000000000     0.09421162
## residual.sugar          0.08902070       0.06428606  0.094211624     1.00000000
## chlorides               0.02308564       0.07051157  0.114364448     0.08868454
## free.sulfur.dioxide    -0.04939586      -0.09701194  0.094077221     0.29909835
## total.sulfur.dioxide    0.09106976       0.08926050  0.121130798     0.40143931
## density                 0.26533101       0.02711385  0.149502571     0.83896645
## pH                     -0.42585829      -0.03191537 -0.163748211    -0.19413345
## sulphates              -0.01714299      -0.03572815  0.062330940    -0.02666437
## alcohol                -0.12088112       0.06771794 -0.075728730    -0.45063122
## quality                -0.11366283      -0.19472297 -0.009209091    -0.09757683
##                        chlorides free.sulfur.dioxide total.sulfur.dioxide
## fixed.acidity         0.02308564        -0.0493958591          0.091069756
## volatile.acidity      0.07051157        -0.0970119393          0.089260504
## citric.acid           0.11436445         0.0940772210          0.121130798
## residual.sugar        0.08868454         0.2990983537          0.401439311
## chlorides             1.00000000         0.1013923521          0.198910300
## free.sulfur.dioxide   0.10139235         1.0000000000          0.615500965
## total.sulfur.dioxide  0.19891030         0.6155009650          1.000000000
## density               0.25721132         0.2942104109          0.529881324
## pH                   -0.09043946        -0.0006177961          0.002320972
## sulphates             0.01676288         0.0592172458          0.134562367
## alcohol              -0.36018871        -0.2501039415         -0.448892102
## quality              -0.20993441         0.0081580671         -0.174737218
##                          density            pH   sulphates     alcohol
## fixed.acidity         0.26533101 -0.4258582910 -0.01714299 -0.12088112
## volatile.acidity      0.02711385 -0.0319153683 -0.03572815  0.06771794
## citric.acid           0.14950257 -0.1637482114  0.06233094 -0.07572873
## residual.sugar        0.83896645 -0.1941334540 -0.02666437 -0.45063122
## chlorides             0.25721132 -0.0904394560  0.01676288 -0.36018871
## free.sulfur.dioxide   0.29421041 -0.0006177961  0.05921725 -0.25010394
## total.sulfur.dioxide  0.52988132  0.0023209718  0.13456237 -0.44889210
## density               1.00000000 -0.0935914935  0.07449315 -0.78013762
## pH                   -0.09359149  1.0000000000  0.15595150  0.12143210
## sulphates             0.07449315  0.1559514973  1.00000000 -0.01743277
## alcohol              -0.78013762  0.1214320987 -0.01743277  1.00000000
## quality              -0.30712331  0.0994272457  0.05367788  0.43557472
##                          quality
## fixed.acidity        -0.113662831
## volatile.acidity     -0.194722969
## citric.acid          -0.009209091
## residual.sugar       -0.097576829
## chlorides            -0.209934411
## free.sulfur.dioxide   0.008158067
## total.sulfur.dioxide -0.174737218
## density              -0.307123313
## pH                    0.099427246
## sulphates             0.053677877
## alcohol               0.435574715
## quality               1.000000000
```

We notice, for example, that *density* and *residual.sugar* are strongly correlated, with *r=0.8389*. We will take this information into account in the later phases of improving the model, which we must first build.

4.4.6 Predictive Tasks

We will build the predictive model, verify the assumptions, and validate the model. These preparatory steps will ensure that the model can reliably predict the quality of a wine, given the set of independent variables. Upon completing the prediction, we will measure the residuals to assess the accuracy of the model.

4.4.7 Data Pre-processing

As with other predictive models, we will now split the data into a *training* and *testing* set, using a ratio of 70:30:

```
library(caTools)
set.seed(123)   # to reproduce the sample

sample <- sample.split(wine.df$quality, SplitRatio = 0.7)

wine.df.train <- subset(wine.df, sample==TRUE)
wine.df.test <- subset(wine.df, sample==FALSE)

head(wine.df.train)

##    fixed.acidity volatile.acidity citric.acid residual.sugar chlorides
## 1            7.0             0.27        0.36           20.7     0.045
## 3            8.1             0.28        0.40            6.9     0.050
## 6            8.1             0.28        0.40            6.9     0.050
## 7            6.2             0.32        0.16            7.0     0.045
## 9            6.3             0.30        0.34            1.6     0.049
## 10           8.1             0.22        0.43            1.5     0.044
##    free.sulfur.dioxide total.sulfur.dioxide density   pH sulphates alcohol
## 1                   45                  170  1.0010 3.00      0.45     8.8
## 3                   30                   97  0.9951 3.26      0.44    10.1
## 6                   30                   97  0.9951 3.26      0.44    10.1
## 7                   30                  136  0.9949 3.18      0.47     9.6
## 9                   14                  132  0.9940 3.30      0.49     9.5
## 10                  28                  129  0.9938 3.22      0.45    11.0
##    quality
## 1        6
## 3        6
## 6        6
## 7        6
## 9        6
## 10       6

tail(wine.df.train)

##      fixed.acidity volatile.acidity citric.acid residual.sugar chlorides
## 4887           6.2            0.210        0.28           5.70     0.028
## 4889           6.8            0.220        0.36           1.20     0.052
## 4890           4.9            0.235        0.27          11.75     0.030
## 4896           6.5            0.240        0.19           1.20     0.041
## 4897           5.5            0.290        0.30           1.10     0.022
## 4898           6.0            0.210        0.38           0.80     0.020
##      free.sulfur.dioxide total.sulfur.dioxide density   pH sulphates alcohol
## 4887                  45                  121 0.99168 3.21      1.08   12.15
## 4889                  38                  127 0.99330 3.04      0.54    9.20
## 4890                  34                  118 0.99540 3.07      0.50    9.40
## 4896                  30                  111 0.99254 2.99      0.46    9.40
## 4897                  20                  110 0.98869 3.34      0.38   12.80
## 4898                  22                   98 0.98941 3.26      0.32   11.80
##      quality
## 4887       7
## 4889       5
## 4890       6
## 4896       6
## 4897       7
## 4898       6
```

4.4.8 Build the Predictive Model

We will use the *lm()* function in R to build an initial regression model, in which all variables are used as predictors of the outcome variable, *quality*:

```
qualityModel <- lm(quality ~., data = wine.df.train)
summary(qualityModel)
##
## Call:
## lm(formula = quality ~ ., data = wine.df.train)
##
## Residuals:
##     Min      1Q  Median      3Q     Max
## -3.9027 -0.4910 -0.0470  0.4555  3.1082
##
## Coefficients:
##                        Estimate Std. Error t value Pr(>|t|)
## (Intercept)           2.087e+02  2.707e+01   7.710 1.64e-14 ***
## fixed.acidity         1.058e-01  2.734e-02   3.869 0.000111 ***
## volatile.acidity     -1.926e+00  1.343e-01 -14.342  < 2e-16 ***
## citric.acid           1.586e-01  1.125e-01   1.410 0.158506
## residual.sugar        9.836e-02  1.022e-02   9.620  < 2e-16 ***
## chlorides            -5.806e-01  6.455e-01  -0.899 0.368454
## free.sulfur.dioxide   3.758e-03  9.981e-04   3.765 0.000169 ***
## total.sulfur.dioxide -9.553e-05  4.578e-04  -0.209 0.834701
## density              -2.093e+02  2.743e+01  -7.632 2.97e-14 ***
## pH                    8.381e-01  1.333e-01   6.286 3.68e-10 ***
## sulphates             7.390e-01  1.186e-01   6.233 5.12e-10 ***
## alcohol               1.219e-01  3.421e-02   3.563 0.000371 ***
## ---
## Signif. codes:  0 '***' 0.001 '**' 0.01 '*' 0.05 '.' 0.1 ' ' 1
##
## Residual standard error: 0.7434 on 3417 degrees of freedom
## Multiple R-squared:  0.2983, Adjusted R-squared:  0.296
## F-statistic:   132 on 11 and 3417 DF,  p-value: < 2.2e-16
```

As we examine the regression output, note that the *p-value* = *2.2e-16*, which is the threshold against the *p*-values of each variable must be examined. We will remove from the model all variables with a higher *p*-value than the threshold, namely *citric.acid, chlorides,* and *total.sulfur.dioxide.*

We will thus construct a new regression model, using only the remaining variables:

```
qualityModel.significantVars <- lm(quality ~ fixed.acidity + volatile.acidity + residu
al.sugar + free.sulfur.dioxide + density + pH + sulphates + alcohol, data = wine.df.tr
ain)
qualityModel.significantVars

##
## Call:
## lm(formula = quality ~ fixed.acidity + volatile.acidity + residual.sugar +
##     free.sulfur.dioxide + density + pH + sulphates + alcohol,
##     data = wine.df.train)
##
## Coefficients:
##         (Intercept)        fixed.acidity     volatile.acidity
##           210.84997              0.11365             -1.97116
##      residual.sugar  free.sulfur.dioxide              density
##             0.09953              0.00368           -211.58968
##                  pH            sulphates              alcohol
##             0.84043              0.74613              0.12446
```

Let us inspect the new model and verify that all predictors are significant:

```
summary(qualityModel.significantVars)

##
## Call:
## lm(formula = quality ~ fixed.acidity + volatile.acidity + residual.sugar +
##     free.sulfur.dioxide + density + pH + sulphates + alcohol,
##     data = wine.df.train)
##
## Residuals:
##     Min      1Q  Median      3Q     Max
## -3.9202 -0.4890 -0.0465  0.4591  3.1178
##
## Coefficients:
##                       Estimate Std. Error t value Pr(>|t|)
## (Intercept)          2.108e+02  2.570e+01   8.203 3.28e-16 ***
## fixed.acidity        1.137e-01  2.664e-02   4.266 2.04e-05 ***
## volatile.acidity    -1.971e+00  1.290e-01 -15.284  < 2e-16 ***
## residual.sugar       9.953e-02  9.779e-03  10.179  < 2e-16 ***
## free.sulfur.dioxide  3.680e-03  7.908e-04   4.654 3.38e-06 ***
## density             -2.116e+02  2.603e+01  -8.130 5.96e-16 ***
## pH                   8.404e-01  1.304e-01   6.443 1.33e-10 ***
## sulphates            7.461e-01  1.183e-01   6.309 3.18e-10 ***
## alcohol              1.245e-01  3.378e-02   3.685 0.000233 ***
## ---
## Signif. codes:  0 '***' 0.001 '**' 0.01 '*' 0.05 '.' 0.1 ' ' 1
##
## Residual standard error: 0.7433 on 3420 degrees of freedom
## Multiple R-squared:  0.2978, Adjusted R-squared:  0.2961
## F-statistic: 181.3 on 8 and 3420 DF,  p-value: < 2.2e-16
```

Indeed, the *p-value* of each value is smaller than the *p-value* of the model, 2.2e-16. An initial interpretation of this model is that (for example) an increase of *fixed.acidity* by 1 unit, results in 0.1137 units increase in the quality of the wine. Similarly, an increase of 1 unit of density, results in the decrease of quality by 0.02116 units.

The number of the fitted values in the model is given by:

```
# The number of fitted values in the model
length(qualityModel.significantVars$fitted.values)

## [1] 3429
```

4.4.9 Initial Verification of the Model

A first step in auditing the model we just created, is to calculate the difference between predicted and observed values:

```
# The fitted values by the training set

predicted.train <- qualityModel.significantVars$fitted.values
head(predicted.train)

##        1        3        6        7        9       10
## 5.490332 5.788104 5.788104 5.438504 5.186689 5.722458

predicted.train.df <- data.frame(predicted.train)

# Calculate residual values

predicted.train.df.residuals <- qualityModel.significantVars$residuals
head(predicted.train.df.residuals)

##         1         3         6         7         9        10
## 0.5096682 0.2118956 0.2118956 0.5614960 0.8133114 0.2775417
```

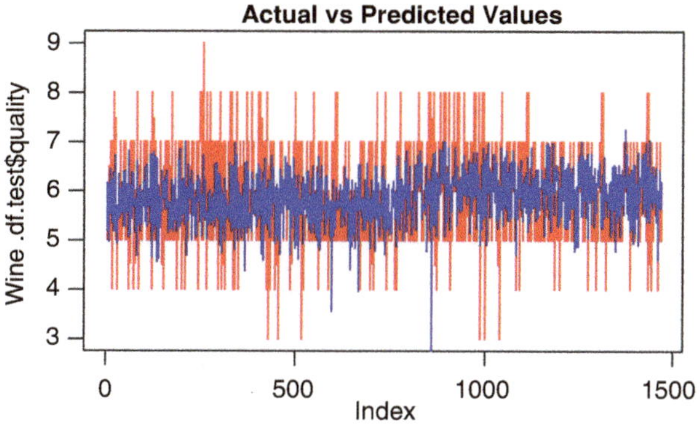

Fig. 23 The difference between actual and predicted values of wine quality

Although only a handful of *residuals* are shown (the reader should inspect all of them), they are all positive. Since the *residuals* = *actual* – *predicted values*, we conclude that the actual values are *greater* than the predicted ones.

We can now proceed and apply the model to the testing set we created earlier.

```
predicted.test <- predict(qualityModel.significantVars, newdata = wine.df.test)
head(predicted.test)

##        2        4        5        8       13       15
## 5.186689 5.786826 5.786826 5.490332 6.161208 5.611991

predicted.test.df <- data.frame(predicted.test)
```

The first six values are shown, and they indicate the predicted quality of the wine. It is helpful at this point to visualize the difference between actual and predicted values, which previously we found to be positive (Fig. 23):

```
# Plot actual values vs predicted values

plot(wine.df.test$quality, col="red", type="l", lty=1.8, main = "Actual vs Predicted V
alues")
lines(predicted.test.df, col="blue", type="l", lty=1.4)
```

It is evident from the plot that the actual values (in red) are greater than the predicted values (in blue).

4.4.10 Further Model Validation

An important step in the validation of every predicted model, is the verification of its assumptions. To verify the assumptions of the linear regression model, we will use the *which* parameter in the *plot()* function, whose values (1, 2, 3, and 5) are mapped

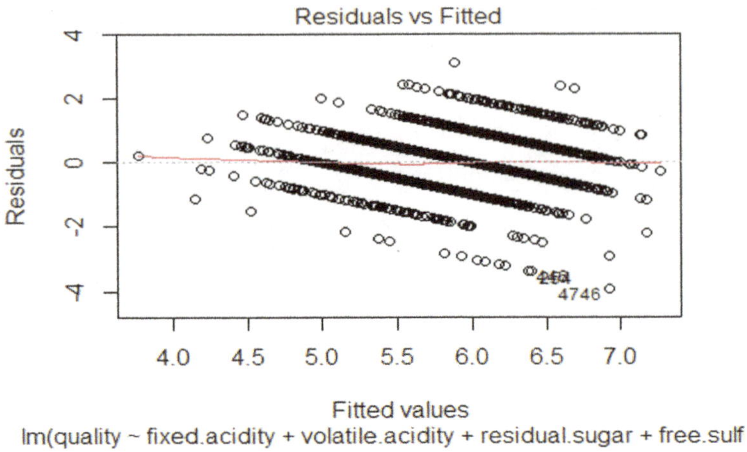

Fig. 24 Random spread of residuals indicates linearity

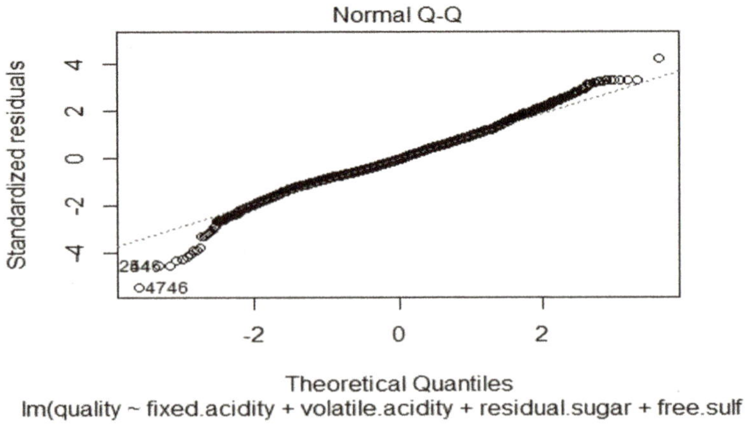

Fig. 25 Residuals are normally distributed

to invoke the different characteristics of residuals we wish to measure. We will first compare the residuals and fitted values to verify *linearity* (Fig. 24):

```
# Plot residuals vs fitted values to verify linearity
plot(qualityModel.significantVars, which=1)
```

It is evident in the plot that the residuals are scattered without any discernable pattern. Therefore, we conclude that the linearity assumption is satisfied.

Next, we need to verify that the *residuals are normally distributed* (Fig. 25):

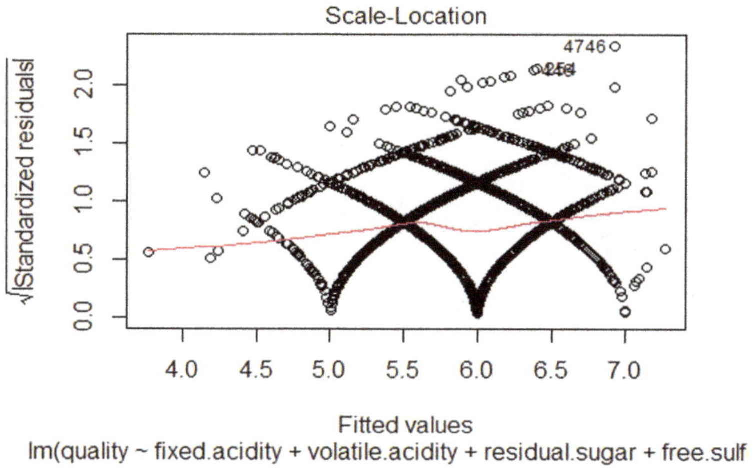

Fig. 26 Homoscedasticity—random spread of residuals

```
# Verify that the residuals are normally distributed
plot(qualityModel.significantVars, which=2)
```

Since the plot approximates a straight line, we conclude that the residuals are indeed normally distributed. An additional validation is the verification of the spread of the residuals (Fig. 26). The focus on residuals is since we have actual results, therefore the best way to measure how accurate are the predictions, is to ensure that they only differ minimally from the actual values. When they do, we need to verify that this is random and there is no pattern (i.e., a variable working "behind the scenes"). This assumption is the homoscedasticity of residuals, meaning that the random error in the difference between predicted and actual value remains approximately constant across all observations.

```
# Verify that the residuals are randomly spread
plot(qualityModel.significantVars, which=3)
```

In Fig. 26, besides two values (2544 and 4746), the residuals are satisfactorily spread about the red line, confirming homoscedasticity. However, there seems to be some pattern in the residuals spread, and homoscedasticity must be further verified (Fig. 27). We will use the *Cook distance*, to measure how significant is the impact of outliers.

```
# Assess the presence of significant outliers that could skew the results
plot(qualityModel.significantVars, which=5)
```

There are three outlier observations, 1932, 1664, and 4746, but they are not crossing the Cook's distance line, which means they do not significantly impact the model.

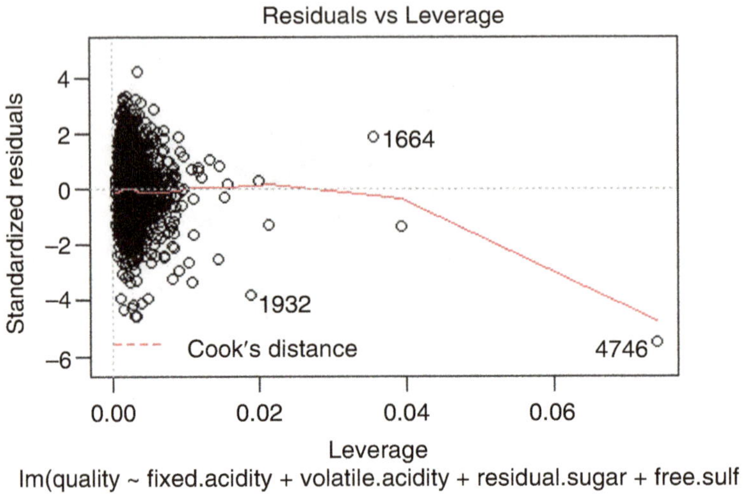

Fig. 27 Homoscedasticity—random spread of residuals verified by calculating the *Cook distance*

One final set of tests will further strengthen the model, by testing residuals independence (i.e., not auto-correlated) using the Durbin-Watson test, and another test for homoscedasticity, using the Non-Constant Variance Score test (NCV):

```
# Verify that the residuals are independent (i.e. not auto-correlated)

library(car) # companion to applied regression

## Loading required package: carData

# Test for independence using the Durbin-Watson Test
durbinWatsonTest(qualityModel.significantVars)

##  lag Autocorrelation D-W Statistic p-value
##    1       0.1733352      1.653117       0
##  Alternative hypothesis: rho != 0
```

Since the *p-value* in the Durbin-Watson test is 0, we cannot reject the null hypothesis, meaning the residuals are not auto-correlated (i.e., they are independent).

```
# Test homoscedasticity using the Non-Constant Variance Score test (NCV)
ncvTest(qualityModel.significantVars)

## Non-constant Variance Score Test
## Variance formula: ~ fitted.values
## Chisquare = 24.32978, Df = 1, p = 8.1174e-07
```

The NCV test returns a p-value = 8.1174e-07, which is smaller than 0.001. This means the null hypothesis cannot be rejected outright, and just to cover our bases, we would state that there is reason to believe that homoscedasticity is not fully confirmed. Since may be some cause of concern, we will also test the collinearity of the predictors, as measured by the *Variance Inflation Factor (VIF)*. We expect the $\sqrt{\text{VIF}}$ (i.e. the standard deviation) value for each predictor to be greater than 5.

```
# Test Collinearity using Variance Inflation Factor (VIF)
vif(qualityModel.significantVars)

##      fixed.acidity   volatile.acidity     residual.sugar free.sulfur.dioxide
##           3.181119           1.049281          14.605641           1.147416
##            density                 pH          sulphates             alcohol
##          35.236265           2.403267           1.150223           10.804521

# Test that SQRT(VIF) > 5

sqrt(vif(qualityModel.significantVars)) > 5

##      fixed.acidity   volatile.acidity     residual.sugar free.sulfur.dioxide
##              FALSE              FALSE              FALSE               FALSE
##            density                 pH          sulphates             alcohol
##               TRUE              FALSE              FALSE               FALSE
```

Since all tests have returned **FALSE**, we conclude that there is no collinearity.

4.4.11 Results Interpretation

After building a multilinear regression model with significant predictors and confirmed that the discrepancies between predicted and actual values are random, lack a pattern, and independent, we can accept with a high degree of confidence the determination of wine quality generated by the model. Here are again the first 20 predicted wine qualities in the test set, which as you recall amounts to 30% of the original data:

```
predicted.test <- predict(qualityModel.significantVars, newdata = wine.df.test)
predicted.test.df <- data.frame(predicted.test)
head(predicted.test.df,20)

##    predicted.test
## 2        5.186689
## 4        5.786826
## 5        5.786826
## 8        5.490332
## 13       6.161208
## 15       5.611991
## 17       4.959925
## 20       5.473400
## 28       5.855804
## 30       6.437969
## 33       5.972844
## 34       5.701604
## 39       5.627041
## 42       5.431163
## 44       5.501018
## 47       5.373176
## 53       6.230720
## 55       5.328904
## 56       6.122070
## 58       5.728106

# Show only the top 20 wines

head(as.matrix(sort(predicted.test.df$predicted.test, decreasing=TRUE)), 20)

##           [,1]
##  [1,] 7.238255
##  [2,] 7.018194
##  [3,] 7.012078
##  [4,] 6.994071
##  [5,] 6.990888
##  [6,] 6.990176
##  [7,] 6.976816
##  [8,] 6.974335
##  [9,] 6.955107
## [10,] 6.953865
## [11,] 6.950063
## [12,] 6.920023
## [13,] 6.873633
## [14,] 6.871852
## [15,] 6.870578
## [16,] 6.865694
## [17,] 6.863794
## [18,] 6.861919
## [19,] 6.860095
## [20,] 6.846164
```

Different training vs testing splits, different thresholds in the construction of the model, make cause results to differ from one analyst to another. Whatever the stakeholder decides to do with the knowledge of top 20 highest quality wines (as predicted by this model) it is beyond the scope of this chapter.

4.4.12 Conclusion

We predicted the quality of wine, but the same process could have been applied to choose the best stocks to invest, houses to purchase, employees to hire, or vegan recipes for those who suffer from acid reflux. The abstract mathematical and statistical tools are the same, but it is the human analyst who adds context and meaning to the interpretation of data and what it reveals. The reader is encouraged to examine the references provided and identify ways to expand and refine the multilinear regression model presented here and apply it to data from a variety of sources.

4.5 Predictive Model 5: RFM Segmentation with k-*means*

4.5.1 Foundation

This is a combination of two models, *Recency, Frequency, Monetary (RFM)*, and the *k-means* clustering model. RFM ranks customers in terms of time of last purchase(s), number of return visits, and amount of money spent. The *k-means* algorithm identifies categories of customers within the (top selected) group. The idea is that is a retailer can predict who will walk through the door in the near future, when will they shop, and how much they will spend, then special advertising campaigns or sales can be tailored to this specific group. The RFM segmentation technique is a key component in studies presented by Zhang et al. (2015), Carrasco et al. (2019), and Güçdemir and Selim (2015).

The RFM model is based on a combination of three tables (sets) of information:

- *Recency*—Time since last purchase
- *Frequency*—Number of previous purchases over a period
- *Monetary*—Amount of money spent over a period

Unlike other predictive models, *RFM* is very simple from a mathematical standpoint, easy to implement, and thus very popular with marketing companies. It essentially amounts to sorting information in a table of historical data, then assign values of 1–4 (for example) depending of the segment in which the customer fits. For example:

- A customer who has not visited the store for a while has an $R = 1$, while one who visited last week has an $R = 4$.
- A customer who frequents the store every week, has an $F = 4$, while one who visits every month has an $F = 3$.
- A customer who spends a moderate amount each time, may be assigned an $M = 2$, while a big spender would be an $M = 4$.

The values differ in meaning based on the type of business. Shopping for diamonds is different than shopping for groceries. The RFM model stops with assigning each individual customer a value (R, F, M), for example (1, 4, 3) to a frequent, fairly high spender who has not made a purchase in a while. However, this designation is insufficient to efficiently segment the market.

The *k-means* model adds more sophistication by employing an unsupervised learning method for segmenting a dataset. Given the dataset $D = \{(R_1, F_1, M_1), (R_2, F_2, M_3), \ldots (R_n, F_n, M_n)\}$, the model clusters the elements in the set into k groups, where k is assigned by the analyst. The choice of k should be refined through repeated experimentation, until the analyst is satisfied with the results.

The algorithm of k-means is straightforward. Since RFM implies a 3D vector space:

1. *Initially*, randomly pick k centroids (or points that will be the center of the clusters) in 3D space. Make them near the data but different from one another.
2. Assign each data point to the closest centroid.
3. Move the centroids to the average location of the data points assigned to it.
4. Minimize variation within the cluster k with centroid C_k, members $x_i = (R_i, F_i, M_i)$, and mean μ_k, using:

$$\text{Within Variation}(C_k) = \sum_{x_i \in C_k} (x_i - \mu_k)^2$$

5. Repeat steps 2–4 until the assignments do not change or change very little.

The ultimate objective of the *RFM k-means* combination is to analyze and monetize customer value.

4.5.2 Advance Organizer

Figure 28 depicts a high-level review of the main steps of constructing and using an *RFM k-means* model.

4.5.3 Objective

Given a dataset of online retail customers and their purchase history, predict who are the best customers.

4.5.4 Data Source

The data is freely available at https://www.kaggle.com/somesh24/customer-segmentation. The dataset includes a list of 541,909 transactions with the following information: *InvoiceNo, StockCode, Description, Quantity, InvoiceDate, UnitPrice, CustomerID, Country.*

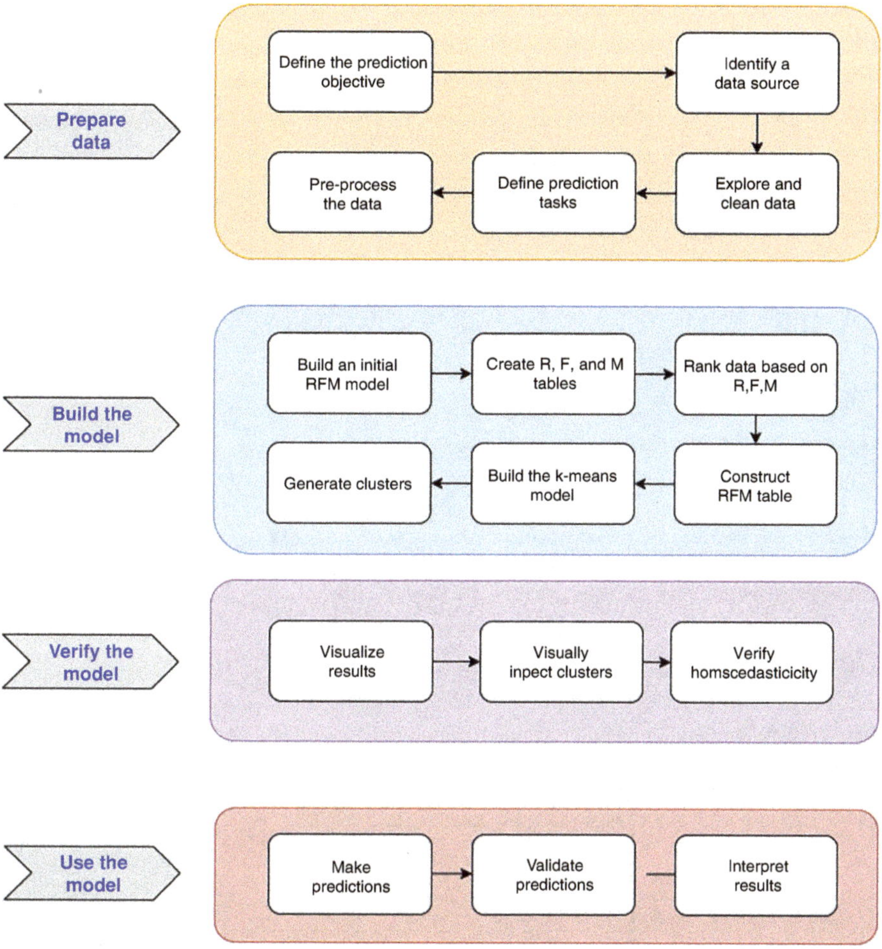

Fig. 28 Overview of the RFM *k*-means process

4.5.5 Data Exploration and Cleaning

We will first inspect the data and its structure.

```
# Initial data acquisition and exploration
customers <- read.csv("Online Retail.csv")
customers.df <- data.frame(customers)
head(customers.df)

##   InvoiceNo StockCode                         Description Quantity
## 1    536365    85123A  WHITE HANGING HEART T-LIGHT HOLDER        6
## 2    536365     71053                 WHITE METAL LANTERN        6
## 3    536365    84406B      CREAM CUPID HEARTS COAT HANGER        8
## 4    536365    84029G KNITTED UNION FLAG HOT WATER BOTTLE        6
## 5    536365    84029E      RED WOOLLY HOTTIE WHITE HEART.        6
## 6    536365     22752        SET 7 BABUSHKA NESTING BOXES        2
##      InvoiceDate UnitPrice CustomerID        Country
## 1 12/1/2010 8:26      2.55      17850 United Kingdom
## 2 12/1/2010 8:26      3.39      17850 United Kingdom
## 3 12/1/2010 8:26      2.75      17850 United Kingdom
## 4 12/1/2010 8:26      3.39      17850 United Kingdom
## 5 12/1/2010 8:26      3.39      17850 United Kingdom
## 6 12/1/2010 8:26      7.65      17850 United Kingdom

tail(customers.df)

##        InvoiceNo StockCode                         Description Quantity
## 541904    581587     23256         CHILDRENS CUTLERY SPACEBOY         4
## 541905    581587     22613         PACK OF 20 SPACEBOY NAPKINS       12
## 541906    581587     22899        CHILDREN'S APRON DOLLY GIRL         6
## 541907    581587     23254       CHILDRENS CUTLERY DOLLY GIRL         4
## 541908    581587     23255 CHILDRENS CUTLERY CIRCUS PARADE          4
## 541909    581587     22138       BAKING SET 9 PIECE RETROSPOT         3
##            InvoiceDate UnitPrice CustomerID Country
## 541904 12/9/2011 12:50      4.15      12680  France
## 541905 12/9/2011 12:50      0.85      12680  France
## 541906 12/9/2011 12:50      2.10      12680  France
## 541907 12/9/2011 12:50      4.15      12680  France
## 541908 12/9/2011 12:50      4.15      12680  France
## 541909 12/9/2011 12:50      4.95      12680  France

# The data structure
str(customers.df)

## 'data.frame':    541909 obs. of  8 variables:
##  $ InvoiceNo  : chr  "536365" "536365" "536365" "536365" ...
##  $ StockCode  : chr  "85123A" "71053" "84406B" "84029G" ...
##  $ Description: chr  "WHITE HANGING HEART T-LIGHT HOLDER" "WHITE METAL LANTERN" "CR
EAM CUPID HEARTS COAT HANGER" "KNITTED UNION FLAG HOT WATER BOTTLE" ...
##  $ Quantity   : int  6 6 8 6 6 2 6 6 6 32 ...
##  $ InvoiceDate: chr  "12/1/2010 8:26" "12/1/2010 8:26" "12/1/2010 8:26" "12/1/2010
8:26" ...
##  $ UnitPrice  : num  2.55 3.39 2.75 3.39 3.39 7.65 4.25 1.85 1.85 1.69 ...
##  $ CustomerID : int  17850 17850 17850 17850 17850 17850 17850 17850 17850 13047 ..
.
##  $ Country    : chr  "United Kingdom" "United Kingdom" "United Kingdom" "United Kin
gdom" ...

names(customers.df)

## [1] "InvoiceNo"   "StockCode"   "Description" "Quantity"    "InvoiceDate"
## [6] "UnitPrice"   "CustomerID"  "Country"
class(customers.df)

## [1] "data.frame"
```

Let us examine the structure of the data and look for missing values, given the large data size:

```
summary(customers.df)

##   InvoiceNo           StockCode          Description           Quantity
##  Length:541909      Length:541909      Length:541909      Min.   :-80995.00
##  Class :character   Class :character   Class :character   1st Qu.:     1.00
##  Mode  :character   Mode  :character   Mode  :character   Median :     3.00
##                                                           Mean   :     9.55
##                                                           3rd Qu.:    10.00
##                                                           Max.   : 80995.00
##
##  InvoiceDate          UnitPrice           CustomerID        Country
##  Length:541909      Min.   :-11062.06   Min.   :12346   Length:541909
##  Class :character   1st Qu.:     1.25   1st Qu.:13953   Class :character
##  Mode  :character   Median :     2.08   Median :15152   Mode  :character
##                     Mean   :     4.61   Mean   :15288
##                     3rd Qu.:     4.13   3rd Qu.:16791
##                     Max.   : 38970.00   Max.   :18287
##                                         NA's   :135080

# Check for missing values
sum(is.na(customers.df))

## [1] 135080
```

Since there are 135,080 observations with missing customer ID, there is no way to verify who they are. Given the stated objective of customer segmentation, the most appropriate course of action is to remove these observations, especially since there are plenty left to process, 406,829 observations.

```
library(dplyr)

##
## Attaching package: 'dplyr'

## The following objects are masked from 'package:stats':
##
##     filter, lag

## The following objects are masked from 'package:base':
##
##     intersect, setdiff, setequal, union

# Omit all rows with n/a values
customers2.df <- na.omit(customers.df)
head(customers2.df)

##   InvoiceNo StockCode                         Description Quantity
## 1    536365    85123A  WHITE HANGING HEART T-LIGHT HOLDER        6
## 2    536365     71053                 WHITE METAL LANTERN        6
## 3    536365    84406B      CREAM CUPID HEARTS COAT HANGER        8
## 4    536365    84029G KNITTED UNION FLAG HOT WATER BOTTLE        6
## 5    536365    84029E      RED WOOLLY HOTTIE WHITE HEART.        6
## 6    536365     22752        SET 7 BABUSHKA NESTING BOXES        2
##      InvoiceDate UnitPrice CustomerID        Country
## 1 12/1/2010 8:26      2.55      17850 United Kingdom
## 2 12/1/2010 8:26      3.39      17850 United Kingdom
## 3 12/1/2010 8:26      2.75      17850 United Kingdom
## 4 12/1/2010 8:26      3.39      17850 United Kingdom
## 5 12/1/2010 8:26      3.39      17850 United Kingdom
## 6 12/1/2010 8:26      7.65      17850 United Kingdom

# Check again for missing values
sum(is.na(customers2.df))

## [1] 0
```

4.5.6 Predictive Tasks

Build the components of the RFM model and assign the (R_i, F_i, M_i) scores to each customer. Then, use the scores as input for the *k*-means algorithm to compute the clusters, i.e., perform customer segmentation.

4.5.7 Data Pre-processing

We have confirmed that all rows with missing values have been removed. Next, we need to modify the timestamp information in the *InvoiceDate* variable, since it cannot be used in computations in its current format. In addition, define *NOW* = *2020-12-12*:

```
# Check again for missing values
sum(is.na(customers2.df))

## [1] 0

# Modify the format of InvoiceDate so it can be processed in calculations

customers3.df <- customers2.df %>%
  mutate(InvoiceDate = as.Date(InvoiceDate, "%m/%d/%Y %H:%M"))
NOW <- as.Date("2020-12-12 12:00", "%Y-%m-%d")
NOW

## [1] "2020-12-12"

customers3.df <- customers2.df %>%
  mutate(InvoiceDate = as.Date(InvoiceDate, "%m/%d/%Y %H:%M"))
NOW <- as.Date("2020-12-12 12:00", "%Y-%m-%d")
NOW

## [1] "2020-12-12"

str(customers3.df)

## 'data.frame':    406829 obs. of  8 variables:
##  $ InvoiceNo  : chr  "536365" "536365" "536365" "536365" ...
##  $ StockCode  : chr  "85123A" "71053" "84406B" "84029G" ...
##  $ Description: chr  "WHITE HANGING HEART T-LIGHT HOLDER" "WHITE METAL LANTERN" "CR
EAM CUPID HEARTS COAT HANGER" "KNITTED UNION FLAG HOT WATER BOTTLE" ...
##  $ Quantity   : int  6 6 8 6 6 2 6 6 6 32 ...
##  $ InvoiceDate: Date, format: "2010-12-01" "2010-12-01" ...
##  $ UnitPrice  : num  2.55 3.39 2.75 3.39 3.39 7.65 4.25 1.85 1.85 1.69 ...
##  $ CustomerID : int  17850 17850 17850 17850 17850 17850 17850 17850 17850 13047 ..
.
##  $ Country    : chr  "United Kingdom" "United Kingdom" "United Kingdom" "United Kin
gdom" ...
##  - attr(*, "na.action")= 'omit' Named int [1:135080] 623 1444 1445 1446 1447 1448 1
449 1450 1451 1452 ...
##   ..- attr(*, "names")= chr [1:135080] "623" "1444" "1445" "1446" ...

head(customers3.df)

##   InvoiceNo StockCode                         Description Quantity InvoiceDate
## 1    536365    85123A  WHITE HANGING HEART T-LIGHT HOLDER        6  2010-12-01
## 2    536365     71053                 WHITE METAL LANTERN        6  2010-12-01
## 3    536365    84406B      CREAM CUPID HEARTS COAT HANGER        8  2010-12-01
## 4    536365    84029G KNITTED UNION FLAG HOT WATER BOTTLE        6  2010-12-01
## 5    536365    84029E      RED WOOLLY HOTTIE WHITE HEART.        6  2010-12-01
## 6    536365     22752        SET 7 BABUSHKA NESTING BOXES        2  2010-12-01
##   UnitPrice CustomerID        Country
## 1      2.55      17850 United Kingdom
## 2      3.39      17850 United Kingdom
## 3      2.75      17850 United Kingdom
## 4      3.39      17850 United Kingdom
## 5      3.39      17850 United Kingdom
## 6      7.65      17850 United Kingdom
```

4.5.8 Build RFM Model

As its name implies, the RFM model is based on three tables, containing *Recency*, *Frequency*, and *Monetary* data about the transactions of each customer. Our first step is to create these tables, by extracting the pertinent information from the dataset.

```
# Build the R, F, and M tables
recencyTable <- aggregate(InvoiceDate ~ CustomerID, customers3.df, FUN = max)

head(recencyTable)

##   CustomerID InvoiceDate
## 1      12346  2011-01-18
## 2      12347  2011-12-07
## 3      12348  2011-09-25
## 4      12349  2011-11-21
## 5      12350  2011-02-02
## 6      12352  2011-11-03

recencyTable$R <- as.numeric(NOW - recencyTable$InvoiceDate)

frequencyTable <- aggregate(InvoiceDate ~ CustomerID, customers3.df, FUN = length)

monetaryTable <- aggregate(Quantity ~ CustomerID, customers3.df, FUN=sum)
```

The three tables can now be combined to form one data frame, which will serve as the data foundation for the RFM model. The first six observations in the dataset are displayed:

```
# Merge the data sets

RFM.df <- merge(recencyTable, frequencyTable, by.x = "CustomerID", by.y = "CustomerID"
)
RFM.df <- merge(RFM.df, monetaryTable, by.x = "CustomerID", by.y = "CustomerID")

names(RFM.df) <- c("CustomerID", "InvoiceDate", "Recency", "Frequency", "Monetary")

head(RFM.df)

##   CustomerID InvoiceDate Recency Frequency Monetary
## 1      12346  2011-01-18    3616         2        0
## 2      12347  2011-12-07    3293       182     2458
## 3      12348  2011-09-25    3366        31     2341
## 4      12349  2011-11-21    3309        73      631
## 5      12350  2011-02-02    3601        17      197
## 6      12352  2011-11-03    3327        95      470
```

The next task is to rank each customer's recency, frequency, and monetary characteristic. The data in each table is sorted and divided into quantile segments and ranked 0–4. For example:

- In the Recency Table, the value 1 means a more recent visit than a value of 2.
- In the Frequency Table, a value of 4 means a more frequent shopper than one with a value of 3.
- In the Monetary Table, a value of 3 means more money was spent than one with value of 2.

The segment rank is then added to the RFM table:

```
RFM.df$Rsegment <- findInterval(RFM.df$Recency, quantile(RFM.df$Recency,
                   c(0.0, 0.25, 0.5, 0.75, 1.0)))
RFM.df$Fsegment <- findInterval(RFM.df$Frequency, quantile(RFM.df$Frequency,
                   c(0.0, 0.25, 0.5, 0.75, 1.0)))
RFM.df$Msegment <- findInterval(RFM.df$Monetary, quantile(RFM.df$Monetary,
                   c(0.0, 0.25, 0.5, 0.75, 1.0)))
```

All scores are now combined into one column so there is one measure for ranking all customers. The first ten customers are listed:

```
# Combine all scores into one column
RFM.df$TotalScore <- RFM.df$Rsegment + RFM.df$Fsegment + RFM.df$Msegment

head(RFM.df, 10)

##     CustomerID InvoiceDate Recency Frequency Monetary Rsegment Fsegment Msegment
## 1        12346  2011-01-18    3616         2        0        4        1        1
## 2        12347  2011-12-07    3293       182     2458        1        4        4
## 3        12348  2011-09-25    3366        31     2341        3        2        4
## 4        12349  2011-11-21    3309        73      631        2        3        3
## 5        12350  2011-02-02    3601        17      197        4        2        2
## 6        12352  2011-11-03    3327        95      470        2        3        3
## 7        12353  2011-05-19    3495         4       20        4        1        1
## 8        12354  2011-04-21    3523        58      530        4        3        3
## 9        12355  2011-05-09    3505        13      240        4        1        2
## 10       12356  2011-11-17    3313        59     1591        2        3        4
##     TotalScore
## 1            6
## 2            9
## 3            9
## 4            8
## 5            8
## 6            8
## 7            6
## 8           10
## 9            7
## 10           9
```

Since the RFM table has been constructed out of several tables, it is important to examine its structure:

```
# The structure of RFM table
str(RFM.df)

## 'data.frame':     4372 obs. of  9 variables:
##  $ CustomerID : int  12346 12347 12348 12349 12350 12352 12353 12354 12355 12356 ..
.
##  $ InvoiceDate: Date, format: "2011-01-18" "2011-12-07" ...
##  $ Recency    : num  3616 3293 3366 3309 3601 ...
##  $ Frequency  : int  2 182 31 73 17 95 4 58 13 59 ...
##  $ Monetary   : int  0 2458 2341 631 197 470 20 530 240 1591 ...
##  $ Rsegment   : int  4 1 3 2 4 2 4 4 4 2 ...
##  $ Fsegment   : int  1 4 2 3 2 3 1 3 1 3 ...
##  $ Msegment   : int  1 4 4 3 2 3 1 3 2 4 ...
##  $ TotalScore : int  6 9 9 8 8 8 6 10 7 9 ...
```

- Customers with scores $R = 1$, $F = 4$, $M = 4$ are the best customers, since they shopped recently, shopped frequently, and spent a lot of money.
- Customers with scores $R = 4$, $F = 1$, $M = 1$, are the “worst” customers, since it has been a (relatively) long time since the last purchase, they have shopped frequently, and spend only small amounts of money.

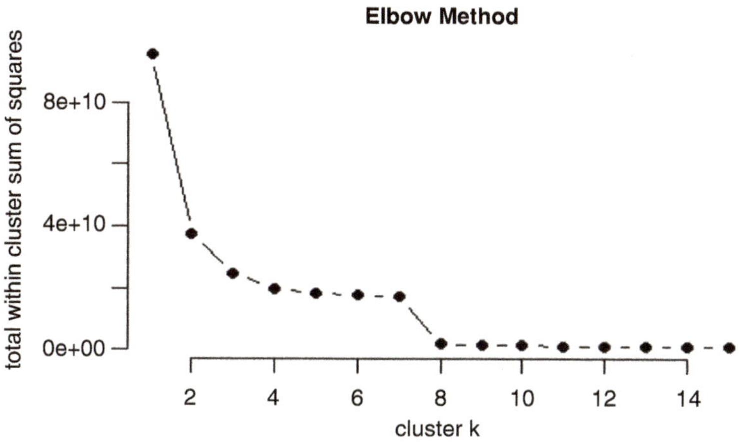

Fig. 29 The elbow method for clustering data

4.5.9 Build the *k*-Means Model

Since the first part of our model, the RFM table is complete, we can now cluster the customers based on their *RFM* scores. To do this, we will create a new data frame, consisting only of the *R*, *F*, and *M* columns in the table:

```
clusters.df <- RFM.df[, c(3,4,5)]  # select only the R, F, and M columns
head(clusters.df)

##    Recency Frequency Monetary
## 1     3616         2        0
## 2     3293       182     2458
## 3     3366        31     2341
## 4     3309        73      631
## 5     3601        17      197
## 6     3327        95      470
```

We will now use the *kmeans()* function in R to generate the clusters, as part of an approach called the *Elbow Method* (Fig. 29):

```
k.max <- 15
wss <- sapply(1:k.max, function(k) {kmeans(clusters.df, k, nstart = 30)$tot.withinss})

plot(1:k.max, wss, type="b", pch=19, frame=FALSE, main="Elbow Method", xlab=" cluster
k ", ylab="Total within cluster Sum of Squares")
```

After examining the "elbow" in Fig. 29, we can conclude that good choices for *k* are 4 or 5. The reader should experiment with different values of *k*, and observe the impact of customer segments allocation. We will again use the *kmean()* function, with a choice of $k = 5$. Notice the structure of the resulting cluster object, the five clusters created and the number of customers in each.

```
set.seed(221)  # For reproducibility

km <- kmeans(clusters.df, centers = 5, nstart = 30)

str(km)

## List of 9
##  $ cluster     : int [1:4372] 4 2 2 4 4 4 4 4 4 2 ...
##  $ centers     : num [1:5, 1:3] 3298 3324 3297 3395 3313 ...
##   ..- attr(*, "dimnames")=List of 2
##   .. ..$ : chr [1:5] "1" "2" "3" "4" ...
##   .. ..$ : chr [1:3] "Recency" "Frequency" "Monetary"
##  $ totss       : num 9.57e+10
##  $ withinss    : num [1:5] 1.00e+09 5.61e+08 1.57e+10 4.72e+08 7.66e+08
##  $ tot.withinss: num 1.85e+10
##  $ betweenss   : num 7.73e+10
##  $ size        : int [1:5] 18 636 9 3615 94
##  $ iter        : int 5
##  $ ifault      : int 0
##  - attr(*, "class")= chr "kmeans"

print(km)

## K-means clustering with 5 clusters of sizes 18, 636, 9, 3615, 94
##
## Cluster means:
##    Recency  Frequency   Monetary
## 1 3298.000 1150.11111 28311.1111
## 2 3323.662  231.29560  2393.9811
## 3 3296.667 1585.66667 80461.4444
## 4 3395.395   51.50097   390.6586
## 5 3312.862  410.38298  7854.5957
##
## Clustering vector:
##     [1] 4 2 2 4 4 4 4 4 4 2 2 4 2 4 4 2 4 2 4 4 2 4 4 4 4 4 4 2 4 4 4 2 4 4 2 4 4
##    [38] 4 4 2 4 4 4 4 4 4 4 2 2 2 5 4 4 4 4 3 2 4 4 4 4 4 4 4 4 4 2 2 4 2 2 5 4 2
##    [75] 4 2 4 4 4 4 4 4 4 4 2 4 5 4 4 4 2 2 4 4 4 4 4 4 4 4 5 2 2 2 4 2 2 4 4 2 2
##   [112] 4 2 4 4 2 4 4 4 4 4 4 2 2 4 4 4 4 4 4 4 4 4 4 4 4 4 4 4 4 4 2 4 4 4 2 4 4
... ... ...
## [4256] 4 4 4 4 4 5 4 4 4 4 2 4 4 4 4 4 4 4 4 4 4 4 4 4 4 4 4 4 4 4 2 4 4 4 4 4 4
## [4293] 2 4 4 4 4 4 4 4 4 4 4 4 4 2 4 4 4 4 4 4 2 4 4 4 4 4 4 4 4 4 4 4 2 4 2 2 4
## [4330] 4 2 4 4 4 4 2 4 4 4 4 4 4 2 4 4 4 4 5 4 4 4 4 4 2 4 4 2 4 4 4 4 2 4 4 4 4
## [4367] 4 4 4 4 2 2
##
## Within cluster sum of squares by cluster:
## [1]  1004260896   561498567 15663777306   471969290   765761574
##  (between_SS / total_SS =  80.7 %)
##
## Available components:
##
## [1] "cluster"      "centers"      "totss"        "withinss"     "tot.withinss"
## [6] "betweenss"    "size"         "iter"         "ifault"
```

The five clusters consist of 18, 636, 9, 3615, and 94 customers, respectively. Each cluster is characterized the mean value of its Recency, Frequency, and Monetary properties.

For example, let us look at Cluster #2 and its properties:

- Total customers: 636
- Mean Recency (rounded): 3224
- Mean Frequency (rounded): 231
- Mean Monetary (rounded): 2394

The clustering vector lists the cluster membership in a cluster (only a partial set of customers are listed). The first is in cluster 2, the next two are in cluster 3, the following 6 are in cluster 4, and so on.

We can now assign clusters to the corresponding data points.

```
km$cluster

##    [1] 4 2 2 4 4 4 4 4 4 2 2 4 2 4 4 2 4 2 4 4 2 4 4 4 4 4 4 2 4 4 4 2 4 4 2 4 4
##   [38] 4 4 2 4 4 4 4 4 4 4 2 2 2 5 4 4 4 4 3 2 4 4 4 4 4 4 4 4 4 2 2 4 2 2 5 4 2
##   [75] 4 2 4 4 4 4 4 4 4 4 2 4 5 4 4 4 2 2 4 4 4 4 4 4 4 4 5 2 2 2 4 2 2 4 4 2 2
##  [112] 4 2 4 4 2 4 4 4 4 4 4 2 2 4 4 4 4 4 4 4 4 4 4 4 4 4 4 4 4 4 2 4 4 4 2 4 4
… … … …
## [4293] 2 4 4 4 4 4 4 4 4 4 4 4 4 2 4 4 4 4 4 4 2 4 4 4 4 4 4 4 4 4 4 4 2 4 2 2 4
## [4330] 4 2 4 4 4 4 2 4 4 4 4 4 4 2 4 4 4 4 5 4 4 4 4 4 2 4 4 2 4 4 4 4 2 4 4 4 4
## [4367] 4 4 4 4 2 2

# within Sum of Squares
km$withinss
## [1]  1004260896   561498567 15663777306   471969290   765761574

# Total Within Sum of Squares
km$tot.withinss
## [1] 18467267633

# Between Sum of Squares
km$betweenss
## [1] 77254009631

# Total Sum of Squares
km$totss
## [1] 95721277263
```

4.5.10 Results Visualization

While these numbers provide accurate, pinpointed information about each customer's membership in a segment, a visualization (Fig. 30) of this outcome always contributes to the overall understanding of what the RFM-k-Means model has produced:

```
library(factoextra)

## Loading required package: ggplot2

fviz_cluster(km, data=clusters.df)
```

We can now complete the task by combining the clusters and display one table with all customer segmentation data we were tasked to find:

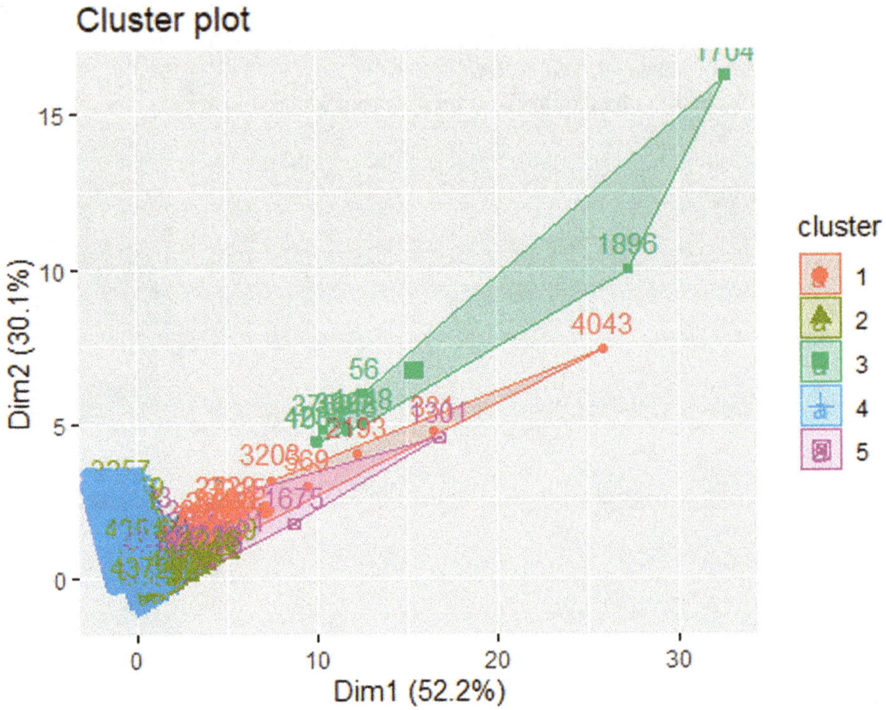

Fig. 30 Visualization of customer segments (cluster)

```
# Combine clusters

combinedClusters <- cbind(clusters.df, km$cluster)
head(combinedClusters)

##   Recency Frequency Monetary km$cluster
## 1    3616         2        0          4
## 2    3293       182     2458          2
## 3    3366        31     2341          2
## 4    3309        73      631          4
## 5    3601        17      197          4
## 6    3327        95      470          4

#Extract customer ID
customerID <- RFM.df[(1)]

# Add customer ID to clusters and display the segments we set out
# to identify in the beginning

clustersWithID <- cbind(customerID, combinedClusters)
head(clustersWithID)

##   CustomerID Recency Frequency Monetary km$cluster
## 1      12346    3616         2        0          4
## 2      12347    3293       182     2458          2
## 3      12348    3366        31     2341          2
## 4      12349    3309        73      631          4
## 5      12350    3601        17      197          4
## 6      12352    3327        95      470          4
```

4.5.11 Results Interpretation

In this model, the results speak for themselves. We were able to segment over 12,000 customers with combined 400,000+ shopping instances into five groups. The model gives us precise information for each individual customer and predicts whether the customer will be a power shopper, visiting the store frequently, or one who occasionally purchases an item. Recall that it was our decision to group the customers into five segments. We could have chosen 4 or 6, depending on our interpretation of the Elbow Method plot. It may seem surprising or counter-intuitive that 12,000 customers who all consider themselves individuals, can be grouped into only five categories. This knowledge can save a lot of advertising money for retailers, while customizing the shopping experience for these customers. This is all very useful information to any retail store and can lead to numerous actions we are familiar with, like coupon offers and target advertising.

4.5.12 Conclusion

We started with a large dataset of customers and their shopping history, and created a taxonomy of these customers, uncovering information that was buried in a dataset of hundreds of thousands of records. As is the case with other models presented in this chapter, the abstract mathematical and statistical tools used can be applied to many different scenarios within the finance discipline and a host of different ones. One can create segments of tourist destinations for traveling agencies, segments of grocery items used in recipes, types of stock portfolios and investor profiles, or even clusters of NBA basketball players and their gameplay characteristics. The reader should explore other fields and applications of this model, as well as many different variants and expansions described in the included bibliography.

5 Future Research Directions

The models, methods, and code presented in this chapter should not be viewed as the definitive approach to developing computational solutions to predictive analytics problems. The reader is encouraged to use them as a springboard towards developing new models, refining existing ones, and exploring other computational tools, like the Python programming language. Every (business) scenario presents unique challenges, expectations, and constraints. The statistical underpinning of the models presented here originate hundreds of years ago, in some cases, when all calculations were manual. Today, with the advent of high-performance computing and soon quantum computers, the rate of increase in the power of brute computational force outpaces the rate of increase of algorithmic efficiency.

The reader is encouraged to peruse Sutor (2019), for a preview of things to come. Just imagine a dataset of one billion Facebook users, segmented based on web browsing habits, in one minute.

6 Conclusion

This chapter surveyed several predictive analytics models that are particularly useful in the field of finance. The combination of linear algebra, calculus, statistics, computer programming, computational thinking, and critical thinking are the mix of skills required to perform predictive analysis. Any deficit in one of these areas, severely hinders the ability to make progress in the discipline. It is worth noting the dichotomy that exists among these skills. While the mathematical concepts have not changed in decades (or centuries) the computing tools are evolving every few months. Those interested in predictive analytics must be willing to spend the time and effort to acquire a strong theoretical foundation, which will serve them well in many years to come. In contrast, analyst must commit to a lifestyle of high-paced continuous learning of computing methods and machines. If one does not sustain a rapid pace of learning, there is a real possibility that newly acquired skills may become outdated (if not obsolete) shortly after one has mastered them.

Acknowledgments I would like to thank all the collaborators on this book project, starting with Dr. Sinem Derindere. Within a few years, the trying times we are currently experiencing due to the COVID-19 pandemic, will have faded away and be replaced by the pressing events of that day. But, in the Winter of 2020–2021, working on this project, offers a glimpse of meaning and purpose to the work we are all carrying in our respective parts of the world.

Key Terms and Definitions

ARIMA Auto-regressive Integrated Moving Average, is one of the two most widely used approaches to time series forecasting. It aims to describe autocorrelations in the data as predictors of future values.

AUC curve Area Under the ROC Curve.

Exponential smoothing One of the two most widely used approaches to time series forecasting. It is based on a description of the trend and seasonality in the data.

Gain and Lift chart A chart used to evaluate the performance of a (classification) model. It shows the difference between making predictions using a model and without the model.

***k*-means** An unsupervised clustering algorithm, where k is the number of clusters, set by the user.

Logistic regression A statistical model that uses the logistic function (sigmoid shaped) to model a binary dependent variable (outcome).

Non-Constant Variance (NCV) test	Computes a score test of the hypothesis of constant error variance against the alternative that the error variance changes with the level of the response (fitted values), or with a linear combination of predictors.
Odd ratio	A measure of association between an independent variable and an outcome. It represents the odds that an outcome will occur given a particular event, compared to the odds of the outcome occurring in the absence of that event.
RFM	Recency, frequency, monetary value is a marketing **analysis** tool, using measures to identify best customers for a business.
ROC curve	Receiver Operating Characteristic curve. It visualizes the ratio between TPR (True Positive Rate) and FPR (False Positive Rate).
Seasonal Variation	A component of a time series which is defined as the repetitive and predictable movement around the trend line in 1one year or less.
Time Series	A set of points collected over a period of time.
Tree pruning	A process to reduce the size of a decision tree, by removing noncritical subtrees.

References

Abreu, R. J., Souza, R. M., & Oliveira, J. G. (2019). Applying singular spectrum analysis and Arima-Garch for forecasting Eur/Usd exchange rate. *Revista de Administração Mackenzie, 20*(4), 1–32.

Ahmar, A. S., & del Val, E. B. (2020). SutteARIMA: Short-term forecasting method, a case: Covid-19 and stock market in Spain. *Science of the Total Environment, 729*.

Carrasco, R. A., Blasco, M. F., Garcia-Madariaga, J., & Herrera-Viedma, E. (2019). A Fuzzy linguistic RFM model applied to campaign management. *International Journal of Interactive Multimedia and Artificial Intelligence, 5*(4), 21.

Chan, N. H. (2010). *Time series: Applications to finance with R and S-Plus* (2nd ed.). Wiley.

Chen, D.-G., & Chen, J. K. (2021). *Statistical regression modeling with R: Longitudinal and multilevel modeling* (Emerging topics in statistics and biostatistics). Springer.

David, S. A., Trevisan, L. R., Lopes, A. M., Machado, J. A. T., & Inácio, C. M. C., Jr. (2017). Dynamics of commodities prices: integer and fractional models. *Fundamenta Informaticae, 151*(1–4), 389–408.

Dixon, M. F., Halperin, I., & Bilokon, P. (2020). *Machine learning in finance: From theory to practice* (1st ed.). Springer.

Güçdemir, H., & Selim, H. (2015). Integrating multi-criteria decision making and clustering for business customer segmentation. *Industrial Management & Data Systems, 115*(6), 1022–1040.

Gul, F., & Khan, K. (2019). An empirical study of investor attitudinal factors influencing herd behavior: Evidence from Pakistan Stock Exchange. *Abasyn University Journal of Social Sciences, 12*(1), 1–11.

Hay-Jahans, C. (2017). *An R companion to linear statistical models* (1st ed.). CRC Press.

Hilbe, J. M. (2018). *Practical guide to logistic regression*. CRC Press.

Kitagawa, G. (2020). *Introduction to time series modeling with applications in R* (2nd ed.). CRC Press.

Kleinbaum, D. G., Kupper, L. L., Nizam, A., & Rosenberg, E. S. (2013). *Applied regression analysis and other multivariable methods* (5th ed.) Cengage Learning.

Kroese, D. P., Botev, Z., Taimre, T., & Vaisman, R. (2019). *Data science and machine learning: Mathematical and statistical methods* (Chapman & Hall/CRC machine learning & pattern recognition) (1st ed.). Chapman and Hall/CRC.

Lantz, B. (2019). *Machine learning with R: Expert techniques for predictive modeling* (3rd ed.). Packt.

Liang, Q., Ling, L., Tang, J., Zeng, H., & Zhuang, M. (2020). Managerial overconfidence, firm transparency, and stock price crash risk: Evidence from an emerging market. *China Finance Review International, 10*(3), 271–296.

McCarthy, R. V., McCarthy, M. M., Ceccucci, W., & Halawi, L. (2019). *Applying predictive analytics* (1st ed.). Springer.

Saha, P., Bose, I., & Mahanti, A. (2016). A knowledge based scheme for risk assessment in loan processing by banks. *Decision Support Systems, 84*, 78.

Seager, H. R. (1900). The economic writings of Sir William Petty, together with observations upon the bills of mortality, more probably by Captain John Graunt William Petty John Graunt Charles Henry Hull. *The Annals of the American Academy of Political and Social Science, 15*, 145–149.

Searle, S. R., & Gruber, M. H. J. (2016). *Linear models* (Wiley series in probability and statistics) (2nd ed.). Wiley.

Shapiro, F. R. (2006). *The Yale book of quotations*. Yale University Press.

Sutor, R. S. (2019). *Dancing with Qubits: How quantum computing works and how it can change the world*. Packt.

Teng, H. -W., & Lee, M. (2019). Estimation procedures of using five alternative machine learning methods for predicting credit card default. *Review of Pacific Basin Financial Markets & Policies, 22*(3), N.PAG.

Turvey, C. G., Kong, R., & Huo, X. (2010). Borrowing amongst friends: the economics of informal credit in rural China. *China Agricultural Economic Review, 2*(2), 133–147.

Ünkaya, G., & Sayin, G. (2019). Halka Açik Finans Dişi Şirketlerde Süreklilik Riskinin Karar Ağaci Modeli İle Öngörülmesi. *Mali Cozum Dergisi / Financial Analysis, 29*(156), 13–28.

Vieira, M., Snyder, B., Henriques, E., & Reis, L. (2019). European offshore wind capital cost trends up to 2020. *Energy Policy, 129*, 1364–1371.

Zhang, Y., Bradlow, E. T., & Small, D. S. (2015). Predicting customer value using clumpiness: From RFM to RFMC. *Marketing Science, 34*(2), 195–208.

Zhao, Y. (2020). Research on personal credit evaluation of internet finance based on blockchain and decision tree algorithm. *EURASIP Journal on Wireless Communications & Networking, 2020*(1), N.PAG.

Prescriptive Analytics Techniques: Theory and Applications in Finance

Isac Artzi

Abstract This chapter examines several key models and techniques associated with prescriptive analytics. They include Sentiment Analysis, Association Rules, Network Analysis, Recommender Systems, and Principal Components Analysis. While these methods are not designed for a particular discipline, they provide a good opportunity for finance professionals and researchers to expand their analytic toolset. An effort was made to encourage the reader to explore applications of these models in other areas, given that mathematics, statistics, and computer programming transcend many disciplines. In some cases, the models used datasets available on free data repositories. In other cases, the datasets were synthetically generated for the examples in this chapter, to highlight certain phenomena. Each example includes a fully developed solution written in the R programming language. Prior knowledge of R is useful but not essential. A reasonable affinity towards computational thinking and experience with other programming languages is a definite plus.

Keywords Sentiment analysis · Association rules · Network analysis · Recommender system · Principal Component Analysis · PCA · Machine learning · R programming

1 Introduction

Prescriptive analysis empowers professionals and researchers across disciplines to make decisions in data-driven scenarios. Given that the abstract mathematical tools, statistical processes, and programming in R transcend disciplines and applications, there is a vast body of knowledge and a pool of topics to draw upon. Due to the

Supplementary Information The online version of this chapter (https://doi.org/10.1007/978-3-030-83799-0_4) contains supplementary material, which is available to authorized users.

I. Artzi (✉)
Grand Canyon University, Phoenix, AZ, USA
e-mail: isac.artzi@gcu.edu

S. Derindere Köseoğlu (ed.), *Financial Data Analytics*, Contributions to Finance and Accounting, https://doi.org/10.1007/978-3-030-83799-0_4

limited scope of this book and this chapter, it is not possible to cover all elements of prescriptive analysis. Rather, topics covered provide a broad scaffolding of the type problems, methods, and tools used by researchers and industry professionals. The reader should keep in mind that methods used in one model are applicable in another in this chapter. In the interest of presenting a broader range of topics and tools, some were covered more in depth in one example but not in another. The reader should perform a "union" of all the models presented and ask two questions: (1) What have I learned from model 1 that might be applicable in model 2? (2) How can this task be accomplished in a different, perhaps better way?

The chapter covers five models: Sentiment Analysis, Association Rules, Network Analysis, Recommender Systems, and Principal Components Analysis. These topics are rarely found in one book, let alone in one chapter. This has contributed to them being chosen. The scenarios and models are presented with moderate mathematical rigor, emphasizing the practical aspect, supported by a complete and detailed R code. While prior knowledge of R is helpful, it is not necessary. A good foundation in statistics and an affinity for computational thinking is expected. Some datasets can be found on public repositories, while others have been created specifically for this project, to highlight certain phenomena.

2 Background

Decisions in data-driven scenarios are subjective. The beauty of the synergy between mathematics and statistics is that mathematics provides very precise tools and concepts, only for statisticians to tell a subjective story, which might differ, sometimes significantly from analyst to analyst. Prescriptive actions form an important topic in the broader analytics field, and thus it is essential to include it in analytics in finance book. Prescriptive analysis, in contrast to predictive, expects models to produce actionable information. Therefore, the nature of models chosen for this chapter is such that they lend themselves to stating clear conclusions. Each scenario can be tackled in multiple ways, both from an analysis standpoint and from an R code implementation. The methods, tools, and programming implementations presented here, follow accepted practices described in academic and professional literature, but should not be viewed as definitive. Furthermore, the diversity of the R ecosystem has resulted in an immense number of libraries that cover almost every concept and method in existence in mathematics, statistics, data science, and machine learning. The solutions and methods proposed here are standard and plausible, but one would probably not have to search too long to find a more efficient or more elegant solution. This chapter attempts to show, present, stimulate, encourage, challenge, puzzle, but not dictate. It is an additional modest contribution to the field, only made possible by the vast body of information already available.

3 Main Focus of the Chapter

3.1 On Prescriptive Analytics

One would be hard-pressed to identify the five representative topics or scenarios in prescriptive analytics. This chapter aims at addressing a broad range of topics, in the attempt to provide a good grasp on what the issue is, how to address it, and how to construct a full solution in code. Every scenario described can be found in multiple disciplines, some not related to finance at all. However, in today's world—and for a very long time to come—everything either produces or consumes data, or both. The methods for analyzing what one thinks about a song on a music app is like finding what a stockbroker thinks about a particular investment. The underlying foundation of both is math, statistics, and computer programming. Each model presented here could have been addressed in many other contexts and disciplines. This is another contributing factor in their selection. Most likely, the title of this book will attract readers from the field of finance and closely related areas. However, it is important to realize that the term *global village*, so often cited in the media, applies to science and technology disciplines as well. It would be very useful for a student of finance to realize and appreciate the methods and tools used by mechanical engineers (for example), as it would for cybersecurity professionals to learn how decisions are being made by marketing executives.

The first model covered is *Sentiment Analysis*. It presents an approach to crowdsourcing feedback about a (hotel) business, to empower business managers to devise a better business strategy. The model uses a dataset of diverse opinions but demonstrates how in the end it presents a clear actionable piece of information: one hotel is better than others and another one is worse. The information can be used to decide what area of the hotel improvement to finance and in general what needs to be addressed. The model does not prescribe what to do, just what is the nature of the problem that needs to be addressed. Human decision-makers must determine the course of action.

The second model discusses *Association Rules*. It presents a method for understanding the shopping habits of customers in a grocery store and produces actionable information that can be used in inventory management, customer acquisition, financial planning, advertising, and others. A basket of groceries is no different than a set of tourist sites, a stock portfolio, or a song list. The method for determining if purchasing bread is associated with purchasing sugar is identical to the one used to detect items association in any field. This empowers finance professionals to focus on elements of the model most relevant to their discipline, with the realization that they can gain insight into the customer's psychology (for example) and not only looking at "dry" numbers.

The third model is *Network Analysis*. The field of *network theory* is not often associated with finance, which is why it was chosen. Everything is connected these days. Whether companies connect on social media, individuals connect in games, countries are bound by treaties, or athletes compete in a team, one can look at almost anything through the lens of network theory. The model focuses on analyzing relationships among business entities, often hidden in plain sight. The premise is that it is essential to acquire knowledge about which companies are influential in a sector, who has partnered with whom, and about the conduits that enable the flow of capital and information. The clearly identifies the leaders and gatekeepers in a network of large companies and provides actionable information about the connections within the network.

The fourth model is a *Recommender System*. The model focuses on analyzing the opinion of individual stockbrokers and uses that information in investment decisions. Rating a stock is no different than rating a movie, a dish in a restaurant, or the suitability of politicians for a job. In this scenario, we explore how seemingly unrelated individuals, who state their opinions about an item, can be viewed as one cohesive unit that expresses its aggregate opinion, as one. The model shows how one can identify trustworthy financial advisors, how to corroborate an opinion, and how to assess similarities among recommenders, as well as among the items they recommend.

The fifth and last model is *Principal Components Analysis (PCA)*. The model was chosen because it is fundamental to improving computational efficiency, data collection, and the construction of *predictive* and *prescriptive* models. The model uses the context of determining the essential factors that explain or predict a phenomenon. It shows how to create artificial, alternative, and fewer predictors that would perform as well as existing ones. As such, it *prescribes* a more efficient course of action, one that requires fewer factors while deciding on an action, thus saving time, resources, and overall streamlining a process. PCA demonstrates how a complex process can result in halving (or better) the number of variables in a model, without sacrificing the amount and quality of information produced.

3.1.1 Programming in R

While prior knowledge of R is not required, an aptitude for reading, writing, and executing computer programs is desired. The programming examples consist mostly of adaptations of mathematical and statistical concepts to the syntax of R, a language created specifically for statistical computing. It is highly recommended to inspect the code and identify the libraries used and install the relevant R packages.

4 Solutions and Recommendations

The following sections cover five different models and approaches commonly used by analysts, data scientists, professionals in a variety of disciplines. It is recommended that readers familiarize themselves with the R programming language and computer programming in general, as presented in Tattar et al. (2016). A good foundation in statistics is highly recommended as is an overall affinity towards computational thinking.

4.1 Prescriptive Model 1: Sentiment Analysis

4.1.1 Foundation

Sentiment Analysis can take many forms. It can describe the attitudes (sentiments) of a group of people towards a person, an idea, a food item, a movie, and many others. It can be stated in a Tweet, in a newspaper article, in a phone call, in an interview, a novel, and others. The main objective is always to identify the public (or crowd) sentiment as reflected in a collection of texts and translate that knowledge into an actionable piece of information.

The main idea behind gauging sentiment is quite simple, as it is powerful. Certain words are known to convey negative sentiments. For example, "sad," "angry," or "disappointment." Other words are known to convey a positive sentiment. For example, "happy," "celebrate," or "pleased." The algorithm for sentiment analysis used in this model consists of a few steps:

1. Acquire a set of text-based data, known to contain expressions of opinions about a common topic.
2. Parse the text to extract a list of all the sentences.
3. Traverse the sentences and search for words associated with a list of words labeled as *positive* or *negative.*
4. Calculate the ratio of positive to negative words.
5. Use the positive/negative ratio to quantify the sentiment expressed in the entire dataset.

The model is based on work described by Liu (2015), who also maintains one of the popular sentiment dictionaries, *bing*. Sentiment analysis has become a driving element in decision-making across disciplines, by individuals and corporations alike. The ubiquity and influence of social media are enabling the generation and dissemination of sentiments (including fake ones), to the point that they can shape public opinion, valuation of a company, attitude towards investment, monetary policy, and decision-making in general. More in-depth coverage of sentiment analysis can be found in Hiremath et al. (2021), Anandarajan et al. (2019), and Bali et al. (2017).

4.1.2 Advance Organizer

Figure 1 reviews the key components in the process of performing sentiment analysis:

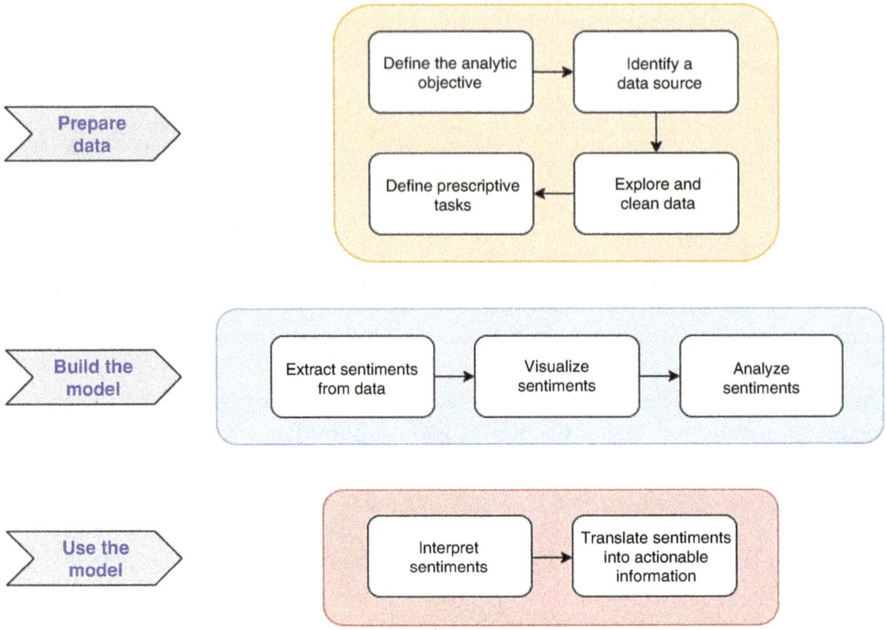

Fig. 1 Key components in sentiment analysis

4.1.3 Objective

Given a dataset of reviews of three hotels, identify which one is most positively reviewed, to update the renovation plans and upcoming marketing campaign.

4.1.4 Data Source

The original dataset is quite large (35,913 reviews, 100+ hotels) and requires a lengthy processing time. In the interest of computational efficiency and without compromising the validity and usefulness of this example, we will be using a subset of the original. First, we need to read the data from three files, *"hotel1.csv,"* *"hotel2.csv,"* and *"hotel3.csv."* Here is a snapshot of the data captured:

```r
library(syuzhet)

data1 <- read.csv("hotel1.csv")
data2 <- read.csv("hotel2.csv")
data3 <- read.csv("hotel3.csv")
data1.df <- data.frame(data1)
data2.df <- data.frame(data2)
data3.df <- data.frame(data3)

# Retrieve raw reviews for each hotel
# Some reviews are not in English, but we will not handle them here.
reviews1 <- data1.df$Reviews
reviews2 <- data2.df$Reviews
reviews3 <- data3.df$Reviews
```

The data is in the form of narrative text, reviews posted by guests at these hotels. You will note that some of these reviews are not in English. Given the large size of the data, we can choose not to treat them in a special way. Here are the first six reviews from each dataset:

```r
head(reviews1)

## [1] "We booked this hostel because it was the cheapest place in the Center area in boston. Whe
n we got there there was a mixup with our reservation and they took care of it right away. Excell
ent customer service at the front desk, very polite and helpful, answered all our questions. The
room was a twin on the sixth floor, very... More"
## [2] "Good place to stay for a few days. Clean rooms, helping staff and clean bathrooms. The co
mmon area is nice and fun with a pool table and a small cinema room. Its the best you can get in
Boston for this price. Good place as well. Might not fit a family but would be great if you are c
oming with... More"
## [3] "Buena localizaciÃ¯Â¿Â½Ã¯Â¿Â½n"
## [4] "The location is perfect for getting to all of the sections and access to subway stops. Ea
sy to figure out and navigate from Berkley location. One must assume that you won't have all the
luxury amenities as the Courtyard Marriott. Taking this into consideration my negative points wer
e was the quality of the beds, the pillow was the worst I... More"
## [5] "I was traveling for work and there was an issue at our hotel so I scrambled for an altern
ative solution and found 40 Berkeley. The lobby was clean and comfortable and the staff was frien
dly. I liked that bed linens and towels were included in the room price so I didn't have to pack
these. The rooms are very bare... More"
## [6] "We arrived to Boston on Amtrak late (11pm) and hustled a car to the hostel. We were quick
ly checked in and put in a larger room as the 2 bed unit we reserved was unavailable. The room wa
s sparse but provided the beds we needed and a mini fridge as a bonus. With no A/C, we used the p
rovided fans... More"

head(reviews2)

## [1] "Breakfast was the best, and the best thing about the stay was the one and only host, grea
t conversations at breakfast and advise on the city. Very nice neighborhood. Only reason that it
did not get 5 stars is that the room has room for improvement, not any fault of the host. This is
bed and breakfast, but not your honeymoon style BB, I would stay here again. Room comfort could i
mprove with a new air conditioning unit, other then that five stars. Sharing the bathroom, never
a problem, and coming in and out with you wanted never a problem. No need to rent a car, easy wit
h public transportation."
## [2] "A nice BB really close to Harvard Square. A little confusing getting there if your walkin
g (very little to no street signs) but ultimately a call to the BB saved me from wondering around
. Quiet neighborhood, bed was comfortable and bathroom was good considering that this is a very o
```

```
ld building so keep that in mind. This is not the Marriot but it is a nice place to rest after a
long day on a plane. The innkeeper (Byron) was very nice and helpful. I didn't stay for the break
fast opting for a bowl of cereal instead due to a busy schedule. Overall a good BB experience and
I would definitely come back if I'm ever in the area. Thank you. A.G."
## [3] "A poor excuse for a BB"
## [4] "This BB couldn't have been more perfect. Great location. Clean rooms, comfortable beds, c
ourteous staff, and breakfast cooked for you at whatever time you request. They even held our bag
s after we checked out so we could go to the natural history museum."
## [5] "We booked for 6 nights but left after 5. BB is old and shoddy. If you choose this place g
et some rose colored glasses like the ones used by other reviewers."
## [6] "Having travelled for 24 hours in total from Ha Noi, Viet Nam to Cambridge, I finally land
ed in the small but cosy BB late in the evening and was wellcomed by Byron Jordan. He gave me the
opportunity to choose the room and advised me which room was less noisy. I immediately felt like
I was at home with care... More"
```

```
head(reviews3)
```

```
## [1] "Relaxing. Nice and peaceful."
## [2] "Room could use upgrades. It is not walking distance to beach.better to pay the extra to s
tay closer to beach and restaurants."
## [3] "The hotel was great for our stay. It was a couples trip for beach week. The only things I
didn't like was the cleanliness of the bathroom. And as a women that's a big part of staying in t
he hotel"
## [4] "Not a bad stay , hotel could use a remodel. .nice to have a 24 hr restaurant on premises.
.pool was nice as well. .I'd book again"
## [5] "Musty smelling bathroom. Continental breakfast was a joke. Bananas were edible."
## [6] "Went to Virginia Beach to pick up our son from deployment. Checked into our hotel on Frid
ay evening. Went to our room, which looked nice at first. Looked under the mattress only to find
a bedbug. Manager tried to say it was a cockroach. They did offer to upgrade our room but I just
wanted a refund. I only got refunded one night and lost my money for the second night. Definitely
would not recommend staying there."
```

4.1.5 Data Exploration and Cleaning

The *syuzhet* package provides the ability to analyze punctuation and convert any text into sentences (Jockers, 2020). It uses the *openNLP sentence tokenizer*. We will now convert the three hotel reviews datasets into sets of sentences:

```
# Extract all the sentences from the text
reviews_sentences1 <- get_sentences(reviews1)
reviews_sentences2 <- get_sentences(reviews2)
reviews_sentences3 <- get_sentences(reviews3)

head(reviews_sentences1)

## [1] "We booked this hostel because it was the cheapest place in the Center area in
boston."
## [2] "When we got there there was a mixup with our reservation and they took care of
it right away."
## [3] "Excellent customer service at the front desk, very polite and helpful, answere
d all our questions."
## [4] "The room was a twin on the sixth floor, very..."
## [5] "More"
## [6] "Good place to stay for a few days."

head(reviews_sentences2)

## [1] "Breakfast was the best, and the best thing about the stay was the one and only
host, great conversations at breakfast and advise on the city."
## [2] "Very nice neighborhood."
## [3] "Only reason that it did not get 5 stars is that the room has room for improvem
ent, not any fault of the host."
## [4] "This is bed and breakfast, but not your honeymoon style BB, I would stay here
again."
## [5] "Room comfort could improve with a new air conditioning unit, other then that f
ive stars."
## [6] "Sharing the bathroom, never a problem, and coming in and out with you wanted n
ever a problem."

head(reviews_sentences3)

## [1] "Relaxing."
## [2] "Nice and peaceful."
## [3] "Room could use upgrades."
## [4] "It is not walking distance to beach."
## [5] "better to pay the extra to stay closer to beach and restaurants."
## [6] "The hotel was great for our stay."
```

This concludes the initial data exploration since the existing R packages are doing all the heavy lifting. The dataset of reviews for each hotel has been converted into a set of sentences. We deliberately lost the attribution of sentences to their authors since we are interested in the content and not in who wrote it. However, other prescriptive tasks, outside the scope of this example, may well be interested in investigating the relationship between author and sentiment. We can now focus on building the model.

4.1.6 Prescriptive Tasks

Calculate the proportion of positive vs negative words in a dataset of text. Use that proportion to identify the overall public sentiment towards a group of hotels.

4.1.7 Build the Prescriptive Model

The first step in building the model is to extract the sentiment expressed in each sentence. The function *get_sentiment()* compares the words in a sentence with one of five vectors of words, labeled as 1 *(positive), 0 (neutral),* and *-1 (negative).* The default sentiment extraction is "syuzhet" (used below), but the reader is encouraged to experiment with the other four: "bing," "afinn," "nrc," and "stanford." These methods are independently created and maintained and can be used with any other NLP package. It is possible to create a custom sentiment dictionary, which is simply a list of words with the labels 1, 0, or -1. (Jockers, 2020) describes the technical details for using this package. Here are the first ten sentiments extracted from each set of sentences, and their structure:

```
# Extract sentiments for each hotel
reviews_sentiments1 <- get_sentiment(reviews_sentences1)
reviews_sentiments2 <- get_sentiment(reviews_sentences2)
reviews_sentiments3 <- get_sentiment(reviews_sentences3)

# Sentiments structure - a vector of numeric values
str(reviews_sentiments1)

##  num [1:705] 0.25 1.8 2.25 0.25 0 0.75 1.25 1.25 0.5 1.55 ...

str(reviews_sentiments2)

##  num [1:255] 2.4 0.5 0.85 1.4 2.3 -0.75 0.8 0.5 0.3 1.6 ...

str(reviews_sentiments3)

##  num [1:367] 0 1.25 0 0 1.1 0.5 0 1 0.25 -0.65 ...

head(reviews_sentiments1, 10)

##  [1] 0.25 1.80 2.25 0.25 0.00 0.75 1.25 1.25 0.50 1.55

head(reviews_sentiments2, 10)

##  [1]  2.40  0.50  0.85  1.40  2.30 -0.75  0.80  0.50  0.30  1.60

head(reviews_sentiments3, 10)

##  [1]  0.00  1.25  0.00  0.00  1.10  0.50  0.00  1.00  0.25 -0.65
```

According to this output, considering only the first 10 sentences for each hotel:

- For **Hotel 1**, the most *positive* is the first sentence, while the most *negative* is the fifth sentence.
- For **Hotel 2**, the most *positive* is the first sentence, while the most *negative* is the sixth
- For **Hotel 3**, the most *positive* is the second sentence, while the most *negative* is the tenth

Here are these sentences:

```
# Show the most positive and negative sentences, among the first 10 for each hotel

reviews_sentences1[c(1,5)]

## [1] "We booked this hostel because it was the cheapest place in the Center area in
boston."
## [2] "More"

reviews_sentences2[c(1,6)]

## [1] "Breakfast was the best, and the best thing about the stay was the one and only
host, great conversations at breakfast and advise on the city."
## [2] "Sharing the bathroom, never a problem, and coming in and out with you wanted n
ever a problem."

reviews_sentences3[c(2,10)]

## [1] "Nice and peaceful."
## [2] "Not a bad stay , hotel could use a remodel."
```

Note the positive and negative words in each sentence:

- **Hotel 1:** The first sentence contains positive words like *cheapest*, while the other two sentences contains the inconclusive negative word *More*
- **Hotel 2:** Positive words are *best* and *great*, while negative flags are *problem*, which clearly is interpreted out of context
- **Hotel 3:** Positive words are *Nice* and *peaceful*, while negative flags are *bad* (out of context) and *remodel* (somewhat negative)

Obviously the above constitute just a small, non-representative sample, which is far from enough to serve as a basis for comparison. The above sentences are displayed simply to illustrate what output can be expected from this model.

After the sentiments have been extracted, it is interesting to investigate some measures of central tendency in each data set, focusing on the *mean*, which is a measure of negativity:

```
# Calculate measures of central tendency (focus on means)

# Hotel 1:
summary(reviews_sentiments1)

##     Min. 1st Qu.  Median    Mean 3rd Qu.    Max.
## -4.0000  0.0000  0.2500  0.4689  0.8500  4.1500

# Hotel 2:
summary(reviews_sentiments2)
##     Min. 1st Qu.  Median    Mean 3rd Qu.    Max.
## -1.2500  0.0000  0.5000  0.6461  1.2500  5.2000

# Hotel 3:
summary(reviews_sentiments3)
##     Min. 1st Qu.  Median    Mean 3rd Qu.    Max.
## -3.0000  0.0000  0.1000  0.2888  0.7500  3.4500

# Standard deviations

# Hotel 1:
sd(reviews_sentiments1)
## [1] 0.8069916

# Hotel 2:
sd(reviews_sentiments2)
## [1] 0.9907964

# Hotel 3:
sd(reviews_sentiments3)
## [1] 0.8456885
```

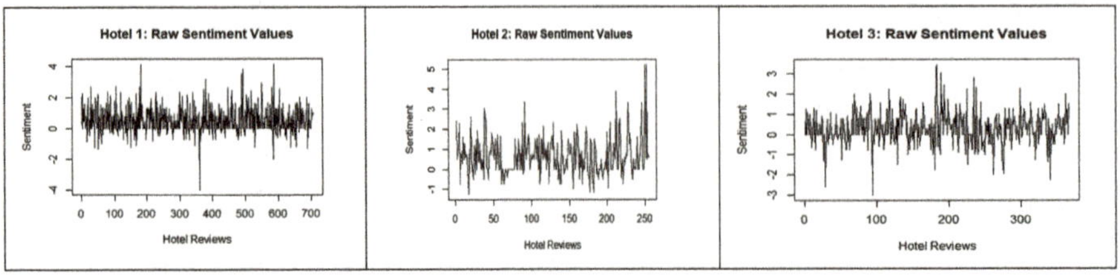

Fig. 2 Raw sentiments

Using the *mean* is a measure of negativity, and it appears that **Hotel 3** has overall the most negative reviews. The *standard deviations* of 0.81, 0.99, and 0.85 reflect the variation in sentiment values, with **Hotel 2** displaying the greater variance.

4.1.8 Results Visualization

We can visualize the raw sentiments using a simple line chart (Fig. 2):

```
# Plot raw sentiments for each hotel
plot(reviews_sentiments1, type="l", xlab="Hotel Reviews", ylab="Sentiment",
     main="Hotel 1: Raw Sentiment Values")

plot(reviews_sentiments2, type="l", xlab="Hotel Reviews", ylab="Sentiment",
     main="Hotel 2: Raw Sentiment Values")

plot(reviews_sentiments3, type="l", xlab="Hotel Reviews", ylab="Sentiment",
     main="Hotel 3: Raw Sentiment Values")
```

It is easier to visually compare these plots by examining their respective trend lines (Fig. 3):

```
# Visualize trends in reviews, where

simple_plot(reviews_sentiments1, title="Hotel 1 Reviews Simple Plot")
simple_plot(reviews_sentiments2, title="Hotel 2 Reviews Simple Plot")
simple_plot(reviews_sentiments3, title="Hotel 3 Reviews Simple Plot")
```

Once *Normalized Narrative Time* curves are generated, it is possible to display all three hotels in the same plot for better comparison (Fig. 4). We will compute the moving averages of sentiments for the three hotels, and rescale the vectors on values (0, 1) so we can chart them on the plot. We will use the *zoo* package for this:

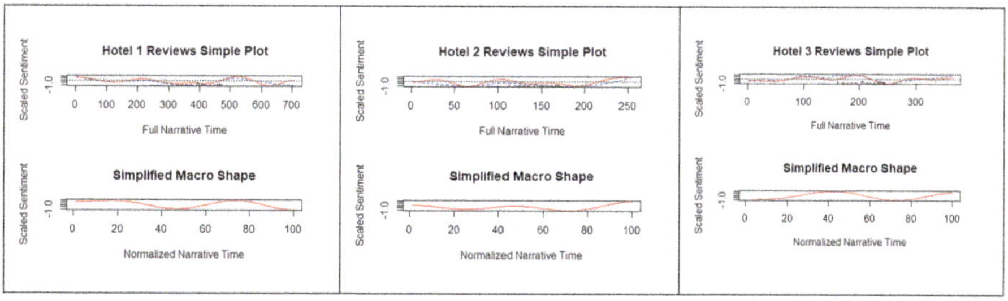

Fig. 3 Normalized Normative Time curves

Fig. 4 Normalized Normative Time curves for all three hotels

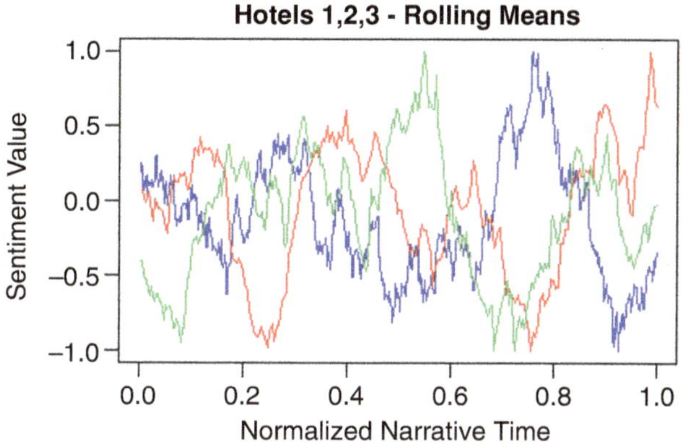


```
library(zoo)

# Use the rollmean function to compute the moving averages of sentiments for the three
hotels

hotel1.window <- round(length(reviews_sentiments1)*.1)
hotel1.rolled <- rollmean(reviews_sentiments1, k=hotel1.window)


hotel2.window <- round(length(reviews_sentiments2)*.1)
hotel2.rolled <- rollmean(reviews_sentiments2, k=hotel2.window)


hotel3.window <- round(length(reviews_sentiments3)*.1)
hotel3.rolled <- rollmean(reviews_sentiments3, k=hotel3.window)

# Rescale the curves by using the x component of the (x,y,z) vector with values (0,1)
returned by the rescale function

hotel1.scaled <- rescale_x_2(hotel1.rolled)
hotel2.scaled <- rescale_x_2(hotel2.rolled)
hotel3.scaled <- rescale_x_2(hotel3.rolled)

# Plot the rescales curves

plot(hotel1.scaled$x, hotel1.scaled$z, type="l", col="blue", xlab="Narrative Time", yl
ab="Emotional Valence", main="Hotels 1, 2, 3 - Rolling Means")
lines(hotel2.scaled$x, hotel2.scaled$z, col="red")
lines(hotel3.scaled$x, hotel3.scaled$z, col="green")
```

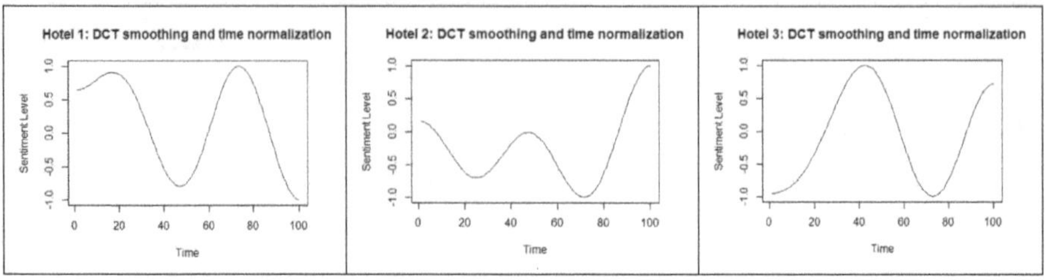

Fig. 5 DCT smoothing and time normalization of each hotel

4.1.9 Results Interpretation

Note that the approach described here takes different meanings when the text represents different topics (e.g., user manuals, literary works, newscasts, etc.). It is more important to focus on the process and model, so it can be applied to other contexts. We will now compare the curves in terms of the progression of reviews, by utilizing their vector characteristics. This is not *time series analysis,* although there is an element of time. We are focusing on the shape of the vector rather than on making a prediction about its future direction. However, this data lends itself to a more complex analysis, using a time series approach, especially comparing changes in sentiment over time, looking simultaneously at different locations. This would make a great follow-up project for the curious reader. In this section, we will focus strictly on the shape of the vectors. To compare two vectors, the method of *cosine similarity* will be used. To accomplish this, we will use *discrete cosine transform (DCT).* The DCT smoothing function produces results on a scale [0, 100], which enables a more meaningful comparison of the three hotels (Fig. 5).

```
hotel1.dct <- get_dct_transform(reviews_sentiments1, scale_range=TRUE)
plot(hotel1.dct, type="l", col="blue", xlab="Time", ylab="Sentiment Level", main="Hote
l 1: DCT smoothing and time normalization")

hotel2.dct <- get_dct_transform(reviews_sentiments2, scale_range=TRUE)
plot(hotel2.dct, type="l", col="blue", xlab="Time", ylab="Sentiment Level", main="Hote
l 2: DCT smoothing and time normalization")

hotel3.dct <- get_dct_transform(reviews_sentiments3, scale_range=TRUE)
plot(hotel3.dct, type="l", col="blue", xlab="Time", ylab="Sentiment Level", main="Hote
l 3: DCT smoothing and time normalization")
```

Next, we will also verify computationally the length of each vector, to confirm it is 100. This will enable to chart all three curves into one plot:

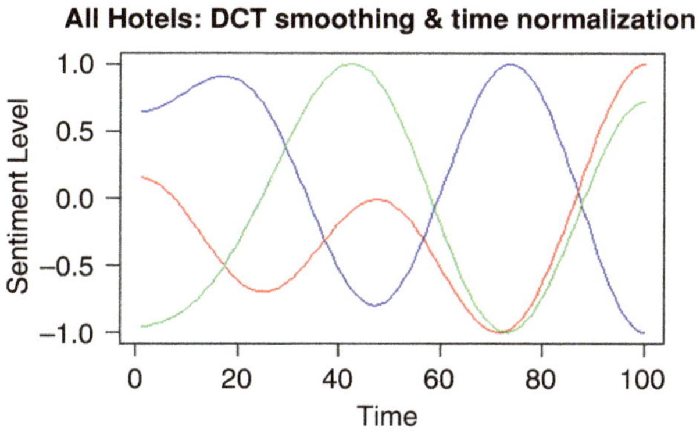

Fig. 6 DCT smoothing and time normalization of all hotels in one plot

```
hotel1.dct.normed <- get_dct_transform(reviews_sentiments1, x_reverse_len = 100,
scale_range = TRUE)
hotel2.dct.normed <- get_dct_transform(reviews_sentiments2, x_reverse_len = 100,
scale_range = TRUE)
hotel3.dct.normed <- get_dct_transform(reviews_sentiments3, x_reverse_len = 100,
scale_range = TRUE)

print("Verify the lengths of the 3 vectors:")

## [1] "Verify the lengths of the 3 vectors:"
length(hotel1.dct.normed)
## [1] 100

length(hotel2.dct.normed)
## [1] 100

length(hotel3.dct.normed)
## [1] 100
```

Now we can view all three curves in one plot (Fig. 6):

The information reflected in the graph can be corroborated by assessing the correlation between each pair of hotels:

```
# The last step is a statistical comparison

cor(hotel1.dct.normed, hotel2.dct.normed)
## [1] -0.6961754

cor(hotel2.dct.normed, hotel3.dct.normed)
## [1] 0.4533065

cor(hotel1.dct.normed, hotel3.dct.normed)
## [1] -0.875713
```

4.1.10 Conclusion

Such an interpretation makes more sense in some cases than in others. The abstract interpretation is that for example, the *sentiments* expressed in reviews for hotels 1 (blue) and 3 (green) are *moderately strongly inverse correlated*, as expressed by $R = -0.696$. In other words, when positive sentiments are expressed about Hotel

1, negative ones are expressed about Hotel 2. Again, this model must be interpreted with a good dose of common sense, since the data was used primarily to provide a visualization of the model. The above result would be meaningful if, for example, Hotels 1, 2, and 3 belonged to different chains but were located in the same areas, and the data was collected in the same time frame. In such a case, the hotel managers would have the necessary information to take steps for improving the customers' opinions about the hotel.

All hotels exhibited fluctuations in their review, which means management must investigate additional factors like season, climate change, environmental factors, and market conditions in order to better understand what happened. Nevertheless, if we were to look at the original much larger set with 100+ hotels, it is possible that some hotels rank consistently high, while others consistently low. This model can be applied to any scenario in which reviews are available. It provides insights into what customers think about a product or service and enables management to act.

The above model basically analyzed text data. As such, it can be used to analyze and compare any type of text – book reviews, restaurant reviews, opinions expressed on social media, peer reviews, diet program reviews, etc.

Additional studies on the uses of sentiment analysis in finance can be found in García-Medina et al. (2018), Hájek (2018), and Wang et al. (2019), and Ranco et al. (2016).

4.2 Prescriptive Model 2: Association Rules

4.2.1 Foundation

Association rules have become a central staple of machine learning and artificial intelligence projects. However, at its core, the concept of association is simply a probabilistic question about the connection between two words, two objects, to people, etc. This example has been inspired by Qiao et al. (2020)

At the heart of the method employed in this example is the *apriori* algorithm. The algorithm receives as input a set of transactions and searches for item associations. For example, if in several transactions, items A and B *are found*, then there is an association between the two. Therefore, if a basket contains item A, there is an expectation that item B should also be included, according to a probability calculated as a proportion of occurrences of the pair $\{A, B\}$ out of all transactions observed.

The set $\{A, B\}$ is then extended to more items. Eventually, one might deduce that whenever items $\{A, B\}$ are in a basket, in a certain number of baskets item C is also present. Therefore, a rule can be created of the form:

$$\text{If } \{A, B\} \text{ then } \{C\}$$

Large datasets with large transactions can lead to the creation of more complex rules of the form:

$$\text{If } \{X_1, X_2, \ldots, X_n\} \text{ then } \{Y_1, Y_2, \ldots, Y_k\}$$

The *apriori* algorithm consists of the following steps:

1. Generate a *candidate set*, by calculating the support of sets (of length n) in the transactional database (i.e., the frequency of occurrence of an itemset).
2. Prune the candidate set by eliminating items with a support less than the given threshold.
3. Join the frequent sets to form sets of size $n + 1$
4. Repeat until no new sets are found.

More in-depth coverage of association rules mining is presented in Binu and Rajakumar (2021), Sharma and Gera (2020), and Zumel and Mount (2019).

4.2.2 Advance Organizer

Figure 7 depicts the key steps in deriving and applying association rules:

4.2.3 Objective

Given a set of transactions, generate a set of association rules for the items observed in those transactions.

4.2.4 Data Source

The data represents a series of 9835 transactions, involving 169 grocery items. Each transaction consists of a list of grocery items purchased. The dataset is *Groceries*, one of the many datasets bundled with RStudio, and widely used.

4.2.5 Data Exploration and Cleaning

We will first load and explore the data, and print a few transactions:

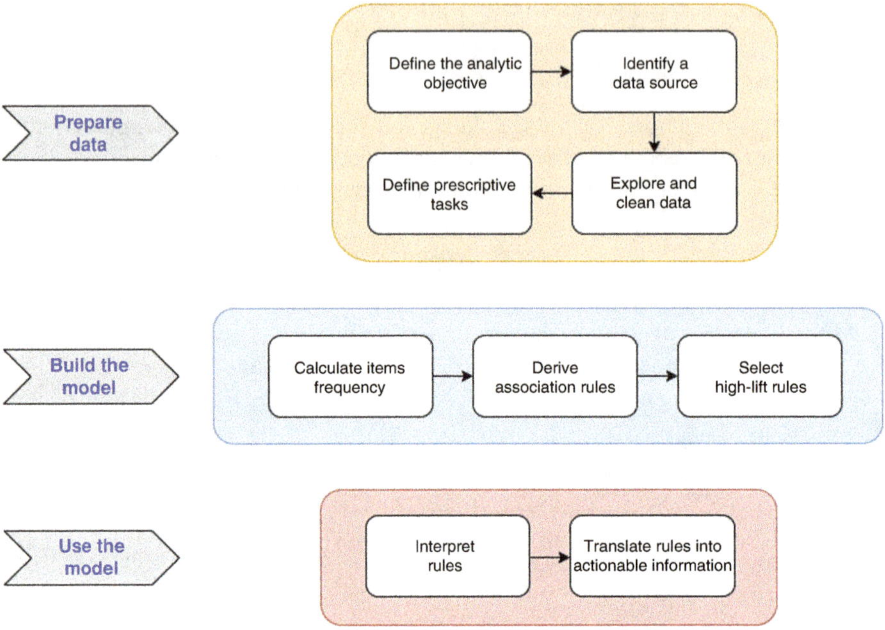

Fig. 7 The key steps in deriving and applying association rules

```
data(Groceries)
class(Groceries)

## [1] "transactions"
## attr(,"package")
## [1] "arules"

inspect(head(Groceries, 3))

##     items
## [1] {citrus fruit,
##      semi-finished bread,
##      margarine,
##      ready soups}
## [2] {tropical fruit,
##      yogurt,
##      coffee}
## [3] {whole milk}
## [4] {pip fruit,
##      yogurt,
##      cream cheese ,
##      meat spreads}
## [5] {other vegetables,
##      whole milk,
##      condensed milk,
##      long life bakery product}
```

4.2.6 Prescriptive Tasks

Inform managers of a retail store about the shopping patterns of their customers to decide on appropriate steps like offer targeted discounts, coupons, and advertising.

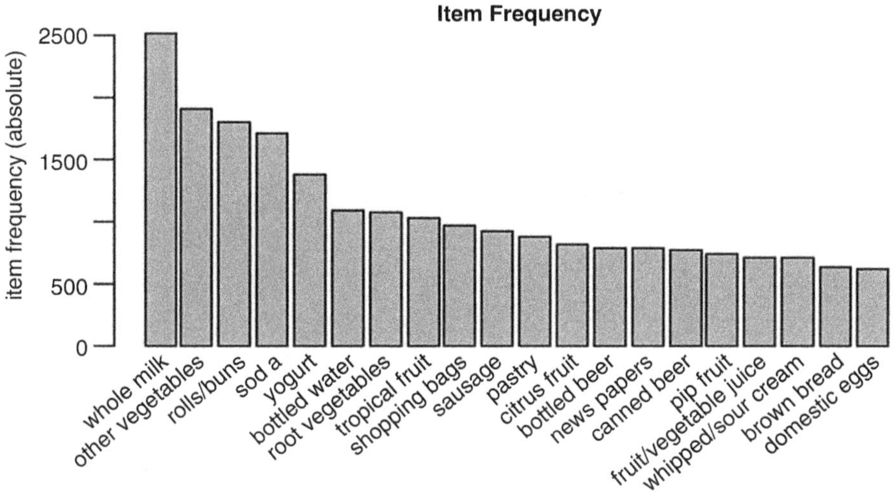

Fig. 8 Most frequent items that occur in at least 7% of transactions

4.2.7 Build the Prescriptive Model

We will use the *arules* package in R, which provides all the functions necessary for building our model.

Our first task is to assess the frequency of items in the dataset, since more frequent items (Fig. 8) are likely members of more transactions, and therefore essential in the construction of association rules. The *eclat()* performs this task. The *support* parameter sets a minimum percentage of transactions that contain a particular item. The *maxlen* parameter limits the number of items in a transaction. The reader should experiment with different values and compare the outcomes:

```
# Calculate support for frequent items
frequentItems <- eclat (Groceries, parameter = list(supp = 0.07, maxlen = 15))

## Eclat
##
## parameter specification:
##  tidLists support minlen maxlen            target   ext
##     FALSE    0.07      1     15 frequent itemsets TRUE
##
## algorithmic control:
##  sparse sort verbose
##       7   -2    TRUE
##
## Absolute minimum support count: 688
##
## create itemset ...
## set transactions ...[169 item(s), 9835 transaction(s)] done [0.00s].
## sorting and recoding items ... [18 item(s)] done [0.00s].
## creating sparse bit matrix ... [18 row(s), 9835 column(s)] done [0.00s].
## writing  ... [19 set(s)] done [0.00s].
## Creating S4 object  ... done [0.00s].

inspect(frequentItems)

##      items                          support    transIdenticalToItemsets count
## [1]  {other vegetables,whole milk} 0.07483477  736                        736
## [2]  {whole milk}                  0.25551601 2513                       2513
## [3]  {other vegetables}            0.19349263 1903                       1903
## [4]  {rolls/buns}                  0.18393493 1809                       1809
## [5]  {yogurt}                      0.13950178 1372                       1372
## [6]  {soda}                        0.17437722 1715                       1715
## [7]  {root vegetables}             0.10899847 1072                       1072
## [8]  {tropical fruit}              0.10493137 1032                       1032
## [9]  {bottled water}               0.11052364 1087                       1087
## [10] {sausage}                     0.09395018  924                        924
## [11] {shopping bags}               0.09852567  969                        969
## [12] {citrus fruit}                0.08276563  814                        814
## [13] {pastry}                      0.08896797  875                        875
## [14] {pip fruit}                   0.07564820  744                        744
## [15] {whipped/sour cream}          0.07168277  705                        705
## [16] {fruit/vegetable juice}       0.07229283  711                        711
## [17] {newspapers}                  0.07981698  785                        785
## [18] {bottled beer}                0.08052872  792                        792
## [19] {canned beer}                 0.07768175  764                        764
```

The algorithm found 19 items that meet the criteria for occurrences in a transaction. It is always a good idea to visualize numeric information.

The next step is to derive the association rules from the dataset. In this case, we set a lower bound for the frequency of occurrence $support = 0.001$, as well as a *confidence* of 0.5, which is the conditional probability.

```
rules <- apriori (Groceries, parameter = list(supp = 0.001, conf = 0.5))

## Apriori
##
## Parameter specification:
##  confidence minval smax arem  aval originalSupport maxtime support minlen
##         0.5    0.1    1 none FALSE            TRUE       5   0.001      1
##  maxlen target  ext
##      10  rules TRUE
##
## Algorithmic control:
##  filter tree heap memopt load sort verbose
##     0.1 TRUE TRUE  FALSE TRUE    2    TRUE
##
## Absolute minimum support count: 9
##
## set item appearances ...[0 item(s)] done [0.00s].
## set transactions ...[169 item(s), 9835 transaction(s)] done [0.00s].
## sorting and recoding items ... [157 item(s)] done [0.00s].
## creating transaction tree ... done [0.00s].
## checking subsets of size 1 2 3 4 5 6 done [0.01s].
## writing ... [5668 rule(s)] done [0.00s].
## creating S4 object  ... done [0.00s].
```

```
summary(rules)

## set of 5668 rules
##
## rule length distribution (lhs + rhs):sizes
##    2    3    4    5    6
##   11 1461 3211  939   46
##
##    Min. 1st Qu.  Median    Mean 3rd Qu.    Max.
##    2.00    3.00    4.00    3.92    4.00    6.00
##
## summary of quality measures:
##     support           confidence        coverage              lift
##  Min.   :0.001017   Min.   :0.5000   Min.   :0.001017   Min.   : 1.957
##  1st Qu.:0.001118   1st Qu.:0.5455   1st Qu.:0.001729   1st Qu.: 2.464
##  Median :0.001322   Median :0.6000   Median :0.002135   Median : 2.899
##  Mean   :0.001668   Mean   :0.6250   Mean   :0.002788   Mean   : 3.262
##  3rd Qu.:0.001729   3rd Qu.:0.6842   3rd Qu.:0.002949   3rd Qu.: 3.691
##  Max.   :0.022267   Max.   :1.0000   Max.   :0.043416   Max.   :18.996
##      count
##  Min.   : 10.0
##  1st Qu.: 11.0
##  Median : 13.0
##  Mean   : 16.4
##  3rd Qu.: 17.0
##  Max.   :219.0
##
## mining info:
##       data n transactions support confidence
##  Groceries           9835   0.001        0.5
```

The algorithm has generated 5668 rules, ranging in size from 2 to 6 items, in both the left-hand side (LHS) and right-hand side (RHS) of the rule. Note the measures of *support*, *confidence*, and *lift* calculated for the entire set. We are not interested in all the rules, but in those with high confidence. Therefore, we must now calculate the confidence of each rule and then sort them in decreasing order of confidence. The first six rules are listed below:

```
#Calculate high-confidence  rules
rules_conf <- sort (rules, by="confidence", decreasing=TRUE)

# Calculate the Support, Lift, and Confidence for all rules
inspect(head(rules_conf))

##     lhs                        rhs                support     confidence    coverage     lift count
## [1] {rice,
##      sugar}                 => {whole milk}       0.001220132          1 0.001220132 3.913649    12
## [2] {canned fish,
##      hygiene articles}      => {whole milk}       0.001118454          1 0.001118454 3.913649    11
## [3] {root vegetables,
##      butter,
##      rice}                  => {whole milk}       0.001016777          1 0.001016777 3.913649    10
## [4] {root vegetables,
##      whipped/sour cream,
##      flour}                 => {whole milk}       0.001728521          1 0.001728521 3.913649    17
## [5] {butter,
##      soft cheese,
##      domestic eggs}         => {whole milk}       0.001016777          1 0.001016777 3.913649    10
## [6] {citrus fruit,
##      root vegetables,
##      soft cheese}           => {other vegetables} 0.001016777          1 0.001016777 5.168156    10
```

Before proceeding with using the set association rules, we will validate them using two measures:

- *Coverage*—measures the probability that a rule applies to randomly selected transactions. It is an estimate of the proportion of transactions that contain the LHS. Hence it is the *support of LHS*
- *Fisher's Exact Test*—whose *p-value* measures the proportion of rules that are more extreme than the test statistic

```
coverage <- interestMeasure(rules, measure="Coverage", transactions="Groceries")
summary(coverage)

##     Min.  1st Qu.   Median     Mean  3rd Qu.     Max.
## 0.001017 0.001729 0.002135 0.002788 0.002949 0.043416
# Calculate Fisher's Exact Test
fisherTest <- interestMeasure(rules, measure="fishersExactTest", transactions="Groceri
es")
summary(fisherTest)

##      Min.   1st Qu.    Median      Mean   3rd Qu.      Max.
## 0.000e+00 5.500e-07 1.549e-05 6.265e-04 2.732e-04 1.610e-02
```

We note that the coverage interval is [0.001, 0.04] with a median of 0.002, which indicates a very low probability that rules apply to randomly selected transactions. Fisher's Exact Test produced a value within the interval [0, 0.0016], which means that the proportion of extreme rules is practically zero.

We can proceed with identifying the *high-lift rules*, calculate their *support*, and list (a first few of) them in decreasing order.

```
rules_lift <- sort (rules, by="lift", decreasing=TRUE)

inspect(head(rules_lift))

##     lhs                            rhs                  support confidence    coverage
lift count
## [1] {Instant food products,
##      soda}                      => {hamburger meat} 0.00122  0.631 0.00193 18.995     12
## [2] {soda,
##      popcorn}                   => {salty snack}    0.00122  0.631 0.00193 16.697     12
## [3] {flour,
##      baking powder}             => {sugar}          0.00102  0.556 0.00183 16.408     10
## [4] {ham,
##      processed cheese}          => {white bread}    0.00193  0.633 0.00305 15.045     19
## [5] {whole milk,
##      Instant food products} => {hamburger meat} 0.00152  0.500 0.00305 15.038     15
## [6] {other vegetables,
##      curd,
##      yogurt,
##      whipped/sour cream}        => {cream cheese }  0.00101  0.588 0.00172 14.834     10
```

4.2.8 Results Interpretation

The output reveals, for example, the purchase of *soda* and *popcorn* is associated with the purchase of a *salty snack*, with a 63% confidence.

At this point, our set of rules is complete, subject to the constraints set earlier. Now we use the rules to make practical decisions, essentially mining them. For example, we might be interested in knowing what items are typically associated with the purchase of *sugar*:

```
LHSrules <- apriori(Groceries, parameter=list(support=0.001, confidence=0.3),
                    appearance=list(rhs=c("sugar"), default="lhs"))

## Apriori
##
## Parameter specification:
##  confidence minval smax arem  aval originalSupport maxtime support minlen
##         0.3    0.1    1 none FALSE            TRUE       5   0.001      1
##  maxlen target  ext
##      10  rules TRUE
##
## Algorithmic control:
##  filter tree heap memopt load sort verbose
##     0.1 TRUE TRUE  FALSE TRUE    2    TRUE
##
## Absolute minimum support count: 9
##
## set item appearances ...[1 item(s)] done [0.00s].
## set transactions ...[169 item(s), 9835 transaction(s)] done [0.00s].
## sorting and recoding items ... [157 item(s)] done [0.00s].
## creating transaction tree ... done [0.00s].
## checking subsets of size 1 2 3 4 5 6 done [0.01s].
## writing ... [12 rule(s)] done [0.00s].
## creating S4 object  ... done [0.00s].

summary(LHSrules)

## set of 12 rules
##
## rule length distribution (lhs + rhs):sizes
## 3 4
## 9 3
##
##    Min. 1st Qu.  Median    Mean 3rd Qu.    Max.
##    3.00    3.00    3.00    3.25    3.25    4.00
##
## summary of quality measures:
##     support           confidence        coverage             lift
##  Min.   :0.001017   Min.   :0.3043   Min.   :0.001830   Min.   : 8.989
##  1st Qu.:0.001017   1st Qu.:0.3233   1st Qu.:0.003025   1st Qu.: 9.548
##  Median :0.001118   Median :0.3411   Median :0.003203   Median :10.074
##  Mean   :0.001305   Mean   :0.3643   Mean   :0.003694   Mean   :10.760
##  3rd Qu.:0.001271   3rd Qu.:0.3732   3rd Qu.:0.003762   3rd Qu.:11.023
##  Max.   :0.002847   Max.   :0.5556   Max.   :0.008439   Max.   :16.408
##      count
##  Min.   :10.00
##  1st Qu.:10.00
##  Median :11.00
##  Mean   :12.83
##  3rd Qu.:12.50
##  Max.   :28.00
##
## mining info:
##       data ntransactions support confidence
##  Groceries          9835   0.001        0.3

#List those rules that lead to the purchase of sugar
inspect(LHSrules)

##      lhs                                     rhs     support     confidence
## [1]  {flour,baking powder}                => {sugar} 0.001016777 0.5555556
## [2]  {margarine,baking powder}            => {sugar} 0.001118454 0.3666667
## [3]  {domestic eggs,baking powder}        => {sugar} 0.001016777 0.3225806
## [4]  {curd,flour}                         => {sugar} 0.001118454 0.3548387
## [5]  {flour,margarine}                    => {sugar} 0.001626843 0.4324324
## [6]  {citrus fruit,flour}                 => {sugar} 0.001016777 0.3125000
## [7]  {root vegetables,flour}              => {sugar} 0.001423488 0.3043478
## [8]  {flour,soda}                         => {sugar} 0.001118454 0.3928571
## [9]  {whole milk,flour}                   => {sugar} 0.002846975 0.3373494
## [10] {root vegetables,whole milk,flour}   => {sugar} 0.001016777 0.3448276
## [11] {other vegetables,whole milk,flour}  => {sugar} 0.001220132 0.3243243
## [12] {whole milk,cream cheese ,domestic eggs} => {sugar} 0.001118454 0.3235294
##      coverage    lift      count
## [1]  0.001830198 16.408075 10
## [2]  0.003050330 10.829329 11
## [3]  0.003152008  9.527269 10
## [4]  0.003152008 10.479996 11
## [5]  0.003762074 12.771691 16
## [6]  0.003253686  9.229542 10
## [7]  0.004677173  8.988771 14
## [8]  0.002846975 11.602853 11
## [9]  0.008439248  9.963457 28
## [10] 0.002948653 10.184322 10
## [11] 0.003762074  9.578768 12
## [12] 0.003457041  9.555291 11
```

We found 12 association rules that indicate an association with sugar, the strongest (*lift* = *16.4*) being the rule *{flour, baking powder}* => *{sugar}*

There are several possible actions a store manager may choose, once this association is revealed, for example: (1) upon adding flour and baking powder to the shopping cart, offer the customer a coupon for sugar; (2) assume that the customer will by sugar anyway, and offer a recipe that includes the items purchased and sugar; (3), etc.

4.2.9 Conclusion

Association rules make up a powerful tool in machine learning in a broad range of fields. Aside from shopping in all its varieties, we can envision marketing plans for tourist attractions based on data about site visitation patterns. A more complex tool could create associations between strategies for balancing a portfolio to maximize yield, the association between professional skills, and many others. Mathematics and statistics are the same, regardless of data. If data can be represented by rules, a prescriptive model can be built, and the rules mined using the apriori algorithm.

Readers interested in delving further into the applications of association rules to finance can find in-depth studies in Liao and Chou (2013), Yang and Koshiyama (2019), and Karpio et al. (2013).

4.3 Prescriptive Model 3: Network Analysis

4.3.1 Foundation

Relationships among entities offer a rich domain for mining valuable information. Whether investigating social networks, political alliances, business networks, or concept networks, there is an opportunity to add a different perspective to any data analysis already performed. For example, the assessment of the valuation of a company would be undoubtedly impacted by the knowledge of its business partnerships, which could lead to new markets for its products or other joint ventures. *Network Analysis.* When looking at a business or finance topic through the lens of network theory, we are treating all entities as *nodes* on a graph. The *edges* of the graph depict the relationships, which could be directed or undirected (Fig. 9). We might have access to SEC filing reports that state: "Company A has partnered with Company B," "Company B has partnered with Company C," "Company D has partnered with Company B," and "Company D has partnered with Company B." It would be difficult to understand exactly who is partnering with whom, but Fig. 9 makes these relationships clear in an instance. The problem is compounded manifold as the number of companies that make up a network increases. Essential concepts, methods, and visualizations of network theory concepts are defined. More in-depth

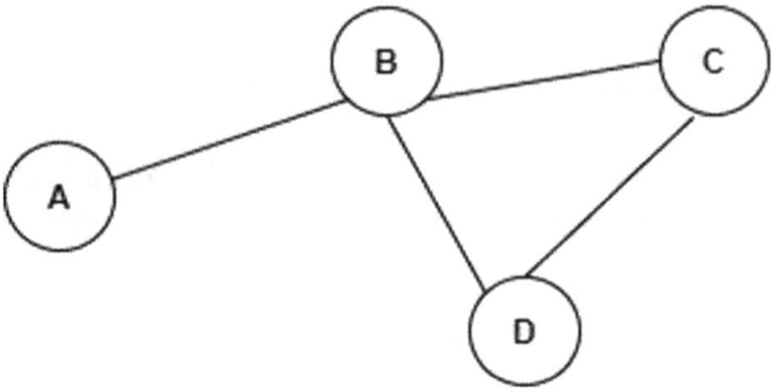

Fig. 9 An example of an undirected network

coverage of network theory and network analysis is available in Scutari and Denis (2021), Crane (2018), and Cranmer et al. (2021).

4.3.2 Advance Organizer

Figure 10 depicts the key steps of a typical analysis of a network.

4.3.3 Objective

Given a network of relationships among corporations, identify all relationships, subgroups, influencers, alliances, and paths to follow in the pursuit of new business relationships.

4.3.4 Data Source

The data is synthetic and depicts financial ties among several large companies, as one could infer from public information and news media. The data consists of a 20 × 20 matrix of companies, with binary values (0, 1) according to the rule:

```
If Financial_ties(Company A, Company B) then
      FinTies[A,B] = 1
Else
      FinTies[A,B] = 0
```

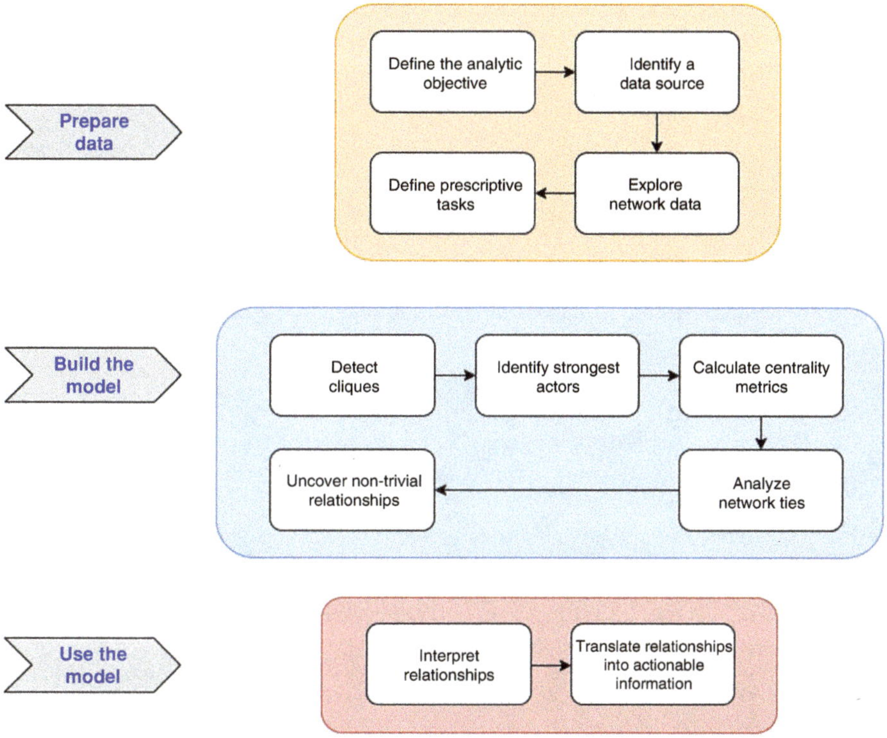

Fig. 10 Network analysis steps

Note: while the company names are real, the relationships depicted are fictitious and the matrix was created specifically for this example. The data is stored in an MS-Excel spreadsheet: *FinancialTies.xlsx*.

```
# Read a network of Financial Ties among companies
FinTies <- read_excel("FinancialTies.xlsx", sheet = 1)

## New names:
## * `` -> ...1

FinTies <- FinTies[, -1]

relationships <- as.matrix(FinTies)
relationships

##       Microsoft IBM Google Facebook Apple Oracle HP Fujitsu Xiaomi Samsung
##  [1,]         0   1      1        1     1      1  1       1      1       1
##  [2,]         1   0      0        1     1      0  0       1      0       1
##  [3,]         1   0      0        0     0      0  0       1      0       0
##  [4,]         1   1      0        0     0      0  0       1      0       0
##  [5,]         1   1      0        0     0      1  1       1      0       0
##  [6,]         1   0      0        0     1      0  0       1      0       0
##  [7,]         1   0      0        0     1      0  0       1      0       0
##  [8,]         1   1      1        1     1      1  1       1      1       1
##  [9,]         1   0      0        0     0      0  0       1      0       0
## [10,]         1   1      0        0     0      0  0       1      0       0
## [11,]         1   0      1        0     1      0  0       1      0       0
## [12,]         1   0      0        0     0      1  0       1      0       0
## [13,]         1   0      0        0     0      0  0       1      0       1
## [14,]         1   1      0        1     0      0  0       1      0       0
## [15,]         1   1      1        1     1      1  1       1      1       1
## [16,]         1   1      0        0     0      0  1       1      0       0
## [17,]         1   1      0        1     0      0  0       1      0       0
## [18,]         1   1      0        0     1      0  0       1      1       0
## [19,]         1   0      0        0     0      0  0       1      0       0
## [20,]         1   1      0        0     0      0  0       1      0       0
##       Siemens SAP SAS Nvidia Amazon Checkpoint Hitachi Dell GE Honeywell
##  [1,]       1   1   1      1      1          1       1    1  1         1
##  [2,]       0   0   0      1      1          1       1    1  0         1
##  [3,]       1   0   0      0      1          0       0    0  0         0
##  [4,]       0   0   0      1      1          0       1    0  0         0
##  [5,]       1   0   0      0      1          0       0    1  0         0
##  [6,]       0   1   0      0      1          0       0    0  0         0
##  [7,]       0   0   0      0      1          1       0    0  0         0
##  [8,]       1   1   1      1      1          1       1    1  1         1
##  [9,]       0   0   0      0      1          0       0    1  0         0
## [10,]       0   0   1      0      1          0       0    0  0         0
## [11,]       0   0   0      0      1          0       0    0  0         0
## [12,]       0   0   0      0      1          0       0    0  0         0
## [13,]       0   0   0      0      1          1       0    0  0         0
## [14,]       0   0   0      0      1          0       0    0  0         0
## [15,]       1   1   1      1      1          1       1    1  1         1
## [16,]       0   0   1      0      1          0       0    0  1         1
## [17,]       0   0   0      0      1          0       0    0  0         0
## [18,]       0   0   0      0      1          0       0    0  0         0
## [19,]       0   0   0      0      1          1       0    0  0         1
## [20,]       0   0   0      0      1          1       0    0  1         0
```

4.3.5 Data Exploration

This example makes use of several R packages, all related to network theory, analysis, and visualization. The first step is to create a graph (Fig. 7) depicting the relationships:

```
FinNetwork <- network(relationships,    directed=FALSE)

ggnet2(FinNetwork, label = TRUE, node.size = 25, node.color = "red", edge.size = 1, ed
ge.color = "blue",label.size = 3, label.color = "black",  size="degree" )
```

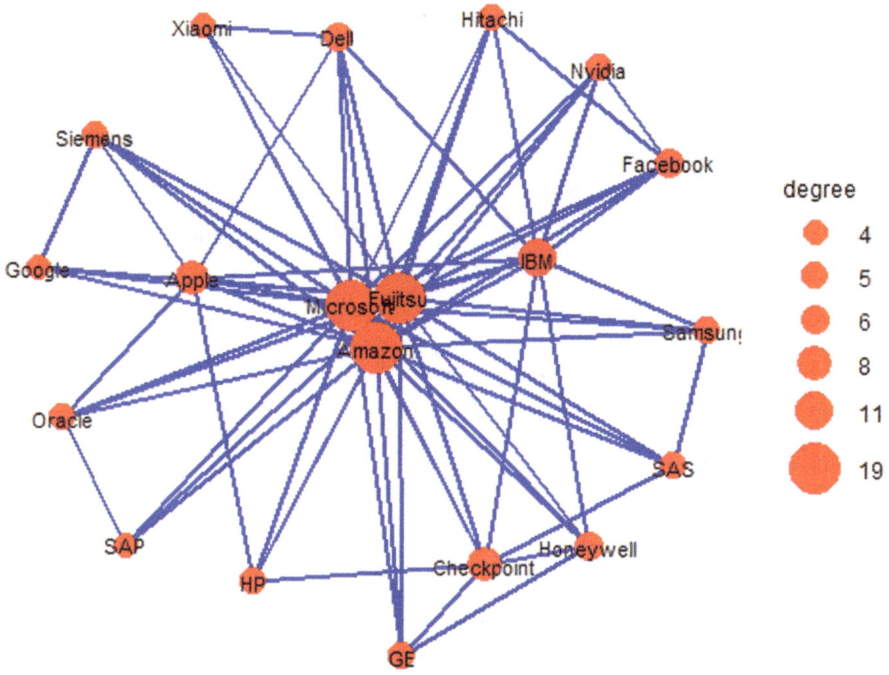

Fig. 11 Financial ties network

The graph (Fig. 11) provides a visualization of the *degree* property of each node, the number of edges. The number of edges impacts the size of each node. For example, Microsoft, Fujitsu, and Amazon have the largest node, since it has ties to five companies (five edges in the graph).

4.3.6 Prescriptive Task

Inform about the financial ties among companies so that company managers can plan a strategy for pursuing specific companies and actions.

4.3.7 Build the Prescriptive Model and Interpretation

Once the graph is built, it becomes the model, and the bulk of the activity is querying the graph to get specific answers. It is less of an interpretation of the result and more being able to accurately define what we are looking for, as demonstrated below. Now we can start mining it for information. For example, we will identify *cliques*, or clusters in which companies are members. A node is a member of a clique if it is connected to every other member of the group at a distance greater than one. The

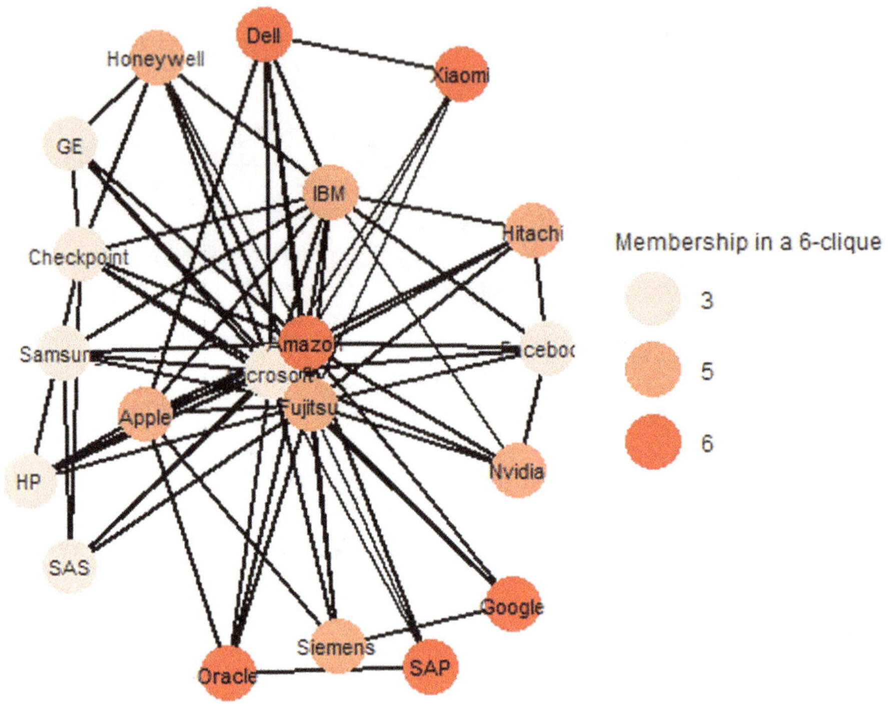

Fig. 12 Clique membership

larger the clique (Fig. 12), the more connections a company has, the more it is a desirable financial partner:

```
FinTies.Graph <- graph_from_adjacency_matrix(relationships, mode = "undirected")
FinTies.Cliques = cliques(FinTies.Graph, 6)
FinTies.Cliques

## list()

# Plot ties

FinTies.Vector = c(0,3,0,1,3,2,3,0,3,2,1,0,0)
FinNetwork %v% "alliance" <- FinTies.Vector

ggnet2(FinNetwork, label = TRUE,  node.color = as.character(FinNetwork %v%
"alliance"), color.palette = "Reds", node.size = 10, edge.size = 1, edge.color =
"black",label.size = 3, color.legend = "Membership in a 6-clique" )
```

Figure 12 shows companies that are members in 6-cliques (e.g., Amazon, Oracle), 5-cliques (e.g., Siemens, Apple), and 3-cliques (e.g., Facebook, SAS). We can ask the mining functions of *igraph* to display this specific information. For example, here are all companies that are members of a *6-clique*, including the companies that make up the clique:

```
FinTies.Cliques = cliques(FinTies.Graph, min=6)
FinTies.Cliques

## [[1]]
## + 6/20 vertices, named, from b370d9f:
## [1] Microsoft IBM       Facebook  Fujitsu   Amazon    Hitachi
##
## [[2]]
## + 6/20 vertices, named, from b370d9f:
## [1] Microsoft  Fujitsu    Amazon     Checkpoint GE         Honeywell
##
## [[3]]
## + 6/20 vertices, named, from b370d9f:
## [1] Microsoft  IBM        Fujitsu    Amazon     Checkpoint Honeywell
##
## [[4]]
## + 6/20 vertices, named, from b370d9f:
## [1] Microsoft IBM       Facebook  Fujitsu   Nvidia    Amazon
##
## [[5]]
## + 6/20 vertices, named, from b370d9f:
## [1] Microsoft IBM       Apple     Fujitsu   Amazon    Dell
```

We can further our analysis and identify who are the strongest actors in a field, or in this context, the companies with the most partnerships. In graph terms, we will count the edges connected to each node:

```
company.degrees <- degree(FinTies.Graph)
company.degrees <- sort(company.degrees, decreasing = TRUE)
company.degrees

##    Fujitsu     Amazon  Microsoft        IBM      Apple Checkpoint   Facebook
##         21         21         19         11          8          8          6
##       Dell  Honeywell     Oracle         HP    Samsung    Siemens        SAS
##          6          6          5          5          5          5          5
##     Nvidia    Hitachi         GE     Google     Xiaomi        SAP
##          5          5          5          4          4          4
```

It turns out that Fujitsu and Amazon have the highest degree of 21 connections (edges), followed by Microsoft with 19. Google, Xiaomi, and SAP have only 4 connections.

Another important metric of a network is its *centrality* and centralities of its nodes. In an undirected graph like the one used in this example, we could be interested in the *closeness centrality* (distance to others in the network):

```
FinTies.Centrality <- centr_clo(FinTies.Graph)
FinTies.Centrality$res <- sort(FinTies.Centrality$res, decreasing = TRUE)
FinTies.Centrality$res

##  [1] 1.0000000 1.0000000 1.0000000 0.7037037 0.6333333 0.6333333 0.5937500
##  [8] 0.5937500 0.5937500 0.5757576 0.5757576 0.5757576 0.5757576 0.5757576
## [15] 0.5757576 0.5757576 0.5757576 0.5588235 0.5588235 0.5588235

FinTies.Centrality.centralized <- centralize(FinTies.Centrality$res, normalized=FALSE)
FinTies.Centrality.centralized

## [1] 6.965848
```

The above result is more meaningful in an interactive application when one can tweak connections, explore alternative scenarios, or compare two subnetworks. The network that has a higher centrality is more time-consuming (expensive) to navigate.

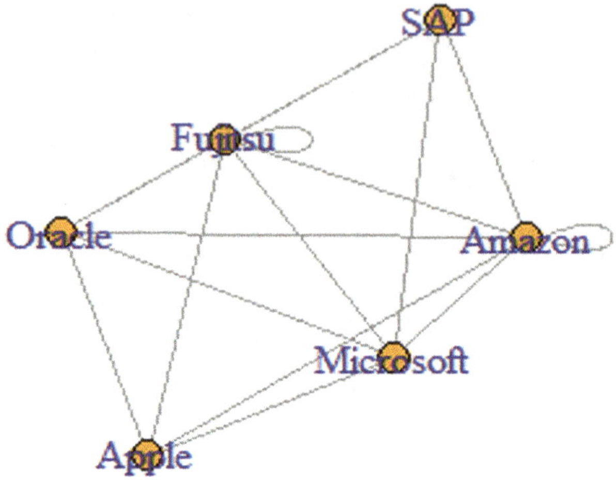

Fig. 13 Immediate neighbors of Oracle

We may also be interested in the immediate neighbors of a node in the graph. This means the companies who are directly connected to a given company, say Oracle (Fig. 13). This would be a question similar to one asks (for example) on LinkedIn—Who do you know? Can you introduce me?:

```
nodeIndex <- as.numeric(V(FinTies.Graph)["Oracle"])

FinTies.neighbors <- graph.neighborhood(FinTies.Graph, order=1)
plot(FinTies.neighbors[[nodeIndex]])
```

4.3.8 Conclusion

Graph Theory and its more concrete incarnation as Network Analytics is a broad field, which is beyond the scope of this chapter. It suffices to say that we have only explored *undirected, unweighted graphs.* The reader is encouraged to peruse the references cited and explore more complex networks. For example, directed networks, in which not all relationships are bilateral. There could be relationships in which information or investment capital only flows one way. There are networks, in which the connections (edges) are *weighted.* This could denote for example, that some connections are stronger, or more expensive, or more difficult to follow. The concepts outlined in this example would be expanded to be adapted to a directed graph with weighted edges. The most important thing is to define what exactly we seek to find, and then devise the appropriate model and implement the appropriate functions to extract that information.

Additional perspectives of the diverse uses of network analysis and network theory in finance can be found in Baker et al. (2020), Cheng and Zhao (2019), and Samitas and Kampouris (2018).

4.4 Prescriptive Model 4: Recommender Systems

4.4.1 Theoretical Foundation

Recommender systems are typically used each time we wish to aggregate the opinions of a group about an item, to decide which action to take about that item. The approach applies to assessing analysts' recommendations regarding the structuring of an investment portfolio, reviewers' opinions regarding a particular movie, or any other type of *crowdsourced recommendation.* The mathematical and statistical tools are identical regardless of data and context. The ensuing decisions are subjective, depending on the context. In this example, we will focus on the recommendation made by a group of independent brokers, regarding which stocks to invest in. The outcome can be used by investors to decide how to structure their investment portfolio.

A recommender system involves a set of users $U = \{u_1, u_2, \ldots, u_m\}$ who communicate preferences (ratings) on a set of items, $I = \{i_1, i_2, \ldots, i_n\}$. The preferences are stored in a *rating matrix,* $R[m \times n]$.

A measure of the similarity of two recommenders a and b, is the Euclidean Distance between them:

$$d_{\text{euclidean}}(a, b) = \sqrt{\sum_{i=1}^{i=n} (a_i - b_i)^2}$$

An alternative method used to corroborate the Euclidean distance is the *cosine distance*, given by

$$d_{\text{cosine}}(a, b) = 1 - \cos(\theta) = 1 - \frac{a \cdot b}{\|a\| \|b\|}$$

Similarly, one can define the Euclidean distance and cosine similarity between two items, in terms of the recommenders that rated them. The main purpose of the recommender is to facilitate decision-making. For example, if an investor is interested in a particular type of company, for which a set of characteristics have been stored in a database, the recommender can find similar companies. If the investor is interested in the opinion of a particular type of advisor, then the recommender can find one with similar opinions, by measuring past activities (ratings). Conversely, we can test whether to items are similar then apply the same action to both. Additional, expanded coverage of recommender systems is available in Kumar et al. (2021), Venugopal et al. (2020), and Falk (2019).

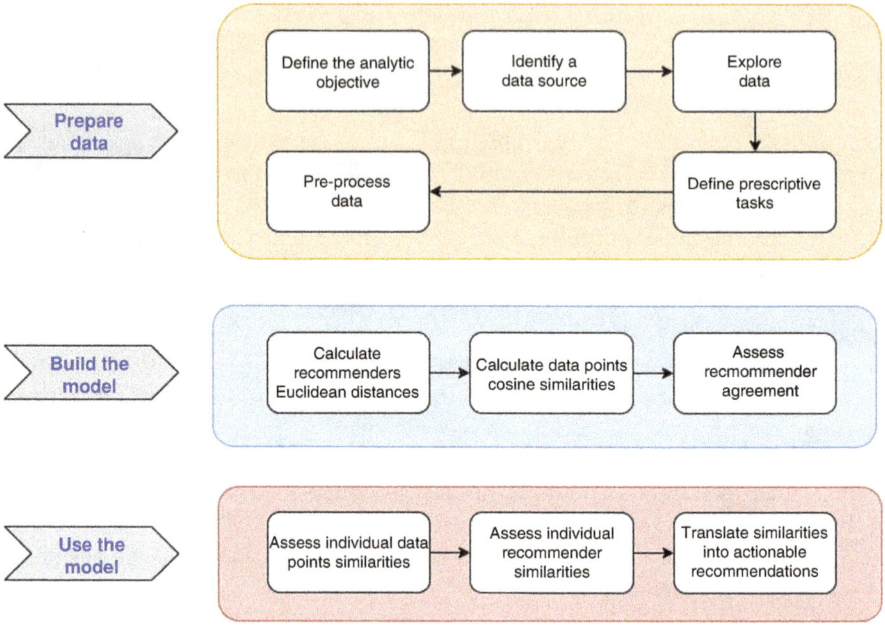

Fig. 14 Main steps in building a recommender system

4.4.2 Advance Organizer

Figure 14 depicts the main steps in building and using a recommender system.

4.4.3 Objective

Given a dataset of company stocks and their ratings by a group of brokers, aggregate their recommendations and decide which stocks to purchase.

4.4.4 Data Source

The data source, created specifically for this example, is the file *SyntheticStockRatings.csv*, which contains simulated ratings of stocks of popular companies, by anonymous investors.

4.4.5 Data Exploration and Cleaning

We will first read the data and convert it into a matrix for subsequent processing:

```
ratings <- read.csv("SyntheticStockRatings.csv")
ratings.df <- data.frame(ratings)

#View(ratings.df)
head(ratings.df)

##   brokerID stockName rating
## 1        1 Microsoft      1
## 2        1       IBM      5
## 3        1    Google      4
## 4        1  Facebook      2
## 5        1     Apple      3
## 6        1    Oracle      5

Create user ratings matrix
head(ratings)

##   brokerID stockName rating
## 1        1 Microsoft      1
## 2        1       IBM      5
## 3        1    Google      4
## 4        1  Facebook      2
## 5        1     Apple      3
## 6        1    Oracle      5
```

4.4.6 Prescriptive Tasks

There is one essential task expected in this example: aggregate the recommendations of a group of brokers and decide which stocks to invest in.

4.4.7 Data Pre-processing

We first need to organize the data matrix, so that each row corresponds to one recommender:

```
library(reshape2)
ratingsMatrix <- dcast(ratings, brokerID ~ stockName, value.var="rating")

head(ratingsMatrix)

##   brokerID Amazon Apple Dell Facebook GE Google Honeywell HP IBM Microsoft
## 1        1      1     3    4        2  4      4         5  4   5         1
## 2        2      1     3    4        2  4      4         5  4   5         1
## 3        3      2     3    3        2  4      5         5  4   3         3
## 4        4      4     4    3        1  4      1         5  3   1         4
## 5        5      2     5    5        5  1      3         2  2   4         4
## 6        6      1     5    3        4  2      5         4  3   3         1
##   Nvidia Oracle Samsung SAS
## 1      4      5       3   1
## 2      4      5       3   1
## 3      3      5       2   1
## 4      3      3       5   5
## 5      2      1       4   1
## 6      5      4       2   3
```

4.4.8 Build the Prescriptive Model

In the first part of this two-part prescriptive model, we will develop a recommendation system based on the agreement among recommenders (stockbrokers). In a preliminary assessment of recommendations, we are interested in measuring the similarities among recommenders. We will measure that in two ways: *Euclidean Distance* and *Cosine Similarity*. First, we will create a similarities matrix using Euclidean Distance. The code below displays the first 6 rows in each matrix:

```
# Calculate all pair-wise distances in the ratings matrix

dist.brokers.Euclidean <- as.matrix(dist(ratingsMatrix, method = 'euclidean'))
head(round(dist.brokers.Euclidean, 2),2)

##    1 2    3    4    5    6
## 1 0 1 4.12 9.00 9.22 7.21
## 2 1 0 3.74 8.72 8.83 6.56

# Calculate similarities of stocks based on ratings from multiple brokers

dist.stocks.Euclidean <- as.matrix(dist(t (ratingsMatrix), method = 'euclidean'))
head(round(dist.stocks.Euclidean, 2))

##          brokerID Amazon Apple Dell Facebook   GE Google Honeywell   HP  IBM
## brokerID     0.00   6.00  2.45 4.80     3.87 6.78   5.57      6.56 5.74 6.63
## Amazon       6.00   0.00  5.83 5.74     5.39 4.90   7.28      7.14 5.20 7.07
## Apple        2.45   5.83  0.00 2.65     3.61 5.29   4.36      4.80 4.12 4.69
## Dell         4.80   5.74  2.65 0.00     3.74 4.36   4.00      4.47 3.16 2.65
## Facebook     3.87   5.39  3.61 3.74     0.00 6.40   4.69      7.21 5.10 4.58
## GE           6.78   4.90  5.29 4.36     6.40 0.00   4.80      3.00 1.73 4.69
##          Microsoft Nvidia Oracle Samsung  SAS
## brokerID      5.20   4.90   7.07    4.90 5.57
## Amazon        2.24   6.00   7.21    3.74 2.65
## Apple         5.00   3.46   5.48    3.46 5.74
## Dell          4.90   3.61   4.80    3.00 6.48
## Facebook      4.69   4.80   6.86    4.80 6.00
## GE            5.39   3.46   2.83    4.00 5.39
```

In the above output, we notice for example, that the distance between Apple and Dell is 2.65, while the distance between Facebook and Oracle is 6.86. The lower the number, the more similar the stock, i.e. the more agreement among the recommenders.

We will now repeat the similarities calculations using the *Cosine Similarity* method:

```
library(proxy)

# Since cosine(0)=1, the closer cosine is to 1, the shorter the distance,
# i.e. the more similar the items

dist.brokers.cosine <- as.matrix(dist(ratingsMatrix, method = 'cosine'))
round(dist.brokers.cosine,2)

##      1    2    3    4    5    6
## 1 0.00 0.00 0.05 0.22 0.24 0.13
## 2 0.00 0.00 0.04 0.20 0.22 0.11
## 3 0.05 0.04 0.00 0.16 0.20 0.09
## 4 0.22 0.20 0.16 0.00 0.22 0.19
## 5 0.24 0.22 0.20 0.22 0.00 0.14
## 6 0.13 0.11 0.09 0.19 0.14 0.00

# Calculate similarities of stocks based on ratings from multiple brokers

dist.stocks.cosine <- as.matrix(dist(t (ratingsMatrix), method = 'cosine'))
# remove the first row and column, which contain broker ID
dist.stocks.cosine <- dist.stocks.cosine [-1,-1round(head(dist.stocks.cosine),2)]

##             Amazon Apple Dell Facebook   GE Google Honeywell   HP  IBM Microsoft
## Amazon        0.00  0.14 0.18     0.32 0.17   0.34      0.16 0.19 0.35      0.04
## Apple         0.14  0.00 0.04     0.05 0.16   0.10      0.10 0.10 0.12      0.12
## Dell          0.18  0.04 0.00     0.08 0.12   0.09      0.08 0.06 0.04      0.14
## Facebook      0.32  0.05 0.08     0.00 0.33   0.12      0.24 0.20 0.13      0.22
## GE            0.17  0.16 0.12     0.33 0.00   0.13      0.01 0.02 0.14      0.24
## Google        0.34  0.10 0.09     0.12 0.13   0.00      0.09 0.05 0.06      0.31
##             Nvidia Oracle Samsung  SAS
## Amazon        0.24   0.27    0.06 0.09
## Apple         0.07   0.15    0.06 0.18
## Dell          0.08   0.12    0.05 0.29
## Facebook      0.16   0.27    0.19 0.38
## GE            0.08   0.03    0.12 0.24
## Google        0.05   0.06    0.22 0.39
```

If we examine the same pairs of stocks, we notice that the similarity of Apple and Dell is 0.04, while that of Dell and Oracle is 0.12. As with the previous method, Apple and Dell appear to be more similar, i.e. there is more agreement among recommenders. These numbers do not represent the recommendation to buy the stock, just that the degree of agreement among recommenders about the stock.

4.4.9 Prescriptive Actionable Information

We can mine the similarities matrix for various types of information. Here are a few examples:

```
#Cosine similarities between stock Facebook and GE
round(dist.stocks.cosine[4,6],2)

## [1] 0.33

# The matrix position of the LEAST similar brokers
# based on Euclidean distance of their ratings
leastSimilar <- which(dist.brokers.Euclidean == max(dist.brokers.Euclidean),
                      arr.ind = TRUE)
leastSimilar

##   row col
## 5   5   1
## 1   1   5

# Use the above returned position as indexes to print the matrix cell at that position
round(dist.brokers.Euclidean[leastSimilar[1,1], leastSimilar[1,2]],2)

## [1] 9.22

# Which user is the LEAST similar to user 1 (based on Euclidean distance)?
# Since the matrix contains 0 values, we'll do a trick: sort all values in ROW 1,
# and pick the second (since the first one is 0 due to measuring against itself)

sortedRow <- sort(dist.brokers.Euclidean[2,])
sortedRow
##        2        1        3        6        4        5
## 0.000000 1.000000 3.741657 6.557439 8.717798 8.831761

# this is smallest number besides 0, i.e. the least similar
# (top is index, bottom is the value)
sortedRow[2]

## 1
## 1

# Which broker is the MOST similar to broker 1 (based on Euclidean distance)?
# We can use the sorted array from above, and display the largest number
print(sortedRow[length(sortedRow)])

##        5
## 8.831761
```

If two brokers are similar (i.e., their recommendations are more alike), then we are more likely to find their recommendations useful and heed their advice.

4.4.10 Conclusion

In summary, we demonstrated the creation of a simple but powerful recommender system that can perform several essential tasks in the process of decision-making:

1. After consulting one advisor, identify similar ones so they can corroborate the first one's opinion. Conversely, identify another advisor, who the recommender has identified as very dissimilar, to hear a counter-argument.
2. Identify an item of interest, then use the recommender to identify additional similar items and perform an action in all of them. Conversely, identify items that are not at all similar, for example, company stocks that exhibit very different behaviors (as rated by advisors), to build a diversified portfolio.

Recommender systems are widely discussed across business- and finance-related disciplines. Readers interested in more specific applications and research will find useful information in Pan et al. (2021), Wang et al. (2016), and Sun et al. (2018).

4.5 Prescriptive Model 5: Principal Components Analysis

4.5.1 Theoretical Foundation

Large datasets are increasingly common, and they include many variables, which poses a significant computational challenge. Principal component analysis (PCA) is a technique for reducing the computational complexity associated with such large datasets. PCA increases computational efficiency, without sacrificing analytical validity. At its core, it replaces existing variables with new, fewer ones (*principal components*), which maximize variance. The core of the PCA method is solving an eigenvalue/eigenvector problem. PCA can be adapted to any domain, any type of data and context, with significant benefits in the field of finance, where the datasets are becoming increasingly large.

The main objective of the PCA method is to determine the minimum number of principal components that account for most of the variation in your data, in key steps (Tattar et al., 2016):

1. Calculate the proportion of variance explained by the components—here we will use the adage "perfect is the enemy of good," in the sense that we will identify key components that explain *most* of the variance. Thus, we gain increased computational efficiency (fewer variables) with minimal loss. *Most* is obviously a subjective measure, but typically 80% of the variance explained by the principal components is acceptable. The model is flexible enough to allow the analyst to make that determination and decide how many components to use.
2. Calculate eigenvalues—as a measure of the significance of each principal component. There are several methods for deciding which component to keep, which will be described in the subsequent sections. The components with the largest eigenvalues will be kept, while the rest discarded.
3. Generate a scree plot—to order the eigenvalues from largest to smallest. Typically, the plot is a steep curve (Fig. 15), followed by a bend, and then a straight line. We keep the components in the steep curve before the bend.
4. Substitution suitability—assess to what extent each component can explain the variance "on behalf" of one or more of the original variables.

To perform PCA, three assumptions must be verified, to ensure that the data lends itself to this process:

- Sphericity *(using Bartlett chi-square test)*—equality of variance of the differences between each pair of values. Test the null hypothesis H_0 that all k variances

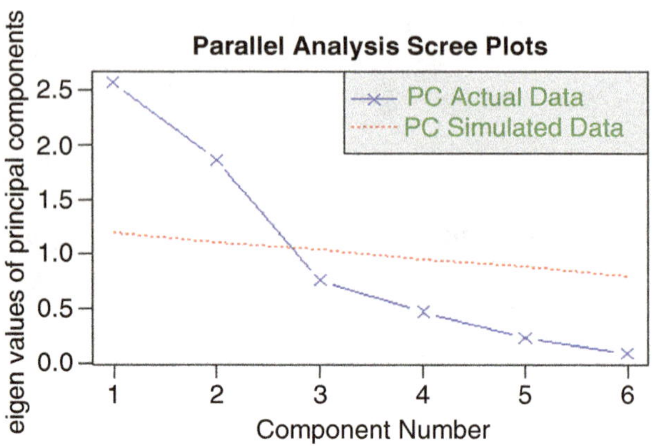

Fig. 15 Scree plot example

are equal and the alternate hypothesis H_1 that at least two are different. The test statistic is χ^2, defined as:

$$\chi^2 = \frac{(N-k)\ln\left(S_p^2\right) - \sum_{i=1}^{k}(n_i-1)\ln\left(S_i^2\right)}{1+\frac{1}{3(k-1)}\left(\sum_{i=1}^{k}\left(\frac{1}{n_i-1}\right)-\frac{1}{N-k}\right)}$$

where:

- k is the number of samples with sizes n_i
- S_i^2 are the sample variances
- N is the sum of all sample sizes n_i
- S_p^2 is the pooled estimate for the variance

- Sampling adequacy *(using the Keiser–Meyer–Olkin or KMO test),* in which the following measure is evaluated:

$$\mathrm{KMO}_j = \frac{\sum_{i\neq j} r_{ij}^2}{\sum_{i\neq j} r_{ij}^2 + \sum_{i\neq j} u}$$

where:

- $R = [r_{ij}]$ is the correlation matrix
- $U = [u_{ij}]$ is the partial covariance matrix
- *KMO* returns values between 0 and 1, which are left to the analyst to interpret, based on experience with the domain. However:

$0.8 \le KMO \le 1.0$ indicates the sample is adequate
$0.5 \le KMO < 0.8$ are left to the discretion of the analyst to decide
KMO close to 0 is an indication of widespread correlation and the sample is not adequate

- Positive determinant of variance-covariance matrix *(calculate determinant of a matrix)*:

$$\mathrm{Det}(C_x) = \prod_{i=1}^{n} \lambda_i \ge 0$$

where:

- C_x is the covariance matrix
- λ_i are the eigenvalues

PCA being a fairly complex topic, additional depth and breadth can be found in Blokdyk (2021), Tanaka (2021), and Naik (2018).

4.5.2 Advance Organizer

Figure 16 highlights the key steps of the complex process of performing principal component analysis.

4.5.3 Objective of the Model

Given a dataset of stocks and several performance metrics, create a model that is more computationally efficient as a preliminary step towards building (a subsequent) model. Note that this example focuses only on the efficiency stemming from reducing the numbers of predictors and not on building a predictive model. This process is commonly known as dimensionality reduction.

4.5.4 Data Source

The data consists of a dataset of 252 observations aggregated over a period of several years. The dataset is freely available here: https://archive.ics.uci.edu/ml/machine-learning-databases/00390/

4.5.5 Data Exploration

We will first read and explore the data:

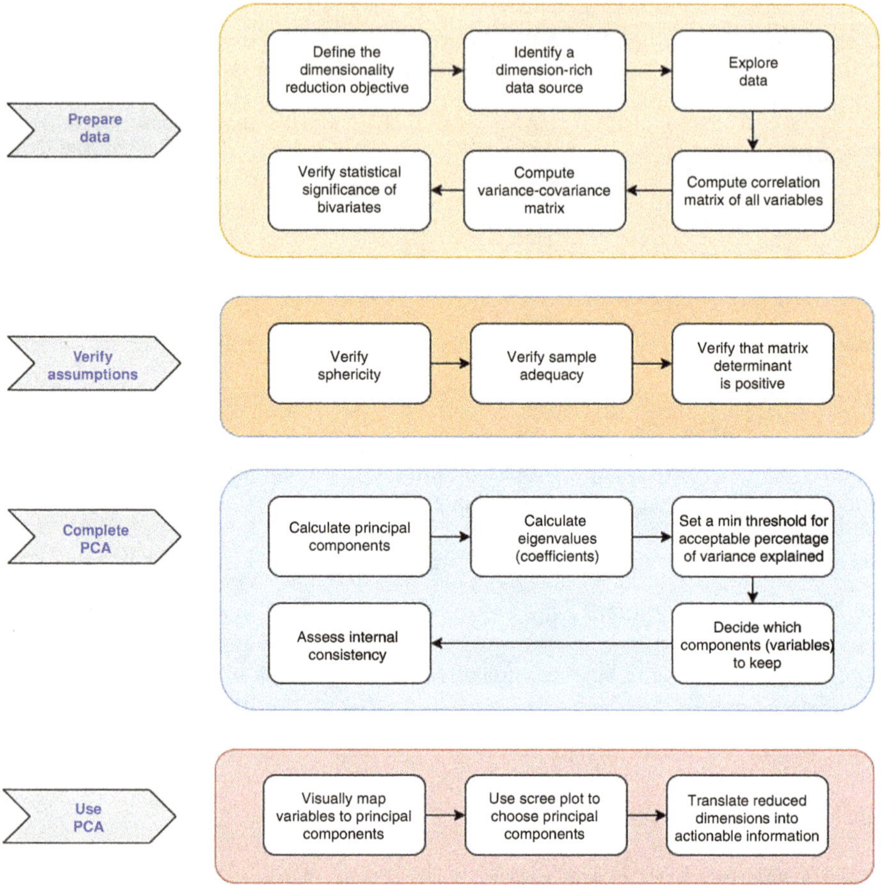

Fig. 16 An overview of the PCA process

```
pca <- read.csv("PCA_stock.csv")
colnames(pca) = c("AnnualReturn", "ExcessReturn", "SystematicRisk", "TotalRisk", "AbsWinRate", "R
elWinRate")
head(pca)

##   AnnualReturn ExcessReturn SystematicRisk TotalRisk AbsWinRate RelWinRate
## 1        0.625        0.714          0.382     0.688       0.56      0.500
## 2        0.599        0.431          0.737     0.634       0.68      0.725
## 3        0.518        0.590          0.443     0.777       0.56      0.200
## 4        0.396        0.320          0.682     0.788       0.32      0.500
## 5        0.219        0.351          0.381     0.200       0.56      0.275
## 6        0.262        0.243          0.620     0.679       0.44      0.350

tail(pca)

##     AnnualReturn ExcessReturn SystematicRisk TotalRisk AbsWinRate RelWinRate
## 247        0.628        0.603          0.401     0.373       0.56      0.533
## 248        0.548        0.522          0.311     0.294       0.56      0.667
## 249        0.544        0.514          0.262     0.257       0.68      0.600
## 250        0.588        0.566          0.391     0.369       0.56      0.467
## 251        0.571        0.542          0.304     0.293       0.68      0.667
## 252        0.638        0.602          0.331     0.312       0.56      0.800
```

The data is a straightforward table of performance predictors for stocks, one stock per row.

4.5.6 Tasks

The key tasks we will perform are to create a variance-covariance matrix, calculate its determinant, derive the eigenvalues, and use those to construct new and fewer components to replace the six predictors. Then we will validate the model and ensure that it indeed performed the task of simplifying the foundation for a subsequent predictive model. Along the way, we will rigorously verify that the assumptions required by PCA are satisfied.

4.5.7 Preliminary Steps in Preparation for PCA

A first preliminary step is to compute the correlation matrix of all six variables. Note that the diagonal is obviously all 1s:

```
pcacor <- cor(pca)
pcacor

##                 AnnualReturn ExcessReturn SystematicRisk   TotalRisk AbsWinRate
## AnnualReturn       1.0000000    0.7841132     0.18529501  0.29913243  0.5604758
## ExcessReturn       0.7841132    1.0000000    -0.12526631  0.14606226  0.5069724
## SystematicRisk     0.1852950   -0.1252663     1.00000000  0.74269266 -0.2637322
## TotalRisk          0.2991324    0.1460623     0.74269266  1.00000000 -0.1017697
## AbsWinRate         0.5604758    0.5069724    -0.26373223 -0.10176967  1.0000000
## RelWinRate         0.5360935    0.3069805    -0.03691824 -0.03619905  0.3180760
##                  RelWinRate
## AnnualReturn     0.53609345
## ExcessReturn     0.30698047
## SystematicRisk  -0.03691824
## TotalRisk       -0.03619905
## AbsWinRate       0.31807604
## RelWinRate       1.00000000
```

Next, we will generate the variance-covariance matrix:

```
pcacov <- cov(pca)
pcacov

##                 AnnualReturn ExcessReturn SystematicRisk     TotalRisk
## AnnualReturn     0.021266832  0.015536521   0.0037909254  0.0063877655
## ExcessReturn     0.015536521  0.018460658  -0.0023877452  0.0029060006
## SystematicRisk   0.003790925 -0.002387745   0.0196815925  0.0152571468
## TotalRisk        0.006387766  0.002906001   0.0152571468  0.0214421411
## AbsWinRate       0.011476913  0.009672189  -0.0051952946 -0.0020925185
## RelWinRate       0.011126237  0.005935957  -0.0007371019 -0.0007543756
##                   AbsWinRate    RelWinRate
## AnnualReturn     0.011476913  0.0111262373
## ExcessReturn     0.009672189  0.0059359571
## SystematicRisk  -0.005195295 -0.0007371019
## TotalRisk       -0.002092518 -0.0007543756
## AbsWinRate       0.019716677  0.0063562979
## RelWinRate       0.006356298  0.0202540950
```

Before proceeding with using the matrix, it is important to verify the statistical significance of the bivariate correlation. Building the PCA model is akin to performing surgery that replaces natural organs with artificial ones. We must ensure, every step along the way, the validity and accuracy of each outcome

```
statSig <- corr.p(pcacor, 252, alpha=.05)
print(statSig, short=FALSE)

## Call:corr.p(r = pcacor, n = 252, alpha = 0.05)
## Correlation matrix
##                 AnnualReturn ExcessReturn SystematicRisk TotalRisk AbsWinRate
## AnnualReturn            1.00         0.78           0.19      0.30       0.56
## ExcessReturn            0.78         1.00          -0.13      0.15       0.51
## SystematicRisk          0.19        -0.13           1.00      0.74      -0.26
## TotalRisk               0.30         0.15           0.74      1.00      -0.10
## AbsWinRate              0.56         0.51          -0.26     -0.10       1.00
## RelWinRate              0.54         0.31          -0.04     -0.04       0.32
##                 RelWinRate
## AnnualReturn          0.54
## ExcessReturn          0.31
## SystematicRisk       -0.04
## TotalRisk            -0.04
## AbsWinRate            0.32
## RelWinRate            1.00
## Sample Size
## [1] 252
## Probability values (Entries above the diagonal are adjusted for multiple tests.)
##                 AnnualReturn ExcessReturn SystematicRisk TotalRisk AbsWinRate
## AnnualReturn               0         0.00           0.02      0.00       0.00
## ExcessReturn               0         0.00           0.19      0.10       0.00
## SystematicRisk             0         0.05           0.00      0.00       0.00
## TotalRisk                  0         0.02           0.00      0.00       0.32
## AbsWinRate                 0         0.00           0.00      0.11       0.00
## RelWinRate                 0         0.00           0.56      0.57       0.00
##                 RelWinRate
## AnnualReturn             0
## ExcessReturn             0
## SystematicRisk           1
## TotalRisk                1
## AbsWinRate               0
## RelWinRate               0
##
##  Confidence intervals based upon normal theory.  To get bootstrapped values, try co
r.ci
##              lower     r upper    p
## AnnlR-ExcsR   0.73  0.78  0.83 0.00
## AnnlR-SystR   0.06  0.19  0.30 0.00
## AnnlR-TtlRs   0.18  0.30  0.41 0.00
## AnnlR-AbsWR   0.47  0.56  0.64 0.00
## AnnlR-RlWnR   0.44  0.54  0.62 0.00
## ExcsR-SystR  -0.25 -0.13  0.00 0.05
## ExcsR-TtlRs   0.02  0.15  0.26 0.02
## ExcsR-AbsWR   0.41  0.51  0.59 0.00
## ExcsR-RlWnR   0.19  0.31  0.41 0.00
## SystR-TtlRs   0.68  0.74  0.79 0.00
## SystR-AbsWR  -0.38 -0.26 -0.14 0.00
## SystR-RlWnR  -0.16 -0.04  0.09 0.56
## TtlRs-AbsWR  -0.22 -0.10  0.02 0.11
## TtlRs-RlWnR  -0.16 -0.04  0.09 0.57
## AbsWR-RlWnR   0.20  0.32  0.42 0.00
```

Note that two *p-values* are quite high, 0.56 and 0.57, and we expect an impact of this relationship, as it is an indication of co-variates. This strengthens the justification for performing PCA to reduce the number of predictors.

Now, we begin the tedious work of verifying the three assumptions required by PCA:

1. Sphericity *(Bartlett Test of Sphericity for covariance matrices)*
2. Sample Adequacy *(Kaiser-Meyer-Olkin Measure of sampling adequacy test)*
3. Positive determinant of the matrix *(det() function)*

First, we will test assumptions 1 and 2, using the *paf()* function, which performs both Bartlett and KMO tests:

```
# coerce data into a matrix and ignore headers
dat <- data.matrix(pca[1:6])
paf.pca <- paf(dat, eigcrit=1, convcrit=.001)
summary(paf.pca)  # Notice Bartlett and KMO values and ignore the rest

## $KMO
## [1] 0.51218
##
## $MSA
##                     MSA
## AnnualReturn    0.50734
## ExcessReturn    0.49672
## SystematicRisk 0.38202
## TotalRisk       0.55243
## AbsWinRate      0.69804
## RelWinRate      0.53850
##
## $Bartlett
## [1] 811.3
##
## $Communalities
##                Initial Communalities Final Extraction
## AnnualReturn                 0.83439          1.15185
## ExcessReturn                 0.74340          0.57841
## SystematicRisk               0.70374          1.00016
## TotalRisk                    0.61743          0.57955
## AbsWinRate                   0.46244          0.43622
## RelWinRate                   0.39180          0.23173
##
## $Factor.Loadings
##                     [,1]     [,2]
## AnnualReturn    1.070070 -0.08243
## ExcessReturn    0.746762  0.14408
## SystematicRisk 0.087504 -0.99625
## TotalRisk       0.241233 -0.72205
## AbsWinRate      0.574084  0.32657
## RelWinRate      0.467036  0.11667
##
## $RMS
## [1] 0.037189
```

Since KMO = 0.51218 we will consider it sufficiently high for the scope and purpose of this example. Other analysts might disagree with using a KMO value less than 0.7, but given certain familiarity with the data and past experiments, we can assert reasonable confidence in the adequacy of the sample size.

Bartlett chi-square = 811.3 does not show a *p-value*. We must thus compute the statistical significance:

```
#Bartlett significance test using correlation matrix

cortest.bartlett(pcacor, n=252)

## $chisq
## [1] 811.3
##
## $p.value
## [1] 0.0000000000000000000000000000000000000000000000000000000000000000000000000000000
0000000000000000000000000000000000000000000000000000000000000000000000000000000000000003
2866
##
## $df
## [1] 15
```

Since p is practically 0, the statistical significance has been established.

The third assumption requires a straightforward calculation of the determinant of the variance-covariance matrix:

```
# Verify that the determinant is positive

det(pcacor)

## [1] 0.038038
```

Since the determinant is positive, we have successfully verified the three assumptions and can proceed with completing the PCA.

4.5.8 Complete PCA

We will now assess the components needed, using the *principal()* function:

```
pca1Component <- principal(pcacor, rotate="none")
# default with 1 component and no scores

pca1Component
## Principal Components Analysis
## Call: principal(r = pcacor, rotate = "none")
## Standardized loadings (pattern matrix) based upon correlation matrix
##                 PC1        h2   u2 com
## AnnualReturn    0.94 0.8811830 0.12   1
## ExcessReturn    0.85 0.7189971 0.28   1
## SystematicRisk 0.00 0.0000008 1.00   1
## TotalRisk       0.20 0.0385368 0.96   1
## AbsWinRate      0.73 0.5279027 0.47   1
## RelWinRate      0.63 0.3982638 0.60   1
##
##                 PC1
## SS loadings     2.56
## Proportion Var 0.43
##
## Mean item complexity =  1
## Test of the hypothesis that 1 component is sufficient.
##
## The root mean square of the residuals (RMSR) is  0.24
##
## Fit based upon off diagonal values = 0.65
```

The eigenvalues are the sum of the h^2 values, with a Proportion Var of 0.43 or 43%. This means that we have yet to explain 57% of the variance. While sometimes one principal component is sufficient because it explains most of the variation, in this case, we need additional principal components.

```
Pca6Components <- principal(pcacor, nfactors=6, rotate="none")
#we calculate all 6 components

pca6Components

## Principal Components Analysis
## Call: principal(r = pcacor, nfactors = 6, rotate = "none")
## Standardized loadings (pattern matrix) based upon correlation matrix
##                 PC1   PC2   PC3   PC4   PC5   PC6 h2                  u2 com
## AnnualReturn    0.94  0.19 -0.01 -0.08 -0.18 -0.21  1  0.0000000000000033 1.3
## ExcessReturn    0.85 -0.05 -0.33 -0.38  0.01  0.16  1 -0.0000000000000111 1.8
## SystematicRisk 0.00  0.94  0.12  0.15 -0.27  0.12  1  0.0000000000000022 1.3
## TotalRisk       0.20  0.91 -0.13  0.04  0.34 -0.05  1  0.0000000000000167 1.4
## AbsWinRate      0.73 -0.34 -0.23  0.55  0.03  0.05  1 -0.0000000000000022 2.6
## RelWinRate      0.63 -0.10  0.76 -0.02  0.11  0.06  1 -0.0000000000000178 2.0
##
##                         PC1  PC2  PC3  PC4  PC5  PC6
## SS loadings            2.56 1.86 0.77 0.48 0.24 0.09
## Proportion Var         0.43 0.31 0.13 0.08 0.04 0.02
## Cumulative Var         0.43 0.74 0.87 0.95 0.98 1.00
## Proportion Explained  0.43 0.31 0.13 0.08 0.04 0.02
## Cumulative Proportion 0.43 0.74 0.87 0.95 0.98 1.00
##
## Mean item complexity =  1.7
## Test of the hypothesis that 6 components are sufficient.
##
## The root mean square of the residuals (RMSR) is  0
##
## Fit based upon off diagonal values = 1
```

The eigenvalues of the components and proportion of variance they explained are given in the code output above:

1. PC1 = 2.56 (43%)
2. PC2 = 1.86 (31%)
3. PC3 = 0.77 (13%)
4. PC4 = 0.48 (8%)
5. PC5 = 0.24 (4%)
6. PC6 = 0.09 (2%)

We can decide which variables we want to keep and what percentage of the variance we are satisfied with explaining (they add up to 100%). Finally, we need to be mindful of the residual error (even if small). We can use the Cronbach alpha reliability coefficient for assessing internal consistency.

```
alpha(pcacor)

## Reliability analysis
## Call: alpha(x = pcacor)
##
##   raw_alpha std.alpha G6(smc) average_r S/N median_r
##       0.67      0.67    0.84      0.25 2.1      0.3
##
##  Reliability if an item is dropped:
##                  raw_alpha std.alpha G6(smc) average_r  S/N var.r med.r
## AnnualReturn          0.46      0.46    0.63      0.15 0.85 0.101 0.055
## ExcessReturn          0.59      0.59    0.74      0.22 1.41 0.108 0.242
## SystematicRisk        0.71      0.71    0.78      0.33 2.48 0.077 0.313
## TotalRisk             0.66      0.66    0.80      0.28 1.92 0.113 0.313
## AbsWinRate            0.66      0.66    0.83      0.28 1.95 0.103 0.242
## RelWinRate            0.65      0.65    0.83      0.27 1.88 0.137 0.242
##
##  Item statistics
##                   r r.cor r.drop
## AnnualReturn   0.91  0.95   0.84
## ExcessReturn   0.71  0.70   0.53
## SystematicRisk 0.41  0.36   0.15
## TotalRisk      0.55  0.49   0.32
## AbsWinRate     0.55  0.44   0.31
## RelWinRate     0.57  0.44   0.34
```

4.5.9 Results Visualization

The above computations are typically sufficient to help us decide how many principal components to keep and avoid diminishing returns. The *Scree Plot* (Fig. 17) provides additional visualization to help with this decision.

```
fa.parallel(pca,n.obs=252, fm="pa", fa="pc")

## Parallel analysis suggests that the number of factors =  NA  and the number of comp
onents =  2
```

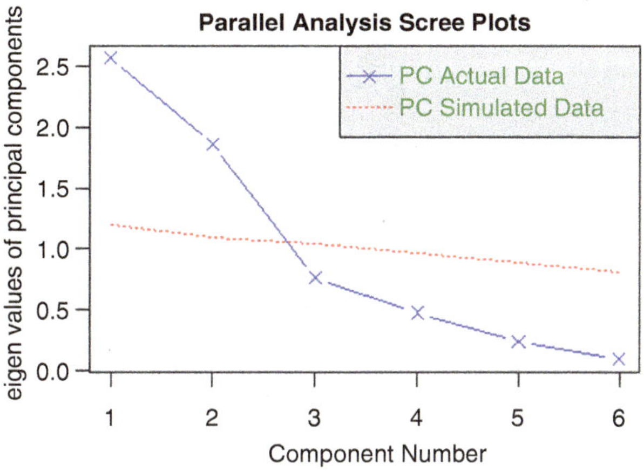

Fig. 17 Scree plot—notice the components before the bend

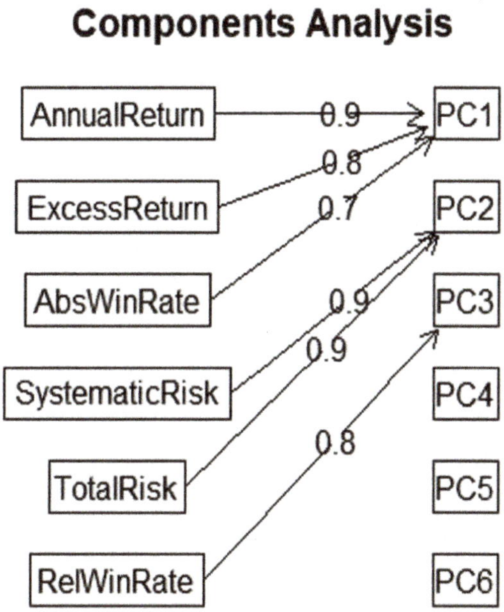

Fig. 18 The component structure of PCA

The Scree plot suggests that the first two components are sufficient. We will corroborate that assessment, by plotting the component structure of the PCA model with 6 components (Fig. 18).

```
fa.diagram(pca6Components)
```

4.5.10 Results Interpretation

The PCA produced results that are subject to interpretations in slightly different ways by different analysts. PC1 and PC2 explained 74% of the variance, which some might consider sufficient. Others may suggest including the third one, PC3, for a combined explanation of 87% of the variance. The choice of three components is supported by the structure in Fig. 18. The choice of components is ultimately a tradeoff between computational efficiency and accuracy. In this case, we will choose the three components, because only the three of them fully map the 6 original variables. Reducing the number of variables from 6 to 3 is already a significant accomplishment. We will now compute the principal components using the first set of weights:

```
pcaDF <- data.frame(pca)     # convert pca matrix to dataframe
attach(pcaDF)                # so we can use variable names

# Coefficients below are the raw alpha values
pcscores <- 0.46*AnnualReturn + 0.59*ExcessReturn + 0.71*SystematicRisk + 0.65*TotalRi
sk + 0.66*AbsWinRate + 0.65*RelWinRate
pcscores <- sort(pcscores, decreasing=FALSE)

pcscores

##   [1] 0.79396 1.18968 1.25669 1.27705 1.28054 1.28185 1.28617 1.28875 1.32440
##  [10] 1.33100 1.35816 1.35954 1.36040 1.36171 1.36395 1.38909 1.38947 1.39209
##  [19] 1.40167 1.40453 1.40933 1.43811 1.43878 1.44404 1.44818 1.45103 1.45367
##  [28] 1.45812 1.45928 1.46834 1.47025 1.47548 1.47569 1.50012 1.50354 1.50916
##  [37] 1.50972 1.51537 1.51777 1.51808 1.52123 1.52256 1.53512 1.54265 1.54330
##  [46] 1.54690 1.54963 1.55129 1.55894 1.56471 1.57429 1.58444 1.58490 1.59046
##  [55] 1.59674 1.60318 1.60396 1.60411 1.60580 1.61021 1.61298 1.61584 1.62093
##  [64] 1.64051 1.64304 1.64577 1.64877 1.65143 1.65855 1.66334 1.68122 1.69103
##  [73] 1.69428 1.69514 1.70424 1.70579 1.70718 1.71091 1.71164 1.72283 1.72680
##  [82] 1.72687 1.72742 1.72955 1.73021 1.73090 1.73195 1.74065 1.74379 1.74402
##  [91] 1.74537 1.74724 1.76284 1.76642 1.77105 1.77512 1.77576 1.79250 1.79325
## [100] 1.79465 1.79503 1.79784 1.79858 1.80217 1.81370 1.81434 1.82378 1.83063
## [109] 1.84551 1.84717 1.84969 1.85424 1.85510 1.85791 1.86009 1.86993 1.87027
## [118] 1.87108 1.87304 1.88419 1.88631 1.88753 1.88786 1.89760 1.90154 1.90253
## [127] 1.90358 1.90556 1.90653 1.90802 1.90902 1.91133 1.91138 1.91584 1.91626
## [136] 1.91951 1.92247 1.92886 1.93587 1.93883 1.94557 1.94925 1.95566 1.95658
## [145] 1.95777 1.95827 1.95902 1.96873 1.97393 1.97482 1.97607 1.97619 1.99766
## [154] 2.00427 2.01213 2.01503 2.01514 2.01830 2.03133 2.03174 2.03272 2.03760
## [163] 2.04007 2.04488 2.04726 2.04819 2.05042 2.05444 2.05879 2.05899 2.06123
## [172] 2.06176 2.06305 2.06447 2.06756 2.06874 2.06986 2.07664 2.07733 2.08211
## [181] 2.08247 2.08274 2.08322 2.08533 2.08683 2.09073 2.09515 2.10007 2.10387
## [190] 2.10877 2.11295 2.12178 2.12475 2.12990 2.13005 2.13311 2.13368 2.13497
## [199] 2.14721 2.14806 2.15408 2.15450 2.15479 2.15871 2.16495 2.16511 2.17310
## [208] 2.17349 2.17470 2.18136 2.18443 2.18795 2.18993 2.19511 2.20014 2.20164
## [217] 2.20209 2.20248 2.22055 2.22862 2.23402 2.23804 2.24354 2.24449 2.25710
## [226] 2.25733 2.26490 2.26497 2.27780 2.28117 2.28778 2.29524 2.30481 2.31726
## [235] 2.31934 2.32190 2.32355 2.32581 2.34491 2.36708 2.37773 2.38525 2.38980
## [244] 2.40454 2.41363 2.44530 2.45668 2.46325 2.51566 2.52239 2.58521 2.65028
```

Since the above scores are difficult to interpret, we will convert them to a 0–100 scale.

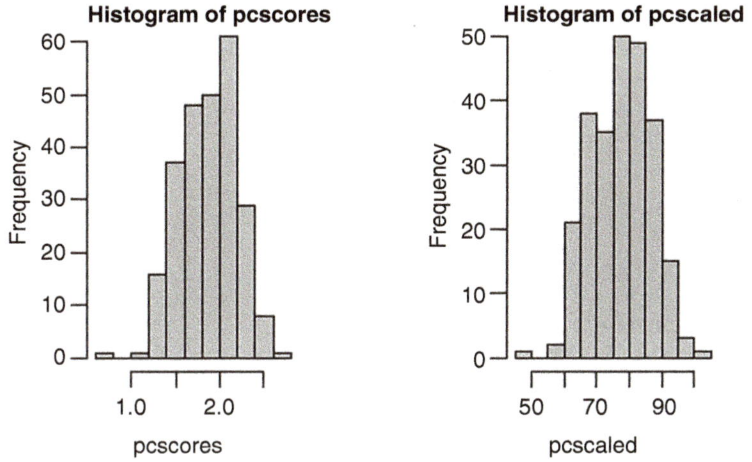

Fig. 19 Equivalence of principal component scores and scaled scores

$$s = 100/(\max - (-\min)) = 100/(2.65028-(-0.79396)) = 29.034$$

$$m = 0-(\min \times s) = -(0.79396 \times 29.034) = 23.052$$

```
pcscaled <- 23.052 + 29.034*pcscores
round(pcscaled,2)

##   [1]  46.10  57.59  59.54  60.13  60.23  60.27  60.39  60.47  61.50  61.70
##  [11]  62.48  62.52  62.55  62.59  62.65  63.38  63.39  63.47  63.75  63.83
##  [21]  63.97  64.81  64.83  64.98  65.10  65.18  65.26  65.39  65.42  65.68
##  [31]  65.74  65.89  65.90  66.61  66.71  66.87  66.89  67.05  67.12  67.13
##  [41]  67.22  67.26  67.62  67.84  67.86  67.96  68.04  68.09  68.31  68.48
##  [51]  68.76  69.05  69.07  69.23  69.41  69.60  69.62  69.63  69.67  69.80
##  [61]  69.88  69.97  70.11  70.68  70.76  70.84  70.92  71.00  71.21  71.35
##  [71]  71.86  72.15  72.24  72.27  72.53  72.58  72.62  72.73  72.75  73.07
##  [81]  73.19  73.19  73.21  73.27  73.29  73.31  73.34  73.59  73.68  73.69
##  [91]  73.73  73.78  74.23  74.34  74.47  74.59  74.61  75.10  75.12  75.16
## [101]  75.17  75.25  75.27  75.38  75.71  75.73  76.00  76.20  76.63  76.68
## [111]  76.76  76.89  76.91  76.99  77.06  77.34  77.35  77.38  77.43  77.76
## [121]  77.82  77.85  77.86  78.15  78.26  78.29  78.32  78.38  78.41  78.45
## [131]  78.48  78.55  78.55  78.68  78.69  78.78  78.87  79.05  79.26  79.34
## [141]  79.54  79.65  79.83  79.86  79.89  79.91  79.93  80.21  80.36  80.39
## [151]  80.43  80.43  81.05  81.24  81.47  81.56  81.56  81.65  82.03  82.04
## [161]  82.07  82.21  82.28  82.42  82.49  82.52  82.58  82.70  82.83  82.83
## [171]  82.90  82.91  82.95  82.99  83.08  83.12  83.15  83.35  83.37  83.50
## [181]  83.51  83.52  83.54  83.60  83.64  83.75  83.88  84.03  84.14  84.28
## [191]  84.40  84.66  84.74  84.89  84.90  84.98  85.00  85.04  85.39  85.42
## [201]  85.59  85.61  85.61  85.73  85.91  85.91  86.15  86.16  86.19  86.39
## [211]  86.47  86.58  86.63  86.78  86.93  86.97  86.99  87.00  87.52  87.76
## [221]  87.91  88.03  88.19  88.22  88.58  88.59  88.81  88.81  89.19  89.28
## [231]  89.48  89.69  89.97  90.33  90.39  90.47  90.51  90.58  91.13  91.78
## [241]  92.09  92.31  92.44  92.87  93.13  94.05  94.38  94.57  96.09  96.29
## [251]  98.11 100.00
```

We can see in the histogram (Fig. 19) the equivalence of principal component scores and scaled scores.

Instead of six variables, we need only use three. We can easily choose 50 as the threshold for assessing who is above or below average:

```
par(mfrow = c(1,2))

hist(pcscores)
hist(pcscaled)
```

4.5.11 Conclusion

We completed a tedious task, in which we successfully reduced the number of performance indicators of stocks from 6 (AnnualReturn, ExcessReturn, SystematicRisk, TotalRisk, AbsWinRate, RelWinRate) to three (PC1, PC2, PC3). Why not all statistical tests passed as robustly as a textbook would advise, we can state with a high degree of confidence that statistically significant bivariations were found. The three assumptions of PCA were successfully tested (sphericity, sample adequacy, positive determinant). PCA revealed that three variables explained 87% of the variance (review table above and Cronbach's alpha) and thus not all 6 are needed. The reader should always keep in mind that statistics is a very subjective discipline and while it is using highly accurate mathematical tools and methods, it is up to the analyst's sound judgment to interpret the results and draw conclusions.

This dataset is now ready for eventual subsequent use in a prescriptive model, benefiting from significantly improved modeling efficiency. While not a predictive or prescriptive model in itself, PCA improves the efficiency of any model, predictive or prescriptive, simply by reducing complexity. In business and finance, this means reduced cost, time for data collection, simpler models, and overall a streamlined process.

There is an abundance of literature on the use of PCA in the context of finance and business applications, which examine pinpointed problems in detail. For example, Song et al. (2019), Juneja (2014), and Bartram and Grinblatt (2021).

5 Future Research Directions

The models, methods, and code presented in this chapter should not be viewed as the definitive approach to developing computational solutions to predictive analytics problems. The reader is encouraged to use them as a springboard towards developing new models, refining existing ones, and exploring other computational tools, like the Python programming language. Every (business) scenario presents unique challenges, expectations, and constraints. Given that data, mathematics, statistics, and computer programming are fundamental to many disciplines, ranging from finance, business, engineering, and many others, it is highly recommended to apply the models presented here to disciplines outside the current scope of the reader. Doing so will help to build bridges across those disciplines and the transfer of ideas and methods, for mutual benefit.

6 Conclusion

This chapter reviewed several key models widely used today in many areas of analytics. While the chapter intended to focus on prescriptive analytics scenarios and tasks, it is important to keep in mind that real-life problems are rarely categorized as predictive or prescriptive, or in any other particular manner. Reality calls for the practitioner, researcher, or student to tap into their analytical toolset and devise mixed approaches that are tailored to the scenario at hand. For example, if one is tasked with identifying the top three portfolio management strategies, then it is most likely that the challenge consists of multiple steps, each suited to a different category of solution. One could use a data mining technique to create a set of portfolio management strategies. Then, use a classifier to categorize them into high-risk, moderate-risk, and conservative strategies. Then, one could use a recommender system to identify other managers faced with the same task and analyze their actions. Finally, the manager could employ a linear regression technique to predict the most likely outcome of pursuing several of the strategies evaluated. In the end, there is an expectation to reach a conclusion, decide, and act. There are predetermined right or wrong decisions. There are decisions that can be backed with a robust set of analytical tools and decisions made based on intuition. Knowledge of multiple methods and more importantly knowledge on when to employ a particular method is the key to successful decision-making, that is supported by sound judgment. However, one should always remember that every model and statistical metric has a value that fluctuates within an interval with a certain distribution. Therefore, it is quite possible that a model will recommend a decision with a very high level of confidence (based on past experiences) and that decision would turn out to not be the best course of action. A good analyst should always be prepared to argue the benefits of a recommendation, warn of potential adverse side effects, and prepare an alternative plan as a backup.

Acknowledgment I would like to thank all the collaborators on this book project, starting with Dr. Sinem Derindere. Within a few years, the trying times we are currently experiencing due to the COVID-19 pandemic will have faded away and be replaced by the pressing events of that day. But, in the Winter of 2020–2021, working on this project, offers a glimpse of meaning and purpose to the work we are all carrying in our respective parts of the world.

Key Terms and Definitions

Apriori algorithm	An algorithm for frequent item set mining and association rule learning over relational databases
Association Rule	A rule-based machine learning method for discovering interesting relations between variables in large databases
Bartlett's Test of Sphericity	Compares an observed correlation matrix to the identity matrix. It checks if there is a certain redundancy between the variables that we can summarize with a few number of factors.
Clique	A sub-structure in which actors are connected with each other in a particular way. Often, they are more densely connected to each other than to other members of the network.
Kaiser-Meyer-Olkin (KMO) Test	A measure of how suited the data is for factor analysis. The statistic is a measure of the proportion of variance among variables that might be common variance.
N-clique	In an undirected graph, a maximal subgraph in which every pair of vertices is connected by a path of length n or less.
Degree Centrality (of a node)	The number of links incident upon a node.
Network theory	The study of graphs as a representation of either symmetric relations or asymmetric relations between discrete objects.
Principal Component Analysis (PCA)	Principal component analysis (PCA) is the process of computing the principal components and using them to perform a change of basis on the data, sometimes using only the first few principal components and ignoring the rest.
Scree plot	A graph that shows the eigenvalues on the y-axis and the number of factors on the *x*-axis.
Sentiment Analysis	A tool that analyzes text to detect positive and negative attitudes

References

Anandarajan, M., Hill, C., & Nolan, T. (2019). *Practical text analytics* (1st ed.). Springer.

Baker, H. K., Kumar, S., & Pattnaik, D. (2020). Twenty-five years of the Journal of Corporate Finance: A scientometric analysis. *Journal of Corporate Finance*, 101572.

Bali, R., Sarkar, D., & Sharma, T. (2017). *Learning social media analytics with R: Transform data from social media platforms into actionable business insights*. Packt.

Bartram, S. M., & Grinblatt, M. (2021). Global market inefficiencies. *Journal of Financial Economics, 139*(1), 234.

Binu, D., & Rajakumar, B. R. (2021). *Artificial intelligence in data mining: Theories and applications* (1st ed.). Academic Press.

Blokdyk, G. (2021). *Principal component analysis a complete guide*. 5STARCooks.

Cheng, X., & Zhao, H. (2019). Modeling, analysis and mitigation of contagion in financial systems. *Economic Modelling, 76*, 281–292.

Crane, H. (2018). *Probabilistic foundations of statistical network analysis* (1st ed.). CRC Press.

Cranmer, S. J., Desmarais, B. A., & Morgan, J. W. (2021). *Inferential network analysis (Analytical methods for social research)*. Cambridge University Press.

Falk, K. (2019). *Practical recommender systems* (1st ed.). Manning.

García-Medina, A., Sandoval, J. L., Bañuelos, E. U., & Martínez-Argüello, A. M. (2018). Correlations and flow of information between the New York Times and stock markets. *Physica A: Statistical Mechanics and Its Applications, 502*, 403–415.

Hájek, P. (2018). Combining bag-of-words and sentiment features of annual reports to predict abnormal stock returns. *Neural Computing & Applications, 29*(7), 343–358.

Hiremath, S., Manjula, S. H., & Venugopal, K. R. (2021). *Efficient techniques for sentiment analysis from social media data*. LAP LAMBERT.

Jockers, M. (2020, November 24). Introduction to the Syuzhet package. Retrieved December, from https://cran.r-project.org/web/packages/syuzhet/vignettes/syuzhet-vignette.html

Juneja, J. (2014). Term structure estimation in the presence of autocorrelation. *North American Journal of Economics and Finance, 28*, 119–129.

Karpio, K., Łukasiewicz, P., Orłowski, A., & Ząbkowski, T. (2013). Mining associations on the Warsaw Stock Exchange. *Acta Physica Polonica, A, 123*(3), 553–559.

Kumar, P. P., Vairachilai, S., Potluri, S., & Mohanty, S. N. (2021). *Recommender systems: Algorithms and applications*. CRC Press.

Liao, S.-H., & Chou, S.-Y. (2013). Data mining investigation of co-movements on the Taiwan and China stock markets for future investment portfolio. *Expert Systems With Applications, 40*(5), 1542–1554.

Liu, B. (2015). *Sentiment analysis (mining opinions, sentiments, and emotions)* (1st ed.). Cambridge University Press.

Naik, G. R. (2018). *Advances in principal component analysis: Research and development* (1st ed.). Springer.

Pan, Y., Huo, Y., Tang, J., Zeng, Y., & Chen, B. (2021). Exploiting relational tag expansion for dynamic user profile in a tag-aware ranking recommender system. *Information Sciences, 545*, 448.

Qiao, X., Liang, L., Yang, J., & Hu, Z. (2020). Intelligent recommendation method of sous-vide cooking dishes correlation analysis based on association rules mining. *International Journal of Performability Engineering, 16*(9), 1443–1450.

Ranco, G., Bordino, I., Bormetti, G., Caldarelli, G., Lillo, F., & Treccani, M. (2016). Coupling news sentiment with web browsing data improves prediction of intra-day price dynamics. *PLoS One, 11*(1), 1–14.

Samitas, A., & Kampouris, E. (2018). Empirical investigation of co-authorship in the field of finance: A network perspective. *International Review of Financial Analysis, 58*, 235–246.

Scutari, M., & Denis, J. -B. (2021). *Bayesian networks with examples in R* (2nd ed.). CRC Press.

Sharma, P., & Gera, U. (2020). *Association rules optimization using ABC algorithm with mutation*. LAP LAMBERT.

Song, Y., Berger, R., Yosipof, A., & Barnes, B. R. (2019). Mining and investigating the factors influencing crowdfunding success. *Technological Forecasting & Social Change, 148*.

Sun, Y., Fang, M., & Wang, X. (2018). A novel stock recommendation system using Guba sentiment analysis. *Personal & Ubiquitous Computing, 22*(3), 575–587.

Tanaka, M. (2021). *Principal component analysis and randomness tests for big data analysis* (1st ed.). Springer.

Tattar, P. N., Ramaiah, S., & Manjunath, B. G. (2016). *A course in statistics with R*. Wiley. ISBN-13: 9781119152729.

Venugopal, K. R., Srikantaiah, K. C., & Nimbhorkar, S. S. (2020). *Web recommendation systems* (1st ed.). Springer.

Wang, C.-S., Lin, S.-L., & Yang, H.-L. (2016). Impersonate human decision making process: an interactive context-aware recommender system. *Journal of Intelligent Information Systems, 47*(2), 195.

Wang, J., Xie, Z., Li, Q., Tan, J., Xing, R., Chen, Y., & Wu, F. (2019). Effect of digitalized rumor clarification on stock markets. *Emerging Markets Finance & Trade, 55*(2), 450–474.

Yang, W., & Koshiyama, A. S. (2019). Assessing qualitative similarities between financial reporting frameworks using visualization and rules: COREP vs. pillar 3. *Intelligent Systems in Accounting, Finance & Management, 26*(1), 16–31.

Zumel, N., & Mount, J. (2019). *Practical data science with R* (2nd ed.). Manning.

Forecasting Returns of Crypto Currency: Identifying Robustness of Auto Regressive and Integrated Moving Average (ARIMA) and Artificial Neural Networks (ANNs)

Sudhi Sharma and Indira Bhardwaj

Abstract The stylized fact of time series is heterogeneity means unequal variance which makes the time series data peculiar and challenging to forecast. The presence of heterogeneity makes the series non-stationary. Predicting such a volatile series requires making series first to be stationary. Investors are specifically interested in prediction prices of asset class that are of time series in nature. Besides, volatility another stylized fact that has been perceived in majority of time series that is time series is auto regressive in nature. Henceforth Auto Regressive Integrated Moving Average (ARIMA) is one of the popular techniques in forecasting time series. Auto Regressive models have been applied on stationary time series and machine learning models provides added advantage over and above econometric models, that are based not based on any assumptions. To mitigate the complexity of AR models, the machine learning models have developed for forecasting of time series. Artificial Neural Networks (ANNs) have been used widely to predict time series on the basis of past values. The study has applied both ARIMA and ANNs to predict the prices of Bitcoin. The study has found a very scant literature on Cryptocurrency and specifically Bitcoin. Thus, the chapter fills the current gap in stock of knowledge. Finally, the chapter also identified the robustness of the models and which model is the best fit for forecasting. The selection of the best suited model among these two models is based on Mean Error (ME), Mean Absolute Error (MAE), and Mean Absolute Squared Error (MASE). The results of the study concluded that ARIMA (4, 1, 1) and ANNs (3, 2) are the best suited models to forecast the prices of Bitcoin. Lastly, it has been captured that ANNs are the robust model to predict the prices.

Keywords ARIMA · ANNs · ME · MAE · MASE

S. Sharma
Apeejay School of Management, Dwarka, New Delhi, India

I. Bhardwaj (✉)
VSBS, Vivekananda Institute of Professional Studies, New Delhi, India
e-mail: indira@dsb.edu.in

S. Derindere Köseoğlu (ed.), *Financial Data Analytics*, Contributions to Finance and Accounting, https://doi.org/10.1007/978-3-030-83799-0_5

1 Background and Motivation of Study

Time series prediction is most challenging given the background of heteroskedastic volatility (see Sharma et al., 2020; Tiwari et al. ; Yadav & Sharma, 2020). The stylized fact about time series is the current prices are auto regressive in nature and volatility of time series is time invariant (Sharma et al., 2020). Henceforth, prediction of time series is always complex and is in the interest of research for investors, policy makers, and regulators. The objective of the univariate time series forecasting is to understand the past behavior and pattern, to formulate the best suited forecasting model to predict the future values of the underlying time series. Time series forecasting, henceforth means forecasting future values based on past behavior (Farooq et al., 2007). Forecasting future values of asset class helps investors to strategize their investment strategies, policy makers and regulators can take strategic decision accordingly. Forecasting of time series is completely dependent on the selection of best predictable model. Henceforth researchers are meticulously involved in finding out the robust model to predict the future values of the underlying asset. Auto Regressive Integrated Moving Average (ARIMA) has been widely accepted by the researchers to predict the future realizations of time series. It is one of the extensive acceptable forms of forecasting that is based on its own lagged values (Box & Jenkins, 1970; Cochrane, 1997; Hipel & McLeod, 1994; Yadav & Sharma, 2020; Zhang, 2003). ARIMA have p, d, and q specifications where p means AR term, d means level of differentiation, and q means MA term. AR term implies that current value of time series depends on previous values and MA term means the current values depends on lagged shock or error term. Auto regressive models are being applied on stationary time series. Time series considered to be stationarity, if the mean, variance, and covariance are constant and time invariant, i.e. not changing with time. Thus, the stationarity of the time series is the prerequisite for the application of AR models. To mitigate the peculiarity of time series, i.e. prediction of non-stationary time series, the machine learning models have been arrived. Machine learning models have been popularly used in forecasting and classification purposes. Artificial Neural Networks (ANNs) have been used extensively to even in nonlinear time series. The model is more dynamic and powerful to forecast the future values of time series. ANNs have been used extensively in various fields of social sciences in general (Tong, 1983; Zhang, 2003, 2007) and financial fields in particular, i.e. banking, investment management companies, institutional investors, etc., for forecasting and classification modeling. The uniqueness of ANNs over and above ARIMA models is that the model is data driven and is not based on any prior assumptions. This makes the model more robust and gaining popularity among practitioners to mimic future based on past values (Tong, 1983; Zhang, 2003; Zhang et al., 1998). A large amount of work has been done on various forecasting models of various asset classes. This study has used both models to predict the unique and emerging asset class that is Bitcoin, a widely used crypto currency.

The study has considered a widely traded Crypto currency, Bitcoin. Crypto currency as an emerging asset class has a strong background. The currency has erupted into a $200 billion industry, sparking a wave of global disruption (Neufeld, 2020). Crypto currency is a digital currency exchanged between investors or owners without the interventions of a third party including a bank or financial institution. Consumers remain digitally connected through a transparent digital process where the values of transactions are revealed without the identities of those conducting them. These exchanges between currencies are conducted through computer networks which act as crypto currency exchanges. These exchanges have the role of preventing the duplication of transactions and reducing digital frauds as far as possible. There are three main categories of Crypto currency which are Bitcoin, Altcoins, and Tokens. BITCOIN (BTC) was the first crypto currency, created and launched in 2009. BITCOIN is the one of the most traded digital currency. BITCOIN's release stimulated the creation of a host of other crypto currencies which were generically called "alternative coins" or "altcoins." Cryptocurrencies are the creation of technology and having no intrinsic value, thus its movement is quite stochastic. The asset is not dependent on any fundamentals of the economy thus predicting the prices is quite arduous. But in the scenario of pandemic, the currency has shown robust growth and thus investors are looking for best prediction model. Limited literature is available to predict the best suited forecasted model for Crypto currency. This chapter analyzes the most suited Model in terms of ARIMA and ANNs models to analyze and compare the robustness of models (Kihoro et al., 2004). The selection of the robust model is based on Mean Error (ME), Mean Absolute Error (MAE), and Mean Absolute Squared Error (MASE). The empirical result of the study has shown that ARIMA (4, 1, 1) is the best suited model. It means the current value depends on its own fourth lagged value, integrated at level one $I(1)$ and depends on its lagged error term. ANNs (3, 2) specification is the best suited model, where p is the input value and q is the hidden value. Lastly, ANNs are considered as the robust model to predict the future value based on ME, MAE, and MASE.

1.1 Historical Background of Bitcoin

BITCOIN was launched in 2009, followed by Litecoin in 2011. Ripple was founded in 2012 and ethereum was launched in 2015. Over a 1000 cryptocurrencies were listed in 2017 and BITCOIN reached the value of US$10,000 followed by a small correction and in July 2020 it hovered around US$9700. Recent trends in crytocurrencies as per Coindesk say that demand has increased for both BITCOIN and Etherum. Annual BITCOIN volatility was at record lows vs. equities, gold, and commodities' crude-oil kin during 2020, indicating that cryptocurrency is maturing on a risk-adjusted basis. Volatility on the benchmark crypto is thus expected to decline further. In case of investments across boundaries, it provides opportunity to the Foreign Institutional Investors (FIIs) to diversify their investments and hedge the country specific risk. Rationale of the study on Predictive Models for Cryptocurrency is explained below.

Crypto currency emerging as a hedging instrument has created a need for its accurate analysis in order to model its future returns. The scant literature on predictive models for crypto currencies provides motivation to study further and select the best suitable model according to Auto regressive and Neural networks. Finally selecting the robust model among two.

The chapter tries to explore the best predictive model to forecast the returns of BITCOIN. Two predictive models have been applied, i.e. Autoregressive Integrated Moving Average (ARIMA) model and Neural Networks (NNs) to predict the returns of BITCOIN. The predictive model has been developed and analyzed step by step, to define the better predictive model among the two on the basis of ME, MAE, and MASE.

The discussions in the chapter are based on a study. The study conducted considered the prices of BITCOIN from 01.10.2013 to 28.12.2020. The data was obtained from www.coindesk.com. R software has been used to predict the prices of Bitcoin. The analytics of time series has been done with the assistance of a variety of packages including fbasics package, tseries package, and forecast package.

2 Methods and Models Used for Analysis

2.1 Descriptive Statistics and Boxplots

The primary visualization of time series data is done through descriptive statistics with the application of R basic package in the context of understanding the mean, median, skewness, and kurtosis in data. The normality needs to be assessed for a better understanding of the pattern and shape of the currency values and returns. Box plots are also used for understanding the pattern and shape of the time series cryptocurrency data.

2.2 Random Walk Model: Augmented Dickey–Fuller Test (ADF Test)

The forecasting model conducted on time series data requires assurance of its stationarity or the non-presence of unit root. It is desirable for the forecasting model that time series is stationary. Stationary data means that mean, variance, and covariance of the series should be equal and not varying with time. If it is not stable, then the presence of unit root ($\sigma \geq 1$) is inferred where $\sigma = (1 + \beta)$. Hence the stationary data set should have rho less than 1, i.e. ($\sigma < 1$) and for this β should be less than 1 and significant at 0.05 level. The stationarity of the series has been analyzed by three versions of random walk model (RWM) that are:

$$\Delta Y_t = \beta_1 Y_{t-1} + \mu_t \tag{1}$$

$$\Delta Y_t = \alpha + \beta_2 Y_{t-1} + \mu_t \tag{2}$$

$$\Delta Y_t = \alpha + \beta_3 Y_{t-1} + \beta_4 T_{t-1}\, \mu_t \tag{3}$$

Equations (1), (2), and (3) are the three versions of RWM, i.e. without drift, with drift, and stochastic trend, respectively. Dickey–Fuller test has been used to check the stationarity. The equation of Dickey–Fuller test is:

$$\Delta Y_t = \alpha + \beta_3 Y_{t-1} + \beta_4 T_{t-1}\, \mu_t \tag{4}$$

Augmented Dickey–Fuller test analyzes the stationarity of time series by providing higher order autoregressive processes by including $\Delta yt - p$ in the Dickey–Fuller model, which improves it over the previous model. The ADF test is used for analyzing the presence of unit root in the time series. The model equation of ADF test has been mentioned hereunder that is:

$$\Delta yt = \alpha + \beta t + \gamma yt - 1 + \delta 1 \Delta yt - 1 + \delta 2 \Delta yt - 2 + \ldots \delta p \Delta yt - p \tag{5}$$

2.3 *Auto Regressive Integrated Moving Average (ARIMA)*

Future Values in time series analysis without stationarity have been forecasted using ARIMA autoregressive integrated moving average (ARIMA) model, which is an extension of autoregressive moving average (ARMA). In case the time series is not stationary, the series have to be made stationary by moving successively towards higher levels of differencing. The specification of ARIMA is in the form of *p*, *d*, *q*; where *p* is autoregressive, *d* is level of stationary, and *q* is dependency on its lagged shocks (MA). The constituents of ARIMA are AR and MA, where AR stands for Auto Regressive which depicts that the future values depend on past values, having both lead and lagged structure pattern and MA stands for Moving average which depicts regression error. ARIMA models can be estimated following the Box–Jenkins approach. Thus the ARIMA Model for cryptocurrency returns can be formulated as:

$$\begin{aligned} C(R)_t = {} & a_0 + a_1 \mathrm{Ret}_{t-1} + a_2 \mathrm{Ret}_{t-2} + \ldots a_n E_{t-n} \\ & + a_{n+1} E_{t-2} \ldots\ldots a_{n+1+m} E_{t-n+1+m} + \varepsilon t \end{aligned} \tag{6}$$

where $C(R)_t$ is Cryptocurrency Return, $\mathrm{Ret}_{t\,-\,1}$ is lagged return, and $E_{t\,-\,n}$ is the lagged error.

2.4 Artificial Neural Networks (ANNs)

Neural Networks are used by the analysts to predict wide range of time series data. It has been considered as a robust model to predict asset class on the basis of past pattern. It has been differentiated the previous models, i.e. ARIMA, as the model is data driven and there is no prior assumptions require to apply the model. The model can be applied even in non-stationary and nonlinear time series. Thus, Artificial Neural Networks (ANNs) are the most popular model to predict time series. The input that has considered in the model that is lagged values of the Bitcoin. The architecture of the ANNs has divided into three layers that are Input layer, hidden layer, and finally, output layer.

The model can be explained in simpler equation form, i.e.

$$Y_t = \alpha_0 + \sum_{j=1}^{q} \alpha_j g\left(\beta_{0j} + \sum_{j=1}^{p} \beta_{ij} y_{t-i}\right) + \varepsilon_t \tag{7}$$

where Y_t is Output or predicted value, y_{t-i} is the lagged values ($i = 1, 2\ldots p$) are the inputs. The integers p, q are the number of input of input and hidden nodes, respectively. $\alpha_j(j = 0, 1, 2\ldots, q)$ and β_{ij} ($i = 0, 1, 2, \ldots, p; j = 0, 1, 2, \ldots, q$) are the connection weights and ε_t is the random shock.

3 Empirical Analysis

The study aimed to analyze the best predictive model for crypto currency, i.e. Bitcoin. To predict the best predictive model of the currency the study has conducted univariate analysis. In univariate analysis of time series, initially ARIMA model has been applied and later Artificial Neural Networks. The section of empirical analysis has been segregated into three subsections, i.e. firstly deals with section related to Forecasting of Bitcoin through ARIMA Modeling; second section includes Forecasting of Bitcoin through Neural Networks, and the third section deals with selecting the best predictive model for the forecasting of Bitcoin.

3.1 Forecasting of Bitcoin Through ARIMA Model

This section deals with predictive modeling in the ARIMA framework. The prerequisite for the forecasting univariate time series model that the series should be stationary. For the stationary time series, the three conditions to present in the series, i.e. mean according to the time should be constant, variance should be constant, and

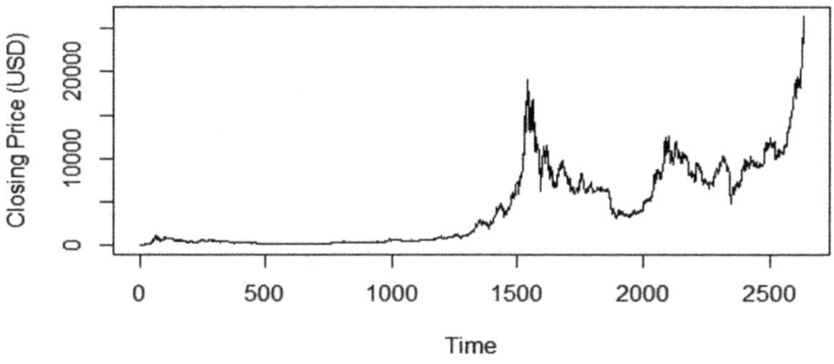

Fig. 1 Plot of Bitcoin

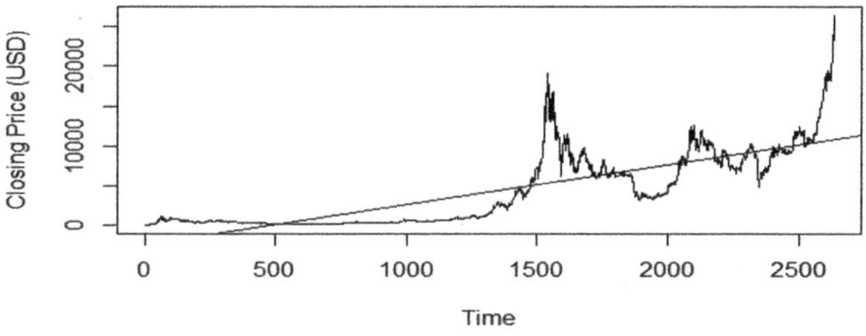

Fig. 2 Trend line on plot of Bitcoin

lastly covariance should not be changing over time. The stationary and non-stationary time series can be visualized as:

The non-stationary time series will provide spurious results and thus the coefficients of the model are unrealistic to predict future. The non-stationary time series means presence of unit root. The presence of root means there is a presence of trend. And the presence of trend in the series is bad for forecasting. For the removal of the trend in the time series detrending is suggested. That has been done through differencing. Hence for the analysis of stationarity of the time series, the preliminary step is to visualize the data through time series plot and to visualize the presence of trend the time series plot has been supported by trend line. Finally the results are analyzed by descriptive and stationarity test.

Below we have visualized the time series under study that is Bitcoin closing prices in a time series plot (see Fig. 1). Figures 1 and 2 are providing certain conclusive interpretations about stationarity of time series and presence of trend. Figure 1 is providing a very clear visualization of non-stationarity of time series and there is a presence of trend. Figure 2 is providing clear evidence of presence of increasing trend by including trend line in the time series plot.

Further the inferences have been complemented with descriptive statistics and ADF test for stationarity check. The descriptive statistics has been encapsulated in Table 1. The descriptive statistics shows 2635 numbers of realizations of time series

Table 1 Descriptive statistics

	Closing Prices _Bitcoin	Ln_Bitcoin
Nobs	2635	2635
Minimum	108.584	4.69
Maximum	26,389.29	10.18
Mean	4293.652	7.50
Median	1644.728	7.41
Sum	11,313,774.67	19,773
Variance	21,501,930.17	2.15
Stdev	4637.017	1.47
Skewness	1.126	–0.020
Kurtosis	1.028	–1.59
ADF Test:		
Dickey–Fuller Test	–0.33	–2.007
P-value	*0.989*	*0.574*

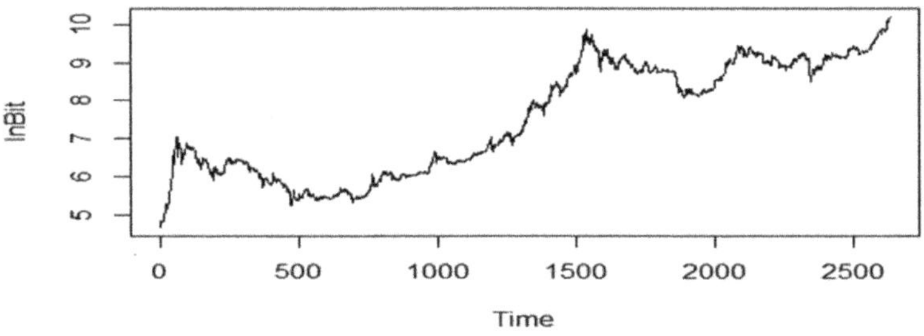

Fig. 3 Plot of Log_Bitcoin Prices

of Bitcoin. The minimum price of the currency is 108.584 and the maximum is 26,389.290. The overall distribution is positively skewed, i.e. 1.126.

It reveals that the prices are tilted towards higher side and the Augmented Dickey–Fuller test showed that the time series is non-stationary. The null hypothesis was "series is non-stationary and there is a presence of unit root." Since the p-value is greater than 0.05 thus, we could not reject the Null Hypothesis and thus it was fairly concluded that the series was non-stationary. Henceforth the preliminary assumptions of time series had been violated. The study then considered log of closing values but the log of closing prices of Bitcoin was non-stationary and was showing trend in them (see Figs. 3 and 4). Moreover, ADF test also showed the presence of unit root, as the p-value was greater than 0.05. Thus, it is an imperative to de-trend the time series of Bitcoin and thus, convert the logarithmic time series of Bitcoin in first order differencing ($Xt - Xt - 1$). Then again the study has applied plot, trend line, and finally complimenting it with descriptive statistics to understand the nature of the Log-differencing/returns data. Figure 5 gives a glimpse of log-differencing prices or returns of Bitcoin. The plot provides the evidences of stationarity of data set having constant mean over the time. Figure 6 shows the inclusion of trend line in the plot of time series. Here it is clearly seen that the overall trend is constant.

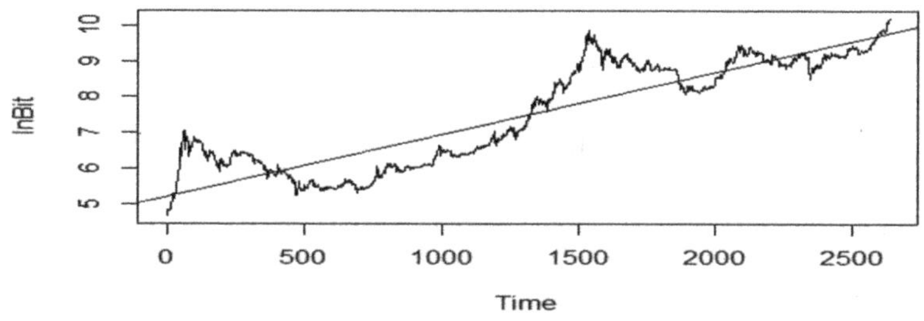

Fig. 4 Trend line on plot of Log_Bitcoin Prices

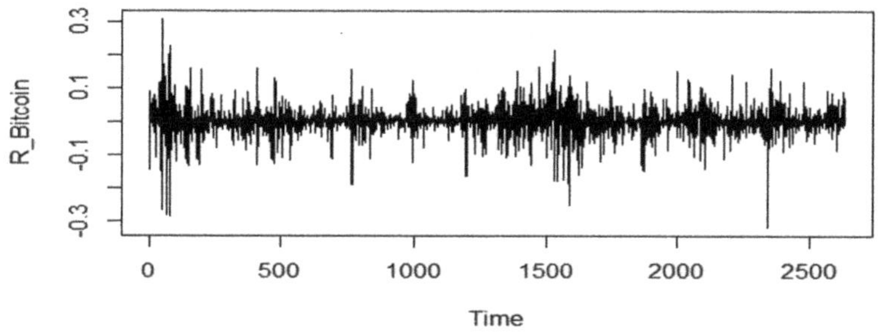

Fig. 5 Plot of Bitcoin returns

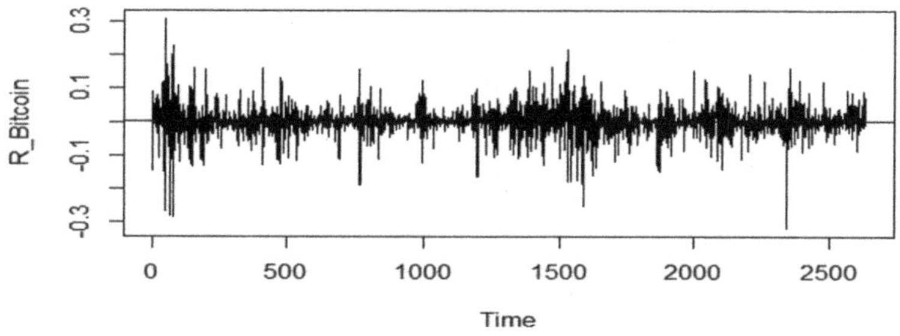

Fig. 6 Trend line on Plot of Bitcoin returns

The results are further strengthened by descriptive statistics and Augmented Dickey–Fuller Test (ADF Test). The results of descriptive and ADF test have been elaborated in Table 2. The minimum returns of Bitcoin generated over the time is –0.316, and the maximum yield is 0.306. The mean return is 0.002. The overall distribution is negatively skewed, i.e. –0.412. The ADF test reveals that the return series of Bitcoin is stationary as the coefficient of Dickey–Fuller is negative and significant at the 0.05 significance level.

Finally at this stage the Bitcoin closing prices series is stationary or integrated at level (1). Thus, the ARIMA order, i.e. *pdq*, *q* component is defining the level of differencing. Since the series is stationary at first-order difference, thus the value of *d* is 1. Now, we have to check the presence of order of ARMA, i.e. *p* and *q*. We have

Table 2 Descriptive statistics of returns of Bitcoin

	Log_Diff_Bitcoin
nobs	2634
Minimum	–0.316
Maximum	0.306
Mean	0.002
Median	0.001
Sum	5.363
Variance	0.002
Stdev	0.042
Skewness	–0.412
Kurtosis	7.336
ADF test:	
Dickey–Fuller test	–11.71
P-value	0.01

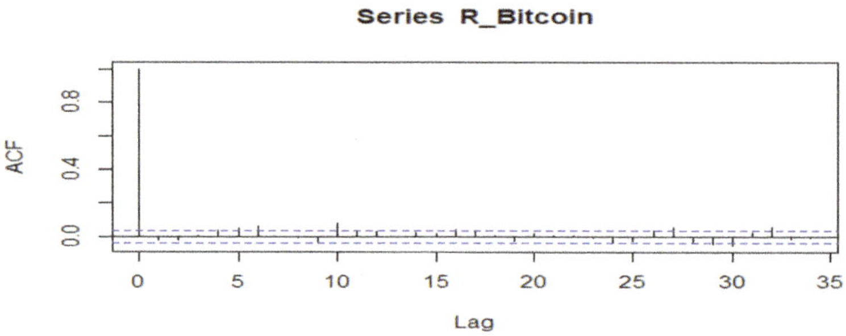

Fig. 7 Plot of ACF of Bitcoin return

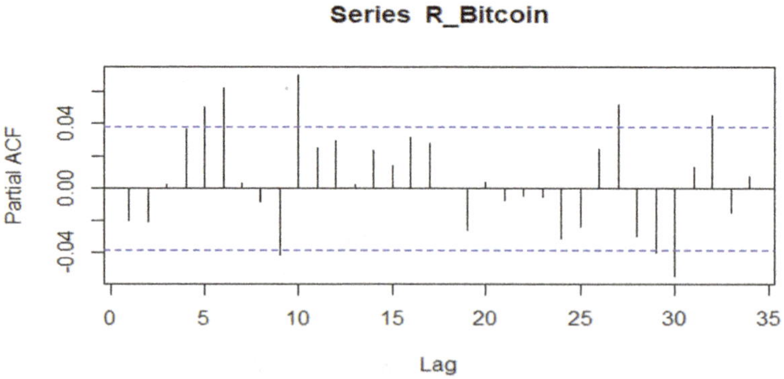

Fig. 8 Plot of PACF of Bitcoin return

to analyze whether the current values depend on its lagged values and error term, for this PACF and ACF, respectively, have to apply. The ACF and PACF plots are given in Figs. 7 and 8. Figure 7 is showing the presence of Auto correlation Function

Table 3 Best fit ARIMA order for Bitcoin

ARIMA(4, 1, 1)				
Coefficients:				
ar1	ar2	ar3	ar4	ma1
0.8445	–0.0026	0.0213	0.0408	–0.8692
s.e. 0.0591	0.0255	0.0256	0.0214	0.0562
sigma^2 estimated as 0.001812: log likelihood = 4579.59				
AIC = –9147.18 AICc = –9147.15 BIC = –9111.92				

Table 4 Robustness of the model

ARIMA(2, 1, 2)	–9139.282
ARIMA(0, 1, 0)	–9132.152
ARIMA(1, 1, 0)	–9130.256
ARIMA(0, 1, 1)	–9131.215
ARIMA(0, 1, 0)	–9128.159
ARIMA(1, 1, 2)	–9127.757
ARIMA(2, 1, 1)	–9140.538
ARIMA(2, 1, 0)	–9140.197
ARIMA(3, 1, 1)	–9149.973
ARIMA(3, 1, 0)	–9141.139
ARIMA(4, 1, 0)	–9141.858
ARIMA(5, 1, 1)	–9151.24
ARIMA(3, 1, 2)	–9137.794
ARIMA(5, 1, 0)	–9145.589
ARIMA(5, 1, 2)	–9149.651
ARIMA(4, 1, 1)	–9156.732
ARIMA(3, 1, 1)	–9150.183
ARIMA(4, 1, 0)	–9137.831
ARIMA(5, 1, 1)	–9149.659
ARIMA(3, 1, 0)	–9136.604
ARIMA(5, 1, 0)	–9142.127

(ACF) that provides the evidences of current prices dependency on previous shocks. On the one hand, Fig. 8 shows PACF, providing the evidences of current prices depend on its lagged values. Figures 7 and 8 are providing the evidences of the presence of auto correlations. The actual order of both p and q was determined later by auto.arima function.

The results of the ARIMA in the form of p,d,q have been derived from the auto arima function, the results are encapsulated in Table 3. Results shows that (4, 1, 1), is the correct form p,d,q. Where p has been elaborated that current log prices depend on its fourth lagged values and d explains integrated at first-order difference, i.e. I (1). Finally q represents that the current log prices of Bitcoin depend on its lagged error term.

The robustness of the model has been encapsulated in Table 4. The best order of pdq has been represented by order (4, 1, 1), as this order is representing the least

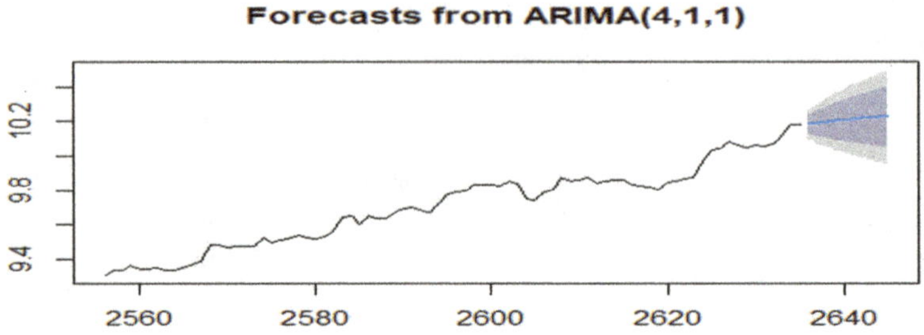

Fig. 9 The forecasts from ARIMA (4,1,1)

Table 5 Result of ANNs

Series: Closing price (USD)
Model: NNAR(3,2)
Call: nnetar(y = 'Closing Price (USD)')
Average of 20 networks, each of which is
3-2-1 network with 11 weights
options were - linear output units
sigma^2 estimated as 78151

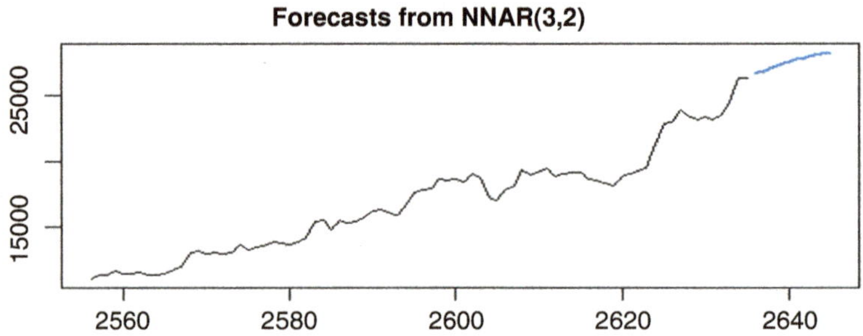

Fig. 10 Forecast from ANNs (3, 2)

Akaike Information Criterion (AIC) value, i.e. –9156.732. The forecasting plot of the model has been shown in Fig. 9.

3.2 *Forecasting of Bitcoin Through ANNs*

Below is the best predictive model of ANN to forecast the prices of Bitcoin and the order of p,q is (3,2). The result of the model is shown in Table 5 and in Fig. 10 the forecasting model through ANNs has been shown for next 10 days.

Table 6 Robustness of ARIMA (4, 1, 1) and ANNs (3, 2)

Criterion	ARIMA (4, 1, 1)	ANNs (3, 2)
ME	0.001517854	–0.7419537
MAE	0.02707254	–0.8451785
MASE	–0.001571626	–1.005213

3.3 Robustness Models Applied

In this section the best predictable model among ARIMA and ANNs has been evaluated on the basis of criterion that is Mean Error (ME), Mean Absolute Error (MAE), and Mean Absolute Squared Error (MASE). According to the results encapsulated in Table 6, it has been captured that ANN is the robust model to predict the prices of Bitcoin.

4 Conclusion

The chapter deals with the prediction of the most traded currency, i.e. Bitcoin. The study has applied two models that are Auto Regressive Integrated Moving Average (ARIMA) and Artificial Neural Networks (ANNs). The empirical results of the study has shown that ARIMA (4, 1, 1) is the best suited model. It means the current value depends on its own fourth lagged value, integrated at level one I (1) and depends on its lagged error term. ANNs (3, 2) is the best suited model, where p is the input value and q is the hidden value. Lastly, ANNs are considered as the robust model to predict the future value based on ME, MAE, and MASE.

The chapter deals with the prediction of the most traded currency, i.e. Bitcoin. The study has applied two models that are Auto Regressive Integrated Moving Average (ARIMA) and Artificial Neural Networks (ANNs). The empirical results of the study has shown that ARIMA (4, 1, 1) is the best suited model. It means the current value depends on its own fourth lagged value, integrated at level one I (1) and depends on its lagged error term. ANNs (3, 2) is the best suited model, where p is the input value and q is the hidden value. Lastly, ANNs are considered as the robust model to predict the future value based on ME, MAE, and MASE.

Relevance of the Chapter in the Financial World
This chapter thus aims to identify the potential of crypto currency as an investment alternative stability and price increase as the parameters for assessment.

References

Box, G. E. P., & Jenkins, G. (1970). *Time series analysis, forecasting and control*. Holden-Day.
Cochrane, J. H. (1997). *Time series for macroeconomics and finance*. Graduate School of Business, University of Chicago, Spring.

Farooq, T., Guergachi, A., & Krishnan, S. (2007). Chaotic time series prediction using knowledge based Green's Kernel and least-squares support vector machines. *Systems, Man and Cybernetics, ISIC, 7*, 373–378.

Hipel, K. W., & McLeod, A. I. (1994). *Time series modelling of water resources and environmental systems*. Elsevier.

Kihoro, J. M., Otieno, R. O., & Wafula, C. (2004). Seasonal time series forecasting: A comparative study of ARIMA and ANN models. *African Journal of Science and Technology (AJST) Science and Engineering Series, 5*(2), 41–49.

Sharma, S., Aggarwal, V., & Yadav, M. P. (2020). Comparison of linear and non-linear GARCH models for forecasting volatility of select emerging countries. *Journal of Advances in Management Research*. https://doi.org/10.1108/JAMR-07-2020-0152. Ahead-of-print.

Tong, H. (1983). *Threshold models in non-linear time series analysis*. Springer.

Yadav, M. P., & Sharma, S. (2020). Analyzing the robustness of ARIMA and neural networks as a predictive model of crude oil prices. *Theoretical and Applied Economics, XXVII* 2(623), 289–300.

Zhang, G., Patuwo, B. E., & Hu, M. Y. (1998). Forecasting with artificial neural networks: The state of the art. *International Journal of Forecasting, 14*, 35–62.

Zhang, G. P. (2003). Time series forecasting using a hybrid ARIMA and neural network model. *Neurocomputing, 50*, 159–175.

Zhang, G. P. (2007). A neural network ensemble method with jittered training data for time series forecasting. *Information Sciences, 177*, 5329–5346.

Report

Neufeld, D. (2020, June 13). *Report on cryptocurrency: Redefining the future of finance*. Visual Capitalist.

Part II
Machine Learning

Machine Learning in Financial Markets: Dimension Reduction and Support Vector Machine

Farshad Noravesh

Abstract The chapter focuses mainly on two aspects of machine learning. The first aspect is based on classification methods such as support vector machine (SVM) and its applications in algorithmic trading based on statistical arbitrage. The second aspect is based on dimension reduction, which is the core of many solutions for problems in modern finance since big data creates its unique challenges. To achieve this goal in this chapter, different paradigms are reviewed, and logical connections between them are mentioned. It is shown how dimension reduction techniques, as well as classification methods such as SVM, is the basis for problems such as portfolio selection and optimization, statistical arbitrage, scenario generation and algorithmic trading.

Keywords Dimension reduction · Machine learning · Financial markets · Big data · Kernel PCA · Support vector machine · Local linear mapping · MDS · Isomap · Laplacian eigenmaps · Portfolio selection · Scenario generation · Algorithmic trading · SVM · SIR · Lasso

1 Introduction

In a world full of asset classes, and each asset class contains countless assets as well as long historical data, the challenges of Big Data arrises. For example, in 2019, there are more than 2096 ETF in the USA. Thus this big data creates new challenges on traditional approaches in both asset management and algorithmic trading, and therefore classical portfolio management theories are not practical anymore and work should be done to scale these theories. In 2013, a new set of machine learning

---

Supplementary Information The online version of this chapter (https://doi.org/10.1007/978-3-030-83799-0_6) contains supplementary material, which is available to authorized users.

F. Noravesh (✉)
Datascientist at Triaset, Selangor, Malaysia

S. Derindere Köseoğlu (ed.), *Financial Data Analytics*, Contributions to Finance and Accounting, https://doi.org/10.1007/978-3-030-83799-0_6

algorithms began to rise which combine neural networks with kernel methods to reduce the dimensionality of the problem by some latent variables. These latent variables are equivalent to factors in financial literature. The author encourages the reader to contemplate why dimension reduction is philosophically so important when dealing with big data in financial markets. An example of why this could be the case would be the method of principal component regression (PCR), where before doing a regression over high-dimensional predictor space, a dimension reduction such as Principal component analysis (PCA) should be done. The problem of dimension reduction can be relaxed by the assumption that this dimension reduction is done so that the reduced model has the same effect on the output variable (response variable) as it has on the original model, and model reduction does not lose any information which is necessary to predict the output. This approach is known as sufficient dimension reduction (SDR) or sometimes known as supervised dimension reduction, since we have supervised information as well. The first known SDR algorithm is proposed by Li (1991)) known as sliced inverse regression (SIR), and later other methods try to remove its problems, such as the method of sliced average variance estimation (SAVE) or generalize it for nonlinear data by utilizing kernel trick and working on Hilbert space by an implicit mapping.

There is a zoo of dimension reduction methods in the literature, but some of the dimension reduction methods are as follows:

1. Variational auto encoder (VAE)
2. Kernel PCA
3. Local linear embedding (LLE)
4. Laplacian Eigenmaps
5. Isomaps
6. Multidimensional Scaling (MDS)
7. t-distributed stochastic neighbor embedding
8. Independent component analysis
9. Linear Discriminant Analysis
10. Latent Dirichlet allocation (LDA)
11. Maximum variance unfolding (MVU)
12. Action respecting embedding (ARE)
13. Sparse probabilistic principal component analysis
14. Supervised PCA
15. Sliced inverse regression (SIR)

Indeed, there are much more methods for dimension reduction, but in this chapter the more widely accepted methods are presented.

2 Background

In this section, some of the methods are discussed very briefly to see different paradigms of solving dimension reduction and observing that many of them are formulated as an eigenvalue problem.

Different methods of dimension reduction are classified into seven classes:

1. Projective methods: PCA, kernel PCA, independent component analysis, linear discriminant analysis, random projection
2. Nonnegative matrix factorization (NMF)
3. Manifold methods: MDS, Isomap, LLE, graphical methods
4. Methods based on neural networks: Self-organizing maps (unsupervised learning), variational autoencoder (supervised learning), generative adversarial neural networks (GANS)
5. Methods based on supervised information such as canonical correlation analysis, partial least squares, Fisher's discriminant analysis, metric learning, sufficient dimensionality reduction, kernel sliced inverse regression, Bair's supervised principal Components and kernel dimensionality reduction based on HSIC (Hilbert Schmidt independence criterion)
6. Methods which first do clustering (such as K-Means or kernel spectral clustering) or classification (such as SVM) and then apply any of the previous approaches
7. Methods based on classical statistics such as LAR (Least angle regression), Forward step regression and Lasso (Least absolute selection and shrinkage operator)

Some important algorithms in machine learning are reviewed here:

2.1 Support Vector Machine (SVM) And Kernel SVM

SVM is one of the biggest achievements in machine learning which is supervised learning for classification and is further developed by the idea of the kernel and is called kernel SVM and has a solid theory in contrast to neural networks.

The problem is to classify data into two separate zones, such as shown in Fig. 1:

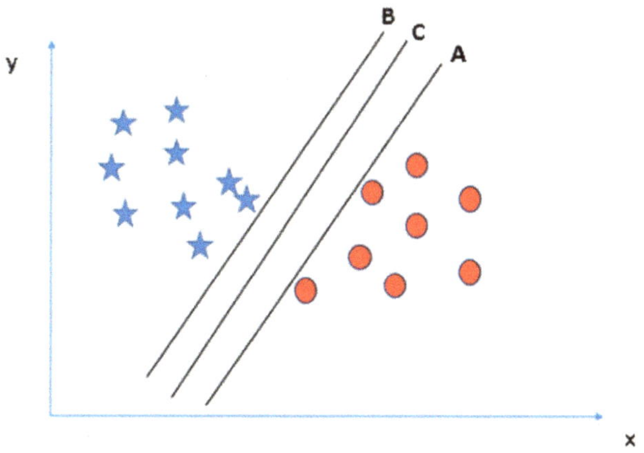

Fig. 1 Classification using support vector machine. Source: Author's Own Creation

The solution is to find a linear decision boundary that has maximum margin to these classes. Hard margin SVM is the case when data is linearly separated. Margin is defined as the distance between the closest point and the hyperplane, and it can be shown that the following minimization problem would maximize the margin:

$$\min \frac{1}{2}|\beta^2|$$

s.t $y_i(\beta^T x + \beta_0) \geqslant 1$

The Lagrangian is as follows:

$$L(\beta, \beta_0, \alpha) = \frac{1}{2}|\beta|^2 - \sum\nolimits_{i=1}^{n} \alpha_i \left[y_i\left(\beta^T x_i + \beta_0\right) - 1\right]$$

derivation with respect to β yields

$$\frac{\partial L}{\partial \beta} = \beta - \sum\nolimits_{i=1}^{n} \alpha_i y_i x_i = 0 \Rightarrow \beta = \sum\nolimits_{i=1}^{n} \alpha_i y_i x_i$$

Also, derivation with respect to β_0 yields:

$$\frac{\partial L}{\partial \beta_0} = \sum\nolimits_{i=1}^{n} \alpha_i y_i = 0$$

Instead of writing Lagrangian in terms of primal variable, it is written in terms of a dual variable.

$$L(\alpha_i) = \frac{-1}{2} \sum\nolimits_{i=1,j=1}^{n} \alpha_i \alpha_j y_i y_j x_i^T x_j + \sum\nolimits_{i=1}^{n} \alpha_i$$

This is a typical quadratic optimization problem that is easy to solve using standard python or Matlab packages or libraries.

What if the problem is not linearly separable? This is why kernel methods shine using kernel trick and mapping data to a high-dimensional space which is a Hilbert space. Thus although the problem may not be separable in the original space, but it can be separated in a higher dimensional space, and nonlinearity will be disappeared. Any function that satisfies the Mercer conditions of positive semi-definiteness can be regarded as a dot product of two points in the mapped space.

$$k\left(x_i, x_j\right) = \Phi(x_i)^T \Phi\left(x_j\right)$$

There are many types of kernels like polynomial kernel, RBF kernel, etc.

Therefore, the Lagrangian is now written as:

$$L(\alpha_i) = \frac{-1}{2}\sum_{i=1,j=1}^{n} \alpha_i \alpha_j y_i y_j k(x_i, x_j) + \sum_{i=1}^{n} \alpha_i$$

2.2 *Lasso*

The idea is popularized by Robert Tibshirani in (1996) and further developed by different approaches such as group lasso in (Yuan & Lin, 2006). The basic idea in the simplest form is minimizing a cost function having an L1 norm and a regularization parameter. When this parameter is zero, it is reduced to OLS (ordinary least square method), and when it is a high value, most of the coefficients are zero. Lasso is extremely powerful when number of features is much higher than the number of samples. A tangible application in finance is dimension reduction of S&P500 (SPX) using a small number of equities. Here the feature size is 505 and is quite big. So the method of Lasso could help in finding which equities are more responsible in tracking this well-known index. Since the problem is intrinsically of high dimension, methods of high-dimensional inference such as sample splitting, POSI (post-selection inference), data carving and randomized response are very important to reduce type I error and increase the power of test.

The selective inference is a broad topic, but the polyhedral lemma explained in (Tibshirani et al., 2014; Lee et al., 2016) is the key idea in post-selection inference. To increase the power of the test, other approaches such as randomized response have been shown to have much higher test power. Sample splitting is always the worst in terms of power since we split the data in half, and we loose power. Data carving is in the middle of POSI and randomized response in terms of the power of test.

2.3 *PCA*

PCA (principal component analysis) is a well-established method for linear dimensionality reduction. Given a set of sample vectors, $x_t \in R^d$, t = 1,. . .,*n*. The first step of PCA is to calculate the sample mean and the sample covariance matrix

$$C = \frac{1}{n}\sum_{t=1}^{n} (x_t - \overline{x})(x_t - \overline{x})^T$$

As C is a symmetric ($d \times d$)-matrix, it is possible to compute its eigenvalues $\lambda_i \in R$, and associated eigenvectors $v_i \in R^d$, i = 1,. . .,*d*, such that:

$$V^T CV = diag[\lambda_1, \ldots, \lambda_d]$$

The number of significant eigenvalues r indicates the intrinsic dimensionality of the data set. A projection of the data into the r-dimensional subspace is given by

$$y_t = V_r^T (x_t - \overline{x})$$

where V_r is the $(d \times r)$ sub-matrix of V containing the first r eigenvectors associated with the r largest eigenvalues as columns.

2.4 Kernel PCA

PCA is discussed so far, but it is, in general, not appropriate for processing data samples from nonlinear manifolds. Therefore, PCA seeks the orthogonal projection of the data onto a lower dimensional linear space such that the variance of the projected data becomes maximal. The idea is to kernelise PCA, that is, to map the data $x_1, \ldots, x_n$ to a higher dimensional space using an implicit nonlinear feature map and then apply PCA. This is the same kernel trick that is common in kernel paradigm such as the support vector machine (SVM) method where data are not linearly separable in the original space, but it becomes separable in the higher dimensional space.

A nonlinear transformation Φ(x) from the original D-dimensional feature space to an M-dimensional feature space is shown below, where usually M ≫ D

$$C = \frac{1}{n}\left(\sum\nolimits_{t=1}^{n} \Phi(x_i) - \frac{1}{n}\sum\nolimits_{t=1}^{n} \Phi(x_t)\right)\left(\sum\nolimits_{t=1}^{n} \Phi(x_i) - \frac{1}{n}\sum\nolimits_{t=1}^{n} \Phi(x_t)\right)^T$$

Its eigenvalues and eigenvectors are given by
$Cv_k = \lambda_k v_k$ where $k = 1,2,\cdots,$M.
Combining the last two equations would result:

$$\frac{1}{n}\left(\sum\nolimits_{t=1}^{n} \Phi(x_i) - \frac{1}{n}\sum\nolimits_{t=1}^{n} \Phi(x_t)\right)\left(\sum\nolimits_{t=1}^{n} \Phi(x_i) - \frac{1}{n}\sum\nolimits_{t=1}^{n} \Phi(x_t)\right)^T v_k = \lambda_k v_k$$

which can be written as:

$$\sum\nolimits_{i=1}^{n} a_{ki}\Phi(x_i)$$

Then substitution makes:

$$\frac{1}{N}\sum_{i=1}^{n}\Phi(x_i)\Phi(x_i)^T\sum_{j=1}^{n}a_{kj}\Phi(x_j) = \lambda_k\sum_{i=1}^{n}a_{ki}\Phi(x_i)$$

By defining the kernel function

$$k(x_i, x_j) = \Phi(x_i)^T\Phi(x_j)$$

and multiply both sides by $\Phi(x_l)^T$:

$$\frac{1}{N}\sum_{i=1}^{n}k(x_l, x_i)\sum_{j=1}^{n}a_{kj}k(x_j, x_i) = \lambda_k\sum_{i=1}^{n}a_{ki}k(x_l, x_i)$$

Thus

$$Ka_k = \lambda_k N a_k$$

and the resulting kernel principal components can be calculated using:

$$y_k(x) = \Phi(x)^T v_k = \sum_{i=1}^{N}a_{ki}K(x, x_i)$$

2.5 *Probabilistic PCA*

PCA is very sensitive to missing data and nonlinearity (Tipping & Bishop, 1999). It is the first attempt to formulate PCA in a probabilistic framework which sheds new light on future progress on PCA and, more generally probabilistic dimension reduction.

Consider the following factor model where t is d-dimensional observation vector and x is an unobserved (latent) q dimensional vector:

$$t = Wx + \mu + \epsilon \quad x \sim N(0, I)$$

where ϵ is a noise modeled by a Gaussian $\epsilon \sim N(0, \Psi)$ and μ is a parameter vector to permit the model to have non-zero mean.

It is easy to show that t is the following Gaussian:

$$t \sim N(\mu, WW^T + \Psi)$$

The use of the isotropic Gaussian noise model $N(0, \sigma^2 I)$ for ϵ implies that the **x**-conditional probability distribution over **t**-space is given by

$$t \vee x \sim N\left(Wx + \mu, \sigma^2 I\right)$$

The marginal distribution for the observed data t is readily obtained by integrating out the latent variables and is likewise Gaussian:

$$t \sim N(\mu, C)$$

where $C = WW^T + \sigma^2 I$ is the covariance matrix and is of size $d \times d$. The log-likelihood function is then

$$L = \frac{-N}{2}\left\{dln(2\pi) + ln\,|C| + tr\left(C^{-1}S\right)\right\}$$

where S is sample covariance matrix of observations t given by

$$S = \frac{1}{N}\sum\nolimits_{n=1}^{N}(t_n - \mu)(t_n - \mu)^T$$

The maximum likelihood estimator for μ is the mean of data while estimates for W and σ^2, can be obtained by iterative maximization of L by any method such as Expectation Maximization (EM) algorithm. It is important that the conditional distribution of x can be calculated using Bayes's rule and is Gaussian as well.

$$x \vee t \sim N\left(M^{-1}W^T(t - \mu), \sigma^2 M^{-1}\right)$$

where M is of size $q \times q$ and is defined as

$$M = W^T W + \sigma^2 I$$

It is easily shown in (Tipping & Bishop, 1999) that the likelihood is maximized when

$$w_{ML} = U_q\left(\Lambda_q - \sigma^2 I\right)^{1/2} R$$

where the q columns in U_q are principal eigenvectors of S with corresponding eigenvalues in the diagonal matrixΛ_q.

It can be shown that the maximum likelihood estimator for σ^2 is given by

$$\sigma_{ML}^2 = \frac{1}{d - q}\sum\nolimits_{j=q+1}^{d}\lambda_j$$

2.6 Sliced Inverse Regression (SIR)

As explained in the introduction, the problem of sufficient dimension reduction is finding minimal subspace that, when conditioned on that, does not lose any information that is essential for the response variable. The first historical attempt to solve sufficient dimension reduction is done by Li (1991)).

Assumption 1 *Let* $\beta \in R^{p \times d}$ be a matrix such that $span(\beta) = \varphi_{Y \vee X}$. It is assumed that $E(X \vee \beta^T X)$ is a linear function of d-dimensional random vector $\beta^T X$

Lemma Suppose $\beta^T \Sigma \beta$ is positive definite. Then

$$E\big(X - E(X) \vee \beta^T X\big) = P_\beta^T(\Sigma)[X - E(X)]$$

Theorem 1 Suppose X is square-integrable and $\Sigma = \ var\ (X)$ is nonsingular. Then, under Assumption 1

$$\Sigma^{-1}(E(X \vee Y) - E(X)) \in \varphi_{Y \vee X}$$

The proof of Lemma and Theorem above are given in (Li, 1991). The following Corollary is the base of SIR to find the central subspace.

Corollary Under the assumption of Theorem 1,

$$span\big(\Sigma^{-1} cov(E(X \vee Y))\Sigma^{-1}\big) \subseteq \varphi_{Y \vee X}$$

In order to use the above corollary, let Λ_{SIR} denote the matrix $cov(E(X \vee Y))$.The column space of $\varphi_{SIR} = span(\Sigma^{-1} \Lambda_{SIR} \Sigma^{-1})$ can be used to recover central subspace. φ_{SIR} is spanned by the set of eigenvectors $\{v : \Lambda_{SIR} v = \lambda \Sigma v, \lambda > 0\}$ in the general eigenvalue problem.

Given the response variable Y and the predictors X(explanatory variables), the SIR algorithm proceeds as follows:

1. Divide Y in h slices and compute $\widehat{p}_j = \frac{1}{n} \sum_{i=1}^{n} I\left[y_i \in s_j\right]$ where I is the indicator function where $p_j = P(Y \in s_j)$

$$\text{Compute } \widehat{m_j} = \frac{1}{n\widehat{p}_j} \sum_{i=1}^{n} x_i I\left[y_i \in s_j\right]$$

2. Obtain the sample covariance matrix $\widehat{\Lambda}_{SIR} = \sum_{j=1}^{h} \widehat{p}_j \left(\widehat{m_j} - \widehat{\mu}\right)\left(\widehat{m_j} - \widehat{\mu}\right)^T$ where $\widehat{\mu}$ denotes the sample mean of x.

A principal component analysis is then applied to $\widehat{\Lambda}$. To extract the eigenvectors related to the *k* highest eigenvalues that are spanning the so-called effective dimension reduction (e.d.r) space.

2.7 Multidimensional Scaling (MDS)

Multidimensional scaling, sometimes known as Principal Coordinates Analysis (PCoA), is a statistical technique originating in psychometrics. The data used for multidimensional scaling (MDS) are dissimilarities between pairs of objects.

The main objective of MDS is to **represent these dissimilarities as distances between points in a low-dimensional space** such that the distances are related as **closely as possible** to the dissimilarities.

The classical algorithm is as follows:

1. Given a matrix D with dimensionality m, calculate for matrix X with the reduced dimension p.
2. From D, compute matrix B by applying a centering matrix to D.
3. Determine the largest eigenvalues and corresponding eigenvectors of matrix B with respect to p.
4. Get the square root of the dot product of the matrix of eigenvectors and the diagonal matrix of eigenvalues of B.

2.8 Laplacian Eigenmaps

The key idea is to preserve only local information, and it is topologically preserving method rather than a distance preserving method. Laplacian Eigenmaps is a subclass of Kernel Eigenmap Method such as kernel PCA. The Original method in (Belkin, 2003) is very interesting. However, when applying it to some real-world data, several limitations have been applied, such as uneven data sampling, out-of-sample problem, small sample size, discriminant feature extraction and selection, etc. Given a set $x_1, x_2, \ldots, x_k$ of k points in R^l, find a set of points $y_1, y_2, \ldots, y_k$ in R^m (m < <l) such that y_i represents x_i. Now assume $x_1, x_1, x_2, \ldots, x_k \in M$ and M is a Manifold embedded in R^l.

First a weighted graph with k nodes is constructed with a set of edges connecting neighboring points, one for each point. Then embedding a map is then provided by computing the eigenvectors of the graph Laplacian. The procedure is stated below:

1. Step 1 (constructing the adjacency graph) put an edge between any two nodes if they are close. There are two variations: (a) ε-neighborhoods. Nodes i, j are connected by an edge if $\|x_i - x_j\|^2 < \varepsilon$ This has geometric motivation. (b) Nodes *i*, *j* are connected by an edge if *i* is among *n* nearest neighbors of *j* or *i* is among *n* nearest neighbors of *j*.
2. Step 2 Choosing the weights. Here as well, there are two variations for weighting the edges. (a) Heat kernel. If nodes *i*, *j* are connected $W_{ij} = e^{\frac{-\|x_i - x_j\|^2}{t}}$ otherwise zero. (b) simple minded: $W_{ij} = 0$.

3. Step 3 Eigenmaps. Assume the graph G, constructed above, is connected. Otherwise, proceed with step 3 for each connected component. Compute eigenvalues and eigenvectors,

$$Lf = \lambda Df$$

where D is diagonal weight matrix and, $D_{ii} = \sum_j w_{ji}$, $L = D - W$ is the laplacian matrix which is symmetric, positive definite matrix. Let $f_0, f_1, \ldots, f_{k-1}$ be the solutions of eq. 1, ordered according to their eigenvalues:

$$\begin{aligned} Lf_0 &= \lambda Df_0 \\ Lf_1 &= \lambda Df_1 \\ &\ldots \\ Lf_{k-1} &= \lambda Df_{k-1} \end{aligned}$$

$$0 = \lambda_0 \leq \lambda_1 \leq \ldots \leq \lambda_{k-1}$$

Leaving out the first eigenvalue, which is zero and use the next m eigenvectors for embedding in m-dimensional Euclidean space:

$$x_i \to (f_1(i), \ldots, f_m(i))$$

2.9 *Local Linear Embedding*

LLE was originally introduced in (Roweis & Saul, 2000). The LLE algorithm has interesting geometric intuitions. Thus, each data point and its neighbors lie on or close to a locally linear patch of the manifold. The local geometry of these patches is characterized by linear coefficients that reconstruct each data point from its neighbors. The following cost function measures reconstruction errors like this:

$$\varepsilon(W) = \sum_i \left| \overrightarrow{X_i} - \sum_j W_{ij} \overrightarrow{X_j} \right|^2$$

To avoid trivial zero solution for this cost function, the following constraint is defined:

$$\sum_j W_{ij} = 1$$

The flexibility of this method comes from the fact that any particular data point is invariant to rotations, rescalings, and translations of that data point and its neighbors. It follows symmetry that the reconstruction weights characterize intrinsic geometric properties of each neighborhood.

In the final step of the algorithm, each high-dimensional observation X is mapped to a low-dimensional vector Y representing global internal coordinates on the manifold. This is originally done by choosing d-dimensional coordinates Y to minimize the cost function for the embedding:

$$\Phi(Y) = \sum_i \left| \overrightarrow{Y_i} - \sum_j W_{ij} \overrightarrow{Y_j} \right|^2$$

By fixing weights, this optimization problem would be solved for Y.

3 Dimension Reduction in Financial Markets

The main focus on this chapter is explaining how dimension reduction can be applied to Finance. Dimension reduction could be regarded as the first building block of any quantitative analysis such as portfolio optimization or algorithmic trading since it helps in managing complex high-dimensional data systematically and makes it more scalable. Since Financial Markets are highly nonlinear, the simple linear approaches such as PCA may not be a good solution to represent the nonlinear structure of these markets, and therefore nonlinear approaches such as kernel PCA and LLE are used in practice.

3.1 Modern Portfolio Optimization

Dimension reduction can be very useful in portfolio optimization methods such as Markowitz which is based on minimum variance. As there are countless assets, the combination of assets to invest is very big and so the decision for the rate of asset allocation is quite challenging. Although contemporary dimension reduction methods are very strong and useful, but there are very few applications like (Tayali & Tolun, 2018) in portfolio optimization methods. Nonnegative matrix factorization (NMF) method could be used since prices are not negative, but their reduction is only on time since the daily price series is huge and can be reduced to a lower time dimension to capture long time dynamics. Another perspective that can be useful for portfolio management is to hedge or immunize a portfolio against moves in the principal components. For example, suppose the goal is to hedge the value of a portfolio against movements in the first k principal components.

It is very known that factor models play an important role in financial models. An example could be the capital asset pricing model (CAPM):

$$r_i = r_f + \beta_i R_M + \varepsilon_i, E(\varepsilon_i) = 0$$

Or the general arbitrage pricing theory model (APT)

$$r_i = \alpha_i + \beta_{1i} F_1 + \ldots + \beta_{ni} F_n + \varepsilon_i$$

Which represents the return of ith risky asset as a linear combination of n risk factors including a constant risk term and an error term. The constant term is riskless and is not influenced by variable risk factors. The betas are called factor sensitivities or factor exposures and are a measure of how sensitive the risky asset is to the known factor. The alpha and betas can be estimated using the ordinary least square method or the lasso method if the number of risk factors is very big.

Sometimes these factors are heuristics such as interest rates or factors in Fama-French Model, which are very tangible in economics. On the other hand, factors can be obtained using PCA without the goal of having a tangible explanation or description. The essence of these principal components will be well understood by introducing the paradigm of risk parity (Aanonsen, 2016). used conditional value at risk as a risk measure and took advantage of the risk parity paradigm and principal component analysis to form a factor model to get the entire return distribution. Risk Parity (RP) is an asset allocation strategy that allocates the weights according to asset classes risk contributions.

The most well-known approach to RP is Equal Risk Contribution Strategy (ERC). The methodology of (Roncalli, 2013) is reviewed. The failure of mean-variance strategy due to estimation errors in the estimated mean lead to researchers and investors to use risk-based strategies that do not have to estimate the expected mean, but only the covariance structure. Therefore, strategies like ERC are generally accepted as robust in the literature due to their good performance over the 2008 financial crisis period, and many Hedge Fund rely on that for its maturity and rigorous theory and, it is highly related to ideas of machine learning in terms of both dimension reduction and classification. Variance is the most popular risk measure due to its computational simplicity and easy interpretation.

Given $\sigma^2(w)$ is the portfolio variance, then

$$\sigma^2(w) = w' \Sigma w$$

Definition Let w be the vector of asset weights and $\sigma(w)$ be the portfolio risk measure, then the marginal risk contribution of the ith asset is the first derivative of the risk measure with respect to its weight

ω_i such that:

$$MRC_i(w) = \frac{\partial \sigma(w)}{\partial \omega_i}$$

MRC gives an infinitesimal change in the whole portfolio risk caused by the *i*th component.

Definition Let σ(**w**) be the portfolio's risk measure. Then the risk contribution of the *i*th component, $RC_i(w)$ is:

$$RC_i(w) = \omega_i MRC_i(w)$$

So, the marginal and total risk contributions of the asset i become

$$MRC_i = \frac{(\Sigma w)_i}{\sqrt{w^T \Sigma w}}$$

$$TRC_i = \omega_i \frac{(\Sigma w)_i}{\sqrt{w^T \Sigma w}}$$

Suppose, there are n asset classes and set the risk budgets $(b_1, b_2, \ldots, b_n)$ and targeted risk contributions are $(TRC_1, TRC_2, \ldots, TRC_n)$ to general risk measure R.

Then the risk budgeting portfolio is given as;

$$TRC_1(\omega_1, \omega_2, \ldots, \omega_n) = b_1$$

$$TRC_2(\omega_1, \omega_2, \ldots, \omega_n) = b_2$$

...

$$TRC_n(\omega_1, \omega_2, \ldots, \omega_n) = b_n$$

Thus, the optimization problem is

$$w_{RB} = argmin \sum_{i=1}^{n} \left(\omega_i \frac{\partial R(w)}{\partial \omega_i} - b_i R(w) \right)^2$$

$$= argmin \sum_{i=1}^{n} \left(\omega_i (\Sigma w)_i - b_i w^T \Sigma w \right)^2$$

subject to the following constraints:

$$\sum_{i=1}^{n} \omega_i = 1, \sum_{i=1}^{n} b_i = 1, \omega_i, b_i \geqslant 0$$

In order to explain the relationship between risk parity and dimension reduction methods such as PCA, a general information about diversified risk parity (DRP) based on the works by Meucci (2010)) is reviewed. This is a special case of risk parity (RP) employing uncorrelated portfolios as risk sources. Applying risk parity strategy to uncorrelated risk sources and maximizing the number of risk sources in a portfolio is known as "diversified risk parity strategy." The overlap of correlations between asset classes leads to poor diversification of RP strategy. Specifically, during the financial crisis, correlations increase significantly, exceeding 90% (Partovi & Caputo, 2004). uses the principal component analysis (PCA) to generate uncorrelated portfolios that are also called uncorrelated risk sources. Contrary to the RP strategy based on asset classes in the previous part, the focus is now on the RP approach that aims for diversification based on the main risk sources (risk factors) driving the asset returns (Partovi & Caputo, 2004). Uses PCA to construct the uncorrelated portfolios, called principal portfolios, which are defined below:

Definition Principal Portfolios (PP). Let Σ be an $n \times n$ covariance matrix. By Applying principal component decomposition to Σ, the relation $E^T \Sigma E = diag\ (\lambda_1, \lambda_2, \ldots, \lambda_n) = \Lambda$ is obtained which is equivalent to $E^{-T} \Lambda E^{-1} = diag\ (\lambda_1, \lambda_2, \ldots, \lambda_n) = \Sigma$. The columns of E are called principal portfolios.

Definition Principal portfolio weights (PPW). Let ω be an $n \times 1$ weight vector of the original portfolio, and E is an eigenvector matrix of covariance matrix Σ of original data. Then unique vectors $\widetilde{\omega}_{PP}$ satisfying: $\omega = E\widetilde{\omega}_{PP}$ are called principal portfolio weights.

Using simple math, it is possible to show that the return, variance of ith principal portfolio, and the total variance of the original portfolio is as follows:

$$\widetilde{r}_{PP,i} = e_i^T R$$

$$\sigma^2(\widetilde{r}_{PP,i}) = e_i^T \Sigma e_i = \lambda_i$$

$$\sigma^2(R) = \sigma^2\left(\widetilde{R}_{pp}\right) = tr(\Sigma) = \sum\nolimits_{i=1}^{n} \lambda_i = \sum\nolimits_{i=1}^{n} \sigma^2\left(\widetilde{r}_{pp,i}\right)$$

where $R = (r_1, r_2, \ldots, r_n)$ is the return of the original portfolio.

Thus, the risk contribution of each principal portfolio to total variance can be written as

$$\frac{\sigma^2\left(\widetilde{r}_{pp,i}\right)}{\sigma^2(R)} = \frac{\lambda_i}{\lambda_1 + \lambda_2 + \ldots + \lambda_n}$$

Thus, the marginal risk contribution of each principal portfolio and the risk contribution of each principal portfolio are written as follows respectively:

$$MRC_{PP} = \frac{\partial\sigma(\widetilde{R}_{PP})}{\partial\omega_i} = \frac{1}{2\sqrt{\sum_{i=1}^{n}\widetilde{\omega}_{PP,i}^2\lambda_i}} 2\widetilde{\omega}_{PP,i}\lambda_i = \frac{\widetilde{\omega}_{PP,i}\lambda_i}{\sigma(\widetilde{R}_{PP})}$$

$$\widetilde{RC}_{PP,i} = \frac{1}{\sqrt{\sum_{i=1}^{n}\widetilde{\omega}_{PP,i}^2\lambda_i}}\widetilde{\omega}_{PP,i}^2\lambda_i = \frac{\widetilde{\omega}_{PP,i}^2\lambda_i}{\sigma(\widetilde{R}_{PP})}$$

Definition Let p be a discrete probability function on given set $z_1, z_2, \ldots, z_n$ with $p_i = p(z_i)$, the entropy of p is given as

$$H = -\sum_{i=1}^{n} p_i \, log \, p_i$$

Definition Exponential entropy of the diversification distribution is defined as

$$N_{PP,Ent} = exp\left(-\sum_{i=1}^{n} p_{PP,i} \, log \, p_{PP,i}\right)$$

Applying risk parity strategy to uncorrelated portfolios and distribute the portfolio risk among uncorrelated risk sources, a diversified risk parity is obtained by allocating the risk among these risk sources uniformly and have maximum risk sources. Thus, the exponential of Shannon entropy should reach its maximum value.

Using the analogy explained so far and ideas in (Meucci, 2010), the following diversification distribution p is given.

$$p_{PP,i} = \frac{1}{\sqrt{\sum_{i=1}^{n}\widetilde{\omega}_{PP,i}^2\lambda_i}}\widetilde{\omega}_{PP,i}^2\lambda_i \quad i = 1, 2, \ldots, n$$

Definition (Diversified risk parity). If the diversification distribution is close to uniform, the strategy is called diversified risk parity.

Diversified risk parity portfolio is the solution of the following optimization problem

$$argmaxN_{PP,Ent}$$

subject to

$$\sum_{i=1}^{n} \omega_{PP,i_i} = 1$$

The full optimization code is written in (https://github.com/farshad-finance/diversified-Risk-parity, n.d.).

3.2 Scenario Generation for Portfolio Theory

Dimension reduction methods could be used for scenario generation, which can be used in both modern and post-modern portfolio theory to generate scenarios. Let $Y = (Y_1...Y_n)^T$ denote the n-dimensional random vector with variance-covariance matrix Σ. Y represents normalized changes in risk factors over some appropriately chosen time horizon. The problem is very general since any kind of risk factor can be used, such as (1) security price returns (2) returns on future contracts (3) changes in spot interest rates of varying maturities. By using any dimension reduction methods such as PCA principal components can be represented as a linear combination of the Y_i 's:

$$P_i := \sum_{j=1}^{n} W_{ij} Y_j \quad \text{for} \quad i = 1, \ldots, n$$

Thus the principal components of **Y** then given by $P = (P_1, \ldots, P_n)$ satisfies:

$$P = \Gamma^T Y$$

Γ^T is called the matrix of factor loading.

Since Γ^T is orthogonal, Y can be written as:

$$Y = \Gamma P$$

Now, if Y is the normalized variable:

$Y_{tj} = \frac{X_{tj} - \mu_j}{\sigma_j}$ where $X_t = (X_{t1}, \ldots, X_{tn})^T$ represents the date t sample observation of returns or yield changes since these observations are from a stationary distribution.

Using a simple rearrangement:

$X_t = diag\,(\sigma_1, \ldots, \sigma_n) Y_t + \mu = diag\,(\sigma_1, \ldots, \sigma_n) \Gamma P_t + \mu$, where P_t is the tth sample principal component vector.

If first k principal components explain sufficiently large amount of total variability, then may partition the $n \times n$ matrix $\mathbf{\Gamma}$ according to $\Gamma = [\Gamma_1 \Gamma_2]$ where Γ_1 is $n \times k$ and Γ_2 is $n \times (n - k)$. So

$$X_{t+1} = diag(\sigma_1, \ldots, \sigma_n) \Gamma_1 P_{t+1}^{(1)} + \mu + \epsilon_{t+1}$$

where

$$\epsilon_{t+1} = diag(\sigma_1, \ldots, \sigma_n) \Gamma_2 P_{t+1}^{(2)}$$

Suppose today is date t, and the goal is generating scenarios over the period $[t, t + 1]$. By applying stress to the above equation, loss scenarios are generated easily.

This method is not scalable for large assets such as large stocks. To organize the stocks in clusters it is common to use a distance metric, between, for example, stock i and j. This clustering idea is also helpful if one is interested to calculate value at risk or any other calculation on large-scale data. Therefore what happens in practice is to utilize clustering methods such as K-Means or spectral clustering and then apply dimension reduction over that. So problems such as large variance-covariance matrix are handled properly. Assume the closing prices for five stocks; Bank of America (BAC), Citibank (C), J.P. Morgan (JPM), Apple (APPL) and Amazon (AMZN) are given. To cluster these stocks based on their correlation with the complete linkage clustering method, calculation of each pair's correlation, ρ_{ij} is done. By defining the following metric, which is a distance between any two stocks, It is now possible to merge assets that have a very high correlation and therefore having a very small distance.

$$d_{ij} = 1 - \rho_{ij}$$

Thus, the big cloud of stocks is just shrunk to their associated clusters. But the problem is still challenging since correlation coefficients describe the linearity of the reality only locally, and they change a lot, and so the clustering results changes! In reality, everything is nonlinear, and distributions have high skewness and kurtosis. In order to develop the model more, one might use the theory of random matrix to overcome the challenge of the varying covariance matrix. An alternative approach to handle nonlinearity is to use nonlinear dimension reduction methods such as kernel PCA. It can be shown that methods such as MDS, IsoMap, LLE, and laplacian Eigenmap can be seen to have a corresponding kernel, and therefore kernel PCA could unify many of these methods.

3.3 Algorithmic Trading

In order to select the most profitable candidates for pairs-trading, kernel PCA can be used to select the most dominant principal components which describe the major cause for dynamics of financial markets. So the dynamics of each ticker is projected on these principal directions. Since markets are highly nonlinear, kernel PCA can decompose these nonlinearities. To further investigate the structure of financial markets, graphical models can be used, which are the cornerstone of modern probability and machine learning. Causality is a deep topic and is deeply investigated theoretically by some of the books of Professor Judea Pearl. Of course, there are many different methodologies, such as Granger's causality, but many researchers argue that Granger's causality does not describe the intrinsic nature of causality and is subjective to the dataset.

A statistical arbitrage model about two assets classes can be expressed as follows:

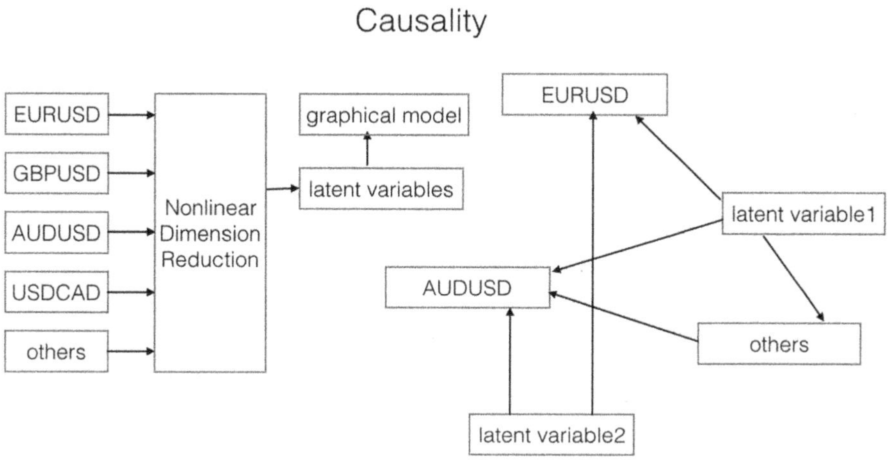

Fig. 2 The first step: dimension reduction of Forex Data. Source: Author's Own Creation

$$\frac{dP_t}{P_t} = \alpha dt + \beta \frac{dQ_t}{Q_t} + dX_t$$

X is a mean-reverting process and P_t and Q_t are respective time series for assets P and Q. Long asset P and short β dollars of stock Q for \$1-worth asset P if X is small, vice versa. In reality, things are not this much simple since mean-reversion may break down over time and hold only in some portion of trading time. To keep track of this relationship throughout the backtesting, several tests are used to constantly evaluate the behaviors of the pair, including the ADF test as described before, Hurst exponent that helps identify whether a time series is trending, mean-reverting, or undergoing a random walk, half-life test from the Ornstein–Uhlenbeck (OU) Process that tests for the mean-reversion speed.

A more general approach is to use dimension reduction to find some factors that have major influences and model the asset returns in terms of these factors. One of the golden achievements in machine learning is the method of support vector machines. On the other hand, methods of statistical arbitrage are very well known among quantitative analysts in investment companies such as Hedge Funds. Here a novel hybrid algorithm is revealed that has got an accuracy of 86% in backtest and 75% accuracy during live Forex Trading.

The first step in algorithmic trading in Forex is illustrated in Fig. 2. As the picture shows, the original space has many variables such as Forex Data, but other variables such as the daily return of Gold and Oil should also be considered, although they have correlations with AUDUSD and USDCAD, respectively. In practice, eight variables are used in the original space, and the reduced space has a dimensionality of only 3, which corresponds to the 3 biggest eigenvalues. The dimension of the data is reduced, and the second step would be the usage of the kernel SVM to do supervised learning to label each point of the factor space as either buy, sell, or

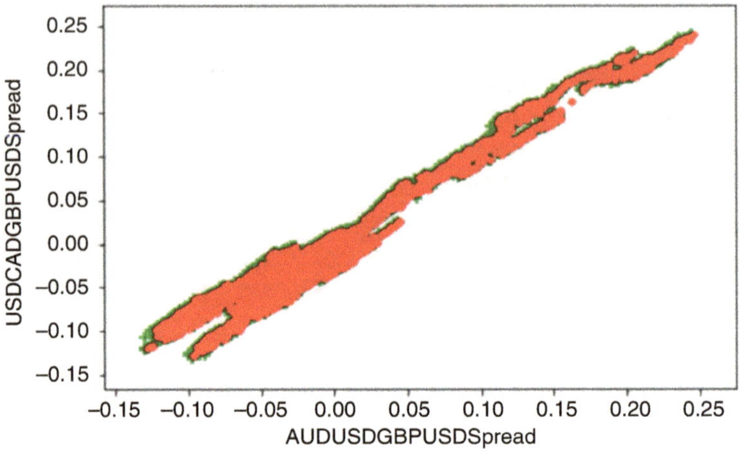

Fig. 3 Regression for spread of USDCAD-GBPUSD and AUDUSD-GBPUSD. Source: Author's Own Creation

DoNothing on the H1 time frame since higher timeframes have low accuracy in SVM. The reason that small times frames such as H1 and M1 have better performance is that inefficiencies of very liquid financial markets such as Forex are easier to capture in these time frames rather than higher time frames such as D1,W1, or higher time frames. So Hedge funds and algorithmic traders can take advantage of these inefficiencies and make money. The following pictures show the classification of data for two-time frames namely H1 and H4 and their associated signal that are taken from historical data. These data are fed up to the SVM classifier to find the classifier and predict out-of-sample data (Figs. 3, 4, 5, 6).

Data is divided into training data and test data to distinguish between sample error and out-of-sample error.

Ordinary PCA showed bad results due to the nonlinearity nature of financial markets.

Gaussian Kernel showed the accuracy of 86.23% during backtesting for out-of-sample test, which was highest among different kernels such as polynomial, Gaussian.

The author summarizes the final algorithm in Fig. 7:

The backtesting accuracy of H1 and H4 timeframes are compared (Fig. 8):

The complete Python code is provided in (https://github.com/farshad-finance/SVM-Forex, n.d.).

3.4 *Future Research Directions*

It is assumed in this chapter that the covariance matrix is constant. In real rigorous portfolio management or algorithmic trading, financial market data should be

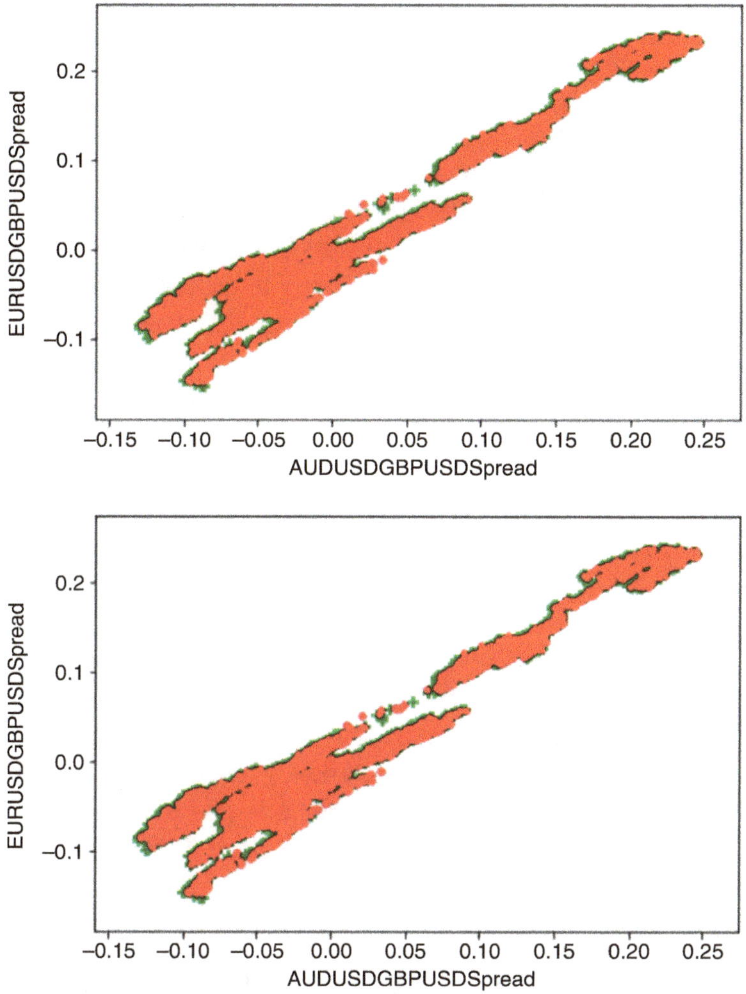

Fig. 4 Regression for spread of EURUSD-GBPUSD and AUDUSD-GBPUSD. Source: Author's Own Creation

separated in a multi-period format. The paradigm of PCA can be generalized by introducing a functional principal component which is a branch of functional data analysis. So instead of having a multivariate point, a multivariate function which is a function of time or any other variable such as inflation or GDP is given. For example, consider a 2-dimensional vector of (EURUSD, AUDUSD), and so the covariance matrix can easily be calculated. But in the functional PCA paradigm, a multidimensional function instead of a vector is given. So this vector has a different value as time, inflation, or GDP changes. The reader is encouraged to think about this dimension since it should be chosen such that it decodes important economic conditions. This variable could even be a behavioral factor (a latent variable) or an supervisorH1.csv

```
AUDUSDGBPUSDSpread,EURUSDGBPUSDSpread,USDCADGBPUSDSpread,GBPUSDOrderType
0.21946016025839987,0.2087497894399999,0.2085596022999998,doNothing
0.21842415707679996,0.2137397590400001,0.20804805309999996,doNothing
0.21852016025839993,0.21292232863999994,0.20798603589999987,doNothing
0.2183506865176015,0.21438424832000003,0.20737416389999996,sell
0.21471705150239995,0.2100102854399999,0.20340167869999992,doNothing
0.21694705150240012,0.2114860593600001,0.20573033390000006,doNothing
0.2174520679480001,0.21121664752000013,0.2039718344999999,doNothing
0.21718356503519987,0.21284680239999987,0.20341180209999998,doNothing
0.21644861437199991,0.21163616767999982,0.20395841329999986,doNothing
0.21632900906639985,0.21147715839999992,0.20342949449999992,doNothing
0.21656376238239994,0.21198963519999992,0.20441951069999997,doNothing
0.21691167325359983,0.21139395407999984,0.2033510006999999,doNothing
0.217015834528,0.21156666304000016,0.20364053269999993,doNothing
0.21761662391680003,0.21172924815999994,0.2034861162999999,doNothing
0.2163700286935999,0.21107048655999971,0.20288466929999993,doNothing
0.21659616344,0.21098591999999994,0.2028809414999999,doNothing
0.2153199958023999,0.21013678687999993,0.2020455030999999,doNothing
0.21430451888000013,0.20891751439999995,0.20171105990000004,doNothing
0.21550298890160002,0.20878923264000004,0.20184401309999989,doNothing
0.2166529560103998,0.21020232863999988,0.20324360429999988,sell
0.21642690295440015,0.2080889694400001,0.2020285316999999,doNothing
```

Fig. 5 Supervisor from historical data in H1 timeframe. Source: Author's Own Creation

economic factor such as interest rates or the return of a special ticker such as Gold that varies between a and b. So EURUSD can have 25 major principal eigenfunctions with respect to Gold, while AUDUSD can have seven major principal eigenfunctions with respect to Gold. Space of functions is infinite dimensional spaces in general, and therefore, it is expected to have infinite eigenfunctions but the first major principal eigenfunctions that have the highest influence are chosen. Let us restrict ourselves to Hilbert space of bounded functions over a finite interval [a, b]. So the equivalence of PCA in functional PCA can be done by substituting vectors and linear algebra equations by continuous functions and integral equations. In addition, eigenfunctions in the functional PCA paradigm are the equivalent of eigenvectors in PCA. This paradigm is discussed in (Ramsay & Silverman, 2005).

supervisorH4.csv

```
AUDUSDGBPUSDSpread,EURUSDGBPUSDSpread,USDCADGBPUSDSpread,GBPUSDOrderType
-0.009528939999999982,0.12084253050000004,0.04437253299999999,doNothing
-0.009039315999999964,0.12116036100000005,0.0461949669999997,doNothing
-0.005594504000000056,0.1262037509999998,0.049047876999999795,sell
-0.012604427999999945,0.11982856450000012,0.04554565499999996,sell
-0.018279916000000007,0.11588592050000002,0.0409456549999998,doNothing
-0.015797360000000094,0.1176215814999999,0.04295507299999968,sell
-0.017859163999999872,0.11566422550000022,0.04187390899999999,doNothing
-0.01654548,0.12184090399999992,0.04347570799999967,doNothing
-0.012055856000000142,0.13158192150000003,0.04535909399999971,doNothing
-0.012235104000000163,0.131992769,0.044647876999999836,doNothing
-0.011442172000000195,0.13245710799999988,0.04565909399999968,sell
-0.019459163999999918,0.12466409100000009,0.03934385599999968,doNothing
-0.01736623199999987,0.12338815850000007,0.040889146999999904,doNothing
-0.017369540000000017,0.12181609050000008,0.04014025799999987,doNothing
-0.017848788000000004,0.11748978500000007,0.04082501999999999,doNothing
-0.014172847999999849,0.12484090400000003,0.04467031099999996,sell
-0.01830397600000011,0.11879751399999994,0.04081740099999975,sell
-0.02046668400000007,0.11504402250000001,0.03681740099999975,doNothing
-0.016236007999999913,0.11849053099999995,0.0401268189999997,doNothing
-0.016560067999999983,0.11296734400000008,0.039096765999999894,doNothing
-0.01700488,0.11306036100000005,0.03869676599999994,sell
```

Fig. 6 Supervisor from historical data in H4 timeframe. Source: Author's Own Creation

4 Conclusion

Two important aspects in machine learning, namely nonlinear dimension reduction and SVM are reviewed and applied to portfolio optimization, scenario generation and algorithmic trading. There are other important paradigms such as deep reinforcement learning, model agnostic meta learning, bayesian networks, and kernel smoothing, which are beyond the scope of this chapter.

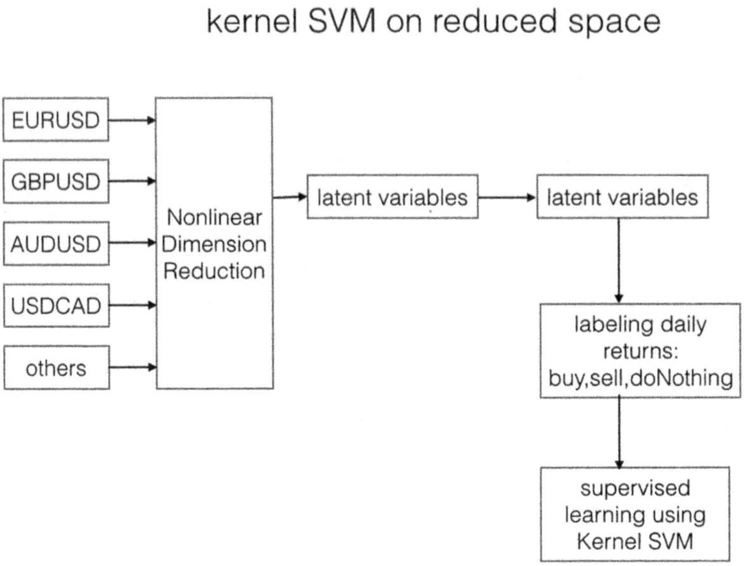

Fig. 7 Layout of the algorithm using a combination of SVM and model reduction. Source: Author's Own Creation

Fig. 8 Accuracy in time frame H1 and H4. Source: Author's Own Creation

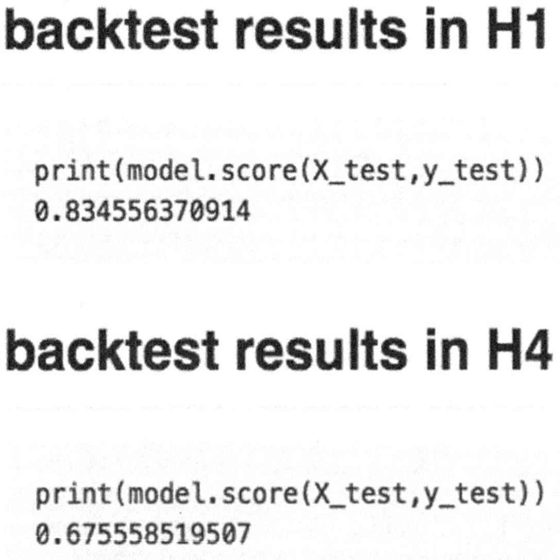

References

Bard O. Aanonsen. (2016). Risk parity stock optimization using principal component quantile Simulation, industrial economics and technology management. Thesis.

Belkin, M. (2003). Partha Niyogi Laplacian eigenmaps for dimensionality reduction and data representation. *Neural Computation, 15*, 1373–1396.

https://github.com/farshad-finance/diversified-Risk-parity

https://github.com/farshad-finance/SVM-Forex

Lee, J. D., Sun, D. L., Sun, Y., & Taylor, J. E. (2016). Exact post-selection inference, with application to the lasso. *Annals of Statistics, 44*(3), 907–927.

Li, K.-C. (1991). Sliced inverse regression for dimension reduction. *Journal of the American Statistical Association, 86*(414), 316–327.

Meucci, A. (2010). Managing diversification. *Risk, 22*(5), 74–79.

Partovi, M. H., & Caputo, M. (2004). Principal portfolios: Recasting the efficient frontier. *Economics Bulletin, 7*(3), 1–10.

Ramsay, J. O., & Silverman, B. W. (2005). Functional data analysis (Chapter 8). Springer.

Roncalli, T. (2013). *Introduction to risk parity and budgeting*. CRC Press.

Roweis, S. T., & Saul, L. K. (Dec 2000). Nonlinear Dimensionality reduction by locally linear embedding. *Science, 290*, 22.

Tayali, H. A., & Tolun, S. (2018). Dimension reduction in mean-variance portfolio optimization. *Expert Systems with applications, 92*, 161–169.

Tibshirani, R. (1996). Regression Shrinkage and Selection via the lasso. *Journal of the Royal Statistical Society. Series B (Methodological), 58*(1), 267–288.

Ryan J. Tibshirani, Jonathan Taylor, Richard Lockhart, Robert Tibshirani (2014) Exact post-selection inference for sequential regression procedures.

Tipping, M. E., & Bishop, C. M. (1999). Probabilistic principal component analysis. *Journal of the Royal Statistical Society, Series B, 61*(Part 3), 611–622.

Yuan, M., & Lin, Y. (2006). Model selection and estimation in regression with grouped variables. *Journal of the Royal Statistical Society. Series B (Statistical Methodology), 68*(1), 49–67.

Pruned Random Forests for Effective and Efficient Financial Data Analytics

Khaled Fawagreh, Mohamed Medhat Gaber, and Mentalla Abdalla

Abstract It is evident that Machine Learning (ML) has touched all walks of our lives! From checking the weather forecast to applying for a loan or a credit card, ML is used in almost every aspect of our daily life. In this chapter, ML is explored in terms of algorithms and applications. Special consideration is given to ML applications in the financial data analytics domain including stock market analysis, fraud detection in financial transactions, credit risk analysis, loan defaulting rate analysis, and profit–loss analysis. The chapter establishes the significance of Random Forests as an effective machine learning method for a wide variety of financial applications. Increasing the efficiency and effectiveness of Random Forests using only a subset of the model (through a process called *pruning*) has been proven successful in two methods, namely, CLUstering-Based Diverse Random Forest (*CLUB-DRF*) and Evolutionary Game Theoretic Approach to Random Forest Pruning (*eGAP*). CLUB-DRF has achieved high pruning levels, while maintaining the model's predictive effectiveness, if not exceeding this of the unpruned Random Forests. On the other hand, eGAP has shown improved predictive effectiveness than CLUB-

Supplementary Information The online version of this chapter (https://doi.org/10.1007/978-3-030-83799-0_7) contains supplementary material, which is available to authorized users.

K. Fawagreh
Prince Mohammad Bin Fahd University, Dhahran, Saudi Arabia
e-mail: kfawagreh@pmu.edu.sa

M. M. Gaber (✉)
Galala University, Suez Governorate, Egypt

Birmingham City University, Birmingham, UK
e-mail: mo-hamed.gaber@gu.edu.eg; Mohamed.Gaber@bcu.ac.uk

M. Abdalla
Galala University, Suez Governorate, Egypt

Alexandria University, Alexandria Governorate, Egypt
e-mail: menatyoussef@gu.edu.eg

S. Derindere Köseoğlu (ed.), *Financial Data Analytics*, Contributions to Finance and Accounting, https://doi.org/10.1007/978-3-030-83799-0_7

DRF at the cost of less pruning levels. Experimentally, we demonstrate the efficacy of these two methods on four financial datasets.

Keywords Machine learning · Random forests · Ensemble pruning · Replicator dynamics · Predictive financial modelling

1 Introduction

The Financial industry, one of the most important and influential sectors in any economy, has witnessed significant changes globally over the past few decades. Characterized by its dynamic nature and the great uncertainties associated with transactions in its diverse segments (banking, insurance, investment, etc.), the financial sector has been widely using digital technology, processing an increasingly large number of online transactions, and offering new products and services (cryptocurrency, fintech, etc.). Moreover, the large number of stakeholders engaged in this sector are involved in various decision-making settings (asset trading, risk management, fraud detection, etc.) (Andriosopoulos et al., 2019). In addition, data available to be processed for problem solving has been unstructured, noisy, and extremely large in terms of volume, variety, and velocity. Hence, big data analytics are more and more used to enhance decision-making efficiency and effectiveness (Andriosopoulos et al., 2019).

Among the many techniques used to help analyze data for decision-making purposes in the financial services industry are algorithms of machine learning (ML), a subset of artificial intelligence that aims to learn patterns in a training data set in order to build models and make accurate predictions using test data accordingly (Provost & Kohavi, 1998). The use of a separate test data set to measure the accuracy of a ML model is a common practice with the objective of ensuring that the trained model is expected to make accurate predictions on deployment. Several ML algorithms (decision trees (DT), artificial neural networks (ANN), support vector machines (SVM), random forests (RF), etc.) have been used to address various decisions for descriptive, predictive, and prescriptive purposes (Andriosopoulos et al., 2019). In particular, RFs, an ensemble of decision trees, have shown superiority in accuracy performance when compared to other ML techniques in a variety of decision-making frameworks (Fernández-Delgado et al., 2014), including financial contexts (Antipov & Pokryshevskaya, 2012; Butaru et al., 2016; Čeh et al., 2018; Khaidem et al., 2016; Kruppa et al., 2013; Sayjadah et al., 2018; Subasi & Cankurt, 2019; Yilmazer & Kocaman, 2020). Random forests, however, have been subject to extensive research to enhance their performance. CLUstering-Based Diverse Random Forest (*CLUB-DRF*) and Evolutionary Game Theoretic Approach to Random Forest Pruning (*eGAP*) are methods for pruning random forests that have shown improved accuracy predictions and speed in regression and classification in healthcare applications (Fawagreh & Gaber, 2020a; Fawagreh et al., 2015a). Since accurate and fast financial decisions are vital for various stakeholders in the industry to prevent financial losses and minimize risks (credit risk, litigation risk, etc.), there is a need to test the performance of pruned random forest extensions as superior financial data analytics. Both pruning methods, adopted in this study, have been experimentally validated, showing efficiency (faster inference time) and effectiveness (more accurate). On the one hand, CLUB-DRF is more efficient, while eGAP is more accurate.

Consequently, this chapter aims to compare the effectiveness and efficiency of pruned random forests, produced by *CLUB-DRF* and *eGAP*, to those of traditional random forests (with the same size as a pruned random forest by eGAP) and parent random forests (before pruning) in the context of four important financial decisions:

(1) Prediction of credit card default, (2) prediction of credit approval, (3) stock portfolio performance analysis, and (4) real estate appraisal. As it can be seen, these applications can benefit from fast decision-making, while maintaining the predictive accuracy of the RF model, or even better—improving it.

The chapter is organized as follows. Section 2 provides an overview of the Machine Learning field, with an emphasis on Random Forests as the basis of the adopted methods in this study. In Sect. 3, applications of machine learning in the financial sector are explored, showing the important role Random Forests played in previous work. Section 4 provides a concise description of the two adopted methods in this study, namely, CLUB-DRF and eGAP. To validate the benefits of using CLUB-DRF and eGAP in the financial sector, a thorough experimental study is presented in Sect. 5. Finally, the chapter is concluded with a summary and pointers to possibilities for future work in Sect. 6.

2 Machine Learning: An Overview

Machine Learning (ML) is a branch of Artificial Intelligence (AI) that focuses on building applications that learn from data without being programmed to do so, resulting in predictive and descriptive models. Initially, computational learning theory in AI and pattern recognition leads to the evolution of ML. Algorithms in ML can be classified as either supervised or unsupervised. A supervised ML algorithm attempts to map a set of input variables X to an output variable Y. Later on, this mapping can be used when making predictions on unseen and new data. A good example of supervised algorithms is classification, which uses labeled data to build models, that are used later to predict unlabeled new data. A training dataset, where all objects have known class labels, is normally used by a classification algorithm to build a model, also called a classifier, as shown in Fig. 1.

Once the model proves its effectiveness to label unseen data in the testing dataset as shown in Fig. 2, it is dispatched to the field.

Unsupervised algorithms, on the other hand, attempt to unveil hidden patterns in unlabeled data without knowing much about their characteristics. A typical example of unsupervised algorithms is clustering which is a technique used to classify

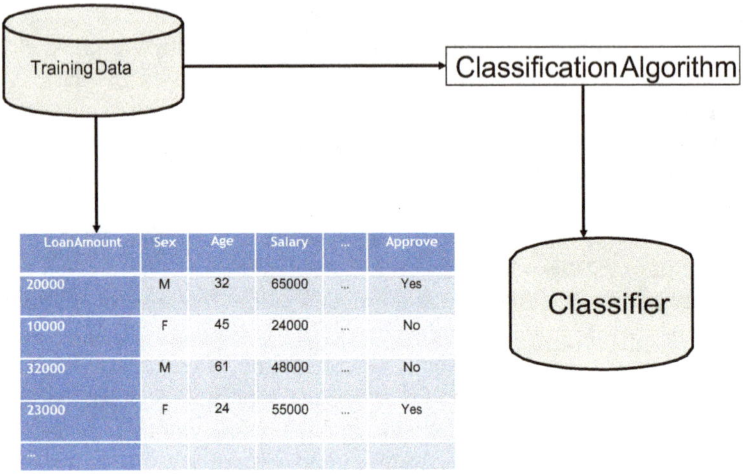

Fig. 1 Classification process—Classifier construction

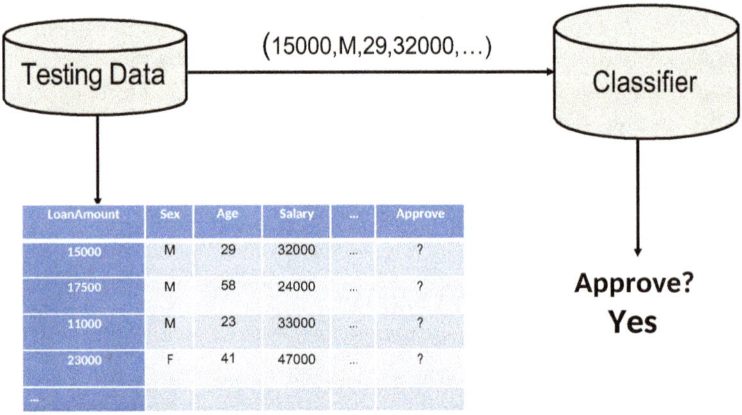

Fig. 2 Classification process—Prediction

objects, whose similarity characteristics are not known ahead of time, by breaking a diversified group of objects into smaller groups of similar objects.

2.1 Machine Learning Algorithms

In this section, we give the readers a quick overview of some commonly used machine learning methods. This is not intended to be a comprehensive discussion of machine learning algorithms by any means. It only serves as pointers to interested readers to explore these methods in more detail in the literature.

Finding a line that best fits the available data instances available, so that the line can be used to predict output values for inputs that are not seen in the data used for the line fitting, assuming that those outputs would lie on the line, or at least nearby it, is called *Linear Regression*. Typically, one target variable/feature is used for the line fitting, while the other features are used as independent variables. Linear regression is simple and easy to interpret.

Logistic regression employs a logistic function to compute a probability value which can later be mapped to two or more discrete classes. Whereas linear regression is used to predict a continuous variable, logistic regression, on the other hand, is used to predict a categorical variable. Hence, linear regression is used best to handle regression tasks, whereas logistic regression is used best to handle classification tasks. Logistic regression is easy to implement and interpret. A *decision tree* acts as a nonlinear predictive model. For each example, the tree is traversed—such that its internal nodes are used to guide the path to a leaf node where the value of the target variable/feature is found. The target variable can either store a discrete value or a continuous value (typically a real number). For the former case, the tree is called a classification tree, and for the latter case, the tree is called a regression tree. The biggest advantage of decision trees is that they are easy to interpret.

Support vector machine (SVM) is a linear model that can be used for classification as well as regression problems. Not only it works well for many practical problems, but it can also solve linear and nonlinear problems. The idea of SVM is an elegant modelling method; it works by finding a decision boundary which is a hyperplane between any two classes in order to separate them or classify them. Support vector machine is very effective even with high dimensional data. Methods like the kernel trick and the soft boundary make it possible for SVM to model nonlinear decision boundaries.

Based on the Bayes' theorem, *Naive Bayes* is a classification technique with an assumption of independence between the features. In other words, a Naive Bayes classifier assumes the absence of feature interaction (i.e., no independent feature affects any other independent feature). Relative to the number of predictors and data points, *Naive Bayes* is known for its scalability. It is also ideal for making real-time predictions.

k-Nearest Neighbor, also known as *k*-NN, is a supervised learning algorithm that can handle regression and classification problems. It is based on the assumption that points belonging to the same class are those that are falling near to each other. In other words, similar things are those that fall near each other. Unlike other algorithms, KNN can easily implement multi-class problems.

k-means is an unsupervised machine learning algorithm for clustering founded by MacQueen et al. (1967) in the late 1960s. Not only it is considered as one of the earliest clustering algorithms, but also the most popular one, mainly due to its efficiency, simplicity, and empirical success (Jain, 2010).

Random Forest (RF) is a supervised ensemble classification and regression technique that has proved its superiority and accuracy over other ensemble techniques. To further enhance and improve its performance accuracy, many researchers developed many extensions of it in order to, using a variety of techniques and strategies, improve certain aspect(s) of it. We have followed this approach in (Fawagreh & Gaber, 2020a, 2020b; Fawagreh et al., 2014, 2015a, 2015b, 2016). An overview of RF is given in Sect. 2.2.

This section provides a quick overview of some of the commonly used shallow machine learning methods, which are still in wide use for small and moderate size datasets. For large size and unstructured datasets, deep learning methods, based on Artificial Neural Networks (ANN) have showed superiority over the last few years.

2.2 *Random Forest*

Random Forest (RF), founded by Breiman (2001), is a supervised ensemble learning method able to solve classification and regression problems. In order to construct a diverse set of decision trees with controlled variation, RF integrates Breiman's bootstrap aggregating (bagging) method (Breiman, 1996), and the random selection of features, developed by Ho (1995, 1998) and Amit and Geman (1997).

Each decision tree in RF is constructed using a sample drawn from the training data. Using bagging, this sample is drawn using sampling with replacement from the training data, hence, statistically speaking, the sample is likely to have approximately 63.2% ($\mathbf{1}\ ^{1}$) of instances appearing at least once in the sample, where e is the Euler's number which can be approximated to be equal 2.71828. Instances that were included in the sample are called in-bag-instances, whereas the remaining instances (about 36.8%), are called out-of-bag (OOB) instances.

To ensure diversity in each decision tree, at each node in all trees, a goodness measure (e.g., Gini index or information gain) is used to select the best split feature from a set of randomly selected features (where n is the total number of features, it is typically $\sqrt{n}$ or $\log n$). Each tree is unpruned and grown to the largest extent possible. However, to prevent trees from growing out of memory particularly in high dimensional datasets, a maximum depth is usually permitted.

2.3 *Machine Learning Applications*

Not only machine learning applications are increasingly playing a role in our daily lives, but also becoming commonplace in many aspects of modern society. They are rapidly growing and now very much cover all industries. In addition to the financial data analytics domain which will be covered in depth in the next section, machine learning applications also include but not limited to medical diagnosis (Alâ'Aref et al., 2019) (Cruz & Wishart, 2006; Lee et al., 2018; Zogheib, 2011), email spam, and malware filtering (Alurkar et al., 2017; Blanzieri & Bryl, 2008; Christina et al., 2010; Guzella & Caminhas, 2009), self-driving cars (Maqueda et al., 2018; Ramos et al., 2017; Stilgoe, 2018) (Rao & Frtunikj, 2018), traffic prediction (Rzeszótko & Nguyen, 2012) (Boukerche & Wang, 2020) (Xu et al., 2017; Zhang et al., 2017), speech and image recognition (Agarwalla & Sarma, 2016; Deng & Li, 2013; Latha & Priya, 2016; Srinivasan et al., 2018), and automatic language translation (Baroni & Bernardini, 2006; Tenni et al., 1999; Zogheib, 2011; Li et al., 2015).

3 Machine Learning in Financial Data Analytics

Financial institutions are working in competitive and dynamic circumstances. In the digital age, they need to handle large amounts and a variety of data and comply with rapidly changing regulations. Hence, among the different computational approaches used, ML methods have been increasingly adopted as powerful data analytics in the financial industry. In practice, banks have used ML algorithms extensively to detect credit card fraud (Van Liebergen et al., 2017). New financial services based on AI "robots" are also introduced. For instance, "rob-advisors" provide investors, in particular, nonprofessional investors, with asset trading recommendations using automated tools (Snihovyi et al., 2018). Also, "chatbots" are more and more used to enhance customer service performance in the financial industry (Okuda & Shoda, 2018; Przegalinska et al., 2019). Moreover, prior research provides evidence that ML-based prediction models improve performance in a multitude of financial decisions, as follows:

- Portfolio management (forecasting the direction of stock returns for trading purposes, etc. (Andriosopoulos et al., 2019; Ban et al., 2018; Paiva et al., 2019; Rapach & Zhou, 2020; Song et al., 2017).
- Real estate valuation (Baldominos et al., 2018; El Hamzaoui & Perez, 2011; Kempa et al., 2011; Trawiński et al., 2017).
- Fraud detection (credit card fraud, insurance claims fraud, financial statement fraud, money laundering, etc.) (Chen et al., 2018; Jullum et al., 2020; Lokanan et al., 2019; Perols, 2011; Raj & Portia, 2011; Ryman-Tubb et al., 2018).
- Risk management (credit scoring, credit card delinquency prediction, bankruptcy forecasting, etc.) (Abellán & Mantas, 2014; Andriosopoulos et al., 2019; Gui, 2019; Kou et al., 2019; Lahmiri, 2016; Mashrur et al., 2020; Sun & Vasarhelyi, 2019; Yang et al., 2018b; Yeh & Lien, 2009).
- Target marketing of financial products (forecasting customer churn and customer loyalty, etc.) (Machado et al., 2019; Mutanen et al., 2006).
- Social media data analysis for financial institution brand support (Saura et al., 2019).
- Regulatory compliance (Lahann et al., 2019; Liu et al., 2020; Van Liebergen et al., 2017).
- Insurance loss reserves prediction (Baudry & Robert, 2019; Ding et al., 2020).

RFs, supervised ML algorithms, have been recently used to develop predictive models for classification and regression in various financial domains. RF models have largely outperformed models based on other algorithms (Kruppa et al., 2013; Sayjadah et al., 2018; Subasi & Cankurt, 2019). Moreover, extant literature suggests that RFs are robust to major characteristics of financial sector data (Antipov & Pokryshevskaya, 2012; Čeh et al., 2018; Lin et al., 2017; Subasi & Cankurt, 2019; Yilmazer & Kocaman, 2020).

3.1 Credit Risk Management

Since the global financial crisis in 2008, the significance of risk management in the financial industry has been emphasized (Butaru et al., 2016). Credit risk, a major risk factor facing many stakeholders, reflects the likelihood that creditors will suffer financial losses as a result of borrowers' inability to pay their obligations (Andriosopoulos et al., 2019). Over the past few decades, the market for credit products (consumer loans, installments, mortgages, credit cards, etc.) has grown largely. With the rising trend for using credit cards in online payments and e-commerce transactions, however, there has been an increasing probability of credit card delinquency (Sayjadah et al., 2018). Credit scoring systems are important credit risk management tools. By classifying customers according to their creditworthiness status, banks, and other lending companies can make more effective and efficient credit analysis decisions when granting loans, credit lines, or installments (Abellán & Mantas, 2014). They can also customize credit products and their limits to customers' credit scoring conditions (Sayjadah et al., 2018). Moreover, predicting the default rate of existing credit allows financial institutions (for instance, by cutting customers' credit lines) and other lenders to mitigate financial debt losses for customers likely to fail to pay their past due debts (Abellán & Mantas, 2014; Butaru et al., 2016).

Logistic regression has been largely used to classify customers according to their default probability (Butaru et al., 2016) until ML techniques, mainly ANN (Sayjadah et al., 2018), have been adopted by numerous researchers to build models to forecast credit card delinquency. Recently, RFs have shown improved accuracy performance compared to other ML classifiers (multilayer perception, SVM, K-NN, Naive Bayes, DT, etc.) to estimate credit card default rates (Sayjadah et al., 2018; Subasi & Cankurt, 2019). Moreover, RFs along with data preprocessing methods, such as SMOTE, can manage the imbalanced distribution of the data sets (Subasi & Cankurt, 2019). Florentin Butaru et al. (2016) compare the classification performance of several models (based on logistic regression, DT and RF) to predict the credit card default rates in six financial institutions. While DT and RF show superior performance compared to logistic regression (Butaru et al., 2016), have not identified one best classifier across all six banks. Jochen Kruppa et al. (2013) estimated installment credit default probability as regression rather than a classification model using RF based on probability estimation trees (RF-PET). In contrast to logistic regression, K-NN and bNN, RF-PET had the highest performance (Kruppa et al., 2013).

3.2 *Financial Fraud Detection*

Financial institutions have successfully used ML-based techniques in order to timely detect and block suspicious credit card transactions (Van Liebergen et al., 2017). Fraud detection in the financial industry is considered a complex classification task as it involves big data analysis and requires significant expert judgment. Available data is usually skewed with a low proportion of fraudulent to non-fraudulent transactions (Álvarez-Jareño et al., 2017; Van Liebergen et al., 2017). With the increasing trend in fraud cases detected, the major losses incurred by many stakeholders, and the greater emphasis placed on corporate governance to maintain public confidence in financial reporting, ML techniques have been utilized to help detect not only credit card fraud but also money laundering and financial statement fraud (Chen et al., 2018; Hajek & Henriques, 2017).

Studies that have used RFs to build models to classify credit card transactions into legal and illegal (i.e., credit card data are stolen and illegally used), though, provide evidence of conflicting performance results. On the one hand, Banerjee et al. (2018) compare the precision and recall of RFs to other statistical and ML classifiers (K-NN, logistic regression, SVM, Naive Bayes, and muti-layer perceptron) and find that SVM model shows the best performance. Also, Dhankhad et al. (2018) suggest that an ensemble meta classifier based on logistic regression outperforms nine other classifiers, including RF (which comes second in terms of performance), in credit card fraud detection. On the other hand, Xuan et al. (2018) show the superior performance of RFs, in particular CART-based RF, to other ML techniques (SVM, NN, and Naive Bayes) in a similar task. Xuan et al. (2018) further suggest the need to improve the RF algorithm.

ML-based techniques have been recently used to detect money laundering (Van Liebergen et al., 2017). In contrast to DT, NN, and logistic regression, RFs with SMOTE data preprocessing more accurately classify transactions into legitimate and illegitimate (Álvarez-Jareño et al., 2017). In addition, RFs show improved accuracy, efficiency, and variable selection performance, relative to other methods, in a financial statement fraud detection task (Liu et al., 2015). Also, ensemble models, including RFs, are highly effective in detecting fraudulent cases when both financial reports (published financial statements and financial analysts' forecasts) and nonfinancial reports, such as management's discussion and analysis reports, are analyzed (Hajek & Henriques, 2017).

3.3 *Portfolio Management*

One of the most important and common financial decisions in practice and research is related to balancing the portfolio of financial investments (stocks, derivatives, funds, etc.) to increase expected returns and reduce investment risk. Tasks, such as portfolio optimization and asset selection, are highly complex nonlinear tasks. They involve significant amounts of unstructured noisy data and a large number of variables (technical indicators, macroeconomic variables, etc.) (Khaidem et al., 2016). Automated tools, primarily SVM and ANN, have therefore been recently introduced to develop predictive classifiers to forecast trends in stock price returns (Andriosopoulos et al., 2019). Selection of assets based on ML algorithms results in a portfolio with higher returns than the market index (Yang et al., 2018a). Khaidem et al. (2016) show evidence of improved performance of RF classification models in predicting the direction of stock prices, highly volatile in nature, compared to other ML-based models. Yet, Abe and Nakayama (2018) find evidence that deep neural networks achieve great accuracy performance in predicting stock price returns, superior to the performance of RF and support vector regression classifiers. In contrast to several ML algorithms including RF, SVM classifiers are more effective in developing an investment strategy for the global stock market using financial network indicators (Lee et al., 2019).

3.4 *Real Estate Valuation*

Real estate values are crucial economic indicators and property appraisal is necessary, among many purposes, for sale, rental, mortgage underwriting, and for the calculation of property taxes (Kok et al., 2017; Yilmazer & Kocaman, 2020). The estimation of real estate prices can be conducted on a large scale or at an individual property level, and the task is very complex involving a large number of independent variables whose characteristics complicate data processing (Yilmazer & Kocaman, 2020). Several studies have used ML-based techniques and Geographic Information Systems (GIS) for mass appraisal of real estate prices. Compared to the most widely used methods in this respect, multiple regression and ANN, RFs showed superior prediction performance of real estate property values across several measures in addition to improved handling of data attributes, such as missing values, outliers, and heteroscedasticity (Antipov & Pokryshevskaya, 2012; Čeh et al., 2018; Yilmazer & Kocaman, 2020).

3.5 *Insurance*

Furthermore, RFs have been used in the insurance industry, along with big data analysis, for more effective insurance products' marketing (Lin et al., 2017) and to detect fraudulent insurance claims (Roy & George, 2017). Insurance companies, important intermediaries in the financial services sector, use traditional inefficient methods to sell life insurance and non-life-insurance policies to customers for premiums. Lin et al. (2017) suggest that ML techniques can be used for target marketing in the insurance sector by determining major characteristics of potential customers. Their experimental results suggest that ensemble RFs result in a more effective and efficient classification of potential customer behavior in the insurance sector, characterized by imbalanced distribution of financial data. Compared to SVM and logistic regression, ensemble RFs achieve more accurate results at less running time, in addition to enhanced performance at the different number of features tested. RF and RF-SMOTE also outperform SVM and logistic regression.

Along with the rising trend to acquire insurance policies, there has been a significant increase in the number of fraudulent claims detected, in particular in vehicle insurance (Roy & George, 2017). Investigating claims for compensations by policyholders for fraud is a challenging task that requires much time and effort. Using a large data set of fraudulent and nonfraudulent vehicle insurance claims, Roy and George (2017) have compared the performance of DT, RF, and Naive Bayes techniques in this respect. Experimental results provide evidence that, compared to Naive Bayes, DT and RF classifiers are better predictors of falsified accident claims not eligible to insurance compensation (Roy & George, 2017).

3.6 Retail Banking

Retail banks can also develop target marketing strategies for their credit products using big data analytics based on ML techniques. In a highly competitive industry, retail banks offering credit products, not highly differentiated, need to customize their products to the customers willing to buy them at the required time. Analyzing large historical transaction data sets for customer purchasing behavior will result in greater success for financial institutions (Ładyżyński et al., 2019). Ładyżyński et al. (2019) build several predictive models for classification purposes using RF, CART, and deep belief networks using multidimensional time series and with or without Boruta algorithm for feature selection. In particular, CART with Boruta feature selection algorithm results in more effective and efficient performance.

In conclusion, RFs compare favorably with other ML algorithms as big data analytics in the financial services industry. They show potential performance advantages with respect to mitigation of credit risk, detection of financial fraud, prediction of trends in stock prices, implementation of effective product marketing strategies and management of data skewness.

4 Pruned Random Forests

In this section, we present two effective pruning methods of RF that we developed and validated. These methods will be used in our experimental study in the following section to investigate their performance in financial decision-making for both effectiveness (i.e., predictive accuracy) and efficiency (i.e., inference time).

4.1 Clustering-Based Diverse Random Forest

The first is called *CLUB-DRF* which stands for CLUstering-Based Diverse Random Forest (Fawagreh et al., 2015a). Using clustering, *CLUB-DRF* is able to find a subset of trees from a standard RF. With only a few of the trees used in RF, in most cases, *CLUB-DRF* is able to provide an even higher classification accuracy. In the area of healthcare analytics, *CLUB-DRF* was used to improve the accuracy of several regression medical datasets (Fawagreh & Gaber, 2020b). *CLUB-DRF* clusters trees based on their similarity of prediction on the training data. Subsequently, the best performing tree is selected from each cluster, forming a pruned RF, where the number of trees selected is equal to the number of clusters.

In a nutshell, the *CLUB-DRF* method can be summarized as follows where *T* refers to the training data set, and *S* refers to the size of the *parentRF* to be created. The constant k refers to the number of clusters to be created, defined as a multiple of 5 in the range 5–50:

- Create an empty super ordered list *All Predictions.*
- Create an empty ordered list $T_{r\ f}$ to represent *parent RF.*
- Create an empty ordered list $T_{clubdr\ f}$ to represent *CLUB-DRF.*
- Using the traditional Random Forest Algorithm, create $T_{r\ f}$ of size *S.*
- For each tree in $T_{r\ f}$, find its predictions on *T* and add it to *All Predictions* (note that each entry in *All Predictions* is associated with a tree).
- Using *k*-means clustering algorithm (*k*-modes is used on classification datasets), cluster *All Predictions* into a set of *k* clusters: $cluster_1 \ldots cluster_k$.
- From the predictions in each cluster, find a representative tree and add it to Tclubdr *f*.

The final step in the list above is to select a representative from each cluster. For this, three variations will be used and are discussed next.

4.1.1 Best Representative on Training CLUB-DRF

In this variation, from each cluster, we loop over the predictions in each cluster and find the accuracy of their corresponding trees on the training data. The representative tree selected from each cluster is the one that has achieved the highest performance on the training data. According to the steps outlined above, the tree will then be added to $T_{clubdr\ f}$ to form *CLUB-DRF*. This is the variation used in the experiments conducted in Sect. 5.

4.1.2 Best Representative on OOB CLUB-DRF

In this variation, from each cluster, instead of picking the tree that has achieved the highest performance on the training data, the tree that has achieved the highest performance on the out-of-bag (OOB) instances is selected instead. These instances account for about 36% of the total number of instances, and represent the instances that were not included in the sample with replacement that was used to construct the tree. Unlike the training data that was seen by the tree when it was constructed, OOB data is considered unseen and therefore, it gives a more accurate and unbiased measure of the tree's predictive accuracy.

4.1.3 Random Representative CLUB-DRF

In this variation, from each cluster, we randomly pick a prediction list and select its corresponding tree without assessing its performance. Since accuracy was not a selection criterion in the selection of the representative in this variation, unlike the previous two variations that have been overfitted on the training and OOB samples respectively, this variation does not suffer from overfitting.

4.2 *eGAP*

eGAP (Fawagreh & Gaber, 2020a), on the other hand, combines the clustering used in *CLUB-DRF* with the evolutionary game theoretic approach Replicator Dynamics (RD) (Schuster & Sigmund, 1983). We have used RD in Fawagreh et al. (2014) to evolve a diversified random forest, through growing (i.e., adding trees) and shrinking (i.e., removing trees) subforests, where each subforest is produced by a randomized subspace (a subset of features drawn randomly). Subforests with better performance are subject to grow, and those with lower performance are subject to shrink. Using RD, a Random Forest ensemble is evolved by *eGAP* in a similar fashion. High-resemblance trees in an initial Random Forest are first clustered. By adding and removing trees using RD, clusters grow and shrink by comparing the predictive accuracy of each subforest, represented as a cluster of trees, with the predictive accuracy of the entire forest. The initial number of trees in each cluster is equal to the number of trees in the smallest cluster. Trees that are not initially sampled are used to grow the clusters.

In a nutshell, the *eGAP* method can be summarized as follows. Assume that the training dataset is referred to as *T*, the size of the *parentRF* to be created is referred to as *S*, the number of clusters to be created is referred to as *k*, and the number of RD iterations that will be applied on the working clusters is referred to as *RDIterations*.

- Create an empty super ordered list *All Predictions*.
- Create an empty ordered list $T_{r\,f}$ to represent *parentRF*.
- Create an empty ordered list $T_{eG\,AP}$ to represent *eGAP*.
- Using the traditional Random Forest Algorithm, create $T_{r\,f}$ of size *S*.
- For each tree in $T_{r\,f}$, find its predictions on *T* and add it to *All Predictions* (note that each entry in *All Predictions* is associated with a tree).

- Using *k*-means (or *k*-modes), cluster *All Predictions* into a set of initial *k* clusters: $cluster_1 \ldots cluster_{k.}$
- From the smallest cluster, find its size *minSize*.
- Create working clusters (*wkClusters*), each of size *minSize*.
- Add *minSize* trees from initial clusters to *wkClusters*.
- Create idle clusters (*idleClusters*).
- Add the remaining trees in each initial cluster to *idleClusters*.
- Loop *RDIterations* times over each working cluster (*nextwkCluster*) in *wkClusters*.
- Calculate the performance of all trees in *wkClusters* (*wkClustersPer f ormance*).
- Calculate the performance of all trees in *nextwkCluster* (*nextwkCluster Per f ormance*).
- If *nextwkCluster Per f ormance* is better than *wkClustersPer f ormance*, the best performing tree in the corresponding idle cluster is chosen and added it to *nextwkCluster*.
- Otherwise, the worst-performing tree in *nextwkCluster* is removed and placed in the corresponding idle cluster.
- After looping *RDIterations* times, trees in *wkClusters* are used to populate the ordered list T_{eGAP} which represents *eGAP*.

Having presented the steps of CLUB-DRF and eGAP, assessing the effectiveness and efficiency of both methods when applied on financial datasets is presented in the following section.

5 Experimental Study

In this section, both the effectiveness and efficiency of the adopted methods: *CLUB-DRF* and *eGAP* are demonstrated through a thorough experimental study on four datasets in the financial sector. Two classification and two regression problems are used.

5.1 Datasets

The choice of the datasets is based on the tasks (classification and regression) the methods are applied to. The datasets are generally of small-to-medium sizes. Consequently, a shallow machine learning model like Random Forests is ideal. This is in contrast to deep learning models that typically require larger sizes datasets to be effective. Table 1 outlines the financial datasets that have been used in the experiments.

The class label for the first two classification datasets is binary. For the default of credit card clients dataset, it indicates whether the customer is likely to default on a

Table 1 Regression datasets

Name	Type	Number of features	Number of instances
Default of credit card clients	Classification	24	30,000
Australian credit approval	Classification	15	690
Real estate valuation	Regression	8	414
Stock portfolio performance	Regression	18	252

payment or not (1 = Yes, 0 = No). The class label is determined based on a collection of inputs like the gender of the applicant, education level, and marital status.

For the Australian credit approval dataset, using a combination of customer input variables, whose actual names and values have been changed to meaningless symbols to protect confidentiality of the data, the class label indicates whether the customer is approved for a credit card or not (1 = Yes, 0 = No).

As for the regression datasets, the target feature in the real estate valuation dataset represents the house price per unit area, given a combination of house input variables like house age, the distance to the nearest Mass Rapid Transit (MRT) station, the latitude and longitude geographic coordinates, etc.

The target feature for the stock portfolio performance dataset is a normalized continuous investment performance indicator. It indicates the total risk associated with investing in stocks of some companies, where the inputs are a combination of stock-picking concepts' weights like book value-to-price ratio (B/P), return on equity (ROE), sales-to-price ratio (S/P), etc.

In all experiments, the size of *parentRF* used is 1000 trees, and since we arbitrarily chose the number of RD iterations to be identical to the size of *parentRF*, during the evolution process, 1000 RD iterations were applied to grow/shrink the clusters.

In addition to comparing the performance of *eGAP* with the *parentRF*, the performance of *eGAP* was also compared with a random forest having identical size to *eGAP* called *RF*, and with *CLUB-DRF*. In the former, the trees are chosen at random from the *parentRF*. The performance comparison was done using the key performance indicator, which is percentage accuracy for classification, and Mean Absolute Error (MAE) for regression.

Though multiples of 5 clusters in the range 5–50 were created in the experiments, it is worth mentioning that results reported in the following subsections correspond to the best performing number of clusters from which *eGAP* was generated.

5.2 Classification Datasets

Table 2 compares the performance of *eGAP* with *parentRF*, *RF*, and *CLUB-DRF* on the classification datasets. Using the key performance indicator (percentage accuracy), it is obvious from this table that *eGAP* was able to outperform all of them. In

Table 2 Performance metrics of eGAP vs parentR, RF, and CLUB-DRF on classification datasets

Dataset	Clusters	Accuracy	AUC	F-Measure	Accuracy	AUC	F-Measure
eGAP					**ParentRF**		
Default of credit card clients	5	**80.78%**	0.63	0.81	80.65%	0.63	0.81
Australian credit approval	10	**87.20%**	0.87	0.87	86.09%	0.85	0.86
					RF		
Default of credit card clients	5	**80.78%**	0.63	0.81	80.61%	0.63	0.81
Australian credit approval	10	**87.20%**	0.87	0.87	85.70%	0.85	0.86
					CLUB-DRF		
Default of credit card clients	5	**80.78%**	0.63	0.81	80.70%	0.63	0.81
Australian credit approval	10	**87.20%**	0.87	0.87	87.11%	0.87	0.87

addition to percentage accuracy, Area Under Curve (AUC), and F-Measure are also reported in the table for both datasets.

5.3 Regression Datasets

Likewise, Table 3 compares the performance of *eGAP* with *parentRF*, *RF*, and *CLUB-DRF* on the regression datasets. For the real estate valuation dataset, as demonstrated in this table, using the key performance indicator (MAE), *eGAP* outperformed the *parentRF* and *RF*, and underperformed *CLUB-DRF* by a tiny negligible fraction. For the stock portfolio performance dataset, *eGAP* had identical performance to *parentRF*, *RF*, and *CLUB-DRF*. For both datasets, in addition to MAE, Mean Squared Error (MSE), Root Mean Squared Error (RMSE), and R Squared are also reported in the table.

5.4 Space and Inference Time Performance

For all datasets, Table 4 depicts the pruning level of *eGAP* relative to the *parentRF*. The reduction ratio between the original ensemble, which we termed *parentRF*, and *eGAP*, is referred to as the pruning level. For example, if the *parentRF* is of size 500 trees, and *eGAP* is of size 50, then $100\% - \frac{50}{500} \times 100\% = 90\%$ is the pruning level that was attained in *eGAP*. Compared with the size of the *parentRF*, this means that *eGAP* is 90% smaller. By taking a closer look at Table 4, we see that *eGAP* achieved high pruning levels on the classification datasets and low pruning levels on

Table 3 Performance metrics of eGAP vs parentRF, RF, and CLUB-DRF on regression datasets

Dataset	Clusters	MAE	MSE	RMSE	R Squared	MAE	MSE	RMSE	R Squared
eGAP						**parentRF**			
Stock portfolio performance	40	**0.05**	0.01	0.08	0.75	0.05	0.01	0.08	0.75
Real estate valuation	50	**5.79**	70.32	8.38	0.60	5.80	70.53	8.39	0.60
						RF			
Stock portfolio performance	40	**0.05**	0.01	0.08	0.75	0.05	0.01	0.08	0.75
Real estate valuation	50	**5.79**	70.32	8.38	0.60	5.80	70.41	8.39	0.60
						CLUB-DRF			
Stock portfolio performance	40	**0.05**	0.01	0.08	0.75	0.05	0.01	0.08	0.75
Real estate valuation	50	5.79	70.32	8.38	0.60	5.72	69.10	8.31	0.60

Table 4 Pruning level of eGAP relative to parentRF

Dataset	Clusters	Pruning Level
Default of credit card clients	5	80.78%
Australian credit approval	10	87.20%
Stock portfolio performance	40	7.50%
Real estate valuation	50	10%

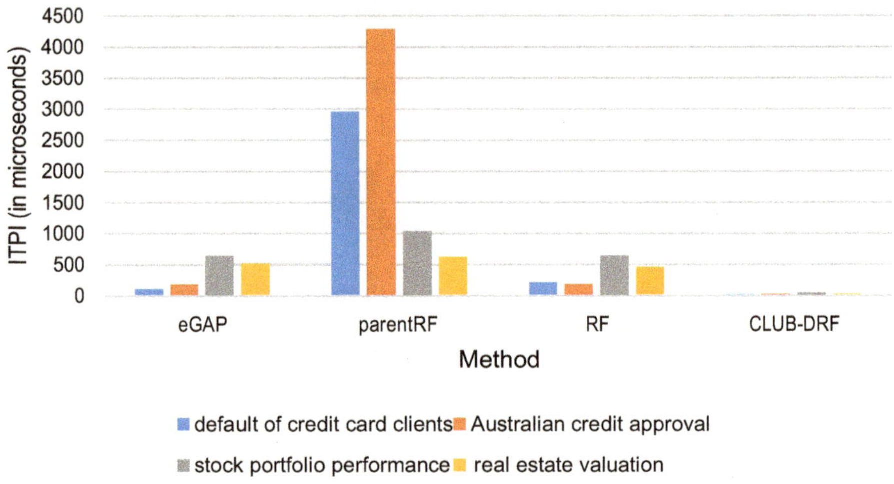

Fig. 3 Inference Time Per Instance (ITPI) in microseconds: eGAP vs parentRF vs RF (same size as eGAP) vs CLUB-DRF

the regression datasets. The achieved pruning levels for *CLUB-DRF* are typically large, as the pruning level is set in advance. Thus, the minimum pruning level is 95% in this study, as 50 trees out of the 1000 trees in the *parentRF* are chosen.

The bar chart in Fig. 3 compares the inference time per instance (ITPI) (in microseconds) of *eGAP* with *parentRF*, *RF*, and *CLUB-DRF*. This refers to the time required to predict all the instances in the testing dataset divided by total the number of instances.

As demonstrated in Fig. 3, it is obvious that for all datasets, *eGAP* achieved faster inference time relative to the *parentRF*, mainly due to its smaller size. As for *RF*, which has an identical size to *eGAP*, *eGAP* achieved faster inference time than the first dataset, identical inference time to the second and third datasets, and slightly slower inference time than the fourth dataset.

As for comparing *eGAP* with *CLUB-DRF*, it is obvious that *CLUB-DRF* performed much better as it attained a much faster inference time. This is expected and comes as no surprise to us, since in the *CLUB-DRF* method, and unlike *eGAP*, only one representative tree was selected from each cluster, producing a much smaller ensemble than *eGAP*.

6 Conclusion and Future Work

The financial services industry involves several participants (investors, lenders, regulators, etc.) who need to take accurate, fast, and informed decisions in several complex and dynamic contexts. With the technological advancements significantly changing this sector, powerful big data analytics are crucial.

In general, ML-based techniques have shown superior computational results in financial decision-making settings. In particular, RFs have outperformed to a great extent other algorithms in terms of accuracy performance. Extant literature suggests room for improvement in RF algorithm. Pruned RF algorithms, *eGAP* and *CLUB-DRF*, are built and show favorable results in healthcare applications. Consequently, the aim of this chapter is (1) to describe the performance of RFs in financial decision-making domains; (2) to adopt *eGAP* and *CLUB-DRF* algorithms for financial modelling; and (3) to provide the experimental evidence in terms of effectiveness and efficiency of using these pruned RF models on four classification and regression financial decisions.

eGAP demonstrates improved performance (compared to *RF*, *parentRF*, and *CLUB-DRF*) in credit risk management settings. The *eGAP* classifier can more accurately predict credit card default and credit approval. For the real estate valuation task, *eGAP* outperforms all models except for *CLUB-DRF*. Yet, all models performed similarly in managing stock portfolios. In terms of efficiency, *eGAP* is faster than *RF* and *parentRF* for three of the decision frameworks while RF (of the same size as *eGAP*) computations are faster for the real estate appraisal decision. Nevertheless, *CLUB-DRF* is the most efficient among all models, including *eGAP*, since it is a smaller ensemble.

Therefore, experimental results imply that *eGAP* and *CLUB-DRF* can improve performance in financial decision-making tasks. Importantly, these pruned RF models are smaller in size and more efficient but not at the expense of their reliability. There is great potential for considering not only RFs but also pruned RF algorithms as useful in financial data analytics. Further research can examine the use of *eGAP* and *CLUB-DRF* to boost accuracy and efficiency in other financial contexts, such as fraud detection (money laundering, insurance fraud, stock market manipulation, financial statement fraud, etc.), stock price crash risk prediction, retail banking, and compliance. The use of *eGAP* and *CLUB-DRF* by financial institutions may not be limited to measuring and mitigating credit risk but also liquidity and operational risks (Leo et al., 2019). Additional research is also necessary to explain why pruned RF models did not have a significant positive impact on accuracy performance when stock portfolio management data were analyzed.

In the digital era, only those entities in the financial industry that cope with technological advancements will be able to compete (Courbe, 2016). Using AI robots and ML methods will be essential to provide faster more innovative and customized services at a lower cost. These approaches are also expected to enhance wealth management, risk management, security, and regulatory compliance (Courbe, 2016). Consequently, studying ML models for being effective and efficient financial data analytics is highly important. In practice, financial institutions have widely used ML techniques for credit card fraud detection and few commercial ML-based applications have been introduced to detect transactions suspicious for money laundering (Chen et al., 2018). Also, fintech startups, providing enhanced digital investment and banking services, have increased competition in the financial services sector (Courbe, 2016). Notwithstanding the potential fast and accurate decisions resulting from the use of ML techniques, their output has long been criticized for not being transparent and hence for being difficult to interpret. RF outputs including those of *eGAP* and *CLUB-DRF*, however, can be easily understood using a collection of high-importance random forest path snippets (CHIRPS) (Hatwell et al., 2020).

References

Abe, M., & Nakayama, H. (2018). Deep learning for forecasting stock returns in the cross-section. In *Pacific-Asia conference on knowledge discovery and data mining* (pp. 273–284). Springer.

Abellán, J., & Mantas, C. J. (2014). Improving experimental studies about ensembles of classifiers for bankruptcy prediction and credit scoring. *Expert Systems with Applications, 41*(8), 3825–3830.

Agarwalla, S., & Sarma, K. K. (2016). Machine learning based sample extraction for automatic speech recognition using dialectal Assamese speech. *Neural Networks, 78*, 97–111.

Alâ'Aref, S. J., Anchouche, K., Singh, G., Slomka, P. J., Kolli, K. K., Kumar, A., Pandey, M., Maliakal, G., Van Rosendael, A. R., Beecy, A. N., et al. (2019). Clinical applications of machine learning in cardiovascular disease and its relevance to cardiac imaging. *European Heart Journal, 40*(24), 1975–1986.

Aakash Atul Alurkar, Sourabh Bharat Ranade, Shreeya Vijay Joshi, Siddhesh Sanjay Ranade, Piyush A. Sonewar, Parikshit N. Mahalle, and Arvind V. Deshpande. (2017). A proposed data science approach for email spam classification using machine learning techniques. In *2017 Internet of things business models, users, and networks*, pp. 1–5. IEEE.

José A. Álvarez-Jareño, Elena Badal-Valero, José Manuel Pavía, et al. (2017). Using machine learning for financial fraud detection in the accounts of companies investigated for money laundering.

Amit, Y., & Geman, D. (1997). Shape quantization and recognition with randomized trees. *Neural Computation, 9*(7), 1545–1588.

Andriosopoulos, D., Doumpos, M., Pardalos, P. M., & Zopounidis, C. (2019). Computational approaches and data analytics in financial services: A literature review. *Journal of the Operational Research Society, 70*(10), 1581–1599.

Antipov, E. A., & Pokryshevskaya, E. B. (2012). Mass appraisal of residential apartments: An application of random forest for valuation and a cart-based approach for model diagnostics. *Expert Systems with Applications, 39*(2), 1772–1778.

Baldominos, A., Blanco, I., Moreno, A. J., Iturrarte, R., Bernárdez, Ó., & Afonso, C. (2018). Identifying real estate opportunities using machine learning. *Applied Sciences, 8*(11), 2321.

Ban, G.-Y., El Karoui, N., & Lim, A. E. B. (2018). Machine learning and portfolio optimization. *Management Science, 64*(3), 1136–1154.

Rishi Banerjee, Gabriela Bourla, Steven Chen, Mehal Kashyap, and Sonia Purohit. (2018). Comparative analysis of machine learning algorithms through credit card fraud detection. In *2018 IEEE MIT Undergraduate Research Technology Conference (URTC)*, pp. 1–4. IEEE.

Baroni, M., & Bernardini, S. (2006). A new approach to the study of translationese: Machine-learning the difference between original and translated text. *Literary and Linguistic Computing, 21*(3), 259–274.

Baudry, M., & Robert, C. Y. (2019). A machine learning approach for individual claims reserving in insurance. *Applied Stochastic Models in Business and Industry, 35*(5), 1127–1155.

Blanzieri, E., & Bryl, A. (2008). A survey of learning-based techniques of email spam filtering. *Artificial Intelligence Review, 29*(1), 63–92.

Boukerche, A., & Wang, J. (2020). Machine learning-based traffic prediction models for intelligent transportation systems. *Computer Networks, 181*, 107530.

Breiman, L. (1996). Bagging predictors. *Machine Learning, 24*(2), 123–140.

Breiman, L. (2001). Random forests. *Machine Learning, 45*(1), 5–32.

Butaru, F., Chen, Q., Clark, B., Das, S., Lo, A. W., & Siddique, A. (2016). Risk and risk management in the credit card industry. *Journal of Banking & Finance, 72*, 218–239.

Čeh, M., Kilibarda, M., Lisec, A., & Bajat, B. (2018). Estimating the performance of random forest versus multiple regression for predicting prices of the apartments. *ISPRS International Journal of Geo-Information, 7*(5), 168.

Chen, Z., Teoh, E. N., Nazir, A., Karuppiah, E. K., Lam, K. S., et al. (2018). Machine learning techniques for anti-money laundering (aml) solutions in suspicious transaction detection: A review. *Knowledge and Information Systems, 57*(2), 245–285.

Christina, V., Karpagavalli, S., & Suganya, G. (2010). Email spam filtering using supervised machine learning techniques. *International Journal on Computer Science and Engineering (IJCSE), 2*(09), 3126–3129.

Julien Courbe. (2016). Financial services technology 2020 and beyond: Embracing disruption. In *PWC*, page 48.

Cruz, J. A., & Wishart, D. S. (2006). Applications of machine learning in cancer prediction and prognosis. *Cancer Informatics, 2*, 117693510600200030.

Deng, L., & Li, X. (2013). Machine learning paradigms for speech recognition: An overview. *IEEE Transactions on Audio, Speech, and Language Processing, 21*(5), 1060–1089.

Sahil Dhankhad, Emad Mohammed, & Behrouz Far. (2018). Supervised machine learning algorithms for credit card fraudulent transaction detection: A comparative study. In *2018 IEEE International Conference on Information Reuse and Integration (IRI)* (pp. 122–125). IEEE.

Ding, K., Lev, B., Peng, X., Sun, T., & Vasarhelyi, M. A. (2020). Machine learning improves accounting estimates: Evidence from insurance payments. *Review of Accounting Studies, 25*(3), 1098–1134.

Youness El Hamzaoui, & Jose Alfredo Hernandez Perez. (2011). Application of artificial neural networks to predict the selling price in the real estate valuation process. In *Proceedings of the 2011 10th Mexican international conference on artificial intelligence*, pp. 175–181.

Fawagreh, K., & Gaber, M. M. (2020a). egap: An evolutionary game theoretic approach to random forest pruning. *Big Data and Cognitive Computing, 4*(4), 37.

Fawagreh, K., & Gaber, M. M. (2020b). Resource-efficient fast prediction in healthcare data analytics: A pruned random forest regression approach. *Computing*, pp. 1–12.

Fawagreh, K., Gaber, M. M., & Elyan, E.. (2014). Diversified random forests using random subspaces. In *International conference on intelligent data engineering and automated learning*, pp. 85–92. Springer.

Fawagreh, K., Gaber, M. M., & Elyan, E.. (2015a). Club-drf: A clustering approach to extreme pruning of random forests. In *International conference on innovative techniques and applications of artificial intelligence*, pp. 59–73. Springer.

Fawagreh, K., Gaber, M. M., & Elyan, E. (2015b). A replicator dynamics approach to collective feature engineering in random forests. In *International conference on innovative techniques and applications of artificial intelligence*, pp. 25–41. Springer.

Fawagreh, K., Gaber, M. M., & Elyan, E. (2016). An outlier ranking tree selection approach to extreme pruning of random forests. In *International conference on engineering applications of neural networks*, pp. 267–282. Springer.

Fernández-Delgado, M., Cernadas, E., Barro, S., & Amorim, D. (2014). Do we need hundreds of classifiers to solve real world classification problems? *The Journal of Machine Learning Research, 15*(1), 3133–3181.

Gui, L. (2019). *Application of machine learning algorithms in predicting credit card default payment*. PhD thesis, UCLA.

Guzella, T. S., & Caminhas, W. M. (2009). A review of machine learning approaches to spam filtering. *Expert Systems with Applications, 36*(7), 10206–10222.

Hajek, P., & Henriques, R. (2017). Mining corporate annual reports for intelligent detection of financial statement fraud—A comparative study of machine learning methods. *Knowledge-Based Systems, 128*, 139–152.

Julian Hatwell, Mohamed Medhat Gaber, & R. Azad. (2020). Chirps: Explaining random forest classification. *Artificial Intelligence Review*.

Ho, T. K.. (1995). Random decision forests. In *Proceedings of 3rd international conference on document analysis and recognition*, vol. 1, pp. 278–282. IEEE.

Ho, T. K. (1998). The random subspace method for constructing decision forests. *IEEE Transactions on Pattern Analysis and Machine Intelligence, 20*(8), 832–844.

Jain, A. K. (2010). Data clustering: 50 years beyond k-means. *Pattern Recognition Letters, 31*(8), 651–666.

Martin Jullum, Anders Løland, Ragnar Bang Huseby, Geir Ånonsen, & Johannes Lorentzen. (2020). Detecting money laundering transactions with machine learning. *Journal of Money Laundering Control*.

Olgierd Kempa, Tadeusz Lasota, Zbigniew Telec, & Bogdan Trawiński. (2011). Investigation of bagging ensembles of genetic neural networks and fuzzy systems for real estate appraisal. In *Asian conference on intelligent information and database systems*, pp. 323–332. Springer.

Luckyson Khaidem, Snehanshu Saha, & Sudeepa Roy Dey. (2016). Predicting the direction of stock market prices using random forest. *arXiv preprint arXiv:1605.00003*.

Kok, N., Koponen, E.-L., & Martínez-Barbosa, C. A. (2017). Big data in real estate? From manual appraisal to automated valuation. *The Journal of Portfolio Management, 43*(6), 202–211.

Kou, G., Chao, X., Peng, Y., Alsaadi, F. E., & Herrera-Viedma, E. (2019). Machine learning methods for systemic risk analysis in financial sectors. *Technological and Economic Development of Economy, 25*(5), 716–742.

Kruppa, J., Schwarz, A., Arminger, G., & Ziegler, A. (2013). Consumer credit risk: Individual probability estimates using machine learning. *Expert Systems with Applications, 40*(13), 5125–5131.

Ładyżyński, P., Żbikowski, K., & Gawrysiak, P. (2019). Direct marketing campaigns in retail banking with the use of deep learning and random forests. *Expert Systems with Applications, 134*, 28–35.

Johannes Lahann, Martin Scheid, & Peter Fettke. (2019). Utilizing machine learning techniques to reveal vat compliance violations in accounting data. In *2019 IEEE 21st conference on business informatics (CBI)*, vol. 1, pp. 1–10. IEEE.

Lahmiri, S. (2016). Features selection, data mining and financial risk classification: A comparative study. *Intelligent Systems in Accounting, Finance and Management, 23*(4), 265–275.

Latha, C. P., & Priya, M. (2016). A review on deep learning algorithms for speech and facial emotion recognition. *APTIKOM Journal on Computer Science and Information Technologies, 1* (3), 92–108.

Lee, Y., Ragguett, R.-M., Mansur, R. B., Boutilier, J. J., Rosenblat, J. D., Trevizol, A., Brietzke, E., Lin, K., Pan, Z., Subramaniapillai, M., et al. (2018). Applications of machine learning algorithms to predict therapeutic outcomes in depression: A meta-analysis and systematic review. *Journal of Affective Disorders, 241*, 519–532.

Lee, T. K., Cho, J. H., Kwon, D. S., & Sohn, S. Y. (2019). Global stock market investment strategies based on financial network indicators using machine learning techniques. *Expert Systems with Applications, 117*, 228–242.

Leo, M., Sharma, S., & Maddulety, K. (2019). Machine learning in banking risk management: A literature review. *Risks, 7*(1), 29.

Yitong Li, Rui Wang, & Hai Zhao. (2015). A machine learning method to distinguish machine translation from human translation. In *Proceedings of the 29th Pacific Asia conference on language, information and computation: Posters*, pp. 354–360.

Lin, W., Wu, Z., Lin, L., Wen, A., & Li, J. (2017). An ensemble random forest algorithm for insurance big data analysis. *IEEE Access, 5*, 16568–16575.

Chengwei Liu, Yixiang Chan, Syed Hasnain Alam Kazmi, & Hao Fu. (2015). Financial fraud detection model: Based on random forest. *International Journal of Economics and Finance, 7* (7).

Liu, B., Wu, M., Tao, M., Wang, Q., He, L., Shen, G., Chen, K., & Yan, J. (2020). Video content analysis for compliance audit in finance and security industry. *IEEE Access, 8*, 117888–117899.

Mark Lokanan, Vincent Tran, & Nam Hoai Vuong. (2019). Detecting anomalies in financial statements using machine learning algorithm. *Asian Journal of Accounting Research.*

Marcos Roberto Machado, Salma Karray, & Ivaldo Tributino de Sousa. (2019). Lightgbm: An effective decision tree gradient boosting method to predict customer loyalty in the finance industry. In *2019 14th International Conference on Computer Science & Education (ICCSE)*, pp. 1111–1116. IEEE.

James MacQueen et al. (1967). Some methods for classification and analysis of multivariate observations. In *Proceedings of the fifth Berkeley symposium on mathematical statistics and probability*, vol. 1, page 14. California, USA.

Ana I Maqueda, Antonio Loquercio, Guillermo Gallego, Narciso García, & Davide Scaramuzza. (2018). Event-based vision meets deep learning on steering prediction for self-driving cars. In *Proceedings of the IEEE conference on computer vision and pattern recognition*, pp. 5419–5427.

Mashrur, A., Luo, W., Zaidi, N. A., & Robles-Kelly, A. (2020). Machine learning for financial risk management: A survey. *IEEE Access, 8*, 203203–203223.

Teemu Mutanen, Jussi Ahola, & Sami Nousiainen. (2006). Customer churn prediction-a case study in retail banking. In *Proc. of ECML/PKDD workshop on practical data mining*, pp. 13–19.

Okuda, T., & Shoda, S. (2018). Ai-based chatbot service for financial industry. *Fujitsu Scientific and Technical Journal, 54*(2), 4–8.

Paiva, F. D., Cardoso, R. T. N., Hanaoka, G. P., & Duarte, W.-d. M. (2019). Decision-making for financial trading: A fusion approach of machine learning and portfolio selection. *Expert Systems with Applications, 115*, 635–655.

Perols, J. (2011). Financial statement fraud detection: An analysis of statistical and machine learning algorithms. *Auditing: A Journal of Practice & Theory, 30*(2), 19–50.

Provost, F., & Kohavi, R. (1998). Glossary of terms. *Journal of Machine Learning, 30*(2–3), 271–274.

Przegalinska, A., Ciechanowski, L., Stroz, A., Gloor, P., & Mazurek, G. (2019). In bot we trust: A new methodology of chatbot performance measures. *Business Horizons, 62*(6), 785–797.

S. Benson Edwin Raj, & A. Annie Portia. (2011). Analysis on credit card fraud detection methods. In *2011 International Conference on Computer, Communication and Electrical Technology (ICCCET)*, pp. 152–156. IEEE.

Sebastian Ramos, Stefan Gehrig, Peter Pinggera, Uwe Franke, & Carsten Rother. (2017). Detecting unexpected obstacles for self-driving cars: Fusing deep learning and geometric modeling. In *2017 IEEE Intelligent Vehicles Symposium (IV)*, pp. 1025–1032. IEEE.

Qing Rao, & Jelena Frtunikj. (2018). Deep learning for self-driving cars: chances and challenges. In *Proceedings of the 1st international workshop on software engineering for AI in autonomous systems*, pp. 35–38.

David E. Rapach, & Guofu Zhou. (2020). Time-series and cross-sectional stock return forecasting: New machine learning methods. *Machine learning for asset management: New developments and financial applications*, pp. 1–33.

Riya Roy, & K. Thomas George. (2017). Detecting insurance claims fraud using machine learning techniques. In *2017 International Conference on Circuit, Power and Computing Technologies (ICCPCT)*, pp. 1–6. IEEE.

Ryman-Tubb, N. F., Krause, P., & Garn, W. (2018). How artificial intelligence and machine learning research impacts payment card fraud detection: A survey and industry benchmark. *Engineering Applications of Artificial Intelligence, 76*, 130–157.

Rzeszótko, J., & Nguyen, S. H. (2012). Machine learning for traffic prediction. *Fundamenta Informaticae, 119*(3–4), 407–420.

Saura, J. R., Herráez, B. R., & Reyes-Menendez, A. (2019). Comparing a traditional approach for financial brand communication analysis with a big data analytics technique. *IEEE Access, 7*, 37100–37108.

Yashna Sayjadah, Ibrahim Abaker Targio Hashem, Faiz Alotaibi, & Khairl Azhar Kasmiran. (2018). Credit card default prediction using machine learning techniques. In *2018 Fourth International Conference on Advances in Computing, Communication & Automation (ICACCA)*, pp. 1–4. IEEE.

Schuster, P., & Sigmund, K. (1983). Replicator dynamics. *Journal of Theoretical Biology, 100*(3), 533–538.

Oleksandr Snihovyi, Vitaliy Kobets, & Oleksii Ivanov. (2018). Implementation of robo-advisor services for different risk attitude investment decisions using machine learning techniques. In *International conference on information and communication technologies in education, research, and industrial applications*, pp. 298–321. Springer.

Song, Q., Liu, A., & Yang, S. Y. (2017). Stock portfolio selection using learning-to-rank algorithms with news sentiment. *Neurocomputing, 264*, 20–28.

Srinivasan, G., Panda, P., & Roy, K. (2018). Spilinc: spiking liquid-ensemble computing for unsupervised speech and image recognition. *Frontiers in Neuro-science, 12*, 524.

Stilgoe, J. (2018). Machine learning, social learning and the governance of self-driving cars. *Social Studies of Science, 48*(1), 25–56.

Abdulhamit Subasi, & Selcuk Cankurt. (2019). Prediction of default payment of credit card clients using data mining techniques. In *2019 International Engineering Conference (IEC)*, pp. 115–120. IEEE.

Ting Sun, & Miklos Vasarhelyi. (2019). Predicting credit card delinquency: An application of the decision tree technique. *Rutgers Studies in Accounting Analytics: Audit Analytics in the Financial Industry (Rutgers Studies in Accounting Analytics), Emerald Publishing Limited*, pp. 71–83.

J. Tenni, A. Lehtola, C. Bounsaythip, & K. Jaaranen. (1999). Machine learning of language translation rules. In *IEEE SMC'99 conference proceedings. 1999 IEEE international conference on systems, man, and cybernetics (Cat. No. 99CH37028)*, vol. 5, pp. 171–177. IEEE.

Bogdan Trawiński, Zbigniew Telec, Jacek Krasnoborski, Mateusz Piwowarczyk, Michał Ta-laga, Tedeusz Lasota, & Edward Sawiłow. (2017). Comparison of expert algorithms with machine learning models for real estate appraisal. In *2017 IEEE International Conference on INnovations in Intelligent SysTems and Applications (INISTA)*, pp. 51–54. IEEE.

Van Liebergen, B., et al. (2017). Machine learning: A revolution in risk management and compliance? *Journal of Financial Transformation, 45*, 60–67.

Yue Xu, Wenjun Xu, Feng Yin, Jiaru Lin, & Shuguang Cui. (2017). High-accuracy wireless traffic prediction: A gp-based machine learning approach. In *GLOBECOM 2017–2017 IEEE global communications conference*, pp. 1–6. IEEE.

Shiyang Xuan, Guanjun Liu, Zhenchuan Li, Lutao Zheng, Shuo Wang, & Changjun Jiang. (2018). Random forest for credit card fraud detection. In *2018 IEEE 15th International Conference on Networking, Sensing and Control (ICNSC)*, pp. 1–6. IEEE.

Hongyang Yang, Xiao-Yang Liu, & Qingwei Wu. (2018a). A practical machine learning approach for dynamic stock recommendation. In *2018 17th IEEE international conference on trust, security and privacy in computing and communications/12th IEEE international conference on big data science and engineering (TrustCom/BigDataSE)*, pp. 1693–1697. IEEE.

Yang, S., Zhang, H., et al. (2018b). Comparison of several data mining methods in credit card default prediction. *Intelligent Information Management, 10*(05), 115.

Yeh, I.-C., & Lien, C.-h. (2009). The comparisons of data mining techniques for the predictive accuracy of probability of default of credit card clients. *Expert Systems with Applications, 36*(2), 2473–2480.

Yilmazer, S., & Kocaman, S. (2020). A mass appraisal assessment study using machine learning based on multiple regression and random forest. *Land Use Policy, 99*, 104889.

Sheng Zhang, Shenglin Zhao, Mingxuan Yuan, Jia Zeng, Jianguo Yao, Michael R. Lyu, & Irwin King. (2017). Traffic prediction based power saving in cellular networks: A machine learning method. In *Proceedings of the 25th ACM SIGSPATIAL international conference on advances in geographic information systems*, pp. 1–10.

Zogheib, A.. (2011). Genetic algorithm-based multi-word automatic language translation. *Recent Advances in Intelligent Information Systems*, 751–760.

Foreign Currency Exchange Rate Prediction Using Long Short-Term Memory, Support Vector Regression and Random Forest Regression

Md. Fazle Rabbi, Mahmudul Hasan Moon, Fahmida Tasnim Dhonno, Ayrin Sultana, and Mohammad Zoynul Abedin

Abstract This chapter aims to predict the foreign currency exchange rate on the basis of the US dollar over twenty-two different currencies. This chapter proposes two machine learning algorithms like Support Vector Regression (SVR), Random Forest Regression (RFR) and one deep learning algorithm named Long Short-Term Memory (LSTM), for the technical analysis of currency exchange rate prediction. The authors use Mean absolute error (MAE), Mean squared error (MSE), Root Mean Squared Error (RMSE), and mean absolute percentage error (MAPE) to measure the performance of the algorithms. Empirical findings specify that the overall performance of the algorithms is outstanding, but the Long Short-Term Memory (LSTM) shows less error than others. This study is useful for the stakeholders to set a wide range of approaches for the foreign exchange market.

Keywords Currency exchange rate prediction · Machine learning · Deep learning · Time series analysis

1 Introduction

The purchasing prediction of one currency with regard to another currency is constantly an exciting topic in the field of financial time series as it highly prevails the trading of different currencies. Fair and accurate predictions of these exchange rates eventually manipulate the international transactions and their global financial market (Dash, 2017). The financial market involves chaotic and nonlinear nature.

M. F. Rabbi · M. H. Moon
Department of Computer Science and Engineering, Hajee Mohammad Danesh Science and Technology University, Dinajpur, Bangladesh

F. T. Dhonno · A. Sultana · M. Z. Abedin (✉)
Department of Finance and Banking, Hajee Mohammad Danesh Science and Technology University, Dinajpur, Bangladesh

S. Derindere Köseoğlu (ed.), *Financial Data Analytics*, Contributions to Finance and Accounting, https://doi.org/10.1007/978-3-030-83799-0_8

Moreover, the exchange rate changes every day due to the trading of foreign currency from one country to another. This changing nature of the exchange rate is not consistent, and sometimes the exchange rate changes dramatically. In the foreign exchange market, a complex relationship between time and exchange rate exists. Therefore, it is a very tough and challenging task to predict the foreign exchange rate accurately. That is why developing more computerized approaches such as hybrid models to foresight the exceptionally nonlinear and non-stationary foreign exchange rates more efficiently is of foremost emphasis in financial markets with exposure to foreign currencies (Dash, 2017). The hybrid forecasting model is a mixture of traditional and current artificial intelligence (AI) techniques that represent improved forecasting capacity than the use of single techniques (Chi et al., 2019). The prediction of the foreign currency exchange rate is important as it is one of the key indicators that determine the level of economic health and economic stability of a country (Kartono et al., 2020). For the massive amount of data, the authors add artificial intelligence to analyze the previous exchange rate of different currencies and predict the future exchange rate. This kind of financial analysis is of two types: fundamental and technical analysis. Fundamental and technical analysis are two key methods in the financial globe, and they utilize technical indicator data and macro-economic data, respectively (Yıldırım et al., 2021). In this chapter, the authors focus on technical analysis and try to find out the best machine learning and deep learning algorithms to predict the foreign currency exchange rate. Deep learning has substantially developed the situation of ordinary language processing, the skill in computer vision, and other fields (Jakob et al., 2020). Accurate prediction of the exchange rate is important as it helps the policymakers and businessmen to improve the quality and quantity of appropriate management decisions. It also helps to plan financial decisions more precisely. Researchers use different kinds of methods to predict the foreign currency exchange rate (Mahmoud & Hosseini, 1994; Arifovic & Gençay, 2000; Colombo & Pelagatti, 2020; Chi et al., 2017). Most of them involve statistical analysis, and overall performance is not satisfactory. Also, researchers have done most of the works based on the relationship between two currencies. So, in this chapter, we take 22 currencies and predict the exchange rate with US dollar. The authors consider three powerful algorithms in this analysis, and the overall performance is better than others. We apply Long Short-Term Memory to predict the foreign currency exchange rate. (LSTM) is a recurrent neural network algorithm. It has a significant impact on deep learning. Furthermore, it performs better than others in time series data. Every neural network involves a predefined architecture. It specifies the number of inputs to the network system and the amount of outputs it generates, the digit of layers, the digit of neurons per layer and the functions of each neuron. But recurrent neural networks have both feed-back and feed-forward connections. They are nonlinear dynamical systems in nature that design temporal problems (Henríquez & Kristjanpoller, 2019). One of the limitations of other neural networks is that the models do not involve any memory and that is a major problem for time series data. LSTM overcomes this issue by generating both a short-term and long-term memory components. The authors also use (*SVR*) and (*RFR*) in this chapter. The prime advantage of support vector machine (*SVR*) is that it involves an excellent generalization capability with high prediction accuracy. A key feature of SVM is that training SVM solves the linearly constrained quadratic programming problem. As a result, the solution of SVM is always distinctive and globally optimal (Moula et al., 2017). Versatility is one of the main advantages of Random Forest. It is one of the most precise learning algorithms. Furthermore, without variable deletion it can handle thousands of input variables and can run efficiently and effectively on large databases. To accurately predict the foreign currency exchange rate, we measure the performance of the algorithms using Mean Absolute Error (*MAE*), Mean Square Error (*MSE*), Root Mean Square Error (*RMSE*) and Mean Absolute Percentage Error (*MAPE*).

2 Related Works

To predict foreign currency exchange rates, many researchers use different statistical time series models, different types of machine learning and deep learning algorithms and try to improve the accuracy of the prediction. An assumption of most of the suggested statistical time series models is that the data are correlated and linear in nature. However, foreign exchange rates rarely assure such assumptions in reality. Therefore, the statistical models are unable to seize the inherent nonlinear and dynamic activities of exchange rates time series data more accurately with fulfillment. In order to deal with the restrictions of time series models and to meet the growing needs for better forecasting models, machine learning and deep learning-based FOREX predictor models (hybrid models) are proposed in the literature Kadilar et al. (2009) use Autoregressive Integrated Moving Average and Different neural network models and they predict the Turkish Lira against US dollar. Their result shows that neural networks are better than ARIMA for financial time series data. Henríquez and Kristjanpoller (2019) utilize (hybrid models) independent component analysis (ICA), and neural networks (NN) to predict the exchange rate. They compare their models with Random Walk, Autoregressive, and Conditional Variance models, Neural Networks, and some other models and show that their model outperforms the other models and significantly improve the accuracy of forecast. Tao and Yang (2020) focus on the real-time changes in financial exchange rates and they use machine learning and complex embedded system. They use different types of sensors, microcontroller, tracker, generator inspection network and by collecting the sensor information, they analyse the data and try to find out the real-time prediction that are displayed on a particular website. A software interface may analyze different input/output processes with machine learning financial changes. By using advanced inserted and Artificial Intelligence (AI), researchers can examine the expectation conversion standard. AI and Machine Learning work on rapid changes in financial transactions and predict the next change (Goncu, 2019). Researchers are divided into two groups; one of the groups use a traditional statistical model and assume that time series data are linear process. Another group uses machine learning models, and they say that machine learning models are successful in financial modeling and forecasting (Kumar & Murugan, 2013; Lee, 2009; Cavalcante et al., 2016; Wang et al., 2011). To forecast exchange rates, researchers accompany a number of studies using neural networks. Sfetsos and Siriopoulos (2005) discover a method by comparing four techniques such as linear regression, auto regression integrated moving average, random walk, and artificial neural network to forecast exchange rate between US dollar and GB pound. But some researchers show that the neural network models are better than the conventional models for predicting foreign exchange rates. The authors scrutinize the predictability of the general regression neural network and contrast its performance with multivariate transfer functions, multi-layered feed-forward network (MLFN), and random walk models. For different currencies, they show that GRNN has both a higher level of prediction accuracy and executes statistically better than other evaluated techniques (Leung et al., 2000). To predict foreign exchange rate, Lubecke et al. (1998) test the usefulness of neural networks as a possible alternative methodology for composite foreign exchange forecasting. Galeshchuk (2016) explains and empirically scrutinize the exploration of artificial neural network with the foreign exchange market data for the economic purposes. They examine panel data of the exchange rates (USD/EUR, JPN/USD, USD/GBP) and optimize to predict the time series with neural networks for the experiment. They find the best neural network with the best prediction abilities on the basis of certain performance measures. Pradhan and Kumar (2010) employ artificial neural network to forecast foreign exchange rate for US dollar, Pound, Euro, and Japanese Yen against the Indian rupee

3 Methodology

3.1 Dataset

The full dataset comes from Kaggle.[1] This is an open-access dataset that comes from the Federal Reserve's Download Data Program. In our dataset, we use twenty-two currency exchange rates against US dollar. In this actual dataset, Australian Dollar, Euro, New Zealand Dollar and United Kingdom Pound are in their units (not in dollar). Therefore, to analyze the data, conversion of all the currencies in a same scales is important. The authors use a converter for this dataset in order to view all rates based on dollar units.

Many researchers use statistical models, machine learning and deep learning models previously and all of them try to improve the rate of prediction. In this research, the authors propose two machine learning and one deep learning algorithm. Furthermore, we measure different types of errors and find out the best model for this dataset.

[1] https://www.kaggle.com/brunotly/foreign-exchange-rates-per-dollar-20002019

3.2 Performance Measures

Errors that we use in this research to measure the performances of the algorithms are:

MAE indicates mean absolute error. The absolute error means the absolute value. It signifies the variance between the actual value and the forecasted value. MAE informs us of the level of significance of an error that we can expect from the average prediction.

$$MAE = \frac{1}{n}\sum_{i=1}^{n}|xi - x|$$

Where:

- n = the number of errors,
- Σ = summation symbol (which means "add them all up"),
- $|x_i - x|$ = the absolute errors.

MSE represents mean squared error. The mean squared error indicates the way that a regression line is adjacent to a set of points. MSE performs this task by detecting the distances from the points to the regression line (these distances are the "errors") and making them squared. The squaring is essential to eliminate any negative signs.

$$MSE = \frac{1}{n}\sum\nolimits_{i=1}^{n}(y - yi)^2$$

Where:

- n = the number of errors,
- Σ = summation symbol (which means "add them all up"),
- y = Actual value,
- y_i = predicted value,

RMSE is the short form of root mean squared error. It is a powerful prediction error (standard deviation of the residuals). Residuals measure the distance between the regression line and data points. RMSE measures the spread out level of these residuals. Particularly, it tells us how the data concentrates around the best fit line.

$$RMSE = \sqrt{\frac{1}{n}\sum_{i=1}^{n}(z - zi)^2}$$

Where:

- n = the number of errors,
- Σ = summation symbol (which means "add them all up"),

- z = Actual value,
- z_i = predicted value,

MAPE represents mean absolute percentage error. For regression problems, authors generally practice mean absolute percentage error as a loss function. It is a measure of prediction accuracy and found by calculating as:

$$\mathrm{MAPE} = \frac{\sum_{i=1}^{n} \frac{|y_i - x_i|}{y_i}}{n} \times 100\%$$

- n = the number of errors,
- Σ = summation symbol (which means "add them all up"),
- y_i = predicted value,

In order to compute the prediction error of exchange rate movements of particular countries, many researchers use different algorithms to choose the best method. This chapter proposes support vector machine, random forests and long short-term memory. The description of these algorithms is given below.

3.3 *Forecasting Algorithm*

3.3.1 Support Vector Machine

Support vector machine is the most used and high-performance algorithm in today's world. This is a supervised machine learning algorithm and used for both classification and regression purposes (Abedin et al., 2019a). Li et al. (2020) propose a regression model on the basis of support vector regression (SVR) and extreme learning machine (ELM) for both noise variances forecasting and smoothing. The purpose of SVM is to form a model based on the training data. This model forecasts the outputs of the target values of the test data that are given in the test data features. Two forms of SVM are available now (i) Linear SVM and (ii) Kernel SVM. In order to solve multiclass problems of large data sets, Linear SVM performs as the extremely fast machine learning algorithm and implements an original proprietary version of an algorithm having illustrated in Fig. 1 (Abedin et al., 2019b).

This algorithm makes a decision boundary based on the support vector point and classifies the data. The accuracy of SVM is higher than other classification algorithms for some special purpose.

Kernel SVM is used for nonlinear data classification because the data are not as simple as shown in the previous figure in the real world. To classify these kinds of data, a modified SVM algorithm called Kernel SVM is essential. There are a number of mathematical functions in the kernel SVM. These functions obtain data as input and convert it into the required form (Hsu & Lin, 2002). The mathematical functions

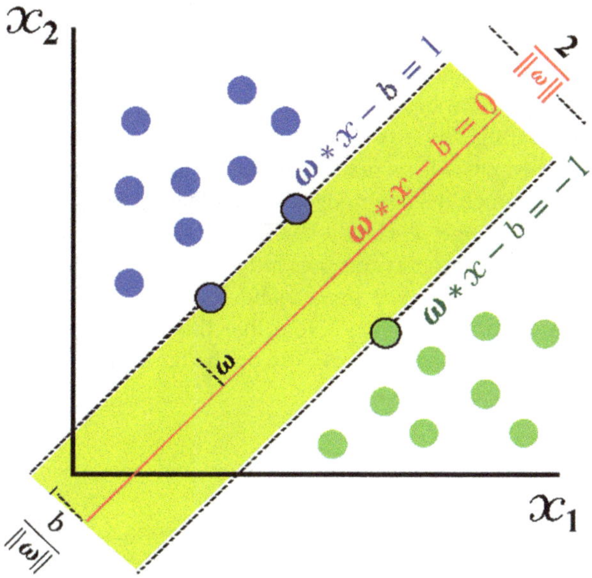

Fig. 1 Graphical representation of SVM (Linear)

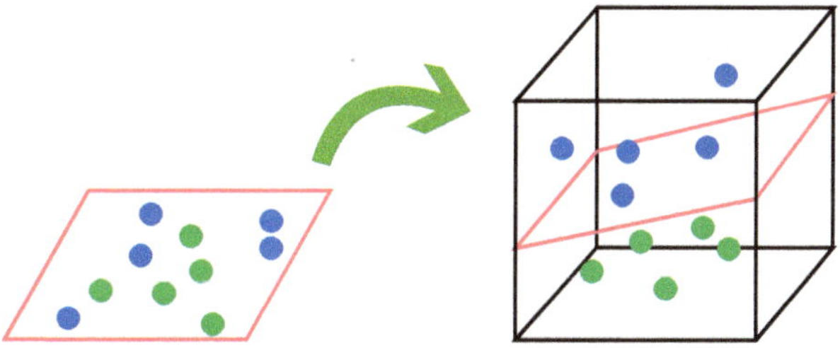

Fig. 2 Graphical representation of SVM (RBF)

involve polynomial, sigmoid, linear, nonlinear, and radial basis functions (RBF) having illustrated in Fig. 2.

3.3.2 Random Forest

Random forest is an ensemble classifier that constructs a group of independent and non-identical decision trees based on the idea of randomization (Provost et al., 2016). This algorithm is used for both regression and classification purposes and is a combination of tree predictors. Each decision tree uses a random vector as a parameter, randomly selects the feature of samples, and randomly selects the subset of the sample data set as the training set (Bradter et al., 2013). The generalization error of a forest of the tree depends on the strength of the individual tree in the forest and the correlation between them. To split each node yields error rates, they use a random selection of features that compare favorably to Adboost. These are more robust with respect to noise (Shakoor et al., 2017). Random Forest is a highly flexible and accessible machine learning algorithm. It yields a great result most of the time, even without hyper-parameter tuning. Moreover, this is a very simple algorithm, so researchers use it mostly. In this chapter, we utilize the regression aspect of this algorithm based on our requirements. Using this random forest regression, we successfully achieve a very high accuracy upon implementation on our dataset. Sk-learn provides a great tool that measures the importance of a feature by looking at how much the tree nodes use that feature to reduce impurity across all trees in the forest (Grange & Hand, 1987). Deep decision trees may suffer from overfitting. Random Forest prevents overfitting by generating random subsets of the features and constructing smaller trees using these subsets most of the time. Afterwards, it combines the sub-trees. Note that this does not work every time and makes the computation slower depending on the number of trees that the random forest builds.

3.3.3 LSTM

LSTM is a kind of recurrent neural network algorithm. It is used in the field of deep learning and designed to learn long-term dependencies more robustly. The LSTM cell is a specially designed logic unit that reduces the vanishing gradient by creating an internal memory state. An interesting concept called forget gate controls the time dependency. It also controls the effect of previous inputs that determine which state are remembered or forgotten. The other two gates, input gate and output gate, are also a feature of the LSTM cell. The line across the top represents the internal memory of an LSTM unit, and the line across the bottom is the hidden state (h), and the acronym is the forget gate, input gate, new memory state and output gate, respectively. When the sigmoid functions take input from last time step h_{t-1} and current input x_t, LSTM primarily determines which information to dump or pass from the cell state at time step t. Here the output 1 means "completely keep" and 0 means "completely dump" and the output is calculated as follows.

$$f_t = \sigma\left(w_f x_t + u_f h_{t-1}\right)$$

Afterwards, LSTM chooses the new finding that is saved in the cell state and brings it up to date, which is calculated as follows.

$$i_t = \sigma(wixt\ uiht - 1)$$

$$\zeta t = \ tanh\,(wnxt\ unht - 1)$$

It is time to update the old cell state ct-1 into a new cell state ζt as follows:

$$ct = ft * ct - 1 + it * \zeta t$$

Finally, LSTM decides which part of the cell state generates output at its output gate. Then, LSTM puts the cell state through the tanh function and multiplies it by the output of the output gate. As a result, LSTM only generates the parts of output it decides, which is calculated as follows.

$$ot = \sigma(w0xt + u0ht - 1)$$

$$ht = ot * tanh\,(ct.)$$

Though the advantage of LSTM over RNN is more due to long-term dependencies it cannot work well when the input sequence is in opposite directions.

4 Result and Discussion

From the Table 1 of performance measurements, it is clear that the performance of LSTM is better than another model. The performance graph in Fig. 3 of the actual and predicted value is the good, and the overall performance of the other algorithms is not bad.

The above graphs clearly show that the performance of LSTM is better than others. The difference between the actual and predicted value is low that clearly indicates that the performance of LSTM is really better than others. The MAE, MSE, RMSE, and MAPE error calculations are given in Table 1.

5 Discussion

The performance errors clearly indicate that the performance of LSTM is higher than others. Sometimes the MAE of SVM is less than LSTM, but the overall perspective LSTM shows less error. The performance of other algorithms is also well. Many previous researchers predict currency exchange rates, and most of them try to discuss the statistical models. The empirical study of Mahmoud and Hosseini (1994) shows that to forecast exchange rates, simple time series methods can perform as well as some complex and expensive techniques. Arifovic and Gençay (2000) use statistical properties of the time series of the exchange rate data where representatives renew their savings and portfolio decisions by means of the genetic algorithm. The time series analysis of the statistics specifies that the dynamic of the exchange rate responds in chaotic. Their findings show that the profit results in chaotic patterns of the exchange rate series. Colombo and Pelagatti (2020) apply creative tools newly projected in the statistical learning methods to forecast the exchange rate in the short and long runs to access the ability of standard exchange rate models. They clarify the procedure of the statistical learning models by developing activity of variable significance. They also investigate the type of association that relates each variable with the result. They find an improved connecting understanding between the exchange rate and economic fundamentals that is complex and categorized by strong

Table 1 Errors calculation from different algorithms

Variable	Algorithms	MAE	MSE	RMSE	MAPE
AUSTRALIAN DOLLAR/US$	LSTM	*0.00700*	*0.00006*	0.00832	0.48547
	SVR (Linear)	0.01024	0.00013	0.01152	2.25615
	SVR (RBF)	0.00968	0.00011	0.01095	2.13208
	SVR (Polynomial)	0.00533	*0.00004*	0.00642	1.16551
	RFR	0.00902	0.00015	0.01243	1.93472
EURO/US$	LSTM	0.00414	*0.00002*	0.00475	0.46196
	SVR (Linear)	0.00604	*0.00005*	0.00716	1.31940
	SVR (RBF)	0.00510	*0.00003*	0.00619	1.11382
	SVR (Polynomial)	1.31940	0.00231	0.04806	10.30038
	RFR	0.00545	*0.00004*	0.00699	1.17382
NEW ZELAND DOLLAR/US$	LSTM	0.01151	0.00017	0.01310	0.75370
	SVR (Linear)	0.04136	0.00174	0.04182	15.28552
	SVR (RBF)	0.03896	0.00155	0.03944	14.40859
	SVR (Polynomial)	0.00679	*0.00006*	0.00828	2.53966
	RFR	0.00591	*0.00005*	0.00741	2.13685
UNITED KINGDOM POUND/US$	LSTM	0.00307	*0.00001*	0.00404	0.39238
	SVR (Linear)	0.01153	0.00022	0.01484	1.33427
	SVR (RBF)	0.00960	0.00016	0.01278	1.11072
	SVR (Polynomial)	0.03945	0.00224	0.04741	4.31878
	RFR	0.01097	0.00019	0.01392	1.24946
BRAZIL—REAL/US$	LSTM	0.02600	0.00110	0.03318	0.65254
	SVR (Linear)	0.01830	0.00044	0.02107	2.02208
	SVR (RBF)	0.02710	0.00087	0.02950	2.98612
	SVR (Polynomial)	0.01657	0.00037	0.01930	1.83479
	RFR	0.01289	0.00026	0.01621	1.43000
CANADIAN DOLLAR/US$	LSTM	0.00708	*0.00006*	0.00790	0.53414
	SVR (Linear)	0.01139	0.00016	0.01271	1.91579
	SVR (RBF)	0.01011	0.00013	0.01147	1.69988
	SVR (Polynomial)	0.04122	0.00172	0.04158	6.99087
	RFR	0.00646	*0.00006*	0.00829	1.09621
CHINA—YUAN/US$	LSTM	0.01171	0.00029	0.01723	0.16897
	SVR (Linear)	0.01968	0.00054	0.02338	5.63159
	SVR (RBF)	0.01791	0.00045	0.02138	5.12330
	SVR (Polynomial)	0.05346	0.00314	0.05604	13.12368
	RFR	0.00636	*0.00007*	0.00874	1.63449
HONG KONG DOLLAR/US$	LSTM	0.00295	*0.00001*	0.00394	0.03768
	SVR (Linear)	0.05527	0.00355	0.05958	6.13942
	SVR (RBF)	0.05819	0.00396	0.06297	6.41549
	SVR (Polynomial)	0.06367	0.00477	0.06912	6.98461
	RFR	0.02229	0.00137	0.03713	2.67761

(continued)

Table 1 (continued)

Variable	Algorithms	MAE	MSE	RMSE	MAPE
INDIAN RUPEE/US$	LSTM	0.61800	0.44499	0.66707	0.87832
	SVR (Linear)	0.04389	0.00198	0.04458	4.93584
	SVR (RBF)	0.04801	0.00237	0.04875	5.39566
	SVR (Polynomial)	0.01388	0.00030	0.01741	1.54251
	RFR	0.00913	0.00013	0.01145	1.03206
KOREA—WON/US$	LSTM	4.91561	37.32682	6.10956	0.41801
	SVR (Linear)	0.03054	0.00100	0.03165	7.73754
	SVR (RBF)	0.03019	0.00097	0.03128	7.64419
	SVR (Polynomial)	0.03227	0.00109	0.03311	8.07118
	RFR	0.00825	0.00011	0.01062	2.02660
MEXICO—MEXICAN PESO/US$	LSTM	0.14996	0.03004	0.17333	0.77973
	SVR (Linear)	0.00629	*0.00007*	0.00858	0.78568
	SVR (RBF)	0.00652	*0.00007*	0.00885	0.81343
	SVR (Polynomial)	0.01419	0.00027	0.01648	1.77482
	RFR	0.00904	0.00015	0.01235	1.13038
SOUTH AFRICA—RAND/US$	LSTM	0.09013	0.01366	0.11688	0.61752
	SVR (Linear)	0.02435	0.00070	0.02659	3.04174
	SVR (RBF)	0.02157	0.00057	0.02408	2.69061
	SVR (Polynomial)	0.00870	0.00012	0.01131	1.09139
	RFR	0.01156	0.00021	0.01481	1.45335
SINGAPORE—SINGAPORE DOLLAR/US$	LSTM	0.00195	*0.00006*	0.00251	0.14291
	SVR (Linear)	0.03424	0.00119	0.03453	13.70571
	SVR (RBF)	0.03180	0.00103	0.03212	12.73728
	SVR (Polynomial)	0.01317	0.00021	0.01465	5.09050
	RFR	0.00426	*0.00003*	0.00559	1.69066
DENMARK—DANISH KRONE/US$	LSTM	0.02317	0.00076	0.02761	0.34623
	SVR (Linear)	0.02310	0.00055	0.02351	4.96489
	SVR (RBF)	0.02320	0.00055	0.02360	4.98501
	SVR (Polynomial)	0.01899	0.00038	0.01949	4.08478
	RFR	0.00695	*0.00007*	0.00845	1.48842
JAPAN—YEN/US$	LSTM	0.28201	0.14041	0.37471	0.25957
	SVR (Linear)	0.01297	0.00020	0.01428	2.27962
	SVR (RBF)	0.01332	0.00021	0.01459	2.34242
	SVR (Polynomial)	0.04643	0.00219	0.04685	8.26688
	RFR	0.00727	*0.00008*	0.00941	1.31057
MALAYSIA—RINGGIT/US$	LSTM	0.01104	0.00015	0.01250	0.26604
	SVR (Linear)	0.03752	0.00144	0.03796	4.81799
	SVR (RBF)	0.03606	0.00133	0.03653	4.62916
	SVR (Polynomial)	0.02160	0.00050	0.02236	2.79100
	RFR	0.00592	*0.00006*	0.00829	0.76350

(continued)

Table 1 (continued)

Variable	Algorithms	MAE	MSE	RMSE	MAPE
NORWAY—NORWEGIAN KRONE/US$	LSTM	0.03618	0.00203	0.04507	0.40980
	SVR (Linear)	0.05422	0.00305	0.05529	6.43643
	SVR (RBF)	0.05351	0.00298	0.05459	6.35085
	SVR (Polynomial)	0.01682	0.00041	0.02044	2.06005
	RFR	0.00881	0.00012	0.01117	1.06121
SWEDEN—KRONA/US$	LSTM	0.03324	0.00182	0.04268	0.34944
	SVR (Linear)	0.01471	0.00028	0.01682	2.04628
	SVR (RBF)	0.01265	0.00022	0.01495	1.75707
	SVR (Polynomial)	0.00745	*0.00009*	0.00977	1.05530
	RFR	0.00941	0.00013	0.01160	1.32738
SRI LANKA—SRI LANKAN RUPEE/US$	LSTM	0.53271	0.39054	0.62493	0.29900
	SVR (Linear)	0.08796	0.00776	0.08812	9.16935
	SVR (RBF)	0.08681	0.00756	0.08700	9.04734
	SVR (Polynomial)	0.04721	0.00225	0.04752	4.93623
	RFR	0.00431	*0.00002*	0.00545	0.45076
SWITZERLAND—FRANC/US$	LSTM	0.00483	*0.00003*	0.00578	0.48732
	SVR (Linear)	0.01149	0.00014	0.01192	4.75302
	SVR (RBF)	0.01099	0.00013	0.01144	4.53995
	SVR (Polynomial)	0.01054	0.00012	0.01134	4.31552
	RFR	0.00333	*0.00001*	0.00437	1.39275
TAIWAN—NEW TAIWAN DOLLAR/US$	LSTM	0.07821	0.00984	0.09919	0.25299
	SVR (Linear)	0.00840	0.00013	0.01180	2.25436
	SVR (RBF)	0.01173	0.00022	0.01514	3.54821
	SVR (Polynomial)	0.01172	0.00023	0.01544	3.56038
	RFR	0.00881	0.00016	0.01268	2.42836
THAILAND—BAHT/US$	LSTM	0.08783	0.01155	0.10750	0.28278
	SVR (Linear)	0.03945	0.00160	0.04009	32.00994
	SVR (RBF)	0.03996	0.00166	0.04075	32.62840
	SVR (Polynomial)	0.04103	0.00187	0.04326	34.74884
	RFR	0.00428	*0.00003*	0.00562	3.23341

nonlinearity. In most countries, the response of exchange rates to unpredictability shocks is categorized by long-memory and symmetry. A probable description for this irregularity is the fear of floating that badly affects the interest rates and inflation which the market considers bad news (Chi et al., 2017). But in this chapter, we discuss machine learning and deep learning algorithms, which is better than the performance of other statistical models. Most of the previous works consider three or four currencies based on US dollar. In this chapter, we consider twenty-two currencies and measure the performance.

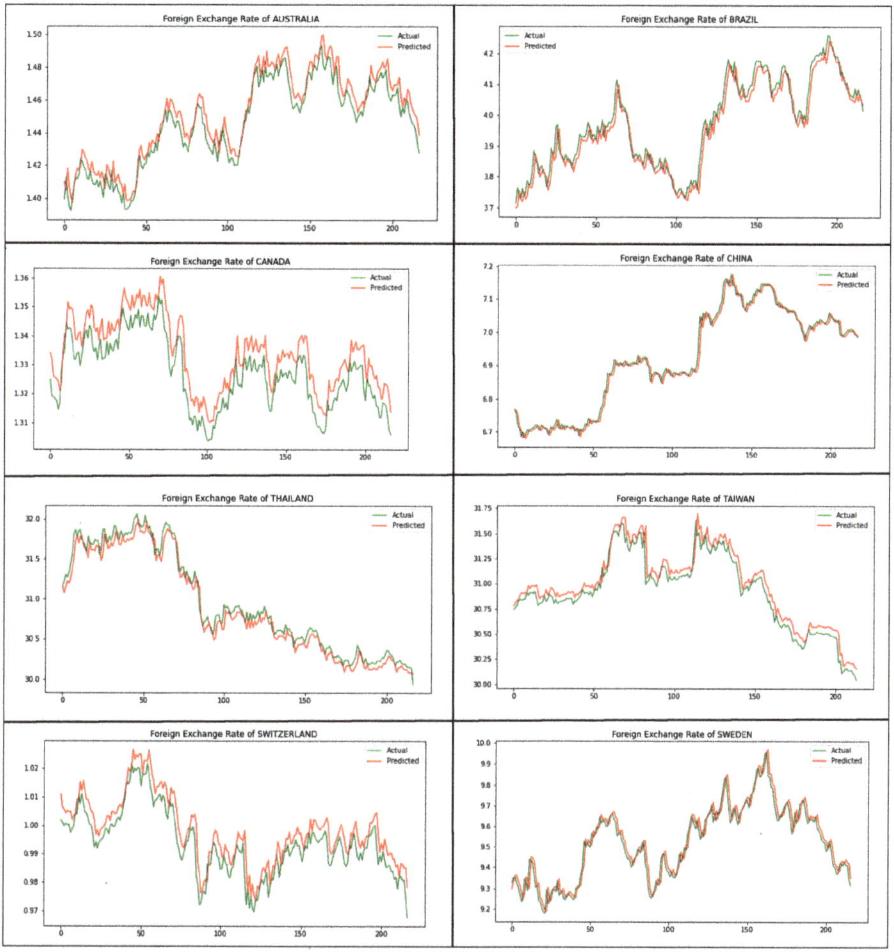

Fig. 3 The actual vs. predicted curve of LSTM

6 Conclusion and Future Works

This research focuses on the exchange rate of twenty-two countries based on US dollar. The overall performance of all machine learning and deep learning algorithms is good, but the performance of deep learning algorithm (LSTM) is better than others. Other algorithms also perform well. In this chapter, the errors to forecast the foreign currency exchange rate prediction are less than others. It specifies that our proposed model is good to predict foreign currency exchange rates. The main obstacles of this study are not to train logit regression and decision tree algorithms.

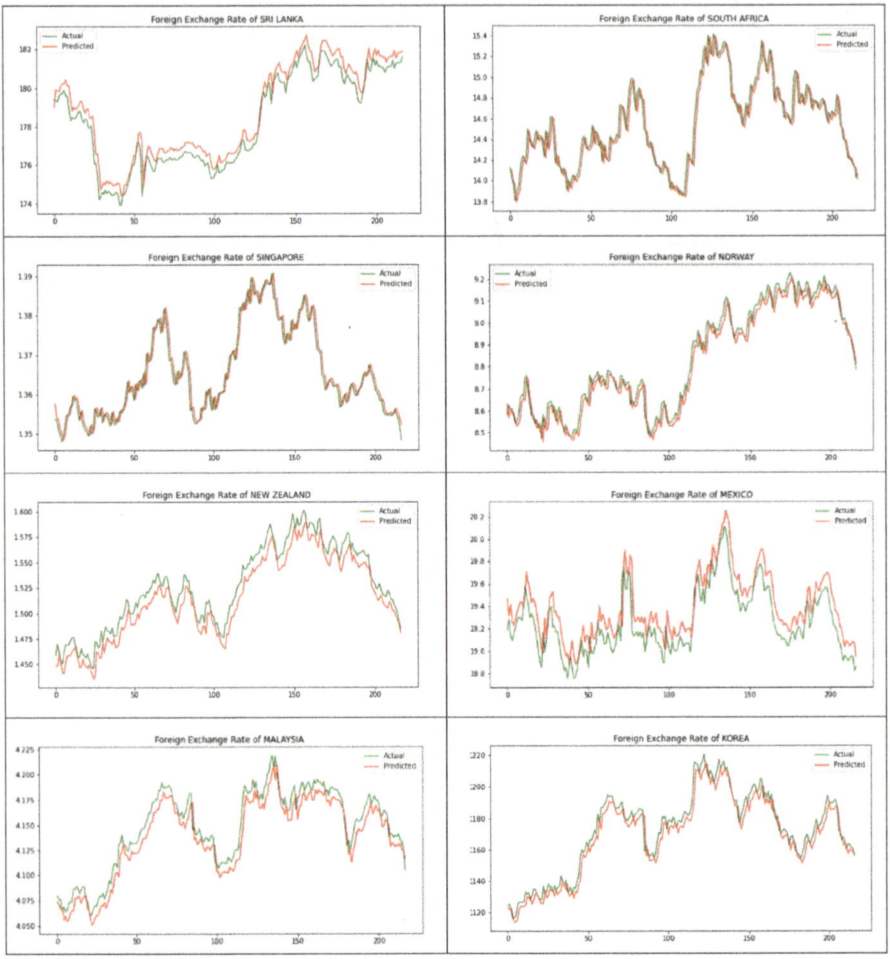

Fig. 3 (continued)

As a future avenue, further study will develop a converter that can predict the exchange rate of any currency on the basis of any currencies in the future. We would like to add more parameters to the input and also minimize the space complexity and time for the models for more precise prediction. Moreover, further study will attempt to prepare application software so that any kind of people may utilize it and they get the real-time exchange prediction.

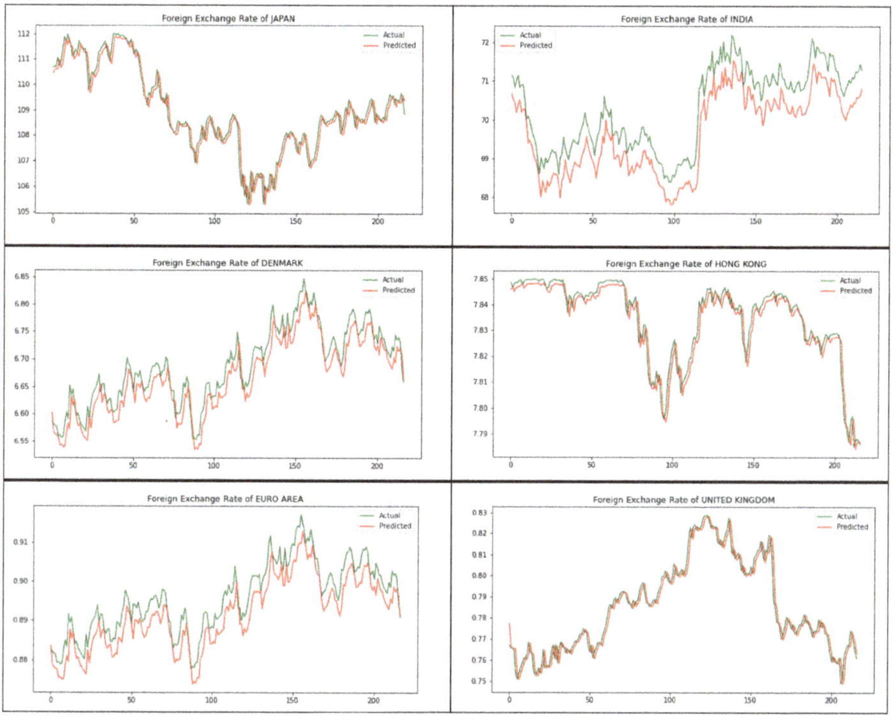

Fig. 3 (continued)

References

Abedin, M. Z., Chi, G., Moula, F. E., Azad, A. S. M. S., & Khan, M. S. U. (2019a). Topological applications of multilayer perceptrons and support vector machine in financial decision support systems. *International Journal of Finance & Economics, 24*, 474–507.

Abedin, M. Z., Chi, G., Moula, F. E., Zhang, T., & Hassan, K. M. (2019b). An optimized support vector machine intelligent technique using optimized feature selection methods: Evidence from chinese credit approval data. *Journal of Risk Model Validation, 13*(2), 1–46.

Arifovic, J., & Gençay, R. (2000). Statistical properties of genetic learning in a model of exchange rate. *Journal of Economic Dynamics and Control, 24*(5–7), 981–1005. https://doi.org/10.1016/S0165-1889(99)00033-0

Bradter, U., Kunin, W. E., Altringham, J. D., Thom, T. J., & Benton, T. G. (2013). Identifying appropriate spatial scales of predictors in species distribution models with the random forest algorithm. *Methods in Ecology and Evolution, 4*(2), 167–174. https://doi.org/10.1111/j.2041-210x.2012.00253.x

Cavalcante, R. C., Brasileiro, R. C., Souza, V. L. F., Nobrega, J. P., & Oliveira, A. L. I. (2016). Computational intelligence and financial markets: A survey and future directions. *Expert Systems with Applications, 55*, 194–211. https://doi.org/10.1016/j.eswa.2016.02.006

Chi, G., Abedin, M. Z., & Moula, F. E. (2017). Modeling credit approval data with neural networks: An experimental investigation and optimization. *Journal of Business Economics and Management, 18*(2), 224–240.

Chi, G., Uddin, M. S., Abedin, M. Z., & Yuan, K. (2019). Hybrid model for credit risk prediction: An application of neural network approaches. *International Journal on Artificial Intelligence Tools, 28*(5), 1–33. https://doi.org/10.1142/S0218213019500179

Colombo, E., & Pelagatti, M. (2020). Statistical learning and exchange rate forecasting. *International Journal of Forecasting, 36*(4), 1260–1289. https://doi.org/10.1016/j.ijforecast.2019.12.007

Dash, R. (2017). An improved shuffled frog leaping algorithm based evolutionary framework for currency exchange rate prediction. *Physica A: Statistical Mechanics and its Applications, 486*, 782–796. https://doi.org/10.1016/j.physa.2017.05.044

Galeshchuk, S. (2016). Neural networks performance in exchange rate prediction. *Neurocomputing, 172*, 446–452. https://doi.org/10.1016/j.neucom.2015.03.100

Goncu, A. (2019). Prediction of exchange rates with machine learning. *ACM International Conference Proceeding Series*. https://doi.org/10.1145/3371425.3371448

Grange, R. I., & Hand, D. W. (1987). A review of the effects of atmospheric humidity on the growth of horticultural crops. *Journal of Horticultural Science, 62*(2), 125–134. https://doi.org/10.1080/14620316.1987.11515760

Henríquez, J., & Kristjanpoller, W. (2019). A combined Independent Component Analysis–Neural Network model for forecasting exchange rate variation. *Applied Soft Computing Journal, 83*. https://doi.org/10.1016/j.asoc.2019.105654

Hsu, C. W., & Lin, C. J. (2002). A comparison of methods for multiclass support vector machines. *IEEE Transactions on Neural Networks, 13*(2), 415–425. https://doi.org/10.1109/72.991427

Jakob, A., Wolfgang, D., Härdle, K., & Lessmann, S. (2020). Forex exchange rate forecasting using deep recurrent neural networks. *Digital Finance, 2*(1), 69–96. https://doi.org/10.1007/s42521-020-00019-x

Kadilar, C., Simsek, M., & Aladag, C. H. (2009). Forecasting the exchange rate series with ann: The case of Turkey. *Istanbul University Econometrics and Statistics E-Journal, 9*(1), 17–29.

Kartono, A., Febriyanti, M., Wahyudi, S. T., & Irmansyah. (2020). Predicting foreign currency exchange rates using the numerical solution of the incompressible Navier–Stokes equations. *Physica A: Statistical Mechanics and its Applications, 560*, 125191. https://doi.org/10.1016/j.physa.2020.125191

Kumar, D. A., & Murugan, S. (2013). Performance analysis of Indian stock market index using neural network time series model. *Proceedings of the 2013 international conference on pattern recognition, informatics and mobile engineering, PRIME 2013*, 72–78. https://doi.org/10.1109/ICPRIME.2013.6496450

Lee, M. C. (2009). Using support vector machine with a hybrid feature selection method to the stock trend prediction. *Expert Systems with Applications, 36*(8), 10896–10904. https://doi.org/10.1016/j.eswa.2009.02.038

Leung, M. T., Chen, A. S., & Daouk, H. (2000). Forecasting exchange rates using general regression neural networks. *Computers and Operations Research, 27*(11–12), 1093–1110. https://doi.org/10.1016/S0305-0548(99)00144-6

Li, Z., Hong, X., Hao, K., Chen, L., & Huang, B. (2020). Gaussian process regression with heteroscedastic noises—A machine-learning predictive variance approach. *Chemical Engineering Research and Design, 157*(1996), 162–173. https://doi.org/10.1016/j.cherd.2020.02.033

Lubecke, T. H., Nam, K. D., Markland, R. E., & Kwok, C. C. Y. (1998). Combining foreign exchange rate forecasts using neural networks. *Global Finance Journal, 9*(1), 5–27. https://doi.org/10.1016/s1044-0283(98)90012-6

Mahmoud, E., & Hosseini, H. (1994). A comparison of forecasting techniques for predicting exchange rates. *Journal of Transnational Management Development, 1*(1), 93–110. https://doi.org/10.1300/J130v01n01_07

Moula, F. E., Guotai, C., & Abedin, M. Z. (2017). Credit default prediction modeling: An application of support vector machine. *Risk Management, 19*(2), 158–187. https://doi.org/10.1057/s41283-017-0016-x

Pradhan, R. P., & Kumar, R. (2010). Forecasting exchange rate in india: An application of artificial neural network model. *Journal of Mathematics Research, 2*(4), 111–117. https://doi.org/10.5539/jmr.v2n4p111

Provost, F., Hibert, C., Malet, J.-P., Stumpf, A., & Doubre, C. (2016). Automatic classification of endogenous seismic sources within a landslide body using random forest algorithm. *Geophysical Research Abstracts, 18*, 2016–15705. https://ui.adsabs.harvard.edu/abs/2016EGUGA..1815705P/abstract

Sfetsos, A., & Siriopoulos, C. (2005). Time series forecasting of averaged data with efficient use of information. *IEEE Transactions on Systems, Man, and Cybernetics Part A: Systems and Humans, 35*(5), 738–745. https://doi.org/10.1109/TSMCA.2005.851133

Shakoor, M. T., Rahman, K., Rayta, S. N., & Chakrabarty, A. (2017). Agricultural production output prediction using Supervised Machine Learning techniques. *2017 1st International conference on next generation computing applications, NextComp 2017*, 182–187. https://doi.org/10.1109/NEXTCOMP.2017.8016196

Tao, X., & Yang, H. (2020). Analysis of real-time changes in financial exchange rates based on machine learning and complex embedded systems. *Microprocessors and Microsystems, November*, 103493. https://doi.org/10.1016/j.micpro.2020.103493

Wang, J. Z., Wang, J. J., Zhang, Z. G., & Guo, S. P. (2011). Forecasting stock indices with back propagation neural network. *Expert Systems with Applications, 38*(11), 14346–14355. https://doi.org/10.1016/j.eswa.2011.04.222

Yıldırım, D. C., Toroslu, I. H., & Fiore, U. (2021). Forecasting directional movement of Forex data using LSTM with technical and macroeconomic indicators. *Financial Innovation*, 1–36. https://doi.org/10.1186/s40854-020-00220-2

Natural Language Processing for Exploring Culture in Finance: Theory and Applications

Jing-Mao Ho and Abdullah Shahid

Abstract Natural language processing (NLP) has found its way into financial data analysis. In this chapter, the authors argue for the prominence of taking NLP approaches to the study of culture in finance. To this end, the chapter first surveys some of the NLP algorithms, including bag-of-words, TF-IDF, sentiment analysis, cosine similarity, word embeddings, and topic models, with the illustration of their implementation in R—an open-source statistical language. Second, the authors demonstrate the usefulness of NLP to finance text mining by analyzing Warrant Buffet's letters to Berkshire Hathaway's shareholders from 1977 to 2019. Results show that there exist identifiable communication patterns in the letters. These findings are crucial for enhancing the understanding of the company's corporate culture and financial decision-making. The chapter is concluded by offering future research directions and opportunities.

Keywords Decision-making · Communication · Text mining · Machine learning · Algorithms · Semantic analysis · Sentiment analysis · Bag-of-words · TF-IDF · Cosine similarity · Word embeddings · Topic models · Letters to shareholders · Warren Buffett · Berkshire Hathaway · R (statistical language)

1 Introduction

Natural language processing (NLP) has come to be increasingly prominent in financial data analysis (e.g., Das, 2014; Fisher et al., 2016; Kumar & Ravi, 2016; Loughran & Mcdonald, 2016; Marco Spruit & Drilon Ferati, 2019). With the

J.-M. Ho (✉)
Utica College, Utica, NY, USA
e-mail: jh2268@cornell.edu

A. Shahid
Cornell University, Ithaca, NY, USA
e-mail: ais58@cornell.edu

S. Derindere Köseoğlu (ed.), *Financial Data Analytics*, Contributions to Finance and Accounting, https://doi.org/10.1007/978-3-030-83799-0_9

massive increase in the amounts of textual data and rapid advances in computational power (Hirschberg & Manning, 2015), scholars now are able to apply NLP tools to test hypotheses and develop theories in finance (e.g., Fligstein et al., 2017; Harmon, 2019). NLP techniques are used for mining a wide array of financial texts, such as corporate annual reports, Securities and Exchange Commission (SEC) filings, business standards and regulations, and online digital documents. More importantly, scholars argue that text mining with NLP can assist in corporate and individual decision-making (Palepu et al., 2020; Sun et al., 2016; Wong et al., 2014).

In this chapter, the authors argue that NLP is of great benefit to the study of culture in finance. More specifically, the chapter stresses that NLP is especially useful for studying communication patterns in corporate finance—processes by which finance and investment decisions are made at both individual and firm levels (Brown & Starkey, 1994; Williamson, 2010). Corporate finance analysts have typically used various financial ratios to understand the implications of managerial choices of firm value. Based on this approach, a variety of influential theories, including but not limited to agency theory (Eisenhardt, 1989) and theories of capital structure (Harris & Raviv, 1991), have been developed. However, the issue of culture has been given relatively little attention in research on finance decision-making (Karolyi, 2016). To shed light on the cultural aspect, the authors advocate taking NLP approaches because human languages are cultural vehicles for expressing and creating "categories of thought that are shared by members of a social group" (Kramsch, 2004, p. 235). Indeed, with the availability of huge amounts of textual data related to firm behavior, students of finance recently have started using NLP tools to not only inductively explore the contents of corporate finance communication but also deductively test theories about corporate finance (e.g., El-Haj et al., 2019; Li et al., 2014, 2020; Matsumoto et al., 2011; Zadeh & Zollmann, 2009).

Against this backdrop, we have the following objectives in this chapter. First, we review the literature on culture in finance and studies of corporate finance communication, aiming at articulating the intrinsic links of culture to natural language processing. Second, we will delve into a selected set of NLP tools and their mathematical foundations and underlying assumptions. We base our selection on the fact that those NLP algorithms have direct applications in finance but have not been extensively applied or explored. Third, we will provide illustrations of the applications of those selected NLP models by analyzing a corpus of text—legendary investor and CEO of Berkshire Hathaway Warren Buffett's letters to shareholders, which are cultural artifacts carrying important information about the past and the future of the firm, as understood, envisioned, and communicated by the chief executive. This illustration will demonstrate how NLP tools can be used as unsupervised machine learning algorithms to help finance scholars to better understand the cultural dimension of corporate finance.

2 Background

Recent work has called for more attention to the role of culture in finance (Carr & Tomkins, 1998; Karolyi, 2016; Stulz & Williamson, 2003; Williamson, 2010). Researchers have pointed out the significance of culture for financial and investment decision-making. For example, Carr and Tomkins (1998) explore the relationship between culture and business strategies by comparing cases in Britain, Germany, the US, and Japan. Karolyi (2016) studies the role of culture in economic decision-making, finding that cultural distance is negatively associated with the investment. Stulz and Williamson (2003) investigate whether or not national and religious culture is correlated with the protection of shareholder rights.

But how does culture affect financial decision-making? To answer this question, one needs to first address the question of what culture is. Williamson (2010, p. 633) defines culture as the "transmission from one generation to the next, via teaching and imitation, of knowledge, values, and other factors that influence behavior." This processual definition highlights the dynamic, malleable characteristic of culture, echoing sociologists' point of view. Swidler (1986) contends that culture matters to decision-making because it provides a toolkit for social actors while dealing with problems in everyday life. DiMaggio (1997) argues that culture enables and constrains humans' cognition while making decisions. On the basis of this understanding, Williamson (2010) explains that culture shapes financial decision-making through three mechanisms: religion, membership in social organizations, and language.

Language is essential for communication in business and finance. Li et al. (2014) analyze firm conference call transcripts, finding that communication is significantly associated with knowledge; specifically, CEOs speak less when knowing less about the topic they are addressing. Luo and Donthu (2006) find that there is a positive correlation between communication productivity and shareholder value. Kohut and Segars (1992) investigate firms' shareholder letters and discover a significant statistical association between communication strategies and company performance. Similarly, Anwar (2015) examines communication patterns in business leaders' letters to shareholders and concludes that heterogeneous communication patterns result from a variety of factors, including corporate cultures, business environments, and available information. Geppert and Lawrence (2008) also analyze letters to shareholders, finding that reputations of firms are associated with the content of letters to their shareholders. Hadro et al. (2017) find that corporations controlled by foreign shareholders are more likely than their counterparts to spend time engaging in impression management in their shareholder letters.

Building on this literature, the remainder of this chapter will demonstrate the usefulness of NLP to research on culture in finance, especially corporate communication patterns and strategies. Although scholars have applied machine learning techniques to analyze financial text data, some NLP algorithms, such as word embeddings and topic models, have not been deployed to analyze shareholder letters. Therefore, in the next section, the authors will provide an overview of certain important NLP techniques for mining financial texts.

3 NLP Algorithms for Studying Culture in Finance

3.1 Basics

Since NLP is a field in itself (Manning & Schutze, 1999), the chapter focuses only on the tools that have shown valuable for knowledge discovery based on mining unstructured textual data in finance. The authors use statistical language R to illustrate the implementation of the NLP algorithms.[1] First of all, when a researcher is to analyze a text, one of the most basic and straightforward modeling frameworks is a "bag-of-words," which assumes that the text is a combination of a number of words without taking into account their sequence, order, and grammar. To create a "bag-of-words," one needs to tokenize the original text. Tokenization is a fundamental NLP process that breaks a text into tokens (words). A tokenized text can be represented by a co-occurrence matrix of tokens appearing in the text; it also can be represented by a matrix of counts for each token in the text, where a count is the number of tokens within the text (vectorization). In R, one can convert a text file (which is named "text" in the example below) into a vectorized corpus by using the "Corpus" function provided by the "tm" package (Feinerer, 2020)[2]:

```
> library(tm)
> corpus <- Corpus(VectorSource(text))
```

Second, researchers usually need to take additional steps to preprocess the corpus, including the removal of stop words, numbers, and punctuations. Stop words are words that do not convey context-dependent meanings, such as "the," "a," and "and." One can use the following R code to remove stop words, numbers, and punctuations:

```
> corpus <- tm_map(corpus, removeWords, stopwords('english'))
> corpus <- tm_map(corpus, removeNumbers)
> corpus <- tm_map(corpus, removePunctuation)
```

Finally, if a corpus contains multiple documents, each of the documents can be thought of as a "bag" full of words, as explained above. In practice, a bag-of-word

[1]R is an open-source programming language for statistical computing. See its official website (https://www.r-project.org/) for more information.

[2]The text file contains all Warrant Buffett's letters to shareholder from 1977 to 2019. Each letter is named "[year].txt." For example, the letter of 1997 is named "1997.txt."

can be represented as a document-term-matrix (DTM) or a term-document-matrix (TDM):

```
> corpus_dtm <- DocumentTermMatrix(corpus)
> corpus_tdm <- TermDocumentMatrix(corpus)
```

In R, one can simply type the names of the DTM ("corpus_dtm") and TDM ("corpus_tdm") to show what a DTM and a TDM are about:

```
> corpus_dtm
<<DocumentTermMatrix (documents: 43, terms: 10520)>>
Non-/sparse entries: 67859/384501
Sparsity           : 85%
Maximal term length: 20
Weighting          : term frequency (tf)

> corpus_tdm
<<TermDocumentMatrix (terms: 10520, documents: 43)>>
Non-/sparse entries: 67859/384501
Sparsity           : 85%
Maximal term length: 20
Weighting          : term frequency (tf)
```

The output shows that either the DTM or TDM contains 43 documents and 10,520 unique words (terms).

3.2 *Sentiment Analysis*

Sentiment analysis has been one of the most common NLP approaches to financial text analysis (Kearney & Liu, 2014). Using pre-established lexicons which categorize words into different sentiments, such as positive and negative, scholars have applied this approach to analyze a wide array of documents, such as typical financial disclosures (Kravet & Muslu, 2013; Rogers et al., 2011), news (Day & Lee, 2016), and online digital footprints like tweets (Bollen et al., 2011; Smailović et al., 2013). Sentiment analysis can capture the changes or differences in a text's tones and emotions. For instance, Rogers et al. (2011) find that optimistic plaintiffs focus more on optimistic statements in lawsuits. Day and Lee (2016) document that financial sentiment has significant impact on investors and their investments. Bollen et al. (2011) find statistical evidence for the correlation of sentiment and stock market returns. Smailović et al. (2013) show that sentiments are predictors of stock price movements.

To conduct sentiment analysis in R, one can use the following code:

```
> library(tidytext)
> library(dplyr)
> corpus_tidy_tdm <- tidy(corpus_tdm)
> corpus_tidy_dtm <- tidy(corpus_dtm)
> corpus_tidy_sentiments <- corpus_tidy_tdm %>%
+   inner_join(get_sentiments("bing"), by = c(term = "word"))
```

Note that two other packages, "tidytext" (Silge & Robinson, 2016) and "dplyr" (Wickham, 2020) are imported before running the code for sentiment analysis. Now "corpus_tidy_sentiments" is a table showing sentiments of all the words in the corpus. One can take a look at the first ten rows in the output table by simply typing its name—"corpus_tidy_sentiments:"

```
> corpus tidy sentiments
# A tibble: 11,887 x 4
   term        document count sentiment
   <chr>       <chr>    <dbl> <chr>
 1 achievement 1977.txt     1 positive
 2 adequate    1977.txt     1 positive
 3 advantage   1977.txt     2 positive
 4 attractive  1977.txt     1 positive
 5 bargain     1977.txt     1 positive
 6 capable     1977.txt     1 positive
 7 casualty    1977.txt     7 negative
 8 comfort     1977.txt     1 positive
 9 commonplace 1977.txt     1 negative
10 crisis      1977.txt     1 negative
# ... with 11,877 more rows
```

There are four columns in this table: "term," "document," "count," and "sentiment." The "term" column has all of the words in the corpus. The "document" column has the names of all documents in the corpus. The "count" column records word frequencies. The "sentiment" column indicates if a term is of positive or negative sentiment.

3.3 *TF-IDF*

While a document-term matrix can tell us information about term frequencies, raw frequencies can be very skewed (Jurafsky & Martin, 2008). In addition, if a term appears very frequently in the corpus, it might be the case that this term only appears in some, instead of all, documents in the corpus. To remedy these two problems, one can use the TF-IDF algorithm, where TF refers to the term "frequency" and IDF "inverse document frequency." TF is measured simply using a raw term count. IDF is measure by this function: $\mathrm{IDF_t} = \log \frac{N}{DFt}$. N is the total number of documents in the corpus, and $\mathrm{DF_t}$ is the number of documents in which term t appears. If a term appears in only a few documents, then $\mathrm{IDF_t}$ will be high. By contrast, if a term appears in many documents, then $\mathrm{IDF_t}$ will be low. Taken together, TF and IDF contribute to the calculation of TF-IDF, which is the weighted frequency of a term in the corpus: $W_{t,d} = \mathrm{TF_{t,d}} \times \mathrm{IDF_t}$.

To compute TF-IDF, one can use the following R code:

```
> library(tidyverse)
> tf_idf <- corpus_tidy_tdm %>%
+   bind_tf_idf(term, document, count)
```

Note that another package, “tidyverse” (Wickham, 2019) should be loaded in. The “tf_idf” variable now stores information about all terms’ TF, IDF, and TF_IDF. One can type the variable’s name to examine the first couple of rows:

```
> tf_idf
# A tibble: 67,859 x 6
   term        document count       tf    idf    tf_idf
   <chr>       <chr>    <dbl>    <dbl>  <dbl>     <dbl>
 1 abegg       1977.txt     1 0.000737 2.37   0.00175
 2 ability     1977.txt     1 0.000737 0.124  0.0000912
 3 accept      1977.txt     1 0.000737 0.235  0.000173
 4 accompany   1977.txt     1 0.000737 0.670  0.000494
 5 account     1977.txt     2 0.00147  0      0
 6 achieve     1977.txt    11 0.00811  0.0235 0.000191
 7 achievement 1977.txt     1 0.000737 0.817  0.000602
 8 acquire     1977.txt     2 0.00147  0.0476 0.0000702
 9 acquisition 1977.txt     3 0.00221  0.0235 0.0000521
10 actively    1977.txt     1 0.000737 1.97   0.00145
# ... with 67,849 more rows
```

3.4 Cosine Similarity

To measure semantic similarities between documents, scholars often use one of the most widely applied metrics—the cosine function: $\text{cosine}(\boldsymbol{V},\boldsymbol{W}) = \frac{\boldsymbol{V}\cdot\boldsymbol{W}}{\|\boldsymbol{V}\|\|\boldsymbol{W}\|} = \frac{\sum_{i=1}^{n} \boldsymbol{V}_i \boldsymbol{W}_i}{\sqrt{\sum_{i=1}^{n} \boldsymbol{V}_i^2}\sqrt{\sum_{i=1}^{n} \boldsymbol{W}_i^2}}$ (Jurafsky & Martin, 2008). The cosine similarity function is based on the inner product of two vectors, ***V*** and ***W***, divided by the product of their lengths ($\|\boldsymbol{V}\| \; \|\boldsymbol{W}\|$). ***V*** and ***W*** are two separate document-term matrices. The cosine similarity score is bounded by 0 and 1. The more elements ***V*** and ***W*** have in the same direction, the greater the score is. When ***V*** and ***W*** are parallel and in the exact same direction, the score is 1. A high cosine similarity score can be interpreted as that documents ***V*** and ***W*** are similar. By contrast, when ***V*** and ***W*** are orthogonal to each other, the score is 0. A low cosine similarity score can be interpreted as that documents ***V*** and ***W*** are dissimilar.

One can use the “pairwise_similarity” function offered by the “widyr” package (David Robinson et al., 2020) to calculate documents’ cosine similarity score:

```
library(widyr)
cosine_sim <- tf_idf %>%
              pairwise_similarity(document, term, count, upper = FALSE, sort =
TRUE)
```

The output is a table that contains all documents’ pairwise cosine similarity scores:

```
> cosine_sim
# A tibble: 903 x 3
    item1    item2    similarity
    <chr>    <chr>         <dbl>
  1 2011.txt 2013.txt      0.908
  2 2012.txt 2013.txt      0.907
  3 2013.txt 2015.txt      0.904
  4 2013.txt 2014.txt      0.899
  5 2010.txt 2011.txt      0.892
  6 2011.txt 2012.txt      0.889
  7 2012.txt 2015.txt      0.889
  8 2010.txt 2013.txt      0.886
  9 2010.txt 2015.txt      0.884
 10 1996.txt 1997.txt      0.883
# ... with 893 more rows
```

In addition to using raw frequencies of all the terms in a document, one also can use weighted frequencies (TF-IDF) to compute cosine similarity:

```
cosine_sim_w <- tf_idf %>%
                pairwise_similarity(document, term, tf_idf, upper = FALSE, sort
  = TRUE)
```

On can notice that the cosine similarity scores based on weighted frequencies are lower than the ones based on raw frequencies:

```
> cosine_sim_w
# A tibble: 903 x 3
    item1    item2    similarity
    <chr>    <chr>         <dbl>
  1 2015.txt 2016.txt      0.417
  2 2013.txt 2015.txt      0.403
  3 2012.txt 2013.txt      0.395
  4 2011.txt 2012.txt      0.361
  5 2014.txt 2015.txt      0.361
  6 2011.txt 2013.txt      0.354
  7 2016.txt 2017.txt      0.349
  8 2013.txt 2014.txt      0.346
  9 2012.txt 2015.txt      0.327
 10 1978.txt 1979.txt      0.325
# ... with 893 more rows
```

3.5 *Word Embeddings*

Cosine similarity assumes that a document is a "bag-of-words." In this regard, any token is a single word with a frequency. This kind of a bag-of-words is called uni-gram. If a token is a two-consecutive-word combination, then the collection is called bi-gram. In general, an n-gram is a bag-of-words in which a token is a combination of n consecutive words. By contrast, a skip-gram is a bag-of-words in which a token does not need to be the combination of consecutive words; rather, it allows for skipping words. This approach serves as a useful basis for taking into account contexts in in which a word appears in a document.

The skip-gram plays a fundamental role in the word embeddings algorithm because context matters to the meanings of a word. The intuition is that the meanings of a word are determined by the contexts in which the word is embedded. One of the most popular word embeddings algorithms is *word2vec*, which was developed by Mikolov and colleagues (Mikolov et al., 2013a, 2013b). The algorithm of *word2vec* is based on the idea that a target word's neighboring words serve as its context. Each of these neighboring words is labeled as 1, while a word in a randomly selected collection is labeled as 0. Using logistic regression, *word2vec* is able to estimate the coefficients of all the words for predicting the probability of the target word appearing in the corpus. Coefficients are thought of as embeddings. Therefore, an embedding can be an indicator for evaluating how likely a word is in the target word's semantic context (Jurafsky & Martin, 2008). While the word embeddings approach has been rarely applied in studies of finance, Li et al. (2020) have demonstrated its analytical advantages in exploring the corporate culture.

To implement the *word2vec* algorithm in R, first, one needs to load in the "word2vec" package (Wijffels, 2020) and train a model:

```
> library(word2vec)
> embedding_train <- word2vec(x =corpus_tidy_tdm$term,
+                              type ="skip-gram", dim =15,iter =20)
```

Second, choose a target word and run the trained model to predict its context. Take the target word "profit" for example,

```
embedding_predict <- predict(embedding_train,c("profit"),type ="nearest",top_n =10)
```

Finally, list five of the context (neighboring) words for the target word "profit" (in the column of "term2"):

```
> embedding_predict
$profit
   term1      term2 similarity rank
1 profit occurrence  0.9997763    1
2 profit    renewal  0.9997099    2
3 profit      prime  0.9985220    3
4 profit      venue  0.9983308    4
5 profit    holding  0.9982160    5
```

3.6 *LDA Topic Models*

Recently, Bayesian probabilistic topic models have become one of the most commonly used statistical approaches to the semantic analysis of text data (Blei, 2012; Blei & Lafferty, 2006). Topic models treat textual data as "arising from a generative process that includes *hidden variables*" (Blei, 2012). Every hidden variable is assumed to have a probability distribution, which is used to calculate the posterior distribution of the hidden variables, given that the observed variables are known. The simplest topic model is *latent Dirichlet allocation* (LDA) (Blei et al., 2003).

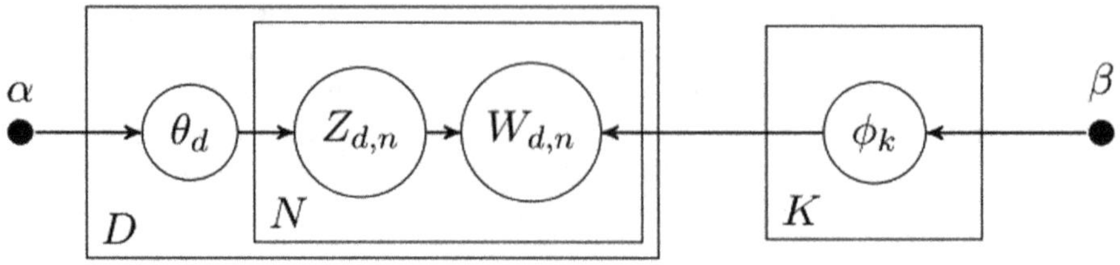

Fig. 1 The graphical presentation of the LDA topic model

LDA topic models have been applied to explore hidden topics and their distributions in a variety of finance text data (Hannigan et al., 2019; Khadjeh Nassirtoussi et al., 2014). Bao and Datta (2014) apply topic models to analyze textual risk disclosures in 10-K forms, discussing how different risky types influence investors' risk perceptions. Similarly, Dyer et al. (2017) use topic models to examine 10-K forms and find three types of disclosures—fair value, internal controls, and risk factor disclosures—account for changes in textual disclosures over time. Brown et al. (2020) also examine 10-K disclosures using topic modeling. In addition, topic models have been used to study other finance documents. Fligstein et al. (2017) use topic models to analyze the Federal Open Market Committee's (FOMC) discourse, aiming at answering the question of why the Federal Reserve was slow to recognize the 2008 financial crisis. Huang et al. (2018) examine analyst reports and corporate disclosures, finding that analysts play an intermediary role in the process by which financial information is shaped. Ryans (2020) explore hidden topics in SEC comment letters and find evidence for associations between innocuous letters and earning credibility increase. Bellstam et al. (2020) use topic models to construct firms' innovation measures by analyzing their analyst reports, concluding that those measures are strong predictors of better firm performance.

The LDA topic model is methodologically useful because it is not only computationally efficient but also conceptually simple (Blei, 2012). LDA is a statistical model with the assumption that a document is composed of multiple topics. In mathematical terms, a topic is a statistical distribution over a set of words. With this assumption, LDA is able to treat a document as a result of a generative process by which topic-related words in the document are chosen based on the corresponding distributions (topics). Figure 1 is a graphical presentation of the LDA topic model.

Assume that the total number of words is $\boldsymbol{N}$, the total number of documents is $\boldsymbol{D}$, and the total number of topics is $\boldsymbol{K}$. $\boldsymbol{W}_{d,n}$ is the nth observed word in document d. $\boldsymbol{Z}_{d,n}$ is the topic assigned to the nth observed word in document d. $\boldsymbol{\theta}_d$ is the topic proportion of the dth document. $\boldsymbol{\alpha}$ is a proportion parameter, which is the prior of the Dirichlet distribution of $\boldsymbol{\theta}_d$. ϕ_k refers to topic k, which is the distribution over a set of words. $\boldsymbol{\beta}$ is a proportion parameter, which is the prior of the Dirichlet distribution of $\boldsymbol{\theta}_d$. T he joint probability of the model can be written down as $\mathrm{P}(\boldsymbol{W},\boldsymbol{Z},\boldsymbol{\theta},\phi;\boldsymbol{\alpha},\boldsymbol{\beta}) = \prod_{i=1}^{K}\mathrm{P}(\phi_i;\beta)\prod_{d=1}^{D}\mathrm{P}(\theta_d;\alpha)\prod_{n=1}^{N}\mathrm{P}(Z_{d,n_d})\mathrm{P}\left(W_{d,k_{Z_{d,k}}}\right)$.R offers a package dedicated to topic modeling—"topicmodels" (Bettina Grün et al., 2020). For example, after importing the package, one can use the "LDA" function to fit an LDA topic model with the aim of finding five hidden topics:

```
> library(topicmodels)
> corpus_lda <- LDA(corpus_dtm, k = 5, method="Gibbs", control=list(iter = 100,
  verbose = 25))
K = 5; V = 10520; M = 43
Sampling 100 iterations!
Iteration 25 ...
Iteration 50 ...
Iteration 75 ...
Iteration 100 ...
Gibbs sampling completed!
```

One can list all topics and ten corresponding words which constitute each of the five topics by using the "terms" function:

```
> terms(corpus_lda, 10)
      Topic 1       Topic 2     Topic 3       Topic 4       Topic 5
 [1,] "berkshire"   "business"  "billion"     "million"     "berkshire"
 [2,] "business"    "company"   "million"     "business"    "company"
 [3,] "earnings"    "earnings"  "operation"   "manager"     "business"
 [4,] "purchase"    "price"     "berkshire"   "profit"      "share"
 [5,] "company"     "capital"   "home"        "shareholder" "earnings"
 [6,] "charge"      "insurance" "asset"       "owner"       "cost"
 [7,] "account"     "market"    "shareholder" "price"       "investment"
 [8,] "stock"       "industry"  "contract"    "change"      "time"
 [9,] "shareholder" "return"    "price"       "risk"        "purchase"
[10,] "acquisition" "bond"      "manager"     "day"         "charlie"
```

4 Solutions and Recommendations

4.1 Overview

To demonstrate the usefulness of NLP to the study of culture in finance, the authors present results of NLP text analysis of Warrant Buffett's letters to Berkshire Hathaway's shareholders from 1977 to 2019 (34 letters in total) (BERKSHIRE HATHAWAY INC., 2020). Figure 2 shows the pairwise cosine similarities of all 34 letters. One can see that letters written in years close to each other are more similar than those written in years that are far apart. Table 1 shows the top 50 words that appear most frequently in the letters. For instance, "business" is mentioned 4437 times (rank 1), "berkshire" 4309 times (rank 2), "tax" 1609 times (rank 10), "capital" 932 times (rank 30), and "financial" 722 times (rank 50). Taken together, Fig. 2 and Table 1 provide an overview of the corpus.

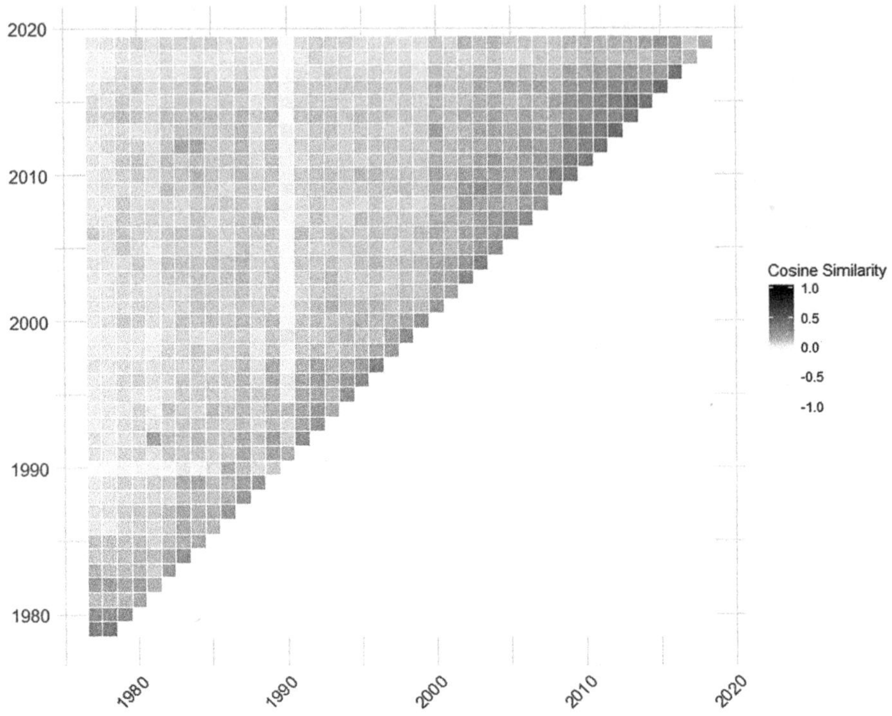

Fig. 2 The cosine similarity matrix of all 34 letters

4.2 Semantic Analysis

Figure 3 shows the distribution of words' positive or negative sentiment expressed in the shareholder letters. Interestingly, Buffett apparently uses more positive words, such as "gain," "goodwill," "worth," "contribution," and "lead," than negative words, such as "loss," "bad," "mistake," and "decline." These words are also commonly seen in financial documents. These observations suggest that it may be Buffett's communication strategy that is positive about the messages conveyed in his letters to the shareholder.

Table 2 presents word embeddings (context words) of the top 10 most frequently mentioned terms (target words) in Buffett's letters to shareholders. These embeddings provide contexts in which each of the target words is mentioned. For example, when Buffett uses the word "business," he appears to focus on some of his companies (i.e., Furniture Mart), people he admires (i.e., Adam Smith and Edgar Lawrence Smith), his colleagues (i.e., Michael Goldberg), or relevant concepts (i.e., society and competitor). When he uses the term "company," some of his companies are likely to appear nearby, such as Borsheim and Burlington Northern Santa Fe (BNSF). In addition, when the word "shareholder" is mentioned, terms such as "Charlie," "GEICO," and "management," are common context words. These

Table 1 The top 50 frequently mentioned words in all Warren Buffett's letters to shareholders

Rank	Word	Count	Rank	Word	Count
1	business	4437	26	pay	1025
2	berkshire	4309	27	operate	1019
3	company	3035	28	meet	1013
4	earnings	3008	29	loss	963
5	purchase	1973	30	capital	932
6	million	1938	31	buy	929
7	share	1879	32	charlie	926
8	stock	1844	33	asset	914
9	shareholder	1754	34	cash	896
10	tax	1609	35	major	884
11	price	1525	36	result	873
12	investment	1460	37	increase	867
13	report	1451	38	rate	847
14	insurance	1429	39	goodwill	839
15	account	1351	40	geico	828
16	cost	1303	41	economic	817
17	time	1264	42	book	782
18	sell	1235	43	annual	776
19	operation	1147	44	return	771
20	acquisition	1123	45	underwrite	770
21	charge	1113	46	management	747
22	manager	1101	47	industry	745
23	market	1098	48	furniture	734
24	gain	1039	49	deal	733
25	billion	1030	50	financial	722

embeddings are heuristically useful because they provide the authors with a basic understanding of the semantics of typically used terms in the letters. They also provide guidance on further analysis and interpretation. Based on this semantic overview, the authors next turn to topic modeling.

Figure 4 shows the results of topic modeling of the corpus with 15 topics. The authors experimented with different numbers of topics, including 5, 10, 12, 15, 20, and 25 topics. The choice of 15 topics was based on two interrelated concerns: first, the authors considered whether the words representing the topics lead to interpretable categories (i.e., topic labels). This can help researchers to formulate research hypotheses. Second, the authors took into account whether there were topics dependent on specific contexts. This concern is important because it can help researchers to discover hidden, unknown patterns in the data, leading to a closer and more contextualized reading of the corpus. As a result, 15 topics seemed the most informative ones.

The 15 topic labels presented in Fig. 4 are (1) financial positions, (2) railroad business, (3) insurance business, (4) housing market, (5) business decisions, (6) business (in general), (7) news business, (8) board of directors, (9) management,

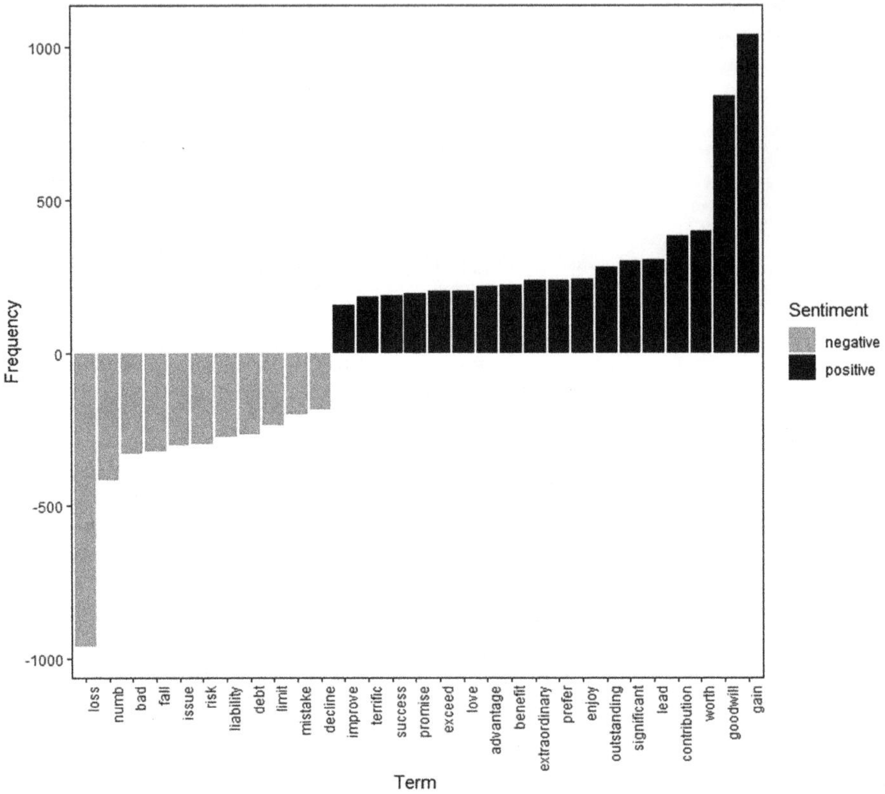

Fig. 3 Sentiment Analysis of all Warren Buffett's letters to shareholders

(10) textile business, (11) company operations, (12) banking, (13) shoe business, (14) economy, and (15) arbitrage/securities. As expected, one can see that Buffett spends most of the time discussing Berkshire Hathaway's businesses, operations, and earnings. For example, Buffett states in his letters in 2011: "Our major businesses did well last year. In fact, each of our five largest non-insurance companies—BNSF, Iscar, Lubrizol, Marmon Group and MidAmerican Energy—delivered record operating earnings. In aggregate, these businesses earned more than $9 billion pre-tax in 2011. Contrast that to seven years ago, when we owned only one of the five, MidAmerican, whose pre-tax earnings were $393 million. Unless the economy weakened in 2012, each of our fabulous five should again set a record, with aggregate earnings comfortably topping $10 billion." It is very common to see statements like this in the letters, which explain the company's financial positions.

Topic modeling results show that Buffett mentions a variety of the businesses that Berkshire Hathaway is involved in, which are revealed in topics (2), (3), (4), (7), (10), (13), and (15). For example, Berkshire Hathaway owns insurance company GEICO, which is one of its major businesses. Berkshire Hathaway also engages in mortgages, bond trading, and arbitrage regularly. Some other major businesses

Table 2 Word embeddings of the top 10 most frequently mentioned words in the letters

Target word	Business	Berkshire	Company	Earnings	Purchase
Context word 1	Mart	Disappoint	Borsheim	Distinction	Match
Context word 2	Smith	Gate	Craft	Financials	Rationally
Context word 3	Goldberg	Couple	See	Pleasure	Extol
Context word 4	Underwriter	Rata	Chairman	Industry	Authorize
Context word 5	Society	Comfortably	Santa	Lodge	Inter
Context word 6	Competitor	Guinness	Year	Expenditure	Venue
Context word 7	Reserve	Personal	Dairy	Daughter	Smooth
Context word 8	Magazine	Fit	Shake	Ebitda	Attribute
Target word	Million	Share	Stock	Shareholder	Tax
Context word 1	Bias	Payable	Bank	Charlie	Release
Context word 2	Practice	Duration	Fireman	Today	Assessment
Context word 3	Designate	Commandment	Insurer	Indemnity	Raw
Context word 4	Optimism	Requirement	Capitalist	Geico	Seek
Context word 5	Criticize	Mid	Gillette	Management	Fix
Context word 6	Dearly	Interpublic	Usair	Alternatively	Prudent
Context word 7	Slow	Notch	Manager	Double	Exemplar
Context word 8	Aggressively	Typically	Allen	Complaint	Flip

include railroad (BNSF), beverage (Coca-Cola), news (The Baffalo News), textile, shoes (Dexter Shoe), and arbitrage/securities.

More importantly, when Buffett mentions his company's businesses, he often explains why he made the decisions. For example, in the 2013 letter, Buffett states: "Late in 2009, amidst the gloom of the Great Recession, we agreed to buy BNSF, the largest purchase in Berkshire's history. At the time, I called the transaction an "all-in wager on the economic future of the United States." That kind of commitment was nothing new for us: We have been making similar wagers ever since Buffett Partnership Ltd. acquired control of Berkshire in 1965. For a good reason, too. Charlie and I have always considered a 'bet' on ever-rising U.S. prosperity to be very close to a sure thing. Indeed, who has ever benefited during the past 237 years by betting against America? If you compare our country's present condition to that existing in 1776, you have to rub your eyes in wonder. And the dynamism embedded in our market economy will continue to work its magic. America's best days lie ahead." In this passage, Buffett apparently addresses his company's investment in very positive tones, which is consistent with the results of the sentiment analysis discussed earlier. This finding provides useful insights into Buffett's communication style.

There is also a significant amount of mention in relation to the board of directors, as topic (8) reveals. This is expected because Buffett is the chairman and CEO of Berkshire Hathaway. The independence of board members has been a prominent feature of corporate governance. For example, in his 2014 letter to shareholders, Buffet notes: "To further ensure continuation of our culture, I have suggested that my son, Howard, succeed me as a non-executive Chairman. My only reason for this

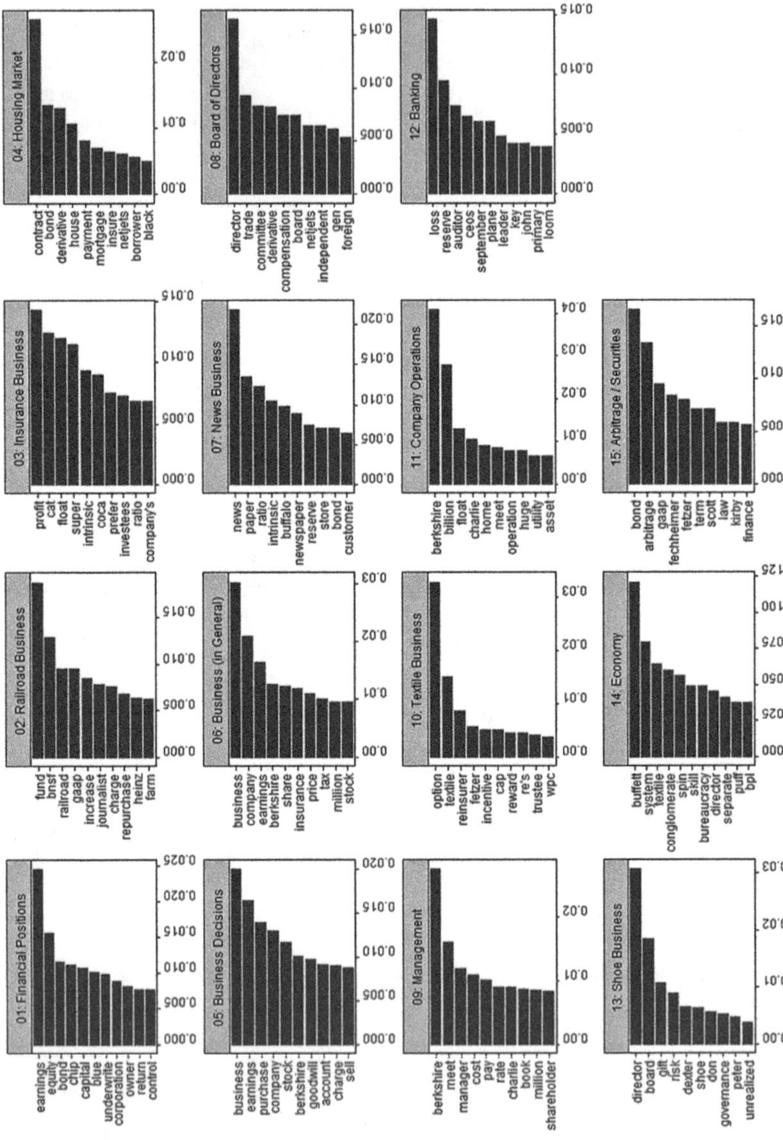

Fig. 4 Findings of topic modeling with 15 topics

wish is to make change easier if the wrong CEO should ever be employed and there occurs a need for the Chairman to move forcefully. I can assure you that this problem has a very low probability of arising at Berkshire—likely as low as at any public company. In my service on the boards of nineteen public companies, however, I've seen how hard it is to replace a mediocre CEO if that person is also Chairman. (The deed usually gets done, but almost always very late.)" This statement shows that Buffett attempts to explain his vision for and ideas about his company's board of directors, which is a critical part of the corporate culture.

Similarly, as topics (9) and (11) imply, Buffett also tends to highlight his view of management and corporate governance in letters to shareholders. For example, in the 1977 letter, Buffet responds to question about staying in the textile business by elaborating his view of management and corporate operation: "A few shareholders have questioned the wisdom of remaining in the textile business which, over the longer term, is unlikely to produce returns on capital comparable to those available in many other businesses. Our reasons are several: (1) Our mills in both New Bedford and Manchester are among the largest employers in each town, utilizing a labor force of high average age possessing relatively non-transferable skills. Our workers and unions have exhibited unusual understanding and effort in cooperating with management to achieve a cost structure and product mix, which might allow us to maintain a viable operation. (2) Management also has been energetic and straightforward in its approach to our textile problems. In particular, Ken Chace's efforts after the change in corporate control took place in 1965 generated capital from the textile division needed to finance the acquisition and expansion of our profitable insurance operation. (3) With hard work and some imagination regarding manufacturing and marketing configurations, it seems reasonable that at least modest profits in the textile division can be achieved in the future." Another similar example is that, in the 2014 letter, Buffett states: "Choosing the right CEO is all-important and is a subject that commands much time at Berkshire board meetings. Managing Berkshire is primarily a job of capital allocation, coupled with the selection and retention of outstanding managers to captain our operating subsidiaries. Obviously, the job also requires the replacement of a subsidiary's CEO when that is called for. These duties require Berkshire's CEO to be a rational, calm and decisive individual who has a broad understanding of business and good insights into human behavior. It is important as well that he knows his limits. Character is crucial: A Berkshire CEO must be "all in" for the company, not for himself. (I am using male pronouns to avoid awkward wording, but gender should never decide who becomes CEO.) He cannot help but earn money far in excess of any possible need for it. But it is important that neither ego nor avarice motivates him to reach for pay matching his most lavishly compensated peers, even if his achievements far exceed theirs. A CEO's behavior has a huge impact on managers down the line: If it is clear to them that shareholders' interests are paramount to him, they will, with few exceptions, also embrace that way of thinking." Taken together, these examples are qualitative evidence consistent with what topics (9) and (11) show.

The culture of teamwork and leadership appears to be critical for Berkshire Hathaway. Evidence is that "Charlie" is mentioned frequently and is one of the significant words in topics (9) and (11). This shows that Buffett likes to mention the vice chairman, Charlie Munger, in his statements about management and company operations. For example, in a letter as early as in 1982, Buffett emphasizes the importance of the role of Munger: "He designated-contributions idea, along with many other ideas that have turned out well for us, was conceived by Charlie Munger, Vice Chairman of Berkshire and Chairman of Blue Chip. Irrespective of titles, Charlie and I work as partners in managing all controlled companies. To almost a sinful degree, we enjoy our work as managing partners. And we enjoy having you as our financial partners." Similarly, in another letter (of 1983), Buffett stresses: "Although our form is corporate, our attitude is partnership. Charlie Munger and I think of our shareholders as owner-partners, and of ourselves as managing partners. (Because of the size of our shareholdings we also are, for better or worse, controlling partners.) We do not view the company itself as the ultimate owner of our business assets but, instead, view the company as a conduit through which our shareholders own the assets." Apparently, Buffett tends to highlight his good working relationship with Munger and present an image to shareholders that the corporation has a culture of shared governance and teamwork.

Results shown in Fig. 4 also indicate that Buffett tends to put small businesses together for discussion. For example, he sometimes puts a few businesses to describe their earnings. In addition, the authors find that Buffett attempts to promote Omaha (the headquarters of Berkshire Hathaway) as a "cradle of capitalism" and to advocate for local businesses and encourage shareholders to purchase local products while attending an annual shareholder meeting. It should be noted that letters to shareholders can also serve as an invitation to the company's annual meetings where the board and CEOs explain earnings and business to the shareholders and other stakeholders (e.g., business analysts in Wall Street). In brief, these findings demonstrate ways in which Buffett manages the impression of his company and communicates with shareholders.

In sum, the topic models of Buffett's shareholder letters present a clear cultural pattern of Berkshire Hathaway's corporate governance. The 15 topics show that Buffett tends to focus on his company's major investment and businesses and convey an impression that he always has his philosophy of and vision for the operation and management of the corporation. These findings reveal not only the ways in which Buffett make financial decisions but also the rationale behind the corporation's decision-making processes.

5 Future Research Directions

The authors have used a variety of NLP algorithms to analyze Buffett's letters to shareholders. While the findings provide insights into Berkshire Hathaway's corporate culture and Buffett's communication strategies, further research can link these findings to other aspects of the company, such as its financial positions, stock prices, investments, and procurement strategies. These findings are informative in that, on the basis of it, researchers can further explore whether the corporation's culture and communication patterns contribute to variations in other domains of the organization. For example, one can address the question of whether Buffet's communication reflects or affects Berkshire Hathaway's stock prices.

Moreover, future research can compare Buffett's communication patterns with other CEOs' or corporations' ones. Because interpretations of NLP text analysis are context-dependent, one can include other corpuses of shareholder letters from different businesses and industries or ones of distinct communication styles. Similarly, future research can also compare the case presented in this chapter with cases in different countries or cultures. Such comparative studies will largely enhance the understanding of how culture works in and matters to finance.

In practice, the findings have important implications for facilitating individual and corporate decision-making. First, one can link the cultural aspect of corporate governance to investment portfolios. In finance, there is a long-standing tradition of understanding whether any specific combination of the portfolio of investments can generate higher returns that is warranted by the traditional risk factors, such as a firm's market risk or beta, size, book-to-market, and momentum (Fama & French, 2012). With the growing social consciousness of cultural and ethical appropriateness of company activities, various aspects of culture can be explored as to whether their absence or presence indicates different riskiness of firms and, therefore, different returns. In such explorations, the combination of firms with different cultures may be examined for any systemic return patterns on the cultural portfolio of investments. Second, one can connect corporate culture with extra-institutional entrepreneurs. Various cultural aspects of a firm can draw attention from various activist investors and the general public, who have been dubbed as extra-institutional entrepreneurs in administrative sciences (King & Soule, 2007). A detailed measurement of various cultural aspects through the methods that the authors have indicated in this chapter can facilitate the managerial and investor understanding of the expectations of various stakeholders of firms. Third, understanding corporate culture matters to managerial communication. Any firms listed newly in a home country or foreign country stock exchange can gain a deeper understanding of the communication styles that are normative in nature in a specific market. Such understanding can help managers to avoid any inadvertent communication gaffe, which is costly.

6 Conclusion

The burgeoning textual data on finance are not only a challenge but also an opportunity for finance scholars to play a critical role in studying culture in finance. To this end, NLP serves as a methodological fit for unraveling cultural dynamics in the finance domain. NLP algorithms, including but not limited to bag-of-words, TF-IDF, cosine similarity, sentiment analysis, word embeddings, and topic models, are of great benefit to researchers because those algorithms can be efficiently and effectively applied to analyze a variety of financial texts, such as annual reports, SEC documents, business standards and regulations, online digital footprint, and letters to shareholders. Analyzing Buffett's communication strategies deployed in his letters to Berkshire Hathaway's shareholders, the authors have demonstrated how NLP models can help scholars identify and discover hidden cultural patterns in finance textual data. The authors also have pointed out further research directions and opportunities. Last but not least, the authors hope this chapter will inspire more finance scholars to engage with NLP methods.

References

Anwar, S. T. (2015). Communicating with shareholders in the post-financial crisis period: A global perspective. *International Journal of Commerce and Management, 25*(4), 582–602. https://doi.org/10.1108/IJCoMA-02-2013-0017

Bao, Y., & Datta, A. (2014). Simultaneously discovering and quantifying risk types from textual risk disclosures. *Management Science, 60*(6), 1371–1391. https://doi.org/10.1287/mnsc.2014.1930

Bellstam, G., Bhagat, S., & Cookson, J. A. (2020). A text-based analysis of corporate innovation. *Management Science*. https://doi.org/10.1287/mnsc.2020.3682.

BERKSHIRE HATHAWAY INC. (2020). https://www.berkshirehathaway.com/

Blei, D. M. (2012). Probabilistic topic models. *Communications of the ACM, 55*(4), 77–84. https://doi.org/10.1145/2133806.2133826

Blei, D. M., & Lafferty, J. D. (2006). Dynamic topic models. *Proceedings of the 23rd international conference on machine learning*, 113–120. https://doi.org/10.1145/1143844.1143859.

Blei, D. M., Ng, A. Y., & Jordan, M. I. (2003). Latent dirichlet allocation. *Journal of Machine Learning Research, 3*(January), 993–1022.

Bollen, J., Mao, H., & Zeng, X. (2011). Twitter mood predicts the stock market. *Journal of Computational Science, 2*(1), 1–8. https://doi.org/10.1016/j.jocs.2010.12.007

Brown, A. D., & Starkey, K. (1994). The effect of organizational culture on communication and information. *Journal of Management Studies, 31*(6), 807–828.

Brown, N. C., Crowley, R. M., & Elliott, W. B. (2020). What are you saying? Using topic to detect financial misreporting. *Journal of Accounting Research, 58*(1), 237–291. https://doi.org/10.1111/1475-679X.12294

Carr, C., & Tomkins, C. (1998). Context, culture and the role of the finance function in strategic decisions: A comparative analysis of Britain, Germany, the U.S.A. and Japan. *Management Accounting Research, 9*(2), 213–239. https://doi.org/10.1006/mare.1998.0075

Das, S. R. (2014). Text and Context: Language Analytics in Finance. Now Publishers Inc.

Day, M., & Lee, C. (2016). Deep learning for financial sentiment analysis on finance news providers. *2016 IEEE/ACM International Conference on Advances in Social Networks Analysis and Mining (ASONAM)*, 1127–1134. https://doi.org/10.1109/ASONAM.2016.7752381.

DiMaggio, P. (1997). Culture and cognition. *Annual Review of Sociology, 23*, 263–287.

Dyer, T., Lang, M., & Stice-Lawrence, L. (2017). The evolution of 10-K textual disclosure: Evidence from latent dirichlet allocation. *Journal of Accounting and Economics, 64*(2–3), 221–245. https://doi.org/10.1016/j.jacceco.2017.07.002

Eisenhardt, K. M. (1989). Agency theory: An assessment and review. *Academy of Management Review, 14*(1), 57–74. https://doi.org/10.5465/amr.1989.4279003

El-Haj, M., Rayson, P., Walker, M., Young, S., & Simaki, V. (2019). In search of meaning: Lessons, resources and next steps for computational analysis of financial discourse. *Journal of Business Finance & Accounting, 46*(3–4), 265–306. https://doi.org/10.1111/jbfa.12378

Fama, E. F., & French, K. R. (2012). Size, value, and momentum in international stock returns. *Journal of Financial Economics, 105*(3), 457–472. https://doi.org/10.1016/j.jfineco.2012.05.011

Feinerer, I. (2020). *Introduction to the tm Package Text Mining in R.*

Fisher, I. E., Garnsey, M. R., & Hughes, M. E. (2016). Natural language processing in accounting, auditing and finance: A synthesis of the literature with a roadmap for future research. *Intelligent Systems in Accounting, Finance and Management, 23*(3), 157–214. https://doi.org/10.1002/isaf.1386

Fligstein, N., Brundage, J. S., & Schultz, M. (2017). Seeing like the fed: Culture, cognition, and framing in the failure to anticipate the financial crisis of 2008. *American Sociological Review, 5*, 879. https://doi.org/10.1177/0003122417728240

Geppert, J., & Lawrence, J. E. (2008). Predicting firm reputation through content analysis of shareholders' letter. *Corporate Reputation Review, 11*(4), 285–307. https://doi.org/10.1057/crr.2008.32

Bettina Grün, Kurt Hornik, David M. Blei, John D. Lafferty, Xuan-Hieu Phan, Makoto Matsumoto, Takuji Nishimura, & Shawn Cokus. (2020). *Topicmodels package | R Documentation.* https://www.rdocumentation.org/packages/topicmodels/versions/0.2-11

Hadro, D., Klimczak, K. M., & Pauka, M. (2017). Impression management in letters to shareholders: Evidence from Poland. *Accounting in Europe, 14*(3), 305–330. https://doi.org/10.1080/17449480.2017.1378428

Hannigan, T. R., Haans, R. F. J., Vakili, K., Tchalian, H., Glaser, V. L., Wang, M. S., Kaplan, S., & Jennings, P. D. (2019). Topic modeling in management research: Rendering new theory from textual data. *Academy of Management Annals, 13*(2), 586–632. https://doi.org/10.5465/annals.2017.0099

Harmon, D. J. (2019). When the fed speaks: Arguments, emotions, and the microfoundations of institutions. *Administrative Science Quarterly, 64*(3), 542–575. https://doi.org/10.1177/0001839218777475

Harris, M., & Raviv, A. (1991). The theory of capital structure. *The Journal of Finance, 46*(1), 297–355. https://doi.org/10.1111/j.1540-6261.1991.tb03753.x

Hirschberg, J., & Manning, C. D. (2015). Advances in natural language processing. *Science, 349*(6245), 261–266. https://doi.org/10.1126/science.aaa8685

Huang, A. H., Lehavy, R., Zang, A. Y., & Zheng, R. (2018). Analyst information discovery and interpretation roles: A topic modeling approach. *Management Science, 64*(6), 2833–2855. https://doi.org/10.1287/mnsc.2017.2751

Jurafsky, D., & Martin, J. (2008). *Speech and language processing* (2nd ed.). Prentice Hall.

Karolyi, G. A. (2016). The gravity of culture for finance. *Journal of Corporate Finance, 41*, 610–625. https://doi.org/10.1016/j.jcorpfin.2016.07.003

Kearney, C., & Liu, S. (2014). Textual sentiment in finance: A survey of methods and models. *International Review of Financial Analysis, 33*, 171–185. https://doi.org/10.1016/j.irfa.2014.02.006

Khadjeh Nassirtoussi, A., Aghabozorgi, S., Ying Wah, T., & Ngo, D. C. L. (2014). Text mining for market prediction: A systematic review. *Expert Systems with Applications, 41*(16), 7653–7670. https://doi.org/10.1016/j.eswa.2014.06.009

King, B. G., & Soule, S. A. (2007). Social movements as extra-institutional entrepreneurs: The effect of protests on stock price returns. *Administrative Science Quarterly, 52*(3), 413–442. https://doi.org/10.2189/asqu.52.3.413

Kohut, G. F., & Segars, A. H. (1992). The President's letter to stockholders: An examination of corporate communication strategy. *Journal of Business Communication, 29*(1), 7–21. https://doi.org/10.1177/002194369202900101

Kramsch, C. (2004). Language, thought, and culture. In *The handbook of applied linguistics* (pp. 235–261). Wiley. https://doi.org/10.1002/9780470757000.ch9.

Kravet, T., & Muslu, V. (2013). Textual risk disclosures and investors' risk perceptions. *Review of Accounting Studies, 18*(4), 1088–1122.

Kumar, B. S., & Ravi, V. (2016). A survey of the applications of text mining in financial domain. *Knowledge-Based Systems, 114*, 128–147. https://doi.org/10.1016/j.knosys.2016.10.003
Li, F., Minnis, M., Nagar, V., & Rajan, M. (2014). Knowledge, compensation, and firm value: An empirical analysis of firm communication. *Journal of Accounting and Economics, 58*(1), 96–116. https://doi.org/10.1016/j.jacceco.2014.06.003
Li, K., Mai, F., Shen, R., & Yan, X. (2020). *Measuring corporate culture using machine learning* (SSRN Scholarly Paper ID 3256608). Social Science Research Network. https://doi.org/10.2139/ssrn.3256608.
Loughran, T., & Mcdonald, B. (2016). Textual analysis in accounting and finance: A survey. *Journal of Accounting Research, 54*(4), 1187–1230. https://doi.org/10.1111/1475-679X.12123
Luo, X., & Donthu, N. (2006). Marketing's credibility: A longitudinal investigation of marketing communication productivity and shareholder value. *Journal of Marketing, 70*(4), 70–91. https://doi.org/10.1509/jmkg.70.4.070
Manning, C. D., & Schutze, H. (1999). *Foundations of statistical natural language processing*. MIT Press.
Matsumoto, D., Pronk, M., & Roelofsen, E. (2011). What makes conference calls useful? The information content of managers' presentations and analysts' discussion sessions. *Accounting Review, 86*(4), 1383–1414.
Mikolov, T., Chen, K., Corrado, G., & Dean, J. (2013a). Efficient estimation of word representations in vector space. *ArXiv Preprint* ArXiv:1301.3781.
Mikolov, T., Sutskever, I., Chen, K., Corrado, G. S., & Dean, J. (2013b). Distributed representations of words and phrases and their compositionality. *Advances in Neural Information Processing Systems, 26*, 3111–3119.
Palepu, K. G., Healy, P. M., Wright, S., Bradbury, M., & Coulton, J. (2020). *Business analysis and valuation: Using financial statements*. Cengage AU.
David Robinson, Kanishka Misra, & Julia Silge. (2020). *widyr: Widen, Process, then Re-Tidy Data version 0.1.3 from CRAN*. https://rdrr.io/cran/widyr/
Rogers, J. L., Van Buskirk, A., & Zechman, S. L. C. (2011). Disclosure tone and shareholder litigation. *The Accounting Review, 86*(6), 2155–2183.
Ryans, J. P. (2020). Textual Classification of SEC Comment Letters. *Review of Accounting Studies*. https://doi.org/10.1007/s11142-020-09565-6.
Silge, J., & Robinson, D. (2016). tidytext: Text mining and analysis using tidy data principles in R. *The Journal of Open Source Software, 1*(3), 37. https://doi.org/10.21105/joss.00037
Smailović, J., Grčar, M., Lavrač, N., & Žnidaršič, M. (2013). Predictive sentiment analysis of tweets: A stock market application. *International workshop on human–computer interaction and knowledge discovery in complex*. Unstructured, Big Data, 77–88.
Marco Spruit & Drilon Ferati. (2019). Applied Data Science in Financial Industry: Natural Language Processing Techniques for Bank Policies. *Research & Innovation Forum 2019: Technology, Innovation, Education, and Their Social Impact*, 351. https://doi.org/10.1007/978-3-030-30809-4_32.
Stulz, R. M., & Williamson, R. (2003). Culture, openness, and finance. *Journal of Financial Economics, 70*(3), 313–349. https://doi.org/10.1016/S0304-405X(03)00173-9
Sun, A., Lachanski, M., & Fabozzi, F. J. (2016). Trade the tweet: Social media text mining and sparse matrix factorization for stock market prediction. *International Review of Financial Analysis, 48*, 272–281. https://doi.org/10.1016/j.irfa.2016.10.009
Swidler, A. (1986). Culture in action: Symbols and strategies. *American Sociological Review, 51*(2), 273–286. https://doi.org/10.2307/2095521
Wickham, H. (2019). *Tidyverse packages*. https://www.tidyverse.org/packages/
Wickham, H. (2020). *Dplyr package | R Documentation*. https://www.rdocumentation.org/packages/dplyr/versions/0.7.7

Wijffels, J., BNOSAC, & Fomichev, M. (2020, November 26). *word2vec: Distributed representations of words*. https://CRAN.R-project.org/package=word2vec

Williamson, R. (2010). The role of culture in finance. In H. K. Baker & J. R. Nofsinger (Eds.), *Behavioral finance: Investors, corporations, and markets* (pp. 629–645). Wiley. https://doi.org/10.1002/9781118258415.ch34

Wong, F. M. F., Liu, Z., & Chiang, M. (2014). Stock market prediction from WSJ: Text mining via sparse matrix factorization. *2014 IEEE International Conference on Data Mining, Data Mining (ICDM), 2014 IEEE international conference on*, 430–439. https://doi.org/10.1109/ICDM.2014.116.

Zadeh, R. B., & Zollmann, A. (2009). *Predicting market-volatility from federal reserve board meeting minutes NLP for finance*.

Part III
Technology-Driven Finance

Network Modeling: Historical Perspectives, Agent-Based Modeling, Correlation Networks, and Network Similarities

Cantay Caliskan

Abstract Network modeling offers a highly mathematical path to capture holistic interpretations of the economic and financial relationships between different kinds of actors. This chapter is an attempt to accomplish several goals to present a variety of resources to researchers and practitioners. The discussion begins with an overview of theoretical and empirical research in the field and continues with a more in-depth review of three key areas in network modeling: agent-based models, correlation-based stock networks, and methods to compute network similarities. The theoretical discussion is complemented by two easily digestible empirical applications. The goal of the chapter is to demonstrate a few possibilities of translating the theory of network science into applications.

Keywords Economic networks · Financial networks · Correlation-based stock networks · Network similarities · Agent-based modeling

1 Introduction

Economics and finance have been widely studied from the perspective of researchers studying network analysis. The emphasis on complex networks has increased in social, natural, and engineering sciences over the last decades (Newman, 2010; Barabasi, 2016; Latora et al., 2017). Some of the main factors behind the rise in the popularity of network analysis in the last two decades include the continuing strengthening of global connections that now include world-wide nets such as Internet and social media, greater availability of data that came with an increasing transparency and the development of public data culture, an increasing belief in the

Supplementary Information The online version of this chapter (https://doi.org/10.1007/978-3-030-83799-0_10) contains supplementary material, which is available to authorized users.

C. Caliskan (✉)
Goergen Institute for Data Science, University of Rochester, Rochester, NY, USA
e-mail: cantay.caliskan@rochester.edu

S. Derindere Köseoğlu (ed.), *Financial Data Analytics*, Contributions to Finance and Accounting, https://doi.org/10.1007/978-3-030-83799-0_10

meaning of social connections, and the availability of more powerful computers that can handle more complicated tasks faster.

Most of contemporary network science deals with complex networks. A complex network is a system of relationships with a large number of nodes and connections between nodes (Albert & Barabási, 2002). A closer look at the existing literature on networks reveals that the field is characterized by its interdisciplinary nature (Barrat et al., 2004; Newman, 2010; Boccaletti et al., 2006; Cohen & Havlin, 2010; Helbing, 2013). Examples from the literature on complex networks look at the importance of connections include the sociological analysis of finding a job (Granovetter, 2018), network of sexual partners (Liljeros et al., 2001), Internet and WWW (Faloutsos et al., 1999; Barabasi & Albert, 1999; Pastor-Satorras & Vespignani, 2007), citation networks (Radicchi et al., 2012), networks of policymakers (Teets, 2018), digital humanities (Knappett, 2013; Jänicke et al., 2017), social media (Recuero et al., 2015; Plotkowiak & Stanoevska-Slabeva, 2013), protein networks (Milo et al., 2002; Sendiña-Nadal et al., 2011), climate networks (Yamasaki et al., 2008; Ludescher et al., 2014), transportation networks (Lämmer & Helbing, 2008; Li et al., 2015), and others. These different realms of applied network research have several conceptual components in common.

Acknowledging the fact that it is hard to make generalizations in the field, most applied network research investigates the results of an "action" leading into "reaction," such as flows, failures, bubbles, crises, positive and negative shocks influencing the actors in a system some of whom are responsible for creating this action. In the field of applied network research, the direction of reasoning usually goes from local phenomena to global observations (and back to local phenomena); thus, individual changes in the elements of a system bring a change to the network, which ultimately changes the local elements. This way of thinking also applies to network research in economics and finance: people, the interactions between people and groups of people create a cooperative behavior setting that ultimately influences the individual behavior. The typical example for this bottom-up and top-down behavior are the bank runs that has occurred during many crises, including the Great Depression and the Global Financial Crisis in 2008. As mentioned by Kanik (2020), the network effect of bank runs have been first exemplified by Thornton (2017)[1] and Bagehot (1873).[2]

In addition, the study of networks from the perspective of economics and finance is also affected by the interdisciplinary nature of the study. The highly mathematical

[1]"If any one bank fails, a general run on the neighboring ones is apt to take place, which if not checked at the beginning by a pouring into the circulation a large quantity of gold, leads to very extensive mischief." (Thornton, 2017, p. 113).

[2]"A panic, in a word, is a species of neuralgia, and according to the rules of science you must not starve it. The holders of the cash reserve must be ready not only to keep it for their own liabilities, but to advance it most freely for the liabilities of others. They must lend to merchants, to minor bankers, to "this man and that man," wherever the security is good. In wild periods of alarm, one failure makes many, and the best way to prevent the derivative failures is to arrest the primary failure which caused them." (Bagehot, 1873, pp. 51–2).

nature of the field has attracted researchers from a wide variety of quantitative disciplines including economics, finance, mathematics, physics, data science, and computer science. Perhaps due to this wide variety of disciplines, it is difficult to find scientific literature that provides an all-encompassing and up-to-date perspective on the developments in this field.[3]

This chapter aims to serve the purpose of providing a review on the different topics studied in this area (i), and to demonstrate easily digestible applications of some of the network models that will be discussed in this review (ii). To accomplish these tasks, the chapter looks at the applications of agent-based modeling, different ways of creating correlation networks between stock prices, and the use of network similarities to make sense of correlation networks. The most significant contribution of the application section of the chapter is the combination of correlation-based measures and similarity measures, which has not yet been considered in the literature. The goal of the chapter is to translate theoretical concepts associated with financial analysis into practical results. The chapter also provides hints on where the practitioners should look, if they would like to review some of the applications more deeply.

2 Financial Networks Literature: Historical Overview

The field of network analysis studies the existing and the predicted structure and geometry and the flow of measurable phenomena. The measurable phenomena can exist in the form of recorded and predicted exchanges (such as money transactions between two bank accounts, imports and exports between two countries, etc.), but also can be unrecorded and identified purely through observation (examples include the spread of epidemics, opinions, innovations, trends, and others).

Like in other fields, network analysis for economics and finance requires a set of observations that can be represented in the format of relationships between units that can be considered in an equal or hierarchical relationship with respect to each other. For this reason, a data-driven financial network study should ideally begin with modeling the real world as a set of connections. The modeling process is followed by the interpretation and the analysis of the structure of hand in a static (a) (for instance, the memberships of companies to a trade union) or temporal way (b) (for instance, Bitcoin transactions in the last year); and also, by looking at issues of interest at the micro-scale (i) (for instance, a LinkedIn ego-network with professional connections), meso-scale (ii) (for instance, the financial connections of a national car industry to foreign buyers), or global scale (iii) (for instance, the dealer network of a global technology supplier).

---

[3] A valuable example that brings together the different perspectives in the discipline is a book titled *Network Models in Economics and Finance* (edited by Kalyagin et al., 2014).

Network analysis has affected the advancement of research in economics and finance in many dimensions. The literature on financial networks has reached its apex in the late 2000s and the early 2010s; and the last few years have witnessed some downward trend in the amount of research output. Some of the early works in the field look at currency and cash management problems. The earliest known example is by Rutenberg (1970) who indicated that the monetary value in another currency can be calculated by using arc multipliers. Rutenberg's network model had multiple periods with linear costs on the arcs. The nodes represented the currencies in a specific period and the arcs were edges weighted by the amount of cash moving from one period to the next. Barr (1972), Srinivasan (1974), and Crum (1976) contributed to the literature by looking at the cash management problem. In their models, the edges in the network represented the possible cash flow patterns and were weighted by different costs associated with cash transfers. The network model on cash management has later been further developed in subsequent works (Crum et al., 1979, 1983 Crum and Nye. 1981).

Later approaches to the use of networks in finance can be grouped into the behavioral assumptions associated with the members of the system and the stability, efficiency, and resilience of the financial systems. Examples focusing on the behavioral assumptions have looked at the evaluation of the penetration or contagion effects (Garas et al., 2010; Kenett et al., 2012; Li et al., 2014), the evaluation of the impact of the disappearance of one of the members in the system (Jackson, 2010; Battiston et al., 2012). Gai and Kapadia (2010) discuss the trade-offs in the degree of connectivity. Elliott et al. (2014) develop a contagion model and look at the effects of diversification and integration on the contagion. Acemoglu et al. (2015) show the types of networks that can be broken as a result of contagious effects and the magnitude and the number of shocks affecting the network would be the key determinants behind the failure.

Under the second group, one can talk about the research on connections between banks, interbank networks. In this group, researchers have so far investigated the topological properties of the networks, the effects of artificially-induced shocks on the system, and remedies to lessen the negative effects of such shocks (Inaoka et al., 2004; Soramäki et al., 2007; Galbiati & Soramäki, 2012; Cabrales et al., 2017). Hüser (2015) indicates the literature on interbank have considered two main channels of risk contagion in the banking system: (i) direct interbank liability linkages between financial institutions, and (ii) contagion through changes in bank asset values. These issues have been extensively studied in the past two decades, both theoretically (Wells, 2002; Furfine, 2003; Upper & Worms, 2004; Elsinger et al., 2006; Nier et al., 2007) and also empirically by mapping out the network of claims and liabilities between institutions in different countries (Boss et al., 2004; Elsinger et al., 2006; Langfield et al., 2012; Cont & Moussa, 2010).

Network models are further used to describe relationships that can be quantified as "flows." In particular, movements of economic actors, goods, currency, and objects of monetary value can be represented as links connecting the units in the system. Li et al. (2014) analyzed the network of sectors connected to each other through the flow of money. This allowed them to uncover the network structure to identify and rank the industries according to their level of influence. Similarly, Minoiu and Reyes (2011) look at the properties of the global banking system formed by 184 countries and their quarterly direct investment flows. The authors found that advanced economies are the major players in the global banking market with ten times more flows between them than to developing or emerging countries. Their analysis of the 1978–2009 period showed that the interconnection between countries is unstable and connectivity decreases during periods of crisis.

There is also a significant amount of literature on the use of correlation-based networks in finance—which constitutes the main methodological component of this chapter. As will be mentioned in greater detail in a separate section, correlation-based networks are helpful for analyzing financial time series, the impact of endogenous variables and exogenous shocks on the system, the identification of lead-lag relationships, and the estimation of causality. For this reason, they are particularly useful in commercially oriented financial applications.

The book written by Kalyagin et al. (2014) gives an overview of the dominant methodological approaches to studying economic and financial networks. The themes covered in the book include advancements in game theory, stock correlation networks, interbank networks, multi-dimensional aspects of financial modeling, agent-based modeling, network centrality, contagion during financial crises, dynamic networks, and the synchronization of business cycles.

As explained in more detail above, network models used in financial analysis are helpful for understanding agent-level and system-level phenomena. These include the behavior of individual consumers, buyers, and sellers; but also, the behavior of collective systems like banks, monetary institutions like World Bank and IMF, and also financial constructs such as stock markets. In contrast to other fields of social sciences, financial analysis is both grounded in explaining the mechanisms, but also slightly more strongly tilted towards making predictive explanations. As such, agent-based modeling and correlation networks are two methodological choices that offer an opportunity to cover multiple aspects emphasized in the financial analysis literature. Specifically, agent-based modeling looks at the behavioral aspects that is heavily studied in the literature, as well as providing an opportunity to consider agent-level phenomena. Correlation networks, on the other hand, emphasize the system-level phenomena and study financial constructs (rather than real actors).

3 Agent-Based Modeling in Economics and Finance

As in other fields of social sciences such as sociology and psychology, agent-based models have been widely used in economics starting from the 1970s and reached a peak interest in the 1990s. An agent-based model (ABM) is a mathematical model that uses a rationally-bounded and usually computationally-induced simulation to understand various dynamics in a society. The connection of ABM to network analysis is the holistic perspective that the aggregated properties of agents in a system have a bigger meaning than a mere collection of individual properties of these agents. With properties that can be traced back to the Von Neumann machine, the assumptions are that the agents in this society are interacting with each other (i), these interactions happen as a result of the individual characteristics of the agents (ii), and the system as a whole exhibits emergent properties (iii). Agents can represent people (consumers, sellers, voters, etc.), institutions (banks, states, alliances, etc.), social groups (families, communities, neighborhoods, etc.).

ABM is closely related to game theory in that researchers need to make assumptions about agents and their interactions with other agents. In turn, the researcher can study large-scale phenomena that cannot be put under scrutiny using inductive or deductive reasoning. Thus, ABM provides a simplified version of the real world that is dictated by rigid rules to help us understand the dynamics in a society under certain constraints. In addition, the researcher can understand why some large-scale processes persist despite the fact there is no top-down enforcement mechanism. Examples include law enforcement, trade networks, philanthropy, and social norms.

Early examples focusing on the use of agent-based models in economics include Thomas Schelling's segregation model (1971). Schelling presents a simulation in which individual members of two clearly identifiable groups distribute themselves in neighborhoods with reference to their own locations. His model had a great impact on understanding segregation in the United States[4]: Even if (hypothetically) there is no top-down control mechanism to impose segregation on the whole population, "mild" in-group preferences may lead to a highly segregated society. In Schelling's model, agents take turns to decide what action they will take based on their immediate surroundings (such as the ratio of other agents with a particular characteristic), and their location.

Some of the mechanisms that influence the decisions of agents in studies based on Schelling's model are the *economic* differences between agents (Hatna & Benenson, 2010); irregular partition of space that provides members of each group a different baseline for taking actions (Flache & Hegselmann, 2001; Laurie & Jaggi, 2002, 2003); asymmetric relations that involve a varying set of preferences and more than two groups (Portugali et al., 1994; and Portugali & Benenson, 1995); and the exchange of places between agents (Pollicott & Weiss, 2001; Zhang, 2004) among other considerations.

Early ABM models often assumed that agents make rational choices—nevertheless, in the real world, decisions made by the agents can often be affected, constrained, or bounded by the lack of resources or inadequate information (Bell et al., 1988; Simon, 1997). This reasoning motivated researchers to update the ABM by introducing the concept of "bounded rationality" to the field. This idea has been underlined repeatedly in the field indicating that agents tend to seek satisfactory results and are at the same time aware of the fact they are not making the optimal decisions (Kulik & Baker, 2008).

[4]A helpful source to understand segregation in the United States is "The Changing Bases of Segregation in the United States" by Massey et al. (2009).

ABM is particularly useful because they allow the researchers to model individual decision making, but also incorporate heterogeneity, interaction, and feedback (Gimblett, 2002). With ABM, researchers can easily model the social/ecological processes, structures in a system, norms and institutional factors (Hare & Deadman, 2004).

4 *Application:* Applying Schelling Model to Renting Decisions

One of the results of the latest Covid-19 pandemic was that there was a considerable amount of change in real-estate prices, especially in big cities, which ultimately have led to significant "re-shuffling" of tenants. This process has been accelerated by the realization that the near future will bring many updates with itself, such as more flexible work hours, more widely accepted practices of tele-work, smaller office spaces, and possibly larger homes and more investment in home offices due to the greater amount of time spent at home. This drastic change can be modeled using the classical Schelling Model of segregation. Initial indicators show that there has been a significant amount of decrease in rent prices in major cities of the USA.

One of the applications of agent-based modeling under the umbrella of `Python` language is provided through the `Mesa` module. The example below demonstrates the capability of this module to develop Schelling simulations quite easily:

> Let's evaluate the situation for a middle-income city dweller in New York City (around 50% of residents in New York City are middle-income residents, which brings the fraction of similar agents in the system to 50%). Assuming that 90% of all apartments in New York City are already taken, our agent is deliberating whether he/she should move out of the city. If there is no significant decrease in the rent our agent pays, he/she will become unhappy and our perfectly rational and happiness-seeking agent will move out. In fact, Robert Frank from CNBC (November 12, 2020) has reported that the average rent price in New York City has dropped by 19% compared to 2019. Let's also assume that our agent would be unhappy if a fraction of his/her neighbors (let's assume 25% of our agent's neighbors) are paying less than our agent. How many moves would it take for our agent to be happy again, if he/she wants to make sure that only less than 25% of his/her neighbors are paying less rent?
>
> The ten-fold re-run of the simulation with a population of 360 agents indicates that it would take our agent an average of *three (3) moves* to maximize their happiness. However, marginally speaking, the first move brings much greater happiness than the last two moves. Nevertheless, it is a costly decision (Fig. 1).

5 Correlation-Based Stock Networks

An important substantial application of the networks in the realm of economics and finance is the study of stocks. Network models are suitable to analyze stock prices, since it is widely believed and the prices of stocks influence each other. Scholars who study stock markets think that stock prices are determined by characteristics

Fig. 1 Agent-Based Modeling and Renting Decisions

intrinsic to the company who represents the stock, and by the movement in the prices of other stocks—the *extrinsic* factors. Network science is especially useful if one is interested in the *extrinsic* factors. Kukreti et al. (2020) indicate that correlation-based stock networks can help us to understand the patterns of complex interactions among stocks at a given period of time (for instance, the cross-correlations based on the aggregated co-movement of prices over a given month). Using this structural information, we can uncover which stocks are particularly helpful in determining the price levels of other stocks, and thus classify some stocks as "core" and others as "periphery."

The literature finds correlation-based stock networks highly intriguing, because they allow the investors and the researchers to monitor the health and fragility of the financial markets (Kukreti et al., 2020) and to find the relationship between socio-political developments and stock market fluctuations (Faccio, 2006, 2007; Mitchell & Joseph, 2010; Yusoff et al., 2015). These system-level dynamics can ultimately be used for practical applications such as portfolio management and risk optimization (Kukreti et al., 2020). As evidenced by some examples in the literature (Onnela et al., 2003, 2004; Bonanno et al., 2003), correlation-based stock networks are easy to understand by the outsiders and provide data that can easily be transformed into meaningful visual representations.

Stocks and their prices can be converted into network structures by treating stocks as nodes in a network, and the price co-movements as edges symbolizing the relationship between two different stocks over a period of time. The most frequently used types of correlation-based stock networks in the literature that use this network structure are: (raw) cross-correlation matrices (Tumminello et al., 2010), mutual-information based networks (Guo et al., 2018), minimum spanning trees (MST) (Mantegna, 1999a, b; Aste et al., 2005; Gilmore et al., 2010), threshold networks (Kumar & Deo, 2012), and planar maximally filtered graphs (Tumminello et al., 2005). In the stock networks covered in the literature by the four types of networks mentioned above, actors are exclusively represented as equal; thus, bipartite networks or other topologies are not used. The main goal in obtaining a network using these options is to have a unique representation of the relationships between stocks in that given time frame, and to increase computational efficiency by capturing the most important subset of the network. These four types of correlation-based networks can be constructed in the ways described below.

1. (Raw) Correlation-based networks:

To construct a correlation-based network to represent N stocks, first a correlation matrix $C(\tau)$ is calculated by taking the closing price of two stocks S_i and S_j for a time unit τ by calculating the Pearson correlation coefficient for all stock pairs in the data. Then, a transformation is applied to convert the correlation matrix into a distance matrix $D(\tau) = \sqrt{2(1 - C(T))}$..

2. Minimum spanning trees:

A minimum spanning tree is constructed by using the strengths of relationship between two stocks d_{ij} from the distance matrix $D(\tau)$. By definition, a minimum spanning tree is a subset of the the network system constructed from $D(\tau)$ such that all N nodes in the network are connected with N-1 edges assuring that the distance between all stocks is minimum (or that the correlation between them is the highest) (Bonanno et al., 2003, 2004; Tumminello et al., 2010). Minimum spanning trees (MST) are obtained by using the Kruskal or Prim algorithms.[5] MSTs have several advantages: they provide a unique identifier for the network at hand (i), this identifier is much smaller than the actual network and therefore computationally easier to manage (ii). Nevertheless, one important disadvantage of MST are that minor

[5]For an example, see the `networkx` package in Python.

changes in the network leads to changes in MST. This means that the order and classification of nodes in a cluster of MST is not robust. MSTs have in the past widely been applied in empirical research to investigate the currency crises and the foreign exchange market (Jang et al., 2011), global foreign exchange dynamics (McDonald et al., 2005), and the identification of different sectors by sector classification (Onnela et al., 2004) among other works.

3. Mutual-information-based networks:

There are articles that indicate the use of Pearson correlation coefficient is not good enough to describe the relationship between the stocks because of the linearity assumption that comes with it (Guo et al., 2018). Some empirical studies in finance that use mutual information-based networks, as well (Kenett et al., 2010, 2012). Similar to Pearson correlation coefficient, mutual information measures the statistical dependence between two random variables, and it is particularly useful to measure nonlinear relationships. One advantage of this method is that it allows to analyze both small and high-dimensional datasets (Wang & Huang, 2014; Villaverde et al., 2014). Mutual information is related to Shannon's entropy theory and it provides a generalized correlation measurement. As exemplified by Guo et al. (2018) and minding the lack of space to go through the formula in detail, mutual information translates into:

$$I(S_i, S_j) = H(S_i) + H(S_j) - H(S_i, S_j)$$

…where $H(S_i)$ is the entropy of a stock and $H(S_i,S_j)$ represents the joint entropy of two stocks. The entropy of a stock is approximated from the probability distribution of a particular stock from an interval that contains the relevant stock's log-returns. For the joint entropy, comparably, a multivariate probability distribution is constructed based on the squares of the log-returns of both stocks.

4. Threshold networks

Threshold networks are created from the (raw) correlation-based networks by applying a threshold value to the correlations (C_{ij}) or distance (d_{ij}) in the adjacency matrix by filtering out the longest distances (d_{ij}). Setting the distances equal to 2 gives the fully-connected graph, whereas distances lower than 1 provide computationally manageable networks with lower density, as shown by empirical evidence (Kukreti et al., 2020). Similar to minimum spanning trees, threshold networks can only be created with "loss of information," since some nodes and edges need to be discarded. Again, similar to MSTs, small changes in the raw network structure can lead to significant changes in the threshold networks.

5. Planar maximally filtered graphs

By definition, planar maximally filtered graphs (PMFGs) are constructed in a way such that there are no intersecting connections in the network. Assuming that there are *N* stocks, this leads to the creation of 3(N-2) connections between stocks. MST is a subset of PMFG (or, PMFG is an extended version of MST). PMFG is unique to each network, and leads to less information loss than MST. PMFG can be combined with threshold networks in empirical studies (Nie, 2017).

6 *Application:* Topological Properties of Correlation Networks

Correlation networks allow the researchers to extract a variety of features about the dynamics of the stock market. These dynamics include the stock-level properties, most importantly the predictability of a stock price based on the behavior of other stocks, and the global properties of the network such as sectoral tendencies, booms, and busts. The literature provides a rich set of alternatives to analyze the topological properties of these networks.

Yahoo Finance provides one of the most comprehensive resources on stocks including prices aggregated by seconds, days, months, and years.[6] In this chapter, stock data from all available stocks starting from the year 1985 has been used. The 1985–2020 period offers an interesting empirical background, since the world economy experienced shocks to the stock market a lot more frequently in the last few decades than in previous years (Yahoo Finance, 2021). The data downloaded from *Yahoo* has grown over the years, along with the number of companies in existence. The figure below shows the number of companies available in the dataset starting from 1985 (the number of data available has grown from a few hundred companies to close to 7000 companies over the years) (Fig. 2).

The graphs below show the threshold networks created from the (raw) correlation-based networks for 3 years characterized by global financial crisis (Black Monday (1987), Burst of the Dot-Com Bubble (2001), Global Financial Crisis (2008)). For the threshold networks, all stocks that have a correlation of at least 0.8 have been taken into account, and other relationships have been removed. Despite the fact that most of the connections have been removed, the threshold networks still possess a very high density (Figs. 3, 4, and 5).

Using correlations, one can analyze the topological properties of a network, as well. A widely used measure is the *average clustering coefficient* as defined by Watts and Strogatz (1998). The clustering coefficient for a node in a network is the proportion of connections between the nodes within its neighborhood divided by the number of all possible connections between this node and its neighborhood. This calculation is repeated for every node in the network and an average is taken. A similar measure is the network density—which gives the ratio of actual connections to all possible connections in a network. Using the threshold networks for each year (only connections with weights bigger than 0.8 are taken into account), the graph below provides the *average clustering coefficient* and *network density* over years.

---

[6]To download stock data, take a look at the `yahoo-finance` package in Python.

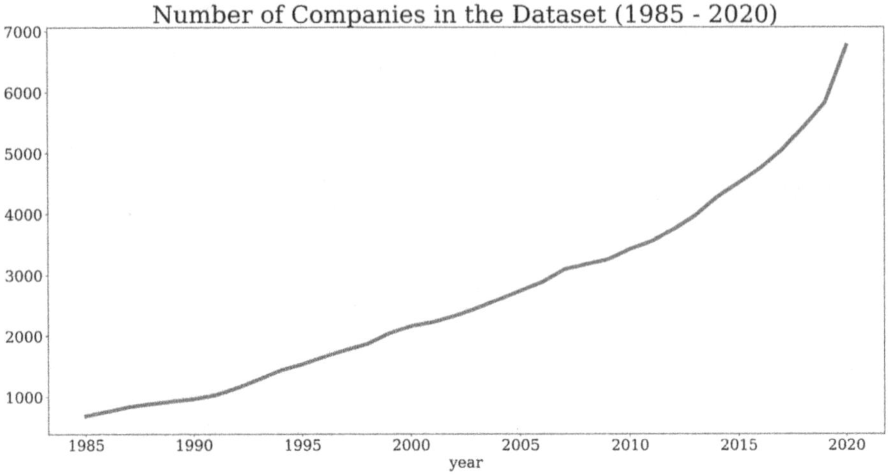

Fig. 2 Number of Companies Over Time (1985–2020)

The vertical dashed lines show four different global economic downturns happened in the last four decades. From the graph, it seems that economics shocks do not have a strong impact on the topological properties (Fig. 6).

Another method to analyze the data at hand is to look at the distribution of the weights in the networks. The distribution of weights is widely used in applications that look at entropy-based measures to compare networks. Distributions provide information about how much of the stocks move together. The ridge plot below shows the distributions over years (1985–2020). The data indicates that in some years, the tendency to move together was greater than others. The years that stand out are 1986, 1997, 2003, 2008, and 2009. Again, as in the example above, it is difficult to tie this variation to different economic downturns in history (Fig. 7).

7 Network Similarities Literature

As mentioned in the introduction, network analysis has the flexibility to handle different levels of analysis. If the interest is in getting a dynamic understanding of the data at hand, being able to compare two (or more) networks is particularly useful. The researcher (or the analyst) may be interested in a dynamic picture, if the trends extracted from the financial data can be helpful for understanding other social phenomena (or vice versa), or financial phenomena related to the data at hand. The latter aspect is especially of interest if the goal is to make predictions about the future by training an algorithm that can handle this task. Thinking about economic and financial systems, this aspect is especially useful, since it is widely believed that similar economic and financial phenomena should be related to each other in terms

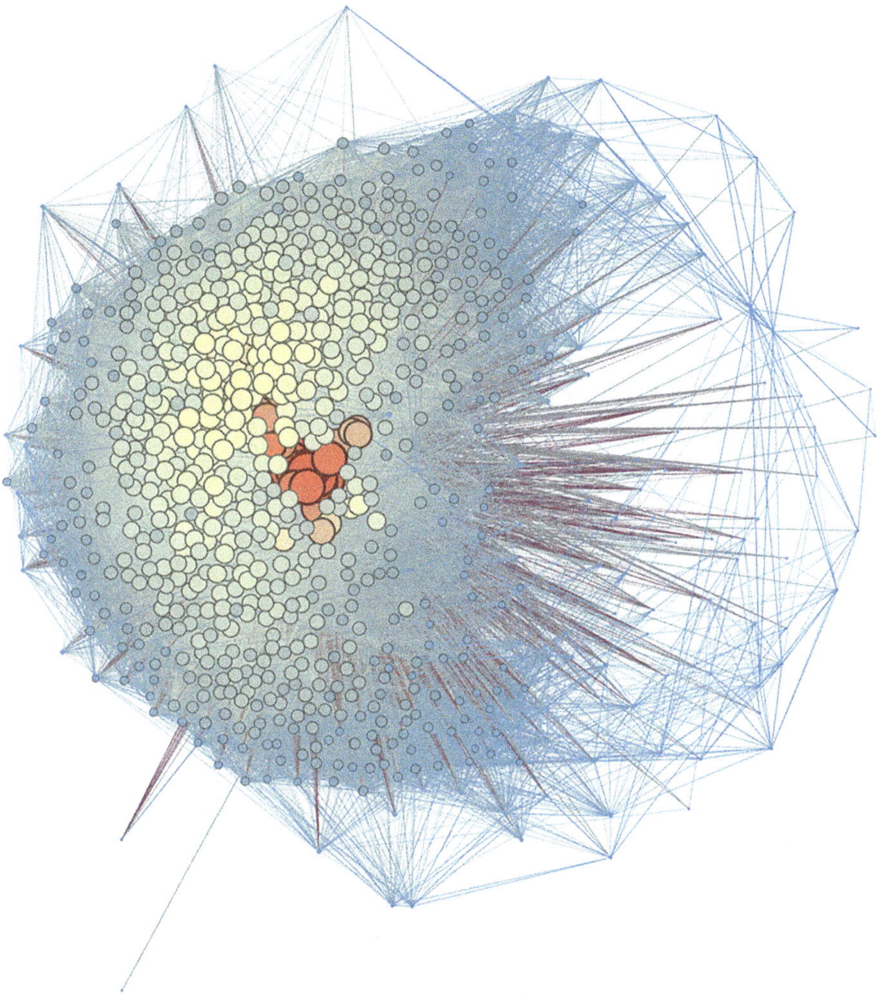

Fig. 3 Threshold Network (1987)

of how agents behave. Thus, it is expected that stock prices will correlate in times of booms and bust.

Partly due to the rich literature on network similarities that spans over several decades of work, the metrics obtained when comparing two graphs may give greatly different results. Earlier attempts to calculate similarities between networks have started in the 1960s and the 1970s (see Sussenguth, 1964; Vizing, 1968; Zelinka, 1975). Zelinka (1975) made the first attempt to quantify the distance between graphs. Analyzing the structures of patterns, or patterns of exchange has been of interest in many applied fields such as linguistics, web indexing and mining (Kleinberg, 1999), political science, and economics and finance (Kanik, 2020).

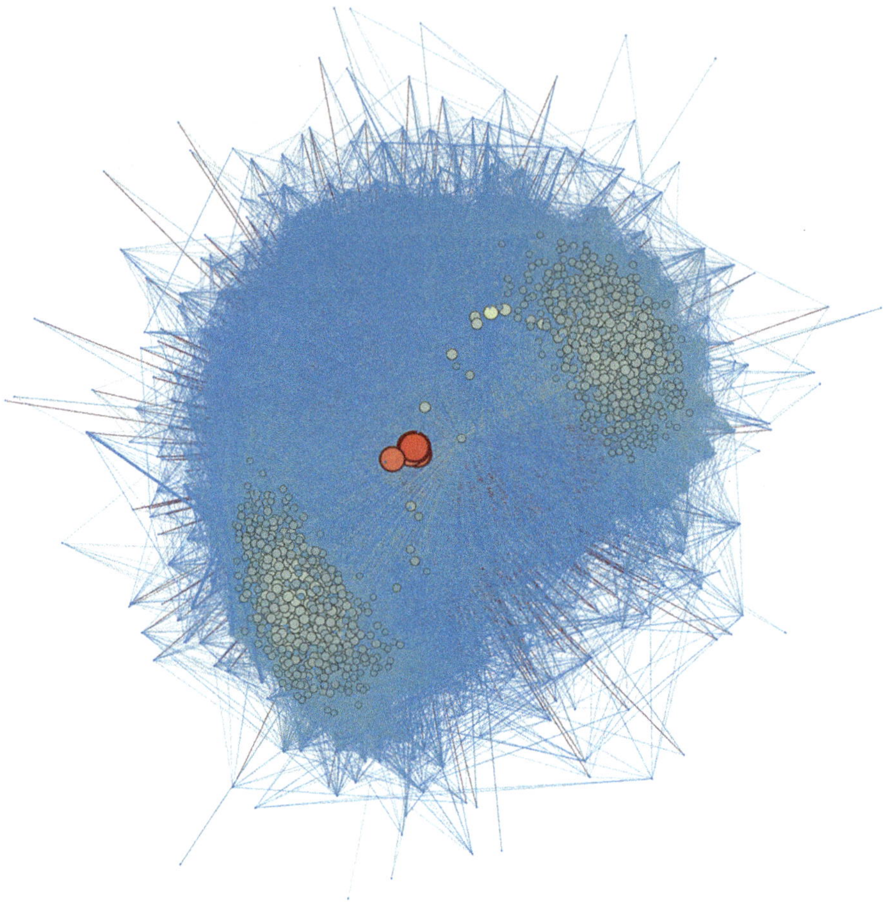

Fig. 4 Threshold Network (2001)

Most of the tools that can be used to compute similarities between networks are designed for undirected and unweighted networks; and, only a few of them are capable of calculating the similarity between directed and/or weighted networks (Tantardini et al., 2019). This section of the chapter will highlight some of the possibilities to compare networks by looking at how three different similarity algorithms perform over time for the correlation data at hand. Specifically, *Frobenius Distance*, *NetLSD Distance*, and *QuantumJSD Distance* will be put into practice. One important advantage of these three techniques is their ability to handle disconnected graphs.

All similarity algorithms that are used to compare networks need a key component: a distance metric with which the nodes in a network can be compared to each other. Deciding on which metric to use is a critical task, and the decision to choose a suitable metric is a trade-off between computational power, interpretability, and the

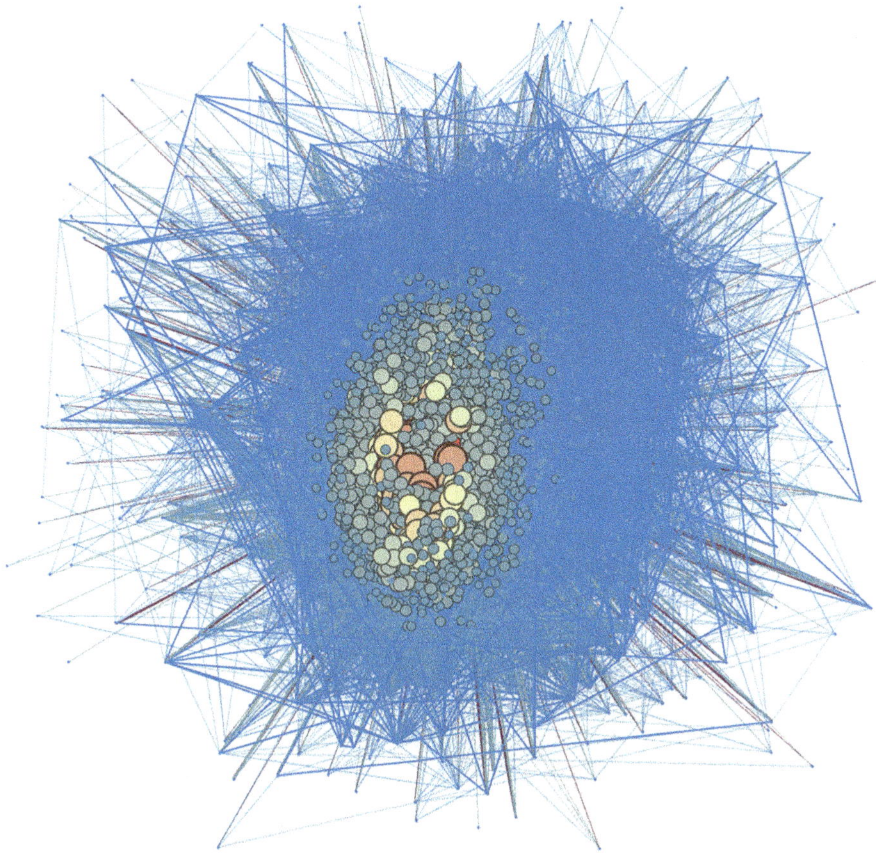

Fig. 5 Threshold Network (2008)

domain knowledge. There are a few important works in the literature that provide a comparative analysis of the similarity algorithms for networks (Tantardini et al., 2019; Soundarajan et al., 2014; Emmert-Streib et al., 2016; Donnat & Holmes, 2018).

The difficulty in comparing two networks can be connected to the *graph isomorphism* problem. Two graphs $G1(V1, E1)$ and $G2(V2, E2)$ are *isomorphic* or identical if the sets of nodes in these two graphs (V1 and V2) are the same, and the connections between these sets of nodes (E1 and E2) are the same, as well. Checking if two graphs are in fact the same graph is a computationally difficult problem (Toda, 1999) and the focus of the researchers interested in studying *exact graph matching*. Nevertheless, since networks are complex structures, and dynamic networks change over time, attempting to do an *exact graph matching* to obtain a binary result about the similarity is often not very practical and rational. As in case with financial and economic networks, a more effective comparison can be done by using an *inexact graph matching*. In this case, a continuous value is obtained to compare two graphs

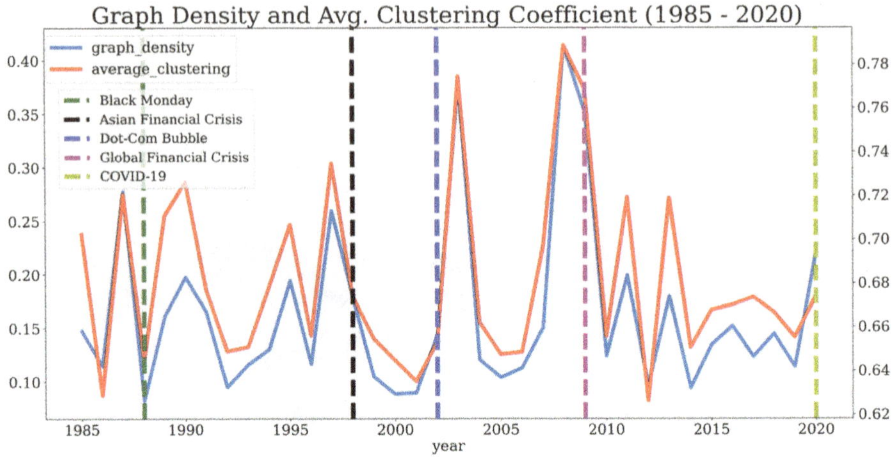

Fig. 6 Graph Density and Average Clustering Coefficient

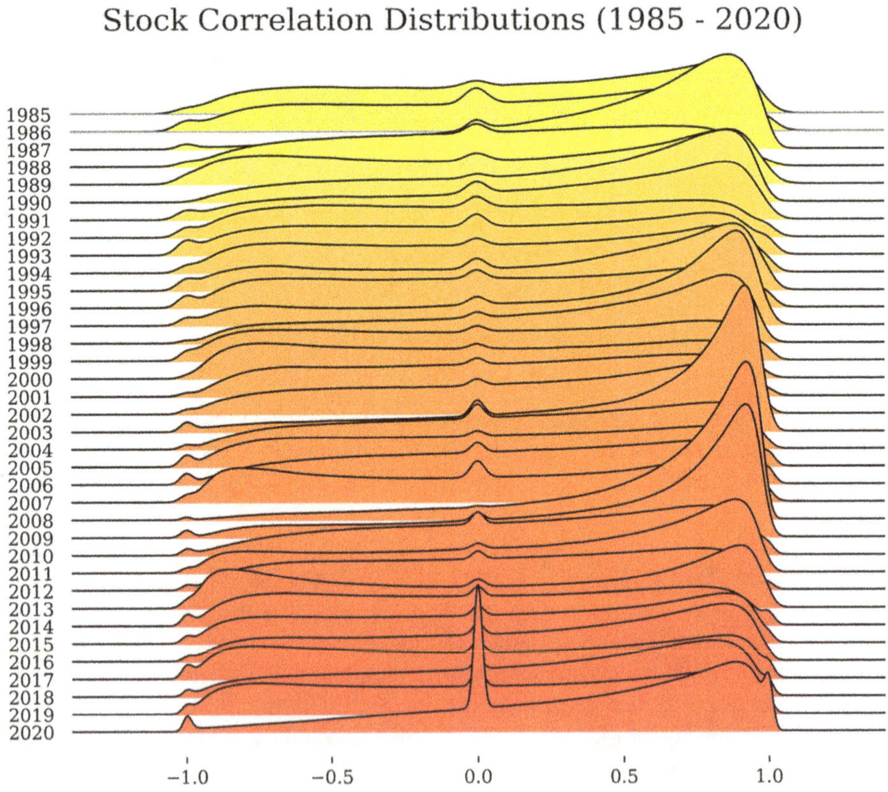

Fig. 7 Stock Correlation Distributions Over Time

and the distance between more *isomorphic* networks is close to zero (Tantardini et al., 2019).

To be able to show that two graphs are isomorphic, we need to have perfect information about the set of nodes and the set of edges that are part of the network. Furthermore, if we are interested in purely comparing the sets of connections in two different graphs to each other, we need to have the same set of nodes. Especially in complex graphs, where the number of nodes and connections is great, this is a hard task to accomplish. In cases where we are interested in calculating a global similarity score by using a one-to-one match between the nodes and their connections between two graphs, we have a "*known node-correspondence*" (KNC) problem. In comparisons where the nodes, sizes, and connections within the networks are different from each other and/or not considered in the calculation of the similarity metrics, we are dealing with an "*unknown node-correspondence*" (UNC) problem. For the case of financial and economic networks, we are usually dealing with the latter case: these types of networks usually look at some type of transaction and/or relationship between an economic entity, such as bank accounts, banks, companies, stocks, countries, etc. If we look at each possibility, it is clear that these entities may appear or disappear in time: bank accounts and banks may be opened or closed, companies may be founded or go bankrupt; and although less likely, new countries can be formed, as well.

7.1 Known Node-Correspondence (KNC) Methods

The majority of the research in this field has been produced in the 2000s. The most straightforward method to calculate a KNC method-based similarity score is comparing the distance between two actors in two different graphs. For this purpose, different distance metrics can be used, such as Jaccard, Frobenius, Canberra, Hamming, and others (Ioffe, 2010). These techniques are not used frequently for practical purposes; however, they have computational advantages in applications of massive networks.

More advanced techniques use local and global criteria at the same time. One important recent example is the *Delta-Con Distance* proposed by Koutra et al. (2013) and Onion Divergence by Hébert-Dufresne et al. (2016). A comparable method is the *Cut Distance* that is frequently used in computer science in the context of community detection algorithms (Liu et al., 2018).

Other more advanced techniques use KNC-based and UNC-based measures at the same time. One example is the *Hamming–Ipsen–Mikhailov Distance* that looks at the local and global measures at the same time (Jurman et al., 2015). A closer explanation of some of these metrics have been provided below.

1. Frobenius distance

Frobenius Distance is one of the more straightforward techniques to look at the similarity between two graphs. It only makes a "local" comparison between two graphs by looking at individual connections between pairs of nodes.

If $a_{i,j}$ and $b_{i,j}$ represent the connections between two nodes *i* and *j* coming from two different graphs *G1* and *G2* such that $a_{i,j}$ is in *G1* and $b_{i,j}$ is in *G2*, Frobenius distance *d(G1, G2)* is the following:

$$d(G1, G2) = \sqrt{\sum_{i,j} \|a_{ij} - b_{ij}\|}$$

2. Delta-Con distance

Delta-Con is a more sophisticated method to compare two networks. It is a KNC-method (hence the graphs that are compared need to have the same set of nodes), so it looks at the similarities between all node pairs in the two graphs. To calculate the *Delta-Con Distance*, a similarity matrix *S* needs to be calculated:

$$S = \left[I + \varepsilon^2 D - \varepsilon A\right]^{-1}$$

In this formula, *I* represents the identity matrix, *A* represents the adjacency matrix, $D = diagonal(k_i)$ is the degree matrix, k_i is the degree of node *i*, and $\varepsilon > 0$ represents a small constant. The similarity matrix is inverted using a fast belief propagation (FBP) algorithm, which is a computationally costly process and has no guaranteed results (the small constant is added to increase the chances that the matrix is invertible). The use of similarity matrix formula has the effect that some edges have greater importance than others. Thus, individual entries in *S* for a node pair, $s_{i,j}$, depend on all of the different paths connecting the nodes *i*, *j*. For each graph, a separate similarity matrix is created and finally, the *Matusita* distance (Dabboor et al., 2014) is computed. Suppose that we have two similarity matrices *S1* and *S2* where $s^1_{i,j}$ is in *S1* and $s^2_{i,j}$ is in *S2*:

$$d(G1, G2) = \left(\sum_{i,j=1}^{N} \left(\sqrt{s^1_{ij}} - \sqrt{s^2_{ij}}\right)\right)^{1/2}$$

The formula above brings a few advantages: similarity matrices with disconnected graphs receive a penalty and therefore are considered as more distant. With regard to the changes made to the graph, bigger changes lead to even bigger increases in distance, and expectedly changes made in lower density graphs have greater impact on the distance than the changes made in higher density graphs. In 2016, the originally proposed algorithm has been extended to be able to find the edges and nodes that are responsible for the differences between two graphs (Koutra et al., 2016).

3. Cut distance

Cut Distance can be used both for unweighted and weighted (which is usually the case with networks in finance). A cut weight is defined as the minimum sum of all edge weights for the edges that need to be removed to be able to create two sub-graphs with disjoint node sets. This methodology can also be applied to calculating the distance between two graphs such that:

$$d(G1, G2) = \max \frac{1}{|V|} \left| e_{G_1}\left(S, S^C\right) - e_{G_2}\left(S, S^C\right) \right|$$

...where S^C represents the matrix that complements S, and S and S^C together make up a graph. The formula indicates that two networks are similar if the cut weight is similar for all possible network bipartitions. The cut distance allows the researcher to compare weighted networks to each other; nevertheless, it is computationally highly expensive.

7.2 *Unknown Node-Correspondence (UNC) Methods*

As with KNC, there is a high number of basic and more advanced methods that can be used here. Some simple network statistics such as the diameter, the clustering coefficient, or the average distance between nodes can serve as UNC methods. The problem with these methods is that they are usually very reactive to small changes in the network and usually disregard the importance of local features. Nevertheless, they offer less computational burden.

The more up-to-date methods in this area are the *spectral* methods. These methods use the spectrum of the representation of a matrix in adjacency or the Laplacian formats. By definition, the spectrum of a matrix is the set of its eigenvalues (Kreyszig, 2015), and provides a unique identifier for a graph. These methods rely on the comparison of spectra of two matrices. More straightforward spectral methods offer the calculation of Euclidean distances between two spectra (Wilson & Zhu, 2008) or they look at a non-parametric test to get a binary result on whether two graphs are different from each other (Gera et al., 2018). Some newer methods generalize well to weighted graphs, as well. These include *NetLSD* (Network Laplacian Spectral Descriptor) by Tsitsulin et al., 2018, *Quantum JSD* (Quantum Jensen–Shannon Divergence) by De Domenico et al., 2016, and *Portrait Divergence* (Bagrow & Bollt, 2019) among many others. A more detailed look at these measures have been provided below.

1. NetLSD distance

The *NetLSD Distance* generalizes to weighted graphs, as well. The method calculates the solution of "heat equation" ($\partial ut/\partial t = - Lu_t$) where u_t is an N-dimensional vector and $L = I - D^{-1/2}AD^{-1/2}$ is the Laplacian matrix in the normalized form. Using eigendecomposition, the Laplacian matrix can be further transformed into $L = \Phi \Lambda \Phi^T$ and the kernel for the heat equation can be provided by the following:

$$H_t = e^{-Lt} = \Phi e^{-\Lambda t} \Phi^{\mathrm{T}}$$

The elements of this equation $(H_t)_{ij}$ are the "heat" transferred from node *i* to *j* at time *t*. The trace of the matrix *H* for a graph *G* forms the NetLSD:

$$h(G) = \{h_t\}_{t>0} = \mathrm{trace}(H_t)$$

Finally, the distance between two graphs can be calculated by taking the "norm" of the vector difference between h(G1) and h(G2). One important advantage of *NetLSD* is that with a time complexity of $O(N^3)$, it is comparably faster than rival algorithms (Tantardini et al., 2019).

2. Quantum JSD distance

Instead of using a "heat matrix," *Quantum JSD* compares the spectral entropies of the density matrices. This is done by calculating the "Quantum" Jensen–Shannon divergence between two graphs. The authors create a connection-based density matrix to calculate the von Neumann entropy of a network. The algorithm proposed uses the whole network, instead of a subset of network features. Most importantly, the algorithm allows the authors to quantify the distance between "complex" networks. Classical algorithms attempt to quantify the amount of information about a probability distribution (entropy), and *Quantum JSD* expands this definition by introducing divergences (also known as quantum relative entropy). The distance is calculated by using a generalized Jenson–Shannon divergence between two graphs:

$$J_q(\rho \parallel \sigma) = S_q\left(\frac{\rho + \sigma}{2}\right) - \frac{1}{2}\left[S_q(\rho) + S_q(\sigma)\right]$$

In the equation above, ρ and σ represent the density matrices and q represents the order parameter. The density matrix looks like the following:

$$\rho = \frac{e^{-\beta L}}{Z}$$

where:

$$Z = \sum_{i=1}^{N} e^{-\beta \lambda_i(\mathrm{L})}$$

and λ_i(L) represents an imaginary diffusion process *i*, over the network with time parameter $\beta > 0$.

3. Portrait divergence

Portrait Divergence is a newly developed method that compares the "portraits" of two graphs to each other. According to Bagrow and Bollt (2019), the network portrait is a matrix B with l x k dimensions such that B_{lk} is the number of nodes that have k nodes at distance l. The biggest value l can take is the diameter (d) of the network (by definition) and—since loops are excluded—k can at most be equal to N - 1 (where N is the number of nodes in the graph). The matrix B offers several advantages as it captures important topological properties such as the number of nodes, the degree distribution, the distribution of the next-nearest neighbors, the shortest path distribution, and the graph diameter. Each graph G has a unique portrait B. Assuming that we have graphs $G1$ and $G2$ with corresponding portraits $B1$ and $B2$, we can compute the *Portrait Divergence* in the following way:

First, we create a matrix C for each graph that includes the cumulative distributions of B by row:

$$C_{l,k} = \frac{\sum_{j=0}^{k} B_{l,j}}{\sum_{j=0}^{N} B_{l,j}}$$

Then, a Kolmogorov–Smirnov test statistic K_l is calculated between corresponding rows of $C1$ and $C2$ associated with $G1$ and $G2$. This test allows us to check whether the rows of the portraits come from the same underlying distributions.

$$K_l = max\left|C1_{l,k} - C2_{l,k}\right|$$

In the last part of the calculation, the test statistics are aggregated by using a weighted average, where each alpha (α) represents a weight chosen to increase the impact of more heavily weighted sets of connections.

$$dist(G1, G2) = dist(B1, B2) = \frac{\sum_l \alpha_l K_l}{\sum_l \alpha_l}$$

8 *Application:* Network Similarities of Correlation-Based Stock Networks

This last application is an attempt to extract information from correlation-based stock networks using more advanced techniques. In the previous application section, average clustering coefficients and graph densities were calculated for stock networks associated with different years. Although being not robust identifiers for networks, these measures can still be used to compare these networks to each other. The two heatmaps below have been calculated by looking at the absolute differences between these two topological properties. Each network has been compared to the other networks by finding the common set of stocks represented by these two graphs. Blue colors indicate comparisons where the distances are big (similarities are small), and red colors show cases where there is greater similarity. Figures 8 and 9 provide rather inconclusive results about the comparisons. The only 2 years that stand out are 2008 and 2009.

Unlike Average Clustering Coefficient and Graph Density that look at global statistics, *Frobenius Distance* is a naive method to compare each connection between two given nodes to each other. The results indicate that networks have become less similar over time (Fig. 10).

Further advanced methods consider local and global statistics at the same time. As explained in the theoretical section on similarities above, both NetLSD and QuantumJSD use the spectra of matrices (another unique identifier associated with correlation-based adjacency matrices). One interesting observation is that the results are quite different. NetLSD Distances indicate that the 1993–1995 period offered difficult terms for predictability. Comparably the QuantumJSD Distances show that the last two decades have provided a rather difficult ground in terms of making time-based predictions (Figs. 11 and 12).

9 Conclusion

Economics and finance offer wide opportunities to do empirical and theoretical research using network theory. This chapter had the goal to provide two easily digestible theoretical discussions from the field: agent-based modeling and network similarities. The field offers vast opportunities to connect academic discussions to real-life applications—an issue that parties from both ends of the career spectrum use to criticize the other. As in many other areas of data analytics, small empirical evidence provided in this chapter suggests that it is hard to find "one unifying explanation" in this field. In other words, techniques that can be used to achieve similar goals can yield vastly different results.

If the researcher is looking for a field to specialize in quantitative applications of economics and finance, the extensive variety of methods can be a barrier to overcome when making decisions. Like in other fields, some popular methods lose their popularity over time and they may regain or never regain their fame again. Additionally, the increasing computational capabilities of individual researchers may lead them to explore new fields that they have technologically not been capable of discovering before. As such, agent-based modeling, correlation networks, and network similarities literature offer a convincing "middle-ground" for the junior researcher and the practitioner. Mathematically, they offer opportunities to build upon the existing literature. Computationally, they offer easily accessible paths to quantitative analysis. These are advantages for people interested in studying network modeling. With the vast theoretical background of the field and the multitude of

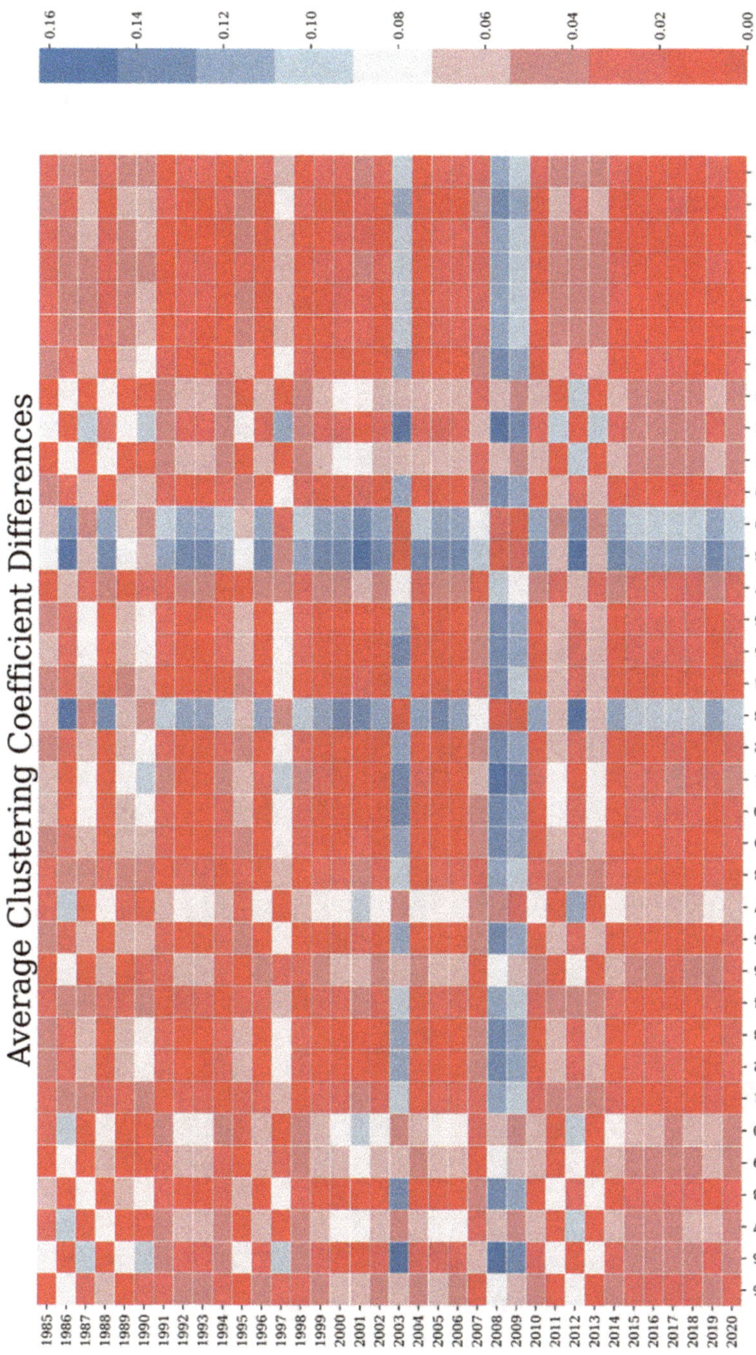

Fig. 8 Differences Between Average Clustering Coefficients

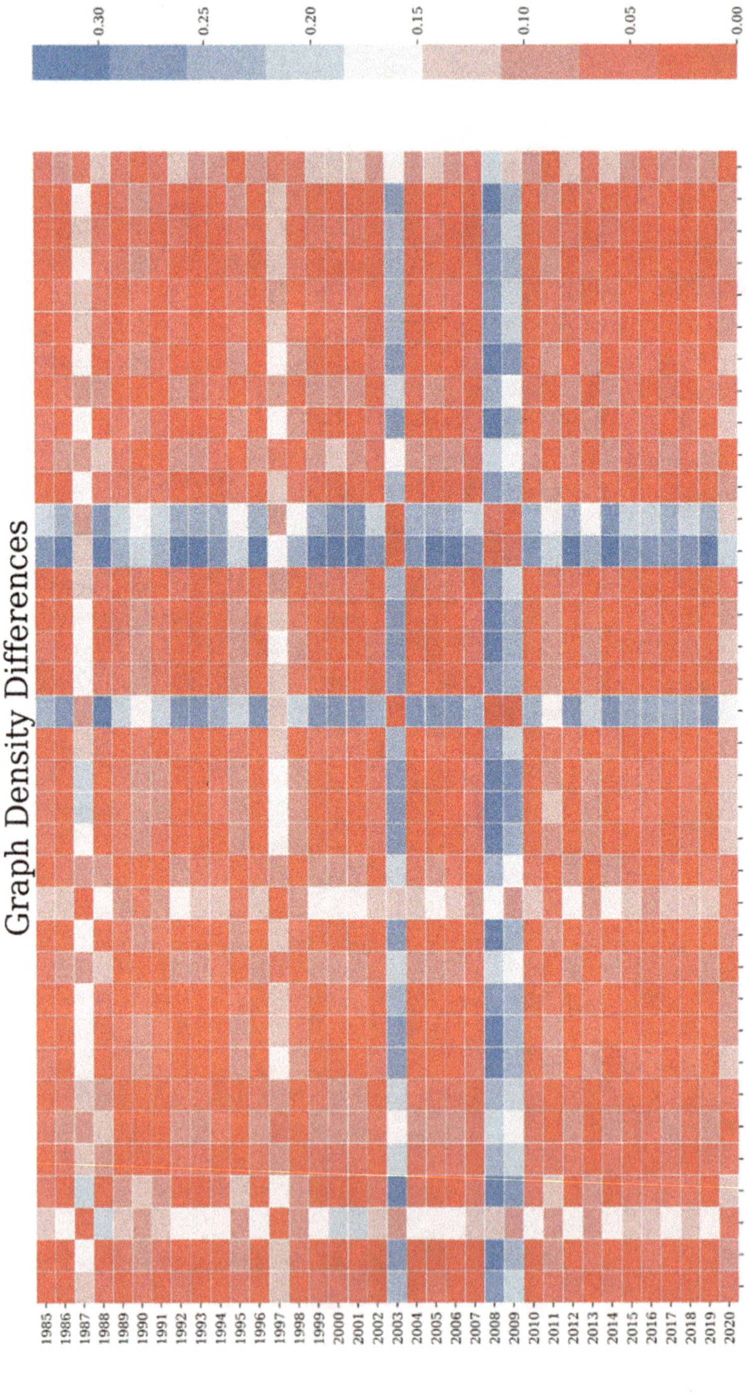

Fig. 9 Differences Between Graph Densities

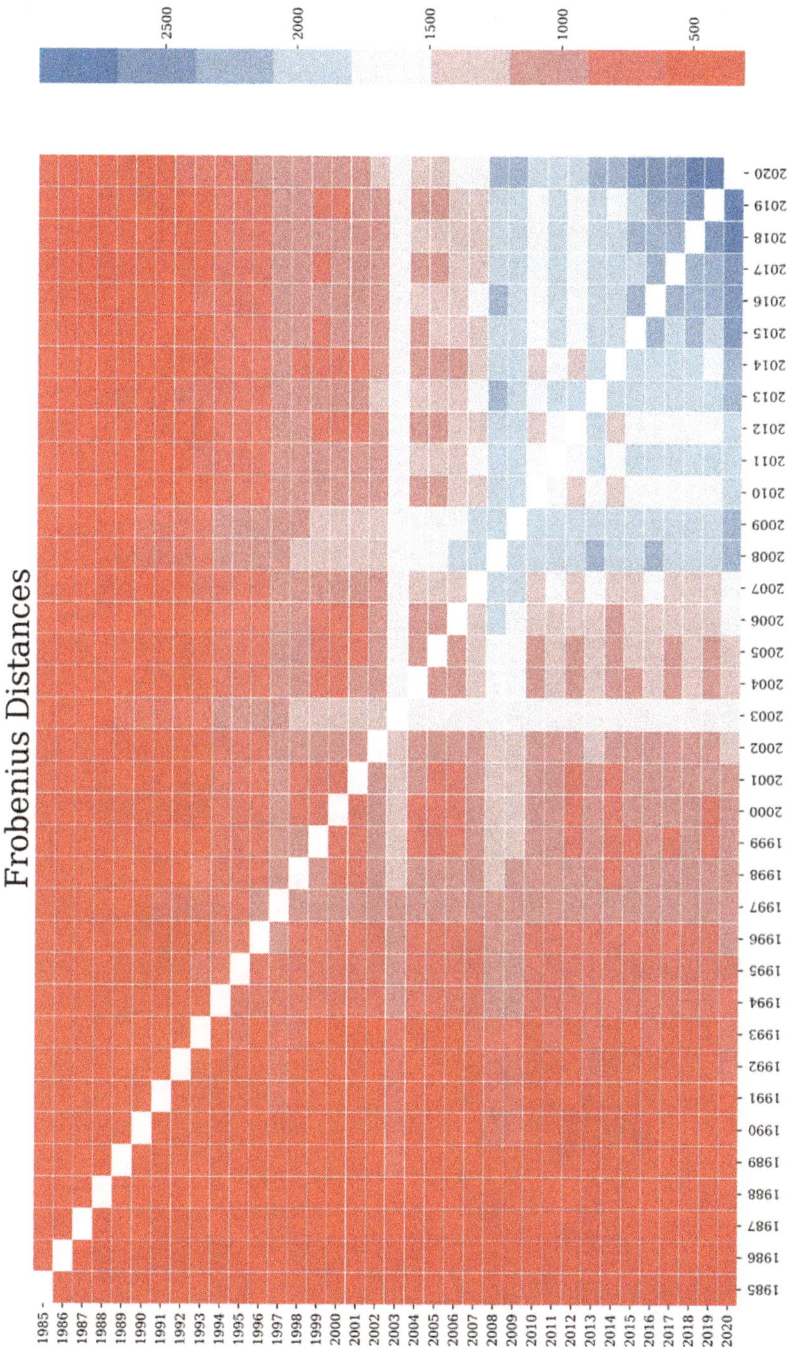

Fig. 10 Frobenius Distances

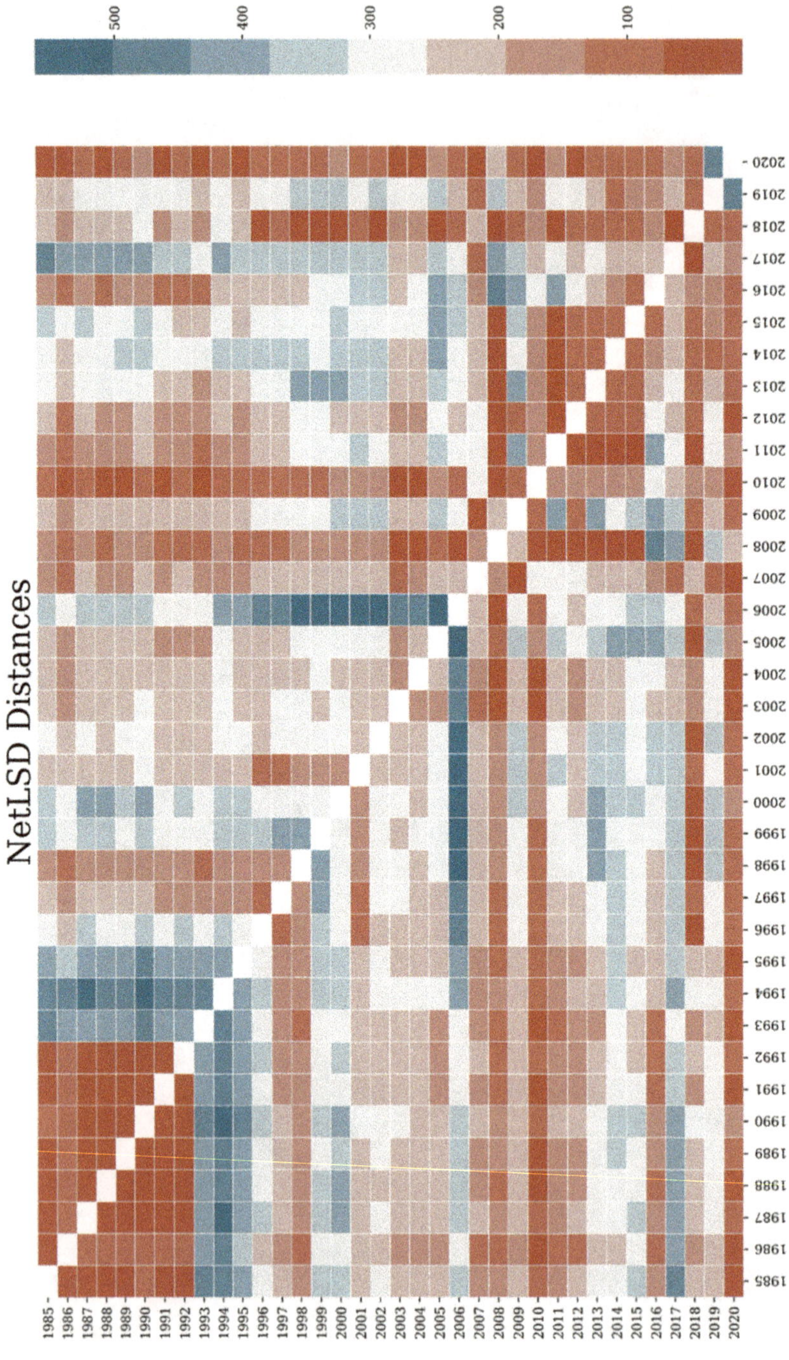

Fig. 11 NetLSD Distances

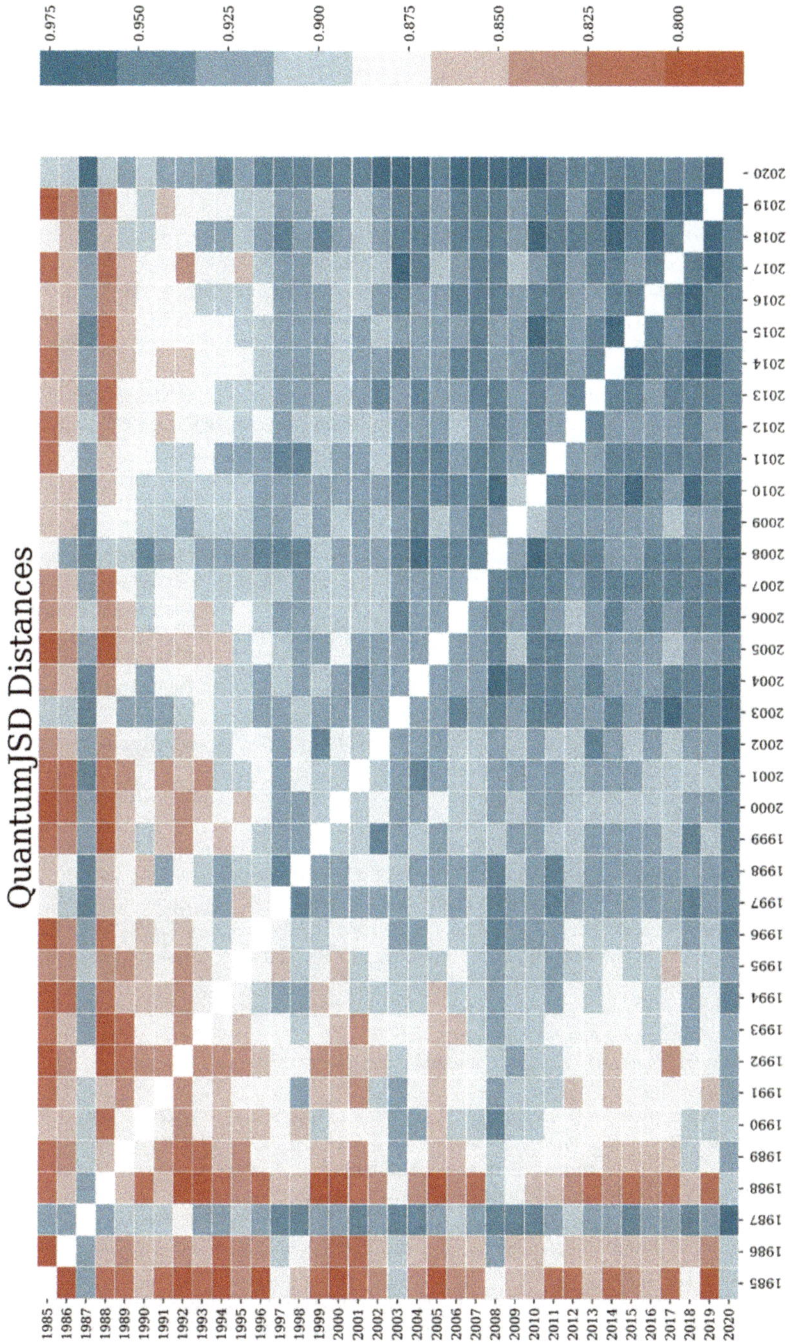

Fig. 12 QuantumJSD Distances

datasets that can be used to provide holistic pictures of the economic and financial world, network modeling continues to offer rich resources to discuss, test, and analyze.

References

Acemoglu, D., Ozdaglar, A., & Tahbaz-Salehi, A. (2015). Systemic risk and stability in financial networks. *American Economic Review, 105*(2), 564–608.

Albert, R., & Barabási, A.-L. (2002). Statistical mechanics of complex networks. *Reviews of Modern Physics, 74*(1), 47–97. https://doi.org/10.1103/RevModPhys.74.47

Aste, T., Di Matteo, T., & Hyde, S. T. (2005). Complex networks on hyperbolic surfaces. *Physica A: Statistical Mechanics and its Applications, 346*(1–2), 20–26.

Bagehot, W. (1873). *Lombard street: A description of the money market Scribner*. Armstong &.

Bagrow, J. P., & Bollt, E. M. (2019). An information-theoretic, all-scales approach to comparing networks. *Applied Network Science, 4*(1), 45.

Barabasi, A.-L. (2016). *Network science (1st edition)*. Cambridge University Press.

Barabasi, A.-L., & Albert, R. (1999). Emergence of scaling in random networks. *Science, 286* (5439), 509–512.

Barr, R. S. (1972). The multinational cash management problem: A generalized network approach. *Work-Ing Paper, University of Texas, Austin.*

Barrat, A., Barthelemy, M., Pastor-Satorras, R., & Vespignani, A. (2004). The architecture of complex weighted networks. *Proceedings of the National Academy of Sciences, 101*(11), 3747–3752.

Battiston, S., Puliga, M., Kaushik, R., Tasca, P., & Caldarelli, G. (2012). Debtrank: Too central to fail? Financial networks, the fed and systemic risk. *Scientific Reports, 2*, 541.

Bell, D. E., Raiffa, H., & Tversky, A. (1988). *Decision making: Descriptive, normative, and prescriptive interactions*. Cambridge University Press.

Boccaletti, S., Latora, V., Moreno, Y., Chavez, M., & Hwang, D.-U. (2006). Complex networks: Structure and dynamics. *Physics Reports, 424*(4–5), 175–308.

Bonanno, G., Caldarelli, G., Lillo, F., & Mantegna, R. N. (2003). Topology of correlation-based minimal spanning trees in real and model markets. *Physical Review E, 68*(4), 046130.

Bonanno, G., Caldarelli, G., Lillo, F., Micciche, S., Vandewalle, N., & Mantegna, R. N. (2004). Networks of equities in financial markets. *The European Physical Journal B, 38*(2), 363–371.

Boss, M., Elsinger, H., Summer, M., & Thurner, S. (2004). Network topology of the interbank market. *Quantitative Finance, 4*(6), 677–684.

Cabrales, A., Gottardi, P., & Vega-Redondo, F. (2017). Risk sharing and contagion in networks. *The Review of Financial Studies, 30*(9), 3086–3127.

Cohen, R., & Havlin, S. (2010). *Complex networks: Structure, robustness and function*. Cambridge university press.

Cont, R., & Moussa, A. (2010, December 1). Network structure and systemic risk in banking systems. *Edson Bastos e, Network Structure and Systemic Risk in Banking Systems*.

Crum, R. (1976). Cash management in the multinational firm: A constrained generalized network approach. In *The University of Florida Gainesville Working Paper*.

Crum, R. L., Klingman, D. D., & Tavis, L. A. (1979). Implementation of large-scale financial planning models: Solution efficient transformations. *Journal of Financial and Quantitative Analysis*, 137–152.

Crum, R. L., Klingman, D. D., & Tavis, L. A. (1983). An operational approach to integrated working capital planning. *Journal of Economics and Business, 35*(3–4), 343–378.

Dabboor, M., Howell, S., Shokr, M., & Yackel, J. (2014). The Jeffries–Matusita distance for the case of complex Wishart distribution as a separability criterion for fully polarimetric SAR data. *International Journal of Remote Sensing, 35*(19), 6859–6873.

De Domenico, M., Sasai, S., & Arenas, A. (2016). Mapping multiplex hubs in human functional brain networks. *Frontiers in Neuroscience, 10*, 326. https://doi.org/10.3389/fnins.2016.00326

Donnat, C., & Holmes, S. (2018). Tracking network dynamics: A survey of distances and similarity metrics. *ArXiv Preprint ArXiv, 1801, 07351.*

Elliott, M., Golub, B., & Jackson, M. O. (2014). Financial networks and contagion. *American Economic Review, 104*(10), 3115–3153.

Elsinger, H., Lehar, A., & Summer, M. (2006). Risk assessment for banking systems. *Management Science, 52*(9), 1301–1314.

Emmert-Streib, F., Dehmer, M., & Shi, Y. (2016). Fifty years of graph matching, network alignment and network comparison. *Information Sciences, 346*, 180–197.

Faccio, M. (2006). Politically connected firms. *American Economic Review, 96*(1), 369–386.

Faccio, M. (2007). The characteristics of politically connected firms.

Faloutsos, M., Faloutsos, P., & Faloutsos, C. (1999). On power-law relationships of the internet topology. *ACM SIGCOMM Computer Communication Review, 29*(4), 251–262.

Flache, A., & Hegselmann, R. (2001). Do irregular grids make a difference? Relaxing the spatial regularity assumption in cellular models of social dynamics. *Journal of Artificial Societies and Social Simulation, 4*(4).

Frank, R. (2020, November 12). *Big drop in Manhattan apartment prices begins to lure back younger renters*. CNBC. https://www.cnbc.com/2020/11/12/big-drop-in-manhattan-rental-prices-lures-back-younger-residents.html

Furfine, C. H. (2003). Interbank exposures: Quantifying the risk of contagion. *Journal of Money, Credit and Banking*, 111–128.

Gai, P., & Kapadia, S. (2010). Contagion in financial networks. *Proceedings of the Royal Society A: Mathematical, Physical and Engineering Sciences, 466*(2120), 2401–2423.

Galbiati, M., & Soramäki, K. (2012). Clearing networks. *Journal of Economic Behavior & Organization, 83*(3), 609–626.

Garas, A., Argyrakis, P., Rozenblat, C., Tomassini, M., & Havlin, S. (2010). Worldwide spreading of economic crisis. *New Journal of Physics, 12*(11), 113043.

Gera, R., Alonso, L., Crawford, B., House, J., Mendez-Bermudez, J. A., Knuth, T., & Miller, R. (2018, January 1). Identifying network structure similarity using spectral graph theory. *Applied Network Science; SpringerOpen.* https://doi.org/10.1007/s41109-017-0042-3

Gilmore, C. G., Lucey, B. M., & Boscia, M. W. (2010). Comovements in government bond markets: A minimum spanning tree analysis. *Physica A: Statistical Mechanics and its Applications, 389*(21), 4875–4886.

Gimblett, H. R. (2002). *Integrating geographic information systems and agent-based modeling techniques for simulating social and ecological processes*. Oxford University Press.

Granovetter, M. (2018). *Getting a job: A study of contacts and careers*. University of Chicago Press.

Guo, X., Zhang, H., & Tian, T. (2018). Development of stock correlation networks using mutual information and financial big data. *PLoS One, 13*(4), e0195941.

Hare, M., & Deadman, P. (2004). Further towards a taxonomy of agent-based simulation models in environmental management. *Mathematics and Computers in Simulation, 64*(1), 25–40.

Hatna, E., & Benenson, I. (2010). The Schelling model of ethnic residential dynamics: Beyond the integrated - segregated dichotomy of patterns. *Journal of Artificial Societies and Social Simulation, 15*(1), 6.

Hébert-Dufresne, L., Grochow, J. A., & Allard, A. (2016). Multi-scale structure and topological anomaly detection via a new network statistic: The onion decomposition. *Scientific Reports, 6* (1), 31708. https://doi.org/10.1038/srep31708

Helbing, D. (2013). Globally networked risks and how to respond. *Nature, 497*(7447), 51–59.

Hüser, A.-C. (2015). Too interconnected to fail: A survey of the interbank networks literature.

Inaoka, H., Ninomiya, T., Taniguchi, K., Shimizu, T., & Takayasu, H. (2004). Fractal Network derived from banking transaction–An analysis of network structures formed by financial institutions. *Bank Jpn Work Pap*, 4.

Ioffe, S. (2010). Improved consistent sampling, weighted minhash and l1 sketching. In *2010 IEEE international conference on data mining* (pp. 246–255).

Jackson, M. O. (2010). *Social and economic networks*. Princeton University Press.

Jang, W., Lee, J., & Chang, W. (2011). Currency crises and the evolution of foreign exchange market: Evidence from minimum spanning tree. *Physica A: Statistical Mechanics and its Applications, 390*(4), 707–718.

Jänicke, S., Franzini, G., Cheema, M. F., & Scheuermann, G. (2017). Visual text analysis in digital humanities. *Computer Graphics Forum, 36*, 226–250.

Jurman, G., Visintainer, R., Filosi, M., Riccadonna, S., & Furlanello, C. (2015). The HIM glocal metric and kernel for network comparison and classification. In *2015 IEEE international conference on data science and advanced analytics (DSAA)* (pp. 1–10).

Kalyagin, V. A., Pardalos, P., & Rassias, T. M. (2014). *Network models in economics and finance*. Springer International Publishing. https://doi.org/10.1007/978-3-319-09683-4

Kanik, Z. (2020). *From lombard street to wall street: Systemic risk, rescues, and stability in financial networks* (SSRN Scholarly Paper ID 3057615). Social Science Research Network. https://papers.ssrn.com/abstract=3057615

Kenett, D. Y., Preis, T., Gur-Gershgoren, G., & Ben-Jacob, E. (2012). Dependency network and node influence: Application to the study of financial markets. *International Journal of Bifurcation and Chaos, 22*(07), 1250181.

Kenett, D. Y., Tumminello, M., Madi, A., Gur-Gershgoren, G., Mantegna, R. N., & Ben-Jacob, E. (2010). Dominating clasp of the financial sector revealed by partial correlation analysis of the stock market. *PLoS One, 5*(12), e15032.

Kleinberg, J. M. (1999). Hubs, authorities, and communities. *ACM Computing Surveys (CSUR), 31* (4es), 5–es.

Knappett, C. (2013). *Network analysis in archaeology: New approaches to regional interaction*. Oxford University Press.

Koutra, D., Shah, N., Vogelstein, J. T., Gallagher, B., & Faloutsos, C. (2016). Deltacon: Principled massive-graph similarity function with attribution. *ACM Transactions on Knowledge Discovery from Data (TKDD), 10*(3), 1–43.

Koutra, D., Vogelstein, J. T., & Faloutsos, C. (2013). Deltacon: A principled massive-graph similarity function. In *Proceedings of the 2013 SIAM international conference on data mining* (pp. 162–170).

Kreyszig, E. (2015). *Advanced engineering mathematics, 10th Ed, Isv* (10th ed.). Wiley.

Kukreti, V., Pharasi, H. K., Gupta, P., & Kumar, S. (2020). A perspective on correlation-based financial networks and entropy measures. *Frontiers in Physics, 8*, 323. https://doi.org/10.3389/fphy.2020.00323

Kulik, B. W., & Baker, T. (2008). Putting the organization back into computational organization theory: A complex Perrowian model of organizational action. *Computational and Mathematical Organization Theory, 14*(2), 84–119.

Kumar, S., & Deo, N. (2012). Correlation and network analysis of global financial indices. *Physical Review E, 86*(2), 026101. https://doi.org/10.1103/PhysRevE.86.026101

Lämmer, S., & Helbing, D. (2008). Self-control of traffic lights and vehicle flows in urban road networks. *Journal of Statistical Mechanics: Theory and Experiment, 2008*(04), P04019.

Langfield, S., Liu, Z., & Ota, T. (2012). Mapping the UK interbank system,. *Bank of England*. working paper.

Latora, V., Nicosia, V., & Russo, G. (2017). *Complex networks: Principles, methods and applications*. Cambridge University Press.

Laurie, A. J., & Jaggi, N. K. (2002). Physics and sociology: Neighbourhood racial segregation. *Solid State Physics (India), 45*(183), 183–184.

Laurie, A. J., & Jaggi, N. K. (2003). Role of 'vision' in neighbourhood racial segregation: A variant of the Schelling segregation model. *Urban Studies, 40*(13), 2687–2704.

Li, D., Fu, B., Wang, Y., Lu, G., Berezin, Y., Stanley, H. E., & Havlin, S. (2015). Percolation transition in dynamical traffic network with evolving critical bottlenecks. *Proceedings of the National Academy of Sciences, 112*(3), 669–672.

Li, W., Kenett, D. Y., Yamasaki, K., Stanley, H. E., & Havlin, S. (2014). Ranking the economic importance of countries and industries. *ArXiv Preprint ArXiv, 1408*, 0443.

Liljeros, F., Edling, C. R., Amaral, L. A. N., Stanley, H. E., & Aberg, Y. (2001). The web of human sexual contacts. *Nature, 411*(6840), 907–908.

Liu, Q., Dong, Z., & Wang, E. (2018). Cut based method for comparing complex networks. *Scientific Reports, 8*(1), 1–11.

Ludescher, J., Gozolchiani, A., Bogachev, M. I., Bunde, A., Havlin, S., & Schellnhuber, H. J. (2014). Very early warning of next El Niño. *Proceedings of the National Academy of Sciences, 111*(6), 2064–2066.

Mantegna, R. N. (1999a). Hierarchical structure in financial markets. *The European Physical Journal B, 11*(1), 193–197. https://doi.org/10.1007/s100510050929

Mantegna, R. N. (1999b). Information and hierarchical structure in financial markets. *Computer Physics Communications, 121–122*, 153–156. https://doi.org/10.1016/S0010-4655(99)00302-1

Massey, D. S., Rothwell, J., & Domina, T. (2009). The changing bases of segregation in the United States. *The Annals of the American Academy of Political and Social Science, 626*(1). https://doi.org/10.1177/0002716209343558

McDonald, M., Suleman, O., Williams, S., Howison, S., & Johnson, N. F. (2005). Detecting a currency's dominance or dependence using foreign exchange network trees. *Physical Review E, 72*(4), 046106.

Milo, R., Shen-Orr, S., Itzkovitz, S., Kashtan, N., Chklovskii, D., & Alon, U. (2002). Network motifs: Simple building blocks of complex networks. *Science, 298*(5594), 824–827.

Minoiu, C., & Reyes, J. A. (2011, April 1). *A network analysis of global banking: 1978–2009*. SSRN Scholarly Paper. Social Science Research Network. https://doi.org/10.2139/ssrn.1808447.

Mitchell, H., & Joseph, S. (2010). Changes in Malaysia: Capital controls, prime ministers and political connections. *Pacific-Basin Finance Journal, 18*(5), 460–476.

Newman, M. (2010). *Networks: An introduction* (1st ed.). Oxford University Press.

Nie, C.-X. (2017). Dynamics of cluster structure in financial correlation matrix. *Chaos, Solitons & Fractals, 104*, 835–840.

Nier, E., Yang, J., Yorulmazer, T., & Alentorn, A. (2007). Network models and financial stability. *Journal of Economic Dynamics and Control, 31*(6), 2033–2060.

Onnela, J.-P., Chakraborti, A., Kaski, K., Kertesz, J., & Kanto, A. (2003). Dynamics of market correlations: Taxonomy and portfolio analysis. *Physical Review E, 68*(5), 056110.

Onnela, J.-P., Kaski, K., & Kertész, J. (2004). Clustering and information in correlation based financial networks. *The European Physical Journal B, 38*(2), 353–362.

Pastor-Satorras, R., & Vespignani, A. (2007). *Evolution and structure of the internet: A statistical physics approach*. Cambridge University Press.

Plotkowiak, T., & Stanoevska-Slabeva, K. (2013). German politicians and their twitter networks in the bundestag election 2009. *First Monday*.

Pollicott, M., & Weiss, H. (2001). The dynamics of Schelling-type segregation models and a nonlinear graph Laplacian variational problem. *Advances in Applied Mathematics, 27*(1), 17–40.

Portugali, J., & Benenson, I. (1995). Artificial planning experience by means of a heuristic cell-space model: Simulating international migration in the urban process. *Environment and Planning A, 27*(10), 1647–1665.

Portugali, J., Benenson, I., & Omer, I. (1994). Sociospatial residential dynamics: Stability and instability within a self-organizing city. *Geographical Analysis, 26*(4), 321–340.

Radicchi, F., Fortunato, S., & Vespignani, A. (2012). Citation networks. *Models of Science Dynamics*, 233–257.
Recuero, R., Zago, G., Bastos, M. T., & Araújo, R. (2015). Hashtags functions in the protests across Brazil. *SAGE Open, 5*(2), 2158244015586000.
Rutenberg, D. P. (1970). Maneuvering liquid assets in a multi-national company: Formulation and deterministic solution procedures. *Management Science, 16*(10), B–671.
Sendiña-Nadal, I., Ofran, Y., Almendral, J. A., Buldú, J. M., Leyva, I., Li, D., Havlin, S., & Boccaletti, S. (2011). Unveiling protein functions through the dynamics of the interaction network. *PLoS One, 6*(3), e17679.
Simon, H. A. (1997). *Models of bounded rationality: Empirically grounded economic reason* (Vol. 3). MIT Press.
Soramäki, K., Bech, M. L., Arnold, J., Glass, R. J., & Beyeler, W. E. (2007). The topology of interbank payment flows. *Physica A: Statistical Mechanics and its Applications, 379*(1), 317–333.
Soundarajan, S., Eliassi-Rad, T., & Gallagher, B. (2014). A guide to selecting a network similarity method. In *Proceedings of the 2014 Siam international conference on data mining* (pp. 1037–1045).
Srinivasan, V. (1974). A transshipment model for cash management decisions. *Management Science, 20*(10), 1350–1363.
Tantardini, M., Ieva, F., Tajoli, L., & Piccardi, C. (2019). Comparing methods for comparing networks. *Scientific Reports, 9*(1), 1–19.
Teets, J. (2018). The power of policy networks in authoritarian regimes: Changing environmental policy in China. *Governance, 31*(1), 125–141.
Thornton, H. (2017). *An enquiry into the nature and effects of the paper credit of Great Britain.* Routledge.
Toda, S. (1999). Graph isomorphism: Its complexity and algorithms. In *International conference on foundations of software technology and theoretical computer science* (pp. 341–341).
Tsitsulin, A., Mottin, D., Karras, P., Bronstein, A., & Müller, E. (2018). Netlsd: Hearing the shape of a graph. In *Proceedings of the 24th ACM SIGKDD international conference on Knowledge Discovery & Data Mining* (pp. 2347–2356).
Tumminello, M., Aste, T., Di Matteo, T., & Mantegna, R. N. (2005). A tool for filtering information in complex systems. *Proceedings of the National Academy of Sciences, 102*(30), 10421–10426.
Tumminello, M., Lillo, F., & Mantegna, R. N. (2010). Correlation, hierarchies, and networks in financial markets. *Journal of Economic Behavior & Organization, 75*(1), 40–58.
Upper, C., & Worms, A. (2004). Estimating bilateral exposures in the German interbank market: Is there a danger of contagion? *European Economic Review, 48*(4), 827–849.
Villaverde, A. F., Ross, J., Morán, F., & Banga, J. R. (2014). MIDER: Network inference with mutual information distance and entropy reduction. *PLoS One, 9*(5), e96732.
Vizing, V. G. (1968). Some unsolved problems in graph theory. *Russian Mathematical Surveys, 23* (6), 125–141. https://doi.org/10.1070/RM1968v023n06ABEH001252
Wang, Y. R., & Huang, H. (2014). Review on statistical methods for gene network reconstruction using expression data. *Journal of Theoretical Biology, 362*, 53–61.
Watts, D. J., & Strogatz, S. H. (1998). Collective dynamics of 'small-world'networks. *Nature, 393* (6684), 440–442.
Wells, S. (2002). UK interbank exposures: Systemic risk implications. *Financial Stability Review, 13*(12), 175–182.
Wilson, R. C., & Zhu, P. (2008). A study of graph spectra for comparing graphs and trees. *Pattern Recognition, 41*(9), 2833–2841.
Yahoo Finance—Stock Market Live, Quotes, Business & Finance News. (2021). Retrieved January 13, 2021, from https://finance.yahoo.com/

Yamasaki, K., Gozolchiani, A., & Havlin, S. (2008). Climate networks around the globe are significantly affected by El Nino. *Physical Review Letters, 100*(22), 228501.

Yusoff, W. S., Salleh, M. F. M., Ahmad, A., & Idris, F. (2015). Short-run political events and stock market reactions: Evidence from companies connected to Malaysian bi-power business-political elite. *Procedia-Social and Behavioral Sciences, 211*, 421–428.

Zelinka, B. (1975). On a certain distance between isomorphism classes of graphs. *Časopis pro Pěstování Matematiky, 100*(4), 371–373.

Zhang, J. (2004). Residential segregation in an all-integrationist world. *Journal of Economic Behavior & Organization, 54*(4), 533–550.

Optimization of Regulatory Economic-Capital Structured Portfolios: Modeling Algorithms, Financial Data Analytics, and Reinforcement Machine Learning in Emerging Markets

Mazin A. M. Al Janabi

Abstract This chapter examines from a regulatory portfolio management standpoint the application of liquidity-adjusted risk modeling techniques in obtaining optimal and investable economic-capital structures for the Gulf Cooperation Council (GCC) stock markets. The observed market-microstructures patterns and the obtained empirical results are quite interesting and promising for practical optimization techniques, portfolio management purposes, and operations research models in financial institutions management, particularly in the wake of the aftermaths of the 2007–2009 financial crisis. The proposed quantitative portfolio management techniques and optimization algorithms can have important uses and applications in expert systems, financial data analytics, machine learning, smart financial functions, and financial technology (FinTech) in big data environments. Likewise, it can aid in the development of regulatory technology (RegTech) for the global financial services industry.

JEL Classifications C10 · C13 · G20 · and G28

Keywords Al Janabi Model · Economic-Capital · Emerging Markets · Financial Crisis · Financial Data Analytics · Financial Risk Management · GARCH-in-mean · GCC Financial Markets · Liquidity Risk · Liquidity-Adjusted Value-at-Risk (LVaR) · Optimization · Portfolio Management · Reinforcement Machine Learning · Regulations

M. A. M. Al Janabi (✉)
Finance & Banking and Financial Engineering, Tecnologico de Monterrey, EGADE Business School, Mexico City, Mexico
e-mail: mazin.aljanabi@tec.mx

S. Derindere Köseoğlu (ed.), *Financial Data Analytics*, Contributions to Finance and Accounting, https://doi.org/10.1007/978-3-030-83799-0_11

1 Introduction

In assessing market risk of financial trading portfolios, one method advanced in the academic literature involves the application of Value-at-Risk (VaR) models (Hull, 2009; Jorion, 2007). This regulatory technique determines how much the value of a trading portfolio would diminish, in monetary terms, over a given period with a given probability as a result of changes in market prices. While VaR is a very popular measure of market risk of financial trading portfolios, it is not a panacea for all risk assessments and has several drawbacks, limitations, and undesirable properties (Sanders, 2002; Al Janabi, 2012).[1]

From a portfolio market risk point of view, VaR faces some major difficulties. Three of the most researched and discussed issues are the non-normal behavior of market returns, volatility clustering, and the impacts of illiquid assets under crisis markets outlooks (Al Janabi, 2013). The effect of the latter on regulatory portfolio risk management, investable portfolios, and dynamic economic-capital allocation under market liquidity constraints (as a result of a financial crunch) is the principal motivation of this comprehensive research case study.

Some relevant studies have tackled the issues of liquidity risk but not necessarily within the context of trading portfolios. Their main focus, in fact, was on modeling transaction costs (that is, the widening of the bid-ask spread), however the effects of adverse market price impact have not been studied rigorously, though Al Janabi (2013), Al Janabi et al. (2017), and Al Janabi et al. (2019) are an exception. For the sake of brevity, we discuss below a concise description of some of the suggested modeling techniques, detailed as follows: Within the VaR technique, Jarrow and Subramanian (1997) provide a market impact model of liquidity by considering the optimal liquidation of an investment portfolio over a fixed horizon. On the other hand, Bangia et al. (2002) approach the liquidity risk from another angle and provide a model of VaR adjusted for what they call exogenous liquidity—defined as common to all market players and unaffected by the actions of any one participant. It comprises such execution costs as order processing costs and adverse selection costs resulting in a given bid-ask spread faced by investors in the market. In a different vein, Almgren and Chriss (1999) present a concrete framework for deriving the optimal execution strategy using a mean-variance approach, and show a specific calculation method. On another front, Al Janabi (2013, 2011a, b) tackles the issue of adverse market price impact on liquidity trading risk using a liquidity-adjusted parametric VaR methodology. His adverse price unwinding approach comprises a

[1]In fact, the general recognition and use of large-scale VaR models has initiated a considerable literature including statistical descriptions of VaR and assessments of different modeling techniques. For a comprehensive review of the different VaR methodologies, empirical analysis and techniques, one can refer to Jorion (2007) and Abad et al. (2014).

liquidation multiplier (add-on) that can adjust the impact of unfavorable price movement throughout the closeout period.[2]

Set against this background and to address the above deficiencies in the conventional regulatory VaR method, this research case study builds on the theoretical foundations and optimization parameters of Al Janabi model (Al Janabi, 2012; 2013; Madoroba & Kruger, 2014) and it includes new empirical testing and optimization results that were not evident in Al Janabi (2013) paper. To that end, in this chapter we characterize potential risk exposures and determine optimal and investable portfolios of emerging equity markets by using a multivariate Liquidity-Adjusted Value-at-Risk (LVaR) method that focuses on the modeling of optimum LVaR under the notion of illiquid and adverse market conditions. As such, the overall aim of this research case study is to construct different structured equity portfolios, which comprise certain stock markets indices of the Gulf Cooperation Council (GCC) region, and to estimate the risk characteristics and structures of these portfolios besides examining an optimization algorithm process for assessing regulatory economic-capital's optimal and investable market portfolios under crisis-driven market circumstances.[3]

In effect, the obtained empirical results are quite interesting and promising for practical optimization techniques, portfolio management purposes, and operations research models in financial institutions management, particularly in the wake of the aftermaths of the 2007–2009 financial crisis. In addition, the proposed quantitative portfolio management techniques and optimization algorithms can have important uses and applications in expert systems, machine learning, financial data analytics, smart financial functions, and financial technology (FinTech) in big data ecosystems (Al Janabi, 2020). Likewise, it can aid in the development of regulatory technology (RegTech) for the global financial services industry, and can be of interest to professionals, regulators, and researchers working in the field of financial engineering and FinTech; and for those who want to improve their understanding of the impact of

[2]For other relevant literature on liquidity, asset pricing and portfolio choice and diversification one can refer as well to Madhavan et al. (1997); Hisata and Yamai (2000); Le Saout (2002); Angelidis and Benos (2006); Berkowitz (2000); Takahashi and Alexander (2002); Amihud et al. (2005); Cochrane (2005) and Meucci (2009), among others. Furthermore, with the objective of avoiding repetitions of literatures and to keep the size of this chapter within a reasonable number of pages, we refer the readers to the full and comprehensive literature reviews in Al Janabi (2013) research paper. For other recent relevant literature on liquidity, internal risk models, asset pricing and portfolio choice and diversification one can refer as well to Al Janabi (2021a); Al Janabi (2021b); Al Janabi (2021c); Asadi and Al Janabi (2020); Arreola-Hernandez and Al Janabi (2020); Grillini et al. (2019); Al Janabi et al. (2017); Al Janabi et al. (2019); Arreola-Hernandez et al. (2017); Arreola-Hernandez et al. (2015), among others.

[3]For further details on the definition of economic-capital (or risk-capital), we refer the readers to Al Janabi (2013) research paper. Moreover, in this chapter the concept of investable market portfolios refers to rational portfolios that are contingent on meaningful financial and operational constraints. In this sense, investable market portfolios do not lie on the efficient (optimum) frontiers as defined by Markowitz (1959), and instead have logical and well-structured long/short-sales asset allocation proportions.

innovative quantitative risk management techniques and optimization algorithms on regulatory challenges for financial services industry and its effects on global financial stability (Al Janabi, 2020).

The rest of the chapter proceeds as follows. Section 2 reviews the theoretical foundations and modeling parameters of Al Janabi model, which are used in portfolio optimization and machine learning process. Section 3 analyzes the overall results of the different empirical tests and reflects on the construction of optimal and investable regulatory economic-capital portfolios. Section 4 remarks on conclusions, possible practical applications, and other recommendations.

2 Review of Theoretical Foundations and Modeling Parameters Using Al Janabi Model[4]

In essence, VaR is intended to quantify, with a given probability and degree of confidence, the largest expected amount of money a trading portfolio could lose under normal market conditions and over a given time horizon. Assuming the return of a financial asset follows a normal distribution, linear pay-off profile and a direct relationship between the underlying asset and income, VaR measures the potential risk of trading income, which results from the volatility of the different markets, for a certain confidence level. To estimate VaR using a closed-form parametric technique, the volatility of every risk factor is obtained from a pre-defined historical observation period and can be assessed, for instance, using a generalized autoregressive conditional heteroskedasticity (GARCH) in-mean model (i.e., GARCH-M (1,1), Engle, 1995) under the possibilities of crisis market settings. The potential influence of each asset component on the overall portfolio value is then determined. As such, for a single trading asset the absolute value of VaR in monetary terms can be determined following Al Janabi model as follows (Al Janabi, 2013):

$$VaR_i = |(\mu_i - \alpha * \sigma_i)(Asset_i * Fx_i)| \quad (1)$$

where μ_i is the expected return of the trading asset, α is the confidence level (or in other words, the standard normal variant at confidence level α), and σ_i is the

[4] The concise theoretical foundation and mathematical approach presented in this section are largely drawn from Al Janabi (2013 and 2012) research papers. For further details on the mathematical derivation, we refer the readers to Al Janabi (2013) research paper, as our intention in this section is to include only the final mathematical formulas that summarize the theoretical foundation, modeling algorithms, and optimization parameters. The LVaR model applied here is based on that proposed by Al Janabi (2013) and Al Janabi et al. (2017). For further discussion on LVaR literature and models, see Madoroba and Kruger (2014). In their paper, Madoroba and Kruger (2014) review and compare ten recognized liquidity risk VaR models, including Al Janabi model. For further details on the mathematical derivation and rational usefulness of Al Janabi model, refer to Al Janabi (2008, 2013, and 2014) and Al Janabi et al. (2017) research papers.

conditional volatility of the return of each asset and can be predicted, for instance, by means of a GARCH-M (1,1) model. *The* $Asset_i$ is the mark-to-market value of the trading asset, and specifies the amount of monetary investment in asset i. Finally, Fx_i denotes the unit foreign exchange rate of asset i.

Portfolio trading risk in the presence of multiple risk factors is determined not only by the magnitudes of the individual risks but also by their correlations. For structured portfolios of multiple assets, VaR is a function of the risk factor of each asset and the correlation factor $[\rho_{i,\ j}]$ between the returns of all assets, detailed as follows:

$$VaR_P = \sqrt{\sum_{i=1}^{n}\sum_{j=1}^{n} VaR_i\, VaR_j \rho_{i,j}} = \sqrt{[VaR]^T\,[\rho]\;[VaR]} \tag{2}$$

In fact, formula (2) is a typical one for the computation of VaR for any portfolio irrespective of the number of trading assets. It should be noted that the second term of the above formula is rewritten in terms of matrix-algebra (i.e., a matrix and two vectors).

In this research study, we adapt and build on the Al Janabi model developed by Al Janabi (2012 and 2013) for calculating a closed-form parametric Liquidity-Adjusted Value-at-Risk (LVaR). The model can be used for the calculation of liquidity trading risk and in the assessment coherent regulatory economic-capital and investable portfolios. The recommended method implies that the trading position is closed out linearly over t-days (i.e., assets have to be liquidated throughout the holding period) and hence it employs the logical notion that losses due to illiquid trading positions over t-days of operations are the sum of losses over each trading day. To that end and in order to implement LVaR under illiquid market conditions we define the following (Al Janabi, 2013):

$$LVaR_{adj} = VaR\sqrt{\frac{(2t+1)\,(t+1)}{6t}} \tag{3}$$

where VaR denotes Value at Risk under liquid market settings and; $LVaR_{adj}$ stands for Value at Risk under illiquid market situations. The latter equation indicates that $LVaR_{adj} > VaR$, and for the special case when the number of trading days to liquidate the entire assets is reduced to one day, then we have the particular case at which $LVaR_{adj} = VaR$. It is also critical to indicate that Eq. (3) can be used for the calculation of LVaR for any time horizon subject to imposing a constraint on the total estimated LVaR results. In this case, the overall estimated LVaR figure for the entire portfolio should not exceed at any market setting the nominal exposure (or in other words the total trading volume of the portfolio).

The choice of the liquidation horizon (t) can be appraised from the total trading position size and daily trading volume that can be unwound into the financial market without significantly disrupting equity market prices; and in concrete financial markets practices it is generally estimated as:

$$t = |\text{Total Trading Position Size of Asset}_i/\text{Daily Trading Volume of Asset}_i|, s.t.\ t \geq 1.0 \tag{4}$$

In order to compute LVaR for the full trading portfolio under illiquid market conditions ($LVaR_{P_{adj}}$), the above mathematical formulation can be extended, with the aid of Eqs. (2) and (3), into a matrix-algebra form to yield the following:

$$LVaR_{P_{adj}} = \sqrt{\sum_{i=1}^{n}\sum_{j=1}^{n} LVaR_{i_{adj}} LVaR_{j_{adj}} \rho_{i,j}} = \sqrt{\left[LVaR_{adj}\right]^T [\rho] \left[LVaR_{adj}\right]} \tag{5}$$

The above mathematical arrangement (in the structure of two vectors and a matrix, $[LVaR_{adj}]^T$, $[LVaR_{adj}]$ and $[\rho]$) can simplify the programming process of algorithms so that the portfolio manager can specify different liquidation days for every specific trading asset and/or for the whole portfolio according to the necessary number of days to liquidate the entire assets fully. The latter can be accomplished by specifying an overall benchmark liquidation horizon (unwinding period) to liquidate the entire constituents of the portfolio completely.

Finally, the annual regulatory economic-capital necessary to support trading activities under illiquid normal and severe market settings is examined in this research case study and can be defined (using an internal risk management model) from Eq. (5) as[5]:

$$\begin{aligned}\text{Economic Capital } (EC) &= \left(\frac{\alpha_{EC}}{\alpha}\right)\sqrt{H}\sqrt{\rho_{BU}}\sqrt{\sum_{i=1}^{n}\sum_{j=1}^{n} LVaR_i LVaR_j \rho_{i,j}} \\ &= \left(\frac{\alpha_{EC}}{\alpha}\right)\sqrt{H}\sqrt{\rho_{BU}}\sqrt{\left[LVaR_{adj}\right]^T [\rho] \left[LVaR_{adj}\right]}\end{aligned} \tag{6}$$

where α_{EC} is the economic-capital quantile of 3.43, α is the daily LVaR quantile as explained in Eq. (1), H is the number of active trading days in the year, ρ_{BU} is the correlation factor required to account for the diversification benefit provided by having the equity trading risk unit as one of a number of diversified financial businesses (i.e., it is the correlation factor between business units).

[5]When calculating economic-capital (using an internal model as defined by Basel II and III capital adequacy requirements), we want to use the same time horizon and confidence level for all asset risk exposures. The time horizon is usually 1 year ahead (assuming 260 active business trading days in the year) and the confidence level is often chosen as 99.97% (or 3.43 quantile) for an AA-rated financial institution (Al Janabi, 2013).

The elements of the vectors of Eq. (6), i.e. $LVaR_{iadj}$, for each trading asset can now be calculated with the aid of Eqs. (1) and (3) in this manner:

$$LVaR_{iadj} = \left| (\mu_i - \alpha * \sigma_i)(\text{Mark-to-Market Value of Asset}_i * Fx_i)\sqrt{\frac{(2t_i+1)\,(t_i+1)}{6t_i}} \right| \tag{7}$$

To end with, we can define the ultimate two vectors $[LVaR_{adj}]^T$ and $[LVaR_{adj}]$ as follows:

$$\left[LVaR_{adj}\right]^T = \left[LVaR_{1_{adj}}\;\; LVaR_{2_{adj}}\;\; \ldots\ldots\;\; LVaR_{n_{adj}}\right] \tag{8}$$

$$\left[LVaR_{adj}\right] = \begin{bmatrix} LVaR_{1_{adj}} \\ LVaR_{2_{adj}} \\ \ldots\ldots\ldots\ldots \\ LVaR_{n_{adj}} \end{bmatrix} \tag{9}$$

3 Scenario Optimization Framework of Structured Regulatory Economic-Capital Portfolios

In this research case study, we use a dataset of returns of the main indices of the seven GCC stock markets before and during the most severe period of the latest financial crisis. The time series are daily and the sample period spans from 17/10/2004–22/05/2009. Thus, the dataset accounts for the austere part of financial scenarios revolving around the 2007–2009 global financial crisis. To that end, historical database of more than 6 years of daily closing index levels is implemented for the structuring of input parameters for the risk engine and optimization algorithms. The historical database of daily stock market indices is drawn from Reuters 3000 Xtra Hosted Terminal Platform and Reuters-Thomson's Datastream datasets. The number of stock market indices implemented in this research study is nine, detailed as follows:

DFM General Index (Dubai Financial Market General Index, Country: United Arab Emirates); ADSM Index (Abu Dhabi Stock Market Index, Country: United Arab Emirates); BA All Share Index (All Share Stock Market Index, Country: Bahrain); KSE General Index (Stock Exchange General Index, Country: Kuwait); MSM30 Index (Muscat Stock Market Index, Country: Oman); DSM20 Index (Doha Stock Market General Index, Country: Qatar); SE All Share Index (All Share Stock Market Index, Country: Saudi Arabia); Shuaa GCC Index (GCC Stock Markets Benchmark Index, Provider: Shuaa Capital in UAE); and Shuaa Arab Index (Arab Stock Markets Benchmark Index, Provider: Shuaa Capital in UAE).

Moreover, for this specific research study, we have chosen a confidence interval of 95% (or 97.5% with "one-tailed" loss side) and several liquidation time horizons (closeout periods) to compute regulatory LVaR. Furthermore, in this chapter, severe or crisis market conditions refer to unexpected extreme adverse market situations (as a result of a financial crunch) at which losses could be several-fold larger than losses under normal market situation. Stress-testing technique is usually used to estimate the impact of unusual and severe events as a consequence of a financial crisis.

To test for the association between the expected returns of stock market indices and volatility, we have employed a conditional volatility GARCH-in-mean (GARCH-M (1,1)) approach to control for the risk parameters that are required for the risk engine and for the assessment of investable economic-capital. Indeed, the time-varying pattern of stock market volatility has been widely acknowledged and modeled as a conditional variance within the GARCH technique, as initially originated by Engle (1982, 1995). As a result, we estimated the assets return distribution dynamic and conditional volatility using a GARCH-M (1,1) model and tested for normality as indicated in Table 1.

Accordingly, Table 1 depicts the necessary risk analysis dataset and basic statistics along with the results of testing for non-normality. In essence, Table 1 includes volatility under normal and crisis market conditions, maximum daily positive/negative returns and its dates of occurrence, beta sensitivity factor as well as the results of non-normality testing using Jarque–Bera test. The analysis of dataset, scenario optimization parameters, and discussions of relevant findings are organized and explained as follows:

3.1 Nonlinear and Dynamic Optimization of Regulatory Economic-Capital Optimal & Investable Portfolios Using LVaR Modeling Algorithm

3.1.1 Variable Dynamics and Constraints for Scenario Optimization

One of the central challenges of applied finance for portfolio management practices is the optimal selection of assets, with the goal of maximizing future returns and constraining risk by appropriate measures (Markowitz, 1959; Al Janabi, 2013). However, optimized portfolios do not generally function as well in practice as one would expect from theory and the optimum could turn out in the end to be not optimal at all (see, for instance, Jobson & Korkie, 1981; Jorion, 1991; Al Janabi, 2013 and 2012; Michaud, 1989).

In this research study, we apply the economic-capital model discussed earlier for optimizing portfolio risk-return with regulatory economic-capital constraints using typical operational and financial scenarios commonly practiced in actual portfolio management. We then conduct different case analyses on optimizing stock market portfolios of the seven GCC financial markets in light of the aftermaths of the

Table 1 Risk Assessment Dataset, Basic Statistics and Test for Non-Normality

Stock Market Indices	Volatility (Normal Market)*	Volatility (Crisis Market)	Expected Return*	Maximum Positive Return (Gain)	Date of Occurrence	Maximum Negative Return (Loss)	Date of Occurrence	Sensitivity (Beta) Factor	Skewness	Kurtosis	Jarque-Bera (JB) Test
DFM general index	1.81%	12.16%	0.14%	9.94%	23/1/2008	−12.16%	14/3/2006	0.58	0.01	7.86	955**
ADSM index	1.32%	7.08%	0.07%	6.57%	09/5/2005	−7.08%	22/1/2008	0.40	0.12	7.26	734**
BA all share index	0.58%	3.77%	0.04%	3.61%	24/1/2006	−3.77%	13/8/2007	0.06	0.43	10.24	2142**
KSE general index	0.71%	3.74%	0.08%	5.05%	16/3/2006	−3.74%	14/3/2006	0.14	−0.18	8.38	1173**
MSM30 index	0.79%	8.70%	0.10%	5.22%	16/10/2007	−8.70%	22/1/2008	0.10	−0.57	18.40	9617**
DSM20 index	1.48%	8.07%	0.07%	6.22%	04/2/2008	−8.07%	22/1/2008	0.31	−0.11	5.59	273**
SE all share index	1.86%	11.03%	0.01%	9.39%	13/5/2006	−11.03%	21/1/2008	0.98	−0.97	8.47	1361**
Shuaa GCC index	1.30%	8.10%	0.08%	11.14%	13/5/2006	−8.10%	21/1/2008	1.05	−0.66	14.00	4949**
Shuaa Arab index	1.15%	7.57%	0.10%	9.43%	13/5/2006	−7.57%	21/1/2008	1.00	−0.61	13.79	4758**

Notes: 1) Asterisk ** Denotes Statistical Significance at the 0.01 Level
2) Asterisk * Denotes Estimation of Conditional Volatility and Expected Return Using GARCH-M Model
3) Downside Risk Under Crisis Market Conditions is Simulated as the Conditional Volatility of the Maximum Negative Daily Return (Loss)
Source: Designed by the author using an in-house built software

2007–2009 global financial turmoil. The different case analyses indicate that the optimization algorithm, which is based on quadratic programming techniques, is very effective in handling different conditional volatilities, the choices of long/short-sales positions, trading volume, liquidity horizons, and correlation factors.

Basically, our applied modeling technique is a robust generalization and improvement on the classic Markowitz (1959) mean-variance approach, where the fundamental risk measure, variance, is substituted by LVaR and economic-capital algorithms. The optimization is achieved here by minimizing the economic-capital objective function, while demanding a minimum expected portfolio return subject to imposing quite a few financially meaningful operational constraints under crisis-driven market circumstances. Therefore, by considering different expected portfolios returns, we can generate an optimal economic-capital frontier under adverse crisis outlooks. To that end, the optimization process of the objective function and constraints is formulated as follows:

From Eq. (6), it is reasonable to compute the minimum optimal amount of regulatory economic-capital required to maintain existing trading operations by solving for the following quadratic programming objective function:

$$\text{Minimize: Economic Capital } (EC) = \left(\frac{\alpha_{EC}}{\alpha}\right)\sqrt{H}\sqrt{\rho_{BU}}\sqrt{\sum_{i=1}^{n}\sum_{j=1}^{n} LVaR_{i_{adj}} LVaR_{j_{adj}} \rho_{i,j}} = \left(\frac{\alpha_{EC}}{\alpha}\right)\sqrt{H}\sqrt{\rho_{BU}}\sqrt{\left[LVaR_{adj}\right]^{T}[\rho]\left[LVaR_{adj}\right]} \tag{10}$$

The above objective function can be minimized subject to the following operational and financial budget constraints as specified by the risk and/or portfolio managers:

$$\sum_{i=1}^{n} R_i x_i = R_P; l_i \leq x_i \leq u_i \quad i = 1, 2, \ldots, n \tag{11}$$

$$\sum_{i=1}^{n} x_i = 1.0; l_i \leq x_i \leq u_i \quad i = 1, 2, \ldots, n \tag{12}$$

$$\sum_{i=1}^{n} V_i = V_P i = 1, 2, \ldots, n \tag{13}$$

$$[LHF] \geq 1.0; \forall_i \; i = 1, 2, \ldots, n \tag{14}$$

Here R_P and V_P represent the target portfolio mean expected return and total portfolio volume, respectively, and x_i the percentage (weight) of asset allocation for each trading asset. The values l_i and u_i, $i = 1, 2, \ldots, n$, denote the lower and upper constraints for the portfolio weights x_i. If we select $l_i = 0$, $i = 1, 2, \ldots, n$, then we have the condition where no short-sales of assets are allowed. Furthermore, [*LHF*] indicates an (*n*1*) vector of the specific liquidity horizon of each asset (for all $i = 1, 2, \ldots, n.$), and LHF_i for each trading asset can be expressed using Eq. (3) in this manner:

$$LHF_i = \sqrt{\frac{(2t_i + 1)\ (t_i + 1)}{6t_i}} \geq 1.0; \forall_i \ i = 1, 2, \ldots \ldots, n \tag{15}$$

3.1.2 Empirical Constrained Scenario Optimization of Regulatory Economic-Capital: The Case of Long and Short-Sales Structured Portfolios

In this research methods case study, the optimization algorithm is based on the delineation of regulatory economic-capital as the minimum likely loss over a definite time horizon within a particular confidence level. The iterative-optimization modeling algorithm resolves the problem by finding the market positions that minimize the loss, subject that all enforced constraints are fulfilled within their initial boundary values. Furthermore, in all optimization cases under examination the liquidation horizons (closeout periods) are assumed constant during the course of the optimization process, as follows:

DFM General IndexLiquidation Horizon = 3 days
ADSM IndexLiquidation Horizon = 3 days
BA All Share IndexLiquidation Horizon = 4 days
KSE General IndexLiquidation Horizon = 3 days
MSM30 IndexLiquidation Horizon = 5 days
DSM20 IndexLiquidation Horizon = 6 days
SE All Share IndexLiquidation Horizon = 3 days
Shuaa GCC IndexLiquidation Horizon = 1 day
Shuaa Arab IndexLiquidation Horizon = 1 day

In the interest of restraining the optimization algorithm and then its analysis, a volume trading position limit of ten million AED is assumed as a maximum constraint—that is the operating equity trading entity must keep a maximum overall market value of assorted equities of no more than ten million AED (between long and short-sales positions and by disallowing both long-only positions and borrowing constraints). In this chapter, the optimal portfolio selection is accomplished by relaxing the short sale constraint for the different stock markets, using a 97.5% confidence level, and under crisis market conditions (Al Janabi, 2013).

On the other hand, optimal portfolios cannot always be reached (e.g., short-sales of assets without realistic lower boundaries on x_i) in the day-to-day real-world portfolio management operations and, hence, the portfolio manager should determine active investable portfolios under realistic and restricted dynamic budget constraints (Al Janabi, 2013), detailed as follows: (1) Total investable portfolio

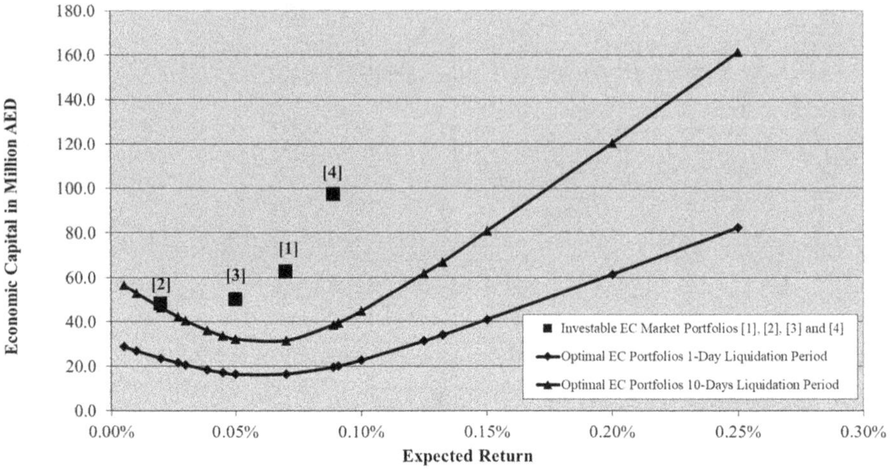

Fig. 1 Optimal and Investable Economic Capital Portfolios with LVaR Technique (Case of Long and Short-Sales Positions under Crisis Market Conditions). Source: Designed by the author using an in-house built software

trading volume (between long and short-sales equity trading positions) is ten million AED; (2) Investable portfolio asset allocation for long equity trading position fluctuates from 10% to 100%; (3) Investable portfolio asset allocation for short-sales equity trading position varies from −10% to −60%; (4) The liquidity horizons for all assets are kept constant according to the values indicated above. Furthermore, volatilities under crisis market notions are estimated as the maximum historical-simulation events with the highest downside risk (Al Janabi, 2013). These conditional volatilities are kept constant throughout the optimization process and in accordance with the values indicated in Table 1.

At this stage, the proportions of asset allocations (weights) are permitted to assume negative or positive values. However, since arbitrarily high or low proportions have no financial logic, we decided to set lower and upper boundaries for the weights and in line with rational trading practices. Furthermore, for comparison purposes and since the attempt in this research study is to minimize regulatory economic-capital subject to particular portfolio expected returns, we determined to plot regulatory economic-capital versus expected returns and not the opposite, as is commonly done in the variety of portfolio management literature. In view of that, it is appealing that the four benchmark portfolios (investable portfolios [1], [2], [3], and [4]) are noticeably located (albeit, with few exceptions) far away from the optimal frontiers as indicated in Fig. 1. This is due to the fact that financially and operationally real-life investment concerns make it unlikely that a trading portfolio will perform accurately as the theory forecasts and predominantly on account of an adverse financial crisis. In addition, Fig. 1 depicts the efficient frontiers of optimal economic-capital portfolios under 1-day and 10-day unwinding periods.

Thus, this empirical analysis is substantially a robust generalization and improvement on the Markowitz (1959) classical model. Therefore, this analysis permits portfolio managers to determine the asymmetric aspect of risk and above all as a result of a severe financial crisis. In any case, the benefit of portfolio optimization critically relies on how correctly the applied economic-capital risk measure is forecasted under adverse market settings.

4 Concluding Remarks

Because conventional mean-variance optimizers (Markowitz, 1959) have serious financial shortcomings, which could often lead to financially worthless "optimal" portfolios (Jobson & Korkie, 1981; Jorion, 1991; Michaud, 1989; Al Janabi, 2013), in this research methods case study we investigate how to determine the optimal and investable economic-capital portfolio choices for an equity portfolio manager under the assumption of various unwinding horizons and by applying dissimilar scenarios of long and short-sales trading strategies. While this chapter builds on Al Janabi (2013) theoretical foundations and optimization parameters, it differs in the sense that it contains new empirical testing and optimization results during the 2007–2009 global financial crisis that were not evident in Al Janabi (2013) paper.

The empirical results we disclose in this empirical research case study indicate that putting into practice LVaR and regulatory economic-capital into an active asset allocation model permits the portfolio manager to focus attention on downside risk for the assessment of investable portfolios, especially in the wake of the 2007–2009 global financial crunch. The empirical results indicate that our implemented technique operates better than the typical mean-variance VaR model (Markowitz, 1959) in terms of the optimum portfolio's selection process as well as in defining the portfolio manager's regulatory economic-capital and investable portfolios.

The proposed quantitative portfolio management techniques and optimization algorithms can have important uses and applications in expert systems, machine learning, financial data analytics, smart financial functions, and financial technology (FinTech) in big data environments. Likewise, it can aid in the development of regulatory technology (RegTech) for the global financial services industry, and can be of interest to professionals, regulators, and researchers working in the field of financial engineering and FinTech; and for those who want to improve their understanding of the impact of innovative quantitative risk management techniques and optimization algorithms on regulatory challenges for financial services industry and its effects on global financial stability.

References

Abad, P., Benito, S., & Lopez, C. (2014). A comprehensive review of value at risk methodologies. *The Spanish Review of Financial Economics, 12*(1), 15–32.

Al Janabi, M. A. M., Ferrer, R., & Shahzad, S. J. H. (2019). Liquidity-adjusted value-at-risk optimization of a multi-asset portfolio using a vine copula approach. *Physica A: Statistical Mechanics and its Applications, Volume, 536*, 122579.

Al Janabi, M. A. M., Arreola-Hernandez, J. A., Berger, T., & Nguyen, D. K. (2017). Multivariate dependence and portfolio optimization algorithms under illiquid market scenarios. *European Journal of Operational Research, 259*(3), 1121–1131.

Al Janabi, M. A. M. (2021a). Is optimum always optimal? A revisit of the mean-variance method under nonlinear measures of dependence and non-Normal liquidity constraints. *Journal of Forecasting, 40*(3), 387–415.

Al Janabi, M. A. M. (2021b). Multivariate portfolio optimization under illiquid market prospects: A review of theoretical algorithms and practical techniques for liquidity risk management. *Journal of Modelling in Management, 16*(1), 288–309.

Al Janabi, M. A. M. (2021c). Optimization algorithms and investment portfolio analytics with machine learning techniques under time-varying liquidity constraints. *Journal of Modelling in Management*. EarlyCite: https://doi.org/10.1108/JM2-10-2020-0259

Al Janabi, M. A. M. (2020). Risk Management in Emerging and Islamic Markets in light of the subprime global financial crisis: Optimization algorithms for strategic decision-making under intricate market outlooks. In N. Naifar (Ed.), *Impact of financial technology (FinTech) on Islamic finance and financial stability* (pp. 98–127). IGI Global,, USA.

Al Janabi, M. A. M. (2014). Optimal and investable portfolios: An empirical analysis with scenario optimization algorithms under crisis market prospects. *Economic Modelling, 40*, 369–381.

Al Janabi, M. A. M. (2013). Optimal and coherent economic-capital structures: Evidence from long and short-sales trading positions under illiquid market perspectives. *Annals of Operations Research, 205*(1), 109–139.

Al Janabi, M. A. M. (2012). Optimal commodity asset allocation with a coherent market risk modeling. *Review of Financial Economics, 21*(3), 131–140.

Al Janabi, M. A. M. (2011a). Dynamic equity asset allocation with liquidity-adjusted market risk criterion: Appraisal of efficient and coherent portfolios. *Journal of Asset Management, 12*(6), 378–394.

Al Janabi, M. A. M. (2011b). A generalized theoretical modeling approach for the assessment of economic capital under asset market liquidity risk constraints. *The Service Industries Journal, 31*(13 & 14), 2193–2221.

Al Janabi, M. A. M. (2008). Integrating liquidity risk factor into a parametric value at risk method. *Journal of Trading, 3*(3), 76–87.

Almgren, R., & Chriss, N. (1999). *Optimal execution of portfolio transaction*. Working Paper, Department of Mathematics, The University of Chicago.

Amihud, Y., Mendelson, H., & Pedersen, L. H. (2005). Liquidity and asset prices. *Foundations and Trends in Finance, 1*(4), 269–364.

Angelidis, T., & Benos, A. (2006). Liquidity adjusted value-at-risk based on the components of the bid-ask spread. *Applied Financial Economics, 16*(11), 835–851.

Arreola-Hernandez, J., & Al Janabi, M. A. M. (2020). Forecasting of dependence, market and investment risks of a global index portfolio. *Journal of Forecasting, 39*(3), 512–532.

Arreola-Hernandez, J., Hammoudeh, S., Khuong, N. D., Al Janabi, M. A. M., & Reboredo, J. C. (2017). Global financial crisis and dependence risk analysis of sector portfolios: A vine copula approach. *Applied Economics, 49*(25), 2409–2427.

Arreola-Hernandez, J., Al Janabi, M. A. M., Hammoudeh, S., & Nguyen, D. K. (2015). Time lag dependence, cross-correlation and risk analysis of U.S. energy and non-energy stock portfolios. *Journal of Asset Management, 16*(7), 467–483.

Asadi, S., & Al Janabi, M. A. M. (2020). Measuring market and credit risk under solvency II: Evaluation of the standard technique versus internal models for stock and bond markets. *European Actuarial Journal, 10*(2), 425–456.

Bangia, A., Diebold, F., Schuermann, T., & Stroughair, J. (2002). Modeling liquidity risk with implications for traditional market risk measurement and management. In S. Figlewski & R. M. Levich (Eds.), *Risk management: The state of the art, the new York University Salomon Center series on financial markets and institutions* (Vol. 8, pp. 3–13).

Berkowitz, J. (2000). *Incorporating liquidity risk into VaR models.* Working Paper, Graduate School of Management, University of California, Irvine.

Cochrane, J. H. (2005). *Asset pricing*. Princeton University Press.

Engle, R. F. (1995). *ARCH selected readings, advanced texts in econometrics*. Oxford University Press.

Engle, R. F. (1982). Autoregressive conditional heteroscedasticity with estimates of the variance of UK inflation. *Econometrica, 50*(1), 987–1008.

Grillini, S., Sharma, A., Ozkan, A., & Al Janabi, M. A. M. (2019). Pricing of time-varying illiquidity within the Eurozone: Evidence using a Markov switching liquidity-adjusted capital asset pricing model. *International Review of Financial Analysis, 64*, 145–158.

Hisata, Y., & Yamai, Y. (2000). Research toward the practical application of liquidity risk evaluation methods. In *Discussion paper, Institute for Monetary and Economic Studies*. Japan.

Hull, J. C. (2009). *Risk management and financial institutions* (2nd ed.). Prentice Hall, Pearson Education.

Jarrow, R., & Subramanian, A. (1997). Mopping up liquidity. *Risk, 10*(12), 170–173.

Jobson, J. D., & Korkie, B. M. (1981). Putting Markowitz theory to work. *Journal of Portfolio Management, 7*, 70–74.

Jorion, P. (2007). *Value at risk: The new benchmark for managing financial risk* (3rd ed.). McGraw-Hill.

Jorion, P. (1991). Bayesian and CAPM estimators of the means: Implications for portfolio selection. *Journal of Banking and Finance, 15*, 717–727.

Le Saout, E. (2002). *Incorporating liquidity risk in VaR models*. Working Paper, Paris 1 University.

Madhavan, A., Richardson, M., & Roomans, M. (1997). "Why do security prices change"? A transaction-level analysis of NYSE stocks. *Review of Financial Studies, 10*(4), 1035–1064.

Madoroba, S. B. W., & Kruger, J. W. (2014). Liquidity effects on value-at-risk limits: Construction of a new VaR model. *Journal of Risk Model Validation, 8*, 19–46.

Markowitz, H. (1959). *Portfolio selection: Efficient diversification of investments*. John Wiley.

Michaud, R. O. (1989). The Markowitz optimization enigma: Is `Optimized' optimal? *Financial Analysts Journal, 45*(1), 31–42.

Meucci, A. (2009). Managing diversification. *Risk, 22*(5), 74–79.

Sanders, D. R. (2002). The role of value-at-risk in purchasing: An application to the foodservice industry.*The Journal of Supply Chain Management*, Spring Issue, pp. 38–45.

Takahashi, D., & Alexander, S. (2002). Illiquid Alternative Asset Fund Modeling. *Journal of Portfolio Management, 28*(2), 90–100.

Transforming Insurance Business with Data Science

Wayne Huang

Abstract This chapter introduces readers to data science practices in the insurance industry. The author discusses how these practices have transformed the industry in actuarial and underwriting operations as well as in sales and marketing. The chapter first gives an overview of data science's role in an insurance company. Then, the data science challenges in each stage of an analytics project life cycle are described. The author draws from his experience to provide solution frameworks for each of the challenges. In the end, an example is demonstrated to showcase a complex business challenge in managing the entire customer journey and calculating customer lifetime value in a life insurance company. Ethical considerations of machine learning models are also discussed.

Keywords Data Science · Machine Learning · Predictive Model · Insurance · Pricing · Underwriting · Claims · Marketing · Customer Journey · Lifetime Value · Project Management

1 Introduction

Insurance is a critical component of modern financial infrastructure. Modern insurance started in seventeenth century Europe when the need arose to protect an owner's interest in an important asset such as real property or a ship (Bernstein, 1998). Since then, the industry has grown immensely over the centuries. Many insurance products were created to cover different types of risks over time. The most popular insurances to the general public are health and life insurance, property and casualty insurance, general liability insurance, and other specialty insurances. A 2020 EY report stated the total premium in 2018 for the life sector was $718 billion while the non-life sector was $1 trillion in the U.S. and Americas (EY, 2020).

W. Huang (✉)
Stevens Institute of Technology, Hoboken, NJ, USA
e-mail: whuang@stevens.edu

S. Derindere Köseoğlu (ed.), *Financial Data Analytics*, Contributions to Finance and Accounting, https://doi.org/10.1007/978-3-030-83799-0_12

In an insurance company, the core business functions consist of operations such as claims and underwriting; distributions such as product, sales, and marketing; and actuarial including pricing, valuation, and assumption. A data scientist needs to learn insurance business domain knowledge in each function in order to provide suitable analytic solutions for challenges and opportunities faced by these functional departments.

Actuaries have been playing an indispensable role in the insurance industry. Actuarial science was developed as a discipline to help organizations assess risk. In recent decades, the science of estimating insurance risk has advanced greatly with the development of new statistics and machine learning algorithms. Both deterministic and stochastic modeling methods are used by actuaries. Data scientists take a different approach to estimate risk. For example, to price an insurance product, it is necessary to estimate the expected probability and the financial impact of a risk in terms of incidence and severity. To be able to calculate the incidence rate, an actuary would first conduct assumption study and collect historical data for assumption variables that may affect the incidence rate. Then the actuary will go through each variable in the dataset and attempt to create a factor table for that variable when the number of records shows enough credibility. Using age variable as an example, the factor for each age band will be decided by observing the relative incidence rate across the age bands. Once all variables are reviewed, some factors will be adjusted to make the overall actual versus expected value (A/E) as close as possible. Finally, the assumptions will be created incorporating the rating (factor) tables, and then the pricing manual/book will be developed for underwriting purpose.

For a data scientist, once the historical dataset is ready, it will first go through the univariate process to determine if a variable has the predictive power, meaning the variable is significantly correlated to the target variable. For all variables that showed initial predictive power, they will be used as the input variables for the multivariate machine learning model. Generalized Linear Model (GLM) is the preferred choice for insurance pricing models due to the algorithm formula's conformity with the actuarial pricing approach and its ability to explain pricing assumptions to regulators. Once a model is built and validated with satisfactory results, data scientists can extract the rating tables from the model and work with actuaries to develop assumptions and underwriting guidelines to produce a pricing manual. Another algorithm "Generalized Additive Models plus Interactions" (GAM) has increased its use due to its ability to produce a more accurate model than GLM while maintaining the benefit of interpretability (Lou et al., 2013).

More and more insurance companies have been using machine learning to assist traditional actuarial pricing and valuation work (Frees et al., 2014) using GLM (Haberman & Renshaw, 1996). Also, new machine learning applications have been developed and enabled operations to automate underwriting decisions by learning from the decision patterns of historical underwriting data. In marketing applications, customer segmentation models and customer acquisition propensity predictive models can significantly improve distribution's ability to conduct effective marketing campaigns and increase sales considerably compared with traditional marketing approaches. Extreme Gradient Boosting (XG Boost) can produce more accurate models than GLM and sometimes GAM. XG Boost has been used in underwriting and marketing applications, while Decision Tree is useful to identify key drivers for a smaller dataset. Deep Learning has been used in some insurance applications as well (Agrawal, 2020).

The surge of big data has further enhanced insurance companies' ability to get a better understanding of customer behavior from social media activities as well as data collected from IoT. The growing availability of third-party data from data aggregators also provides insurers an alternative to better estimate an insurance applicant's risk. The convergence of new machine learning tools with big data and third-party data allows InsurTech startups to create new business models in one or more insurance value chain activities. Traditional insurance carriers and brokers, not wanting to be left behind, are also aggressively embracing data science as a source of innovation.

2 Data Science Challenges

Given the importance of data science, many insurance companies have made significant investments in data analytics. However, similar to the "Productivity Paradox" phenomenon (Brynjolfsson, 1998), not all companies have received expected return on investment (ROI). The author tries to address this issue by providing frameworks that will help guide data science managers from the very beginning of creating a data science vision to managing the data science team's daily operations.

When a data science team is first established, the team leader needs to create an analytics vision along with strategies that are aligned with the company's strategies. To realize the analytics strategies, the manager should work with stakeholders to develop a multi-year project roadmap to guide the data science team with a clear vision and direction. As an example, suppose the company's strategy is driving profitable growth while reducing operational cost. After discussions with actuarial and underwriting leaders, the potential analytics projects could include: (1) developing a pricing predictive model to improve risk selection of profitable customers; (2) enabling underwriting automation with a predictive model to reduce cost and offer superior customer experience.

Strategy and project roadmap only provide the direction. To truly develop an enterprise data science capability and maturity, it is important to think from the perspective of analytics project portfolio and project management. In each portfolio selection and project management stage, there are different challenges. In the following sections, we will discuss these challenges and proposed solutions.

2.1 Explore Analytics Opportunities

The first challenge of a new data science team lies in where to find meaningful projects that can create business value. Here, the author suggests four approaches to find new analytics project ideas. Each approach will be explained through one or more data analytics use cases.

2.1.1 Find the Diamond

The advancement of information technology since the 1980s has propelled workflow automation, which has dramatically improved office productivity. However, these automation works were mostly focused on well-defined human activities that could be coordinated or replaced by computers. Human decisions in many of these "improved workflows" became bottlenecks that created friction in the business. A machine learning model can learn from human decision history data and identify decision patterns to make similar or better-quality decisions. In a process map, these human decisions are typically represented by the diamond symbol. Finding the diamonds and replacing them with analytics solutions can alleviate operational inefficiency.

For example, a life insurance application first requires an applicant to answer 20 to 30 questions about his/her medical condition and history. If an applicant checks any red-flag questions, s/he will be subjected to additional application steps. The insurer will often request the applicant to go through a medical examination and request medical records from the applicant's physician. The application approval or denial decision will not be made until the underwriter receives the examination results and medical records. This process can take an average of 30 days to complete. In this case, the human decision step is the diamond that slows down the process. In the age where customers are used to the two-day "Amazon Prime Service," many applicants choose to drop out of the application during the process. This results in a significant revenue loss for a company. In the author's experience, a machine learning model can be built to learn from past underwriter decisions by using only the answers on the application form and other third-party data that might require the applicant's consent. The predictive model was able to automatically approve 25% to 30% of applications without asking the applicants to go through a medical exam or requesting medical records while keeping the underwriting risk at the same or lower level.

2.1.2 Leverage New Data

Traditional risk assessment methods often are limited by the availability of quality transactional data. This limitation creates the possibility of over or underestimating a risk. The emergence of many third-party data providers helped mitigate the data gap.

For example, the U.S. government census data provides a rich source of zip code level data for many aggregated personal or household characteristics such as average household income, personal educational level, marital status, etc. This third-party dataset can be used as a proxy to represent the characteristics of the individuals in the model dataset when the transactional data does not contain these potentially important variables. Companies such as Equifax and Experian can provide a more targeted dataset that includes a variety of aggregated household financial wealth data and credit indexes at a more granular zip code+4 level. These data provide opportunities for data scientists to create new and better machine learning models. Other specialty companies such as Milliman can provide a prescription history based risk score for a predictive underwriting model if the applicant has consented to the release of prescription history on the application form. Many other third-party data providers offer interesting data that could be useful for a particular machine learning project. One interesting source is the alternative data, which tracks non-traditional company, personal, geospatial, and time-based data from the Internet and other sources.

2.1.3 Predict the Next Move

The purpose of a predictive model in many cases is to foretell what a customer's next move will be. Will a marketing campaign recipient respond to a direct mail and request for more insurance product materials or go to the insurer's website to search for the product information? Will the prospective customer purchase the insurance product after reading the materials? Being able to predict a consumer's propensity to go through the sales funnel and execute an effective marketing campaign are critical to the success of the sales department. For operations, it is critical to be able to predict the claim volume, who is more likely to stay on a disability claim longer, or who is more likely to have his/her insurance policy lapse. This knowledge will allow the business to take preventive actions or develop contingency plans.

2.1.4 Reduce Uncertainty

Uncertainty creates risk. To be profitable and competitive in the insurance business, a company first needs to be able to price the risk of the product correctly. Some insurance products have fewer variables that drive risk, such as basic group life contracts. The basic group life mortality risk is mostly driven by limited variables such as age, gender, income, plus a few other variables because the product is priced at the group level. In contrast, individual life mortality risk has to consider many more variables, including age, gender, income, medical history, and biometric data because it is priced at the individual level. The additional complexity of medical history and biometric data makes the mortality risk much more difficult to estimate. A machine learning model can help identify which variable is a more impactful predictor than the others. When facing a high uncertainty decision with a large set of variables, machine learning is a good solution to help reduce the uncertainty.

2.2 *Evaluate Analytics Solutions*

Once a good analytics project opportunity is identified, the proposed solution should go through a rigorous evaluation process before a major investment of time and resources is committed to the project. Design thinking offers a good evaluation framework for analytics project proposals. Design thinking focuses on the design idea's desirability, feasibility, and viability (Brown, 2009). To evaluate a potential analytics project, we will focus on the operational feasibility and financial viability of the analytics solution.

2.2.1 Operational Feasibility

To assess the operational feasibility of an analytics solution, we first need to know how it will be implemented operationally. It starts with having a good understanding of the current process. Then, it is possible to identify process activities that will be impacted by the proposed solution. Through discussions with the process owner, a redesigned process map should be conceptualized to incorporate the proposed solution. One should assess the impact on operational changes. The framework of process innovation change levers—people, structure, information, tool (Davenport, 1993) offers a good foundation for the assessment. The author will add risk as an additional dimension for consideration. For the people dimension, we need to evaluate what are the role and responsibility changes and determine if new training is required. For the structure dimension, we need to consider the feasibility of the new process design and new functional department change required by the solution. For the information dimension, what new data would be required by the new analytics model? Would any of them need real-time data that may require IT infrastructure changes? For the new analytics tool, how easy is it to be integrated with the existing system? For the risk dimension, are there any compliance and regulatory concerns that need to be addressed before implementing the solution? Are there any operational change requirements that may not be feasible? Each of the feasibility concerns should be discussed and answered with an agreement from stakeholders.

2.2.2 Financial Viability

The ROI should be considered for any project requiring a significant investment of time and resources. The first question is what value can the analytics solution bring? Existing business metrics offer a good direction for consideration. For example, can the solution reduce operating cost, increase sales revenue, or improve profit? Even when a strong value proposition is proposed for an analytics solution, it is not always easy to quantify the value. Here are some examples of how to quantify the values. In the category of cost saving, we can calculate how much labor cost can be saved from

Table 1 Project ROI calculation

	Year 1	Year 2	Year 3	Year 4	Year 5	ROI
Cashflow	-$1 M	$1 M	$1 M	$1 M	$1 M	
NPV (10% IRR)	-$909 K	$826 K	$751 K	$683 K	$621 K	**$1.973 M**

automating decisions after using the new analytics tool. Also, other cost savings may be possible if implementing the new tool would eliminate the need for traditional data acquisition. On the flip side, we also need to consider the cost of new data if required by the new tool as well as the cost of any new risk the new tool may introduce. In the previously predictive underwriting project example, we know the new model can help automate underwriting decisions. Any life insurance application being approved by the model represents saving from an underwriter's labor cost. Additional savings also come from skipping costly medical exams and medical records. However, new costs may incur as a result of acquiring prescription history data if used in the model. We should also include the cost of risk from using a predictive model. Since no model is perfect, an incorrect approval decision based on the prediction (a Type I false-positive error) could increase future claim cost. In the category of improved profit, it is not difficult to multiply the estimated sales revenue increase by the profit margin. If the analytics solution also helps acquire new customers, the value calculation can be the estimated number of new customers acquired multiplied by the lifetime value per customer.

We also need to estimate the analytics project investment cost to calculate the ROI. It should not be too difficult for an experienced data science manager and IT manager to create an estimate that is within a reasonable range of the actual project cost. When the estimated value and cost are both obtained, we can calculate the ROI using a 5-year discounted cash flow projection. The example in Table 1 shows an analytics project having an estimated investment cost of $one million. The project would take one year to complete. After that, the project can bring in $one million in savings or profits per year. From the cashflow perspective, the total investment is $one million, and the total return is $four million. When using a 10% internal rate of return (IRR) discount rate, the total net present value (NPV) for the ROI becomes $1.973 million. Having a positive ROI allows the project to move forward. The next step is to decide this project's priority by comparing this project with other potential projects. In the next section, we will discuss a project evaluation framework with the consideration of ROI and other factors.

2.3 *Prioritize Analytics Projects*

2.3.1 Evaluation Framework

Since organizations have resource and budget constraints, even when an analytics project shows promising operational feasibility and financial viability, it needs to be

Table 2 Analytics Project Evaluation Framework

Project	Value (ROI)	Analytics Solutions	Data Availability	Process Integration	Other Supports	Project Ease
A. Pricing predictive model	$3 M	Complex	Partial	Medium Difficulty	Not fully available	4
B. Claims analytics	$2 M	Medium Complexity	All	Medium Difficulty	Available	3
C. Customer journey analytics	$1 M	Simple	All	Easy	Available	1
D. Predictive underwriting	$3 M	Medium Complexity	Partial	Medium Difficulty	Available	3
E. Prospect prioritization	$1 M	Complexity	Partial	Difficult	Not available	5
F. Campaign response model	$1 M	Simple	Partial	Easy	Available	2

compared with other analytics opportunities to determine its priority. Here, the author introduces an evaluation framework specifically for analytics projects. Let us assume there are 6 potential analytics project opportunities, all showing a positive ROI and various levels of operational feasibility. See Table 2. In this framework, we have four criteria to determine project ease. The first determinant is the analytics solution complexity. This is how complex it is to design the analytics model and provide a solution. The level of complexity can range from simple, medium complexity, to complex. The second determinant is data availability. The availability of data can have a significant impact on the success of an analytics model. Sometimes, we may be lucky to have all or most of the data available for model development. Other times, only partial or incomplete data are available. The data scientist will need to identify third-party data sources to supplement the insufficient dataset. The third determinant involves whether the analytics tool can be successfully integrated into the current or redesigned workflow process. The integration work could range from easy, medium difficulty, to difficult. The last determinant is other support requirements. It represents the level of operational readiness for the new business process when incorporated with the new analytics tool. The consideration includes the readiness of related IT systems, regulatory compliance, management support, and employee training, whichever is required to implement the new analytics solution.

After these four criteria are rated, we can give a project ease rating from 1 to 5, with 1 being the easiest and 5 being the most difficult project. The rating could be subjective; however, an experienced analytics manager should be able to discern the various degree of difficulty among competing projects and come up with reasonable and explainable ratings. For project examples in Table 2, let us review Project A-Pricing Predictive Model first. Its $three million ROI is positive and significant, which is great. Then, we review the analytics solution. It is complex because this insurance product has many product features that could impact pricing. Besides, other macroeconomic factors could impact the product risk. Adding to the difficulty, not all the potentially predictive data are available in the claims and policy systems.

Some will need to come from third-party data. The process integration could experience medium difficulty because a new pricing tool would require an underwriting process change. Other support would be needed due to the required underwriting application change and the regulatory approval of a new pricing structure. In comparison, Project C-Customer Journey Analytics Project also shows a positive ROI of $one million although at a lesser amount. However, it does not require a sophisticated predictive model, the penalty of a less accurate model is small. As a result, we can rate the analytics solution in the simple category. The customer interaction history data are available in the CRM system. After the model is developed, the predicted propensity score should be easy to use in the marketing campaign design. All the other support infrastructures are already in place. Therefore, we would rate Project A as 4 and Project C as 1 in terms of project ease.

2.3.2 Project Selection Heuristic

Having the project ease ratings will help determine project priority. Here, the author introduces a heuristic for project selection. The goal of the heuristic is to maximize the ratio of the ROI value to project ease. Assuming the analytics department's annual budget is $three million, not all 6 projects on the list can be selected this year. Table 3 illustrates how the heuristic works.

By now we already have estimated cost, ROI value, and project ease ratings for each project. We can obtain the ratio using the value column divided by the ease column, which gives us the initial ratio for project priority ranking. The author believes it is also important to consider whether an analytics project's goal is aligned with the organizational strategy. 50% additional weight is added to the strategic projects' ratio, which applies to Projects A, D, E. The new ratio is displayed in the strategic column. Using the new ratios, we can rank the projects. Project D-Predictive Underwriting has the highest ratio of 1.5, hence the highest ranking. Project A-Pricing Predictive Model has the second-highest ratio of 1.13, therefore ranked number 2. Using the ranking, we can start selecting the projects and also adding up the project cost. After selecting Projects D, A, C, B, the total cost is $2.75 million. If we were to select one more project, Project F, the total cost would be $3.25 million. It will exceed the $three million budget, so we stop here. After this exercise, Projects A, B, C, D were selected.

Table 3 Project selection heuristic

Project	Cost	Value	Ease	Ratio	Strategic*	Rank
A. Pricing predictive model	$750 K	$3 M	4	0.75	1.13*	2
B. Claims analytics	$500 K	$2 M	3	0.66	0.66	4
C. Customer journey analytics	$500 K	$1 M	1	1	1	3
D. Predictive underwriting	$1 M	$3 M	3	1	1.5*	1
E. Prospect prioritization	$500 K	$1 M	5	0.20	0.30*	6
F. Campaign response model	$500 K	$1 M	2	0.50	0.50	5

2.3.3 Project Sequencing

After projects are selected, the next question is: when can they start and when will they be completed? In project management, critical chain (Goldratt, 1997) is an important concept and practice. The data science, information technology, and operations resource constraints need to be thoroughly evaluated to identify any bottlenecks. If the data science team only has resources to work on two projects at a time and assume it takes an average of two quarters to develop a machine learning model from start to finish, then the team can only work on Projects D and A in the first half of the year, followed by Projects C and B in the second half of the year. Assuming IT and Operations have the necessary resources to implement two analytics models in two quarters, we can plan the project sequence as in Fig. 1.

2.4 *Manage an Analytics Project*

After priority projects are selected, each project will go through a formal predictive model development life cycle. CRISP-DM (Shearer, 2000) is often used as the structure to manage a data science project. It includes six phases: business understanding, data understanding, data preparation, modeling, evaluation, and deployment. In this section, the author describes a predictive model development life cycle framework that is more aligned with insurance industry practice. See Fig. 2. In this framework, the project life cycle starts with defining the scope and creating hypotheses for the model. Based on the scope and hypotheses, relevant data will be collected. Then it is followed by feature engineering, univariate, multivariate model development, evaluation, and deployment. It is also important to measure

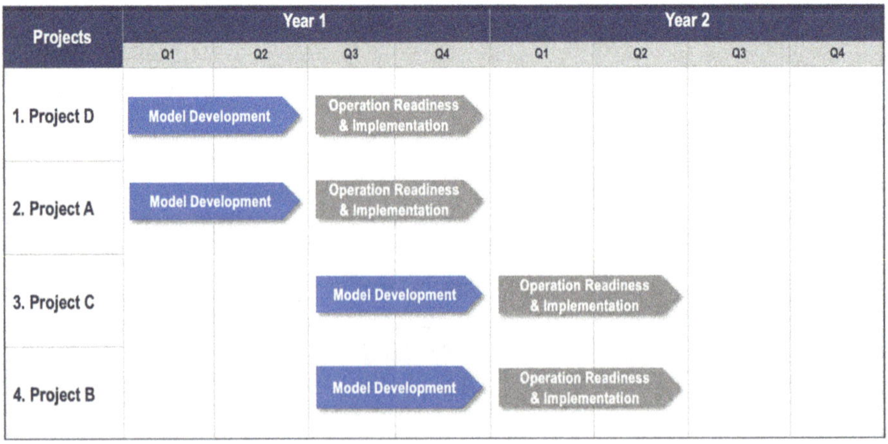

Fig. 1 Project sequence

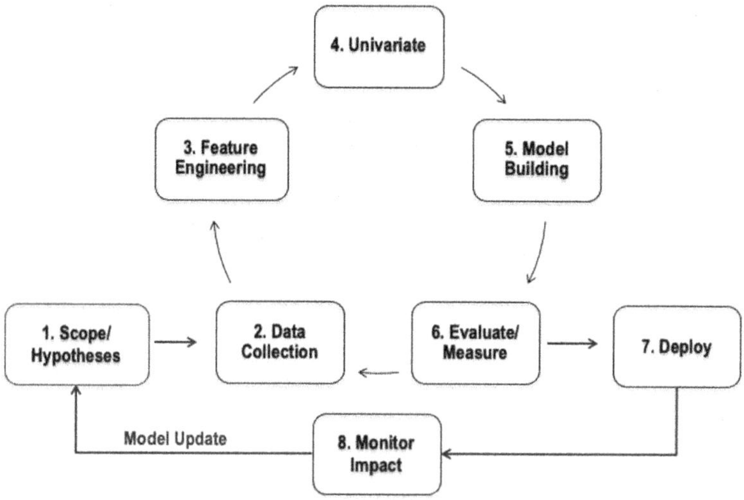

Fig. 2 Predictive model development life cycle

the model's impact on business outcomes after model deployment. These stages will be explained in more detail in the following sections.

2.4.1 Scope and Hypotheses

After the previous project evaluation process, the objectives of a project should be clear. The scope of using an analytics model to solve a specific business problem should have been defined. For example, the scope could be building a mortality predictive model that can predict the mortality risk of pension participants. With a clear scope, data scientists can then start forming hypotheses. A hypothesis is a supposition of a possible causal relationship between an input variable and the target variable. For example, we can hypothesize a person's income level may affect his/her mortality. This is based on general observations and our ability to come up with a reasonable explanation about the casual relationship. There is an interesting distinction between actuarial and data science approaches to identify potential predictors. An actuary may try to find both the correlation and explanation to form a hypothesis, whereas a data scientist may look for any possible correlated input variables first, and then seek the explanation. The author's preference is to follow the actuarial approach for pricing and underwriting models, and the data scientist approach for other types of models. This is because models used for pricing and underwriting may be subjected to state regulations in the U.S. and would require interpretability. The requirement also affects the type of machine learning algorithms to choose from. The availability of data also drives decisions of hypothesis forming.

2.4.2 Data Collection

After hypotheses are created, the next step is to collect relevant data. For most insurance predictive models, internal experience data from transactional systems are used. For example, for a disability pricing predictive model, the billing system would have the policyholder data, and the claims system would have the claimant data. The data would include features such as gender, date of birth, date of disability, occupation, and salary data. However, it may not have the person's education level, marital status, household size, and other personal data that might have an impact on disability incidence and severity. To develop a disability predictive model, a data scientist would need to acquire relevant third-party community characteristic data to supplement the transactional data to improve model accuracy. The other important consideration is to decide the dataset record granularity. For example, in a disability predictive model, the risk exposure is measured by per person life-year. It means that each record in the dataset represents one insured person-year that is covered by a disability insurance policy. For an incidence predictive model dataset, each record should have a target variable column that indicates whether the person had incurred disability or not in the year of the record. Once the initial data features from the transactional systems are collected to build the initial master dataset, all other features defined in hypotheses can be appended to the master dataset one by one.

2.4.3 Feature Engineering

Most transactional data contain some level of data quality issues. This is because transaction systems were initially developed to handle business transactions and were not designed for analytics purposes. For a transactional system, as long as a premium can be billed or a claim can be paid, not every data field in a system is required to be populated. For example, missing or incorrect educational level data in a claimant's record in a disability claims system is not necessarily critical from a claim examiner's perspective as long as the claim can be adjudicated and paid. Consequently, missing values and outliers are constant challenges in an analytics model dataset. These data issues need to be addressed before model development. During the hypothesis stage, data scientists could also create a new variable by combining two different variables that could form a new hypothesis. For example, considering that people who have higher disability risk may choose higher disability policy coverage amount, the ratio of disability policy amount to the policyholder's salary could be a good predictor for disability incidence. By going through the list of available variables, a data scientist may discover new features as the above example for the model.

2.4.4 Univariate

Sometimes, the initial number of selected variables in the hypotheses could reach hundreds. We do not want to start building a model by entering all the hundreds of input variables into the model without knowing the predictive power of each variable. The reason being, first, the machine learning tool may not be able to handle a large number of variables in building a multivariate model. Second, the weak or non-predictors may create too much noise in the initial multivariate model which diminishes the impact of top predictors. A better approach is to conduct univariate first. Univariate is to run each variable on its own to see if it is predictive of the target variable. In deciding which variables to keep in the univariate process, we look at three criteria. First, is the correlation statistically significant? That means is the p-value less than 0.05. and is the Chi-Square or the F-value high enough? Second, we look at if the correlation is consistent over time in either a positive or negative correlation. The third is does the correlation make sense, is it explainable? This is where the data scientist's judgment would come in. Once a variable passes all three criteria, it can be added to the multivariate model.

2.4.5 Multivariate Model Development

This stage is where the data scientist can select the machine learning algorithms suitable for the intended model, be it a binary classification, a regression, or a time-series forecasting problem. Many statistical packages provide built-in machine learning algorithms. In the commercial space, SAS, SPSS, Tibco Data Science are three popular options. In the open-source space, Python and R remain the most popular languages. On the AutoML front, major leaders include DataRobot and H_2O.ai (Gartner, 2020).

The first step is to split the dataset into three parts: train, validate, and test. A typical split is 30–30-40. When there are less records, we may adopt a 40–40-20 split. The test dataset is also called a holdout sample. If the use case has a huge dataset with multiple millions of records, we can sample a percentage of the records, say one million records to build the model. The sampling method can be either random sampling or stratification sampling if the dataset distribution followed a particular pattern.

There are many machine learning algorithms to choose from when building a model. As discussed in the introduction section, GLM and GAM are the preferred choice for pricing and underwriting applications due to its conformity to actuarial approach and its interpretability. GLM differs from linear regression by introducing a link function to the linear predictor with a particular probability distribution. For readers who are interested in learning more about GLM, an excellent paper by Ewald and Wang (2015) provides a walkthrough of the theory and a practical use case.

2.4.6 Model Evaluation

With different machine learning algorithms, different sets of input variables, and different dataset splits, one can build different version of models for a project. Although Log Loss, RMSD, Confusion Matrix, etc., are frequently used measures for model performance, the author prefers to use the lift chart and lift table to decide whether a predictive model is acceptable. See Table 4 for a lift table example. This example is from a model that predicts the probability of a policyholder lapse. The table shows the predicted results using a holdout sample. The average lapse rate is 6.35%. In this example, we first sorted the records by predicted lapse probability from high to low. Then, we divided the records into ten equal count groups. Column A shows the group number. Column B shows the number of insured records in a group. Column C shows the number of insured who has lapsed in a group. Column D shows the average lapse rate in a group. Column E shows the sum of the predicted lapse probability in a group. Column F provides the model lift of that group compared to the average predicted lapse rate. Usually, if the average lift of the top three groups is above 200%, it is a good enough model. Column G shows the actual vs. expected value. This is the most important column. The rule of thumb is to check whether each group's A to E is within a 10% deviation from 100%. Any group with an A/E that deviates more than 10% is considered not acceptable. In which case, the model needs to be fine-tuned or rebuilt. Column H and I show the cumulative actual number of lapsed records and percentages. For groups 1 to 4 in column I, it shows by using this predictive model we can capture 79% of policy lapses by focusing on 40% of policyholders. In this application, if group 10 showed 120% or 80% A/E, the model will still be acceptable since we will only focus on the top 40% of high potential lapsed policyholders. This is an exception to the A/E 10% range rule of thumb consideration.

There are two other considerations in model evaluation and implementation. In a binary classification predictive model, we often need to decide the threshold for the true or false of predicted scores. Typically, 0.5 is used as the threshold. The confusion matrix can help us decide how to move the threshold up or down for the model to provide an optimized financial return if we knew the economic value of a correct prediction, as well as the penalty of a false positive and a false negative prediction. The other consideration is how to reduce the financial impact of type 1 and type 2 errors. We can use other variables such as the policy coverage amount to limit the risk exposure by not using the model to underwrite any life insurance application that is more than, for example, 500,000 dollars.

2.4.7 Model Deployment

After a model is accepted and selected as the final model, the next step is model implementation. There are several ways to deploy a model. First, the model can reside in the model development tool's production environment. The incoming

Table 4 Predictive model evaluation

Group (A)	Record # (B)	Actual # (C)	Actual % (D)	Predicted % (E)	Model Lift (F)	A/E (G)	Cumulative Actual # (H)	Cumulative Actual % (I)
1	100,000	24,902	24.90%	24.20%	378%	102.90%	24,902	39%
2	100,000	11,893	11.89%	12.20%	191%	97.48%	36,795	58%
3	100,000	7710	7.71%	8.20%	128%	94.02%	44,505	70%
4	100,000	5798	5.80%	5.90%	92%	98.27%	50,303	79%
5	100,000	4312	4.31%	4.30%	67%	100.28%	54,615	86%
6	100,000	3195	3.20%	3.20%	50%	99.84%	57,810	91%
7	100,000	2389	2.39%	2.30%	36%	103.87%	60,199	95%
8	100,000	1705	1.71%	1.60%	25%	106.56%	61,904	97%
9	100,000	1099	1.10%	1.10%	17%	99.91%	63,003	99%
10	100,000	511	0.51%	0.50%	8%	102.20%	63,514	100%
Total / Avg.	**1,000,000**	**63,514**	**6.35%**	**6.40%**		**99.24%**		

Note: F1 = E1/E11, F2 = E2/E11, etc. G1 = D1/E1, G2 = D2/E2, etc.

production case data can be fed into the model and produce the prediction on demand. Second, the model algorithm can be coded into the company's workflow system. When a case is being processed in the workflow, the case data can run through the embedded model algorithm to obtain the prediction. Third, some machine learning tool provides a model deployment facility where a workflow system can call the model remotely through a URL with the required input variable data. It will return the prediction to the workflow system. There are many books and articles about the machine learning operations (MLOps) topic that readers can read if interested.

2.4.8 Measure Business Impact

Once a model is deployed, it is important to measure the value that the model brings from a business standpoint. Specifically, does it match the expectation of the original financial viability assessment? We can monitor the business performance variance between the pre- and post-implementation, or between the experimental group and the control group to validate the model efficacy. See Figs. 3 and 4. Figure 3 compares the before and after predictive underwriting model implementation case processing volume. The bar chart on the left shows the pre-implementation case volume, where the underwriting decisions were all made by human underwriters. The bar chart on the right shows the effect of the model implementation, where a significant percentage of underwriting decisions were automated (striped bars). Also, the quarter-over-quarter processing volume was increased consistently as a result of a lower applicant dropout rate, which translated into higher revenue. The comparison shows that the model implementation was successful.

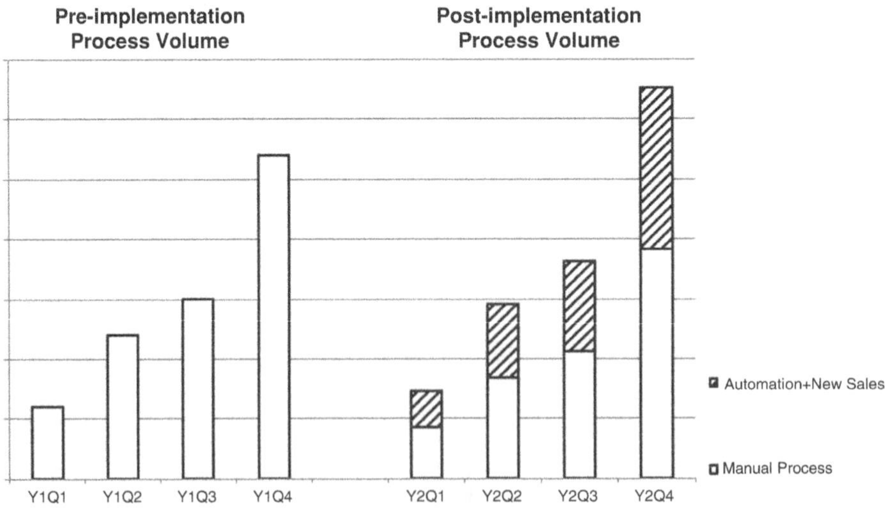

Fig. 3 Pre and post model implementation comparison

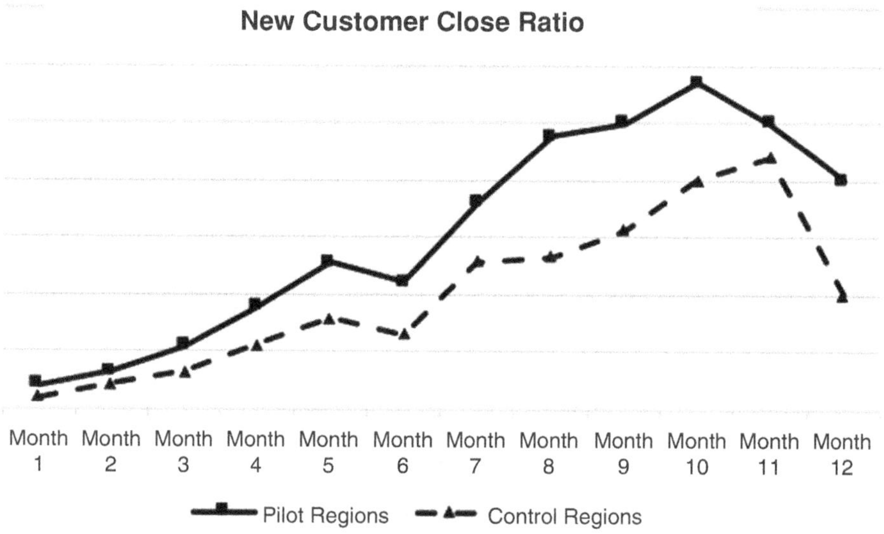

Fig. 4 Comparison between experimental and control groups

Figure 4 compares the new customer close ratio between the pilot sales regions that implemented a predictive model and the control regions that conducted business as usual. The close ratio is defined as the number of new customers acquired per one hundred prospective customers. The result shows the pilot regions experienced a consistently higher close ratio month after month during the one-year pilot period. As a result of the strong evidence, the model was implemented nationwide. In addition to measuring the efficacy of the model, collecting business metric data throughout the model implementation period can provide insights for model refresh and new model development in the future.

3 Build a Data Science Team

3.1 Data Science Functions

Patil (2011) described his experience in building a data science team at LinkedIn when it was a startup. He discussed various functions a data science team plays and the role of a data scientist. At a startup, a data scientist could wear multiple hats including being a data engineer and a project manager. Whereas in an established large insurance company, the functions are more divided. The roles and responsibilities are more segregated due to more refined data science activities, audit control requirements, and a broader stakeholder base. Based on case studies conducted by Saltz and Grady (2017), a data science organization's functions include, but not limited to data collection, model development and evaluation, and model

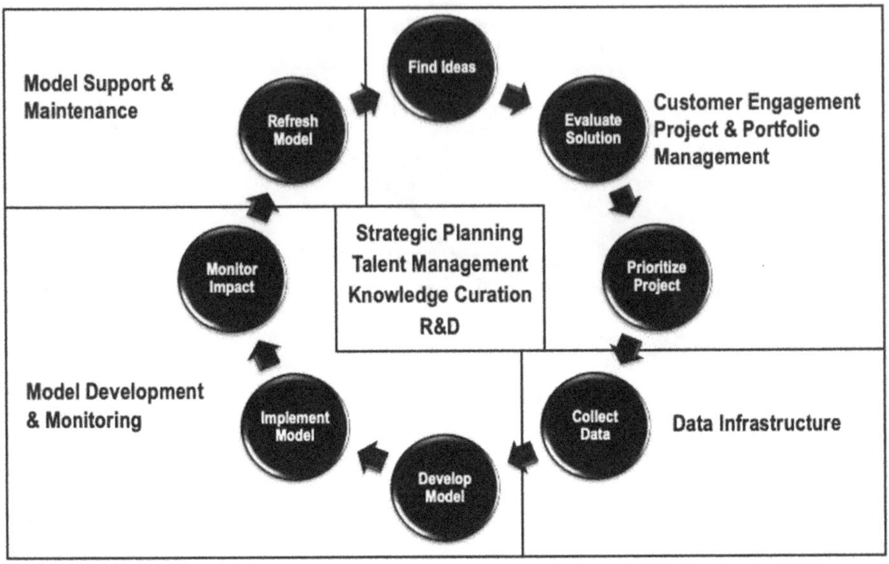

Fig. 5 Data science team functions

interpretation and deployment. The key roles include data engineer, data scientist, and data analyst. Viewing from the entire project life cycle perspective, the author would propose a data science organization should include the following 5 functions as displayed in Fig. 5.

1. The customer engagement and project & portfolio management function is to collaborate with business partners to explore analytics opportunities, evaluate solutions, prioritize projects, and manage project activities.
2. The data engineering function is to create and maintain a data infrastructure to provide quality data for model development and model refresh. It also includes creating and supporting a model deployment facility.
3. The modeling function is to develop, evaluate, and deploy models as well as monitoring business impact.
4. The model support and maintenance function is to provide production support to models used by business operations and keep models up to date. When new case data starts to drift from the historical data that was used to build the model, the model should be refreshed.
5. The management function is to lead strategic planning, talent management, knowledge curation of the model portfolio, and research and development activities.

3.2 *Data Science Organization*

To support the data science functions, 5 different roles are recommended for a data science team as shown in Fig. 6. Each of them is responsible for several functional activities described above.

1. The head of the team is to lead the strategic planning, talent management, knowledge curation, and R&D activities.
2. A relationship and project manager is to engage business partners with team lead and data scientists to discuss analytics opportunities, evaluate solutions, prioritize projects, and manage project activities.
3. A data scientist is to identify analytics ideas, evaluate analytics solutions, develop and interpret models, and monitor post model implementation business impact.
4. A data engineer is to collect and prepare data, support model deployment, provide data for a model refresh, support data infrastructure, and conduct research to improve data and model deployment infrastructure.
5. A data analyst can provide production model support, work on model refresh, build simple model, and provide data visualization using tools such as Tableau, Qlik, and Power BI.

4 Analytics Applications

With all the potential applications of machine learning models, let us use customer journey management and customer lifetime value calculation in a life insurance company to demonstrate the broad impact of data science on business. To be a

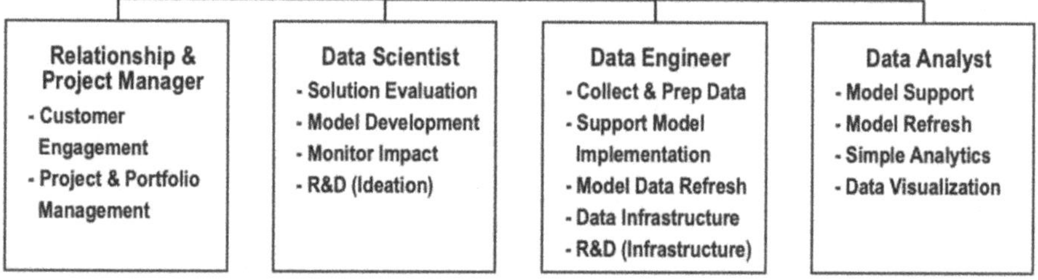

Fig. 6 Data science team organization

successful life insurance company, it is critically important to manage the sales funnel and customer journey effectively. The customer journey for a life insurance product has four stages: prospect journey, visitor journey, applicant journey, and customer journey. It starts with identifying high propensity prospective customers for a product. At the prospect journey, based on previous marketing campaign results, a company can develop a campaign response predictive model to target high propensity customers. A good predictive model can help reduce the campaign operating cost and increase the response rate. The prospective customers who are attracted by the company's campaign may go online as a visitor to the company's website or request product information offline to learn more about the product. At the visitor journey, the company can conduct web analytics to improve the website design to increase the conversion rate and reduce the abandon rate. If a visitor finds the product meets his/her needs, s/he will apply for the insurance product. As an insurer, it is important to provide a convenient application process and be able to differentiate high-risk applicants from low-risk applicants. The traditional underwriting process requires human underwriters to make the approval or denial decision. This human decision step associated with required medical exam and medical records often becomes a bottleneck in the application process, which causes customer dissatisfaction and high cost. At the applicant stage, a predictive underwriting model can estimate the risk, assign the applicant to the right risk class, and set the premium according to the risk level. Most low-risk applicants can be automatically approved, which allows human underwriters to focus on the high-risk applicant underwriting decisions. Once the application is approved, the company will send out the premium bill to the applicant. When the premium is received, the applicant becomes a customer—a policyholder. During the customer journey, a customer may stop paying the premium and cause a lapse in coverage. A policyholder lapse predictive model can help operations identify customers having a high probability of lapse. The company can take proactive action to prevent or reduce lapses, such as sending out a newsletter to remind customers of the importance of continuous insurance coverage before the premium bill is due. At some point during the customer journey, a covered incident may occur, and a claim will be submitted. A successful company needs to provide a fast and accurate claim service to a customer. A claim triage predictive model can help expedite common low-risk claims. A claim duration predictive model can also be developed to help operations manage claims with a long duration, such as worker's comp and long-term disability claims.

When combining all the previously discussed predictive models in the entire customer journey, we can create a powerful customer lifetime value (CLV) predictive model to measure a customer's CLV as early as when the customer is still a prospect. The CLV model could include the following sub-models.

1. Propensity-to-buy predictive model—the model predicts the probability (Pp) that a prospect will buy an insurance product.
2. Predictive underwriting model—the model predicts the approval probability (Pu) for underwriting an applicant.

3. Premium predictive model—the model predicts the insurance coverage amount (*Ap*) that a prospect will purchase.
4. Policyholders lapse predictive model—the model predicts the lapse probability (*Pl*) of a policyholder. The number of years that a policyholder will stay is $T = 1/Pl$.
5. Claim incidence predictive model—the model predicts the probability (*Pc*) that an incident will occur, and a claim will be filed by a given customer.
6. Claim severity predictive model—the model predicts the amount (*Ac*) will be paid out when a claim is received.

Assume the company's internal rate of return is *Irr* and the selling, general, and administrative (SG&A) expense ratio for acquiring a customer is *Ra.* The formula to calculate a prospective customer's CLV is as the following:

$$CLV = Pp\ x\ Pu\ x \left(\sum_{n=1}^{T} \frac{Ap}{(1 + Irr)^{(n-1)} x\ (1 + Pl)^{(n-1)}} - Pc\ x\ Ac - Ra\ x\ Ap \right)$$

The CLV represents the NPV of the total profit that can be received from a prospective customer. First, it considers the probabilities of converting the prospect into an applicant and from an applicant into a customer. Second, it accounts for the NPV of all future premium cashflow discounted by the internal rate of return and predicted lapse rate for a given prospect. Third, claims and SG&A costs are deducted.

Being able to calculate the CLV at the prospect stage means that the company can use the insights to make many quantifiable decisions throughout the customer journey. For example, how much expense should be spent on sales-related campaigns and promotional activities for a particular group of prospects? Which group of applicants has lower risk and should receive higher priority from the underwriting department? Consequently, companies that can truly decode the CLV and understand the behavior drivers at each customer journey stage will be able to make better business decisions and take proactive actions to increase revenue and profit while reducing operational costs.

5 Ethical Considerations

Decision automation and advisory tools powered by machine learning algorithms can help managers make faster and better decisions. However, a decision tool may bring unintended bias if it was not carefully reviewed. The concern for an insurance machine learning model is whether the model would raise an ethical concern or inflict a discriminatory effect on a particular class of prospects or customers. Besides the moral judgment of fairness and discrimination, Loi and Christen (2019) provided a framework to conduct an ethical analysis of discrimination to guide the use of predictions. They suggested reviewing algorithms that may cause direct discrimination, indirect discrimination, and disparate mistreatment. Insurance regulators in the United States have started raising concerns in this area. For example, the New York State Department of Financial Services issued a letter (2019) to authorized life insurers in New York State, stating that "an insurer should not use external data sources, algorithms or predictive models in underwriting or rating unless the insurer has determined that the processes do not collect or utilize prohibited criteria and that the use of the external data sources, algorithms or predictive models are not unfairly discriminatory."

In addition to regulatory compliance, no company wants its reputation to be tarnished by having a questionable predictive model publicized by media. Duhigg (2012) provided a vivid example of how a retail company's use of predictive models to drive customer behavior was uncovered. Consequently, there is a strong incentive to build a governance process into the machine learning model development life cycle. At a large insurance company in the United States, two control points were established in the model development life cycle to ensure the concern is addressed. After the hypothesis stage and before the data collection work starts, the list of variables defined in the hypotheses would be sent to a corporate attorney who specialized in machine learning and privacy regulations for review. Once the data scientist received the legal approval and built the model, the final list of predictors as well as the proposed model implementation method would be sent to the attorney again for a final review. The legal review would comment on each predictor used in the model, data access method and usage of data, and limitations that should be considered when using the model. Although the additional process steps may not cover all angles, having data scientists working with legal counsels should reduce ethical concerns.

6 Summary

Data science increasingly plays an important role in all aspects of operations in an insurance company. As discussed in this chapter, there are many applications where machine learning models can speed up decisions, enable new capabilities, and reduce uncertainty. In today's competitive business environment where customers are used to fast response time and customized services, insurance companies need to develop new analytics capabilities to meet new customer expectations and to grow the business profitably. Property and casualty insurers were the frontrunners in applying data science to business operations. This is followed by health and life insurers. Retirement and annuity insurers have started picking up the speed. This trend of using analytics to transform the insurance business will only deepen into every business function within an insurance company and spread across the industry over time.

References

Agrawal, N. (2020). *5 Deep learning use cases for the insurance industry*, Retrieved from https://www.mantralabsglobal.com/blog/deep-learning-use-cases-insurance/

Bernstein, P. L. (1998). *Against the gods: The remarkable story of risk*. Wiley.

Brown, T. (2009). *Change by design: How design thinking transforms organizations and inspires innovation*. Harper Business.

Brynjolfsson, E. (1998). *Beyond the productivity paradox: Computers are the catalyst for bigger changes*. Communications of the ACM.

Davenport, T. H. (1993). *Process innovation: Reengineering work through information technology*. Harvard Business School Press.

Duhigg, C. (2012). How companies learn your secret. *The New York Times Magazine, 16*, 2012. https://www.nytimes.com/2012/02/19/magazine/shopping-habits.html

Ewald, M., & Wang, Q. (2015). Predictive modeling: A modeler's introspection.. Society of Actuaries.

EY. (2020). *2020 US and Americas insurance outlook,* Retrieved from https://assets.ey.com/content/dam/ey-sites/ey-com/en_gl/topics/insurance/insurance-outlook-pdfs/ey-global-insurance-outlook-us-americas.pdf

Frees, E. W., Derrig, R. A., & Meyers, G. (2014). *Predictive modeling applications in actuarial science* (Vol. 1). Cambridge University Press.

Gartner (2020). Magic quadrant for data science and machine learning platforms., Retrieved from https://www.forbes.com/sites/janakirammsv/2020/02/20/gartners-2020-magic-quadrant-for-data-science-and-machine-learning-platforms-has-many-surprises

Goldratt, E. M. (1997). *Critical chain*. North River Press.

Haberman, S., & Renshaw, A. E. (1996). Generalized linear models and actuarial science. *Journal of the Royal Statistical Society: Series D (The Statistician), 45*(4), 407–436.

Loi, M., & Christen, M. (2019). Insurance discrimination and fairness in machine learning: An ethical analysis. *Available at SSRN, 3438823*.

Lou, Y., Caruana, R., Gehrke, J., & Hooker, G. (2013). *Accurate intelligible models with pairwise interactions, proceedings of the 19th ACM SIGKDD international conference on knowledge discovery and data mining, 2013*. IL, USA.

New York State Department of Financial Services. (2019). RE: Use of external consumer data and information sources in underwriting for life insurance. *Insurance Circular Letter No., 1*. Retrieved from https://www.dfs.ny.gov/industry_guidance/circular_letters/cl2019_01

Patil, D. J. (2011). *Building data science teams*. O'Reilly Media.

Saltz, J. S., & Grady, N. W. (2017, December). The ambiguity of data science team roles and the need for a data science workforce framework. *2017 IEEE International Conference on Big Data* (pp. 2355–2361). IEEE.

Shearer, C. (2000). The CRISP-DM model: The new blueprint for data mining. *Journal of Data Warehousing, 5*, 4.

A General Cyber Hygiene Approach for Financial Analytical Environment

Waleed M. Ead and Mohamed M. Abbassy

Abstract Ideally, users must have a good level of cyber hygiene. Many people have bad cyber hygiene. They openly exchange passwords and share private information on social networks. This chapter will include a technical survey to investigate the cyber hygiene behaviors of end-users which will promote the creation of more successful approaches in the financial analytical climate. It will include aspects to allow the company to improve its cyber hygiene approaches due to the various forms of access to financial solutions in the area.

Keywords Cyber Hygiene · Financial Analytical · Cloud computing · Cloud Security · Open source-based services · Payment System

1 Introduction

Cyber hygiene habits will maintain data safe and well-protected. The activity and measures used by users of computers and other devices to preserve system health and improve online safety may be subject to cyber hygiene. Healthy cyber hygiene is the biggest problem for users. We might understand the need to take the time to develop passwords and the need for a software update. Several users are more likely to have weak cyber hygiene. They share passwords freely and easily share private information via social networks. Attackers know that stealing user details is the fastest way into the system.

The Ponemon Institute's Second Annual Cost of cybercrime has shown that the financial impact of U.S. cybercrimes is beyond Japan. Since 2014, 98% of organizations experienced malware-related attacks. Phishing and social engineering organizations that suffered attacks rose by 8 percent from 2015 to 2016. Specific end-users often face substantial risks because of these safety violations, writes

W. M. Ead (✉) · M. M. Abbassy
Faculty of Computers and Artificial Intelligence, Beni-Suef University, Beni-Suef, Egypt
e-mail: waleedead@bsu.edu.eg

S. Derindere Köseoğlu (ed.), *Financial Data Analytics*, Contributions to Finance and Accounting, https://doi.org/10.1007/978-3-030-83799-0_13

Shashank Joshi. He says users must enhance their understanding of cyber hygiene and their reactions to their behavior.

The FBI's IC3 (Internet Crime Complaints Center) includes data reported by Americans on cybercrimes. During 2017, 288,012 cybercrime reports were issued by the FBI and over 40% were economic losses. The overall number of losses reported in 2017 amounted to $2,070,711,522; the average loss report was $8421. males 50–59 years of age have the largest number of victims with 31.473 victims.

The real value of a cyber hygiene program for organizations is the advantages it will offer. This may be as basic as advertising for customers and customers that defense takes it seriously. This study will investigate the cyber hygiene knowledge of concepts. The knowledge of threats, and the behaviors of end-users. The present research and approaches provide a survey to explore the cyber hygiene habits of end-users.

2 Background

End-users have access to security tools, such as antivirus systems, firewalls, and intrusion detection systems. Many people tend not to be paying attention to the distinction between firewalled and antivirus software. Either the program up-to-date or occasionally even antivirus was not installed in 67% of survey participants. The firewall was not fully calibrated at 72 percent. A further survey stated that 97% of non-trainers use antivirus receipts, 72% use firewall security, 38% use anti-phishing tools, 75% use anti-spyware, and 18% use an intrusion detection system (Talib et al., 2010).

Ovelgönne et al. (Dhillon et al., 2018) gathered data on antivirus malware attacks from computers and found the most frequently attacked web developers. A protection action and risk management analysis showed that participants were more vigilant than using firewalls to use antivirus applications to download security product patches.

Authentication is one of the key security functions of the network (Anderson & Agarwal, 2010). The analysis of Sensitive Infrastructure and Main Services incidents in Dawson and Stinebaugh (Bullo et al., 2017) reveals that bad keys and other technological problems are a significant cause of network weakness (e.g., vulnerabilities because of bypassing a firewall). It is advised that users chose strong passwords to prevent attack (Konieczny et al., 2015; Singh et al., 2020; Furnell et al., 2006; Ovelgönne et al., 2017; Gratian et al., 2018). Strong passwords of at least eight characters (van Schaik et al., 2017) have been established. The eight characters should include numbers, letters, and symbols, or include the letters, numbers, and special characters of the upper and lower case. Any personal or dictionary information (Ovelgönne et al., 2017; Dawson & Stinebaugh, 2010) shall be included.

Earlier study has found that phishing emails have very high response times. 500 military cadets were found in 2004, 80% clicked on an embedded link. In

2005, 10,000 New York State workers were phished and 15 percent of them started to enter personal details before they were alerted (Hoonakker et al., 2009). Dodge et al. (Cain & Still, 2018) have taught organization participants how to avoid responding to phishing emails. The researchers have recently sent participants virtual Phishing emails to test their response patterns. Simulation model phishing emails included malicious connections, malicious attachments, and sensitive information requests. A link to the Website was given to 50%, a link opened 38% of the participants and sensitive learning was provided by 46%. Caputo et al. (Florêncio et al., 2007) also trained an organization to prevent from answering suspicious email.

Following training, the study identified drop rates and records for phishing emails. After preparation, the click rate for embedded links was 60%. Holm et al., (2013) have tested responses in the electric power domain to virtual phishing emails. A malicious link was sent to the researchers. The email was in English or Swedish, regardless of the native tongue of the workers. The link to the email in English was used by 7.5 percent of the participants and the link was made available in Swedish by 30.2 percent.

Personal information can also be hacked as people share it on social networking sites. 59% of the participants surveyed reported their true name on social networks, 62% reported that they were divulgent, and 45% reported their birth date and full names being dissociated (Talib et al., 2010). 77% of users said their privacy preferences would be restricted (http://www.ponemon.org/, n.d.). In attacks on social technology, such as spell phishing, personal information will be used to expand the possibilities for response (Florêncio et al., 2007), even in fake emails.

There are different forms of cyber hygiene activities between users. Even though 43% of adults have reported security training, only 19% of university students report receiving safety training (Dodge Jr et al., 2007), the seniors have been found to be a significant indicator of their inability to apply best practices to cyber hygiene (Ashford, 2009). Less relevant, recognizable and technology-related knowledge may be attributed to older users' failings in upholding best standards and their increased risk of sharing their personal data such as passwords (Konieczny et al., 2015).

To address this, we will adopt a cyber hygiene strategy emphasizing the importance of routine, low-impact protection measures. This would reduce the risk that cyber-attacks may spread to other organizations or the effects of a cyber-attack. Today, with each Member Country providing its own initiatives or guide, there is no universal standard or generally accepted approach to cyber hygiene in Europe. Most of these systems are coordinated or guided in, and at varying maturity stages, the national cyber security policies issued by each Member State 6. Three programs are listed as adequately established in the public records to provide organizations with specific advice.

This program can identify measures that can be applied by organizations with limited or no dedicated IT security staff and assess a requirement for good practice. It is not possible to expect a small firm to employ a coding professional to deploy tailor-made scripts for monitoring and alert and this level of detail for the essential standard is excessive.

Good practice monitoring may look at behavior that can be done by major operating systems or software or limited business processes. For organizations facing a more powerful attack, infrastructure may be improved, but changes to functionality can be optional.

The key value of a cyber hygiene program for many organizations is the advantages it will offer. It would be as easy as advertising to clients and customers that they take security seriously, acting as either a market differentiator or as complex to simplify the safety elements of due diligence inspections. The last word decision consideration for any company that proposes a cyber hygiene program will definitely be the cost. Cost. Though this lifetime expenses of any program, it is also impossible that small enterprises that are thinking with their actual profits may suffer from a violation.

In practical Terms, there are Three Aspects to the Value of a Scheme

Cost of Implementation: This cost would affect any organization seeking to follow by and is included in any necessary new technologies. It is difficult to predict what this could be, but this can be reduced by reducing the need for application or resources.

Cost of Accreditation: In the United Kingdom, the accreditation of an organization wasting a five-digit government contract costs £300 (around EUR 350) per annum. In the final review, the price of accreditation is controlled by the value of the credential product.

Cost of Ongoing Maintenance

This is often a required benefit for needing care for the scheme to stay in effect. Often this is really a long-term responsibility Combined Public and personal Sector Engagement.

Many of the organizations were unaware of the cyber hygiene schemes developed by the Government. Cyber Essentials were thus not adequate to interest them. The main considerations that foster healthy cyber security are to make sure that they are enshrined in inevitable commitments. The more mature an organization becomes in cyber security terms, the more likely it will force security restrictions through the supply chain. Governments of the Member States should be encouraged to define minimum viable safety conditions an organization should take.

Lack of Cloud Security Controls

Cybersecurity hygiene programs focus heavily on physical infrastructure management and protection. Most controls assume that the organization operates the assets directly. This provides a drag for organizations that want to conform to guidance but have adopted a cloud-based service offering. For smaller organizations without any advanced tools, this is much less possible. While Security professionals may quickly realize the way to adapt the programs to service environments. As a result, there is a requirement for a typical approach to cyber hygiene that covers the subsequent main topic areas. Such typical approach was recommended by the European Union Agency for Network and Information Security (ENISA) (https://www.enisa.

europa.eu, n.d.). This might give scope for individualization by the Member States or industry sectors, while retaining the facility to work out compliance regimes.

1. Protect the perimeter
2. Protect the network
3. Protect individual devices
4. Use the cloud during a secure manner
5. Protect the availability chain

Based on these five areas, one approach, almost like the prevailing regimes, would be to interrupt down into 10 action points:

1. Have a record of all hardware so you recognize what your estate seems like.
2. Have a record of all software to make sure it is properly patched.
3. Utilize secure configuration/hardening guides for all devices.
4. Manage data in and out of your network.
5. Scan all incoming emails.
6. Minimize administrative accounts.
7. Regularly copy data and test it are often restored.
8. Establish an event response plan.
9. Enforce similar levels of security across the availability chain.
10. Ensure suitable security controls in any service agreements (including cloud services).

3 Proposed Methodology

This research would explore the concepts of cyber hygiene. The understanding of risks and the behavior of end-users in a thorough and modified manner, spanning from cloud services to security measurements. In addition, no traditional or systematic solution to cyber hygiene is currently available. They are designed to educate the consumer and his/her organizations' actions based on processes and behavior. The KSA presented a 2030 strategic strategy to establish the operational structure for KSA government institutions' migration to cloud computing paradigms.

In this research, they wish to suggest in KSA government entities a general framework that is different from other cyber hygiene systems in other countries for good cyber hygiene. In addition, through the 2030 corporate cloud computing strategic plan the new KSA cyber hygiene/Framework will analyze KSA's customers and organizations for best practices.

The aim is to promote a cybersecurity strategy that both complies with international standards and can be readily implemented in domestic terms such as economies of scale, society, customers' behavior, corporate processes, local regulatory requirements, etc.

The KSA new cyber hygiene policy aims to sensitize the public to cyber-risk, Internet security and cyber-exposure resistance (crime and attack, external and internal). However, factors such as expense, market competences, developments in business, government, or regulation play a major role in its growth, if it is for the commercial, public and government sectors. It reflects on the market needs and importance of KSA government agencies, core properties of an organization such as customers, computers, and data storage. The defense pillar includes the simple protected configurations of computers, firewalls, and gateways and improves the security of data by monitoring data and handling account/password.

The proposed KSA cyber hygiene approach will cover the protection to the following.

- Cloud Providers.
- Amazon Web Services.
- Google Cloud Computing Platform.
- Microsoft Azure.

Here a short description for KSA cyber hygiene principles for cloud provider such as google cloud platform. Such principles will contain the important security considerations when designing your infrastructure on Google Cloud Platform that depends on your project level. Such principles will include (not limited):

- Know the project level and its Users.
- Identity and Access Management.
- Logging and Monitoring.
- Networking.
- Virtual Machines.
- Storage.
- Cloud SQL Database Services.
- Kubernetes Engine.

3.1 Cloud Computing Services

The amount of cloud computing services (CCSs) is rising fast and is now one of the key buzzwords. Many large computing market players like Microsoft are also attending the cloud service event (Long, 2013; Taneski et al., 2014; Europe, 2008; Aytes & Conolly, 2003) as are other heavyweights in Internet innovations, like Google and Amazon. Many firms, even companies which do not have a technical focus, want to pursue cloud computing's capabilities and advantages (Holm et al., 2013). Cloud storage resources have become rare (Choong & Greene, 2016; Europe, 2008) and any provider of cloud infrastructure uses numerous technology, protocols, and formats. There are no uniform services. In addition, most clouds are highly unclear regarding the internal functioning. All this makes it impossible to interoperate with different systems or switch to new services. There is also a major marketing buzz in the world of cloud computing where Internet service providers are re-branding their offerings as part of the cloud revolution. Due to the large number of

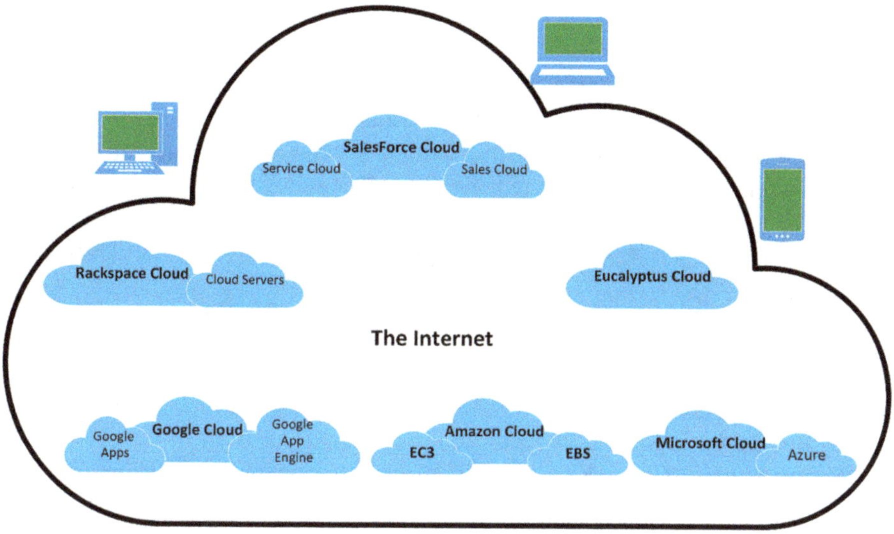

Fig. 1 Cloud computing services (Lebek et al., 2014)

different cloud computing providers, it is impossible to compare and find the correct one. The huge number of cloud computing services and, therefore, the absence of common concepts and specifications cause the question that cloud computing services are mostly graded for simple comparability during a taxonomy. There are, however, table-based analyses with cloud infrastructure systems, which are primarily for commercial use and thus the level of detail is somewhat different. But it is not a way of categorizing and contrasting emerging and potential cloud services but trying to find the powers, shortcomings, and threats of current cloud systems. In addition, the cloud system offers state-of-the-art and analysis problems. However, there is still no means of categorizing current and future cloud infrastructure resources.

A cloud is often used as a scalable platform enabling and connecting many cloud services; see Fig. 1.

The cloud itself consists "of a set of interconnected and virtualized computers that are dynamically provisioned and presented together or more unified computing resource(s)" (Lebek et al., 2014). The clients who use their home or work machine or other Internet connected device to connect with and use the cloud computing resources are the consumers of cloud computing services. Service-level contracts typically cover the provision of cloud services.

In (Long, 2013; Bank, 2005) are defined the major features which distinguish cloud computing from conventional solution:

- The infrastructure and software fundamental principle is summarized and delivered as a service.
- Focus on an infrastructure that is flexible and scalable.
- On-demand customer delivery and service quality assurances (QoS).

- Purchase of computer services by cloud customers without advance commitment.
- Multi-tenant and shared.
- Accessible.

Cloud infrastructure systems are state-of-the-art and analysis problems and include greater detail on the cloud infrastructure and, consequently, technology. Virtualization infrastructure offering versatile and modular computing platform, web services and repair of Oriented Architecture (SOA) systems to handle the cloud and remote backup storage and worldwide data connectivity is the underlying technology.

The National Institute of Standards and Technology (NIST) proposed the next definition of cloud computing: “Cloud computing could also be a model for enabling convenient, on-demand network access to a shared pool of configurable computing resources (e.g., networks, servers, storage, applications, and services) which can be rapidly provisioned and released with minimal management effort or service provider interaction. This cloud model promotes availability.” (Chaudhry & Rittenhouse, 2015). This term is used because cloud computing systems and conventional Internet services are distinguished. Three service models, such as web-based email, Platform-as-a-service (PaaS), which enable customers to implement their own applications as well as Infrastructure-as-a-Service (IaaS), are currently differentiated (Chaudhry & Rittenhouse, 2015), and three services models are being deployed in an online manner that provides, as an example, power or stowage delivery. Other service models, such as Service-as-a-service (Holm et al., 2013) and Data-as-a-service (Hoonakker et al., 2009) or Storage-as-a-service (Hoonakker et al., 2009), were considered in previous works, but these models may usually be grouped with the three existing ones. Even so, some categories are not considered in the existing descriptions in comparison to these service types.

3.2 Current Services for Cloud Services

The key differences between the deployed cloud infrastructure systems refer to the types of services available, such as (1) storage and computing capacity, (2) own software deployment frameworks, or (3) online software apps, from Web Email to business analytics tools. Based on these variations, three major groups of cloud computing providers have already been proposed to NIST (Chaudhry & Rittenhouse, 2015). The three models of service are shown in Fig. 2. A few cloud providers in any type will be discussed in this section to provide an overview of the current services. For this summary, existing taxonomies (Taneski et al., 2014) and related work shape a collection of emerging cloud computing resources.

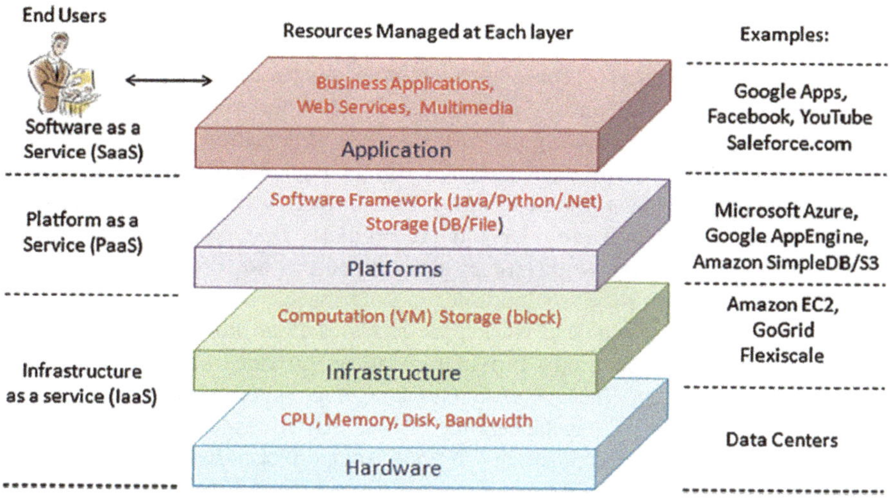

Fig. 2 Cloud Networking providers' three key categories (Taneski et al., 2014)

3.3 Infrastructure as a Service

Usually, cloud providers provide virtualization platforms known for a long time now, which are an extension of private virtual server offering (Taneski et al., 2014). Rather than having to allocate the computers, equipment, and space of the data center themselves, purchasers buy the resources and buy the resources supported. They launch and monitor and maintain the applications on your virtual machines. The simulated instances also have to be leased out for the duration of an hour. Often to achieve clients' needs, the numbers of instances are scaled dynamically. Time and additional resources are dependent on this amount, such as additional storage space. Providers also have data centers in many places that enable easy connectivity around the globe. Web interfaces allow cloud service monitoring. Some providers make it easy to connect virtual instances via VPN to the network of the company, and it seems like it is one huge flexible IT infrastructure for the company's corporate network.

These approaches are called hybrid clouds, which link the (interior) private cloud of the business to the IaaS provider's public cloud. Amazon is a leader around power generation and computing (Almeida et al., 2017). One of the most deployed infrastructure platforms (Taneski et al., 2014) is the Amazon Elastic Compute Cloud (EC2). ServePath's GoGrid (van Schaik et al., 2017) and thus Rackspace Cloud are both common virtualization services. The IBM Smart Business Cloud (Grawemeyer & Johnson, 2011), Oracle Cloud Computing, GigaSpaces (Gratian et al., 2018), RightScale, and Nimbus service services are also supported. The IaaS category for Online Storage and Recovery Facilities. Although different storage systems are designed for organization use like most virtualization systems, special facilities are also provided to private people. Corporate facilities vary from time to time and from general additional storage capacity to internal capabilities, to storage services for database-structured material. These latter facilities are paid not only for disk space used, but also for the number of data requests. In addition, especially built services expand the data volume with regular instances of virtualization. Cloud computing and backup services for individuals are increasingly available. The manufacturers of laptops and netbooks also promote OS providers for extra web storage. Data also are backed up on servers of a provider and can regularly be recovered from various locations to sync several workstations since resources are often available even through web browsers, such as CloudFiles in Rackspace.

For enterprise and private use, Rackspace provides cloud storage. Nirvanix (Toth & Paulsen, 2016) is also a data provider. Amazon provides the Amazon Elastic Block Store (EBS) and the Amazon Quick Storage Facility (S3) data storage facilities or splits their EC2 instances free (Aloul, 2012), respectively. As with the Amazon SimpleDB (Almeida et al., 2017), Amazon also has unique database solutions.

3.4 Platform as a Service

PaaS providers are able to design and deliver groups of software applications and facilities using the supported tools, environments, and programs frameworks, in a managed high-level software architecture. The offering covers the usage of the underlying resources, such as servers, networks, computing facilities, or operating systems that the customer has no influence over, provided that the infrastructure is excluded from below the platform (Taneski et al., 2014; Chaudhry & Rittenhouse, 2015).

Platform providers often concentrate on those areas, such as web applications creation, and rely on the language of programming. To verify and build or deploy their software indefinitely, customers get a different environment. Google's development engine focuses on standard Java or Python web applications (Dawson & Stinebaugh, 2010). The Google Software Engine is free for small non-scaling apps. Applications can be built with the.NET libraries on the Microsoft Azure platform (Long, 2013).

Microsoft uses its cloud offerings to sell its own bundles of software (Taneski et al., 2014). Bungee Link is developed primarily for creating and delivering cloud apps (Konieczny et al., 2015). Force.com (Ovelgönne et al., 2017) is a special domain PaaS, which helps businesses, including Salesforce.com, to create personalized software apps.

3.5 *Software as a Service*

Cloud computing offers usually unique programs that have already been built on a cloud platform. The web-based email is a very popular SaaS. Many cloud-based computing providers are web-based applications that, like an Internet browser, can be accessed from multiple customer devices with an intricate client interface. The users of such platforms do not manage or control the core technology and application platform; it is only possible to provide minimal user configurations. Features that provide Internet-based storage in standard, nonremote device applications are also treated as part of SaaS' offerings. Salesforce.com, which delivers Customer Relationship Management (CRM) solutions, is a cloud-based computing services for enterprise use. Another domain-specific SaaS is Appian Anywhere that provides tools for the management of business processes. Google Apps are also popular web utilities for personal use. The fact that it is still included in the Google Docs package (Ashford, 2009; Florêncio et al., 2007), which enables access and exchange of documents, tablets, and presentations is included in this calendar, email contacts, and chat capability. Box.net (Anderson & Agarwal, 2010) is another service for document sharing and backup. SmugMug is designed and uses Amazon S3 in video and picture sharing.

3.6 *Open Source-Based Services*

Even though some providers use open-source technologies or platforms, the underlying frameworks are largely exclusive. But there are a few fully open-source systems, primarily IaaS cloud providers, as software and tools. These tools allow you to track the virtual instances, handle them, and control them. Sadly, most open-source cloud applications are available at the level of infrastructure or networks and there is few open-source SaaS software. Furthermore, Linux operating systems which restrict the customer community to those operating systems are supported in most open-source platforms (Toth & Paulsen, 2016). The Cloud Eucalyptus attacks private clouds in particular (Coventry et al., 2014). Groundwork is an open-source cloud computing management system running with Amazon's EC2 (Pelgrin, 2014). Open Nebula can be used for the Amazon EC2 service and a "standard open-source toolkits for creating private, public and hybrid clouds." Additionally, the Nimbus project is based on an open source. It is preserved and developed for science calculations by the University of Chicago.

3.7 Main Characteristics of Cloud Computing Services

There are several cloud providers, as seen above. The most noticeable distinction has been discussed, the form of service available. The common characteristics of cloud providers such as Iaas, Paas, and SaaS are discussed in this section. More unique functionality would then be addressed for each type. However, the chosen features make finer distinctions at each stage of the taxonomy. The list is likely to be extended further.

3.8 Common Characteristics

The common aspects include the type of license, the targeted customer community, the protection provided, the structured arrangements between the supplier and the customer, payment mechanisms, interoperability, and enforcement. Each of this functionality is discussed in the following chapter.

3.9 License Type

Many cloud computing platforms use tools and certificates of their own. However, many suppliers of cloud computing use open-source tools and frameworks. Amazon uses the open-source Xen technology (Almeida et al., 2017) and the Python open-source programming language for Google PaaS (Dawson & Stinebaugh, 2010), but their core cloud storage resources and additional services are maintained closed-source. Much open-source applications and smaller cloud storage platforms are used for cloud monitoring, as small companies frequently lack the capacity and leverage to sell proprietary software (Taneski et al., 2014). In technology and platform level facilities, license forms also play a role. When renting the virtual servers out without installed operating systems IaaS providers do not suffer from difficulties with software licensing. This may also contribute to possible issues with how the user can be paid with the use over a short time span by including operating systems and software bundles. Additional devices use costs are also payable. Additional platforms use only applications like Microsoft Azure. The current challenge to cloud computing in (Long, 2013; Taneski et al., 2014) has been software licenses.

3.10 Intended User Group

Any applications in the cloud discriminate between enterprise and private use. The majority of IaaS and PaaS deals are for enterprises, while SaaS offers for companies, private individuals, or both are available, like Google Apps (Ashford, 2009). This does not, though, mean that business resources cannot be bought by individuals. A division may be made between mobile and fixed users within the corporate and private user classes. Mobile users access cloud computing applications from anywhere, regardless of whether they are at home, at work, on a tablet, laptop, or by hand. Right users are stationary and usually link to the service using the same unit. Once cloud platforms for mobile phones and other resource-effective devices are available, a new category may be considered based on this form of hardware.

3.11 Security and Privacy

The security and privacy issues are significant, especially when important data are on the servers of the cloud. Data losses or data theft is not only liable for the loss of sales but also for court proceedings (Aytes & Conolly, 2003). Certain provisions, including Directives 2002/58/EC (Furnell et al., 2006) and 95/46/EC (Bullo et al., 2017), can relate in particular to the processing of personal data. For example, EU regulation on data security specifies that only countries with sufficient protection should save data, and with such details the physical location of data, which is not always available for cloud-based systems, must be identified. Owing to the lack of requirements, each vendor treats each other differently regarding cloud storage, data protection and ownership. In general, all cloud providers should be secured and authenticated. For example, encryption will protect against interception on network level between virtual machines. For taxonomy, protection initiatives can be divided into external protection that considers confidentiality, guarantees cloud connectivity, and addresses the internal security mechanisms provided by cloud to separate and stable virtual instances and customers in the cloud. Most cloud providers can be accessed through web browsers; for connecting to the cloud, the basic HTTP (Hyper Text Transmission Protocol) is used. The SSL/TLS (Secure Socket Layer/Transport Layer Security) is used to provide encryption and secure identification. The PKI (Public Key Infrastructure) and X.509 SSL certificates are additionally used for authentication and authorization. These processes must, however, be correctly applied. For authentication, the Amazon EC2 uses public keys. VPNs are found in hybrid clouds. This is achieved by the Amazon Virtual Private Cloud provider (Amazon VPC) (Almeida et al., 2017).

3.12 Payment Systems

One of the distinctive features is the billing system for cloud storage services. The key distinction is that true cloud providers are paid depending on dynamic use (Taneski et al., 2014). The consumer spends only the services that are used instead of paying a set monthly or annual rate. Resources could include a variety of virtual cases, the volume and width of the data stored, the time and resources of the machine (CPU or RAM), and transactions, as well as variations of these (measured in database Gets and Puts). Different payment mechanisms can also be used by cloud machines, depending on their tools. The pricing model most used is the pay-per-use method in which units or units are connected to fixed value (resource) per time. If competitive or shifting pricing is used, price, for example as auction or negotiation, is set because of dynamic supply and demand. Dynamic pricing uses Zimory.com. Some cloud providers are available without charge such as Google Docs and the Google App Engine (Dawson & Stinebaugh, 2010). (http://www.ponemon.org/, n. d.). The services used based on a pay-per-use model are paid monthly for Amazon EC2 customers (Almeida et al., 2017). GoGrid consumers may opt between payment as you-go billing, i.e., customers pay only for their services, or prepaid plans for which customers receive "a prepaid cloud server resource allocation at a discounted rate at a fixed monthly price."

3.13 Specific Characteristics

The main aspects of cloud storage platforms are discussed earlier. As far as the general features are concerned, more complex features of cloud infrastructures, networks, and applications often do not permit consistent variations in the chosen function, hence only a few features are discussed below.

3.14 IaaS-Specific Characteristics

The licensed operating systems and applications/frameworks are the characteristics to remember since this could be relevant for prospective customers. Most IaaS providers support Linux, but others support Windows and Open Solaris. The Apache HTTP Server and MySQL database program are commonly supported programs. Another essential feature for developers is when and what software resources the provider offers. This could require an API or special resources in the command line. Digital instance facilities can be further separated by virtualization technologies. Most providers are currently using Xen (Such et al., 2019).

3.15 PaaS-Specific Characteristics

The programming languages and environments are supported by a significant platform level feature. For example, Google's App Engine currently supports only Python and Java environments. A relevant functionality can also be supported to operating systems and applications.

3.16 SaaS-Specific Characteristics

The cloud providers with information differ considerably. The customer/application domain of the provided service is an attribute to be considered. This field may be client partnerships or other fields of company administration, workplace software, social networking, and data sharing.

4 Conclusion

Users must have a good degree of cyber hygiene. Poor cyber security is expensive to society. Attackers know that the easiest way to gain into a device is to steal information from a user or find a technological vulnerability. This chapter would include a technical survey mostly on cyber hygiene practices of end-users. It will also encourage the development of more successful practices in the financial analytical environment. It will also provide aspects that allow the company to improve its cyber hygiene approaches due to the various forms of access to financial solutions in the financial environment.

References

Almeida, V. A., Doneda, D., & de Souza Abreu, J. (2017). Cyberwarfare and digital governance. *IEEE Internet Computing, 21*, 68–71.

Aloul, F. A. (2012). The need for effective information security awareness. *Journal of Advances in Information Technology, 3*, 176–183.

Anderson, C. L., & Agarwal, R. (2010). Practicing safe computing: A multimedia empirical examination of home computer user security behavioral intentions. *MIS Quarterly, 34*, 613–643.

Ashford, W. (2009). Millions of web users at risk from weak passwords. Computerweekly.

Aytes, K., & Conolly, T. (2003). A research model for investigating human behavior related to computer security. AMCIS 2003 Proceedings, p. 260.

Bank, D. (2005). Spear Phishing Tests educate people about online scams. [Online]. The Wall Street Journal.

Bullo, A., Stavrou, E., & Stavrou, S. (2017). Transparent password policies: A case study of investigating end-user situational awareness. *International Journal on Cyber Situational Awareness (IJCSA), 2*, 85–89.

Cain, A. A., & Still, J. D. (2018). Usability comparison of over-the-shoulder attack resistant authentication schemes. *Journal of Usability Studies, 13*.

Chaudhry, J. A., & Rittenhouse, R. G. (2015). Phishing: Classification and counter measures. In *Multimedia, Computer Graphics and Broadcasting (MulGraB), 2015 7th International Conference on* (pp. 28–31).

Choong, Y.-Y., & Greene, K. K. (2016). What'sa special character anyway? Effects of ambiguous terminology in password rules. In *Proceedings of the Human Factors and Ergonomics Society Annual Meeting* (pp. 760–764).

Coventry, L., Briggs, P., Jeske, D., & van Moorsel, A. (2014). Scene: A structured means for creating and evaluating behavioral nudges in a cyber security environment. In *International conference of design, user experience, and usability* (pp. 229–239).

Dawson, L. A., & Stinebaugh, J. (2010). *Methodology for prioritizing cyber-vulnerable critical infrastructure equipment and mitigation strategies*. Sandia National Laboratories.

Dhillon, G., Torkzadeh, G., & Chang, J. (2018). Strategic planning for is security: Designing objectives. In *International Conference on Design Science Research in Information Systems and Technology* (pp. 285–299).

Dodge, R. C., Jr., Carver, C., & Ferguson, A. J. (2007). Phishing for user security awareness. *Computers & Security, 26*, 73–80.

Europe, I. (2008). *Women 4 times more likely than men to give passwords for chocolate*. Press Release.

Florêncio, D., Herley, C., & Coskun, B. (2007). Do strong web passwords accomplish anything? *HotSec, 7*.

Furnell, S. M., Jusoh, A., & Katsabas, D. (2006). The challenges of understanding and using security: A survey of end-users. *Computers & Security, 25*, 27–35.

Gratian, M., Bandi, S., Cukier, M., Dykstra, J., & Ginther, A. (2018). Correlating human traits and cyber security behavior intentions. *Computers & Security, 73*, 345–358.

Grawemeyer, B., & Johnson, H. (2011). Using and managing multiple passwords: A week to a view. *Interacting with Computers, 23*, 256–267.

Holm, H., Flores, W. R., & Ericsson, G. (2013). Cyber security for a smart grid-what about phishing? In *Innovative smart grid technologies Europe (ISGT EUROPE), 2013 4th IEEE/PES* (pp. 1–5).

Hoonakker, P., Bornoe, N., & Carayon, P. (2009). Password authentication from a human factors perspective: Results of a survey among end-users. In *Proceedings of the Human Factors and Ergonomics Society Annual Meeting* (pp. 459–463).

http://www.ponemon.org/. (n.d.)

https://www.enisa.europa.eu.

Konieczny, F., Trias, E., & Taylor, N. J., (2015). *Seade: Countering the futility of network security.*, air and space power Journal maxwell AFB Al.

Lebek, B., Uffen, J., Neumann, M., Hohler, B., & Breitner, M. H. (2014). Information security awareness and behavior: A theory-based literature review. *Management Research Review, 37*, 1049–1092.

Long, R. M. (2013). *Using phishing to test social engineering awareness of financial employees.*

Ovelgönne, M., Dumitraş, T., Prakash, B. A., Subrahmanian, V., & Wang, B. (2017). Understanding the relationship between human behavior and susceptibility to cyber attacks: A data-driven approach. *ACM Transactions on Intelligent Systems and Technology (TIST), 8*, 51.

Pelgrin, W. (2014). A model for positive change: Influencing positive change in cyber security strategy, human factor, and leadership, ed.

Singh, D., Mohanty, N. P., Swagatika, S., & Kumar, S. (2020). Cyber-hygiene: The key concept for cyber security in cyberspace.

Such, J. M., Ciholas, P., Rashid, A., Vidler, J., & Seabrook, T. (2019). Basic cyber hygiene: Does it work? *Computer, 52*(4), 21–31.

Talib, S., Clarke, N. L., & Furnell, S. M. (2010). An analysis of information security awareness within home and work environments. In *Availability, reliability, and security, 2010. ARES'10 international conference on* (pp. 196–203).

Taneski, V., Hericko, M., & Brumen, B. (2014). Password security—No change in 35 years? In *Information and Communication Technology, Electronics and Microelectronics (MIPRO), 2014 37th International Convention on* (pp. 1360–1365).

Toth, P. R., & Paulsen, C. (2016). Small business information security: The fundamentals.

van Schaik, P., Jeske, D., Onibokun, J., Coventry, L., Jansen, J., & Kusev, P. (2017). Risk perceptions of cyber-security and precautionary behaviour. *Computers in Human Behavior, 75*, 547–559.

GPSR Compliance
The European Union's (EU) General Product Safety Regulation (GPSR) is a set of rules that requires consumer products to be safe and our obligations to ensure this.

If you have any concerns about our products, you can contact us on

ProductSafety@springernature.com

In case Publisher is established outside the EU, the EU authorized representative is:

Springer Nature Customer Service Center GmbH
Europaplatz 3
69115 Heidelberg, Germany

www.ingramcontent.com/pod-product-compliance
Lightning Source LLC
Chambersburg PA
CBHW072113160625
28292CB00003B/64
9783030837983